Unique and Unknown

The Story of Biathlon
in the United States

Arthur Stegen

ISBN: 978-0-578-49033-5
Library of Congress Control Number: 2019903789

published by
Arthur Stegen
New Paltz, NY 12561

produced and designed by
Grace Peirce
Great Life Press
Rye, NH 03870
www.greatlifepress.com

Pictures in this publication are used with permission of the United States Biathlon Association and the individual contributors.

Front cover photos (clockwise from top), by Nordic Focus, courtesy of the U.S. Biathlon Association.

Back cover photos of Art Stegen, courtesy of the author.

To my wife Susan and daughters Solveig and Annika,
who graciously supported my passion, often watching in
the cold and enduring my absences on many long trips
away from home.

Contents

Seen here shooting prone at one of the four shooting ranges, Jim Mahaffey won the first biathlon race held in the U.S. at Camp Hale, Colorado in 1956.

Maurice "Gus" Paquette achieved an 8th place finish at the 2nd World Biathlon Championships in 1959.

Preface

Growing up in New Paltz, New York, a small town surrounded by a great environment provided for many outdoor activities. The historical Mohonk Mountain House hotel in the local Shawangunk mountains had many trails for hiking, running and skiing. The nearby village of Rosendale had a Nordic ski center with an active ski club of a Scandinavian heritage. My high school years in the early 1960s focused on running and I dreamt of becoming a successful runner. I followed the world's best runners and their achievements with great interest. It was also with some interest that I became involved with alpine and cross-country skiing while working weekends at Mohonk's small Bonticou ski hill. I enjoyed outdoor winter activities and cross-country ski racing but never considered myself a real committed ski racer and did it only for activity and enjoyment during the season away from running. I became aware of biathlon during those years when the U.S. Army's biathlon team visited Rosendale for training and racing prior to their annual trip to international competitions in Europe.

After a few years away attending college through an athletic scholarship for running I returned home and began what I thought would be a teaching career in foreign languages. I continued to train and participated in the local running races during that time. I also reconnected with an older ski club member who had spent time in Alaska at the U.S. Army's Modern Winter Biathlon Training Center and participated in the 1968 Winter Olympic Games in France. As we trained together preparing for the Boston Marathon he convinced me to take skiing more seriously. Due to my enjoyment of winter, and without running activities to occupy my attention, I embraced cross-country ski racing whole-heartedly. My fitness levels from running helped find success and I soon found myself traveling to weekend racing throughout the winter.

However, it was the military draft in 1970 that sent my life in a totally unplanned direction. Basic training exposed my physical abilities and I became noticed by the deputy sports director for the Department of the Army, who also happened to be secretary of the U.S. Modern Pentathlon and Biathlon Association. Shortly after basic training I was sent directly to Alaska, assigned to the U.S. Army's Modern Winter Biathlon Training Center. I joined a small group of cross-country skiers who were also serving in the U.S. Army. This training center and its small group of exceptional athletes was the core of what became the heart of America's international participation in biathlon and its evolution of what the sport has become today.

My years at the army's biathlon training center changed my life. I loved the sport from the beginning. One of the most important aspects of this exciting sport was the fact that it is more than just ski race time that determines the outcome. Unlike cross-country skiing or running in which the clock becomes the difference between winning or losing, it requires another skill where perfection is possible. Although biathlon is still a race against the clock, it is also a test of marksmanship that provides an additional path to success. Like bowling or golf where it is possible to manage a perfect score, so too does biathlon by hitting every target. Biathlon provided a race experience where achievement and satisfaction comes from the skills you've developed through training and an appreciation of the drama and the narrative of each particular race.

The unique balance between skiing and shooting is what captivated my interest and generated my enthusiasm. This book is about biathlon; explaining what it is; what it takes and how it's done and an historical perspective of the sport in the United States. It is also a tribute to the small group of dedicated participants, coaches, administrators and supporters who made contributions to its evolution from its beginning to the dynamic and exciting sport that it has become today. Without their contributions of pictures, scrapbooks and memories this effort would not have been possible.

Art Stegen
January 2019

PART I.

"What is Biathlon?"

The high premium placed on today's competitive sports is as old as human existence. It began as a form of human survival where the ability to survive the natural world depended on one's adeptness to overcome the lack of natural protection and to avoid extinction through strength, endurance, agility and intelligence. In the fight for survival, humans run, jump, climb, swim and fighy for their lives. They also dream and strive. Their curiosity is their glory and their pain. They climb mountains, cross uncharted seas and explore outer space for reasons other than material benefit. They thrive on challenges. Seekers of laurels, they especially measure themselves in competition with fellow humans. Where there is no contest, they create one. From deep within, and from millennia past, comes the impulse for athletic competition. In northern climates, they overcame snow and ice by making crude skis, snowshoes and skates. Some distinguished themselves as superior to others, eventually leading to competitive sport among the ancient Olympic Games of Greece.

Biathlon is the unique modern Winter Olympic sport, and generally unknown by the American public. Unlike the familiar sports that are played out on athletic fields and gymnasiums across the American landscape, biathlon takes place in a relatively few locations, during the cold winter environment and with few spectators. Biathlon is unique in sports in that the demands of this "combined" undertaking is such that success requires the pinnacle of physiological fitness as well as the calmness required for solid accuracy. Despite sharing the unique and inherent values characteristic of American culture, biathlon as a competitive sport is not fully in the awareness of the public.

Regardless of the particular form they take, there are three most critical elements for the success of any sport, especially in modern times. They are: having athletes with the inherent talent, including physical and intellectual abilities, personality, health and motivation; providing those individuals with support and management of resources, including the right opportunities in the correct environment for participating in training and competition; and providing them with the right guidance through coaching, planning, and direction.

Although the athletes would seem to be the primary element as those actively participating in the sport, this first section begins the story of biathlon in the United States by reviewing the second of these; those who organize, formalize, manage, and govern the sport. Focusing on this element allows for an explanation of how it began and how the bureaucracy behind it developed biathlon into today's dynamic and exciting Winter Olympic sport.

CHAPTER 1

Beginnings

The Greek name "biathlon," meaning a dual test, has been given to the modern sport combining nordic skiing and target shooting. Known in Scandinavia as *skiskytting* or *ampumahiihto* this exhausting effort required by nordic skiing and the steadiness and control demanded in marksmanship may at first seem an unlikely combination; but in fact, biathlon has a more realistic basis in history than many other sports, combining physical skills and accuracy. Hunting on skis, the utilitarian forerunner of biathlon required the same coupling of effort and concentration as the exciting Winter Olympic sport of today. The Rødøy rock-paintings portray the use of skis for hunting in prehistoric Norway and Norwegian bogs have preserved skis dating from the Bronze Age. The prehistoric hunting on skis, like so many of the original Olympic sports finds its foundations in the human struggle for survival. Like the javelin throw of athletics, or running and swimming, each, unlike modern "thrill sports," which often seem to have little practical value, have their basis in utilitarian human efforts. Just as any sport today, those purposeful hunter's and warrior's skills evolved from the primitive hunting and warring activities that were necessary for survival. Those who demonstrated the most successful abilities became admired and these activities eventually evolved into contests and competitions.

Although the concept of skiing and marksmanship can be traced to prehistoric Scandinavia, its role in military planning and strategies came at a much later time and it can be said that the early Scandinavian military ski troops are the true origins of this modern-day exciting sport. While it would appear the deployment of lightly armed ski detachments in winter campaigns would seem a natural thing, the apparently obvious was not so easy to put into practice. The earliest account of ski troops is found in the writings of Danish historian, Saxo Grammaticus, who wrote of the defeat of Ragnar Lodbrok about 850 A.D. by a group from Finnmark who came on skis.

There are many other written historical references to soldiers on skis. A few important ones were the accounts of the battle at Oslo on March 6, 1200, when King Sverre dispatched ski scouts to reconnoiter and report back as quickly as possible the position and strength of the enemy. This is probably the first reference to the use of skis in a planned military action. In a letter dated 1536, Gustav Vasa (for whom the Vasa Race in Sweden is held in memory) points out that skis could be used with convoys and by the intelligence service, and that good skiers could cover 185km in a day. When the Swedes invaded Norway in 1564, things went badly for the Norwegians because, unlike the Swedes, they did not have any skiers. In neighboring Finland, an army unit defeated a Russian unit in 1555 mostly because of its mobility on skis. In the Gyldenløve War (1675-79), there were many accounts of ski troops and this was the first war in which skiers were included in the units. The first occasion skiers played an important role was during the Great Scandinavian War (1700-1718), when ski companies were organized under the system of district-supported soldiers operating in connection with conscription to the army.

The first set of rules for the military use of skis was drawn up (in German) by Captain Emahusen in 1733 and replaced by a new set (in Danish) in 1774. The first regular ski detachments were introduced into the Norwegian Army in 1742. The equipment supplied by every district which maintained soldiers was fixed as follows: one pair of skis with stick and fittings, one pair of homespun gaiters, one calfskin knapsack with leather strap, and a canvas backpack with leather strap. The army had no standard type of skis, so the soldiers wore the kind of skis to which they were accustomed at home. These skis were made of hardwood; birch, mountain ash, and sometimes ash. Next to elm skis, ash skis have always been considered the fastest. Those made of elm had such speed that scarcely anyone dared to use them since their speed was considered dangerous.

The austere equipment of the ski-runner detachments bears little relation to the success of the early prize races run by the army. The very fact that such competitions were organized shows that there was great interest. The first recorded ski race was held in 1767. This competition was the first ski race of any type to be historically recorded and was to have four classes: shooting at a target at full speed, downhill race in wooded country, downhill race without riding one's stick to brake and without falling, and a long-distance race on flat ground. These races became regular events by 1792, with monetary prizes for the winners. Although the use of ski-runner detachments had disappeared following the reduction of the Norwegian armed forces after its union with Sweden in 1814, stories and memories of first-rate skiers who had distinguished themselves in military service and military skiing continued to be handed down.

Biathlon skills were kept alive in the 1800s through military exercises but also through the formation of ski clubs in Norway. The Trysil Rifle and Ski Club was organized in 1861 promoting cross-country skiing and rifle shooting with the purpose of preparing soldiers for national defense. In 1865 Norwegian military officer Oscar Wergeland wrote a book of military ski drills titled *Skiløbningen, Dens*

Historie of Krigsanvendelse. In 1912 the Norwegian military rekindled an interest in competitions by organizing the annual 17 kilometers "Førvarsrennet" in Oslo. This was the first "individual" competition that resembled today's disciplines in that this race featured two bouts of shooting in between the skiing for which two minutes of time was subtracted from the ski time for each target hit. In 1918 the Norwegian King's Guard organized the annual 30 kilometers "Military Langrenn" which favored skiers since only 10 shots were fired at targets of random distance up to 200 meters. Another important race in Norway was the "Vardevaktrennet," first held at Lillehammer in 1938. Athletes of all ages competed for the same cup in this 12km race with the different age groups handicapped by penalizing one to three minutes per missed target.

The Winter War of 1939-1940 between Finland and the Soviet Union revealed the greatest example of skiing and shooting skills in the military environment. Following independence from Russia in 1917, the Finnish Home Guard that evolved from the White Guard after a brief civil war, became active in numerous areas of Finnish life, including the organization of sports activities. It was the period when Finnish athletes dominated distance running in track and field. Finland's historic sports personality Lauri Pihkala, known as "Tahko" and the inventor of pesäpallo, the Finnish variant of baseball, was responsible for encouraging biathlon races throughout the 1920s which recorded approximately 14,300 competitions involving over 240,000 participants between 1921 and up to the Winter War in 1939. He had developed a set of rules for biathlon competitions that introduced targets with scoring rings for determining shooting accuracy. This undoubtedly provided the Finnish soldiers with cross-country ski skills that allowed their inferior numbers to take advantage of their speed, tactics and economy of force against the overwhelming numbers of the Soviet army that suffered large losses due to the extreme cold weather and poor tactics.

Biathlon skills gradually became a genuine international competition in the form of the military patrol race. Because of their training and fitness, value patrol competitions started in the Soviet Union and other nations by 1924. Patrol teams consisted of four soldiers who skied a distance of 30 kilometers with army rifles, backpacks and 8 kilograms of gear. The team was headed by an officer and included a sergeant and two soldiers. The officer carried only a pistol and did not fire at the shooting range but directed the soldiers who fired at targets up to 200m distance. The event was long and grueling, often taking nearly four hours. The military ski patrol race was included in the program of the inaugural Winter Olympic Games at Chamonix in 1924, as well as at St. Moritz in 1928, at Garmisch-Partenkirchen in 1936 and again in St. Moritz in 1948. The Finnish patrol team placed second in all these competitions, while Switzerland, Norway, Italy and again Switzerland respectively were the winners. The Winter Olympic Games of 1940 and

1944 were suspended because of WWII, however, the limiting factor that only military personnel could participate in the event, along with the anti-war sentiment following World War II caused it to be excluded from the Winter Olympic Games program after 1948.

In the ten years following the exclusion of the Military Patrol from the Winter Olympic Games, biathlon was without an international event, but due to its military nature, this period coincided with the development of the Conseil International du Sport Militaire (CISM). CISM was founded by five European Nations in France in February 1948. The United States Armed Forces became a member in 1951. The Military Patrol found a natural place in the aims and desires of the military mission of CISM; to develop friendly relations between the Armed Forces of member nations and to meet in sports competitions instead of battlegrounds, with the ideal and goal of "Friendship through Sports."

CHAPTER 2

A Winter Olympic Games Event

The Military Patrol can be considered the forerunner of present day biathlon, however its exclusion from the Winter Olympic program in 1948 did not minimize interest in the skills of combining skiing with shooting. After World War II Sweden took the leadership role in helping biathlon develop into an international event. The first Swedish Championships in "Skidfeltskytting" were held in 1944. Skidfeltskytting was a ski competition in which the athletes skied a 20 kilometers distance and stopped to shoot five bouts of shooting of six shots at silhouette targets placed at random distances. Finland held similar competitions in 1945 and by 1956 the Scandinavian nations were sending representative teams to compete in Scandinavian "skifeltskytting" competitions.

However, it was another military sport that also played an important role in developing biathlon into an international event. The Modern Pentathlon is a combined discipline sport comprising the contemporary sports of pistol shooting, fencing, swimming, equestrian cross-country riding and running, which embraced the spirit of its ancient counterpart. The founder of the Modern Olympics, Baron Pierre de Coubertin had great admiration for the Pentathlon and tried to have the event re-introduced into the Olympic program. De Coubertin believed that it would be this event, above all others, that "tested a man's moral qualities as much as his physical resources and skills, producing thereby the ideal, complete athlete." It was introduced to the Olympic Games at Stockholm in 1912 and was a modernized version of the ancient Pentathlon from the Greek Olympiad in 708 B.C., consisting of running the length of the stadium, jumping, throwing the spear, throwing the discus and wrestling. The Pentathlon held a position of unique importance in the ancient Games and it was considered to be the climax, with the winner ranked as "Victor Ludorum."

It was this concept of the "complete athlete" that led to a proposal before the International Olympic Committee (IOC) that a combined sport, "a sport for the complete man," be included in the program of the Winter Olympic Games. The proposed competition included equestrian riding, fencing, pistol shooting, a 3 kilometers downhill ski race and a 12 kilometers cross-country ski race. A test event was held at Gstaad, Switzerland in 1942 between Sweden and Switzerland and it was a demonstration event at the 1948 Winter Olympics at St. Moritz. Fourteen athletes participated in the event which was won by Gustave Lindh of Sweden who would later become the secretary general of the International Modern Pentathlon and Biathlon Union (UIPMB). However, the IOC decided to discontinue the event at future Winter Olympic Games.

It was due to the leadership efforts of the Union Internationale de Pentathlon Moderne (UIPM), especially Presidents Gustav Dyrssen and Sven Thofelt of Sweden, that biathlon became organized internationally and eventually introduced into the Olympic movement. The UIPM was organized during the 1948 Olympic Games at London with the task of establishing rules and organizing international competitions. At the same time, it was suggested that the IOC not give up on the "complete man's" multiple sport event in the Winter Olympic program. The Swiss Olympic Committee made a proposal to the IOC session in London that the Modern Winter Pentathlon should be introduced into the Olympic program especially since an international federation was being formed to govern it.

Discussions to have a winter pentathlon event were continued, but the discussions gradually shifted to one that included sports entirely on ice or snow. Avery Brundage of the USA suggested a competition comprised of cross-country skiing, downhill skiing, figure skating, tobogganing and ski jumping. Because such an event would be so "facility and logistically demanding" and only a few organizers could host such an event, the discussion turned to skiing and shooting and the idea of a winter pentathlon was abandoned. Perhaps incorrectly, because the sport of skiing and shooting was not a true multi-sport event with a series of competitions of different disciplines, but rather a contest of two diametrically opposed skills in a single competition, the sport was named "Biathlon."

The next step to include the Winter Biathlon into the Winter Olympic Games was taken by the UIPM President Sven Thofelt. He had to convince the president of the International Olympic Committee (IOC), Avery Brundage. Brundage felt that biathlon was an artificial sport, designed purely to suit the military. He felt that sports should be open to all participants. Since nearly all competitors in the biathlon related competitions taking place were in the military, he did not feel biathlon should be an Olympic sport. At the same time as the CISM Ski Games were being organized in 1953 which seemingly gave the military its own international event, Sven Thofelt shifted his argument by telling Brundage the story of the ancient man going out to hunt with his weapon on foot or on skis in order for his family to survive. This seemed to sway Brundage's thinking and he agreed to help get biathlon on the Winter Olympic program.

In 1957 after both the International Shooting Union (UIT) and the International Ski Federation (FIS) showed no interest in biathlon, the UIPM declared itself to be responsible for biathlon and made a motion to the IOC at a meeting in Sofia, Bulgaria, to have an individual biathlon race in the Winter Olympic Games as an official competition. The motion passed, and it was later confirmed at its meeting in Tokyo the following year, however with the condition that its continuation in the Olympic program was subject to the experience from the 1960 Winter Games. The decision was helped by the fact that the 1960 Winter Olympic Games could not hold a bobsled competition and Brundage saw biathlon as a replacement. Rules for the event were established, creating the men's individual 20 kilometers competition with four bouts of shooting five shots each at targets, from the prone position, at 250, 200, and 150 meters and one at 100 meters from the standing position with large bore, centerfire rifles. The shooting penalty for each missed target was two minutes added to the ski time.

In preparation for the first Winter Olympic Biathlon event the UIMP scheduled the first World Championships for Biathlon on March 2, 1958 at Saalfelden, Austria. A total of seven nations participated, including the U.S. Swedish athletes were the most successful in the first World Biathlon Championships at Saalfelden as well as the 1960 Olympic Winter Games at Squaw Valley because of their success on the shooting range. Despite the success of these early World Championships and Olympic events, biathlon was still not assured a place in the future Olympic program and at the 1960 IOC session in Rome discussion again surfaced that biathlon looked too much like a military sport and should not be continued. A vote taken resulted in favor of eliminating biathlon. At the next IOC session in Athens, the UIPM asked to reintroduce the sport and an exceptional vote was taken in favor of including it again, with the condition that the UIPM make the event more interesting. The question of Olympic participation continued and was raised once again during the 62nd IOC session at Innsbrück in 1964 and again a favorable vote was taken, keeping it in the Olympic program.

In the interest of self-protection, the UIMP took additional steps to make biathlon more interesting and acceptable. In 1965, it changed the scoring to include 1- and 2-minute penalties for shooting and changed the shooting to a single range of 150 meters. The shooting format was also changed to alternating two shooting bouts each from prone and standing positions. These changes made for greater convenience to the organizer and spectators. Also in 1965, a test relay event was held that created a more interesting and exciting event and it was made official in 1966. This exciting addition to the World Championships program tested the skills of a four-man relay team over a 7½ kilometers distance for each man, with two bouts of shooting, one from each position at breakable targets. The competitors were required to break five glass targets and had 3 spare or reserve rounds to do it. The penalty for each unbroken target was an added skiing distance of a "penalty lap" of 200 meters. This event eventually replaced the team scoring used in prior World Championships.

The 1964 vote to keep biathlon in the Winter Olympic Games did not end the debate which came up again during the 1972 Sapporo Winter Olympic Games. At that time anti-war sentiment due to the ongoing war in Vietnam had grown. Avery Brundage again felt biathlon was too "military" and in a concealed effort to phase it out, the number of starters at the 1976 Winter Games in Innsbrück was reduced. Sven Thofelt and the UIPMB again countered Brundage's passive opposition by first introducing the 10 kilometers sprint race with two shooting bouts at prone and standing breakable targets with penalty laps of 150 meters for missed targets. The penalty for the relay race was also reduced to 150 meters to make the competition closer and finally by voting to reduce the shooting distance to 50 meters with .22 caliber rimfire rifles. This change made biathlon more accessible to the public and more easily organized. The number of participating nations went from 17 at the 1976 Winter Olympic Games to 27 at the World Championships in 1978. After adding the sprint race to the Winter Olympic program in 1980, changing from paper targets to immediate response targets and introducing women to the sport with the 1st World Biathlon Championships for women in 1984, it became hard to justify removing it from the Winter Olympic program. Biathlon became the international winter ski event with the highest number of participating nations and it has since evolved to become the very dynamic Winter Olympic sport for both men and women with high public interest with ever-increasing excitement.

CHAPTER 3

The International Biathlon Union

T he Union Internationale de Pentathlon Moderne (UIPM) assumed international responsibility for biathlon in 1957 and appointed its first technical
committee to help define and organize the sport. Biathlon was officially
integrated in the UIPM as a second sport alongside modern pentathlon. From that
time on, biathlon was supported and further developed within the UIPM, and in
1968 the federation was renamed *Union Internationale de Pentathlon Moderne et
Biathlon* (UIPMB) after biathlon had successfully been established. By the 1980s
a few officials from the UIPMB representing biathlon started openly debating
about whether it was positive for the further development for biathlon to be
represented in an international federation promoting a winter sport and a summer
sport at the same time. Dissatisfaction with the development of biathlon, the
under-representation of biathlon on the UIPMB executive board and the dissatisfaction with the work of the UIPMB administration in the area of biathlon were
also reasons making more and more biathlon functionaries within the UIPMB
consider biathlon going a separate way. This also coincided with the improvement
of financial health due to the rapidly growing broadcasting rights for biathlon.

As the opportunities for an independent world biathlon federation were
explored there were positive examples of new national biathlon federations being
founded, emerging from national ski federations or national pentathlon federations and this lent momentum to the desire to have an independent world federation. In the U.S. the Amateur Sports Act essentially mandated that the USOC
end multiple sport governing bodies and the U.S. Biathlon Association was one of
the early products of this federal law. Since discussions to this effect were taking
place throughout the functionary ranks and the UIPMB member federations, the
UIPMB executive could not help but notice that something was happening. At
that time, the strong, universally-recognized UIPMB president, Sven Thofelt, who
had built up the Union into an undivided whole over many years had fallen ill
and did not have any personal influence upon the way things progressed. Despite
the efforts of the serving vice-president, Igor Novikov, who was publicly against
separation, those who advocated a disbanding of the UIPMB were aware that they
could not afford to harm either of the sports and that each sport had to have a

basis upon which to develop further in sporting and financial terms. They also had to ensure that the IOC would accept such a separation and that both disciplines would remain on the program of the Olympic Games.

The immense developments in the political arena that led to the demise of the Eastern European Communist nations brought about considerable repercussions which also impacted biathlon and the UIPMB and diverted attention away from actions to separate from the UIPMB. However, by 1991 the presidents of some UIPMB member federations were invited by Secretary General of the Norwegian Biathlon Federation Anders Besseberg, to Munich for a session of discussions about the development of the sport for the future. Several UIPMB member federations then submitted a motion to the 1992 UIPMB Congress to leave the UIPMB. Thirteen member federations took up the invitation. Following a discussion on the fundamentals for separation, thirteen viable arguments for leaving the UIPMB were developed. The authorized representatives of the national federations spoke in favor of separating from the UIPMB and for the creation of an independent international biathlon federation. Voting was to be held on remaining or separating from the UIPMB at the 1992 UIPMB Biathlon Olympic Congress in Les Saisies, France and an extraordinary biathlon congress was called for the following day in the event of a decision in favor of separation. Ten UIPMB member federations (AUT, CAN, CZE, FIN, GER, ITA, NOR, SWE, USA, YUG) submitted a motion to leave the UIPMB and form an independent world biathlon federation at the 1992 UIPMB Congress. At the UIPMB Congress on February 13, 1992 in Les Saisies, there was heated discussion about the motions and voting was not held until Greece and Cyprus submitted a motion for secret ballot voting. 26 of the 32 votes were in favor of leaving the UIPMB.

Anders Besseberg was elected conference chairman from among the representatives of the 24 national biathlon federations present at Les Saisies. As a first step, two biathlon representatives were selected to join the UIPMB statutes commission with the mandate of drafting a constitution for an independent world biathlon federation outside the UIPMB by the end of June 1992. A working group was then formed comprising Anders Besseberg as chairman and members Howard Buxton of the USA, Zdenek Vojtisek of the Czech Republic, Georgios Patieridis of Greece, John Leaning of Great Britain and Secretary Peter Bayer of Germany. The group's primary tasks for further action included calling all the national biathlon federations to a conference on November 27, 1992 in Amélie-Les-Bains, France, one day before the UIPMB annual general meeting. A constitution proposal for an international biathlon federation and a constitution proposal for an umbrella organization governing this international biathlon federation and the international federation for modern pentathlon were presented at that conference, at which representatives from 23 national biathlon federations participated.

The umbrella organization was to initially represent both federations to the IOC and the international Olympic sports federations. The name International Biathlon Federation (IBF) was used as a working term.

At the intense Amélie-Les-Bains meeting, two congresses, biathlon and modern pentathlon, convened separately and 22 biathlon federations voted in favor of, with two against, a complete separation from and dissolution of the UIPMB at the biathlon congress. The pentathlon delegates at the UIPMB annual general assembly delayed a decision to vote on leaving the UIPMB *and* on a new, separate constitution at the next biathlon congress on February 10, 1993 at Borovetz, Bulgaria, and to then call an extraordinary annual general assembly in the summer of 1993 at London, during which voting would be held in the first part of the meeting on the issue of separation of both sports and on a dissolution of the UIPMB. Then in part two, the international biathlon federation would hold its first congress based on its own constitution. The annual general meeting voted almost unanimously in favor of retaining the umbrella organization UIPMB with two autonomous federations for biathlon and modern pentathlon. The 1993 UIPMB biathlon congress in Borovetz adopted the constitution of the IBF with a two-third majority.

At the UIPMB extraordinary annual general meeting July 2, 1993 in London, the agenda item of the reorganization of the UIPMB passed by a vote of 77 out of 85 in favor of two separate international federations for biathlon and modern pentathlon under the umbrella organization of the UIPMB. A day later the biathlon's founding congress took place in London, and they named their federation the International Biathlon Union (IBU). Elections took place, and Anders Besseberg was elected the first president of the IBU and Salzburg, Austria was decided upon as the seat of the International Biathlon Union. The first regular Congress of the IBU followed in June 1994 in Salzburg. The ensuing period was devoted to developing the sport of biathlon, increasing the Union's assets by entering lucrative TV and marketing contracts, and modernizing the event and competition rules. The UIPMB Executive Board, which consisted of the presidents and secretary-generals of both the UIPMB and the IBU, met as and when required, whereby the president of the UIPMB or the president of the IBU chaired the meeting in alternate, two-year intervals.

Due to the very positive development of biathlon internationally, certain people in the biathlon field began to get more vocal, demanding that the IBU leave the UIPMB once and for all. Talks with various IOC members, such as its president, Marquis Juan Antonio Samaranch, showed that the IOC would accept the IBU leaving the UIPMB if the move were in conformity with the statutes, would recognize the IBU as well as the UIPM and retain both disciplines on the Olympic program. However, according to the UIPMB statutes, a decision to leave the UIPMB required a two-third majority at two consecutive Congresses. At the 1996 IBU Congress, 21 delegates voted in favor of withdrawal and five were against; at the 1998 IBU Congress, 30 delegates voted in favor of withdrawal and five were against. The withdrawal of the IBU from the UIPMB thereby became effective, based on the UIPMB statutes, on September 25, 1998. The president of the IOC was informed of the withdrawal. IOC President Samaranch advised on August 21, 1998 that the IOC executive had acknowledged the IBU's withdrawal from the UIPMB at its meeting on August 20, 1998 and recognized the International Biathlon Union as an international Olympic winter sports federation. The IOC president sent a certificate of recognition to that effect that is on display at the IBU Headquarters.

Thus, the era of good cooperation and positive development lasting since 1957 within the UIPMB on behalf of the sport of biathlon had ended. The new international Olympic winter sports federation for biathlon had yet to hold a formal constitutional congress to legalize its seat in Austria based on the Austrian law of associations. It took place on September 25, 1999 in Minsk, Belorussia and ended with all the participants signing a declaration that the seat of the IBU had been founded in Salzburg/AUT.

The separated partners, biathlon and modern pentathlon, survived the dissolution very well. Both of the two disciplines have experienced an extremely positive development since then, and biathlon has been able to progress from being a marginal discipline to a popular one with great broadcast and audience following. Throughout the early years the questions of the sport's viability, whether it was an artificial sport or too "military," were continually and ably answered by the UIPMB President Sven Thofelt by recounting human history and hunting on skis. Although there are clearly historical and modern applications for the military, biathlon was indeed a very natural sport with very old traditions. It has been described as the only combined natural test yet included in international competitions, and the well-known physiologist, Sweden's Per-Olaf Åstrand once commented that, "Biathlon is a fascinating event combining demands of power, endurance, skill on various levels and tactics in an unusually advanced mix."

CHAPTER 4

The U.S. Army

The solution for traveling over snow during the winter hunt by native Americans found a different path than Europe's ancient hunters. Rather than skis, they improvised and developed the slower method of travel by snowshoes. The introduction of skis to North America came via European immigrants, especially those from Scandinavia. The development of skiing in North America is well known and documented with stories of mail-carrying Norwegians who were mistakenly called by such names as "Snowshoe Thompson" and although there were undoubtedly hunts on skis, there is no real clear documentation of the first efforts of the skills related to today's biathlon. However, what is clearly known is that the development of biathlon in the U.S. followed a similar pattern in Scandinavia through its military applications by the U.S. Army.

In November 1939, during the Soviet Union's invasion of Finland, Russian efforts were frustrated following the destruction of two armored divisions by Finnish soldiers on skis. This conflict attracted global attention as the outnumbered and outgunned Finnish soldiers used the difficult local terrain to their advantage, severely hampering the Soviet attacks and embarrassing their military. Upon seeing the effectiveness of these troops, Charles Minot Dole, then the president of the National Ski Patrol, began to lobby the War Department of the need for a similar unit of troops in the United States Army, trained for fighting in winter and mountain warfare. In September 1940, Dole presented his case to General George Marshall, the U.S. Army Chief of Staff, who agreed with Dole's assessment, deciding to create a "Mountain" unit for fighting in harsh terrain. Having learned the lessons of the Winter War between Finland and the Soviet Union, the U.S. Army understood the value of "ski-soldiers." The alpine ski troops of the Axis Powers during the Second World War prompted the U.S. Army to establish the 10th Mountain Division in 1943 and put approximately 20,000 young men on skis at Camp Hale, Colorado. Many of those soldiers became lifelong skiers, and the backbone that amounted to the future of American skiing. It also provided the starting point of biathlon skills in the United States when a group of Finnish veterans of the Winter War were brought to Camp Hale as instructors in winter tactical training on skis. Primary instruction at Camp Hale was focused on alpine ski skills and mountaineering, after the models of the middle European nations of the Alps, but it was the arrival of the group of 40 Finnish junior officers who had escaped Soviet capture that became the catalyst for the introduction of biathlon in the United States.

The 1947 arrival of Lieutenant Colonel Erkki Lahdenpera, one of the key figures in the Weapons Cache Case in which a large number of Finnish Army weapons was hidden around the country in case of another Soviet invasion, is perhaps most responsible for bringing biathlon to life in the United States. He had received his military education and served as a regimental and an infantry battalion commander in Finland during the Finnish-German campaign, where winter warfare tactics made a substantial difference. Like many other Finnish officers, he had narrowly escaped Soviet captivity by fleeing to Sweden as he was about to be arrested at his home in Rovaniemi, and eventually made his way to the United States with his family. After joining the U.S. Army, he was assigned to Ft. Carson, Colorado for duty with the Mountain Training Command at Camp Hale and later in Alaska where he was a technical advisor for winter exercises. A good friend of Finland's historic sports personality Lauri Pihkala, and "Godfather" to his son Peter (Pekka), Colonel Lahdenpera was familiar with the efforts Pihkala had made in training the Finns in biathlon skills and the impact it had in Finland's wars with the Soviet Union. While at Camp Hale he introduced cross-country ski races among the troops for more appropriate winter tactical training and often used his young son Peter to demonstrate proper ski technique. Peter later played an important role in the development of biathlon in the U.S. both as an Olympic competitor and administrator. After the U.S. Army's unpreparedness for winter conditions and strategies in the Korean War, Colonel Lahdenpera was later assigned to the U. S. Army Command and General Staff College where he wrote the U.S. Army training doctrine on Winter Warfare and he could be viewed as the person who introduced biathlon to the U.S. Army through the winter training doctrine.

While the Finnish advisors were having an impact on the training at Camp Hale, the actual organizational foundation of biathlon in the U.S. was set in motion by the first Inter-Service Sports Council (ISSC) meeting held in November of 1947. Representatives of the U.S. Army, Navy and Air Force Occupational Forces in Europe met and agreed to form the ISSC with the objectives of promoting inter-service sports championships, esprit de corps, physical fitness, cooperation, understanding and good will among the U.S. Armed Forces. The famous General Omar Bradley approved the agreement and officially established the ISSC in February 1948. Among the many sports competitions between the U.S. Forces occupying Europe, the ISSC hosted ski championships in the Alps. It was also in February 1948 that the Council of International Military Sport (CISM) was created with the U.S. joining in June of 1951 and the U.S. CISM Executive Agency operating out of U.S. Army Europe (USAREUR). The U.S. Delegation to CISM Championships came primarily from U.S. Armed Forces personnel stationed in Europe.

Following the deactivation of the 10th Mountain Division, the U.S. Army left a smaller group at Camp Hale and created the Mountain and Cold Weather Training Command (MCWTC) in 1952. Although their task was to teach skiing, rock climbing and outdoor survival to various military units, they also had ski races and began biathlon training. Soldiers who had skiing experience at the inter-service championships in Europe were reassigned to Camp Hale as instructors and they encouraged competitions among the troops. In 1956, they organized the first biathlon race in the U.S. to choose a team to compete in a CISM competition in Switzerland. That race on December 18th, 1956 was part of a Nordic Weekend; an open meet in which college skiers from the region were also invited. The events included a 15 kilometers cross-country ski race, ski jumping and a biathlon race. The biathlon race was won by Jim Mahaffey of Western State College at Gunnison, Colorado who beat his college teammate and the best cross-country skier at the time, Mac Miller. Mahaffey's ski time for the 20 kilometers race was one hour, 38 minutes, 29 seconds and he missed seven targets which added 14 minutes to his ski time for a total of one hour, 52 minutes, 29 seconds. Miller missed 16 of his 20 targets adding an additional time of 32 minutes to his ski time to finish 36 seconds behind Mahaffey. Mahaffey, who had previously served in the U.S. Air Force prior to attending Western State College had participated in alpine and two military patrol races during his military service which gave him better familiarity with shooting and skiing.

A second biathlon race was also held at Camp Hale on April 11th, 1957 and was restricted to soldiers in the U.S. Army Mountain and Cold Weather Training Command (MCWTC) who used the military's M-1 Garand rifles. This race was won by Master Sergeant Stanley Walker who skied the course in 1 hour, 34 minutes and 21 seconds, missing 12 targets which added 24 minutes for a total of 1 hour, 58 minutes and 21 seconds. The best ski time of 1 hour, 23 minutes was made by Specialist Third Class Gerald Jenson, however he hit only two targets and thus added an additional 36 minutes to his final time, enabling Walker to win by 39 seconds. In each of the first two U.S. Biathlon races the better shooter was able to defeat the faster skier and from the military standpoint, offered a high incentive for good marksmanship. With the main requisite of a good infantryman being the ability to move and shoot, the biathlon implication for military training was obvious. Along with those training benefits, the logistics of biathlon race organization, physical setup and ranges as well as the manpower required were not normally available within civilian ski organizations but ideal for a military presence. With the re-introduction of biathlon on the Winter Olympic program in 1960, the U.S. Army took a major role in the development of the sport for the nation.

Based on the results of the Camp Hale race of 1957 the U.S. Army named what can be generally regarded as the first U.S. Biathlon team. The race served as the team selection for the group that participated in the International Military Ski Championships (CISM) at Andermatt, Switzerland. Included on that team was Lt. Fritz Holt and MSgt Stan Walker, who both had previous experience in military ski competitions in Europe. German born Hans Wagner who emigrated to the U.S. in 1935 and served as a first sergeant in the 10th Mountain Division at Camp Hale and in Italy, and later employed as a civilian with the USAREUR and the MCWTC as a ski instructor, was selected to be their coach.

After their initial efforts at putting together military ski teams, the U.S. Army considered creating a better organizational structure for recruiting and training soldiers in skills needed for biathlon for the growing number of military competitions, the upcoming scheduled World Biathlon Championships and the reintroduction of biathlon into the Winter Olympic Games in 1960. In 1958 the MCWTC was relocated to Ft. Greely in Alaska and the army made plans to create the U.S. Army Modern Winter Biathlon Training Center (USMWBTC) there. It began to assemble personnel for the project and assigned Colonel Ken Floto to be the commander. Floto, who had learned to ski in the Lake Tahoe area of California and had extensive experience with the 10th Mountain Division during World War II, was given the mission of starting an army biathlon team to compete against the Scandinavian teams. Hans Wagner was hired to be the coach and Captain Arvo Vikstrom, a native of Finland and one of the 40 veterans of the Winter War was assigned as the assistant and rifle coach. The army then issued Army Regulation 28-50 that outlined the requirements and procedures for membership in a training group for biathlon. It stated that candidates "should be expert riflemen who are capable of covering a 13½ mile cross-country ski course in approximately 90 minutes." It gathered up 23 candidates for the team from among the known outstanding skiers and marksmen from Army commands all over the world and transferred them to Ft. Richardson rather than Ft. Greely, where the USMWBTC was decided for its final location. After Hans Wagner and Colonel Floto visited Ft. Greely looking for skiers, runners and all-around athletes, training began in September of 1958, on the Ft. Richardson golf course.

After their initial training at Ft. Richardson the group was narrowed down and sent to Camp Hale for additional training and selection of the team members. They were to participate in the 1st World Biathlon Championships at Saalfelden, Austria. That first U.S. team included 1st Lt. Frederick Holt, MSgt Stanley Walker, Cpl Gunnar Jansen, Pvt Walter Jackson, Pvt Richard Mize and PFC

Lawrence Damon. The team and coaches were to meet up for training with skiers chosen from Europe (USAREUR and USAFE) at Berchtesgaden, Germany for the 1958 CISM Championships at Bardonecchia, Italy before going to Saalfelden. At Bardonecchia the patrol team of Lt. Jack Armstrong, A1C Kaarlo Jokela, along with Mize and Jackson finished 13th in the 25 kilometers race. Following the CISM Championships and before the World Biathlon Championships in Austria the team trained and raced in the Rauschberg-Lauf in Ruhpolding, Germany, long before Ruhpolding became one of the most popular biathlon venues.

At the first championships in Austria, the U.S. team was one of 7 participating nations with 28 athletes starting the single 20 kilometers race. The winner was Sweden's Adolf Wiklund who missed three targets and finished with a time of 1 hour, 33 minutes and 13 seconds. His countryman Olle Gunneriusson was 2nd, also missing three targets to finish only 28 seconds behind Wiklund. The Soviet Union's Viktor Butakov was 3rd, missing 6 targets to finish 33 seconds behind Gunneriusson. Lawrence (Larry) Damon was the top U.S. finisher in 20th place with Richard (Dick) Mize finishing 24th, Walter Jackson 26th and Gunnar Jensen 28th. None of the U.S. competitors were able to hit more than 5 targets which left them with substantial penalty minutes for poor marksmanship added to their ski time. A factor contributing to their poor shooting results was a lack of shooting slings on the military rifles as well as the method of carrying the rifle on the ski course.

After the many learning lessons and working out the details of 1958, the next year showed lots of improvement. News began circulating of the army's biathlon ski team and Colonel Floto began to actively recruit college skiers who were facing mandatory military service of that period. He wanted to make sure college skiers knew of the option before they entered military service and wanted the army to have notice of their skills. Colonel Floto also had the help of Ft. Greely's MCWTC, especially that of legendary MSgt William "Bill" Brown who earned a Silver Star during the 10th Mountain Division's actions in Italy during World War II, a championship racer in the Army ski championships of the U.S. Occupational Forces in Europe and eventual member of the U.S. Ski and Snowboard Hall of Fame. Brown, or "Sarge" as he was known, was the MCWTC First Sergeant and impressed every soldier in the MCWTC with his discipline and challenging physical training. Always looking for ski talent he helped the MCWTC provide seven members of the 1956 U.S. Winter Olympic ski team at Cortina. He also recognized the talent of a young high school skier who was assigned at Ft. Greely. Maurice Paquette was a four-event high school skier from Plymouth, New Hampshire and was taken under Brown's wing. After leading the MCWTC to victory in the USARAL ski championships, Paquette was assigned to the USMWBTC at Ft. Richardson where he qualified for the 1959 CISM

Championships and the 2nd World Biathlon Championships in Bardonecchia, and Courmeyer, Italy. The team's training became more advanced with a new site at Arctic Valley and they used the military M-1 30-06 caliber rifles. At the World Championships "Gus," as Paquette was known to his teammates, achieved an 8th place finish that would not be bested until 1987. Hitting 15 of his 20 targets, the same as the winner Vladimir Melanin, he was only seven minutes, 38 seconds behind. MSgt Brown, who had by then become the chief of mountain operations for the ROTC at Dartmouth College praised his performance and said he was definitely the best skier on the U.S. Biathlon team. The other team members showed improvement as well.

Upon their return to the U.S. the 1959 World Championships team traveled to Squaw Valley for the North American Biathlon Championships that was also to serve as a test run for the upcoming 1960 Winter Olympic Games. This competition attracted the best U.S. athletes from the initial biathlon years as well as a few international competitors. The race, held on March 3rd, 1959 was both a success and an introduction for the U.S. skiers, many who would later become important contributors that helped to foster the growth of the sport. Larry Damon won the race in 1 hour, 48 minutes and 3 seconds, hitting 13 targets, more than six minutes ahead of 2nd and 3rd places. The Army's Dick Mize was 2nd ahead of Swede Klas Lestander who would become the first Olympic Biathlon Gold Medalist the following year. John Burritt was 4th, and the winner of the very first U.S. Biathlon race at Camp Hale in 1956, Jim Mahaffey finished 5th. Gustave Hanson finished 6th, and Maurice Paquette was 7th. University of Utah skier and ROTC student William Spencer finished 8th after hitchhiking his way to California. There was a total of 19 finishers in the race.

Trials for the 1960 U.S. Winter Olympic Biathlon team were held on a course laid out at the top of Tennessee Pass, over 10,000 ft. high near Camp Hale and Leadville, Colorado. Prior to the trials the USMWBTC held a training camp there and invited civilians to attend, including Jim Mahaffey, for his early success in the previous years. The team was selected from a three-race series and consisted of John Burritt, Dick Mize, Gustave Hanson, Peter Lahdenpera and Larry Damon. On the 21st of February 1960, the 20 kilometers race was held at McKinney Creek with 30 starters from 9 nations. Of the five-man U.S. team Burritt had the best result in 14th place hitting 15 of his targets for a total time of one hour, 46 minutes, 36 seconds. Mize was 21st, Hanson 23rd and Damon 24th. Lahdenpera, who qualified for both the cross-country and biathlon teams was forced to decide between the two and did not race the biathlon race, choosing instead the 15 kilometers cross-country race where he finished in 46th place and the 4 x 10 kilometers relay team which was 11th. Sweden's Kas Lestander recorded the 15th best time over the 20-kilometer course but was perfect on each of his 20 rifle shots to win the 1st Winter Olympic Biathlon gold medal with a total time of 1 hour, 33 minutes and 21 seconds. Antti Tyrvaninen of Finland and Alexander Privalov of the Soviet Union were the Silver and Bronze medalists. As in the first two World Biathlon Championship races, two distinct theories emerged regarding tactics in the biathlon competitions; the Soviets and Finns counted heavily on skiing ability while the Swedes relied mainly on shooting skills. With their emphasis on accuracy the medalists were those with the best shooting results and the Swedes were the dominant force during the first years, but the Soviets quickly improved their marksmanship and became a significant power ever since.

After the 1960 Winter Olympic Games, the U.S. Army further developed the USMWBTC center at Ft. Richardson and Colonel Ken Floto continued to contact college skiers encouraging them to join the "Unit" as it was being called by those serving in it. Despite the disbelief among the army recruiters and basic training instructors, Colonel Floto reassured potential members that he could have them transferred to the Unit, as soon as they enlisted in the Army and completed basic training. He had help from George Wilson who was developing and managing sports programs for the U.S. Army and Department of Defense in Washington, DC. Wilson was an assistant professor at the University of Oregon, and then Northwestern University, when the War Department recruited him to develop new sports programs for the occupation forces in Europe starting in 1946. After 11 years of establishing outstanding programs in Europe for the Armed Forces he became deputy sports director for the Department of Army and eventually director of the Interservice Sports Committee Secretariat for the Department of Defense. Of all the amateur sports he helped develop, he was most fond of the U.S. Modern Pentathlon and Biathlon Association, for which he served as secretary from 1961-1972, and eventually as president from 1973-1980. Following the lead of the UIMP and its responsibility for biathlon he encouraged the natural fit for the U.S. Modern Pentathlon Association (USMPA) to include biathlon within the organization, becoming the U.S. Modern Pentathlon and Biathlon Association (USMPBA) as both were "military" multiple discipline sports. Colonel Floto's direct communication to Wilson facilitated orders issued directly from the Pentagon for assignment to the USMWBTC.

In the 1960s the Army's Biathlon Unit at Ft. Richardson, as it became known in the skiing community, was essentially the only place a skier could continue to train and ski seriously outside of a college program. The training became full-time with helicopter visits to local glaciers for summer ski training and visits to Ft. Benning, Georgia for marksmanship training with the army's shooting team. When the change was made to the more accurate, specially fitted Winchester model 70 .243 caliber rifles with customized, glass bedded stocks it was said that if the bullet couldn't find the target, the problem was not with the rifle. In

1961 a new ski coach, Sven Johanson took over the team's training. MSgt Marvin Fitzpatrick, who was the rifle coach since 1959 and the Olympic coach in 1960 continued in that role. Johanson, originally from Korpika, Sweden was North American Ski champion for cross-country in 1955, later winning the national ski title in 1957 and becoming a member of the 1960 U.S. Olympic Team at Squaw Valley after being denied membership on the 1956 team because of his citizenship status. As the participation in the World Biathlon Championships was growing so was the team's international schedule and at the 3rd World Biathlon Championships at Umeå, Sweden, Dick Taylor finished 11th. Colonel Floto took the team of Taylor, Lahdenpera, Wilson, along with Bobby Cragg, Dusan Samardzic and Stanley Zalewki on a training and competitive tour in Scandinavia during the winter of 1961 where Taylor was 6th in an international race at Kuopio, Finland, Lahdenpera finished 11th in the Finnish Championships at Kuovala and Joe-Pete Wilson captured 10th place at the Swedish Championships.

The World Biathlon Championships of 1962 and 1963 saw the Soviet Union and Finland dominate the medal standings with the best U.S. competitors finishing in the mid-20s. In 1962 the same group of Lahdenpera, Wilson, Taylor along with Charles Akers and Marty Hall made an extensive European tour participating in all the big races in Scandinavia. Colonel Floto explained in an interview with the Norwegian newspapers while attending the Norwegian Championships at Elverum, while the Scandinavians were experiencing a dramatic interest and participation in biathlon, "There aren't more than a few participants in the U.S., however there was growing interest in cross-country skiing. Our boys ski fast enough but need to improve their shooting. They only have a few races at home and we are optimistic that our racing here in Norway and Sweden will prepare us for the World Championships in Finland." He went on to say, "We haven't come here for sightseeing, but to learn. The tracks are fine, and the team is in bed at 10 o'clock. The Elgstua won't be selling much beer while we are here. Our team is disciplined and serious with high hopes for the future." In those Norwegian championships Peter Lahdenpera finished 5th behind the future World Champion Olav Jordet and later was 10th in the Finish Championships at Rovaniemi. At the famous Forvarsrennet at Oslo, out of 225 starters all of the American team finished in the top 26 places, causing a stir among the Norwegian press when it was discovered Joe-Pete Wilson with 16 hits had missed his chance for a top finish when he broke a ski, but still finished 22nd.

However, at the 1964 Winter Olympic Games with 14 nations and 54 competitors participating, Charles Akers, who was the NCAA ski champion twice (1959 and 1961) and a member of the 1960 Olympic Nordic team finished 16th at Innsbrück with 18 hits. While at the University of Maine, he had been invited by Colonel Floto to join the biathlon team in Alaska following his college graduation. As an indication of the quality of the USMWTC athletes during that time, Joe-Pete Wilson and Peter Lahdenpera both skied in the 1960 Olympic Nordic races. Lahdenpera was later a member of the 1964 Olympic Biathlon team, while Dick Taylor did not qualify for the biathlon team but raced in the Nordic races at Innsbrück. The members of the Army's Biathlon Unit were a collection of the best cross-country skiers in the nation at the time and during the 1964 Olympic trials many were trying to qualify for both the biathlon and cross-country teams. Also racing for the U.S. at Innsbrück were William Spencer who raced in the 1959 North American and Pre-Olympic test at Squaw Valley as a University of Utah college skier and Paul Renne who had recently graduated from Montana State University in Bozeman. Renne who had skied at MSU was also a winner of the Junior National Small-bore Rifle Championships and became a member of the All-Army Rifle team in 1966.

The period between the 1964 and 1968 Winter Olympic Games saw the USMWBTC continue to provide the basis for U.S. Biathlon and a place for collegiate skiers to continue their ski careers while serving in the military. Improvements in training better prepared the U.S. teams for ever-improving international competition. Sven Johanson's tough and innovative training principles and knowledge from Sweden turned the biathlon training at Ft. Richardson's Arctic Valley site into a highly effective center. The early ski training at the abandoned Independence Mines in the Talkeetna Mountains near Palmer were legendary and became a common thread to which the alumni of the biathlon unit held dear. Johanson brought the first roller skis from Sweden which were at the time simply wooden skis with wheels. He also designed and fabricated early ski trail grooming systems that helped improve ski technique. The USMWTC office expanded to include its own arms room and gunsmith, a supply sergeant, sports medic, a logistics sergeant and clerk. It also had use of an indoor range in the basement of the building that housed the athletes.

The mid 1960s also began a time when former USMWBTC athletes continued biathlon after their release from the army and broke into the biathlon community as civilians. This at first presented a problem since army funding, which had up until that time provided all the resources necessary for international competition, could not fund civilians. This first occurred during the first U.S. National Championships at Rosendale, New York when Charles Kellogg, who had been discharged from the army just three weeks before, won the race. As a civilian he was not able to accompany the team to Europe since no other funding was available. Kellogg went on to race in the 1968 Winter Olympic Games at Grenoble in the cross-country ski events, however this situation of civilians eventually prompted the USMPBA to greater involvement with the biathlon side of the organization.

Despite being in Europe for the annual CISM competition, military funding shortages prevented the U.S. team from participating in the 6th World Biathlon Championships at Elverum, Norway. The following year at Garmisch-Parten-kirchen the team of Ed Williams, John Ehrensbeck, Allan Small and William Spencer participated in the individual race that had been revised to a single range at 150 meters with two stages of shooting from the prone position and two from the standing position. Spencer, Williams, Ehrensbeck and Gary Varnam also finished 11th in the first World Biathlon Championships relay. At the height of the Cold War era, the U.S. also did not send a team to the 1967 Championships at Altenburg in Eastern Germany.

The 1968 Winter Olympic Games at Grenoble, France represented a return to normalcy for the U.S. team. The number of participating nations had climbed to 16 with 77 starters for the individual race. Ralph Wakely led the U.S. athletes with a 27th place while William Spencer, Ed Williams and Jon Chaffee finished 37th, 45th and 49th. Williams, a former Dartmouth skier was joined by Wakely, Spencer and John Ehrensbeck on the U.S. team's highpoint with an 8th place finish in the relay. A rule change reducing the penalty lap to 150 meters helped to make the relay race more exciting.

As the next quadrennial towards the 1972 Winter Olympic Games began, the team switched to a smaller, high velocity .223 caliber rifles, the same ammunition that was being used in the army's M-16 standard rifle. Larger calibers were not necessary for the shorter-range distance and the .223 caliber was faster and more accurate, later becoming popular in international competitions. As the Vietnam War continued, ever-increasing numbers were being drafted and many colle-giate skiers and high school skiers were included in the massive numbers being inducted into the Armed Forces. A continuous supply of new athletes appeared at the Army's Biathlon Unit in Alaska. Many were ROTC graduates which required a longer term of service than the two-year draft commitment. Also, after being released from service and training at the USMWBTC some athletes continued to participate in the sport. The 1969 World Championship team was an example in which two prior members, Ed Williams and Jay Bowerman qualified for the team and this expanded the financial problem of civilians. Other members of that team were USMWBTC members Peter Karns, a University of Utah skier, John Morton and Dennis Donahue, both Middlebury skiers.

Donahue, Morton and Karns were joined on the 1970 World Championships team by Terry Aldrich, a University of St. Lawrence skier and Bill Kendall who were also assigned to the Army Biathlon Unit. By this time the Armed Forces Sports Program began to assign skiers from the other branches of military service to the unit also, so airmen and even a sailor from the U.S. Navy were included in the training. One of the most unique was a Navy UDT (later renamed SEALS) team member, John Hall who was a high school skier from upstate New York.

Nicknamed "Frogman" by his teammates at the Unit, he became the subject of many cherished stories among the alumni from that period. That time also saw the intensity of the war in Vietnam begin to have an impact on both the military and society in general and the USMWTC did not escape its impact. Although the skiers assigned to the Army Biathlon Unit were essentially guaranteed avoiding the war, however, due to their military career requirements the officers were less safe than the enlisted soldiers. Immediately following the 1968 Winter Olympic Games in France, William Spencer who had spent more time at the unit in Alaska than anyone, was reassigned to Vietnam just after the famous Tet Offensive by the North Vietnamese. In the spring of 1970 John Morton was also sent to Vietnam for a year. For the most part, the assignment in Alaska to the USMWBTC was an extraordinary duty and a great experience for those with a ski background. Even collegiate skiers like University of Wyoming's Tom Ruhkala who had already served 6 months in Vietnam was able to contact his congressman while home on leave and get reassigned to the USMBTC, and then qualify for the 1972 CISM team after only a month of training in Alaska.

The number of participating athletes at the World Biathlon Championships of 1971 had increased to a total of 93, making the event even more competitive. It was also the first time that the Soviet Union had to face serious competition from within their sphere. Although the Soviets still were the dominate force, the Norwegians and Finns saw East Germany's (DDR) Deiter Speer win the gold medal which might have been considered an advance look at the future. The East Germans eventually became a powerful nation in the sport. The U.S. team of Dexter (Terry) Morse, Dennis Donahue, Terry Aldrich and Mike Romine finished in the middle of the field with Morse having the best individual finish at 28th. The same team finished 11th in the relay race.

Back in Alaska the members of the USMWBTC began to feel the impact of negativity against the military for the ongoing war in Vietnam. It was a microcosm for what was happening nationwide, and this caused some pressure on the athletes both within the public and within the army. Many in the regular forces saw the biathlon team as not "real soldiers" and escaping the sacrifice expected of those involved in Vietnam. They were often criticized by the leadership who felt that the athletes seen running around the Ft. Richardson base in their blue training uniforms were exempt from normal "army" duties. They were not allowed to enter base track and field championships after having won nearly every race for many years. Even some local civilian running and ski races created a separate "military" competitor class to prevent them from winning the top prizes in the traditional races such as the Equinox marathon, Gold Discovery race and the Mt. Marathon hill climb, events they traditionally still won. In addition to the changes in the general atmosphere towards the military, the USMWBTC began to lose the internal support of the military leadership. The advocates such as MSgt Brown, Colonel Floto and those that followed such as Captain Vikstrom and Major Helinski were activists that had developed the USMWBTC, retired, and were replaced by leaders without ski or biathlon experience and lacked the passion of the early promoters. By the time the Vietnam War was winding to its conclusion so too did the Army's interest in keeping the USMWBTC vibrant and functional.

The 1972 Olympic season represented the final year of the USMBTC's success. After bringing home Maj William Spencer from Vietnam to be the team leader, the trials for the team were held at Jackson, Wyoming. Just before the trials were to begin, the U.S. Army's fast withdrawal of troops from Vietnam suddenly required a drastic reduction of forces and offered many drafted soldiers an early release. Several of those assigned at the unit took the offer and left, with only a few of the new civilians attending the trials. However, there were several other former members who did try out successfully for the team as a part of the U.S. Olympic Biathlon Training Squad which was funded by the USOC. Three of them, Peter Karns, Dennis Donahue and Jay Bowerman came from that group. Additionally, Peter Lahdenpera who had been inactive in biathlon since 1964 returned and qualified along with two members of the unit, Dexter Morse and John Morton. Lahdenpera found the 150 meter single range much easier than the four ranges and four different target distances prior to 1965, to his liking. The mix of athletes on the Olympic team came from the 1972 trials procedure that was a deliberate attempt to focus on the relay at Sapporo, Japan and a complicated system of overlapping between four races, two of which were "relay format" races and two individual races. John Morton was the only athlete chosen from the individual races, but the team did experience success when the U.S. team of Karns, Morse, Donahue and Bowerman finished in 6th place, 5 minutes and 40 seconds behind the Soviet Union with only one penalty. Peter Karns also equaled John Burritt's U.S. 1960 best U.S. Olympic result at 14th place.

In early 1972 the military draft was suspended and by the summer of 1972 nearly all the former college and experienced skiers had left the army. The USMBTC now lacked access to a pool of drafted skiers to replace them. With only a few remaining officers and enlisted left, it sought to find potential athletes within the ranks of the 172nd Infantry (Artic Ranger) companies at Ft. Richardson. By the start of the 1973 winter season, there were no previous members of the unit left and only one new experienced skier, West Point graduate and Idaho junior skier, Lyle Nelson assigned to it. With the World Biathlon Championships to be held at Lake Placid that year, the unit came to the trials with mostly inexperienced skiers just recently introduced to biathlon. Only two qualified for the team in the junior category, which the U.S. entered for the first time. Marvin Macabe, a Navaho Indian from Arizona and Bob Beaman, an excellent shooter from Ohio qualified for the team. The senior team of Dennis Donahue, John Morton, Jay Bowerman, Ken Alligood, George Tuthill and Art Stegen were all civilians but former members of the Unit from previous years. The 1973 winter season was the final effort by the USMBTC.

CHAPTER 5

The National Guard

Upon their return to Alaska in the spring of 1973 the leadership and remaining members of the USMWBTC learned that the army was considering a decision to discontinue and disband the "unit." This news was disheartening to not only those who were still assigned there, but those who had also served in the program. Walter Williams of Rosendale, New York, who had organized the first U.S. National Biathlon Championships at his resort hotel and was at the time the vice president of the U.S. Modern Pentathlon and Biathlon Association (USMPBA), acted immediately with the hope of saving the program. George Wilson, the USMPBA president who was also the director of the Inter-Service Sports Committee Secretariat for the Department of Defense could not be helpful due to his conflict of interest between his military employer and his USMPBA status.

In a lengthy letter of May 23, 1973 to Secretary of the Army Howard Callaway, Mr. Williams outlined the history of the "unit" and its contribution to the U.S. Winter Olympic biathlon teams stating that "no civilian not a product of the USWBTC had ever qualified for a senior international team" and that biathlon, "more than any sports, requires skills that the Army seeks to develop in every soldier: strength, endurance, stamina, rifle marksmanship and the ability to perform well under pressure." He received a reply from Major General Verne Bowers that gave little hope by saying that economics, including the important factor of personnel and other influences had dictated special consideration of the overall subject of continuing support of the USMWTC, a clear reference to the army's inability to recruit the necessary talented individuals to sustain the program. He also stated that a final decision would be forthcoming.

A second letter from Major General Verne on September 7, 1973 stated "It was determined that the activity was not supportable in view of diminishing financial and manpower resources. Accordingly, the USMWBTC activities were discontinued effective September 1st, 1973." The current members of the unit were reassigned back to their previous units and Lyle Nelson was reassigned to Ft. Carson, Colorado. Once again Mr. Williams immediately acted, suggesting that the army relocate the center to be jointly administered by the U.S. Army and the

USMPBA at Ft. Douglas and Park City, Utah. This proposal was also met with rejection, however, concerning the question of the biathlon supplies and equipment at Ft. Richardson, the army was willing to donate to the USMPBA those items, which included 20 biathlon rifles.

Prior to the announcement of the discontinuation of the USMWBTC in Alaska in the fall of 1972 former members of the unit, Dennis Donahue and George Tuthill were looking for a training location in Vermont for their preparations for the 1973 World Biathlon Championships tryouts at Lake Placid. The Vermont National Guard had been in the process of establishing its own biathlon program when Art Gibbs, a Vermont state legislator, suggested Ethan Allen Firing Range. When the Middlebury resident who was familiar with many of the former Middlebury ski team athletes who had been members of the USMWBTC, became aware of the U.S. Army's plans to discontinue the program in Alaska, he contacted Major General Reginald M. Cram, Vermont's National Guard Adjutant General, suggesting the National Guard support a biathlon program. Considering the heightened interest in Vermont skiing following the success of the Cochran family, including the gold medal performance of Barbara in 1972, Major General Cram invited Gibbs to his office along with the two local Vermont former members of the USMWBTC, Donahue and Tuthill. At that meeting the Vermont National Guard's facilities manager Major Howard Buxton invited the athletes chosen to represent the USA for the World Championships for some pre-championship training at the Ethan Allen Firing Range (EAFR) at Jericho, Vermont where he had a rudimentary range constructed for that training.

In late September Walter Williams began another step in helping to move the biathlon program from the U.S. Army a to new home. After learning of the meeting with MG Cram and the Vermont legislator Gibbs, he began correspondence and coordination of the transfer of the former USMWBTC's equipment and rifles. At an emergency meeting of the USMPBA on September 30th, 1973 in Washington, Mr. Williams suggested that the USMPBA take ownership of the USMWBTC equipment, however there was the issue of a site to store and manage the equipment and supplies. Aware of the growing interest in Vermont, he wrote to MG Cram suggesting that it become the custodian for the equipment with ownership remaining with the USMPBA. MG Cram responded very favorably on October 25th with an official invitation for the national team to train at EAFR and suggested that the Vermont National Guard was considering building a biathlon training site on its 11,000 acres of varied and challenging terrain.

At the same time as the events were developing at EAFR in Vermont, Camp Ripley in Minnesota, in conjunction with its Winter Ops program, was also developing a biathlon site. The Winter Ops program included a two-week exchange with the Norwegian Home Guard, which alternated between Camp Ripley and a

Norwegian site. During this exchange, biathlon training and competition gained the attention of Colonel Clinton "Buck" Johnson who was an avid skier and who organized shooting matches at Camp Ripley. As an offshoot of the Winter Ops program a biathlon range and ski course were developed at Camp Ripley for biathlon training with the Norwegian troops. At that time, the facilities at Camp Ripley were somewhat better than EAFR, however despite Minnesota's interest, Vermont provided the early leadership for National Guard biathlon development. The direction of biathlon activities immediately had to struggle over the issue of rules. Biathlon was still a large bore (caliber) event and this caused problems for the National Guard program since the specialized biathlon rifles were rare. Some pushed for using military rifles and equipment, however it was clear that they were inadequate for the demands of biathlon accuracy and participation. The UIPMB's 1976 decision to change to small bore (caliber) by 1978 helped to determine the future direction for the National Guard program.

Promoted to Colonel, Howard Buxton became the Vermont Army National Guard's Facilities manager and immediately set out to build the site Major General Cram had earlier suggested to Walter Williams. He also took control of the former USMWBTC's equipment at Camp Johnson, the Vermont National Guard's headquarters. The USMPBA needing a site and organizer for the 1974 World Championships team trials, Colonel Buxton offered EAFR as the site and the National Guard as the race organization. Also, in 1974 at the Adjutant General's Conference in Washington, D.C. Major General Cram issued a challenge to New Hampshire and Maine to compete in a biathlon race at EAFR. The Minnesota adjutant general overheard the conversation and wanted to be involved also. Major General Cram tasked Colonel Buxton to plan it. Colonel Buxton spread the word at NGB Headquarters and met with Utah's chief of staff, who also wanted to be involved. Casual conversation at the AG level gradually spread interest in the challenge.

During the winter of 1974 Colonel Buxton prepared for the Vermont National Guard to host the U.S. team trials and National Championships at EAFR however poor snow conditions forced the relocation of the event to Burke Mountain in northeastern Vermont. He arranged for the transportation of targets and constructed a temporary range near the alpine ski area and housed the team at the ski area accommodations. Prior to travel to the World Championships at Minsk in the Soviet Union, the team stayed at the National Guard's old helicopter hanger, Bldg. 890 at the Burlington airport and left for Europe from Montreal. Without the National Guard's help, and the last-minute efforts by USMPBA President George Wilson to find the funding resources for the trip, it would most likely not have happened. Later that winter EAFR hosted an unofficial National Guard Championships with five states attending. In 1975 after making improvements to its site and developing a new small-bore biathlon range on West Hill, the Vermont National Guard again hosted the U.S. National Championships and team trials and the first official National Guard Championships with seven states (VT, MA, NH, MN, UT, MT, OR) participating.

The growth and development of the National Guard's role in biathlon was also greatly helped by its involvement in the 1980 Olympics. Coinciding with the closing of the USMWBTC and the early development of National Guard biathlon, the IOC and USOC were in the planning stages for the 1980 Winter Olympic Games at Lake Placid. The Lake Placid Organizing Committee began a search for a chief of competition and event support for the biathlon events. Due to the lack of cohesion within the USMPBA, Al Merrill who was responsible for all the Nordic events, proposed Colonel Buxton to be that person. Colonel Buxton and the New York Army National Guard's involvement, which provided range and medical support for the biathlon events at the 1980 Winter Olympic Games, raised the visibility of the National Guard's role in the development of biathlon and a role in the creation of the United States Biathlon Association, separate from Pentathlon. Upon the separation from the USMPBA in 1980, Colonel Buxton was elected president of the new national governing body.

As the level of biathlon development accelerated following the establishment of the National Guard Championships, Colonel Homer Pearson, the NGB marksmanship coordinator began to take an interest in the biathlon program and in 1979 moved towards providing the first full-time staff support through the creation of an NGB biathlon coordinator as an AGR (Active Guard and Reserve) position in Vermont. Former USMWBTC and two-time Olympic team member LTC William "Bill" Spencer was selected for that position. This gave full-time direction to the National Guard's biathlon program. From 1975 to 1985 part-time ADSW (Active Duty Special Work) coaching was made available with the primary focus on developing biathlon programs within the states, however 1986 was to become the pivotal year for the National Guard biathlon program.

Between 1974 and 1985 the U.S. Armed services did not participate in the annual CISM Ski Games. During that time, the active duty branches and Armed Forces Sports vigorously opposed participation and representation in CISM by the National Guard and Reserve forces. By 1985 international pressure and a favorable legal opinion sought by Colonel John Abair, the VTARNG (Vermont Army National Guard) training officer, that was favorable to reserve participation, helped to end that opposition and in 1986 the National Guard sent its first team to the CISM Games at Ruhpolding, Germany. This international mission gave legitimacy and justification for many elements of the National Guard program and the appropriate funding that then permitted it to grow and become a true replacement for the former USMWBTC.

1986 was a pivotal year for National Guard biathlon for more than just its CISM participation. The previous year John Abair, a major at the time and the director of the National Guard Biathlon program took a team of National Guard athletes to a competition and training as guests of the Norwegian Home Guard at Camp Terningmoen in Norway. Much of Norway's biathlon program was in fact mostly organized by their Home Guard and biathlon was aligned with their shooting federation. That team participated in a few local club races and Olympic team veteran Lyle Nelson, a captain at the time, won most of the races. While in Norway the team was invited to participate in a World Cup event at Holmenkollen. After achieving sanction from the USBA, the team enjoyed the "once-in-a-lifetime experience" of racing at the top level of the sport. Nelson finished just outside the top 50 in both the individual and sprint races. During that trip, the National Guard athletes and coaches experienced a new level of the sport, including lighted ski trails, club programs that included youth shooting from Styrofoam rifle rests and brought back with them three important well-illustrated manuals: Manual for Race Organizers, Manual for Coaches and Training Manual for Athletes. Upon return, Abair commented that the experience gained from the trip had better prepared the National Guard for their eventual participation in CISM. That trip to Norway, along with several other coincidental factors converged at the same time, helping to promote the growth of the National Guard program. Although it wasn't the primary factor, the international mission of CISM encouraged recruitment of talented athletes, hiring of additional administrative and coaching staff, improvements to facilities, development of a more refined program with direction and clearly defined goals, and the emergence of an infrastructure that supported the National Guard's collective biathlon mission.

In 1983 a National and Olympic team member and one of the last members of the USMWBTC, Lyle Nelson had joined the National Guard and within the next few years other Olympic and National team members joined. In 1986 the top U.S. junior athlete Curtis Schreiner joined, and this group of athletes became the core of what would lead to the drastic improvement by National Guard athletes from the participatory level to higher "performance" levels and would be the heart of the teams that competed in CISM during the late 1980s and early 1990s. It also served as the catalyst for other talented athletes to join the National Guard that included women. Pam Nordheim, who was one of the earliest women members of U.S. National Biathlon team and first U.S. Winter Olympic Biathlon team that included women became the first U.S. medalist in biathlon at the 1986 CISM Games.

In 1988 updated Army Regulations 215-2, Army Sports Program and 350-10, Training/Competitive Biathlon, gave the National Guard regulatory authority for biathlon in the military. These documents allowed for funding athletes and resourcing of equipment, supplies, facilities and authorization of state-level teams. A major deciding element for athletes to join the National Guard was the fact that at the same time as athletes were being funded for their biathlon activities, a program with coaching and international participation had also emerged, along with continued development and improvements to facilities, including such innovations as the first roller-ski loop connected to the shooting range. Full-time training was permitted at EAFR with housing provided. Full-time coaches were also hired, and the National Guard Sports office was expanded to include an important administrative sergeant, and a secretary.

In the years between 1983 and 1990 as the newly-created U.S. Biathlon Association struggled to establish the required resources necessary for success, the National Guard biathlon program continued to improve both in quality and quantity and became the dominant force in U.S. Biathlon. In 1992 former USMWBTC, World Championships team member and Olympic team coach Art Stegen was hired as the National Guard coach and the numbers and abilities of the athletes in both the state and international programs improved steadily. At the 1988 Winter Olympic Games there were two members of the National Guard's biathlon program on the U.S. team. By 1998 at Nagano and 2002 at Salt Lake there were five National Guardsmen on the team of eight. The National Guard athletes were successful in winning medals on 9 occasions during the period between 1987 and 2002. In 1989, 1993 and 2001 the Vermont National Guard hosted the CISM Games at EAFR in Jericho, Vermont. Prior to the wars in Iraq and Afghanistan the National Guard Championships, which was rotated between Camp Ripley and EAFR, became the largest biathlon race in the country with more than 125 competitors from 33 states. The National Guard also led the way in range development at other locations and became a leader in the certification of biathlon officials. Through the efforts of Howard Buxton who had been promoted to general and was a member of the U.S. Olympic Committee and the IBU Working Group for separation from the UIMPMB, Major General Donald Edwards, Adjutant General of the Vermont National Guard who also served as the president of the U.S. Biathlon Association, and Colonel Alan Nye, the VTARNG facilities manager, the National Guard provided considerable assistance to the development of the U.S. Biathlon Association, moving both the quality and quantity of athletes and programs to higher levels.

The National Guard biathlon program made continual and constant progress towards accomplishing its mission and achieving its objectives. Much of the efforts by Colonel Buxton, Colonel Abair, Colonel Nye and Major General Edwards were directed towards securing the three most important elements for that progress: athletes, opportunity and guidance, and ensuring that the adequate resources were available. They clearly understood these needs when they charted the program's direction, enhanced its operational budget, acquired its human resources and developed the facilities at EAFR. However, despite the consistent progress, setbacks and temporary interruptions were always potential threats to the program and the most dangerous threat was interrupted or inadequate funding, a constant struggle for the USBA program. They understood that improvements in performance and achievement of the organizational goals were impossible if funding was problematic. The most immediate consequence of limited financial resources is a reduction of the training and racing opportunities for the athletes and can have multiple consequences: fewer supported training days in a specific training environment with appropriate facilities, less supervised and specific training, with fewer rounds fired, causing a gradual reduction in training effectiveness, becoming more generalized, less specific and without the motivating group influences such as peer evaluation, introduction of personal economic and social distractions, and changes in priorities and commitment, all of which would result in reductions in performance and performance potential. Furthermore, these results would compound themselves into more serious potential outcomes, such as a team becoming a transitory group instead of a functional team, the important role of developing a "culture" for success the leadership and motivation become unsupportive of that success, the personal and team performance fails to improve or declines, apathy sets in and organizational support weakens and as the organizational support weakens, interest in the program and its mission also weaken, making recruiting more difficult, and rising questions about the value of program, which increase funding difficulties.

Once athletes no longer see a mutual exchange of benefits or mutually shared goals between themselves and the program, losing the belief that their association or membership in the program will be useful in achieving their personal goals, it leaves little reason for them to remain in it. Despite the fact that the functional authorities at HQ USARAL were not completely supportive or were unclear about the mission and purpose of the USMWBTC, seeing it as not a traditional military unit and its members were not performing traditional military jobs, and despite the fact that its members were soldiers of unique abilities, the greatest contributing factor to the USMWBTC never really being able to fully realize its potential was the suspension of the military draft in 1972, losing its access to its source of athletes required for success. As their program expanded, the National Guard recognized this, providing their athletes opportunity, guidance, and ensuring that the adequate resources were available. As the leader of the Vermont National Guard, Major General Edwards stated his program guidance was "to put National Guard athletes on the Olympic Team. My vision for biathlon is that the United States become a recognized world biathlon power. We will accomplish this through continual improvement by U.S. biathletes in international competitions, culminating with medal performances in the Winter Olympics. We must be convinced that we can achieve this national objective through the organization and infrastructure provided by the National Guard."

Nonetheless the wars in Iraq and Afghanistan eventually began to have an impact on the National Guard's efforts. The National Guard faced the very same problems in acquiring athletes, as did the USMWBTC in 1973. Individuals with such abilities do not normally exist in the traditional National Guard population. Without athletes of high performance standards, accomplishing the biathlon mission was impossible and therefore unlike the draft of the 1960-70s it required efforts to recruit them. Since 1986 the National Guard enjoyed a steady flow of athletes into the program, mainly for the quality of its program and the benefits made available. Recruiting was mainly about providing opportunities for the few athletes available by getting them into or keeping them in the sport and its systems, and to grow within the system, by helping them to improve and develop their abilities to their full potential. Providing the appropriate opportunities to the athletes was the most important element to recruiting, and within the National Guard structure, critical to getting them at all. In addition to having the climate, facilities, and equipment necessary for the pursuit of the sport, the athletes also need opportunity in terms of time and money. Biathlon is a sport that is particularly environmentally and equipment intensive, and without access to the appropriate snow and weather conditions, on a timely and consistent basis or the required specific equipment, skills development will be prevented or delayed substantially. The National Guard was able to offer those resources to aspiring athletes.

Once the National Guard fell under heavy reliance for mobilization to the wars in the Middle East, numbers fell dramatically at the National Guard Championships and recruiting athletes for biathlon became increasingly difficult. Although most of the active athletes were protected from deployment, some retiring and a few others who were left unprotected and those without high level skills were deployed. At the same time the USBA was improving its funding resources so that many aspiring athletes no longer saw the need to join the National Guard for the support it could offer, especially considering the perceived risk of deployment. The National Guard's role gradually shifted from that of a primary to secondary one, becoming mainly a bridging program for developing younger athletes from junior to senior levels and from domestic to international performance standards. Although the National Guard continues to put its athletes on the National, World Championships and Winter Olympic teams its focus in recent years has been the National Guard Championships and supporting the various annual international military competitions in Italy, Germany, Spain, Argentina, and Chile. It also continues to send representative teams to the CISM Ski Championships and

CISM quadrennial World Military Games.

Although the National Guard has been the center of biathlon activity in the military, in 1996 the U.S. Army decided to increase its support for competitive sports as a public relations effort. Noticing the success of the National Guard biathlon program it created the Army's World Class Athlete Program (WCAP) at Ft. Carson, Colorado. Although the army had always supported high performance within the ranks on an individual case basis, the WCAP was a more formalized attempt to organize and centrally manage the best soldier-athletes with the specific goal of qualifying as many as possible for selection to U.S. Olympic teams. Managed through the Moral, Welfare and Recreation (MWR) Command in Washington it assigned athletes meeting the program standards of National and International competitive levels and recommendations from the National Governing Body for the sport for two years of temporary duty to the WCAP office at Ft. Carson for full-time training. Recognizing that coaching and facilities dependency was critical for the program to be successful most athletes were then assigned temporary duty with their sport's national teams and coaches in the best environment for reaching the Olympic team goals.

As the WCAP related to biathlon, it recognized that the National Guard was already successful at the same goals. The MWR command and the National Guard worked out an agreement to mobilize National Guard athletes to regular full-time military status with temporary assignment to the National Guard biathlon office for management, coaching and training. Since the National Guard coaches were in an active duty reserve status (AGR) the National Guard did not want to lose those assets following the two-year temporary duty with the WCAP so another agreement between the MWR and the National Guard assigned a National Guard coach to the WCAP group and assigned a WCAP coach, who would be temporary, recommended by the National Guard to take over the National Guard program. It was also agreed that after first referring to the WCAP athletes as U.S. Army athletes in all the media information, the WCAP would identify those athletes as National Guard soldiers as well. Biathlon became the most successful of all the sports in the WCAP program when 5 athletes qualified as Winter Olympic team members and raced at Nagano, Japan in 1998 and again at Salt Lake City, Utah in 2002. However, as the National Guard's role shifted, so too did the WCAP program. By 2010 at Vancouver, Canada, Jeremy Teela was the only military member of the U.S. Olympic Biathlon team and at Sochi, Russia, there weren't any. By then the primary program for biathlon had shifted to the U.S. Biathlon Association.

CHAPTER 6

The Pentathlon and Biathlon Association

Every sport needs an organizational body that governs its rules and standards. Just as the international governing body evolved from local military leadership to the IOC, UIPMB and the IBU responsibility, the development of biathlon in the United States followed a similar pattern. When the U.S. Army held the first-ever biathlon race at Camp Hale, there was no specific National Governing Body (NGB), which had authority for biathlon. The army organized the race under the rules that had been developed in Sweden. After the UIPM 1957 declaration for responsibility for biathlon and the 1958 decision to include it in the Winter Olympic Games in 1960, the general rules were universally established. But in the beginning, there was no other governing authority for biathlon in the United States other than the U.S. Army. For the 1959 pre-Olympic test race and North American Championships at Squaw Valley, the National Ski Association provided guidance and technical assistance through what might be considered a "quasi-sanction" of the event. During the 1960 Winter Olympic Games the IOC and UIPM were the authority and regulatory bodies, however from 1961 until 1965 it was again the U.S. Army that acted as the governing body, and organizing the team trials and providing support for the U.S. team that participated in the World Championships and 1964 Winter Olympic Games.

The first steps on the path towards developing a National Governing Body for biathlon in the U.S. could be considered taken when Walter Williams of Rosendale, New York proposed hosting the first U.S. National Championships for biathlon at his resort hotel. The Williams Lake resort had already a long ski history. With his Finnish heritage, Walter's father Gust Williams was chiefly responsible for establishing skiing in Rosendale by bringing together a group of Scandinavians, mostly Norwegians, in 1936 and formed the Telemark Ski Club. They began racing on trails at Williams Lake and ski jumping at nearby Joppenbergh in 1937. Although ski activity fell dormant during and following WWII, Walter reorganized the club as the Rosendale Nordic Ski Club in 1963. His son, Edward, became a member of the Dartmouth College Ski team and was enrolled in the ROTC program where he met MSgt William "Bill" Brown, the former sergeant in charge of the MCWTC of Camp Hale and Ft. Greely, and USAREUR ski champion who then headed the ROTC mountain operations at Dartmouth College. He advised Ed about the biathlon program and eventually recommended him for assignment to the USMWBTC.

In 1965 Captain Norman Helinski, the USMWBTC commander contacted Al Merrill, the ski coach at Dartmouth College and indicated that he wanted to have the trial races for that year's biathlon team in the northeastern part of the country. Merrill, a U.S. ski team coach had been the co-chief of course for the nordic events at Innsbrück, Austria for the 1964 Winter Olympic Games where Captain Helinski had met him. Knowing Walter Williams through his son Ed, who was assigned to the unit in Alaska, Merrill contacted Walter and put him in touch with Helinski. Recognizing that the U.S. Army was essentially the controlling authority for biathlon and there had never been recognized or sanctioned National Championships for the sport, Walter Williams put the wheels in motion to hold the first biathlon National Championships by inviting the USMWBTC to hold its team trial race at Rosendale with the dual purpose of also holding a National Championships for biathlon. For official recognition of the event he turned to the U.S. National Ski Association (NSA), which then established a biathlon committee with Capt. Norman Helinski of the USMWBTC as the chairman. Also a member of the nine-man committee was George Wilson, deputy sports director for the Dept. of the Army and secretary of the U.S. Modern Pentathlon Association. The ski association provided technical support for the ski part of the competition; designating Tauno Pulkkinen and John Wictorin, both well-known within the NSA as the chief of course and chief of timing. Birger Torrissen acted as the technical delegate, having previously served in that role for the 1960 Winter Olympic Games at Squaw Valley.

The NSA had no experience in the shooting part and therefore did not appear to have a strong interest in biathlon. For the range functions and marksmanship scoring Walter recruited Sergeant Major Alfred O'Neill, the marksmanship coach at the U.S. Military Academy at West Point to be chief of range, target scoring and safety. On January 31st, 1965 17 athletes that included 8 current and 5 former members from the USMWBTC in Alaska, 2 from the U.S. Military Academy at West Point and 2 civilians participated in the first U.S. National Biathlon Championships. Three of the competitors were members of the 1964 Winter Olympic team.

Charles Kellogg, who had been released from the U.S. Army and the USMWBTC in Alaska just three weeks prior to the event was victorious over his former teammates by winning the first National Biathlon Championship title. A former Williams College skier, Kellogg used superior marksmanship, missing only 4 targets, combined with the 3rd fastest ski time to finish ahead of Lt. William Spencer of the USMWBTC, who also missed 4 targets in 2nd place and Ford

Hubbard, who had the best shooting score of 3 misses in 3rd. Hubbard had also recently been released from the U.S. Army and the USMWBTC as well. The fastest skier of the day finished with a time of 1 hour, 18 minutes, 35 seconds, just over two minutes faster than Kellogg, but he hit only 5 of his targets for a total penalty of 30 minutes to finish 7th overall. Once again, as in most of the early biathlon races, the fastest skier was not able to win. Among the others participating in the race was former USMWBTC member Marty Hall who later became the well-known coach of the U.S. Ski Team. Walter Williams' son Ed had the second fastest ski time of the day but finished 9th after he hit only 4 of the 20 targets.

Important questions followed the completion of the first National Biathlon Championship race that would not find immediate answers but did open the door to an issue that would need to be answered in the near future. The first question of who would support civilian athletes that qualified for a world championship team led to the primary one; that being, who would have regulatory authority and responsibility as a National Governing Body for biathlon. The question of civilian support was delayed since the USMWBTC had not planned to attend the 1965 World Biathlon Championships at Elverum, Norway, but only the CISM Games that year. The primary question of national governance still remained. Despite having set up a biathlon committee within the National Ski Association, the ski association was clearly not interested in biathlon. A major factor in their disinterest may have been the same as what surfaced at the international level; the fastest skiers were not able to win the biathlon races due to poor marksmanship, and those in the ski community may not have been overly thrilled to see a ski race that did not reward the fastest skiers.

The hosting of the 1965 National Biathlon Championships at Rosendale went so well, including the festivities surrounding the competition, the USMWBTC asked the Rosendale Nordic Ski Club to host the 1966 trials and national championships again. With that year's World Biathlon Championships scheduled for Germany, it made for easy logistical planning since Rosendale was within an easy distance from New York City's international airport. However poor snow conditions that year required the races to be relocated to Lake Placid's Whiteface golf course since there was no real cross-country facility there at the time. With 20 participants that included 6 Canadian military athletes, the race was won by William Spencer with John Ehrensbeck and Ed Williams finishing second and third.

Following the 1965 National Championships, during which a biathlon committee within the National Ski Association was established, the National Ski Association made it known that it was not interested in continuing a relationship or supporting biathlon within their organization. George Wilson and Walter Williams began to seek another route to solving the lack of an official authority for biathlon and since the majority of competitors were from the U.S. Army's USMWBTC, and the only place where biathlon training was taking place, they followed the example of the UIMPB structure and considered approaching the U.S. Modern Pentathlon Association. Pentathlon was the other multi-discipline sport strongly supported by the U.S. Army at Ft. Sam Houston, Texas. The president, Byron Nishkian of the National Ski Association that later became the U.S. Ski Association, was in favor of this and appointed Walter Williams as the U.S. Ski Association's representative to the USMPA to accomplish joining biathlon with the pentathlon organization. With the help of George Wilson, the USMPA secretary who was also the director of the Interservice Sports Committee Secretariat for the Department of Defense, they persuaded the USMPA, although reluctantly, to accept authority for biathlon and changed its name to the U.S. Modern Pentathlon and Biathlon Association (USMPBA).

In the years between 1966 and 1968 there was no budget for biathlon within the USMPBA and there apparently was no need for one since all the funding for attending the World Championships came from the Army Forces Sports program through the military biathlon training center in Alaska. The team trials and National Championships in 1966 at Lake Placid and 1967 at Marquette, Michigan did not see any civilians qualify for the team so there was no concern for finding funding for civilians. However, in 1968 at the trials and National Championships at Upson, Wisconsin, a civilian and former member of the USMWBTC Ed Williams, qualified for the 1968 Olympic Winter Games team. Due to the Olympic year, the USOTC was the funding source for civilians on the team.

It was at the National Championships and team trials in 1969 that the USMPBA had to finally find a way to support biathlon when Ed Williams and another former USMWBTC member Jay Bowerman, son of the famous track coach, Nike founder and 10th Mountain Division soldier during World War II, Bill Bowerman. As now civilians they qualified for the World Biathlon Championships team at Zakopane, Poland. USMPBA did find the funding, however the reluctance of the partnership within the organization became clear and an ongoing struggle for biathlon.

The USMPBA as the governing body for biathlon in the United States was also a member of the UIPMB and became responsible for the participation and representation of the USA in the Olympic Games, the Pan American Games and the World Championships in both Modern Pentathlon and Biathlon. Accordingly, it was also responsible for discovering, training and assisting any and all athletes interested in those events, and in holding annual national and, as appropriate, sectional championships in the U.S.; exercising jurisdiction, either directly or through its members or committees, over all matters pertaining to the participation in international competitions. At the time, the greatest portion of USMPBA membership was made up of those primarily interested in modern pentathlon and most of any biathlon issues at the USMPBA annual meetings were handled on a one-to-one basis between Walter Williams and George Wilson who acted as either the secretary of the USMPBA or from the U.S. Army Sports Branch.

For each sport in the Olympic or Pan American Games program the board of directors of the U.S. Olympic Committee elected a "Games Committee" composed of representatives nominated by the member organizations to serve for one quadrennial with the task of organizing and managing the selection of athletes to represent the USA in the Olympic Games. This committee was also provided a token budget from USOC funds for accomplishing its task. As the national governing authority for biathlon those funds went to the USMPBA. Under the structure of the USMPBA, the board of directors was constructed of a representative of the Army, Navy, Marine Corps, Air Force, Fencing Association, Horse Association, Pistol Association, AAU, the U.S. Ski Association and the NRA. There was also a director from pentathlon and one from biathlon in addition to directors from various classes of paid members defined in its constitution. In addition to the lack of autonomy with the USMPBA for biathlon, the constitution provided that the representative for biathlon on the USOC's Executive Board had to be elected by the USMPBA Board of Directors from among its own officers. Under that provision someone from biathlon would first have to be elected to the USMPBA Board before being elected to the USOC's Executive Board, perhaps impeding the strongest voice for biathlon within the USOC or the USMPBA. With USOC and USMPBA funding for biathlon being handled by the USMPBA treasurer, biathlon had lacked both efficiency and autonomy to approve and audit expenditures for the sport. This situation reached a near crisis point following the closure of the USMWBTC in Alaska and the loss of the U.S. Army's support.

Throughout the 1970s the USOC provided a meager budget for training and competition of about $10,000 per year. For the build-up to the 1980 Winter Olympic Games bid, the Lake Placid organizing committee wanted to host a world championship for many of the winter sports for experience and approached the USMPA for its help. It delegated Walter Williams as the one to go to Sapporo in 1972 to make the bid for a Biathlon World Championships and provided him with only $600 for the trip. He was successful in outbidding Norway and the 1973 World Championships was secured for Lake Placid. The original budget for those championships came from the Town of North Elba and was only $10,000. The USOC funding provided the U.S. team with limited support during the team trials and championships. It would be the following year's World Championships, scheduled for Minsk in the Soviet Union that would bring the funding resources issue to a critical point.

The fact that no apparent effort was forthcoming from the USMPBA for financial resources for participation in the 1974 World Biathlon Championships created a situation that at first looked like a U.S. team did not have ability to meet the required expenses for the trip. It then took a semi-coordinated effort by several individuals to develop a plan and find the resources to successfully participate in the first big international winter sport championships inside the U.S.S.R. At the height of the "Cold War" there were many political motives for both sides of the political spectrum. George Wilson who was then the president of the USMPBA and had many contacts through the pentathlon association, began to look for a benefactor while Peter Lahdenpera who had established a very successful sports business in Colorado worked towards finding the clothing and equipment for the team. Bill Spencer, who would be the team leader, worked with Art Stegen who was living in Norway at the time, for accommodations, training and racing possibilities prior to going to the Soviet Union. The Soviet's had offered to fly the Scandinavian teams and Great Britain from Oslo to Minsk on a charter flight, so Spencer had coordinated that part of the travel to link up with the charter flight. Stegen had arranged for the U.S. team to stay first at Sirdal in a Norwegian Home Guard Camp for a race with local competitors from that region and then move by train to Oslo where they stayed at the Norwegian Sports Institute (NIH) at Sognsvatn and participated in the Østlandsmeisterskap (Eastern Biathlon Championships) with the Norwegian and British teams. After securing the visas at the Soviet Embassy in Oslo the team left from the Gardermoen Air Base on the chartered Aeroflot Soviet era Tupolev 134 for Sweden to pick up the Swedish team and then on to Minsk.

For the 1974 team trials, Colonel Buxton of the Vermont National Guard hosted the races, which were moved to Burke Mountain. After the team was selected, they returned to Burlington spending a few days at the National Guard's Building 890, which was a helicopter hanger, waiting to learn if the team had secured the resources to make the trip. At the last minute, George Wilson found Patricia "Tish" Hewitt, who would later become a board member of the USMPBA and the biathlon committee, a benefactor who was a descendant of the Deere family from Moline, Ill. She was the great-great-granddaughter of John Deere, who founded Deere & Co., the agricultural equipment manufacturing business, and the wife of William A. Hewitt, the former chairman and chief executive officer of Deere and former ambassador to Jamaica. With the gift of adequate resources and new team uniforms the team flew out of Montreal for Oslo and eventually Minsk. What looked like a patient on the deathbed, biathlon was revived at the last minute to contemplate its future.

The 1975 World Biathlon Championships were scheduled for Antholz/ Anterselva in the German speaking South Tyrolean Alps of Italy. Having the experience of the 1974 funding issues, new strategies were developed by Howard Buxton, Peter Lahdenpera, Walter Williams and George Wilson to avoid the near cancellation of 1974. The first of these was to engage a greater interaction within the USMPBA by biathlon advocates. Peter Lahdenpera was elected vice president for biathlon and greater efforts were made to attend the annual meeting and provide information for the USMPBA newsletter. Lahdenpera also established the first "equipment pool" for biathlon for which potential suppliers would pay a fee to enter the pool and then provide equipment; skis, poles, boots, clothing, etc. to the team and its members in return for indirect advertising to an ever-increasing public interest in nordic skiing. Colonel Buxton integrated the team's training into the National Guard's developing program and Wilson and Williams worked on finding financial resources. In advance of the 1976 Winter Olympic Games the USOC improved its developmental funding and with those individual efforts the World Championships at Antholz appeared to be a turning point towards a better future.

The funding issues of 1974 were occurring in the backdrop of ever-increasing athlete activism of the 1970s. This activism had a strong impact on biathlon and all amateur sports in the U.S. The Vietnam War and the presidential abuses of the Nixon administration had made the public skeptical, and questioning of authority became somewhat of a norm. The small biathlon community was not immune and there was a general awareness of the struggles amateur athletes faced against the monolithic Amateur Athletic Union (AAU), which exercised autocratic control over many Olympic sports. The leading track and field athletes Frank Shorter and Steve Prefontaine became public focal points of the inequities imposed by the amateur rules that forced them into complete amateur compliance while the officials and administrators enjoyed the fruitions of the athletes' success. Although there had been criticism for many years the activism among the athletes surfaced again just prior to the 1972 Summer Olympic Games when they began questioning governance decisions, such as how the team flag bearer was selected. Responding to the inquiries, then U. S. Olympic Committee Executive Director F. Don Miller arranged for a meeting in Munich for the team captains to hold the first election of a U.S. flag bearer for Olympic Games. At the Sullivan Awards that followed, many athletes who had been in Munich, were again together and expressed the need to have a real voice in governance of sports in the USA. Don Miller provided the resources for athletes to meet and created the Athletes' Advisory Committee (AAC) in 1973. At the beginning, it had no formal structure within the USOC, no internal structure within their own organization and voice but no vote at the board of directors meeting. Shortly afterward Tenley Albright, the 1956 Olympic figure skating champion, a prominent surgeon and a member of the Executive Committee of the U.S Olympic Committee moved towards formalizing the AAC in 1974 by requesting national governing bodies to nominate representatives of their sport at the AAC. George Wilson nominated Edward Williams, who had served in the New York district attorney's office and had become a practicing lawyer at a prestigious firm in New York City, to be the biathlon representative.

With increasing pressure on the AAU for what was seen to be exploitation of the athletes and its arbitrary rules, which prohibited women from participating in running events, and prohibited any runner from racing an event as a runner with a shoe-company sponsorship, along with the continuing battles over jurisdiction with the NCAA, President Ford organized the President's Commission on Olympic Sport, which led to Congress passing legislation in 1978 called the Amateur Sports Act giving athletes both voice and vote in the governance process of Olympic sports. Prior to the adoption of the Act, which became Public Law 95-606 on November 8th, 1978, Ed Williams who had been elected chair of the AAC, Gary Johansson, the legal advisor for the Commerce Committee and Mike Scott, the NCAA lawyer drafted the Athletes' Rights section of the Amateur Sports Act. The law amended the corporate charter of the Olympic Committee giving the USOC sole authority over amateur sports. It can charter only one national governing body (NGB) for each sport. This was the clear signal that biathlon and pentathlon would have to split into separate governing bodies.

CHAPTER 7

The U.S. Biathlon Association

In a February 12, 1980 edition of a *New York Times* article titled "A Revolution Aimed at 1980," which was a story about USOC financing the winter sports at the 1980 Winter Olympic Games at Lake Placid, it explained that the USOC had expanded its commitment to winter sports by authorizing a record total $627,100 in development funds for the seven Olympic winter sports which was four times that spent for the 1976 Games. The share of those funds for biathlon was $54,400, which was an increase up from $10,000 in 1976. Far less than the state subsidized program in the Soviet Union or the German Democratic Republic (East Germany), the article highlighted the plight of the biathlon competitors who lacked any significant support following the elimination of the military draft. Lyle Nelson described the problem in terms of support by saying, "I don't think that the public has any perception of us at all." Called "the last of the amateurs" by the *Times* the athletes were said to feel "doubly damned" because the military was no longer involved, and the team received no arms or ammunition from rifle manufacturers while at the same time other companies were reluctant to involve themselves in a sport that entails the firing of rifles despite the clean image of biathlon.

In the late 1970s the few athletes participating in biathlon faced similar problems as those subjected to the arbitrary rules of the AAU in finding the financial resources to continue their participation and sustain a livelihood. In 1972 Avery Brundage, the IOC president led the effort to prevent "professional" athletes from competing in the Olympic Games with his "amateurs-only" efforts and the removal of Austrian ski racer Karl Schranz. In his last effort against allowing athletes any income from sport, he failed to understand changes that were needed to provide for the normal daily and professional needs of athletes. As the USOC began to address the need for supporting athletes' training and sustainment it began a program of broken time reimbursement and job opportunity programs that compensated missed employment and provided corporate part-time subsidized jobs for Olympic athletes. The athletes increasingly found themselves at a disadvantage when competing against the state-supported athletes of the Eastern European nations and the concepts of broken time payments or job opportunity programs seemed to be a "half-answer" to creating a level playing field. Once the military support ended, many found part-time jobs in construction or other labor-intensive occupations while others opted for teaching positions that allowed more time for training with shorter work days, but limited time away during the competitive winter months. As Peter Lahdenpera's equipment pool for biathlon began to provide increasing revenue for biathlon activities, they began to seek compensation, demanded funding changes and began to market themselves directly with suppliers, which immediately forced questions of funding within amateur status and the relationship between the two sports within the USMPBA. At about the same time the USSA was facing the same issue, Lahdenpera found a solution to indirectly support the athletes by funneling money from pool suppliers through the NGB in a system whereby the athletes would submit their training and competition expenses to the NGB and be reimbursed with that money.

The passage of the Amateur Sports Act in 1978 brought some of the problems that created difficultly within the USMPBA to the surface. Ed Williams, who was the vice president for administration, found his role compromised between his membership on the executive committee, which was taking up to 80% of his time and the pentathlon athletes who were asking for his help as a member of the USOC's Athletes Advisory Council. He eventually resigned when a question of embezzlement and a lawsuit claiming slander went to an arbitration hearing and the USMPBA Board of Directors disavowed Williams' expenses on his defense of the USMPBA when called to San Antonio to testify before an arbitration board under the Amateur Sports Act provisions. Other biathlon members of the USMPBA became increasingly frustrated as they listened patiently when pentathlon problems of horse thievery and embezzlement were discussed and when it came time for a short presentation of biathlon, nearly everyone left the room. At a December 8th, 1979 meeting when it came time for Peter Lahdenpera to give his biathlon report, biathlon advocates blocked the isle so no one could leave, but when conversations began throughout the room, Peter eventually interrupted his report to ask, "Hey, are you guys listening to me or am I talking to myself."

In his letter confirming his resignation from the USMPBA Executive Committee and board of directors on October 8th, 1979 Ed Williams listed among his reasons; the USMPBA's demonstrated insensitivity to the various requirements of both the Amateur Sports Act and the USOC Constitution, and its failure to recognize and appreciate that the overwhelming majority of the USMPBA who were associated with biathlon desired to seek complete autonomy and the administration of the sport. After another scandal hit the USMPBA over doping allegations and an investigation of U.S. participants at the World Pentathlon Championships of 1979 in Hungary, Walter Williams began a serious attempt towards separation with a questionnaire circulated among the biathlon community which was intended to ask for approval for separation of the two sports into their own governing bodies. After receiving near total approval, he wrote a proposal and forwarded it to George Wilson and asked to present it to the USMPBA Board of Directors. His questionnaire asked if biathlon and pentathlon should each be represented in the USOC by separate national governing bodies and listed several key issues as to why he believed it to be in the best interest of biathlon. It was clear that the participants, athletes and officials of one sport had little or no interest in the other. He also felt that it was inappropriate for the USMPBA Board of Directors or executive committee, which was composed of a mix of representatives of each sport, to make decisions and rulings in behalf of the other.

After notifying George Wilson, the USMPBA president of his proposal, Walter attended the USMPBA Annual Meeting with his proposal for separation. The proposal asked for USMPBA approval in principle for the formation of an autonomous corporation by individuals primarily associated with biathlon in order that it could seek recognition by the USOC and UIPMB as the National Governing Body for biathlon in the United States and that the USMPBA, its officers and members support the new corporation in its applications to the USOC and UIPMB for recognition. A vote on the proposal was taken and the proposal was overwhelmingly rejected.

George Wilson had responded in a letter on December 7th, 1979 to Walter Williams' proposal suggesting separation at that time could possibly influence the legality of entries in the 1980 Winter Olympic Games and felt that the question of separation needed broad consideration by the membership and pursued within the requirements of the USMPBA By-laws and all the legal attention necessary. He therefore proposed the appointment of a committee headed by Peter Lahdenpera to study the feasibility and to develop the necessary organizational requirements to be presented to the membership at its meeting in 1980. The following day he selected Bill Askins, Howard Buxton, Walter Williams and one other appointed by Lahdenpera as members of the committee with the task to make a feasibility study. Since the USOC rules could only consider a new NGB within a year after the close of the Olympic Games, Walter pointed out that that date would be for February 22nd, 1981 as a completion deadline for separation. With the date of November 8th, 1980 on the horizon, two years after the Amateur Sport Act was signed into law the USMPBA would be in violation of that law. With the USOC Development Committee's request for a preliminary budget for the next quadrennial by April 1st, 1980 and with the USOC House of Delegates meeting coming up on April 11-13th, 1980, Walter Williams stressed the urgency of action on the part of the biathlon community.

While at the 1980 Winter Olympic Games in Lake Placid, Walter took the opportunity to make a presentation to a biathlon committee meeting on February

14th, 1980. In his lengthily oral and written presentation he explained the reasons he concluded it necessary for separation and outlined the process by which it had to follow. With the committee finalized when Lahdenpera appointed retired General William Martin of Salt Lake City, a date for a report from the Feasibility Committee was to be concluded for the USMPBA Board of Directors meeting by June 1st, 1980.

The Feasibility Study Committee presented its report to the group of USMPBA members attending the USOC House of Delegates meeting in Colorado Springs on April 12th, 1980. The report began by stating the task issued by President George Wilson that the committee "study the feasibility of a separate biathlon governing body and to report to the USMPBA Board of Directors at a meeting sometime in the time frame of April 15th to June 1st. If the subject was considered feasible by the board of directors, the Feasibility Study Committee would then develop the necessary organization, recommended by corporate structure and by-laws and operational guidelines for final consideration by the membership at the 1980 meeting." The unanimous conclusion of the study was that the separation of the sports into two NGBs was feasible and beneficial to each sport. Among the many considerations examined by the committee the most important were that the sports were geographically separated with little crossover value as each sport was conducted and administrated differently, each sport had individual requirements and base for fund-raising, making neither dependent upon the other for resources, and biathlon was growing to a point where it needed the identity and direct guidance where volunteers and supporters would be more willing to work for their cause. However, it was the Amateur Sport Act which gave the USOC authority over each sport as a national governing body, but only one for each sport that was the most compelling reason for separation. The report also developed a ten-step sequenced plan to accomplish the separation that it felt could be accomplished prior to the November 8th, 1980 date by which all National Governing Bodies had to file membership applications with the USOC.

The Feasibility Study Committee outlined ten actions that were necessary to implement a path to a separate governing body for biathlon. Those "steps" were:

- Approval by the USMPBA Board of Directors of the concept of forming a separate governing body for biathlon,
- Creation of a Biathlon Standing Committee by the USMPBA Board of Directors to provide the nucleus for a new biathlon governing body and to act in a dual capacity under the USMPBA for as long as necessary before the transfer of responsibilities,
- That a Standing Committee be directed to formulate the necessary plans

and by-laws for review and become effective after an affirmative vote for separation by the general membership in August 1980.

- The executive board appoint a committee representing each sport to investigate and determine the terms of dividing the legal and financial responsibilities and assets when the final separation takes place.
- Vote by the general membership at the August 1980 quadrennial meeting.
- If the vote is affirmative, resolutions from the USMPBA should be voted and directed by the USMPBA to the USOC and the UIPMB supporting the recommending recognition of the new biathlon national governing body.
- The new association should hold a properly notified organizational meeting to approve the by-laws, elect officers and incorporate.
- Application should be made for tax exempt status, USOC membership and finally, UIPMB membership.
- The dual status of the USMPBA Biathlon Standing Committee should continue until all necessary approvals and recognitions are received and at that time formal transfer of responsibilities in accordance with paragraph D would take place.
- The USMPBA will take steps to be prepared to delete reference to biathlon in its by-laws and change its organizational structure at the time of separation.

The ten steps were to be accomplished well before the November 8th, 1980 date by which all national governing bodies must have filed applications with the USOC. Following the presentation of the report, Walter Williams once again swung into action and at the suggestion of Dennis Donahue, he got together with his son Edward and put together an action plan to accomplish the steps outlined in the feasibility study.

Shortly after the meeting of the USOC House of Delegates in Colorado Springs, a decision by the board of directors approved the concept of forming a separate national governing body for biathlon at the May 18th, 1980 meeting in Washington, D.C. The vote was 9 in favor and 1 opposed. On June 8th Ed Williams forwarded a letter to all persons interested in biathlon that announced the members of the Standing Committee for Biathlon. Those members were Peter Lahdenpera, the vice president of the USMPBA for Biathlon; four athletes that were elected by the athletes, Ken Alligood, Dennis Donahue, John Morton and Bill Spencer; a representative elected by other coaches, trainers and officials, Art Stegen; and five individuals selected by Peter Lahdenpera and approved by the USMPBA Board of Directors, Howard Buxton, William Martin, Kent Mills,

Walen Porter and Walter Williams. The first meeting of this committee was scheduled to take place at Williams Lake Hotel in Rosendale, New York on the weekend of June 13-15th, 1980.

At that meeting on June 14th, Walter Williams' action plan was put in place. It included the framework of a new organization with the various positions and responsibilities of officers and directors and the organization would create membership groups with voting strength of the various categories agreed upon by a new Biathlon Association that could be formed informally without incorporation as an Ad Hoc group of interested people among whom a constitution and by-laws would be drafted and circulated for agreement on final draft. Once a constitution and by-laws were agreed upon, application could be made for incorporation as a "Not for profit Corporation" to the state of incorporation as agreed upon by the ad hoc association. A letter from the Internal Revenue Service certifying the new corporation would then be sought for "tax-exempt" status. The membership categories proposed in the plan included 9 recognized biathlon clubs that were actively sponsoring and conducting races, individuals interested in biathlon, and corporate contributors. The National Rifle Association and the U.S. Ski Association would not be members but technical advisors without vote. The board of directors would be elected by the membership categories with 20% athlete membership according to the guidelines of the Amateur Sports Act.

At what might be considered the birth of the new U.S. Biathlon Association, the meeting at Rosendale on June 14th, a resolution was made by those attending to accept the recommendations of the Biathlon Standing Committee. Signed by William Spencer, William Martin, Howard Buxton, Walter Williams, John Morton, Kent Mills, Dennis Donahue, Art Stegen and Chairman of the USMPBA Biathlon Feasibility Study Committee and vice president for Biathlon, Peter Lahdenpera forwarded the document "Procedures for developing a separate National Governing Body for Biathlon" to USMPBA President and Secretary Guy Troy requesting the actions outlined be included on the agenda for the August 16th, 1980 USMPBA Annual and Special Meeting.

On July 16th, after the Standing Committee's meeting at Rosendale, Howard Buxton wrote an important letter of explanation and support for separation to George Wilson. Buxton had for many become the leading spokesman within the biathlon community and as the chief of competition for biathlon at the 1980 Lake Placid Winter Olympic Games had earned high respect within the U.S. Olympic environment for his organizational abilities, his vision and opinions concerning amateur sport and the status of biathlon. His letter summarized the feeling of many who saw biathlon in a caretaker status since the loss of military support and that the momentum built up during the 1980 games was in jeopardy. He acknowledged that progress had been made but not as a result of the USMPBA.

Other than only a few; President George Wilson, Secretary Guy Troy, Treasurer Dan Steinman and Board Member Tish Hewitt who had become an interested biathlon supporter, there was little interest in biathlon from the USMPBA. In fact, he pointed out that much of the progress was made due to the improved funding and training support with the U.S. Olympic Training Center at Squaw Valley and not because of any strong or singular effort made by the USMPBA to support biathlon. He felt that many matters concerning biathlon were handled through inaction rather than action by the USMPBA due to the multi-layered superstructure within the organization. He concluded that biathlon was surviving mainly through the efforts of Peter Lahdenpera and a handful of people who had put personal differences aside and overlooked organizational shortcomings for the common goal of improving U.S. Biathlon for the 1980 Winter Olympic Games, but sensed that those individuals, including himself were not willing to continue in that manner.

Buxton's letter had identified a major key in the need for separation that was beneath the surface of all the obvious reasons. He explained how, in putting together the organization for the 1980 Games, an effort was made to include as many people as possible with past connection in biathlon and that effort sparked a lot of enthusiasm and general atmosphere of a reunion during the games, a fact that he admitted he was slow to recognize. But he felt that he saw a door opening with that enthusiasm by people who were sitting on the sidelines but were now excited and wanted to help very much. It was clear to him that they would support and work for a separate biathlon organization and that the future would lie in a grassroots base from which many of them were a part. With non-biathlon members of the USMPBA rarely attending meetings or competitions, the apathy of the pentathlon side of the organization clearly visible to the biathlon community, Buxton felt it was time for the USMPBA to "get in step" with the situation so they can make the appropriate decisions. He concluded his letter by saying that for the future of biathlon he saw no other scenario other than a separate organization.

The first issue of the *Biathlon Bulletin* was circulated to the biathlon community in October of 1980. The first page of this newsletter was a message from the newly-elected president announcing the new national organization for biathlon, the United States Biathlon Association. The first official meeting of the new organization was held at Rosendale, New York on September 13-14, 1980 and although the "Association" had not completed the full list of organizational requirements, the initial steps of adopting an incorporation certificate, a set of by-laws and election of the officers by the attendees had taken place. The meeting was the culmination of years of work by a variety of people who believed the interests of biathlon could be better served by a single association. As of September 13th, the new U.S. Biathlon Association assumed responsibility for biathlon in the United

States, pending final approval by the USMPBA, USOC and the UIPMB. The first annual meeting was set for late February 1981, and the elected officers, President Howard Buxton, Vice President William Martin, Treasurer Walter Williams and Secretary Dennis Donahue, would serve a term to end at that time. At an earlier USMPBA meeting on August 16th, the biathlon representatives were pleased to learn that the newly-elected president, Dan Steinman was prepared to make the final arrangements for separation and the terms were acceptable to all, however since the U.S. Biathlon Association (USBA) had not yet received tax exempt status, financial arrangements were to become a subsidiary of the USMPBA. In November 1980, the new by-laws were submitted to the USOC for review along with the application for recognition as the national governing body for biathlon.

Following recognition by the USOC, the final step in gaining sole jurisdiction over biathlon occurred at the UIPMB Congress meeting in Lahti, Finland, during the World Biathlon Championships held there in February 1981 when recognition of the U.S. Biathlon Association as the national governing body at its Congress was approved. The first annual meeting of the USBA took place during the National Biathlon Championships weekend at Bozeman, Montana on February 28th, 1981. With 43 members present, Howard Buxton called the meeting to order and after some opening remarks and the treasurer's report the election for the remaining three years of the quadrennial was held. The current officers were elected at the organizational meeting for a one-year term only. After a motion to continue with the current officers as candidates, nominations from the floor were opened. There were no further nominations and the current officers were re-elected to continue through 1984. The membership broke into caucusing groups and elected their representatives on the USBA Board of Directors and before the adjournment of the meeting Howard Buxton announced that he would appoint the various committees before the next meeting in May. He also announced that since separation, the new association membership had increased by more than three times and was a good sign that there was greater interest and that the sport was growing. This trend was also demonstrated in the athlete participation levels in that the National Championships included 34 racers and the National Guard Championships had climbed to a total of 94 participants. The newly established 1980-81 USBA National Points list or ranking of competitors listed 140 men and 25 women. The 1981-82 season saw that list grow to a total of 240, but also important it showed that the quality of racers was also improving with the number of athletes with higher point values increasing as well.

The final step of the process in establishing sole authority for biathlon by the newly formed U.S. Biathlon Association happened on September 24th, 1981 when it was fully recognized as a 501 (C) (3) "Not for Profit" Corporation by the Internal Revenue Service. Incorporated in the State of New York, this tax-exempt status completed the final step in the process of becoming the national governing body for biathlon in the United States and removed the last obstacle to raising its own funding. Adequate funding had been an ongoing issue ever since the U.S. Army ended its support. The USOC's four-year "Games Committee" which had become known as the Olympic Biathlon Committee submitted funding requests to the USOC's Sports Budget/Development Committee and this provided minimal funding for travel and accommodations for designated training team members and coaches. The first year without military support following the closure of the USMWBTC in Alaska, with the 1973 World Championships being held at Lake Placid that funding was adequate. However, for 1973-74 Ed Williams submitted a budget request for $43,221 that was included with a total of $1,327,000 from 30 sports. The USOC had only $400,000 to work with and granted biathlon only $10,000 for the season leaving the biathlon financial status very precarious and participation in the 1974 World Championships at Minsk in jeopardy. The financial situation gradually improved as the 1980 Winter Olympic Games approached and the USOC opened its training center at Squaw Valley, however it did not immediately solve the constant shortage of financial resources.

In 1981 the board of directors decided it was necessary to have a full-time program director and Art Stegen was hired for this position. He, along with the efforts of Peter Lahdenpera made progress in securing better financial and valuable in-kind resources, including air-travel and equipment. That along with the assets available at the USOC's training center, helped to develop a more professional and positive environment for biathlon to grow. However, the need to find the financial support for the increasing international biathlon competitions and a pathway to improving performance at the top levels of the sport were continually thwarted. President Buxton pointed out that the new association would be in critical need and a high priority, in the plans to send a team to Minsk, USSR for the 1982 World Championships and extending the trip to the newly-established World Cup races.

The number of athletes above 90 on the USBA points ranking list remained the same between its initiation in 1979 through 1982. With the establishment of the World Cup for biathlon in 1981 the best athletes were pushing for participation in these international races in addition to the World Biathlon Championships, however in a message to the members in the U.S. Biathlon's newsletter, *Biathlon Bulletin*, during the summer of 1982 President Howard Buxton wrote:

> This year's National Program will largely depend upon available funds. The economic climate has had a disastrous effect on our ability to raise funds as well as how far we have been able to stretch our existing monies. We are very dependent upon USOC development funding.

To date, the USOC has experienced the same difficulties in their own fund-raising program... To best use our existing money, the board has decided to limit support to a men's A and B team... After attending the pre-games in Sarajevo, a four-man team would continue to the World Championships. If sufficient funding is available as of 1 December, the Board committed itself to send a women's team to the World Cup races.

The issue of adequate funding became even greater following the 1982 season at the annual meeting during the National Championships in Bemidji, Minnesota. At that meeting President Buxton announced to the membership in the summer *Biathlon Bulletin* that the board of directors decided to terminate the staff contracts. Although efforts were made, sufficient fund raising would not meet appropriate requirements. That action meant that most of the USBA administration and coaching would take place on a volunteer level. Buxton asked for understanding from the membership saying that this step was necessary to protect its competitive program with the hope that the situation would only be temporary. This also coincided with the closure of the USOTC at Squaw Valley. Along with the loss of a program director and part-time coaching, 1983 represented a period of retrenchment for biathlon.

Adding to the situation, a poor winter made 1983 a difficult year. Secretary Dennis Donahue carried most of the administrative responsibilities and made several pleas for help. The USBA managed to stretch its resources to send a team to the World Biathlon Championships and attend their first World Cup events. The events did however indicate that the competitiveness of the U.S. team was not improving and there had been considerable loss of momentum that showed only a minor increase of the USBA membership.

Things however looked brighter for the near future since the USOC development funding would increase with the upcoming 1984 Winter Olympic Games at Sarajevo and the opening of the USOTC at Lake Placid would once again provide badly needed resources. At the June 3rd, 1983 USBA annual meeting, President Buxton highlighted the key issue from the previous annual meeting in Minnesota was the lack on sufficient funds to support the position of a program director which put a strain of the Association's officers. Due to the efforts of several individuals and volunteers there had been some financial gains, but Treasurer Walter Williams warned that there were unpaid bills which would require every penny of any unspent USOC development funds for the remainder of the year. Since 1984 would bring USOC team preparation money and it would also be the first time that the UIPMB would hold a World Championships for women, Buxton felt that USBA fiscal status would improve. With that optimism, it was announced that the positions of salaried part-time (October to March) Ski and Rifle Coach would be solicited along with that of a team leader for the 1984 Winter Olympic Games at Sarajevo, Yugoslavia would be for a paid expenses volunteer. Former competitor Ken Alligood and well-known shooting coach Marie Alkire were hired for those positions.

Following the Olympic and Women's World Championship team trials at Lake Placid in January 1984, the board of directors once again felt confident that it could support a full-time position for an Administrator in addition to the part-time coaches. Dale Rogers filled the administrative position and was later followed by Jed Williamson. It was an important turn mostly because the team of Kari Swenson, Julie Newnam and Holly Beattie earned the first World Championships medal by a U.S. team at the 1st Championships for women at Chamonix, France. The men's results at the Olympic Winter Games also showed a noticeable improvement from the previous two years with a penalty-free 20th place finish by Willie Carrow in the sprint race and a 26th place in the individual race by come-backing Lyle Nelson who had sat out 1983. The Winter Olympic Games and Women's World Championships appeared to have an impact on the domestic interest in biathlon as well. Impressive increases were seen in both the number and participants in local club races and the number of participants in the National Guard Championships reached a high point of 141 participants from 28 states.

Following the 1984 Winter Olympic Games there were momentous changes in both the organization of competitions and the nature of the sport due to the evolution of the traditional skiing technique to faster "skating" technique. Starting at the international levels there was some disagreement both at the FIS (Federation Internationale du Ski) and the UIMPB about whether this should be allowed. At the board of directors meeting of the USBA in June 1985 a decision was made to follow the decision of the UIPMB, which had not yet been made at that time. Another important decision made at that meeting was the hiring of Sigvart Bjontegaard of Elverum, Norway to be the assistant coach under Jim Young who previously served as the domestic development coach for the U.S. Ski Team. Along with Major John Abair's leadership the National Guard's program was increasing its budget and its athletes were entering in international competitions for the first time. Funding from the USOC's multiple sources such as development, sports medicine, sports equipment and technology, international travel and Olympic Foundation grants were another important reason that biathlon in the United States was seeing an impressive improvement in all areas.

The 1984 Summer Olympic Games at Los Angles was a commercial success and the USOC granted additional funds to each of the National Governing Organizations. The USBA Board of Directors decided to divide up their grant between immediate needs and saving for the future. This decision helped turn 1987 into a banner year when, at that year's World Biathlon Championships at Lake

Placid, Josh Thompson captured the first-ever individual World Championships medal with his second-place finish in the 20 kilometers event. Josh Thompson had shown his abilities in the previous year's 1986 World University Games and under the coaching leadership of Tracy Lamb and Sigvart Bjontegaard the entire team enjoyed remarkable improvement. Going into the 1988 Winter Olympic Games there were high hopes for the first-ever Olympic medal, however it was not to be. Under intense media pressure, the relay team managed a 9th place finish and was not able to finish in the top 20 places of the individual races.

Despite the success of 1987 and high expectations of 1988, funding issues still plagued the USBA. In April 1988 President Howard Buxton highlighted those issues by reviewing the situation in a letter to the board of directors. Having preserved $350,000 of the USOC Los Angeles principal which was thought to generate a regular cash flow of $2,000 per month, and an average of $185,000 per year from USOC grants for the three previous years, changes in the USOC formula that would centralize funding into one annual grant that was to be calculated on factors such as size of Olympic team, medals available and success, number of registered athletes administered by the sport and a comprehensive plan for development would most likely reduce annual funding to between $150,000 and $175,000. In addition, since the women's biathlon events were not yet part of the Olympic program, USOC funding could not be used for supporting women, which meant that if the IOC Executive Committee meeting on April 30th, 1988 did not decide to include women's events, support could only come from pure USBA sources. Also, the IOC decision to alternate Winter Games and Summer Games every two years would place an additional funding burden on the USBA as there would be a need to support two Olympic Games within six years rather than eight. In addition to the USOC funding, Buxton proposed expansion of the USBA marketing program managed by Marty Rudoph that had succeeded in raising $60,000 to $80,000 per year and to initiate a "special major sponsor effort" to locate a major four-year sponsor against a need of $300,000 per year.

During the years between the 1988 and 1992 Winter Olympic Games the USBA entered into two separate contracts with fund-raising agents to help solve the financial problems, however each of those efforts failed to generate any significant sources of new funding. Two other initiatives did help to keep things going in a positive direction; the first was the sudden interest in a growing summer biathlon program headed up by Lyle Nelson which helped to bring the National Shooting Sports Foundation's Executive Director Bob Delfay to the USBA Board of Directors, and the other was the hiring of Max Cobb as the domestic race series coordinator. Bob Delfay brought grants from the NSSF to support both winter and summer biathlon and put together NSSF fund-raising sources to help USBA. Max Cobb was a former Dartmouth racer and 1987 graduate who received the

Dean's Award for outstanding administration skills. He also had established and directed the Upper Valley Nordic Club in New Hampshire where he managed a 15-person elite ski racing team as well as directing the club's programs, raising funding and managing its budget.

In his April 19th, 1988 letter to the members of the Board of Directors, President Howard Buxton tried to present an accurate picture of the situation at the time. Three unexpected funding sources had helped the Association recover from a deficit funding situation. The first was an additional grant from the Olympic Foundation that covered the women's international race expenses; the second was a gift from the Auburn Ski Club obtained by Lyle Nelson to cover the men's international competitions and the third was an unanticipated $37,200 from the Olympic Committee to support the 1988 Olympic team after the team selection. Buxton also wrote that Olympic funding had been received from multiple sources such as: development funds, sports medicine funds, sports equipment and technology funds, international travel funds and Olympic Foundation grants. Averaging a total of about $185,000 per year this amount was the result of a complicated formula developed over the years and was intended to help small sports, but also reward success. However, on January 1st, 1989 the USOC had made the decision to go to centralized funding, eliminating all the separate funding categories and granted each sport one annual grant based on a formula similar to the previous development funding that included the factors of the size of the Olympic team, gold medals available and the number of registered athletes administered by the sport. His estimate of what biathlon could expect was $150,000 to $175,000 and although below previous levels, it would provide more flexibility as to how the money was spent. He pointed out also that with the new plan, there would be more accountability, in that progress would be measured against a comprehensive plan that the Association had to develop.

Still facing a known need of a minimum of $300,000 per year Buxton encouraged continuation of finding a "major four-year sponsor" and that it would not happen if the Association did not have a specific plan and approach. At a minimum, he estimated that the current USBA organization and central office effort would require $100,000, the current development efforts $50,000 and a one-coach, 10 athlete team for two weeks of fall training and two weeks of international competition $100,000. His "bare-bones" estimate was also complicated by the serious cash flow problem from July to January due to the fact that the new USOC fiscal year began on January 1st.

The new program director, Jed Williamson, who was a former member of the USMWBTC in Alaska and who had helped Sven Johanson write the first biathlon training manual, immediately assessed his role and the status of the USBA. He began his position at a time when there were high expectations for the Calgary Olympic Games, but at the same time there was a sense that the organizational structure was "just holding things together." Carefully and methodically he analyzed the organizational needs of the Association, including the goals and working structure, the financial status, personnel needs, including a new head coach and administrative assistant, a bookkeeper, restructuring the programs, taking control of the inventory, and office space considerations. Feeling a strong need for organizational reforms, especially in financial matters, he made several suggestions for the board of directors to make the Association more professional.

At the time Jed Williamson assumed his position, the U.S. Biathlon Association had established its office in Building 5 of the Vermont National Guard Headquarters at Camp Johnson in Colchester, Vermont. It was also the location of Howard Buxton's office for his National Guard Duties. The small office where Betty Law served as secretary quickly became inadequate and was not conductive to a good working environment. In addition to the issue of inadequate office space, the most pressing issue for the Association was that of potential financial deficits and the trimming of athlete programs. In May of 1987, in light of the success of Josh Thompson's medal winning result at Lake Placid, Treasurer Walter Williams submitted a proposal to help meet the Association's primary goal of winning a medal in Calgary that, although it caused a severe drain on the financial resources, $200,000 be withdrawn from the USOC investment pool and that the remaining $350,000 be preserved in an endowment fund controlled by an investment committee. He also asked that beginning in May 1988, projected expenditures be based on funds raised rather than funds projected to be raised and that future budgets be balanced. This proposal got to the heart of the problems that had been facing the U.S. Biathlon Association ever since its formation and would continue to do so well into the 1990s.

At the July 9-10, 1988 board of directors meeting at Bolton Valley, Vermont important decisions were taken to move the Association in a more professional direction. Howard Buxton stated in his opening address to the members that the time had come, with a competent staff, for the Directors to move from program management to that of setting policy. A previously appointed staff selection committee reported the need for a program director, head coach, women's assistant coach, development director/coach, regional coaches, marketing support, bookkeeping support and secretarial support with an estimate cost of $225,000. Two budgets were proposed, an optimal one of $424,000 and a minimal one of $376,000. The group approved the minimal budget. To accommodate Buxton and the staff selection committee's proposals, a by-law change approved the title for the full-time staff person to be changed from that of program director to executive director with check signing ability. The members also approved naming President Howard Buxton to be the U.S. Biathlon Association's representative on the USOC

Executive Board which would later pave the way for him to play a significant role within the USOC as well at the UIPMB Congress. The members also approved the first domestic race series. The U.S. Biathlon Association was reported to be 777 members.

The annual membership meeting the following March 1989 at Royal Gorge, CA had shown some signs of the professional improvements sought following 1988, however there remained many of the problems that were still unsolved. The most important issue that had been resolved was that audits for 1986 through 1988 had finally been completed. Also, in the interim, a USOC requirement for a 4-year plan of operation had also been completed and with the introduction of women's biathlon for the 1992 Winter Olympic Games there would be an increase of money from the USOC. However, questions from the floor about the by-laws, determination of authority to "run the USBA" and making changes in membership classifications seemed to signal developing problems.

By the June 10-11th, 1989 board of directors meeting membership in the Association had dropped to 695 and only a single club had registered. After the budget was approved for $444,250 a discussion developed over the percent budget allocations to the administration (24%), "grass-roots" development (8%), National team (22%) and elite programs (46%). An attempt by motion to increase the allocation to development by those involved with that aspect was defeated and questions of these percentages lingered. Other issues that had been brewing were that of regionalism and coaching. Athletes were demanding increased coaching contact and there seemed to be an "east-coast vs. west-coast" issue. John Morton, who chaired the Training and Competition Committee proposed a trials schedule for two western races prior to Christmas and three in the east following Christmas with the National championships held in the midwest. After many opinions on coaching and centralized training at one location a motion to hire a qualified head coach and two assistants barely passed. The coaching issue continued, following the motion over whether the head coach should be a European. Dennis Donahue and Bill Spencer filled those rolls at the time. Another troublesome issue that surfaced was 11 male athletes were sent letters offering team positions when in fact there were only eight positions authorized, which once again caused skepticism among the athletes about the Association's professional ability. The remainder of that meeting was spent hammering out trials and team criteria and athlete's support levels, which exposed a serious problem that Howard Buxton had earlier tried to resolve and that was with the organizational structure of the Association. This issue would not be resolved until the same problems would later require reforms of USBA governance as well.

With over 80% of the Association's budget coming from the USOC there was an urgent need to increase other funding sources. The various marketing efforts had not met expectations and supplier pool fees had become increasingly difficult to tap for direct fees as suppliers were more willing to supply their product on an annual basis and channel support directly to individual team members. Other demands pressing the Association in the fall of 1989 were a possible relocation of the USBA office and resolving the coaching situation. Dennis Donahue, the head coach at the time was unable to fulfill the wishes of the athletes who were expressing a need for daily contact with a coach and moving towards the concept of centralized team training. The period between 1989 and 1990 saw the role of the National Guard support improved in many direct and indirect ways, the development of a strong National Races and North American Cup series led by the Domestic Race Series Director Max Cobb, and the efforts of Jed Williamson helped to send the USBA in a more positive direction.

Following the disintegration of the Soviet Union the Association hired Lithuanian Algis Shalna to be a full-time coach in 1991 to work along with German Walter Pichler who had been hired as team trainer in June of 1990, replacing John Ruger. Both were Olympic medalists and brought high performance level coaching skills to the team leading into the 1992 Olympic Winter Games. With obvious language and cultural knowledge deficits by the coaches, Max Cobb was moved to the program director's position to focus on the needs of the National team. This new crew helped to focus on Olympic goals, especially since it was also the first time that women would be participating.

However, the expected Olympic results were less than anticipated and following the Games at Albertville the Association once again found itself facing a host of both old and new problems. The first was the May resignation of Executive Director Jed Williamson. He had originally agreed to serve 5 years when hired, to get through the quadrennium. Somewhat discouraged by the Association's inability to find any private sector interest in financial support there was growing tension within the organization over finding a "home base." There were continuing struggles between development and high-performance efforts, but Jed agreed to stay on until September. Shortly after his resignation the USOC's Member Services Committee's decision to "downgrade" the USBA from its previous classification of an "emerging" sport to an "underdeveloped" sport forewarned a significant impact on USOC funding. Newly elected for the short two-year period between the 1992 and 1994 Winter Olympic Games, President Ed Williams called a USBA Executive Committee meeting on July 12th, 1992 at Salt Lake City.

At that meeting Williams announced that the executive director and staff were to take immediate steps to improve the performance of the USBA in the areas that led to the USOC decision. Among those steps were no renewal of any employment contracts or requests for salary increases of staff except for coaches Walter Pichler and Algis Shalna until a new executive director had been hired.

This, along with a list of other cost cutting measures sent shock waves among those deeply involved within the biathlon community.

The re-evaluation of biathlon as an underdeveloped sport in 1992 also came at a time when the USOC began to tie its financial support to the performance of the athletes. It had created a system of stipend and incentive programs that would make funds available only to clearly defined elite athletes rather than the organization. Four athletes (Josh Thompson, Anna Sonnerup, Joan Guetschow and Beth Coats) met the qualification standard of finishing in the top 20 at the World Cup level which provided slightly over $40,500 for various projects involving those athletes and a potential of $12,000 for each of those athletes as incentives for performance at any World Cup or World Championships for the 1992-93 season. The USOC also awarded biathlon $151,571 from its Team 94 program. This new system of USOC support amounted to less than previous year's totals and took much of the financial flexibility away from the Association.

In an August 2nd, 1992 letter to the members, President Ed Williams announced that the U.S. Biathlon Association's office would move from Essex Junction, Vermont to the USOC's Training Center at Lake Placid, New York. He also announced Jed Williamson's resignation and a search for a new executive director. Without mentioning the change in USOC funding support, he also announced a membership and fund-raising drive. Shortly after the letter to members from Williams, Max Cobb forwarded a letter to the board of directors highlighting the progress made between 1991 and 1992 which saw the men's and women's IBU Nations Cup standing improved from 20th to 8th for the men and from 11th to 6th for the women. He also suggested that with the USOC grant money down to its lowest level in over 4 years, a 100% turnover of the office staff (Williamson, Law and Donahue) and unknown replacements, and moving the office to Lake Placid would destabilize all the U.S. Biathlon Association programs, setting them back at a time when the next Winter Olympic Games was just 18 months away.

Following the letter from Max Cobb, Jed Williamson sent a letter to the board members outlining his concerns, suggesting disgruntled employees and athletes were unhappy with the efforts of the Executive Committee. An emergency meeting of the board of directors was called on September 3rd which responded quickly to the conditions of growing instability within the Association. From this meeting was announced that the office would not move in that fiscal year, continued employment for Betty Law, Dennis Donahue and bookkeeper Lisa Hughes would be offered through the fiscal year and that a Board member not on the Executive Committee would be involved in the search for a new executive director. It was also established as policy that the Executive Committee would consult with the entire board of directors on all matters which could potentially be controversial, prior to or as soon as possible after taking action to insure strong board of directors support.

The October 10th, 1992 meeting of the board of directors at the famous Hotel Fontainebleau in Miami Beach restored some sense of optimism and confidence among the members which later filtered down to the general membership. Despite the USOC's denial of a request for reconsideration of its decision to downgrade biathlon's status to an underdeveloped sport and the resulting loss of funding, there were many other developments that gave cause for optimism. Much of that came from the Search Committee's recommendation and the Board's approval of Duane "Dusty" Johnston as the new executive director. Dusty's background in marketing positions with IBM along with a background in skiing seemed to suggest that he would be capable of solving the USBA's continual financial difficulties at a time when it was most needed. It was also at this meeting that other issues seemed to be resolved in a positive manner. Since Dennis Donahue did not change his mind about resignation, he was replaced by John Morton who had left his Dartmouth College ski team coaching position and agreed to step down as a member of the board and assume the program director's responsibilities on a temporary assignment. John had always been viewed as an advocate for the athletes and good program manager which were qualities that pleased the athletes. At the meeting, the National Guard also announced that it had completed development of a roller-ski loop at its Jericho biathlon training site and invited unlimited use of the site for the National team. With his announcement as the new executive director, Dusty outlined his vision and objectives and asked the board for help in defining USBA objectives. A discussion for the development of "Centers of Excellence" led by Max Cobb also generated new enthusiasm among those concerned with development. One development that helped restore optimism was the USOC's grant of $50,000 to USBA. It supported the program at the Northern Michigan University Education Center and the rapid growth of the summer biathlon program with a proposal of a three-year financial support agreement of $200,000 annually.

As the USBA began focusing on the 1994 and 1998 Lillehammer and Nagano Winter Olympic Games there was a serious effort on the part of the Executive Director Dusty Johnstone to move the organization to a more "committee" based structure with clearly defined goals, tasks and expectations. For the most part, the board of directors were favorable to the committee structure and were pleased with the efforts of Johnstone in developing a "vision" for the Association and a "Organization Self-appraisal" Four Year Plan. The 1994 Strategic Plan for International Success and revised USBA mission statement evolved out of the events between 1992 and 1994. It was during that period that the USBA, like many National Governing Bodies had to cope with the ever-increasing demands for high performance in the face of decreasing financial resources. The USBA was feeling the USOC pressure for "medal winning" performances at the international levels at the same time it was trying to cope with decreasing USOC financial support. Despite the financial optimism during the previous board of directors meeting at West Yellowstone, Montana on December 14th, 1992; two frustrating problems surfaced, one recurrent and one completely new.

After the competitive season in an April 8th, 1993 letter to the National Team athletes, Dusty Johnstone explained that expenses had exceeded revenue by over $100,000, creating a severe budget deficit that required immediate action. Support levels to the National team members was severely reduced and for many eliminated. These harsh measures also brought back the issue about where best to allocate resources; on development or high-performance, and introduced a source of disgruntlement among the athletes. It also exacerbated growing tensions between the athletes and the leadership of the organization. The budget imbalance also came at a time when the National Guard budget had expanded to provide excellent support for its athletes, had constructed and improved biathlon sites and facilities and educated and supported many race officials and staff to the point where USBA was heavily dependent of National Guard resources. A letter from the adjutant general of Vermont and USBA member of the board of directors, Major General Donald Edwards to Dusty Johnstone questioned the decision for the athletes to bear the burden of reducing costs and asked for a summary and explanation of the budget shortfall.

Facing the pressure of improving international results became an even more critically serious issue when the UIMPB's Technical Committee made a proposal to restrict the number of athletes that may participate in World Cup, World Championships and Olympic events. Their proposal would limit the number of participants in international events by a quota defined by each nation's team standing earned through Nations' Cup points at World Cup events. This issue collided with the USOC's re-evaluation of biathlon and decision to re-direct financial support to qualified athletes based on their international results. The UIMPB's proposal became a growing concern for the weaker and mostly non-European nations and at the October 10th, 1992 meeting in Miami Beach the board of directors made a motion to send Bill Spencer and Art Stegen to the UIPMB meeting at Amilié-Les-Bains, France to join forces with other nations in supporting a resolution to reverse the direction of UIMPB's Technical Committee's recommendation that would in effect limit U.S. participation and "less competitive" nations in international events. At that meeting, despite the efforts of the group led by the U.S., Canada and Great Britain, there was no impact on the decision, with the UIPMB's attention focused on the issue of separation between biathlon and pentathlon. The new international "quota" system was a clear message that the USBA must produce better training and prepared athletes along with an administration and budget that would support improved international results if it wished to retain a viable place in the international biathlon community. Each of these two issues would have a severe impact on each other.

The UIMPB's Technical Committee's proposed participation quota wasn't the first attempt to reduce the numbers of biathlon participation at the Winter Olympic Games, however it appeared to be for a different reason. It looked like an attempt to reduce the total number while retaining higher participation levels of the "stronger" biathlon nations. The IOC reduced the entries in biathlon from 4 to 3 in 1976, 1980 and 1984 but to meet the growing popularity of biathlon it was again raised to 4 in 1988. However, the response of media attention to the "Eddie the Eagle" ski jumper and "Jamaican Bobsled team" stories at Calgary, IOC President Juan Antonio Samaranch was strongly motivated in his ambition to build the IOC into a powerful global organization and firmly establishing the Olympics as a world sports premier force. Ending amateurism, he worked towards making the Olympic Games the world's favorite sports festival. The directive from the IOC to address controlling the numbers and the competence of the athletes prior to the 1994 Lillehammer Winter Games impacted biathlon and especially teams below the best eight in the Nations cup scoring. Bill Spencer, who was the sole representative from North America on the technical committee, reported that a discussion with Anders Besseberg revealed that the impression concerning Olympic participation under Samaranch's leadership, the Olympic Games were moving away from the theme or philosophy of participation and amateurism to one of "show-casing" the best of the sports world, professionalism, media marketability, and a "money-making spectacle." Any sport that couldn't adjust to the changing times risked being dropped for the Olympic program.

The UIPMB's Technical Committee was poorly represented by nations outside of Europe, and its proposal to limit World Cup, World Championship and Olympic Games participation quotas on the Nations Cup rankings appeared to reflect that condition. The proposal outlined an Olympic participation quota based on the Nations Cup ranking that provided four start positions for the teams ranked 1st through 8th, three for those ranked 9th to 15th, two for those ranked 16th to 20th and only one for any nation ranked 21st or lower. World Championships and World Cup quotas were similar but with 6 start positions for the top nations at World Cup events. The Nations Cup rankings were to be determined from participation in five World Cup events which would place an unfair burden on the teams outside of Europe and it would become nearly mathematically impossible for any nation not ranked in the top 8 to aspire to have full representation at international events, which included the United States. It would certainly increase the difficulty of improving U.S. international results and USOC funding.

After the separation of the UIMPB into two bodies, the new IBU put into place the recommendations of the Technical Committee and the U.S. Biathlon team could only enter two men and three women in the 1994 Winter Olympic Games at Lillehammer. Results for the men were much worse than expected with no result better than 64th place. The women's results had improved over 1992. Confronting what was considered a crisis, the USBA made some assumptions in the 1994 Strategic Plan for International Success that were well-intentioned but led to a reduction in its effectiveness. One of the key assumptions was that the current senior athletes, especially men, were incapable of improvement and did not possess the appropriate physiological or psychological qualities for success. These athletes were viewed as consuming valuable resources and stalling the progression of younger athletes, serving as "blockers" to junior development and quality high performance. Other assumptions that guided the Strategic Plan were that international success at the junior levels would lead to success at the senior levels and the development of Regional Centers of Excellence would fulfill the dual role of recruiting young athletes and augmenting the resources of the national program. With these assumptions guiding the plan a decision was made to devote 1995-96 to "development" and 1997-98 to "high performance."

This was not the first time such a similar critical decision on the best use of limited resources was forced by such a plan. In 1978, when Art Stegen was hired as the National coach he implemented a "regional" philosophy for the development and identification of new talent and finding junior athletes. The pipeline of senior athletes from the U.S. Army's program in Alaska had begun to dry up and although junior athletes began to participate in 1973, they were in small numbers and real support was absent. Regions were drawn up and regional coaches were named (John Morton for the eastern states, John Durben for the central states, Matt Montagne in the Rocky Mountains and Nat Brown in the west). Within a short period, each coach had identified and introduced talented athletes who were named to a new USBA Junior team that became the core of young talent that soon began to challenge the senior athletes, directing their training towards the 1980 Winter Olympic Games at Lake Placid. With a "home" Olympic Games and no international travel, the budget could absorb both junior development and high performance. In the post-Olympic year, the issue about where best to allocate resources again surfaced when the financial well-being weakened.

At the time, the Sports Act gave new-found strength to athlete representatives on the board of directors and they, senior athletes, convinced the directors that the only way to improve international success was more intense European competition. The board decided to eliminate the full-time staff, cut development and junior support and use the savings to support continued exposure to European racing by sending the senior men's team on the European Alpine Cup circuit. The assumption was that increased exposure to quality racing would lead to better skills and therefore translate into better results. The decision eventually had no real impact on the international results, however it did lead to the loss of nearly the entire group of younger athletes with exciting potential for the future (Tom McElroy, Rich McGuire, Stuart Jennings, Greg Cress, and Rody Hagen). There was little progress in the improvement of international results and the lag in development between 1982 and 1986 wasn't corrected until the resources from the successful 1984 Summer Olympic Games began to manifest themselves with better financial health, resulting in better programs, full-time coaching and ultimately success at the 1987 World Championships.

With the assumptions built into the 1994 plan, a decision by the board of directors was made to not send a senior men's team to the World Championships at Antholz in 1995 and only to the final two World Cups, and for the following year, not to send a senior men's team to any World Cups or World Championships in 1996. The logic of this decision was that the limited resources spent on the senior men were better spent on getting the younger athletes ready to replace them. This decision was suddenly put in jeopardy when the IBU adopted the Nations Cup quota system for participation, leaving the men's team with three start positions for 1996. Not attending the 1996 season's events would have left the U.S. men with only a single start position and little chance of improvement leading into the 1998 Olympic Games. This created a critical condition for both UOSC funding potential and difficulty for encouraging the Regional Centers to find and motivate junior athletes facing the potential of a single Olympic start position. After analyzing the situation, Major General Donald Edwards and Colonel John Abair of the National Guard suggested a solution.

At the trials for the 1996 World Championships, National Guard athletes occupied the first four positions (Curt Schreiner, first year senior Dan Westover, Chad Salmela and Robert Rosser). The National Guard proposed to send those athletes and National Guard Coach Art Stegen to the World Cups and World Championships with full funding support from the National Guard. This solution allowed for the men's National team Coach Algis Shalna to be free to work with Junior Coach Cory Salmela towards developing the promising junior men who were viewed as the next generation of quality senior athletes. Despite the assumption of being unable to improve and "blocking" the path for potentially more talented juniors and having been reduced to only two start positions at the 1996 World Championships and three at the World Cups, the National Guard athletes were able to gain back a start position for the 1997 World Championships.

The help of the National Guard, the 1994 Strategic Plan for International Success did lead to some improvement with the emergence of the 1997 World Junior Champion for the Sprint, Jay Hakkinen, however it did not help to gain additional start positions at Japan's 1998 Winter Olympic Games at Nagano. The men were left with two competitors in each individual event while the women retained three. With Hakkinen on the U.S. Olympic team and a member of the World Cup team, they were able to gain back four start positions for the 1999 season with a team of mostly first year senior athletes. Yet despite this turn in a positive direction, there remained a budget crisis that threatened a sustained effort and began to reopen dissention among the athletes and the leadership over budget priorities and decisions. The discord once again manifested itself over the issue of funding developmental efforts versus high performance at the international level as well as some serious athlete criticism and issues with program decisions and coaching.

The issue of funding had been an ongoing problem since the establishment of the U.S. Biathlon Association however, considering the USOC ever increasing expectations for success, both the USBA leadership and the athletes began to see those expectations as unreasonable in face of the constant reductions of financial support. U.S. athletes never enjoyed the full or quasi state supported status of the athletes from the European nations, especially those from the Soviet bloc nations. Although the U.S. Army provided support at the USMWBTC, it was not the same long-term support that was clearly needed to be competitive at the international levels. U.S. athletes of the 1970s and 1980s were essentially amateurs that were sacrificing careers and financial security while competing against professionals. When Howard Buxton, who had become a committee member of the USOC explained at the USBA Board of Directors meeting at Lake Placid on September 18, 1993 that the USOC was rewarding success at the expense of those sports that are not achieving the expected levels of success, he alluded to biathlon's major problem, financial shortcomings. He stated that the USOC had perceptions that were unfair, and it was an unsympathetic audience. Those perceptions were: the staff of USBA was too large and taking up too much resources, the USOC had spent $5,000,000 on biathlon since 1984 with little results in athletic performance, biathlon as an Olympic sport had never received an Olympic medal, the USBA must achieve measurable results for better support and that the USOC wants to see plans for success, with milestones, levels of progress, honest assessment and consistency. This news from Buxton was clear and another call to action for USBA. It highlighted the two plaguing problems, limited resources and lack of athletic success. It precipitated the 1994 Strategic Plan for International Success, but his news also provoked the discord within the organization that would be ongoing over the next few years.

It was hard for the athletes, leadership and general membership of the USBA to accept the situation and not ignore self-examination. At that September 18th, 1993 meeting the members were presented with a breakdown of USBA funding categories that showed 25% of the budget dedicated to administration, 9% to grassroots development, 21% to national and domestic programs and 45% to elite athlete programs. To many this appeared to be the right distribution of resources, however further investigation into the categories of funding showed much of the funding in national/domestic and elite programs included insurance, coaching salaries and staff travel, which some viewed as administrative expenses. The athletes were particularly critical of the limited "athlete subsistence" at the same time feeling somewhat "blamed" for poor performance.

Their criticism soon turned to the coaching staff and USBA administration. President Lyle Nelson sought to answer their criticism and initiated efforts to improve the functioning of the USBA committee structures and identify solutions to remove the anxiety among the athletes. The issue of coaching, appropriate concepts, responsibilities and relationships between the athletes and coaching was not a new issue. Although off-the-record discussions were always taking place and many opinions often stated, Howard Buxton first brought up the issue officially with the board of directors following the departure of Sigvart Bjontegaard and the failure to meet the high expectations at the 1988 Winter Olympic Games. In an April 19th, 1988 memo to the members Buxton wrote that a replacement for Bjontegaard would be necessary and listed the many opinions that were being injected into the developing discussion of what should be a search committee's requirements and priorities. Many opinions were contradictory. Those identified in Buxton's memo included: coaches should have biathlon experience and several years of coaching experience, more emphasis should by placed on shooting, a European coach is necessary, a European coach should be an assistant, there needed to be a continuity beyond a few years, a good coaching staff should take priority over athlete support, the coach should be a manager-type head coach, and the necessity to meet the needs of the elite athletes.

Along with these opinions, Buxton also outlined the feedback he was receiving from the athletes who felt very strongly about the coaching issues and who had the responsibility for poor performance. Much of their concerns were also centered on athlete support that included continuing broken time payments, expanding the domestic racing program, the question of supporting fewer athletes at a higher level or more athletes at a lower level, team members being required to participate in all training events as a condition to receive support and should they be required to furnish part of their support. The issues of coaching personality, technical ability and performance suddenly became a philosophical discussion intertwined with support and responsibility issues among the athletes along with program emphasis. Lyle Nelson provided focus to this discussion at the July 9-10, 1988 board of directors meeting at Bolton Valley, Vermont. He spoke about the purpose and philosophy of the USBA and felt that the philosophical questions fell into three categories: 1) centralized training (training center with athletes and coaches in residence) versus decentralized (club system with athletes and coaches in regions), 2) accountability for performance (who is responsible, athlete, coaches or administration), and 3) emphasis of program (elite athletes or development athletes or should there be equal emphasis). Following Lyle's presentation each board member was asked their opinion on these three areas. The majority favored a decentralized program; felt the performance should be shared equally by all with the athlete finally accountable and the preferred program emphasis should be on the development program, while maintaining an effective elite program.

The board of directors decision on the three philosophical questions and the hiring of Dennis Donahue, and Bill Spencer as the coaching staff did not solve the critical issues of adequate funding or improving international performance. In fact, those issues resurfaced again at the June 10-11th 1989 board of directors meeting at Bolton Valley, Vermont. John Morton, who chaired the Training and Competition Committee, reported that the coaching issue was not resolved. Dennis Donahue reported that the problem was that providing athletes with "hands-on" coaching was impossible in that some athletes wanted every-day coaching. He stated that athletes would need to locate to one area with facilities before such coaching would be possible. Despite the long discussion on the potential of creating centralized elite training, no real solution came from the meeting, however it was narrowly decided to hire a qualified head coach and two other coaches for the next season.

Before the spring board of directors meeting in 1990 Director Jed Williamson outlined the continual difficulty in finding financial stability and a budget that would support both ends of the discussion. It was his first year as director and he said that he had spent much of the year trying to determine where the program and the money to support it was going. At the time, the USBA was fast approaching two Olympic Games within a short period and he reported to the members of board that the "Four-Year Plan" approved by them was constantly being revised due to the USOC requirements for such a plan and USOC's projections of expected funding. He stated that the funding levels from USOC were about one-quarter of what is needed to accomplish the plan's goals and that marketing efforts had been unable to generate any substantial increase. With the intensified demands by the athletes for centralized training and full-time coaching, as well as changes in the way the USOC measures progress, he felt that there were serious challenges for the coming years. At the May 4th, 1991 meeting, hoping to meet the deficit of the over $600,000 budget, the board of directors decided to use the remaining funds from the Los Angeles surplus to support current operating expenses. Attempting to resolve continuing budget deficits while facing continued demands of the USOC and the athletes were a continual major problem facing the organization. The actions of the Executive Committee in July 1992 and the executive director's letter to the athletes in April of 1993 were consequences of the continual disconnection between the efforts to improve performance within the circumstances of budget deficits.

Despite the ongoing budget woes, there was progress in international performance that began to make a difference with the USOC funding. There were several factors that helped make this possible. One of the most important was that of the support from the National Guard. Major General Donald Edwards was elected president and following the resignation of Dusty Johnstone, Colonel Steve Sands, who was serving as the National Guard's Biathlon program director took over Dusty's role at no expense to the Association and provided greater access to the Guard's facilities. This arrangement, which was questioned by many within the organization and the National Guard, provided great budget relief. It was also to the credit of the younger, developing athletes who, with the coaches' direction made great progress in their development and became increasingly competitive at the international levels. However, maintaining continued improvement still required improved financial resources. Progress had also been made with the L.L.Bean support during the period from the Albertville Winter Olympic Games through those at Salt Lake City. The L.L.Bean support of $50,000 per year and national team uniforms and clothing was the first real major sponsorship arrangement that included substantial financial resources as well as team clothing. The sponsorship was developed by Andy Sheppard who worked at L.L.Bean at the time. Andy had earlier served as the coach of the Bowdoin ski team during the same time that John Morton was the coach at Dartmouth. John had helped Andy at the Eastern Ski Carnivals and developed a friendship. When John was named the team captain for the World University Games at Zakopane, Poland he asked if Andy could help to request that L.L.Bean provide uniforms for the team. Seeing a need and opportunity, not long afterwards Andy set up a presentation with Dusty Johnstone proposing the contract for $50,000, team clothing and items. L.L.Bean provided perhaps what were the most attractive and practical team racing uniforms for the team through the 2002 Winter Olympic Games, however their support ended following those games.

Besides the ongoing financial conditions that faced the USBA during the period between 1988 and 2002, another issue began to exert tension on the leadership structure of the USBA. That issue was the effectiveness and efficiency of the organization's programs, coaching and governance structures. It was a condition that was being forced from both below at the "grass-roots" local levels and from above by the USOC. There was also increasing pressure from the athletes over funding issues and the performance of the coaching staff. Combined, these issues were making it difficult for the board of directors, staff, athletes and others with interest within the biathlon community to agree and come together to,wards common goals, assignment of resources and direction of consistent efforts.

As a former four-time Olympian who struggled through the 1970s and 1980s without the support that the current athletes received, Lyle Nelson who was the USBA president between 1992 and 1998 was sensitive to the athletes' interests, first attempted to respond to the growing concern when the athletes brought up their issues at a board of directors meeting on May 16, 1998 at Park City, Utah. The athletes expressed concern about recognition and coaching, saying all coaches must put aside their ego and work together towards unity for the good of the athlete and the association. A competitive nature between the National Guard program and the USBA coaches had developed, and it had even surfaced among the USBA coaches as well. At the next meeting on November 7, 1998 there was a discussion over the need to rewrite a High-Performance Plan for the USOC and submit it by December 1999. A proposal was made for the executive committee to appoint a group to write the plan and demanded that athletes and coaches be included in the group. It was pointed out at that meeting USBA expenses overview had now shown 44% of the 1998 budget went to athlete and race support while 37% to salaries and benefits and 19% for organizational and business costs.

Following the 1999 competitive season the issue of funding and international success was again a major issue at the May 15th meeting at Park City, Utah. Preparation and expectations for the upcoming home Winter Olympic Games at Salt Lake City were increasing the stress on many aspects of the organization. Lyle Nelson opened a discussion at that meeting concerning the role of the USBA Board of Directors and the agenda of how best to generate Olympic success. The discussion exposed general disagreement among the members with some expressing the need for making the philosophy of the board known to the athletes and clearly articulating the Association's goals and process for moving towards success. Even the definition of "success" came under scrutiny. Some saw the board's primary responsibility as fundraising when the question of what should happen when the board makes decisions that members do not support crept into the discussion. In answering the underlying question about universal support of decision making, one member suggested that if decisions were not universally supported once made, members should step down from the board. Considering these questions, a task force to review the USBA's organization and the High-Performance Plan was appointed with a specific goal of reviewing USBA's vision, mission goals and values as it pertained to governing and management.

That task force came back to the next meeting with a recommendation for redesigning the board of directors. Their conclusion was a clear indication that there was a general feeling that the current board was not functioning effectively. This recommendation came at the same time that the USOC had revised its constitution and by-laws and had distributed notice that it intended to do a review of NGB governance and compliance. It was the intention of the USOC to review each National Governing Body every two years to determine the appropriate and effective use of USOC funds, and its financial and managerial competence. Highlighted in the USOC's preliminary NGB governance guidelines were that NGB's should be governed by a board which has sole responsibility for governance, generally 7 to 12 in membership with at least 20% independent directors as well as at least 20% athletes. It also suggested staggered term limits with separation between the role of governance and management, meaning that the NGB should be staff managed and board governed. Although the USBA met most of the USOC's basic standards and guidelines, it clearly was not in alignment with the recommended size, type and separation of governance and management.

The original USBA by-laws and design of the board of directors was developed following its separation from the USMPBA and had seen few changes in the interim. At its original organization, a "widening of the grass roots" through development at club levels was the major strategy, thus a certain "departmentalization" or orderly arrangement of activities and functions that had to be performed by the organization helped to determine its structural design. That included the number and representation of the board membership and since there was no management staff, the board assumed both governance and management responsibilities. Although the by-laws had been amended to meet the requirements for 20% athlete representation, it had essentially retained the same structure with a BOD membership of 25 from various membership categories and a "block voting" structure that was designed to prevent any one group from controlling the organization. The membership groups and number of members on the board were: Clubs (4), Armed Forces (1), Sports Organizations (2), Corporations/Businesses (1), Past Officers (5), WBC/Olympic Athletes (5), Coaches/Officials (2), and At Large (5). The number and nature of the board members created a rather wide "span of control" or horizontal structure that made it difficult to provide leadership and with the various committees having no decision-making authority, the BOD's efficiency and effectiveness was constantly compromised. As the nature of the BOD focus moved away from "grass-roots" towards "high performance" it gradually failed to represent the membership in all its forms which often resulted in less than full support of all the objectives of the organization.

Like other frequent occurrences, the discussion concerning board of directors revision was overwhelmed by the increasing focus on the approaching Salt Lake Winter Olympic Games and little action took place other than Lyle Nelson re-tasking Steve Sands and Ed Williams to provide a model of what might become a recommendation for a change to the board of directors. However, prior to the May 6, 2000 board of directors meeting at Heber City, Utah, Lyle held a Biathlon Summit meeting with the goal focusing on content and priority for the Association in front of the upcoming Olympic Games. The summit resulted in five priorities: athletic performance, public awareness, capitalizing on 2002 funding opportunities, hosting an Olympic biathlon competition of which the Association can be proud and maintaining organizational motivation and vitality following the Olympic Games. In the discussion about these priorities it became clear once again that all board members were not in agreement. Members sparred with each other over the reoccurring issue of grass-roots development and high performance. Some felt the RCE's were being shortchanged while others felt that success at the Olympic games was the highest priority. A short discussion at the November 3, 2001 board of directors meeting about restructuring the board and by-laws revision also took place without anything other than mention in Lyle Nelson's president's report that the USBA has a professional and very competent staff and that it should be the role of the board to set policy during the meeting and leave the execution of any decisions to the full-time staff.

The results achieved by Jay Hakkinen and Jeremy Teela at Soldier Hollow indicated notable progress in international racing and following the Games, attention once again turned towards the financial health of the organization and issues of governance and management. At the October 19, 2002 board of directors meeting, in a discussion of the vision and goals beyond the Salt Lake City Games, financial stability was again the major topic. This was also again an issue that exposed disagreement within the board of directors. There was an attempt to make the directors responsible for fund-raising however the motion to do so was withdrawn. It was clear that some of the board's decisions were not universally accepted and that although the current budget met the business side of things, it did not meet the needs of all the athletes for performing at an expected higher level towards the next Olympic cycle. To meet the budget shortfall, the directors approved the withdrawal of $40,000 from the USOF funds.

Also, at that October 19th meeting there was an agenda item concerning the restructuring of the board of directors. President Lyle Nelson explained why he and the USOC were concerned with improving the responsiveness and governance of the USBA. He felt along with other members of the board that reorganization along the line of the USOC-suggested guidelines would streamline the economy and efficiency of efforts, helping to make the USBA move forward and be "more responsive in a more-timely manner." Supported by other board members, he appointed Art Stegen to chair a committee on restructuring the USBA Board of Directors and to present a recommendation reflecting USOC recommendations and traditional corporate structure that seeks to improve its effectiveness to the board 60 days prior to the next scheduled meeting for the spring of 2003. He also suggested the need to review the USBA by-laws insuring that the committee's work would be in line with those by-laws. This began what would become a very difficult and contentious period for the Association.

At the next board of directors meeting on May 17, 2003 at the impressive new facility at Ft. Kent, Maine, Art reported on the committee's recommendations for restructuring the BOD. Those recommendations were in line with those encouraged by the USOC which recently experienced their own leadership troubles and demands from Congress for more business-like reforms. The committee recommended reducing the number of board members to 11 and explained an analysis behind the motivation for change from the present status, the primary concerns, facts and assumptions and an examination of various organizational characteristics and functions. The committee also stressed that there was a critical need for by-law changes, committee restructure and the responsibility to meet the legal standards of the Amateur Athlete Sports Act and New York State Not-for-Profit Incorporation laws. Vice President Alan Nye made a motion to charge the president to name a committee for proceeding with the development of the board of directors restructuring and by-laws revision. Andy Shepard seconded the motion and a discussion concerning the time-line, the process and what the final BOD would look like followed, but no firm deadlines were identified, and the motion was approved without opposition. Also, at that meeting it was observed that the momentum that is developed after an activity such as a board of directors meeting or an event such as the team trials or National Championships is often lost. Regular communication is an important way to continue the enthusiasm and momentum that takes so much energy to acquire and in June the *Biathlon Bulletin* was resumed and sent by e-mail to the membership.

Another issue brought forward by the athletes at that meeting became entangled with the issue of restructuring the BOD, revising the by-laws and ongoing funding issues. The athletes questioned the team nominations and methods used by the International Competition Committee and they felt that raising the bar of international performance was becoming a negative motivating force rather than a positive one. They saw the team selection criteria as unrealistic and tied to USOC "performance dollars" and unnecessary for naming the National team. Without any alteration, the directors approved the ICC recommendation. This decision did not satisfy the athletes and would have additional future impact. At the next BOD meeting on September 27, 2003 at Colchester, Vermont facing growing discontent within the organization, Lyle found himself urging the members to work together in solving problems. He stated that identifying a problem did not make the person identifying it the problem. He asked the members to recognize the "diversity" of the association and despite the increasing competition for control and widening differences between groups, he felt it should become a cause for cohesion and not create misunderstanding between "competing energies."

Lyle reviewed the recommendations by the Committee for Restructure and gave his view as to how the future board would look and operate. He felt it would be more dependent on committee work and that it would be a "non-constituency" based group. He recommended approval to go forward with the restructuring plan and creating a nominating committee for the election of new officers to fill a two-year term. At that point, an intensive and somewhat contentious discussion gripped the meeting. Much of the discussion centered on the need for a "military" member from Group B. Some saw adequate and more desirable a nine-member board without military representation and the need for one less athlete representative, perhaps partly due to the feeling by some that the National Guard had too much control over the organization. Ed Williams, who now served as legal consul reminded the members the Sports Act required "entity" programs capable of producing Olympic athletes, including the military to have "reasonable direct" representation on the board of directors. Implications of non-compliance could ultimately result in removal of the USBA as the National Governing Body. Some members also had difficulty in understanding and accepting the block voting structure by the categories as outlined in the current by-laws, preferring instead a "one-man, one vote" structure which would clearly create the conditions and ability for one constituency group to dominate the association.

In the developing urgency to reorganize the board of directors some of the members failed to understand the need for a by-law revision before a Board membership election prior to a new board structure taking place. Without any formal written documentation, and purported amendments to the by-laws, it was felt that modification to the structure of the board and the composition of officers provided for a special election. Without any formal approval or discussion about its membership relative to the by-laws there was a willingness by board members to act outside the rules. These flawed actions resulted in naming a Nomination Committee and time-line for the election without attention to by-laws revision. This situation was complicated by the athletes' issues. They felt they faced continual ambiguity or uncertainty of their status, were unhappy about their progress, training, funding and about the administration and organization as a whole. Seeing themselves as the most important part towards achieving the objectives and mission of the USBA, they felt they should be the major part for which the financial resources should be allocated. A serious sense of frustration rather than success had developed. This feeling had been developing ever since the first High Performance Plan of 1994 was developed under perceptions that the athletes were not working "hard" enough, that they were economically secure, had easy life-styles and lacked "winning" attitudes within the organization. Attempting to respond to the athletes, Lyle named an Ad Hoc Committee to address their concerns, however some BOD members seized upon their issues for leverage in the effort to reorganize the structure and by-laws of the Association.

In the haste to change the leadership a Nomination Committee was named, ignoring the warning of Ed Williams about maintaining a balance of constituencies. Three of the members of the committee had strong ties to the Minnesota programs, which gave the appearance of trying to gain control of the board when their recommendations were announced. Then attempts to influence the anticipated vote surfaced with the formation of new clubs and shifting of membership classes. Soon after the Nomination Committee submitted its recommendations, a formal complaint was filed in January 2004 claiming that in accordance with the by-laws and against the advice of Ed Williams, the Nominating Committee was not "generally representative of the various constituencies of the Association" and that there were clear "conflicts of interest" by the individuals recommended by the Nominating Committee.

The previously named Ad Hoc Committee's analysis uncovered a perception of exclusion among the various constituencies that was at the center of the issue and a severe weakness preventing a "culture of success" to become the core or central issue within the Association. This coincided with the anticipated changes in the organizational structure and impending elections. Unqualified statements such as "has by far the largest and most successful junior biathlon program in the U.S.," or "we have been sub-optimized" exposed the fact that there was a sense of limited participation, especially the planning, directing and controlling of USBA activities, even when those issues were not in complete harmony with the "philosophical base" or "fundamental purpose" and outside the financial realities of the organization. The committee provided specific recommendations, the most important of which was making the structural changes in the organization that would make the Association more responsive and active rather than procrastinating and inactive.

The internal turbulence began to take its toll on the organization. In July 2004 Lyle Nelson resigned and at the next board of directors meeting on September 11, 2004 at Colchester, Vermont where the USBA office had relocated back to Vermont from Lake Placid, Vice President Alan Nye chaired the meeting. Alan announced to the members present that he would not seek to serve as interim president and asked that the issue be considered later in the agenda. The meeting took place following actions taken by the Nominating Committee's candidates for the anticipated reorganized board of directors and a formal complaint to the USBA. The complaint alleged that the athlete nominators to the Nominating Committee for the new USBA Board of Directors were not chosen in a forthcoming manner and that there were potential conflicts of interest concerns among those nominees put forth on the ballot. A fact-finding independent committee (Howard Buxton, Mark Muedeking and Erich Wilbrect) was formed and determined there was validity to the complaint, which angered those who were frustrated by that finding and thus delaying the anticipated time-line for elections. However, despite the issues of the complaint and the impact on the reorganization and election, the fact that a by-laws revision was still required prior to either an election of officers or reorganization of the BOD was still generally unrecognized. Coupled with a net loss of $200,000 in basic USOC funding and another $130,000 in performance grants, which represented nearly one-half of total USBA revenues, and the athletes' loss of confidence in the leadership, the USBA found itself in a crisis.

That contentious meeting ended with a delay of the election for the members of the reorganized board of directors until 2006, before the Torino Winter Olympic Games and resulted in naming William (Bill) Lilly, the Chairman of NYSSRA and the Empire Games Biathlon Committee in New York to serve as Interim president. It was also decided that in the time before the next election a by-laws committee would begin work on drafting new by-laws that would meet all the requirements of necessary compliance. A new strategic plan committee was also appointed and directed to work simultaneously. Unfortunately, during an executive committee meeting on December 17th, 2004 a perception that the delay was intentional and accusations that some appeared to want to retain "power" surfaced. This notion appeared to be encouraged by the frustration of trying to put the election in front of the by-laws revision. Also "regionalism" and personalities had been injected into any discussions of thinking within the biathlon community as a whole and how the board might improve the effectiveness and efficiency of its efforts.

Prior to the next regular board of directors meeting to be held in June of 2005, a teleconference meeting was held on January 22, 2005 for presenting a title sponsorship proposal by John Ratoff of BankNorth. Without full knowledge of the entire BOD, Andy Shepard had been working with both BankNorth and the Libra Foundation in Maine for solutions to solve the multiple financial issues faced by the Association. It was at that conference the participating members learned that the proposal would be conditional upon moving the USBA office from Vermont to Maine and the need for a new executive director. The fact that a press conference announcing an agreement had been scheduled, prior to the meeting, was seen as an attempt to pressure immediate signing of an agreement. A draft of this proposal had previously been distributed and it had raised serious questions that were left unanswered. Bill Lilly had suggested that a Memorandum of Understanding be prepared outlining the major areas that needed to be worked on and to find agreement. No action had been taken on the draft proposal and the questions during the teleconference focused on the Memorandum, especially on moving the USBA office to Maine and the retention of Steve Sands as the executive director who had a multi-year contract. There was strong disagreement among the members on these issues however an agreement making BankNorth the title sponsor for U.S. Biathlon was signed on January 24, 2005 which included USBA plans to relocate its headquarters to Portland, Maine following the 2006 Torino Winter Olympic Games. The agreement was to last for six years.

Those issues were still a major topic of the next BOD meeting on June 11, 2005 at Pineland Farms, New Gloucester, Maine. Andy Shepard who had been most responsible for developing the TD BankNorth proposal told the members that moving the office was a condition of the proposal and he had demanded an immediate decision to relocate the USBA office to Pineland Farms to have close contact with TD BankNorth and Owen Wells, CEO of the Libra Foundation. He previously indicated Libra would be donating the office space, equipment and services to the USBA. Two new at-large members, Bill Haggett and Larry Pugh, both from Maine supported the request and explained the relationship of Owen Wells and the Libra Foundation as it applied to the USBA and many other projects, such as the Maine Winter Sports Council. To comply with the previous BankNorth agreement, a motion to relocate was approved and a time-line that had been pre-developed in advance of the meeting was agreed upon with the transfer to be complete on June 30, 2006, which left some members feeling they were ambushed. However, the majority approved the decision and time-line. The other important decision that was achieved was how the reorganized board of directors would look and that a by-laws revision would take place prior to the next election of directors. Alan Nye, who would chair the by-laws revision committee explained that the critical issues concerning the size of the board and the composition and voting strength of the membership groups still needed to be resolved. After discussion of those issues and a decision to combine the military (National Guard) within the organizational group, Larry Pugh who had extraordinary experience with the composition of a board of directors made the motion to reorganize to an 11-member board as suggested by the Committee for Reorganization with the composition and voting strength to be worked out by the by-laws revision committee. The path finally seemed to be set for the future.

The board of directors meeting on September 10, 2005 at Pineland Farms was one of significant progress on what was viewed as a positive step towards resolving the internal issues and a better future. The two most important steps in that direction were a presentation and review of the by-laws and establishing a nominations committee and ethics review committee. The subject of the office relocation remained an issue when it was discovered that lease agreement at Pineland Farms identified fees for rent and other costs. The management of Pineland Farms was by the Libra Foundation. It was explained that Libra would provide the space at no cost by providing a grant, which would not cover "up-front" costs. Larry Pugh agreed to work out the title sponsorship agreement with TD BankNorth to coincide with the relocation. Ed Williams gave a comprehensive report on the by-laws revision highlighting compliance with USOC, Amateur Sports Act and

New York State requirements. He pointed out the revision also met the guidelines issued in the USOC Memorandum of May 6, 2005 concerning "Independent Directors." That memorandum expressed USOC expectations of meeting the conditions of objectivity and independent perspective, balance of voting power among the various constituent groups, ability to focus on the entire organization rather than a particular constituency, diverse experience and skills that may add strength to the current board and access to new circles of influence that may benefit the NGB such as donors, business contacts, etc... Ed also outlined perhaps the most important requirement, the need for the Association to go to the membership for approval of the changes. At that meeting Athlete Representative Chad Salmela also reported that there was now a sense of high spirit, motivation and fitness among the athletes.

In December 2005, the Nominating Committee announced its slate of officers. Two of the candidates, including one who had been a recommendation by the first Nominating Committee and found to have a "conflict of interest" were again found to have a conflict of interest by the Ad Hoc Ethics Committee on December 22, 2005. The conflicts were based on the individual's relationship to the Maine Winter Sport Center. After Andy Shepard removed his named from the nominating process, the candidate for secretary removed himself and was replaced by Art Stegen, and after Larry Pugh resigned from the board of MWSC the election went forward. After 10 years of serving in many roles, Steve Sands resigned as the executive director but would continue to serve as executive director on a consultant basis until his successor was appointed. He was praised for his tireless efforts to make the Association continue to function when financial support began evaporating after the 2002 Olympic Winter Games and was faced with very challenging situations. He supported relocation of the USBA offices to Maine even knowing the potential negative impact on him personally.

As of February 26, 2006, the date of record the vote by the membership to approve the proposed changes in the by-laws and the election of the new officers, it appeared that that the USBA had turned a corner. At the July 2006 meeting of the newly elected board of directors Chairman Larry Pugh announced the appointment of Max Cobb as new executive director. On June 26th Max Cobb announced the hiring of two new National Team coaches, Per Nilsson and Mikael Lofgren. Widely regarded as the best biathlon coaches anywhere in world, the two Swedes were a good fit into the U.S. program.

With the approval of new by-laws, election of a new board of directors and the hiring of a new executive director and National Team coaches, it can be said that USBA began a new era. The number of changes converging at the same time (revised by-laws and board of directors, new coaches and administration, sponsorship agreements and USOC support) was not coincidental, but the work of many who had the vision and success of the sport as their motivation. Bernd Eisenbichler who had begun working for the team as a wax technician in 1999 became the ski service chief, and later the high-performance director in 2007. With what the USOC characterized as a "model for governance" and the charismatic leadership of Larry Pugh, the USOC approved the USBA funding requests. The dynamics of how the BOD and staff functioned changed drastically. The changes in 2004 and 2005 renewed a sense of unity within the biathlon community and believed to be a response and adaptations to the ever-present changes in the sport and specific biathlon environment.

From 1958 to 1973, biathlon was totally managed and supported by the military. This was a natural result of the military origins of the sport and its international governance. During that time, there were no domestic races or development of athletes outside the military environment at the USMWBTC in Alaska. Following the end of the military draft and the closure of the U.S. Army's training center in 1973, the U.S. Modern Pentathlon and Biathlon Association (USMPBA) managed minimal support and volunteer coaches for World Championships participation. The USOC began to improve financial support, but it wasn't until 1978 that biathlon was able to hire a full-time coach, and that was only possible after USMPBA made some changes in its by-laws that allowed biathlon some sense of autonomy. After independence from the USMPBA, the U.S. Biathlon Association and the athletes struggled in what might be considered the "amateur" phase of the sport, yet as Josh Thompson demonstrated by winning the first-ever World Championships individual medal, there was potential to win. As the Association moved from one phase of the sport into one far more demanding of the athletes, it also approached the change with optimism and hope that made 2006 a pivotal year for U.S. Biathlon's future.

The athletes began to show the consequences of the changes almost immediately. Jay Hakkinen achieved the "best-ever" Olympic result with a 10th place in the men's individual race at the Torino Winter Olympic Games and Jeremy Teela followed that with a 9th place at Vancouver. Tim Burke would lead the men's team to finishing in the top ten of the 2007 IBU Nations Cup ranking. The U.S. team began winning World Championship medals again. First at the junior level, when the women were successful in both the individual and relay events at the 2006 World Junior Championships and again with Leif Norgren's bronze medal at the World Junior Biathlon Championships in 2008. After successful seasons, including the first-ever U.S. athlete to wear IBU leader's yellow bid, Tim Burke captured the silver medal at the 2013 World Biathlon Championships. At the 2014 Winter Olympic Games at Sochi Lowell Bailey improved the best-ever Olympic result with his 8th place finish in the individual race. By 2016 the U.S. men's team ranked 6th in the IBU Nations Cup standings and the impressive Sean Doherty who had raced at the Sochi Olympic Games while still a junior became IBU's and the USA's most decorated junior athlete, capturing over 10 individual medals at the World Junior Biathlon Championships. Also, in the far more competitive environment of today Susan Dunklee equaled the 1984 best U.S. women's World Championships finish to 5th place, and the best Olympic finish to 12th while also achieving multiple podium finishes at World Cup events. Susan Dunklee and Lowell Bailey continued their extraordinary efforts by winning a silver and first-ever gold medal at the 2017 World Biathlon Championships.

Looking back over the years of U.S. Biathlon history, it is clear the success of any organization is dependent on three basic elements; its physical, financial and human resources. With world-class facilities and top-level training sites at multiple locations across the country and despite disagreements and varying opinions the association's physical and human resources can be viewed as very defining and positive. The most difficult and ongoing shortcoming for the USBA is always with the financial resources, which can never seem to be maximized. With the goal of winning an Olympic gold medal still unachieved, a collective look at the U.S. Biathlon history must be considered as mostly successful despite being in mere survival mode on many occasions. As the association transitions to the future it is important to remember the paradox of life; although we have complete vision of the past, we have no ability to change it, while at the same time we have complete ability to change the future, but we are unable to see it clearly. The guiding principle and objectives of the board of directors and staff following the reorganization has been to operate from its philosophical base and fundamental purpose, "The U.S. Biathlon Association exists to support and encourage the development of biathlon in the United States and to prepare athletes for international competition, including the Olympic Winter Games."

USBA Organizational Structure as approved June 11, 2005

Individual Memberships				Organizational Memberships		
Group A	Group B	Group C	Group D	Group E	Group F	Group G
Athletes	Coaches Officials	Life Members	General Members	Clubs	Organizations	Sponsors

Rules:
- Members in Group A, B, and C are represented by individuals who have been designated by the head of the organizations involved, in writing to the Secretary.
- Only members (organizational and individual) with fully paid dues are entitled to representation and vote.
- Individuals or organizational delegates may vote only once and as a

member of the Group to which assigned as recorded by the Secretary in the official roll.

- Fractional votes if the members of a group exceed the number of votes for that group.
- If the number of members is less than the group votes, the group votes shall be reduced to that number of members voting.
- No member or delegate may exercise more than one vote.
- No proxy votes are allowed.
- Group A votes will equal 20% of the total votes.
- Groups F and G are entitled to 15 and 5 votes at any meeting of members.
- Note: Total number of votes is 40.
- USBA Board of Directors and responsibilities, approved June 11, 2005.

Executive Committee

Chairman	Vice Chairman	Secretary	Treasurer	Athlete Representative	
USOC/IBU Liaison, Ex-Officio	Personnel, Ethics/Bylaws	Communications, Membership	Budget, Finance	ACC Representative	
Coaches/Official Representative	Organization Member	At Large* Member	At Large* Member	Athlete* Rep	Athlete Rep
Competition, Coaches/Officials Ed, Rules, Safety	Marketing Fund Raising	Development, Awards	Public Relations, Media	Alt ACC Rep	Alumni, ICC

- Non-voting members

Legal Counsel	Executive Director/ CEO
Legal Opinion	Operations, Logistics

Notes:

- Chairman, Vice Chairman, Secretary and Treasurer elected by the membership.
- At least one At Large Member and one ACC Athlete Representative must be female.

CHAPTER 8

The Events and Competition

The first biathlon competition held in the U.S. at Camp Hale, Colorado in 1956 as part of a Nordic Weekend consisted of a one loop course with four separate shooting ranges. Firing was done at the four ranges which were scattered over the ski course between the distances of three to eighteen kilometers. The ranges and target sizes were at 250 meters at a target of 30 centimeters; at 200 meters at a target of 25 centimeters; at 150 meters at a target of 20 centimeters and at 100 meters at a 30 centimeters target. Firing at the first three ranges was from the prone position while the final 100 meters range was from the standing position. The targets were black circular disks with a straight bottom and five centerfire, large caliber rounds were to be fired at each target with the most common being 7.6 mm or 30-06. Each target was marked with a number corresponding to the racer's position on the firing line. The penalty for each missed shot was 2 minutes added to the ski time, which included the time used on the shooting ranges, to complete the course. The winner was determined by the lowest total adjusted time. The early configuration of the single 20 kilometers ski course along with the four separate shooting ranges had been essentially modeled after the military patrol race designed for individual participants. The format made the race difficult to organize, required a large supporting staff and was not especially spectator friendly.

By the time of the first U.S. National Championship biathlon race in 1965 held at Williams Lake in Rosendale, N.Y. the shooting distances were consolidated at a single shooting range with the targets set at the different required distances. This also allowed for a series of ski trails of 3 to 5 kilometers looping back to the single shooting range which made the race more spectator friendly, more convenient for administration and requiring less race supporting man-power. In the following year the UIPMB established new rules for the shooting with the change to a single shooting range of 150 meters and the shooting done alternately from the prone and standing positions. The targets had an aiming black diameter of 25 centimeters and a series of scoring rings of 12.5 and 25 centimeters for prone with a penalty for misses outside the 12.5cm ring of 1 minute and outside the 25cm ring 2 minutes of added time. For standing the scoring rings were 35 cm and 50cm with penalties for misses outside the 35cm ring of 1 minute and outside the 50cm ring 2 minutes. In 1971 the back-aiming circle was expanded to 35 centimeters. When the single range became the norm, the loop configurations also changed to a typical sequence of a minimum of 3 separate loops of 3.75, 5.0, 3.75, 5.0 and 2.5 kilometers that were color coded. The 1966 rule changes were prompted by efforts to make the sport easier to organize as well as making it more attractive to spectators.

That format remained the same until the UIPMB decided in 1976 to adopt the use of small bore (.22 rimfire caliber) rifles and reduce the shooting distance to 50 meters at a target with an 11 centimeters black aiming center. This change in shooting distance also caused a change in the target configuration. Since the inner prone ring was reduced to 4 centimeters, it sometimes became difficult to score the five shots on the target since the shots could be so tightly grouped that it was sometimes impossible to distinguish five separate bullet holes. To make the scoring less difficult a three-target configuration was used for which there was one target and two lower targets in a triangular formation rather than a singular paper target used previously. Competitors were to shoot two shots at any of the three targets and one shot at the remaining target. That resulted in any two targets with two scoring shots and a third with only one, according to the sequence decided upon by the athlete.

The 1980 Olympic Winter Games was the final time paper targets were used for the individual race. In 1981 "immediate response" or metal targets replaced paper targets for the individual 20 kilometers race and the 2 minutes penalty was eliminated. With the introduction of the relay event in 1966, immediate response targets of glass or balloons in a "five-bull" configuration was being used. The relay target at that time looked like a large "5" on a dice. In 1977 Dr. Josef Deflorian, the Austrian member of the UIPMB Technical Committee tested metal mechanical targets for use in the 1978 World Championships sprint and relay competitions. This target system had all five targets in a row on the same frame and registered a hit if the bullet went through a 4.5 centimeters hole in the middle of the aiming circle for the prone stage, or through the entire aiming mark of 11.5 centimeters for standing. The bullet would hit a hinged strike plate which would cause a white plate to fall and cover the aiming circle, indicating a hit. The falling plates would then be reset from the firing point by pulling a rope connected to the resetting mechanism on the target frame. This target system was used at the 1980 Olympic Games at Lake Placid for the sprint and relay races as well. At the 1981 World Biathlon Championships at Lahti, Finland the new metal targets and shooting format of one-minute penalty for missed targets changed the dynamics of the race by reducing the need for butts below the target line for changing paper targets and thus providing the excitement of immediate knowledge of hits or misses by both the competitors and spectators. In the ensuing years additional mechanical targets were developed and at the 1993 World Biathlon Championships at Borovetz, Bulgaria the system included electronic scoring functions and TV graphics and in 1995 a lead catching system was added.

Although the early concept of the 20 kilometers individual biathlon race was based primarily on the military patrol race, there was interest in creating a team competition right from the start at the first World Biathlon Championships in 1958. The winner of the team competition was decided by adding up the best results from each nation's four best competitors. This system was changed to include only the best three up until 1965 when the concept of a separate relay race was proposed to replace the early team competitions. The idea was promoted by Norwegians Jens Kjelsås and General Ole Jacob Bangstad. Their thoughts were that a relay race would be a more exciting type of team competition which would be more interesting to the spectators and television broadcasting and increase the public's acceptance of the sport. The concept was approved by the UIPMB Congress at Seefeld, Austria in 1964 and a test competition was scheduled for the World Biathlon Championships at Elverum, Norway in 1965. At first the competitors were allowed ten shots to hit five targets at each of two bouts of shooting at breakable targets, one from the prone and one from the standing positions, with a penalty lap of 200 meters for each missed target. Following the test race in 1965, the UIPMB approved the rules for the relay event, which reduced the number of reserve or spare rounds to three. Teams were comprised of 4 team members with each skiing 7.5 kilometers and it was added to the official program in 1966 and in 1968 it became a part of the Winter Olympic Games program. The relay competition was the first to use a mass start and because of the ease of following the competition it became the most exciting and popular biathlon event. To make the relay competitions closer at the finish and even more exciting the penalty lap was reduced to 150 meters in 1978.

With the development of breakable targets for the relay competitions, came the concept of the sprint race. Immediate response targets provided both the athletes and the spectators to see the shooting results immediately after each shot, and therefore the concept of requiring the competitors to pay the penalty for poor marksmanship immediately as well was possible and appropriately interesting. After some experience with this type event, at the congress in 1973 at Lake Placid the UIPMB approved the decision to include the sprint race in the 1974 World Biathlon Championships at Minsk, USSR. It was also included in the 1980 Winter Olympic Games program.

As the new biathlon events were being developed and added to the World Championships and Winter Olympic Games programs, another addition came following the addition of the relay event in 1966. The UIMPB Congress (that year seven nations) pledged that they would send a team for the initial competition for junior men at the 1967 World Biathlon Championships at Altenberg in the German Democratic Republic. That year 24 athletes from eight nations were represented at that first junior competition that was open to men less than 21 years of age. Although the USMWBTC had attempted to expand civilian biathlon participation for both seniors and juniors, there was a specific effort to create a modified program for athletes meeting the new UIMPB age group. A U.S. Junior Championships was held in Maine during March 1968. Twenty-one junior athletes participated in a modified event with William Wattles of New Vineyard winning in a time of 1 hour, 08 minutes and 24 seconds. The U.S. didn't send its first junior athletes to the World Championships until 1973 when they were held at Lake Placid. The junior men's distance was set at 15 kilometers with three stages of shooting, two from the prone position and one from the standing. For the junior men's relay, the distance was the same as the senior men, but reduced to only three team members. At the 1980 UIPMB Congress at Sarajevo, Yugoslavia the junior men's age limit was reduced from 21 to 20 and rules for women's biathlon were established.

Women's participation in biathlon began in the Eastern European countries prior to the establishment of international rules for women. There was also some participation in the Scandinavian countries as well as some individual participation in the U.S. and Canada. The start of formal women's national championships appears to have started in 1967 in Czechoslovakia where the women skied a distance of 5 kilometers and shot .22 caliber rifles only once from the prone position. By 1969 the number in this event had grown to include 56 women athletes and included a relay event of 11 teams. In 1970 the Eastern European nations held the first women's international biathlon competitions when the German Democratic Republic, Bulgaria, Poland, Czechoslovakia and the Soviet Union in a "For Friendship and Brotherhood" competition.

At the time women's competitions followed the rules of the individual countries, which were modified and based primarily on the men's rules. In Scandinavia and North America women competed using the men's rules with respect to skiing distance and shooting. Sonja Nehr of Canada competed in the men's class in the 1978 Canadian Championships and is the first woman to compete in Canada. In the U.S. the first woman to compete was Holly Beattie who entered a few early season competitions at Jackson Hole, Wyoming during the 1978-79 season. In the following year a few more women expressed interest so national coaches Art Stegen and Bill Spencer invited women to participate in a training camp at Squaw Valley, California in the spring of 1979. At the 1980 U.S. Olympic team trials which had been relocated to Valcartier, Quebec due to poor snow conditions at the original sites of Lake Placid and Rosendale, New York, several Canadian men and a woman participated in the races. Although women's events were not part of the Winter Olympic Games, the presence of Holly Beattie and Canadian Karina Englebrecht gave a boost to the involvement for women. The rapid growth of women's biathlon in the U.S. was aided by support from the coaches, the U.S. Biathlon Association and the USOC out of general concern for equal opportunity in sports and the Title IX Federal legislation that mandated equal opportunity for women. During the winter of 1981 junior and senior women's classes were included in most of the biathlon competitions in the USA and Canada.

In 1978 Finland and Czechoslovakia requested that women be included in UIPMB competitions. The Technical Committee was tasked to look at it and decided to observe and support the development of national and international events for women. The committee recommended that the targets and ski course be the same as those used by the junior men, that women carry the rifle and that the rules be prepared for the 1980 Congress. The first UIPMB sanctioned event occurred in Jáchymov, Czechoslovakia. Women from Poland, Norway, Sweden and Czechoslovakia participated in a 10 kilometers individual race with three bouts of shooting, prone-standing-prone and a 5 kilometers sprint race with a prone and standing shooting stage. In 1981 the UIPMB Congress made the decision to include women in UIPMB Cup competitions starting in the 1983-84 season, but those plans failed to materialize when the first two competitions in Finland and Norway were cancelled due to the low numbers registering for the events. However, a competition was held at Falun, Sweden on January 7, 1984. The most important event that secured participation for women was the 1983 UIPMB Congress' decision to hold the first World Biathlon Championships for women. It was to be held at Chamonix, France in 1984 in conjunction with the junior men's championships. It also set the age limit for junior women to parallel that of the junior men.

The first World Championships for women in 1984 included 12 participating nations and a total of 37 competitors. The USA was among those participating and the U.S. team of Kari Swenson, Julie Newnam and Holly Beattie captured the first-ever World Championships medal by U.S. athletes after placing 3rd in the relay race. The next step would be to include women in the Winter Olympic program and at the 1984 UIPMB Congress the executive board was tasked with exploring that step. At first there was some apprehension that too few women would participate, however a letter for approving their participation was sent to the IOC, but the item was not put on the agenda of its July meeting. UIPMB Secretary General Willie Grut circulated a survey to the member federations to find out how many women participated and whether a National Championships for women was organized. That information was used to support the letter to the IOC. The IOC reviewed the issue in 1986 and decided not to deal with it until after the 1988 Winter Olympic Games at Calgary.

To further encourage greater women's participation, the UIPMB decided to support the 1986 World Championships for women at Falun, Sweden by providing travel subsidies for up to 3 participants for European athletes from outside of Scandinavia and it continued the assistance for the next two years. At the 1984, 1985 and 1986, proposals to the UIPMP Technical Committee to increase the skiing distances for women were rejected, however at the 1987 Congress the distances of 15 and 7.5 kilometers for the individual and sprint races and a relay of 3 X 7.5 kilometers were established and the number of shooting bouts in the individual race was increased to four. Distances for junior women were also set at 10, 7.5 and 3 X 7.5 kilometers.

Lobbying efforts to get women into the Winter Olympic program was strongly supported at the International Coaching Symposium at Calgary in 1986 when Canadian team member Gail Niinimaa presented a paper entitled "Women in Biathlon" to the 53 delegates from 13 nations. The UIPMB took actions on all the suggestions included in the document and the Administrative Council tasked Dr. Veli Niinimaa during the 1988 Winter Olympic Games to lobby the IOC program committee members to support women's admission into the Olympic Games. He presented the arguments that: 1) There have been international women's competitions since 1980 and World Championships since 1984. 2) There has been rapid growth in women's participation, far surpassing the men's initial participation in both the World Championships and Olympic Games. 3) It would provide an additional women's sport in the Olympic Winter Games and bring about greater equality between men and women. 4) Women's participation would bring in an additional 8 hours of coverage to fill the recently expanded 16-day Olympic program. 5) No additional facilities were needed, nor would additional officials be necessary. 6) Women's biathlon was already practiced in 22 nations on five continents. 7) Women's World Biathlon Championships participation was greater than that of Luge or Speed Skating. 8) The UIPMB had moved in the direction of giving women equal opportunity in competitions.

During the 1988 Olympic Games at Calgary, Bill Spencer, the UIMPB's Technical Delegate had a meeting with IOC President Juan Antonio Samaranch during which he asked Bill if everything was well with biathlon. Bill answered "no," to which Samaranch asked what was wrong. Bill simply said, "there were no women competitors." Samaranch responded by telling him that it would be corrected. At the April 1988 IOC Executive Board meeting, the inclusion of women's biathlon competitions as official medal events was recommended for the 1992 Winter Olympic Games at Albertville, France.

The first World Biathlon Championships for Junior Women was held in 1989 at Voss, Norway with 11 nations participating and at the 1992 Congress an increase of relay team members for women's teams to four was approved for the following season. Except for the distance of the individual and sprint races, which were 75% of the men's distances, which made the duration of the races approximately the same, and although the women's relay distance was later reduced to 6 kilometers, women had essentially gained equality with the men. In 1987 women and men competed in joint World Cup competitions and a Nations Cup scoring was instituted. In 1989 men and women were brought together to compete in joint World Championships at Feistritz, Austria. In 2000 the IBU decided to separate the World Junior Biathlon Championships into Youth and Junior classes, with male and female competitors who have completed their 19th years of age as of December 31st designated as Juniors and those who had not yet reached Junior age and are at least 16 at the cut-off date of 31 December are Youth Men or Youth Women respectively.

Additional race disciplines of a pursuit race and mass start race were added to the World Biathlon Championships in 1997 and in the Olympic Games programs in 1998 and 2002. The start sequence and intervals in a Pursuit competition are based on a qualifying competition, which is normally held the previous day. The basic concept of the Pursuit is that the winner of the qualifying competition starts first, and the others follow in the order and time that they finished behind the winner in the qualifying competition. The Pursuit is highly exciting because at any time it is easy to see who is leading, and due to the psychological thrill of the competitors pursuing the athletes ahead of them. The first competitor to cross the finish line is the winner. The Mass Start Competition begins with a simultaneous start by all the competitors and offers the ultimate in excitement and suspense for both competitors and spectators. The format of the Mass Start is similar to the Individual race except the distances are shorter and shooting follows the sequence of prone, prone, standing, standing. Participation is limited to 30 because each competitor requires a target at approximately the same time due to the simultaneous start. An additional mixed relay event was added to the World Championships and World Cup programs in 2007 and into the Winter Olympic Games at Sochi in 2014. This relay consists of 2 women and 2 men. The two female team members ski 6 kilometers and the two male team members ski 7.5 kilometers with 2 bouts of shooting, one prone and one standing with the women leading off on the first two exchanges. This was also an attractive event in that just like pairs figure skating, women and men were competing together as a team.

Along with the efforts to accept and open biathlon to women and the addition of new race formats, the UIMPB also, like the FIS, had to struggle with the decision about which ski technique would be allowed. The very fast expansion of the free technique or the skating step as it was called at the time, was the one major item on the agenda when the delegates gathered at Landmark hotel in Vancouver, Canada in May 29, 1985, in connection with the FIS Congress, "The future of the Cross-Country sport – to skate or not." Pauli Siitonen from Finland used a technique called the Siitonen step in long ski marathon competitions like Marcialonga in Italy or Dolomitenlauf in Austria. He used only a half-step by pushing off the edge of one ski to the left or right while maintaining the other ski in the track. The step was used on the flat parts of the track. Previously in 1982 this technique was discussed at a FIS meeting and a proposal was made to the Cross-County Committee that where tracks are set, only the classical technique is allowed. It stayed as a proposal and did not become a part of the rules and regulations. By the 1984 Sarajevo Winter Olympic Games, most of the athletes were using this technique and the next step in the development of this new ski technique, the use of the double skating step, where the skis are used similar to skates on ice, occurred in Kiruna, Sweden at their traditional games on April 5, 1984. The Norwegian stars Ove Aunli, who had been disqualified in the Olympic Winter Games at Sarajevo for using the skating step in the finish, and Anette Bø won their competitions in a dominating way by using skis without any kick wax at all. They had waxed the skis only with glide wax like alpine skiing and thus they achieved a higher speed.

The FIS Council agreed that a solution should be found to avoid the skating step technique becoming the dominant technique in the future cross-country skiing, but also agreed that the technique itself shall not and cannot be forbidden. The aim of the FIS was to accept the skating step technique as one of the possible techniques which are used on certain parts of the tracks, but not as the only technique as the tracks are badly damaged by the competitors using this kind of step. Although attempts were made to ban or modify its use, the skating technique dominated the FIS World Championships at Seefield, Austria in 1985. At that event, the FIS Council met with the Cross-Country Committee on January 25th and appointed a Working Group consisting of the executive board of the Cross-Country Committee, medical experts, specialists on the design and preparation of competition courses as well as representatives from coaches and athletes to elaborate on the proposals on the future of cross-country skiing. That Working Group met in April 13-14th, 1985 at Zurich, Switzerland and included the FIS General Secretary, UIPMB representatives and Technical Committee members Peter Bayer, Federal Republic of Germany and Kurt Hinze of the German Democratic Republic. Their proposal was essentially to allow two techniques, preserving the classic technique for some races and allowing skating for others and to establish rules for the two techniques concerning tracks and preparation, control, obstructions etc.

Later that summer the UIMPB decided that for the season 1985/86 all cross-country techniques would be allowed. The final decision for the future would be taken at the Congress 1986, which then also confirmed the proposal and the skating technique became the dominate one used for biathlon. The same happened to Nordic Combined in a 1986 FIS Council decision and somewhat surprisingly also in CISM (military sport) with its old traditions in patrol competitions.

Over time numerous changes have slowly developed the sport as it is known today. In the early years, it was the military that guided its development and it wasn't until the 1950s that a common interest in rules and regulations began to appear and standardization occurred. Improvements in training methodology, technology of equipment, track preparation and the development of ski technique dramatically changed the nature of biathlon, affecting both the skiing and shooting disciplines. The reduction of the two minutes shooting penalty and shortening of the penalty loop along with the 1986 decision to go freestyle or skating ski technique made for faster, closer race finishes and more excitement for both the competitors and spectators. The result of these evolutionary changes had a profound impact on the nature of biathlon but had not altered the fundamental concepts. Today's biathlon race has a very different appearance than the earlier years, however it has been modified so as not to have significantly changed the fundamental tests of endurance, strength, speed and skill combined with accuracy.

The current IBU/USBA Race Formats and Competitor Classes are shown in the following table:

Class of Competitor	Course Length and Competition Type	Standard Start Types and Intervals	Ski Loops	Shooting Bouts and Penalty
Senior Men **21+ years**	20 Km Individual	Single, 30 sec	5 x 4 km	P, S, P, S – 1 minute
	10 Km Sprint	Single, 30 sec	3 x 3.3 km	P, S – 150 m penalty lap
	12.5 Km Pursuit	Pursuit timed start	5 x 2.5 km	P, P, S, S –150 m penalty lap
	15 Km Mass Start	Simultaneous	5 x 3 km	P, P, S, S – 150 m penalty lap
	4 x 7.5 Km Relay	Simultaneous and Tag	3 x 2.5 km	P, S (each) + 3 spare 150 m penalty lap
Junior Men **19-20 years**	15 Km Individual	Single, 30 sec	5 x 4 km	P, S, P, S - 1 minute
	10 Km Sprint	Single, 30 sec	3 x 3.3 km	P, S – 150 m penalty lap
	12.5 Km Pursuit	Pursuit timed start	5 x 2.5 km	P, P, S, S –150 m penalty lap
	15 Km Mass Start	Simultaneous	5 x 3 km	P, P, S, S – 150 m penalty lap
	4 x 7.5 Km Relay	Simultaneous and Tag	3 x 2.5 km	P, S (each) + 3 spare 150 m penalty lap

Class of Competitor	Course Length and Competition Type	Standard Start Types and Intervals	Ski Loops	Shooting Bouts and Penalty
Youth Men **17-18 years**	12.5 Km Individual	Single, 30 sec	5 x 2.5 km	P, S, P, S – 45 seconds
	7.5 Km Sprint	Single, 30 sec	3 x 2.5 km	P, S – 150 m penalty lap
	10 Km Pursuit	Pursuit timed start	5 x 2 km	P, P, S, S –150 m penalty lap
	3 x 7.5 Km Relay	Simultaneous and Tag	3 x 2.5 km	P, S (each) + 3 spare 150 m penalty lap
Senior Boys **15-16 years**	7.5 Km Individual	Single, 30 sec	5 x 1.5 km	P, S, P, S – 45 seconds
	6 KM Sprint	Single, 30 sec	3 x 2 km	P, S – 150 m penalty lap
	7.5 Km Pursuit	Pursuit timed start	5 x 1.5 km	P, P, S, S –150 m penalty lap
	3 x 4.5 Km Relay	Simultaneous and Tag	3 x 1.5 km	P, S (each) + 3 spare 150 m penalty lap
Junior Boys **13-14 Years**	5 Km Individual	Single, 30 sec	5 x 1 km	P, P, P* - 45 seconds
	4.5 Km Sprint	Single, 30 sec	3 x 1.5 km	P, P* – 150 m penalty lap
	5 Km Pursuit	Pursuit timed start	5 x 1 km	P, P, P, P* 150 m penalty lap
	3 x 3 Km Relay	Simultaneous and Tag	3 x 1 km	P, P* (each) + 3 spare 150 m penalty lap
Master Men **40+ years**	15 Km Individual	Single, 30 sec	5 x 4 km	P, S, P, S – 1 minute
	10 Km Sprint	Single, 30 sec	3 x 3.3 km	P, S – 150 m penalty lap
	12.5 Km Pursuit	Pursuit timed start	5 x 2.5 km	P, P, S, S –150 m penalty lap
	12.5 Km Mass Start	Simultaneous	5 x 3 km	P, P, S, S – 150 m penalty lap
	3 x 7.5 Km Relay	Simultaneous and Tag	3 x 2.5 km	P, S (each) + 3 spare 150 m penalty lap
Master Men **50+ years**	12.5 Km Individual	Single, 30 sec	5 x 2.5 km	P, S, P, S – 1 minute
	7.5 Km Sprint	Single, 30 sec	3 x 2.5 km	P, S – 150 m penalty lap
	10 Km Pursuit	Pursuit timed start	5 x 2 km	P, P, S, S –150 m penalty lap
	3 x 6 Km Relay	Simultaneous and Tag	3 x 2 km	P, S (each) + 3 spare 150 m penalty lap

Class of Competitor	Course Length and Competition Type	Standard Start Types and Intervals	Ski Loops	Shooting Bouts and Penalty
Veteran Men **60+ years**	**10 Km Individual**	Single, 30 sec	5 x 2 km	P, S, P, S – 45 seconds
	6 KM Sprint	Single, 30 sec	3 x 2 km	P, S – 150 m penalty lap
	7.5 Km Pursuit	Pursuit timed start	5 x 1.5 km	P, P, S, S –150 m penalty lap
	10 Km Mass Start	Simultaneous	5 x 2 km	P, P, S, S – 150 m penalty lap
	3 x 6 Km Relay	Simultaneous and Tag	3 x 2 km	P, S (each) + 3 spare 150 m penalty lap
Veteran Men **70+ years**	**7.5 Km Individual**		5 x 1.5 km	P, S, P, S – 45 seconds
	5 KM Sprint	Single, 30 sec	3 x 1.5 km	P, S – 150 m penalty lap
	7.5 Km Pursuit	Pursuit timed start	5 x 1.5 km	P, P, S, S –150 m penalty lap
	7.5 Km Mass Start	Simultaneous	5 x 1.5 km	P, P, S, S – 150 m penalty lap
	3 x 4.5 Km Relay	Simultaneous and Tag	3 x 1.5 km	P, S (each) + 3 spare 150 m penalty lap
Senior Women **21+ years**	**15 Km Individual**	Single, 30 sec	5 x 3 km	P, S, P, S – 1 minute
	7.5 Km Sprint	Single, 30 sec	3 x 2.5 km	P, S – 150 m penalty lap
	10 Km Pursuit	Pursuit timed start	5 x 2 km	P, P, S, S –150 m penalty lap
	12.5 Km Mass Start	Simultaneous	5 x 2.5 km	P, P, S, S – 150 m penalty lap
	4 x 6 Km Relay	Simultaneous and Tag	3 x 2 km	P, S (each) + 3 spare 150 m penalty lap
Junior Women **19-20 years**	**12.5 Km Individual**	Single, 30 sec	5 x 2.5 km	P, S, P, S – 1 minute
	7.5 Km Sprint	Single, 30 sec	3 x 2.5 km	P, S – 150 m penalty lap
	10 Km Pursuit	Pursuit timed start	5 x 2 km	P, P, S, S –150 m penalty lap
	10 Km Mass Start	Simultaneous	5 x 2 km	P, P, S, S – 150 m penalty lap
	4 x 6 Km Relay	Simultaneous and Tag	3 x 2 km	P, S (each) + 3 spare 150 m penalty lap

Class of Competitor	Course Length and Competition Type	Standard Start Types and Intervals	Ski Loops	Shooting Bouts and Penalty
Youth Women **17-18 years**	**10 Km Individual**	Single, 30 sec	5 x 2 km	P, S, P, S – 45 seconds
	6 Km Sprint	Single, 30 sec	3 x 5 km	P, S – 150 m penalty lap
	7.5 Km Pursuit	Pursuit timed start	5 x 2.5 km	P, P, S, S –150 m penalty lap
	3 x 6 Km Relay	Simultaneous and Tag	3 x 2 km	P, S (each) + 3 spare 150 m penalty lap
Senior Girls **15-16 years**	**7.5 Km Individual**	Single, 30 sec	5 x 1.5 km	P, S, P, S – 45 seconds
	6 KM Sprint	Single, 30 sec	3 x 2 km	P, S – 150 m penalty lap
	7.5 Km Pursuit	Pursuit timed start	5 x 1.5 km	P, P, S, S –150 m penalty lap
	3 x 4.5 Km Relay	Simultaneous and Tag	3 x 1.5 km	P, S (each) + 3 spare 150 m penalty lap
Junior Girls **13-14 Years**	**5 Km Individual**	Single, 30 sec	5 x 1 km	P, P, P, P* – 45 seconds
	3 Km Sprint	Single, 30 sec	3 x 1 km	P, P* – 150 m penalty lap
	5 Km Pursuit	Pursuit timed start	5 x 1 km	P, P, P, P*–150 m penalty lap
	3 x 3 Km Relay	Simultaneous and Tag	3 x 1 km	P, P* (each) + 3 spare 150 m penalty lap
Master Women **40+ years**	**12.5 Km Individual**	Single, 30 sec	5 x 2.5 km	P, S, P, S – 1 minute
	7.5 Km Sprint	Single, 30 sec	3 x 2.5 km	P, S – 150 m penalty lap
	10 Km Pursuit	Pursuit timed start	5 x 2 km	P, P, S, S –150 m penalty lap
	10 Km Mass Start	Simultaneous	5 x 2 km	P, P, S, S – 150 m penalty lap
	3 x 6 Km Relay	Simultaneous and Tag	3 x 2 km	P, S (each) + 3 spare 150 m penalty lap
Master Women **50+ years**	**10 Km Individual**	Single, 30 sec	5 x 2 km	P, S, P, S – 45 seconds
	6 Km Sprint	Single, 30 sec	3 x 5 km	P, S – 150 m penalty lap
	7.5 Km Pursuit	Pursuit timed start	5 x 2.5 km	P, P, S, S –150 m penalty lap
	7.5 Km Mass Start	Simultaneous	5 x 2 km	P, P, S, S – 150 m penalty lap
	3 x 6 Km Relay	Simultaneous and Tag	3 x 2 km	P, S (each) + 3 spare 150 m penalty lap

Class of Competitor	Course Length and Competition Type	Standard Start Types and Intervals	Ski Loops	Shooting Bouts and Penalty
Veteran Women **60+ Years**	**7.5 Km Individual**	Single, 30 sec	5 x 1.5 km	P, S, P, S – 45 seconds
	4.5 KM Sprint	Single, 30 sec	3 x 2 km	P, S – 150 m penalty lap
	5 Km Pursuit	Pursuit timed start	5 x 1 km	P, P, S, S –150 m penalty lap
	3 x 3 Km Relay	Simultaneous and Tag	3 x 1 km	P, S (each) + 3 spare 150 m penalty lap

*Indicates "rifle not carried and shooting on prone on standing targets"

The Rødøy Petroglyph found in a Norwegian cave depicts a skier from 10,000 years ago.

Despite the fact that biathlon is a relatively new sport, it has a realistic basis in history. The practical use of skis and weapons was undoubtedly the real beginning and like other sports, its practical origins gradually developed into a contest of skills. A race in 1767 among Norwegian ski troops was the first recorded ski race of any type.

For its original logo the Norwegian Ski Association used an ancient skier hunting on skis.

A group of 40 Finnish officers who had escaped Soviet captivity following the Finnish-German campaign made their way into the United States Army where they had an influence on U.S. Army Winter Warfare training doctrine and could be viewed as introducing biathlon to the U.S. Army. Colonel Erkki Lahdenpera introduced cross-country ski races among the 10th Mountain troops at Camp Hale in 1947 for more appropriate winter tactical training.

The military patrol race at the 1936 Winter Olympic Games was won by Italy.

The military application of biathlon skills proved to be of great value during the Winter Wars of 1939-1945 between Finland and the Soviet Union.

The 10th Mountain Division on skis.

Sven Thofelt was instrumental in the development of biathlon as an international sport. A Gold medalist in pentathlon, and President of the UIPM, he convinced the IOC that biathlon was more than a military sport. He helped clear the way for biathlon's entry into the Winter Olympic Games when the UIPM declared responsibility for the sport and held the first World Biathlon Championships in 1958.

The U.S. Army named the first U.S. Biathlon Team in 1957 from among 10th Mountain Division soldiers for the CISM competition in Switzerland. From left to right (back row): Fred Beck (IL), Quintin Golder (MT), Selwyn Presnall (FL), and Stan Walker (NH); (front row) Gunnar Jansen (CT), Gerald Jensen (UT), and Fritz Holt (WA).

Early training on Ft. Richardson golf course in 1958. Ronald Seater and William Rudd, members of the U.S. Army Biathlon Team, in standing firing position; Lt. Phillip Joberd, background, watches through the spotting scope near the club house of the Ft. Richardson golf course. Seater was added as a replacement to the 1960 Olympic team after Peter Lahdenpera was forced to choose between biathlon and cross-country.

Dick Mize, a former NCAA and Western State skier who was among the first to be assigned to the U.S. Army Modern Winter Biathlon Training Center (USMWBTC) at Ft. Richardson, Alaska leaves the start line at the 1st World Biathlon Championships at Saalfeden, Austria in 1958.

Maurice Paquette, (left) accepting an award from Master Sergeant Bill Brown, achieved an 8th place finish at the 2nd World Biathlon Championships (right).

In 1959 the U.S. team participating in the 2nd World Biathlon Championships at Courmayeur, Italy included (left to right) Bob Collins, Dick Mize, Walt Jackson, Maurice Paquette and John Burritt.

In the 1950s ski trails were narrow and often closely lined with trees, unlike the "fine machined grooming" of today. A fall could often break the tip of a wooden ski or shatter the bamboo ski poles of the equipment of the period. This picture shows Walter Jackson finishing the CISM individual race of 1959 with two broken skis, an extraordinary accomplishment as such a fate often resulted in a "DNF" (Did not finish). In those days a CISM competitor had to carry an 18-lb. rucksack and rifle over a ski course that included a downhill section with slalom gates as well as a shooting range of an unknown distance for the marksmanship.

Walter Jackson enjoys compliments from U.S. Coach Hans Wagner for finishing the 1959 CISM race after breaking both of his ski tips. Jackson and Wagner were members of the early U.S. teams that participated in the first two World Biathlon Championships and the 1960 Winter Olympic Games.

Not only did the early competitors have to deal with greater potential of equipment failure, they also did not enjoy the well-groomed, wide ski tracks of today. Dick Mize leads the way up a hill during the 2nd World Biathlon Championships in 1959. The competitor behind Dick can be seen carrying his rifle as if he is on a hunting outing.

Trials for the 1960 Winter Olympic biathlon team were held at Colorado's Tennessee Pass, near Camp Hale, which is over 10,000 feet above sea level. Dick Mize is seen here leaving the start while Peter Lahdenpera awaits behind him. Both were members of the team chosen to participate at Squaw Valley, however Lahdenpera was later forced to choose between biathlon and cross-country, having been selected for both teams.

Many members of the 1960 Winter Olympic cross-country team would later become members of the U.S. Biathlon team. Standing in the rear, left to right are Olavi Hirvonen, and Coach Sven Wiik, In the second row are John Dendahl, Sven Johanson, Mack Miller, and Joe-Pete Wilson. In front are Leo Massa, Karl Bohlin, Charlie Akers, and Peter Lahdenpera.

Colonel Don Hull and the first U.S. Biathlon coach, Hans Wagner (on the right) at the Squaw Valley Winter Olympic Games.

McKinney Creek Stadium officials prepare to start the USSR's Vladimir Melanjin while Jon Istad of Norway awaits behind him. Melanjin had the fastest course time, however only finished 4th because of missed targets. A few years later Jon Istad was a World Champion.

PART II.

"Who Are They?"

In the book published in 1970 by Aschehoug, S*ne-Ski-Skudd, Om Norsk Skiskyter,* Ole Jacob Bangstad who was in charge of biathlon in Norway at the time, wrote in the introduction "There is little use to discussing which sport is the biggest or the most demanding. But many would argue that the biathlon stands strong in this respect. Cross-country skiing and shooting by themselves each require very much from of its athletes. Biathlon demands even more. Biathlon requires the speed, fitness and technique of skiing as well as the shooter's cold nerves, determination and concentration. The distinct ability to combine the shooting results, with the cross-country ski time and the time used on the shooting range affect the end result in a relationship that requires caring and wise calculation alongside of the full physical effort, from start to finish."

He continued: "It is possible that our new Olympic sport is not sufficiently well-established before the large audience. It has hardly helped that our biathletes in recent years have enjoyed a string of victories and medals in major international championships. But strong public attention has not yet been achieved. This will develop, especially when one gets acquainted and the plans such as stadiums for biathlon open opportunities for greater visibility of the events to a great audience. Under all circumstances, it is appropriate that we get complemented and coverage in our domestic media with a book that describes the events in biathlon that led to knowledge about some of this sport's best athletes, and the achievements of young athletes can serve as role models for anyone who seeks for themselves high goals."

Part I explains the origins of the sport, how it was gradually organized, formalized, managed, and the bureaucracies that govern the sport developed its rules and guided its growth into the exciting sport it has become. Like the Norwegian book, which focuses on the early Norwegian athletes, this section will focus on the individuals who have actively played a prominent role in the sport in the United States. It doesn't include everyone but focuses on those athletes who have made outstanding contributions through their competitive efforts, the coaches who have guided and advised them in their achievements and the administrators and organizers who made the events and activities possible for their participation.

Many of these individuals made contributions in multiple areas, often as active athletes, then coaches and finally as administrators and directors.

It is the athletes that stand at the heart of these groups as the most visible to the spectators. It is primarily the athlete, and for the athletes that the real essence of sports exists. It is about those participants doing something supremely well in the face of physical and psychological challenges that brings satisfaction to all of those who support that effort and excites the spectators who watch from the side. Just as it was for Bangstad, there is a relatively small community of interest for this unique sport and the American public is generally unaware of that excitement enjoyed by the athletes, coaches and administrators who played a role in this unfamiliar sport, but they are none-the-less important for their contributions. When viewed over more than 60 years, these individuals who contributed can be grouped into distinct periods and by which they were impacted by the conditions and events imposed on their efforts.

CHAPTER 9

Soldier Athletes

During the summer of 2003 Don Nelson, a former member of the U.S. Army's Modern Winter Biathlon Training Center at Ft. Richardson in Alaska organized a reunion of those who had also served their military obligations at the "unit," as it was known by them, training and competing in biathlon. Prior to the event he circulated a list of many of those athletes for whom he could locate information and asked others to help him complete the list of everyone who had shared that unique experience. The list included 146 names and known addresses of former members and 33 unknowns. The 179 names of those who shared the biathlon unit's experience was similarly unique to many other military experiences of specific units, commands, ships, etc. in that they had all developed a sense of common bonding from that shared experience through their efforts, tasks, locations and friendships that were developed during that service. However, although they shared the military experiences, they also enjoyed a similar sense of a separate uniqueness that was more about their similar athletic paths and the things that surrounded their participation in a truly unique environment in a very specific athletic community.

Approximately half of those who had fulfilled their military obligation by training for biathlon at Ft. Richardson attended that reunion. Some of those were the earliest competitors who hadn't really known others who came later, but they found that they all had much in common. As the athletes, along with their wives circulated among the gathering during the reunion it became clear that there were distinct groups separated by the years they spent together. Those from the same Olympic quadrennial appeared to have the strongest friendships and memories, and it seemed everyone was well known by the others, even if in name only and as they shared their stories it was clear their stories were remarkably similar for those who spent time at the Unit. That same sense of sharing experiences and having the same characteristics continued in the groups and teams in the years that followed including those who participated following the closure of the USMWBTC. Small groups of athletes with the same goals, led by inspired leadership was the heart of biathlon's uniqueness.

However, the earliest athletes who are what can be considered the first U.S.

Biathlon team were never part of the group that assembled for the reunion in 2003. They came before the USMWBTC was established and most were from the small group that remained at Camp Hale following the deactivation of the 10th Mountain Division. That group was the Mountain and Cold Weather Training Command established in 1952. Their assignment was to teach skiing, rock climbing, outdoor survival and military winter skills to various military units following the U.S. Army's winter warfare doctrine written by Colonel Erkki Lahdenpera, a veteran of the Finnish-Russian Winter War. Those who had skiing experience at the inter-service championships in Europe, like the renowned Master Sergeant Bill Brown were reassigned to Camp Hale as instructors and they began to encourage competitions among the troops. In preparation for the international military ski competition, CISM, at Andermatt, Switzerland in 1956, a team was selected from that group and became the first U.S. Biathlon team. It included Fred Beck (IL), Quintin Golder (MT), Selwyn Presnal (FL), Stan Walker (NH), Gunnar Jansen (CT), Gerald Jensen (UT) and Fritz Holt (WA). Gunnar Jansen, a former captain of the University of Denver ski team, Fritz Holt and Stanley Walker were also members of the U.S. team that raced in the 1957 and 1958 CISM championships. That team also included Larry Damon who had competed in the 1956 Olympic Games, the famous Holmenkollen race in Oslo and the Finnish Salpausselka competitions in 1956 and 1957 and was assigned to the U.S. Army's 8th Division in Germany. Walter Jackson and Dick Mize, both of Ft. Devins, Massachusetts were also part of the group. Following the 1958 CISM competitions the team went to Berchtesgaden, Germany to continue training and compete for the final selection of the team that would participate in the 1st World Biathlon Championships at Saalfelden, Austria. While in Germany the team also participated in the famous Rauschberglauf at Ruhpolding, long before it became one of the most the famous biathlon World Cup sites. Those athletes that participated in the early CISM competition were the core members of the USMWBTC that was established in 1958.

One of the earliest competitors, Jim Mahaffey was never actually a member of the USMWBTC but attended the 2003 reunion because of his close relationship with it. Jim was a key figure in the earliest biathlon activities. He was the winner of the first-ever U.S. Biathlon competition held at Camp Hale in 1956. He grew up in Pennsylvania where he liked outdoor activities and was taught to shoot by his dad. After 1949 he spent his time between Colorado and Alaska, and it was while attending Western State College in Gunnison Colorado where he learned to ski and became a member of the Western State ski team and the 1956 NCAA Championship team. Like many on the college ski team, he later served in the military. While most had been members of the 10th Mountain Division, Jim served in the U.S. Air Force at Elmendorf Air Base in Alaska.

The same year that the Western State College ski team won the NCAA championships they also participated in what the Army called a "Nordic Weekend" at Camp Hale that included a 15 kilometers ski race, a jumping event on a 35-meter hill and the biathlon race of 20 kilometers, which Jim won. Because of that first place and a later fifth place in the North American Pre-Olympic race at Squaw Valley in 1959, Jim was invited to join the Army athletes at the pre-Olympic 1959-60 training camp at Camp Hale, however hitting only 13 targets in the trials race for the Olympic team was a disappointment and not good enough to be selected. Years later he revealed that he used a hunting rifle with a factory front sight for hunting, didn't have a biathlon rifle sling and had to carry his ammunition in his pocket. He also admitted that he didn't know enough to slow down on approaching the range. The Western State College skiers, coached by Sven Wiik, took five of the first six places in that race. Jim later became Wiik's assistant coach at Western State and a certified FIS Technical Delegate while working towards his master's degree. Not able to be a member of the USMWBTC and despite hitting 19 of his 20 targets in the final trials race for the first U.S. Olympic Biathlon team in 1960, at 30 years old, Jim felt he could not wait another four years and accepted an assistant professorship at the University of Alaska. He went on to become full college professor and renowned ski coach himself, first at the University of Alaska at Fairbanks and later at Alaska Methodist University in Anchorage. He was a familiar face to all the Unit team members and an important contributor to the skiing community in Alaska, developing many Olympic team members and starting the first women's intercollegiate ski team. In 1963, he created the Equinox marathon and helped Sven Wiik write the first manual for cross-country ski training. He was the assistant chief of course at the 1980 Winter Olympic Games and continued to race in masters competitions that included a bronze medal in the 1992 World Masters Ski Championships.

Larry Damon became involved with the U.S. Army's efforts with biathlon when he enlisted in the army after competing in the 1956 Winter Olympics cross-country ski races at Cortina, Italy. A four-event skier at Burlington High School, in 1951 he won the Vermont State Slalom Championship and came in second in the cross-country race. Learning to ski at the Burlington Golf Country Club, he watched the University of Vermont skiers training there and then later in 1955 skiing for UVM, he won the NCAA Nordic cross-country ski championship. In the army after racing in Europe he was assigned to the group training for biathlon at Camp Hale and then Ft. Richardson and was a member of the team that competed in the first World Biathlon Championships at Saalfelden. He finished 20th and then won the 1959 North American Championships and pre-Olympic test race at Squaw Valley. The following year he qualified for the 1960 Winter Olympic Games cross-country ski team and finished 24th at the Squaw Valley games. After he left the army he continued cross-country ski racing, participating in the 1964 and 1968 Winter Olympic Games. He was also an excellent runner, finishing 10th in the 1962 Boston Marathon with a time of 2:34:05.

Of those Western-state skiers who participated in the first biathlon race along with Jim Mahaffey, four others became members of the USMWBTC at Ft. Richardson when it was first established in 1958. Walter Jackson, Dick Mize, John Burritt and Ken MacLennan were the core group of the athletes who comprised the first members of the U.S. Army's biathlon training group at Ft. Richardson, Alaska. In that period military service was expected and all men were subjected to conscription by their local draft boards. The standard enlistment for draftees was 2 years and those who enlisted usually had more choice of their assignments, but a longer 3-year commitment. Having enlisted, following their basic training at Ft. Carson, Colorado, Dick Mize and Walter Jackson got their original assignments to the Army Security Agency at Ft. Devins, Massachusetts. It was then, before they finished the ASA School that they were released to try out for the 1958 FIS cross-country ski tryouts in McCall, Idaho. They failed to make the team but were able to participate in the trials for the 1958 CISM team at Tennessee Pass near Camp Hale and both Jackson and Mize were successful. Along with Frederick Holt, Gunnar Jansen and Larry Damon they joined up with USAREUR and USAFE skiers from Europe to make up the 1958 CISM team that raced at Bardonecchia-Torino, Italy and would later participate in another set of trials at Berchtesgaden, Germany to determine the team that would represent the U.S. in the first World Biathlon Championships at Saalfeld, Austria. Again, Mize and Jackson were successful, along with Larry Damon and Gunnar Jensen and became the first Americans to race in the first official World Biathlon Championships.

When they returned to Ft. Devins to complete the ASA program they heard that a new biathlon unit would be established in Alaska, so they applied for a transfer. The captain in charge told them since they had been on a vacation skiing in all the championships in Europe they wouldn't be going anywhere before completing the Army Security Agency (ASA) program. After a few phone calls (including from their parents) the army agreed to release them to the new biathlon unit at Ft. Richardson and they, along with Ken MacLennan were transferred to the newly established biathlon training center, which was first scheduled to go to Ft. Greeley in the Fairbanks area, but by the time they received their orders to report to the center it had been relocated to Ft. Richardson.

Dick Mize grew up in Eagle County, Colorado where he began skiing on a small hill behind his home at Red Cliff. He and his dad, along with some neighbors also often drove to Cooper Hill near Camp Hale and the 10th Mountain Division Training Area for weekend skiing. After high school Dick had the unique distinction of participating in the very first NCAA Ski Championships while skiing for Western State College in 1955, finishing 4th, and later finished 2nd in 1956 and 3rd in 1957 when Western State won the NCAA championships. He also participated in the first two World Biathlon Championships at Saalfelden and Courmayeur and the first Winter Olympic Games Biathlon at Squaw Valley. Dick's Western State teammate, Walter Jackson grew up in Leadville, Colorado near Camp Hale and learned to ski also at Cooper Hill, a training site for the 10th Mountain Division where a season pass for youngsters was subsidized by the Leadville Recreation Board. After high school Walt enrolled in Western State College where he competed as a four-way skier. He finished 2nd in the Skimeister event at the 1956 NCAA Ski Championships. He, Mize and Western State teammate John Burritt along with Larry Damon and Gunnar Jensen led the way to becoming the first U.S. international biathlon competitors.

When Dick Mize and Walter Jackson were reassigned to Ft. Richardson they joined their college teammate John Burritt who had also joined the army and was assigned to the "unit." Burritt had also grown up in rural Colorado in a pioneering farming family on Redlands Mesa, where he learned to shoot and hunt. He graduated from Hotchkiss High School in 1952 and went on to Western State College where he was also a member of the cross-country ski team that won the NCAA Cross-country Championship in 1956 and raced in the first biathlon race at Camp Hale. He competed in the 1959 Biathlon World Championships at Courmayeur, Italy, and qualified for the 1960 U.S. Olympic Biathlon Team competing at the Olympics at Squaw Valley where he finished 14th which was the best American finish for the individual event under the rules of the early period. Even though the rules for the shooting penalties were lessened, it took until 2006 to achieve a better U.S. Biathlon Olympic finish.

Gustave Hanson joined Mize and Jackson at the newly established U.S. Army Biathlon training center after Hans Wagner and Col. Ken Floto visited Ft. Greely looking for potential athletes to join the training group at Ft. Richardson. Gustave was born in Pennsylvania in 1934 but returned to Sweden in 1935. In Sweden, he began skiing at the age of 7 when he had to hike or ski to school. He began school ski racing in 1947 and was involved with summer activities of running, orienteering and shooting. He came back to the U.S. in 1953 and began skiing in Colorado before he was drafted into the army in the spring of 1958 and assigned to the Cold Weather Mountain School at Ft. Greely where he was chosen to join the biathlon group training by Hans Wagner. Gustave maintained one of the highest shooting averages and won 2 of the 3 Olympic team trials races in 1960 and finished 23rd at Squaw Valley. Following the Olympic Games and his discharge he remained in Alaska and started an importing business specializing in ski equipment and clothing from Norway, Sweden and Austria.

The former Western State skiers were soon joined by a few others who also played an important role in the early biathlon competitions. Soon after the USMWBTC was established in 1958, Master Sargent Bill Brown at the U.S. Army Cold Weather and Mountain School, which had been relocated to Ft. Greely in Alaska discovered a young skier from New Hampshire who was a natural on skis. Maurice "Gus" Paquette joined the group at Ft. Richardson after an exceptional display of skiing skills in army competitions. Like many skiers of that period, he was both an alpine and nordic skier, and many also did ski jumping as well. From Plymouth, New Hampshire, Maurice grew up in a large family that years earlier had moved across the border from the small Quebec town of Paquetteville. His large family had a history with skiing having helped Herman Johannsen, better known as "Jack Rabbit" develop ski trails in the Laurentians of Quebec. His father, a hard-working farmer, logger and construction excavator along with Maurice's older brother helped build the first ski lift at Waterville Valley, NH in 1955 and went on to work on projects at other ski areas.

Maurice first excelled at hockey but living near a hill with a rope tow near his home in Plymouth he developed ski skills early and later became an accomplished skier who was ranked among the top 30 Alpine skiers in the nation. While working for the ski patrol at Sun Valley, Idaho he received his draft notice in 1957. Once in the U.S. Army he was assigned to U.S. Army Cold Weather and Mountain school at Camp Hale but moved with the U.S. Army's Cold Weather and Mountain School to Ft. Greely, Alaska soon afterwards. Under Master Sergeant Bill Brown's supervision Maurice led a team from Ft. Greely to victory at the Alaskan military championships at Artic Valley by winning the slalom, downhill and combined events and then finished second in the cross-country race. After receiving the overall top honors award from the military officials, Col. L. Meyers, Sports Officer and head of Special Services for the Army had him reassigned to the USMWBTC at Ft. Richardson. In 1958, he was included in the biathlon training group of 23 military skiers selected for training prior to the 1959 World Biathlon Championships at the newly formed USMWBTC. Master Sergeant Brown who had been reassigned to the ROTC at Dartmouth College highly praised Paquette in the New Hampshire newspapers by saying that "he was the best skier of the group having improved in each race and expected him to be the top skier for the U.S. Army." Brown's praise proved to be correct. He was selected for that team and at the 1959 World Biathlon Championships, Maurice finished in 8th place, an American best World Championship result that was not improved until 1987. His shooting score was remarkable because when the team arrived in Italy they learned that the other competitors were using arm slings to steady their rifles. While the U.S. team shot without the aid of arm slings, he tied for the third best shooting score of the race and matched that of the Soviet winner Vladimir Melanin, which combined with the 10th fastest ski time gave him a result that was over 12 minutes faster than his teammates. He led a remarkable improvement of the American team that took 5th place in the team honors and was awarded the Italian Grolla Cup for the most improved team.

Upon the team's return from Italy they traveled to Squaw Valley and rejoined some of the other USMWBTC athletes for the North American Championships and the pre-Olympic test event for the following year's Winter Olympic Games. Larry Damon and Dick Mize finished first and second, ahead of Sweden's Klas Lestander who would become the first Olympic Biathlon Gold medalist in 1960. Maurice finished 7th in that race, hindered by hitting only 13 of the 20 targets. Not long after that race his military commitment was completed and he left the U.S. Army. He attended Western State College for a period but due to limited financial resources he eventually moved to California for employment, never continuing biathlon competition. Still skiing and following the sport, years later he admitted that he perhaps should have stayed in the army through the 1960 Winter Olympic Games, however at the time there was no support system outside of the USMWBTC for athletes, like that enjoyed by the Soviet's Melanin who went on to Olympic success in 1964.

Just as Maurice left the army in 1959, many of the other members of the USMWBTC were also completing their military duty and as they left, the army needed to look for replacements. Two of the first were Peter Lahdenpera and Joe-Pete Wilson, both who had raced in the cross-country events at the 1960 Squaw Valley Winter Olympic Games. Both came from the east and were college skiers at Middlebury College in Vermont and St. Lawrence University in northern New York. Peter was the son of Colonel Erkki Lahdenpera who can be credited with the introduction of biathlon in the U.S. after a group of Finnish veterans of the 1941 Winter War escaped Soviet capture following the Weapons Cache incident and made their way to the United States. As a matter of fact, it was Peter who aided the escape of his father by delaying the Soviet Secret Police at the front door of their home in Rovaniemi while he slipped out the back door and made his way to neutral Sweden. At the age of 12 Peter's family rejoined his father in the U.S. at Ft. Benning, Georgia and followed him around to various military bases, including Ft. Carson, Colorado, Ft. Drum, New York, Ft Leavenworth, Kansas and eventually Ft. Devins, Massachusetts where the family lived in Fitchburg. It was a vibrant Finnish community that offered lots of ski activities at Saima Park. After finishing high school, he attended Middlebury College where he won 6 straight Eastern ski carnivals. Graduating in 1959, he joined the list of alumni who became Olympians competing in the cross-country races at Squaw Valley. In fact, he had been selected for both the cross-country and biathlon teams but was forced to choose between the two. Seeing the potential for multiple cross-country ski races at Squaw Valley rather than the single biathlon race, he chose cross-county and Ronald Seater from the Army's USMWBTC replaced him on the biathlon team. He later earned additional uniqueness in that he again qualified for both teams by attending both trials in 1964. Unlike 1960 trials, which were held following each other at Tennessee Pass and Steamboat Springs, Colorado, the 1964 trials were scheduled concurrently for December 12 to the 19th, 700 miles apart at West Yellowstone, Montana and Spout Springs, Oregon. Some of the athletes attempted to qualify for both teams which required a race at one location followed by 75 miles drive to a train station, an overnight train ride of 550 miles to another 75 miles drive in time for a race. Of those athletes who attempted the double, only Lahdenpera was successful, and even more remarkable was that he was disqualified in one of the biathlon races for an error on the ski course and did not finish one of the cross-country ski races in which the coaches waxed the skis, leaving him with poorly waxed skis for his ski technique style for the difficult conditions during that race.

After qualifying for both biathlon and cross-country and participating in the 1960 and 1964 Olympic Games Peter focused on developing his sports retail business in Fort Collins, Colorado. With the 1972 Olympic trials scheduled for Jackson, Wyoming, he decided to participate, despite not having raced under the new shooting requirements at 150 meters. Without any real expectations of qualifying for the team he drove through a winter storm that had essentially closed the highways and isolated the town for nearly a week. Following a day of practice, he commented that he found the shooting much easier than the old program that had targets out to 250 meters and two minutes of penalty. After postponement of the races and the restless athletes sitting around uncomfortably for a week, eating pasta for "carbo-loading" and waiting each day for some activity, the weather cleared. At first it was relatively cold but gradually grew warmer each day until the final race, which occurred in extremely warm conditions and a light rain. Peter enjoyed another advantage other than the closer targets. Through his sports store, he was the only one who had a new Swix yellow klister that had just been released for sale. Along with his legendary ability in difficult ski conditions, this new wax worked well and at the age of 40 and eight years after Innsbrück he qualified for his third Olympic team by earning one of the relay positions of the selection criteria.

At Squaw Valley, Lahdenpera and Wilson met Colonel Don Hull, the AAU president who worked in the Pentagon and who was the biathlon team leader at the Squaw Valley Olympic Games. Colonel Hull was responsible for finding and placing army athletes where they could train and compete for spots on the 1960 Summer Olympic Games in Rome. A background in boxing gave him insight that enabled him to identify athletic talent, so he had Lahdenpera and Wilson assigned to Ft. Meade with the intention of finding a sport that they might participate in the trials for the summer games. With their orders to report for duty with athletic gear and clothing, they were unclear about what their assignment would be, but later in the summer of 1960 he had them assigned to the Unit in Alaska.

Joe-Pete Wilson was born in Lake Placid and spent his youth on a family farm at nearby Keene, New York. He graduated from Lake Placid High School in 1953 where he was the Ski Meister for four years. In 1954, he attended Vermont Academy for a year and was coached by Warren Chivers. He then attended St. Lawrence University where he was the ski team captain, competing in cross-country, Nordic combined, and Ski Meister. He graduated in 1958 and became a 1st Lieutenant in the United States Army shortly afterwards. In 1959, he was the top U.S. finisher in the cross-country race at the Squaw Valley pre-games test race and together with Lahdenpera was assigned to the USMWBTC in the summer of 1960. He and Lahdenpera were soon joined by Dick Taylor.

Seeing that the U.S. Army's Biathlon Training Center in Alaska was the only place that one could continue to train and ski seriously after college, Dick Taylor joined the U.S. Army for that purpose. He had grown up in New Hampshire and started skiing at the Gilford Outing Club, began cross-country skiing at Holderness School in Plymouth, NH and later continued skiing for Dartmouth College where he was the team captain in 1959. After enlisting and spending his 16 weeks in Georgia, becoming an infantryman, with the help of his senator, he was assigned to the USMWBTC. He arrived at the same time as the new commanding officer, Colonel Ken Floto. Besides Lahdenpera, Wilson and Taylor there were a few others chosen from the battle group stationed at Ft. Richardson, however it was those three who were the heart of the U.S. team that participated in the 1961-62 World Championships. Dick Taylor was the best U.S. finisher in 1961 with an 11th place at the World Championships, but other competitions in Scandinavia that winter also produced some excellent results. Taylor placed 6th in an international race at Kuopio, Finland; Wilson finished 10th in the Swedish National Championships, and Lahdenpera was 11th in the Finnish National Championships at Kuovala. Taylor made the 1964 Olympic Team, but as a cross-country skier. He eventually went back to graduate school and began a teaching career, but never left the ski community and between 1983 and 1987 was a full-time coach with the U.S. Cross-Country Ski Team. He was the author of many articles about skiing and a book in 2002 entitled, *No Pain, No Gain: How Athletes, Coaches and Parents Can Re-shape American Sports Culture*.

After taking command Colonel Ken Floto, a 10th Mountain Division veteran, began to look for college skiers shortly after his arrival at the USMWBTC. One of the first he contacted was Charlie Akers who was skiing for the University of Maine and had taken a year off to compete in the 1960 Winter Olympic Games cross-country where he was an Olympic teammate of Wilson, Lahdenpera and

Taylor. Charlie had grown up in the small town of Andover, Maine and had won the Maine High School ski championships as a sophomore and repeated the following two years. He then went on to the University of Maine in 1957 and competing for their cross-country running team as a way of training for the ski team, he also became an exceptional runner. He won the 1959 NCAA Nordic Ski Championships and after taking the year off for the Olympic Games, he came back to finish college and was the NCAA cross-country champion again in 1961. During his senior year he was contacted by his former competitors (Wilson, Lahdenpera and Taylor) telling him about the "unit" and he was later contacted by Colonel Floto who requested that he join the Unit, offering him help in securing an assignment there. Although no one, including military personnel and recruiters, believed he would have any control over his assignment or that he would "ski" for the army, he enlisted and near the end of his basic training at Ft. Dix, New Jersey the commanding officer, a bit flustered, called him to his office and wanted to know why he thought he would go to Alaska. After explaining what he had been told by Colonel Floto, the officer relaxed and said he had never seen orders issued directly by the Pentagon before. He was assigned to the Unit at Ft. Richardson in 1961 and was there until 1964. Charlie participated in the 1962 and 1963 World Biathlon Championships and achieved the best U.S. result at the 1964 Winter Olympic Games with a 16th place finish. Like Dick Mize before him, Charlie stayed in Alaska following his release from the military and retired from a career in education at Palmer, Alaska.

In the years following Dick Taylor and Charlie Akers' arrival, others steadily began arriving for duty at the USMWBTC. The center was attracting many of the best college skiers in the country. This was clearly apparent during the 1964 Winter Olympic Games when some members who failed selection for biathlon participated in the cross-country events. By 1963 the group included Martin Hall, Jim Shea, Ford Hubbard, Otto Robsahm, Bill Spencer, Herb Thomas, Wayne Fleming, Paul Renee, Linwood Bean, Quentin Skinner, Karl Bohlin, Gerry Varnum, Charlie Kellogg, Jed Williamson and Dick Breen.

Many knew each other, at least in name, from prior ski competitions and shared similar backgrounds as teammates in college skiing like Marty Hall and Jed Williamson or being Olympic teammates like Karl Bohlin who was another Squaw Valley Olympic cross-country skier. Some like Paul Renne were not really known to the others since he did not share the traditional skiing background. He attended Montana State University where his father was the president of the school and was enrolled in ROTC. Although Paul did have some skiing experience, his background came from shooting and during the period when shooting played a greater role in the outcome of biathlon racing, his skills on the range served him well. With the four different distances and the inability to zero the rifles at each range prior to the race the competitors had to have a good sense of how much change the sights needed for each shooting bout. As the winner of the Junior National Small-bore shooting championships he had highly developed shooting skills to go along with his cross-country skiing. In 1961, after a tour with the Infantry Brigade at Ft. Richardson he was assigned to the Unit and after placing second at the 1964 Olympic Trials he finished 39th at Innsbrück. His shooting talent gave him an assignment to the U.S. Army's Advanced Marksmanship Unit at Ft. Benning in 1966 where he became a top competitor with the All-Army team that competed in the National Matches held at Camp Perry. Sadly, Paul died in an automobile accident near Ft. Hayes, Kansas while returning from a rifle match in 1970.

Karl Bohlin was born in the famous ski town of Mora in Dalarna, Sweden and after coming to the U.S. he graduated from North Community High School in Minnesota. He skied for the Minneapolis Ski Club and the University of Minnesota, but later attended Western State College in Colorado. As a freshman at Minnesota, he won the 1958 NCAA cross-country title. After racing in cross-country relay at Squaw Valley he joined the army and was assigned at the USMWBTC. Karl followed the training philosophy encouraged by coach Sven Johanson. After winning the Mt. Marathon race at Seward in 1963, he and Dean Rickerson took 9 hours to ride their bicycles back to Ft. Richardson. He was the top U.S. finisher in 27th place at the 1963 World Biathlon Championships but in 1964 did not qualify for the biathlon team, but instead qualified for the 1964 Winter Olympic cross-country team and raced in the cross-country 15 kilometers race. Rickerson was from New Mexico and joined the USMWBTC as another Western State skier and participated in the 1961 CISM Games in Germany.

Otto Robsahm had a most interesting route to becoming a member of the USMWBTC. A native of Norway, and previously a Lieutenant in the Norwegian army with over 80 free-fall parachute jumps and an impressive list of sports achievements in Norway, when asked why he left the Norwegian army to join the U.S. Army he said, "I have a strong desire to become a U.S. citizen." As a member of the Co. D, 504th Airborne Infantry, he won the 8th Infantry track championship in 1961 and numerous other athletic competitions. After being recognized by King Olav V for finishing 4th out of 350 entrants and the only American participating in the Norwegian Militaerloppet, he was sent to Garmisch-Partenkirchen to participate in the final trials for the U.S. team to compete at the CISM Games. Successful in that effort he was later assigned to the USMWBTC and received his citizenship. Finishing in the top three places on three occasions at the Mt. Marathon race in Seward, he was a member of the 1963 World Championship team that competed at Seefeld, Austria.

After moving to rural New Hampshire from New York City following World

War II, Marty Hall fell in love with skiing. Like most of his "unit" teammates he skied for a college team, the University of New Hampshire. He was a member of the 1962 team that toured Europe and participated in the CISM Games, however illness severely hampered his efforts that year. Marty went on to become the renowned coach of the U.S. Ski Team during the 1970s. New Hampshire native Linwwod Bean, nicknamed "Skip" was a Dartmouth graduate and ski team member who became a member of the USMWBTC team in 1962, and competed with the group in Europe in 1963. Another college skier at the Unit during the period, Charlie Kellogg was originally from Andover, Massachusetts and attended Holderness School in New Hampshire where he began cross-country and alpine skiing. He then attended Williams College in Massachusetts where he competed in cross-country running, track and skiing. Becoming one of the east's top skiers he was the team captain and received the Townsend Award as a senior. Originally thinking of joining the Navy, he switched his direction when Al Merrill, the ski coach at Dartmouth recommended him for the USMWBTC. After basic training at Ft. Dix, Charlie was assigned to the Unit and arrived there in March of 1963. An alternate for the 1964 Winter Olympic team he achieved the best U.S. result in the 1964 CISM competition at Östersund, Sweden and just 3 weeks after his release from the U.S. Army, Charlie won the first U.S. National Biathlon Championships in 1965 at Rosendale, New York. A full-time position with the Data Processing Division of IBM in Cambridge, Massachuestts limited his training time for biathlon, but he continued to train for cross-country skiing. In 1968, he was a member of the Winter Olympic cross-country ski team competing at Grenoble, France and continued as a member of the U.S. National Cross-Country Ski Team until 1973. He stayed actively involved with biathlon as a long-time serving member on the USBA Board of Directors.

Jim Shea came from a great winter sports family, as his father, Jack Shea, won two gold medals in speed skating at the 1932 Lake Placid Winter Olympics. But growing up around Lake Placid, he first focused on ski jumping and later turned to cross-country skiing. One day on a training run he was stopped by Craig Lussi, also from Lake Placid and a member of the Nordic combined team at the Squaw Valley Olympic Games who skied for the University of Denver, and Craig suggested that Jim think about going there too. Jim did, after receiving a ski scholarship, and helped win the 1961 NCAA team title in skiing. In his senior year during the 1960-1961 season, he was named team captain and an All-American. In 1962 two months after graduation Jim was drafted into the U.S. Army assigned first at Ft. Carson and later transferred to the Unit at Ft. Richardson. While there he finished 33rd in the 1963 World Biathlon Championships but was discharged just before the 1964 Winter Olympic Games and returned to the University of Denver to become an assistant coach for Willy Schaeffler. At the trials for the

1964 Olympic team at Spout Springs, Oregon he was selected for both the U.S. Olympic cross-country and Nordic combined teams. At Innsbrück he achieved a 27th place in Nordic combined, 48th place in the 30 kilometers cross-country ski race and was a member of the men's relay team that finished in 13th place. Jim continued to stay active in the ski community and was the U.S. Biathlon coach for the 1972 Winter Olympic Games and the 1973 World Championships at Lake Placid.

William "Bill" Spencer joined the group in April of 1963 and remained assigned there until immediately following the 1968 Winter Olympics at Grenoble. Born in Alabama and then spending early childhood in Bermuda, Bill's family moved to Utah in 1948 when he was 12. While attending South High School, he and his brother spent the winter weekends skiing at Brighton. In high school Bill joined the Junior ROTC which provided him the chance to begin competitive shooting. After high school, he joined the Utah National Guard and attended the University of Utah. He represented the Utah National Guard in national shooting competitions and joined the ski team at the University. After finishing 6th in the 1959 NCAA cross-country ski championships he decided to follow his interest in biathlon by packing up his skis and hunting rifle and took a Greyhound bus to Reno and then hitchhiked to Squaw Valley where he participated in the North American Biathlon Championships which was also the Pre-Olympic test event. He finished in 8th place and was hooked on biathlon. Bill returned for the Olympic tryouts in December but did not make the 1960 team. He also participated in the cross-country trials with some good results but also did not qualify for that team. Determined to continue with biathlon he saw that the only way to do it would be join the U.S. Army and train at its center in Alaska.

What eventually became a 21-year career as an army officer, Bill spent the early part of his years at the USMWBTC and was a two-time national biathlon champion and the second U.S. finisher at both the Innsbrück and Grenoble Winter Olympic games at 30th and 37th places. While still at the 1966 World Championships Bill was approached by the TV producers of the popular game show, *To Tell the Truth,* asking if he would consider staying over in New York on the way back home to be a contestant on the show. He declined saying he had been away for too long and wanted to get home to be with his young family. The producers then offered to bring his wife Judy, and children to New York and be on the show as well if he would agree. The show's premise was a panel of celebrities would have three questions each to discover which of three guests, two of which were imposters, was the one who had a special ability, talent or unusual characteristic. Thinking "biathlon" would be difficult for the celebrity panel to discover was probably a good guess by the producers, however one of the celebrity panelists was a skier and asked if "herringbone" was related to skiing. The contestants were obligated to be honest, so Bill didn't win a lot of money, however he couldn't keep the amount he did win due to the strict amateur rules at the time. Ironically, he donated the money to the U.S. Olympic Association, the organization that imposed and enforced the strict amateur rules.

Because Bill's assignment to Vietnam was delayed so that he could participate at Grenoble, he was immediately reassigned to duty in Vietnam after the 1968 Games and arrived there just after the famous Tet offensive. Bill continued to participate sporadically but essentially became one of U.S. Biathlon's long-time coaches, focusing mostly on the range and shooting. Bill was an athlete, coach or team leader at more than seven Olympic Games and played a major role at the Salt Lake Games in 2002. He also served on the USBA Board of Directors for many years and was the first American elected to the UIMPB/IBU Biathlon Technical Committee where he served until being retired at the age of 60.

The years between 1964 and 1968 saw changes in the race format and addition of the team relay event. It also was a period when some athletes completed their military duty and left the USMWBTC and a new group of skiers began taking their place. With the troop level buildup for the escalating war in Vietnam intensifying the military draft, it also provided access to a pool of athletes with college or high school ski experience. All the USMWBTC and the Army Sports Branch had to do was to identify them and request their assignment to the Unit. Some, like that of Ed Williams, son of Walter Williams and a Dartmouth skier who was also the National 30km cross-country ski champion had helpful recommendations and someone looking out for them. Of Finnish heritage, Ed and his father were involved with skiing at the family's resort hotel in Rosendale, New York. Ever since the Telemark Ski Club was formed there in 1938 and later revived as the Rosendale Nordic Ski Club in the early 1960s, the family was close to the skiing environment. While at Dartmouth, he was able to take time away from college due to advanced classes and tried out for the 1964 Olympic team for cross-country. He won all the Eastern College ski carnivals in his senior year and finished 3rd in the NCAA Championships. While on the ski team at Dartmouth he enrolled in the ROTC program and had the recommendation from both Colonel Elmer Hassett and Master Sergeant Bill Brown, who was assigned to the ROTC program at the time. Colonel Hassett was a skier himself, originally from Minnesota and a veteran of many of the legendary Birkebeiner races in Norway and served as the Commander of the Cold Regions Warfare Center at Ft. Greeley. Following Ed's initial officer training at Ft. Benning he was at first assigned to an Infantry Brigade at Ft. Hood until his father alerted Colonel Alpo Marttinen, one of the famous Finns who had escaped Soviet capture following the Weapons Cache incident. Colonel Marttinen was the youngest Colonel in the Finnish Army and a recipient of its highest military award. He was working in the Pentagon at the time and interceded, having Ed reassigned to the Unit. Ed arrived in Alaska during the late fall of 1964 when there was already snow on the ground. He had the best U.S. finish at the 1965 World Biathlon Championships at Garmisch-Partenkirchen, Germany and after his release from the army he returned to Dartmouth's Tuck School for graduate studies but continued to train for biathlon and succeeded in securing his position on the 1968 Winter Olympic Games at Grenoble. Ed interrupted his studies again and successfully qualified for the 1969 World Biathlon Championships in Poland. After completing law school, Ed had a distinguished career which included a major role in writing the Amateur Sports Act. He served as the president of the U.S. Biathlon Association and its legal counsel for many years. His advocacy for athletes' rights has made him one of the leading legal authorities on specific athlete issues and NGB governance as well as serving on committees for arbitration of international scope.

Shortly after Ed, John "Louie" Ehrensbeck from the Adirondack community of Old Forge, New York arrived in January 1965. He was like many of the early biathlon team members who were "all-round skiers" having a background in all the ski disciplines. Like Maurice Paquette of the 1959 team, he was a natural, an accomplished alpine skier as well as a cross-country skier. His teammates at the USMWBTC saw him as the most talented athlete in the group. Graduating from Old Forge High School in 1963 he captained the high school ski team for his last three years and was a member of the team as early as his freshman year. With an alpine ski hill at the back of the Old Forge School playground, its students were introduced to skiing early, often skiing during their recess and gym classes. During his high school career, he won many trophies and was chosen to represent the East in the National Ski Championships. He was a member of the U.S. Alpine Ski Team in 1961 and the Nordic Team in 1963. Often cited as one of the best technical cross-country skiers in the nation, he joined the U.S. Army in September 1963 and was quickly identified for assignment to the unit and sent to Ft. Richardson immediately after basic training. Following his participation in the 1968 Winter Olympic Games he earned a bronze medal in the CISM triathlon, which was a combination of results from both the individual biathlon race and the alpine slalom.

John Ehrensbeck, Ed Williams, and Bill Spencer were the core of the 1968 Winter Olympic team and the USMWBTC in the period between 1964-68. They were joined by Jon Chaffee, Ralph Wakely and Jay Bowerman on the team at Grenoble, France. Bowerman was from Oregon and the son of the famous Oregon track coach, co-founder of Nike and a 10th Mountain Division alumni, Bill Bowerman and the grandson of the Governor of Oregon. After WWII and his experience in the 10th Mountain Division at Camp Hale, Jay's father returned to Medford, Oregon for a teaching position and regularly took the family skiing at Crater Lake. The family then moved to Eugene where his father began a long illustrious coaching career and continued to take young Jay and the family to Willamette Pass ski area, where they used the classic white military wood skis. As a freshman enrolling at the University in 1961, in the era of an active draft, two years of ROTC was mandatory, with continued participation after the sophomore year optional. After running for his father's team at the University of Oregon he was commissioned in 1966 in the Chemical Corps. He finished Officer Basic Training at Ft. McClellan, (Alabama) with the highest score on record for the PT test when he had learned of the army biathlon program and applied for duty with the Unit. At time of graduation from his Officers Basic Training, however, his first assignment was to stay at Ft. McClellan to become one of the training officers whose job it was to take successive classes and lead them on punishing forced marches and physical training, something he was physically more than prepared to do. He had one week of leave coming between the end of Officers Basic and the beginning of active duty, and it was during that leave time in Oregon that he received a change of orders assigning him to the USMWBTC. Arriving there just as the winter training season at the Independence Gold Mines was beginning, he spent the first year improving his cross-country skills, however once the winter was over and the summer training began, Jay was troubled by Sven's soon to be outdated training philosophy of daily heavy training loads, in contrast to the "hard-easy" training that allowed distance runners to achieve impressive results by his father's runners at Oregon. It was during this period that Sven applied his belief that from his personal experience, one just had to learn to be tough and that came through breaking the body down and learning to overcome whatever challenges were presented, was increasingly unacceptable by the athletes. Despite his difference of opinion on training, Jay was a member of the 1968 and 1972 Olympic teams and a member of the relay team that finished 6th at Sapporo.

A New Hampshire native, Chaffee was a cousin to alpine skier and actress Suzy Chaffee who was also a 1968 Olympic team member for alpine skiing. Despite limited time for ski training at Harvard, he captured a 10th place finish at the 1966 NCAA Championships and scored second place to his Olympic and USMWBTC teammate, Ed Williams in three of the big eastern ski carnivals. He was also a member of the U.S. National "B" cross-country ski team. Following graduation from Harvard in 1966 where he ran cross-country and was the captain of the ski team, Jon entered the U.S. Army and after basic training at Ft. Bragg, he was assigned to the Unit at Ft. Richardson. Many thought Chaffee had the most natural talent as an aerobic athlete and was an excellent runner. Others at the USMWBTC at the time were Pete Ripple, who grew up near Niagara Falls and whose prior athletic achievements had been as a boxer; Juhani Isokangas, a Finn known as Izi, who had grown up in New York City and for whom the others thought he saw biathlon was a way to stay out of Vietnam; and Myron Gallagher, known as Gary, who really improved during his time there and eventually coached college skiing at Northern Michigan University. During early Summer of 1968, the athletes were participating in one of the road races in the Anchorage area, and part of the course was along a gravel road with several sharp curves in it. During the race, some local driver and his buddy were rallying along the gravel road, came around a curve in a 4-wheel drift, and hit Gary Gallagher, pitching him up over the car and cartwheeling him onto the road shoulder. He apparently had jumped upwards and was bounced off the hood and windshield and up over the car. Amazingly, he suffered no broken bones and was back training the next week, but what stood out beyond the fact that he wasn't injured seriously was that Gary was running on the right shoulder of the road and received a citation for running on the wrong side of the road and the driver got off without any admonishment!

Mel Matis, Allan Small and Ralph Wakely were also at the USMWBTC during that period. Wakely came in the summer of 1965 and was there through April of 1968. Like Bill Spencer, Wakely was from Salt Lake City where he started skiing at the age of eight and was an excellent shooter. After good results at Grenoble, he wanted to stay in the military through the next Olympic quadrennial, but the army wanted to send him to Ft. Harrison, Indiana so he left the army to train as a civilian. Before his discharge he was selected to compete with the U.S. Army Alaska Advanced Marksmanship Unit and shooting for USARAL in the 1967 All-Army Championships. He spent the 1970-71 winter in Norway, skiing with a local club in the Oslo area, but suffered a nasty knee injury and never recovered enough to make the 1972 team. Ralph later became a reporter for the United Press International, a news wire service, and was assigned to cover the 1980 and 2002 Winter Olympics and the 1984 Summer Games. Allen Small was perhaps one of the youngest members of the group, growing up in Durango, Colorado and had excellent results as a junior cross-country skier.

Chaffee, Ehrensbeck, Spencer, Williams, and Wakely dominated the 1968 trials for the Winter Olympic Games at Upson, Wisconsin and Bowerman grabbed the final place on the team, but the next generation of athletes also gained their first biathlon experience at those trials and would become the next group of athletes at the "unit" and the core of the 1970s teams. Peter Karns, and Dennis Donahue were the first of the next group of Olympic team members who began their biathlon career by participating in the selection race for the 1968 team at Upson, Wisconsin and would later play important roles as athletes, coaches and administrators. Peter, a fourth generation Jackson Hole, Wyoming native began skiing in 1955 with the Jackson Hole Ski Club as an alpine, cross-country and ski jumper and was the Rocky Mountain Intercollegiate cross-country ski champion in 1967 while skiing for the University of Utah. He finished 3rd in the U.S. Cross-country National

Championship 15km race. An All-American skier, he participated in the Olympic team trials for biathlon at Upson, Wisconsin as an independent competitor and following college, Pete entered the army and was assigned to the Biathlon Training Center at Ft. Richardson where he quickly established himself as the top biathlete of his era. He won the National Biathlon Championships in 1970 and 1972 and was typically the top American internationally, finishing 2nd in the 1969 Swiss Biathlon Championship and 2nd in the 1970 Swedish Biathlon Championships. He was a member of the American team to the 1969 Biathlon World Championships in Zakopane, Poland as well as the 1970 World Championships in Östersund, Sweden. His most impressive biathlon results came after he was released from active duty in 1972 at the Sapporo Olympic Games where he set a U.S. benchmark performance that equaled the 14th place finish of John Burritt from 1960, however, it was a performance in an era when the numbers of nations and competitors made the events more competitive. He was also a member of the 6th place relay team, a best U.S. result that wasn't equaled until the 2018 Olympic Games at Pyeongchang, Korea. Following his impressive legacy of accomplishment at every level of skiing competition, junior, collegiate, national and Olympic he served as a member of the U.S. Olympic Committee from 1973 to 1976, the same years he coached the U.S. Biathlon Team. He coached the U.S. Olympic Biathlon Team in 1976 and was chief of timing for Biathlon during the 1980 Olympic Winter Games in Lake Placid, and during the 2002 Olympic Winter Games in Salt Lake City, he served as chief of forerunners for biathlon events.

Dennis Donahue, like many others involved with biathlon, was an alumnus of Holderness School in New Hampshire and Middlebury College where he was a member of the ski teams. At Holderness, he was a member of the 1960 and 1961 Eastern Prep School Championship teams, competing in all four ski events both there and at Middlebury College. After graduation in 1966 he entered the army and was assigned to the USMWBTC. He was a member of the 1968 CISM team and the World Biathlon Championship teams for 1969 to 1974 and two Olympic teams, 1972 and 1976. Dennis was known as an extremely good marksman and achieved a perfect shooting result at the 1973 World Biathlon Championships at Lake Placid. Always achieving some of the best U.S. results, he was the top American in the 1970 World Championships at Östersund, Sweden, 1973 at Lake Placid and 1974 at Minsk. He later served as the coach of the U.S. National Biathlon team from 1988 to 1991.

John Morton, also a four-event skier originally from New Hampshire, and like others before him, after attending Holderness School he went on to ski four years on the Middlebury College ski team. He was the Eastern Intercollegiate Champion in 1966 and 1968, and the runner-up in the 1968 NCAA Championships. As a ROTC student, he entered active duty and did his officer training at

Ft. Benning. After a personal trip to the Pentagon he was reassigned to Alaska at the USMWBTC, and after participating in the 1969 and 1970 World Biathlon Championships, his military assignment at the USMWBTC was interrupted by a tour of duty in South Vietnam during the 1971 season. After spending that year as an advisor to the Vietnamese forces in the Mekong Delta, he returned to the USMWBTC and resumed his biathlon career by qualifying for the 1972 Winter Olympic Games along with his college roommate and ski team member both at Holderness and Middlebury, Dexter (Terry) Morse who was also assigned at the USMWBTC. Terry was also a member of the 1971 World Championships team while John was in Vietnam.

Upon release from active military service in 1972, John taught and coached high school skiing in Anchorage and continued biathlon training. He qualified for the 1973, 1974, and 1975 World Championships teams and his second Winter Olympic team at Innsbrück in 1976. He returned to Vermont to become the head coach of men's skiing at Dartmouth College in 1978 and was an assistant biathlon coach at the 1980 Olympic Games. John participated in seven Winter Olympic Games as an athlete, a coach, the U.S. Biathlon team leader, and at the Salt Lake City Games, as chief of course for the biathlon events. As the Eastern Regional Biathlon coach, he recruited many future Olympic team members into the sport. He also served as the interim executive director in 1992-93 and was appointed as an international referee by the IBU in 1994. He was the team leader for many other international events and authored two books about biathlon. His business specializing in trail design developed many inspiring trails for private landowners, municipalities, schools and resorts, as well as competition venues for major international events such as the World University Games and Biathlon World Cups. In 2002 John was the chief of course for the Salt Lake Games.

Other former collegiate skiers also found their military assignment to the USMWBTC. Donahue, Karns, and Morton were joined by Terry Aldrich, George Tuthill, Mike Romaine, Ed Schnackenberg, Scott Leake and Mike Devecka. Terry Aldrich grew up skiing in Old Forge, New York and later for New York's St. Lawrence University where he was one of the outstanding collegiate skiers in the East throughout his St. Lawrence career. He was captain of the St. Lawrence team as a senior and demonstrating his overall skiing ability, was second in the Skimeister competition at both the Dartmouth and Middlebury Carnivals. After competing in the 1971 World Biathlon Championships and suffering illness during the 1972 Olympic team trials, Terry went on to become a ski coach at the University of New Hampshire and later from 1977 until 2007 at Middlebury College, where he helped 30 skiers achieve All-American status. He was the Eastern Intercollegiate Ski Association Coach of the Year in 1975 and a member of the NCAA Ski Committee.

Terry's nickname in college was "Coyote" and years later he said he didn't honestly remember how he got it. With three of his ATO fraternity also members in the unit, (Don Simonds, Bruce Crawford, and Dave Pope) the name stuck. Terry was also responsible for finding nicknames for many of the other athletes there at the time. Explaining how they evolved he said, "they were based on experiences at the unit." For example, Don Simonds was terrible in volleyball and always ended up in the net, so he earned the nickname "Spiderman." He named Dennis Nelson as "Pigeon" because during a fall in jumping during his nordic combined days at Cloquet, Minnesota high school he had landed on his head, and his neck was permanently bent and he appeared to walk like a pigeon. Ed Schnackenberg was simply Schnack. Mike Devecka was "Beak" for obvious reasons (he had a prominent nose). Ladd Christianson was "Angle" for he was always able to find a way to get out of things. Dan New was known simply as "Deadwood" because that's where he grew up. George Tuthill was "The Flea" because he was always bouncing around with way too much energy. Bruce Crawford was called "Raccoon" because of the perennial circles under his eyes. Dave Kern was known by everyone as "Kid" because of his age. Pete Karns was the "Chicken Man" because he drove an old silver and red station wagon which everyone called the Chicken Wagon. Mike Romine was called "Boulder Fella" because of where he was from. Beryl Palmer was called "Cowboy" because he really was one and he would quietly, without telling the coaches, enter bronc riding contests in Anchorage and nearby Palmer. Once many team members went to Palmer to watch him ride, where he drew a horse named "Dynamite" and was promptly thrown. He still managed to place second, however on another occasion he was thrown during a competition in Anchorage just before the Gold Discovery race at Fairbanks, which caused him some pain in his hip. He evaded giving Sven Johanson the real reason for not starting the race. Beryl and Peter Hale often had the problem of trying to avoid fully explaining their pains or soreness from "other activities" and in Peter's case it was playing hockey in the Anchorage senior league.

Ed Schnackenberg grew up in Steamboat Springs, Colorado and skied in three Junior Nationals. Later at the University of Wyoming, he finished 2nd in the 1966 NCAA Nordic Combined Championships. Ed's laughter became a legend at the USMWBTC. He loved to make everything a fun experience and there were two stories that were always retold by his teammates. One story came from the last trip back to Anchorage after many weeks of training at Independence mines during the fall and early winter of 1970-71. It was the week before Christmas and finally adequate snow had arrived at Arctic Valley for training there. With everyone anxious to get home for Christmas and looking forward to not making any more trips to the training site at the mines, in Mike Devecka's absence, who was away with the Nordic combined team, Ed became the designated driver of the army's M35 2½-ton long-lived 6x6 cargo truck, commonly referred to as a "deuce and a half" back to Ft. Richardson. Normally most of the enlisted team members rode in the canvas-covered back of truck with all the gear while the coaches and a few ranking officers drove or rode in a jeep. Being tactical vehicles, neither was very fast on the long straight highway through the Matanuska Valley from Palmer to Anchorage, however on this particular day, Schnackenberg managed to get the truck moving at a speed well beyond its expected maximum and left the jeep far behind. Both the jeep riders and the team sitting in the cold winds through the flapping canvas in the back of the truck were incredulous at the speed Schnackenberg achieved with the unwieldy truck on the trip back to Ft. Richardson. The second story that circulated among Ed's teammates was about an incident during one of the Wednesday night relay races that were held at Russian Jack Springs in Anchorage. On his leg of the relay he began to have trouble with his ski bindings and he continually kept losing his ski when it came undone. After a few times of running down his errant ski, he became completely frustrated, losing lots of time. Finally, on a dark corner it came off again he took out his frustration by breaking the wood ski in half over his knee. After claiming to coach Sven Johanson that he didn't finish due to the broken ski, Sven examined the ski and commented that it did not appear to have broken in the usual way and couldn't understand how it could have happened. Eventually someone else revealed they had seen what had happened and hinted to the group the real cause of the broken ski. The following day Sven chastised Ed for "breaking a perfectly good ski."

Like Schnackenberg at Wyoming, Mike Devecka focused on Nordic Combined at Ft. Lewis College in Colorado where he graduated in 1969. Originally from Oregon, Mike had the talent to be a great biathlete as he was both a good shooter and the fastest skier in the unit at the time. He had the best individual result at the 1972 CISM Games and was a member of the Nordic Combined team at the 1972, 1976 and 1980 Olympic Games. After his discharge from the army he was U.S. champion in the Nordic combined in 1972, 1974, 1975, and 1979, and U.S. ski jumping champion on the large hill in 1978. Mike's father built high performance racing engines and Mike also had a fondness for classic cars. He often repaired the unreliable generator engine at Independence Mines whenever the power failed in the building that housed the team during the cold, dark winter nights. He had a lot of talent and was not only the unit's fastest skier but also the fastest runner. He was the first person to break the 3-hour mark by running a record-setting 2 hours 59 minutes in the difficult Equinox marathon at Fairbanks in 1971. His ski success was a product of his admirable motivation, often being the first and last one on the ski trails at Independence, but he was essentially released to travel with the Nordic combined team during the winter for most of his assignment at the USMWBTC.

Scott Leake came from a farm near Bennington, Vermont and was also a four-event skier from his early school days and captained his prep school team at the Darrow School in Lebanon, New York. He was also the captain of the ski team at the University of Vermont in 1967 and was a member of the Eastern X-C Training Squad and the winner of several Nordic combined events at eastern Winter Carnivals. A rather low-key individual, Scott was often left to be the leader of the group when the CISM and World Championships teams left for overseas competitions; however, Scott did qualify and race in the 1972 CISM Games held at an unusual location at the Cedars of Lebanon.

George Tuthill was honored as a Danforth Fellow at Williams College and a Phi Beta Kappa graduate. From Williston, Vermont he began skiing at Edmunds High School in Burlington, Vermont concentrating on cross-country and jumping. As a member of the Williams College team he had good results in Nordic Combined, finishing 2nd in the 1967 National Combined Championships. He also excelled in running, with impressive results in the Boston Marathon. Following graduation, he began PhD studies at M.I.T and continued skiing for the Cambridge Sports Union until he was drafted into the U.S. Army and assigned to the USMWBTC. While in Alaska George earned a reputation for being too serious and while others often played cards or socialized during the evenings at Independence Mines, he was often reading scientific studies. Following his release from military duty, he returned to his advanced studies in physics and continued training. As a civilian he qualified and raced in the 1973 World Biathlon Championships at Lake Placid. Following the 1974 team trials he returned to his studies and after receiving his PhD from M.I.T. he joined the faculty at Montana State University at Bozeman in 1976 where he spent 30 years as an award-winning teacher and physicist recognized for his integration of teaching and research and for his commitment to students. He also served as director of the National Teacher Enhancement Network (NTEN), funded by the National Science Foundation, and associate dean of MSU College of Letters and Science. After moving back to the east, he was named interim associate vice president for the College of Graduate Studies, at Plymouth State University in New Hampshire in 2009.

Others who had not followed the traditional prep school, college ski team path also were being captured by the military draft and found assignment at the USMWBTC. Peter Hale, originally from Minnesota was an ROTC student and track runner at the University of North Dakota and was assigned to the Cold Weather and Mountain School at Ft. Greely where he improved his skiing and was an instructor. At the annual Fairbanks Gold Discovery race, he raced well against the members of the biathlon unit and was invited by Sven Johanson to apply for a transfer to Ft. Richardson. His background in track and cross-country included a 1978 NCAA finalist in the college division for track which prepared him well for skiing when assigned at Ft. Greely. Peter's calm demeanor and approach to training became legendary and made him popular among the group. He earned the nickname "Omar the tentmaker." It developed following an exceedingly long shooting stage, to which Coach Arvil Hunter loudly asked if he was "camping out" on the range. Peter's often lengthy range times made the phrase popular among the athletes when anyone took too much time shooting and "camping out on the range" became the common term for excessive range times. Peter earned the nickname also because he wore a mustache and resembled Omar Shariff, who appeared in the famous movie of the time, "Doctor Zhivago." After leaving the military in 1974 he was one of the organizers of the Minnesota Biathlon Association and was a member of the National Team from 1975 to 1980. He later became well known in the ski industry as a ski representative to many of the nation's top skiers for a succession of Norwegian ski companies.

Dennis Nelson from Cloquet, Minnesota was a high school skier who volunteered for the army and had a slightly longer commitment than the draftees. After high school, where he had competed in the Junior Nationals from 1965 to 1968 he attended the University of Duluth for a year before he joined the army. Most of those who had been drafted were only obligated for two years but were also limited to a rank below that of a sergeant. Dennis was able to advance higher and was eventually the highest ranked enlisted soldier-athlete at the unit. His sergeant status was valuable in the 1972 CISM Games at Lebanon where he was the NCO on a patrol team. Dennis was like Terry Aldrich in that he often liked to "dare" the egos of his teammates like John Hall. Two high school skiers from Colorado, Dave Bristol and Beryl Palmer arrived together in early December during the last big push of military conscription just as President Nixon announced the draft lottery. Both came from Summit High School at Frisco where he and Beryl were coached by the well-known Jim Balfanz. After a year at Colorado Mountain College Dave joined the army and competed in the 1972 CISM Games in Lebanon. Beryl had placed 2nd in the 1967 Junior Nationals and the following year finished 11th at the NCAA cross-country championships while attending Western State College. Beryl was originally assigned to a Ft. Richardson detached missile site at Arctic Valley before being transferred to the USMWBTC. During a warmup for a ski race at Russian Jack Springs in Anchorage Beryl was leading the group around the loop when he stopped suddenly due to the presence of a young bull moose near the edge of the ski track. Dennis Nelson, keeping his tradition of "dares" kept calling from the middle of the group to "get some backbone" and go on. Beryl did start slowly watching the moose carefully until the moose suddenly and quickly advanced towards him. It seemed only a split second, but almost instantly Beryl had climbed up a skinny tree, with his skis and poles, and while holding onto the swaying tree, yelled to the others, "get him off me." The others couldn't believe their eyes as they quickly came to his rescue, waving their ski poles and chasing the moose away. They couldn't contain their laughter as Beryl tried to climb back out of the tree, with skis still on his feet.

At the same time that Devecka, Bristol and Palmer had arrived at the unit, Art Stegen had also been caught in the military draft. Art had attended college on an athletic scholarship for track and cross-country running and was in the middle of his second year of teaching high school French. Although primarily a runner, he had been skiing since high school with the Rosendale Nordic Ski Club near his home in New York and had been a training partner with Ed Williams during the summer before Ed entered the army in 1964. After setting the record for the mile run in combat boots at Ft. Dix for the army's physical fitness test and winning the Battalion, Brigade and Ft. Dix cross-country championships while in basic training, Walter Williams alerted George Wilson at the Armed Forces Sports office in Washington and Wilson had Art's original assignment to the Defense Language Institute in California revoked and changed to go directly to Ft. Richardson. A surprise finish of 3rd place in his first actual biathlon race at the 1972 Olympic team trials and then participating in CISM convinced him that biathlon was his sport. After leaving the army and participating in the 1973 World Championships he relocated to Norway for language studies where he continued training with Norwegian athletes and began a new direction by earning Norwegian coaching certification for biathlon and cross-country skiing. He also participated in the 1974 and 1975 World Biathlon Championships while living in Norway and upon returning to the U.S. built a new home and continued to train along with a few others who he encouraged to take up the sport. He continued racing and along with Veikko Salmela, a cousin of Finland's Pauli Sitonen, who was responsible for the beginning of skating, and Esa Hirvonen, son of Olavi Hirvonen who was a member of the 1960 Olympic team and teammate of Peter Lahdenpera, the trio successfully raced in both biathlon and cross-country skiing for the Rosendale Nordic Club. Esa was named to the U.S. Biathlon Development Team just prior to his tragic death in an auto accident. Art was later hired as the first full-time National Biathlon Coach in 1978 and then in 1981 as the first program director. He returned to teaching following the 1982 season, where he earned high recognition as a high school running and ski coach, with many local championship teams, individual state and national champions for both sports. In 1992, he accepted the position as the coach for the National Guard Biathlon program, from which he retired in 2006. Art was active in many areas, having participated in the formation and signing of the original documents of independence and incorporation of the U.S. Biathlon Association, the formation of NYSSRA Nordic and Biathlon, including biathlon's addition to the Empire State Games and a long-time member of the USBA Board of Directors. He was also an UIPMB/IBU Technical Delegate and was honored by Sven Thofelt for publishing the first book about biathlon written in English.

One of the more interesting athletes during this period was the U.S. Navy's John Hall. The training center was open to athletes from the other service branches and while there were a few airman like Danny New of South Dakota and Western State College, John was from the Navy. He was a high school skier from Johnstown, New York who entered the Navy and became a member of a UDT unit (known as SEAL teams today) at Virginia Beach, Virginia. John was the ultimate "tough" but very congenial guy. Nicknamed "Frogman" he was the center of many stories among the skiers at the unit, especially when it came to telling stories about the sauna at Independence Mines or canoe racing in Fairbanks; he was a tough competitor with a paddle in any kind of boat. John and Terry Aldrich had a habit of challenging each other and John was never one to let a challenge go to waste. Once during the daily sauna at the end of the training day someone suggested seeing who could stay under the very cold water longest in the corner of the sauna where there was an opening to waste-deep running water below. The water usually was iced over, so cold that even after being heated by the sauna, no one could tolerate it longer than a quick dip. Everyone fully expected John to win that challenge. He however made the challenge something of a legend. With the other steaming, naked athletes standing above the ladder he descended into the darkness of the cold water and after more than a minute did not reappear. As the group began to get anxious he quietly and casually walked through the front door and approached the others from behind as they were leaning over the ladder and asked, "did I win?" He swam under the building, broke through the ice and walked around the building in the snow to totally surprise the group.

Two other stories that were frequently retold also added to his legend. One was in the sauna, which was built over a stream. He liked to trick other athletes into believing he had cleared the way for the next to enter the stream by calling out before he himself had entered. He would then submerge himself and grab the ankles of the next person in the very cold water, creating a frightening experience. The other occurred when the team was required to meet the USARAL Headquarters Company Commander, which required them to show up in the basic Army duty uniform known as "fatigues." Both the army and navy used the same uniform at the time; however, the navy was authorized a short-sleeved shirt version. Both uniforms looked identical except for the service tag; and of course, the navy's short sleeves. As the team members stood at attention in a row before his desk the commander immediately noticed John's short sleeves. From behind his desk the army major promptly got up and immediately went to John and without noticing the U.S. Navy service tape on the uniform, wanted to know who authorized him to "cut the sleeves" of his uniform. John answered that it was an authorized uniform, without specifying a "navy" uniform. The major, clearly showing growing frustration, then stated there was no regulation authorizing it and asked who his commander was. John gave the name of the navy "captain" responsible for him at Ft. Richardson, again without specifying "navy." A navy captain is equivalent to a colonel in the army, but in the army a captain is two ranks lower and lower than an army major. The other biathletes could see where the situation was headed, and John was clearly playing with the major's lack of knowledge about the navy and its ranking. The group could hardly hold back their pleasure of seeing the major make a fool of himself. After loudly declaring he wanted someone to get John's commanding "captain" on the phone, his first sergeant interrupted and tried to explain that John was attached to the USMWBTC, as a "sailor," and a navy captain is the equivalent of an army colonel and the navy uniform authorized is short sleeves. Fully embarrassed, the major quickly dismissed the group returning to his desk without looking up and probably heard the laughter of the athletes as they walked down the hall to the biathlon office, having never been told why the visit was necessary. After leaving Alaska John left the Navy for a period but had the unfortunate luck of breaking his big toe just before two different Olympic trials, an injury that made classic skiing terribly painful. John was a member of the 1971 CISM team and did participate in the 1978 World Championships. After a year of coaching the National Guard team he returned to the SEAL team at Virginia Beach as a senior enlisted leader and tragically died in a training accident. Many former team members and USBA Board members attended his funeral.

Another unique member of the USMWBTC during the late 1970s was Ken Alligood. Like Arvil Hunter before him, Ken was originally from the south. His early years were spent in Georgia where his father was serving a career in the U.S. Army but moved to Alaska with his father's assignment at Ft. Richardson. He attended East Anchorage High School and it was there he began skiing. He was a member of the Alaska Junior National team from 1963 to 1966 and the Alaska State High School Champion four years consecutively from 1963 to 1966. After attending Western State College, he joined the army and was assigned to the USMWBTC. He left the army in 1971 but continued to train at the center as a civilian. Like Mike Devecka, Ken was a classic car enthusiastic and had a reputation for his skills at driving any kind of vehicle and like Mike, Ken was often the driver of the army "deuce and a half" tactical truck that drove the team to Independence Mines and Arctic Valley for training and was especially skilled at navigating the primitive road up to the mines in the Talkeetna mountains. He was the U.S. National Champion four times and a member of the 1971 CISM team. As a civilian he was a member of the 1973, 1974, 1975 and 1979 World Championships teams. Very colorful, Ken often entertained other team members with wit and humor as at the 1974 World Championships in the USSR. Every time

Ken entered one of the team's rooms he would go to the telephone, pick up the receiver and bang it on the desk a few times. When asked why he continually did that, he replied that he wanted to wake up the "listeners" in the "bugging room." He also would often make faces and obscene gestures at the light fixtures saying he wanted to entertain the KGB. He had an especially good laugh, when the maid had spent the week trying to wash out the stains from a dirty t-shirt that he had used to clean the klister from his skis. Laughing he said, "it looked like the grey, dull-looking t-shirts" available in the local GUM department store."

In 1977 Ken was named as the coach for the 1977 World Championship team, the last to be held with large caliber rifles. He returned to competition in 1978, and despite finishing 2nd in the National Championships, due to a flaw that made the selection criteria somewhat unfair, he and few others who were thought to have high possibility for selection were unable to earn selection. He returned the following year winning the National Championships and achieved the best U.S. finish at the World Championships at Ruhpolding, Germany. The year after the 1980 Winter Olympic Games he was named as the coach for the National team, World Championships teams and the 1984 Olympic team coach at Sarajevo. Ken returned to Alaska where he became a pilot and established an air service business along with other ventures. Ken was always extremely practical and innovative, especially in finding solutions to problems of many kinds. While sitting around the hotel in Jackson, Wyoming, at one winter's training camp he came up with the idea to make getting into and out of the prone shooting position easier by splitting the arm sling into two pieces; the arm band which remained on the upper arm during skiing and the sling to the rifle stock with a hook that could be quickly coupled and uncoupled to and from the arm band. He visited a local army/navy store and purchased the materials, including light nylon webbing to replace the leather of the old-style sling. He then borrowed a sewing machine and assembled his new system. Not only did it enable faster in and out of the prone shooting position, it also improved consistency of shooting by not having to remove the entire sling from the supporting arm. Most of the team realized the potential and made one themselves or had Ken fabricate it for them. When Europeans saw the American's innovation, the rifle manufacturer Dieter Anschütz quickly mass produced them.

CHAPTER 10

Amateurs

The years after the closure of the USMWBTC in 1973 can be considered "Amateur Years" because although many of the athletes from then and prior to the 1980 Olympic Games had their original exposure and biathlon training during their military service in Alaska, as civilians they had to cope without any organizational, financial and training support in the 1970s. They were essentially left to their own resources and self-direction. In the days before the change to small bore there weren't any viable facilities for training and no access to the training requirements for marksmanship, especially ammunition. Without a site, coaching, and any assembled group for centralized training, those athletes that continued created individual training environments, sometimes with a few others in the best locations that they could support themselves and their training.

These conditions extended well into the 1980s and in an interview with *Fasterskier.com*, Pam Weiss explained in a story "Where are they now?" that focused on the first women competitors; she "lived on the cheap." Her recounting of those years best represented the conditions to which the athletes were subjected. She waitressed constantly and worked as a raft guide on the Snake River. The only way to make biathlon manageable was to join the National Guard, but Weiss wasn't interested. She started her own hat company, Mountain Woolies, and knit ski hats on a knitting machine. In the winters, she would put all her belongings into a storage unit, move out of her housing, and thus avoid paying rent. "I also did many other part-time jobs to save up for the winter traveling and had many very generous friends that helped me out with places to stay," she wrote. "It was a dream to be able to just train, rest and eat and not have to work so many hours. Our counter-parts in Europe certainly weren't working in addition to training."

It was also a time during which there was little organized effort in recruiting. Without any high school programs for biathlon, bringing in new athletes was essentially left to the existing athletes or former athletes themselves. The most promising of the newcomers were junior skiers Rusty Scott and Martin Hagen from Jackson, Wyoming who had been introduced to biathlon after the U.S. National Championships and team trials were there in 1970 and his father, along with a few other locals established a Junior Biathlon Club. Interest was also augmented by the fact that Peter Karns had won the National Championship and was a member of the World Championship team, and later achieved significant Olympic results at Sapporo. After it had been decided that the U.S. would enter juniors in the World Championships for the first time in 1973 at Lake Placid, Peter and Ken Alligood, who had relocated to Jackson began working with Rusty and Martin. The world championships team trials at Lake Placid also revealed the potential of the next dominate athlete, Lyle Nelson who attended the team trials with the final group of USMWBTC athletes.

Although a junior class was added to the Biathlon World Championships in 1967, it wasn't until the 1973 World Championships at Lake Placid that the U.S. would enter its first junior competitors. At the 1973 team trials, which were also at Lake Placid, Rusty Scott and Martin Hagen, high school teammates on the Jackson Wyoming High School ski team dominated the junior races. They were joined on the team by the USMWBTC athletes Bob Beaman of Ohio who was an excellent shooter and Marvin Macabe, a Navajo from Arizona, both who met the age requirements for the junior class. Both Rusty and Martin were exceptionally good junior skiers having earned many honors between them as members of the USSA Intermountain Junior National teams. They must be included in what would be the next generation of athletes with their top junior results in the 1973, 1974 and 1975 World Biathlon Junior Championships. Rusty and Martin achieved a 10th and 14th place at Minsk in 1974 and Martin led the way in 1975 with a 13th place at Antholz. Continuing as a senior racer Martin was a three-time Winter Olympic team member in 1976, 1980 and 1984, despite taking some years away while attending the University of Wyoming. Like Ken Alligood, Martin was also innovative and developed a carrying harness for the biathlon rifle that allowed one to remove the rifle without removing the carrying straps for the shoulders. It was eventually not approved by the IBU Technical Committee because it also could be done without removing the ski pole straps, which the technical committee saw as a potential way of supporting the standing position. Rusty also continued and had the fastest relay leg time for the 1977 World Championships team, however injury a year later limited his hopes and following the 1980 Olympic team trials he focused on ski racing. His impressive junior ski results included winning the 1974 USSA Junior National Championships and top 20 finishes for his class in both the American and Norwegian Birkebeiner ski races.

Lyle Nelson was clearly a promising talent in his first year at the sport, but his ski course errors at the 1973 team trials at Lake Placid denied him a chance to qualify for that team. Lyle was from McCall, Idaho where he was the captain of his ski and track teams and a member of the 1965, 1966 and 1967 USSA Pacific Northwest Junior National teams. He was a graduate of the U.S. Military

Academy at West Point where he also was a four-year member of the ski team and first in his class for physical ability. Commissioned in the U.S. Army he was first assigned to Ft. Carson, Colorado and then transferred to the USMWBTC in the final year before its discontinuation. Had it not been for those errors on the ski course, Lyle surely would have been a member of the 1973 World Championships team. His talent was impressive despite often being compromised by his tendency of occasional distractions. After participating in the 1973 CISM Games, and aside from the years he did not participate, such as 1978 when he earned a graduate degree from the University of Southern California, he became the dominate figure in biathlon from 1974 through the 1980s. A winner of 7 National Championship titles and a four-time Olympian, competing in 1976, 1980, 1984 and 1988 he was elected to be the bearer of the U.S. flag during the opening ceremonies at Calgary. With bests of 19th place finishes in both the World Championships and the Winter Olympic Games, Lyle was often seen as someone who could have been the first "medalist" breakthrough for the U.S. An example of this potential was exposed when he achieved the 2nd fastest first relay leg for the U.S. team at the 1976 Innsbrück Games. His years away from competition and occasional distractions often frustrated his coaches. Among the well-remembered were being late for the zero period and leaving his start bib in the hotel room at the 1975 Seefeld pre-Olympic Games competition. The targets went down just as he arrived at the range. With the team assigned lane 18 for the zeroing, and knowing that most of the team's zeroes hadn't changed, Art Stegen quickly saw the target number "8" was made of two perfect circles about the same size as the target and suggested to coach Bill Spencer to have Lyle shoot five rounds on upper circle of the "8" on the lane number down range. Lyle quickly got into position and fired 5 rounds as the officials came running. It worked perfectly as he put five shots in the center before he was stopped. Then as the competition was about to start he was not allowed into the start area without a number. Peter Lahdenpera made a dash back to the hotel a short distance from the range for the number and Lyle barely made the start line for his opening leg of the relay. Despite such adrenaline producing moments for the coaches and teammates, Lyle's many achievements speak for themselves. He was a thoughtful and supportive informal leader among his teammates and was the force behind the exploding interest in Summer Biathlon (running and shooting) during the 1990s. An innovative thinker, he was instrumental in finding new revenue sources for the U.S. Biathlon Association in the struggle to be financially stable and served as president of the Association at a particularly difficult time.

Peter Dascoulias was another of the final members of the USMWBTC who participated in the 1973 team trials. From Tilton, New Hampshire, he was commissioned into the army following graduation from the University of New Hampshire in 1972. He was a four-year member of the cross-country ski team, cross-country running team and track team at both the Tilton School and University of New Hampshire. A member of the Eastern USSA ski team he was assigned to the USMWBTC in 1972 and was a member of the 1973 CISM team. Following the closure of the training center he was sent to Garmisch-Partenkirchen, Germany, but later released for temporary duty to train for biathlon with the U.S. National Team. He qualified for the 1974 and 1975 World Championships teams and the 1976 Winter Olympic team. Military duty kept him away from biathlon during 1977 but Peter was renamed to the U.S. National team in 1978. Injury hampered his efforts in 1979 and following the 1980 Olympic team trials he returned to his military career as a transportation officer.

Other promising junior athletes that emerged during this period were Bob Foote from Bend, Oregon, Peter Hoag from Minneapolis, Minnesota, and John Harney from Salisbury, Connecticut. Bob went to high school in the middle of track-running-country at Corvallis where he competed in track, swimming and skiing as a member of the Pacific Northwest Junior National team. After high school, he attended Central Oregon Community College where was a member of the ski and track teams. Bend was also where he met Jay Bowerman and was introduced to biathlon. Winning the National Championships junior sprint race in 1977, he also qualified for the World Championship team and finished 11th in the junior race at Vingrom, Norway and raced on the senior relay team. Racing only cross-country skiing in 1978-79, he returned to biathlon for the 1980 Olympic trials where he just missed qualifying for the team.

Peter Hoag graduated from Minneapolis North High School where he was the captain of the cross-country, ski and tennis teams. Introduced to biathlon by senior competitor Peter Hale, he attended the University of New Hampshire where he was a member of the ski team and was named to the National Biathlon team as a junior in 1975 and competed in the World Championships that year at Antholz, Italy. In the final selection race for the 1976 Winter Olympic team Peter edged out more experienced seniors by a tenth of a percentage point to earn his place on the Olympic team. A stable shooter, he went on to a fine competitive career with having the best U.S. finish at the 1977 World Championships sprint race. He was a member of the 1980 Winter Olympic relay team that achieved an excellent 8th place, less than two minutes outside the bronze medal. Peter continued to participate through the 1984 Olympic team trials after which he turned to coaching, first as the women's coach at their first World Championships and then as the National Guard coach, at Montana State University at Bozeman and later he helped to administer the USOC's Education Program at Northern Michigan State University at Marquette.

John Harney also began biathlon competition as a junior. He was a member of the ski team at the Salisbury School and during the summer he trained at the USMWBTC as a junior. While in Alaska he placed first in the junior class in both the Resurrection Pass marathon and the Gold Discovery races. He recorded 2nd place finishes in the New York and Connecticut cross-country ski championships racing with the Salisbury Winter Sports Association. At Williams College in Massachusetts he was a 4-year member of the ski team and a member of the 1975 World Championships team as a junior. After graduation, he was commissioned in the U.S. Marines, however due to his military requirements John was unable to devote full energy to biathlon despite having been named to the 1979 National team and participating in the 1980 Olympic team trials.

One of the first very successful athletes without USMWBTC experience to find his way to biathlon during this period was California's Glenn Jobe. Highly successful as his high school's outstanding track athlete in Alturas, California he then attended the University of Nevada at Reno where he captained the ski team and was the Pacific Coast cross-country ski champion in 1973. As the USSA Far West's outstanding skier in 1973-75, Glenn was named to the National Biathlon team in 1976 and participated in the World Biathlon Championships in 1978 and 1979. He had the fastest relay lap time for the U.S. team in the 1978 World Championships and ended the 1979 season as the top ranked U.S. athlete. At the 1980 Winter Olympic Games Glenn finished 38th in the individual race. Glenn continued involvement in biathlon and skiing, coaching both the Far West USSA Junior National teams and later serving as the Western coordinator for the USBA regional development.

After the struggles of the early 1970s following the closure of the USMWBTC, a more optimistic mood developed within the biathlon community after the UIPMB's decision to switch to small bore (.22LR rim-fire caliber). This came at the same time that the USOC opened the winter sports training center at Squaw Valley, California and Peter Ladenpera's leadership began to make a difference. Serving as team leader in 1975 at the World Championships and the 1976 Winter Olympic Games he felt a strong need to improve the ski speed of the U.S. athletes, who despite generally good shooting were well behind their European competitors in ski time. Since it was generally known to be less productive, more difficult and taking much longer to teach a good shooter to become a good skier rather than teaching a good skier to learn how to shoot well, Peter personally sought out fast skiers, offering them a chance to try biathlon. He recruited three potentially good skiers that each were successful in earning World Championships and Olympic team selections as well as challenging the existing athletes to higher competitive ski speeds. Those three were Glenn Ewing, John Ruger, and Don Nielson.

Glenn Ewing was a three-letter man in high school, excelling in wrestling, for which he received an athletic scholarship to Western State College in Gunnison, Colorado. While attending Western State he was also a member of the ski team, competing in the 1973-75 NCAA championships with a best finish of 6th place. He first tried biathlon in 1976 and did well enough to be named to the National team in 1977 and qualified for the World Championships that year. He qualified again in 1978. After missing selection for the 1979 World Championship team and the 1980 Winter Olympic team by narrow margins Glenn opened a Nordic ski shop in Eagle, Colorado and became a retailer for Boise Cascade.

Like Glenn Ewing, John Ruger was also a high school wrestler, at John Jay High School in Katonah, New York, where he also ran on the track team. After graduation from Rutgers University his rock climbing and mountaineering interests led him to Colorado where he became a successful cross-country skier. Noticed by Lahdenpera for his natural talent and ability to learn quickly he encouraged John to try biathlon. Named to the Development team in 1978 and the National team in 1979, a year later he earned selection to the 1980 Winter Olympic team. Cold weather rifle problems severely impacted his performance in the Olympic 20km individual race, but John came back the following years to race in the 1981-83 World Championships, having the fastest relay leg for the U.S. team in 1983. After his competitive days John served as the USOC's long-time Athlete Ombudsman.

Don Nielsen was one of the U.S. Biathlon's most interesting ventures at development. Always a guess at how a junior athlete or cross-country skier conversion will develop, Peter Lahdenpera took a risk at inviting Nielsen to give biathlon a try. Nielsen had graduated second in his class at Hotchkiss School in Lakeville, Connecticut where he was captain of the ski team and later a magna cum laude graduate from Dartmouth College in 1974 where he was also a 4-year member of the ski team. Named to the U.S. National cross-country ski team in 1974 he was selected to the 1976 U.S. Winter Olympic cross-country team and the FIS World Championship team in 1978. However, continued difficulties with the coaching and the administration of USSA led to his dismissal. Lahdenpera then invited him to try biathlon. Nielsen's ability to learn shooting quickly, coupled with his excellent ski speed helped him to immediately become one of the top U.S. athletes, winning 5 of the 8 World team trial races in 1979, racing in the World Championships that year and scoring the World Cup points for the United States at Antholz. He injected a new sense of importance among the other athletes in their training and racing as well as placing great demands on the coaches and organization. A sprint specialist he was a member of the 1980 Winter Olympic relay that achieved one of the best U.S. finishes, just outside the bronze medal finish time in 8th place. However, his intense criticism, inconsistencies and sometimes troubled relationships with coaches and teammates plagued his performance, bouncing in and out of biathlon for a few years. He did manage to return to the 1984 Winter Olympic team and raced on the relay team at Sarajevo that finished 11th.

Although there was little active recruiting outside of Peter Lahdenpera's efforts the Vermont National Guard began holding regular races at its developing facility in Jericho. Howard Buxton was organizing races in which civilians were always invited. Those races provided an opportunity to introduce skiers to biathlon and many citizen racers seized the chance. Two athletes who began through this route using these races to advance their skills to much higher level were Brian Doxsee and Brent Anderson from Bennington and Charlotte, Vermont. Brian was the Vermont State Rifle Champion at Mt. Anthony Union High School in 1970 and ranked 23rd nationally. While at the University of Vermont he was a member of the ski team from 1973 through 1975 which seemed a natural combination for biathlon. Combining those abilities, he began winning local races at Jericho and was named to the biathlon National Development team in 1976 and participated in the 1977 World Biathlon Championships at Vingrom, Norway. After the 1980 Olympic team trials, Brian retired to operate his family's business in Bennington.

Brent Anderson also found his way to biathlon through shooting and skiing as separate sports. While in high school he was the winner of the Skimeister award and was also the Vermont state champion small-bore shooter in the sub-junior class. Attending St. Lawrence University in New York he was the top shooter on the ROTC rifle team and a member of the ski team. Trying biathlon at Jericho in 1975 he competed in the 1976 Olympic team trials and was later named to the biathlon Development team in 1977. After his college graduation, he began military service and was the National Guard Biathlon Champion in 1979 and participated in the 1980 Olympic team trials. Brent continued his participation in the National Guard program while serving as an officer in the Vermont Army National Guard.

Another big project in 1978 helped to recruit many junior and senior athletes that appeared to give promise to the future. It was the establishment of a regional organization and development for biathlon that began to introduce new athletes to biathlon. Shortly after Art Stegen was hired as the full-time National team coach he recognized the need for recruiting. He proposed dividing the country into regions, each with a volunteer coach who was responsible for organization and development in that region. John Morton served the Eastern Region that included the New England and Mid-Atlantic states. The Central Region included the North Central and Midwestern states with John Durben of St. Paul, Minnesota, a national level marksman and president of the Minnesota Biathlon Association serving as that region's coach. Matt Montagne of Bozeman, Montana was selected for the Mountain Region, including the Rocky Mountain states, and Nat Brown of Edmonds, Washington the Western Region that included the

Pacific Coast states and Alaska.

This project began to have immediate results. Tasked with finding potential junior and young senior skiers who would be interested in biathlon each of the regional coaches searched their areas for athletes that had potential. Among the juniors that were introduced to biathlon and continuing later to become members of World Championships teams of the late 1970s and early 1980s were Tom McElroy, Rody Hagen, Steve Flankey, Richard McGuire, Stuart Jennings and Greg Cress.

One of the most talented juniors, Tom McElroy was named to the National team for the 1978-79 season. From Golden Valley, Minnesota he was the captain of his high school ski team and the regional champion in 1977. A winner of the American Birkebeiner ski race for the 14- to 15-year-old class, he was also a member of the Central Division's USSA Junior National team. A member of the 1979 World Championships team he was the best U.S. finisher in both the sprint and individual junior races. In 1980, after nearly qualifying for the 1980 Olympic team as a junior, he again achieved the top U.S. team finishes at the 1980 World Junior Championships at Sarajevo, Yugoslavia. An unfortunate recurring foot injury limited his further participation and ended his career early.

Rody Hagen of Jackson, Wyoming, Martin Hagen's brother, followed him into biathlon. Like Martin, he was a 4-year member of the ski and track teams and was a state finalist in both sports. He was also a 4-year member of USSA Inter-Mountain Junior National team. In 1979, he finished 2nd in the National Biathlon championship junior race and was a member of the 1979 World Championships team.

Steve Flankey of Cloquet, Minnesota was also a member of the 1979 World Championships team at Ruhpolding, Germany. A 1979 high school graduate, he was a state finalist in three sports, cross-country running, shooting and cross-country skiing. Being a runner-up at the state rifle championships made him a natural for biathlon. Named to the National Biathlon team in 1978, he competed in the 1979 and 1981 World Championships. Steve consistently had the lowest penalty average of any American during his years of participation. Steve went on to become an instructor for the U.S. Army's helicopter pilot training at Ft. Rucker, Alabama.

Stuart Jennings of Bozeman, Montana also graduated from high school in 1979 where he was also a participant in cross-country running, shooting and skiing. A member of the Northern USSA Junior National team he was named to the National Development team as a junior after a 2nd and 3rd place in the 1979 National Biathlon Championships junior races. A member of the 1979 and 1981 World Championships teams, Stuart also maintained a low shooting penalty average. After attending Montana State University, Stuart continued his interest in biathlon and has been involved with the development of biathlon in Montana ever since his competitive days.

Rick McGuire and Greg Cress were two Alaskans with strong backgrounds in cross-country skiing who gave biathlon a try. Rick was a student at Middlebury College of Vermont and had an impressive high school record while attending Service High School in Anchorage where he was the state champion and finished 2nd at the 1977 USSA Junior Nationals. Winning two of the Eastern College Winter Carnivals and 14th in the NCAA Championships as a freshman he gave biathlon a try in 1979 and won the junior sprint and finished 3rd in the National Championships junior races. In his first year as a senior competitor he was a member of the 1981 World Championships team at Lahti where he raced in the sprint and relay races. Greg Cress was the son of 1960 Olympic team member and University of Wyoming ski coach John Cress who was not only an Alaskan state champion in cross-country skiing, but the cross-country running champion too. A graduate of Diamond High School, he won every junior cross-country ski race in Alaska during 1979. Despite finishes of 3rd and 2nd in the biathlon National Championships in 1977 and 1979, Greg chose to focus on cross-country skiing after receiving an athletic scholarship to the University of Vermont.

The years immediately after 1978 also saw several senior athletes from skiing or other backgrounds give biathlon a try. Most notable was Chuck Lyda of Olympic Valley, California. Chuck was a well-known canoe/kayak racer who participated in World Championships and the 1976 Summer Olympic Games at Montreal for those sports and would have raced in the 1980 Summer Olympic Games had the U.S. not boycotted those hosted at Moscow. A well-rounded athlete he won the Squaw Valley triathlon three times and began skiing for training during winter. He gave biathlon a try during the U.S. team's training at the USOTC in Squaw Valley and became a regular competitor following his introduction. As a member of the National Guard, Chuck became well-known in the biathlon community and raced in many National Guard Championships, National Championships and CISM Games. He eventually was hired as the Army's World Class Athlete Program biathlon coach and served many roles with the coaching staff of the USBA.

CHAPTER 11

Hopefuls

By the close of the 1980 Olympic Games there was much optimism about the future of biathlon. Those games had developed and rekindled a lot of enthusiasm as many within the U.S. Biathlon community had come together as volunteers for the events at Mt. Van Hoevenberg and shared their stories, thoughts and vision with each other. Central to this enthusiasm was the anticipated separation from the USMPBA to become an independent national governing body for biathlon. It was also the period that biathlon began to develop into a more modern and competitive sport within the international community, and growing the number of domestic competitions across the country. Hosting the Olympic biathlon events at Lake Placid gave the sport its highest visibility within the ski community ever, which translated into seeing more skiers becoming aware and interested in giving it a try. It was also the first time that women became interested and introduced to the sport. Women's participation created a generation of new hopeful athletes, both men and women looking for Olympic opportunities.

In the fall of 1978, Art Stegen was hired as the first full-time National Team coach. There was only a men's team at the time. Bill Spencer was the rifle coach and in those days the staff was generally a team leader, ski coach and rifle coach. Bill was still in the active military working as the National Guard's first biathlon program director. During the first training camp scheduled the U.S. Olympic Training Center that was located at Squaw Valley, Holly Beattie, a local endurance athlete, watched the training one day and at the end of the session asked if she could try shooting. The athletes were quick to offer help and were willing to spend some time in helping her. The sport had recently changed from large bore rifles to small bore, which facilitated movement towards mass participation. She began to show up at the team's training regularly, partly due to her growing social interest and partly because she was somehow intrigued by the biathlon challenges.

Although there was no program for women anywhere in the sport, Art and Bill did not discourage her, and the men on the team actively encouraged her. She eventually expressed a desire to compete despite the non-existence of a separate class for women. In light of the growing concerns for equal opportunities in sports, due to Title IX legislation, Art and Bill contemplated the prospects and took the opportunity to promote her desires, especially because of the fact that the shooting sports were still suffering from a negative image in the post-Vietnam era. They also felt strongly about equal opportunity and both having daughters increased their support. Peter Lahdenpera also did not oppose her participation nor was there any real resistance from the USMPBA, the national governing body. They did have some concerns about how the USOC might view the inclusion since there were no biathlon events for women in the Winter Olympic program and feared that using the USOTC facilities might cause a problem, however the issue never surfaced.

Holly then traveled to Jackson, Wyoming to try a real biathlon race during the start of the 1978-79 season. She entered the races at Jackson and raced among the men at the same distances and did in fact finish ahead of a few of them. During the pre-race training and racing at Jackson another local athlete, Pam Weiss observed Holly doing biathlon and quickly became interested. For all the first U.S. women to try biathlon, they grew up in a pre-Title IX world. Pam was frustrated in her athletic endeavors as a kid and was even denied training with the boy's track team at high school. Her father was a ski patroller, so she got into alpine ski racing. Attending the University of Vermont where she was a member of the alpine ski team she ran cross-country in her senior year in an attempt to also participate in cross-country skiing. She became the top alpine skier and made a successful transition to nordic, helping UVM to a 3rd place finish at the NCAA Championships in 1976. She then moved to Jackson, Wyoming, where she actively started cross-country skiing, getting fully into racing after winning her first race by 6 minutes. As a regular on the ski trails she was exposed to the shooting on the temporary shooting range and the men, knowing her ability, were eager to introduce her to biathlon. However, lacking any other additional real racing opportunities, that is where things ended that season. It was the next year, 1979-80 that things really began to develop.

During the fall training camp at Squaw Valley, Holly began to take a much more committed approach to biathlon and became a regular in the training despite having no official association to the team. Julie Newnam from Washington State University observed Holly training with the men when her ski team had a training camp at the USOTC. When she returned to her school she contacted the Washington National Guard shooting coach, Dick Domey who began to teach her marksmanship skills and encouraged her to participate in the Washington State National Guard's biathlon races. When the training again moved to Jackson, Wyoming, Holly came along, and since Pam Weiss had maintained interest, Art and Bill included a women's class in the early season races. This attracted the attention of Betty Stroock, a Dartmouth ski team graduate, who was also living nearby at Teton Village. During that year there was also a race in Bozeman,

Montana for which the Canadian team came south to participate. Kosti Uusitar-kano, the Canadian coach was surprised to see the few women race and expressed an interest in getting the Finnish/Canadian female ski racer, Karina Englebrecht, who he was training, to start in a biathlon race among the American women. Later when the U.S. Olympic team trials had to be relocated from Rosendale, New York to Valcartier, Quebec due to limited snow conditions, Kosti brought Karina along with the Canadian men's team who were scheduled to participate in the U.S. trials races. They were disappointed to learn that no American women had come. Although there would be no actual Olympic team for women, Art quickly proposed that if Holly and Pam could come to Valcartier, they would be included on the start list. Only Holly took up the offer and she raced against Karina, who won all the races between them. It was unofficially recognized but represented a real opportunity and opened the door to women's participation despite the non-interest showed by the European coaches during the 1980 Winter Olympic Games at Lake Placid.

In the spring of 1980 Art and Bill decided to take the first semi-official steps and invited women to participate in the spring training camp at Squaw Valley. Despite worries about using the Olympic training facilities for women who did not have an Olympic biathlon program, the invitation was quietly extended through the regional coaches, John Morton in Vermont, John Durben in Minnesota and Matt Montagne in Montana. Several women attended, with the largest group driving a mini caravan from Minnesota to Squaw Valley. That group included Pam Nordheim, Patrice Jankowski, and Rae Hoisve. Holly Beattie, Pam Weiss and Karina Englebrecht from Canada also participated. Following that first training camp, women were included in all team communications and activities, continually promoting their participation. It was shortly afterwards during a summer training camp in Bozeman, Montana that additional women, including Kari Swenson and Diana Tiahrt became interested. At the June meeting of the USMPBA/Olympic Biathlon Committee the final official steps were taken for women's biathlon participation with the naming of the first U.S. National Women's Biathlon team. This inclusion of women was confirmed by the newly independent U.S. Biathlon Association in September 1980 and the ten women, juniors and seniors named to this "development" team were announced in the very first issue of the *Biathlon Bulletin* of the newly formed U.S. Biathlon Association in October 1980. The team included seniors Patrice Jankowski, Pam Weiss, Betty Stroock, Julie Newnam, and Holly Beattie. The juniors were Rae Hoisve, Diana Tiahrt, Kari Swenson, Kelly McDonell and Becky Fuller.

At the same time that the new biathlon association was approving women's participation the National Guard had also begun to encourage women to take part in their growing program. This was helped by the new USBA President Howard

Buxton who was extremely supportive of inclusion of women, as both the USBA leader and his strong influence as a colonel in the Vermont National Guard and essentially the founding father of the Guard program. Laura Freeman was encouraged by her father, a National Guard racer and coach of the Vermont team to take up the sport. She joined the National Guard and earned All-Guard honors (top ten combined finish at the National Guard Championship) even though there wasn't a separate class for women at the annual National Guard Championships.

During the winter of 1981 a women's class was included for most of the races and participation grew rather dramatically and rapidly. Following the rules and distances for junior men, and requiring each regional relay team include a woman, that year's National Championships included women's events for the first time. It was also during the early 1980s that some nations in Europe began to open their races to women competitors. The Czechs, Poles and French were among the first. By 1984 common rules and distances were agreed upon and international competition was initiated for women with the first World Championships for women held at Chamonix, France. The U.S. team of Julie Newnam, Kari Swenson and Holly Beattie achieved the first-ever U.S. World Championships medal with their bronze medal in the relay.

The change to small bore rifles and 50 meter targets, as well as elimination of the 2-minute penalties in the period between 1978 and 1981 did exactly what it was intended. Not only had it encouraged the participation of women it also increased the number of junior and senior men athletes. At Jericho, Vermont the USBA trials for the 1981 World Biathlon Championships at Lahti, Finland witnessed the largest number of competitors ever. There were 18 junior men and 13 women, the highest number ever, despite there being no international event for the women. It was also at those trials that new athletes began to assert themselves. Clearly the 1980 Winter Olympics at Lake Placid stirred greater interest and this manifested itself with the appearance of Nat Lucy, Willie Carow, Glen Eberle, Erich Wilbrecht and Rick McGuire; all eastern collegiate skiers from UNH, Dartmouth College and UVM. Nat Lucy, from New Hampshire made rapid progress from his first introduction to biathlon and was a member of the World Biathlon Championships team in 1981, 82 and 83. Willie Carow, from Vermont was one of a group of Dartmouth skiers recruited by John Morton. Willie and his teammate at Dartmouth, Glen Eberle were eventually Olympic teammates at the Sarajevo Olympic Games. Eberle who was a successful junior skier from McCall, Idaho had previously been introduced to biathlon and was a member of the junior teams competing in the World Championships at Lahti in 1981 and Minsk in 1982. Wilbrecht, from Jackson, Wyoming also had some earlier competitive experience with biathlon before skiing for Dartmouth and was a member of 1987, 90, 91, and 93 World Championships teams and the 1994 Olympic Games team at Lillehammer. He also became one of the top summer biathlon competitors and participated in the IBU's Summer World Biathlon Championships when it was a running event.

Perhaps two of the most important athletes to evolve during the early 1980s were Curt Schreiner and Josh Thompson. Curt came slightly before Josh, emerging as a promising junior and then continued a long competitive career coinciding with that of Josh who accomplished an international breakthrough. Another interesting athlete who also came into biathlon during this period was Raymond Dombrovsky. He came from a completely different background than any other U.S. team member, as a refugee from the Soviet Union. Early one Sunday morning in the spring of 1981 Raymond arrived at the front door of Art Stegen's home in New Paltz, New York with an interpreter. Raymond had been part of the junior biathlon development program in Latvia, which was at the time part of the Soviet Union. Speaking little English, the interpreter helped explain why he had come and was looking for a way to continue biathlon. Raymond's family had been given exit visas from the Soviet Union during the pressure from President Carter's human rights campaign against the Soviet Union's policies towards religious minorities. Raymond's stepfather was Jewish and received permission to leave with the family. After spending some time in Italy, the family was given a choice to relocate to either the U.S. or Australia. Raymond convinced his stepfather to choose the U.S. because, as he said, "I knew the U.S. had a biathlon team, but never heard of an Australian team." After the family had settled in New York City and begun to learn a whole new culture, he spent months before he found anyone who knew anything about biathlon and eventually discovered Art's name in connection to biathlon.

Raymond was most interesting because of his difficulty in adjusting his perceptions to such drastic changes and differences between the sports cultures as well as the society in general. Much like the problems experienced by anyone raised in the Soviet totalitarian system and then relocated to a more open democratic society, his family had to learn a whole new system of banking, economic choices and the most basic freedoms, especially getting over the fear of constant surveillance and state propaganda. Enrolled in an inner-city school, without language skills, he was eventually resourced to a high school equivalency program where he made great progress in acquiring basic language skills while exceeding standards in math and science. He continued his education at the North Country Community College in Saranac Lake, New York while he trained for skiing and biathlon. Following their initial meeting, Art encouraged him to join the Rosendale Nordic Ski Club and during that summer he regularly rode his bicycle 90 miles from New York City to Rosendale for regular training with two National team juniors, Mark and Steve Krivda. Often staying overnight, at first camping out, they would train at the biathlon range at Williams Lake and for the first time, began roller-skiing, something he had never done in Latvia because, as he explained, "the roads were too bad."

At the 1982 team trials for the World Championships at Minsk, Raymond qualified for the team, but due to his citizenship status he was not allowed to be a member of the team nor would the Soviets have granted him a visa for return to the Soviet Union. Raymond would continue competing in biathlon and skiing, winning the National Junior College ski championships, but would have to wait until 1985 before his local congresswomen and future vice-presidential candidate Geraldine Ferraro introduced a bill to Congress granting him early citizenship to compete in that year's World Biathlon Championships at Ruhpolding. He was also a member of the 1986 and 1987 World Championships where he followed the breakthrough performance of Josh Thompson with a 23rd place and the fastest relay leg on the 10th place U.S. relay team. In 1988, he qualified for the U.S. Olympic team but was unable to race at Canmore due to medical recovery following appendicitis at a World Cup event in Austria just prior to the Olympic Games. In 1989, he participated in the World Biathlon Championships in Feistritz, Austria and in 1990 he returned to the Soviet Union and reunited with his Latvian junior coach as a member of the U.S. team at that year's World Biathlon Championships at Minsk. Following the dissolution of the Soviet Union, he returned to Latvia where he developed a high-performance ski training center.

Curt Schreiner was the other athlete who also essentially "showed up" at the front door at Art Stegen's house shortly after the 1980 Winter Olympic Games. At the time Curt was only 12 years old and came with his father and brother Jim. They had watched the biathlon events at Lake Placid and the boys had decided they wanted to try the sport and that began the long-term development of Curt's very successful and long career that included participation in three Olympic Games. Curt and his brother Jim were the sons of Betty and Jim Sr. Their father, Jim Sr. was the son of the head gardener at New York City's Gracie Mansion during three consecutive mayoral terms of the famous Fiorello La Guardia. Jim Sr. attended Manhattan College in New York City on a track scholarship and after the birth of their two sons, he and wife Betty decided they wanted to move away from the city and eventually purchased a large property in the southern Adirondacks near the shore of the Great Sacandaga Lake. There they built a great log building in the shape of an octagon for their home and a smaller one for Jim's mother. With many outdoor recreational activities available at their doorstep Curt and Jim began skiing early in life and became very interested in biathlon after their exposure to the races at Lake Placid Olympic Games.

Jim Sr. took their interest to heart and made the trip with them to visit Art, who had been the coach of the team, and find out how to get started. That visit turned on a passion that resulted in an incredible benefit for the biathlon development of his sons and growth of the sport within New York State.

Curt and Jim participated in nearly every available cross-country ski race in New York State and began to practice shooting at a primitive range their dad had set up on near their house. With crude equipment, they participated in their first biathlon races at Williams Lake in Rosendale in 1981. In 1982, they started the Saratoga Biathlon club along with other juniors, Dan Adams, Tom Burke, and Mike Farah. In the spring of 1983 Jim Sr. invited Art Stegen to visit the property to help with guidance on constructing a biathlon range and adjacent ski trails. Art took local high school ski champion and future U.S. Biathlon junior team member, Mark Krivda with him and together with Curt they "crust skied" around the property laying out potential routes for the trails. Later during that summer Jim Sr. and friends cleared the proposed trails and with an old bulldozer ruffed out a biathlon range and the ski trails. The old bulldozer remains on site because it had to be left running overnight, being so difficult to start. During the night, the oil plug vibrated loose and the engine oil drained out causing the engine to seize up and be destroyed. Fortunately, it was parked off the trail and out of the way and today it still sits where it stopped, barely visible among the brush and weeds.

Curt and his brother Jim attended a small local school that did not have a cross-country ski team, but this did not prevent the development of their ski skills. In 1983 Curt finished third in the Empire State Games behind two of the best junior skiers in New York at the time, Bill Sapp and Mark Krivda. He also finished 2nd to Mark Krivda in the biathlon race. In 1984, he won the Empire Games by over 2 minutes and skied in the Junior Nationals. Before Curt qualified for his first World Biathlon Championship team, he had already achieved international status in flatwater canoe racing and participated in the World Junior Canoe Championships in 1983 at Bydgocz, Poland and again in 1985 at Castel Gandolph, Italy. Living next to the Great Sacandaga Lake had encouraged both Curt and Jim to participate in rowing sports during the summer. Jim participated in the Pan American canoeing events.

The winter of 1985 was Curt's first international experience in biathlon when he qualified for the World Junior Biathlon Championships at Egg, Switzerland as a high school senior. He went 10 for 10 on the range and finished 41st in the sprint race. Graduating first in his high school class Curt earned an academic scholarship to Skidmore College and continued to train for biathlon. At the time, skating was taking over as the new ski technique and he again qualified for the World Junior Biathlon Championships in 1986 at Falun, Sweden. However, following that season and returning to Skidmore, he found himself like many amateur athletes during that period, without any income to cover normal everyday expenses and other necessities such as gasoline and car insurance. In April 1986, he withdrew from Skidmore and enlisted in the Army National Guard and finished his basic training that summer as the "Soldier of the Cycle" just as the National Guard received the CISM mission and the U.S. was making an important turning point. He had joined just at the time that the National Guard had received the international mission of returning to CISM and had begun improving their program in preparation for participation at international levels and which also coincided with USBA's hiring of Norwegian Sigvart Bjontegaard as its National team coach.

Still a junior competitor in 1987, Curt and his new National Guard teammate, Dave Jareckie participated in the World Junior Championships at Lahti, Finland and later in the CISM Games at Autrans, France. The next season, his first as a senior, Curt qualified for the 1988 Olympic Games team at Calgary and had an outstanding 1988 season by earning World Cup points in three different World Cup races at a time when the points were only earned for top 25 finishers. At the 1992 Olympic Games at Albertville he shot clean in the sprint race and only missed 3 targets of the total 40 for the individual, sprint and relay races. After another good year in 1993, Curt competed in his third Olympic Games at Lillehammer and narrowly missed qualifying for the team in 1998 and again in 2002. Curt became well-known for his amazing double-pole starts in relay mass starts. With extraordinary strength from his early canoe days, he often exploded at the start, passing everyone in the start area.

Curt was an important member of the U.S. team at World Cup events and was the top U.S. finisher at the CISM Games from 1994 through 1998 and 2000, and a seven-time National champion. One of Curt's best international performances came at the 2000 CISM Games at Hochfilzen, Austria when he was one of only two competitors to hit all 20 targets in the individual race that earned him a 6th place finish. It was a unique day for him because his wife Deborah Nordyke, who was a member of the 1998 Olympic team at Nagano, was the only other competitor who was without penalty in the women's individual race. At the 1998 Olympic team trials at Jericho his best finish of 3rd in the 4 races did not place him on the team and with a 5th place ranking in the combined criteria points from 3 of the 4 races, he was the alternate for the team. Again in 2002, as a member of the WCAP program, despite a 3rd, 4th and 7th place finishes in the Olympic team trials at Soldier Hollow, his overall percentage points was also just outside the total that would have earned him a place on the team. His final race was at the 2003 National Guard Championships and after mobilization to Iraq he completed a career in the military, earned a master's degree and plays a major role in the New York State Ski Racing Association's biathlon program, coaching high school and improving the biathlon site at the property that was started by his father in 1983.

The most successful athlete of the later 1980s and early 1990s was Josh

Thompson. Josh was the first individual World Championship medal winner for the U.S. team in 1987 at Lake Placid where he captured the silver medal, but his start in biathlon began many years before that. Both his parents were U.S. National Park rangers who moved twice a year for duty at both summer and winter stations. When Josh was 3 years old they were stationed at Yellowstone Park's Old Faithful geyser for the first of multiple assignments there. It was there that he began to ski and at the age of six and in first grade, they were assigned to Yosemite which had the Badger Pass alpine ski area where he spent a lot of time. Back in Yellowstone at Mammoth Hot Springs for grades 5 and 6 he became more interested in cross-country skiing and often used his mother's Norwegian wood BlåSkia skis to ski at Montana's Cook City where the U.S. Ski team held regular training camps. The U.S. Biathlon team also visited there, and Josh recalled what was for him a thrilling experience "fetching used targets for those guys," never imagining that he would know several of them many years later. He also recalled the fun of skiing as fast as he could just to keep Peter Hale in sight ahead as Peter casually glided through the forest.

It was during grades 7-10 when his parents were assigned at Mt. Rainier where Josh began ski racing, both alpine and cross-country. Later another assignment put him in Carbondale, Colorado for his final high school years and with a high school team, coach, a wax bench and skis that were not wood. Coached by former biathlon competitor and Olympic racer Dick Taylor, he raced in the USSA Rocky Mountain Division races at Winter Park and participated in the Junior Nationals where he won some medals in the relay races. In March of 1980 he met Don Nielsen who had just competed at Lake Placid and was training at Devil's Thumb near Winter Park. Don offered to let him try some biathlon shooting. Having only experienced seeing the National team in Montana and watching it on television, after trying it he became "hooked" like so many athletes before him and followed Nielsen around for a week afterwards. However, biathlon would lay dormant for a few years while he attended Western State College and during his first two years he did no biathlon at all. Working for the Western Regional biathlon coach Nat Brown during the summer provided an opportunity to shoot again and during his junior year Western State coach Ken MacLennan allowed him to do a little biathlon training so long as it did not interfere with the cross-country training and racing. MacLennan was an alumnus of the Western State ski team that were coached by Sven Wiik and like many of his college teammates, had served his military duty at the USMWBTC in Alaska. After earning a place on the 1983 World University Games for biathlon, MacLennan let him train for biathlon even more and it paid off with a 12th place (despite cross-firing an entire prone stage) and a 6th place at those World University Games. Following those results, Josh recalled "knowing exactly what I wanted to do" and took the next year off from school to train full time with his friend Brian Wadsworth, a biathlon junior team member. His plan succeeded when he qualified for the 1984 Winter Olympic Games at Sarajevo.

Returning to Western State with a greater experience following the Olympic Games, Josh continued to excel. Without biathlon at the next World University Games, he qualified for the cross-country races just as skating technique was becoming dominant. After some technical help by Todd Boonstra a few days before the 30km race he earned the best U.S. result with a top-ten finish. After graduation, he committed himself to full-time biathlon training in 1986-87, just when the USBA hired Norwegian coach Sigvart Bjontegaard. The 1987 World Championships gave the U.S. team a home-field advantage and Josh made the most of it with a silver medal breakthrough performance. With only one penalty he finished less than 50 seconds behind Frank Peter Roetsch of the German Democratic Republic who also missed only one target. Roetsch went on to double by also winning the sprint in 1987 and repeated the feat at the 1988 Calgary Olympic Games in 1988. Following Josh's excellent result at Lake Placid there was high media anticipation for success at Calgary, however it was not to be. Close to the leaders for most of the individual race, he missed three targets on the final standing stage and fell back to finish 25th, 4 minutes, 56 seconds behind the winner Roetsch. In the sprint race, he finished 27th after missing 4 targets. Relay hopes were also dashed when both Josh and Lyle Nelson had to run a penalty lap for missed prone targets and the team finished 9th.

It was a bitter pill for both Josh and the U.S. Biathlon Association and after much analysis it seemed to have been caused by the constant distractions and hubris leading into and at the Olympic Games. The team had worked well together outside of media scrutiny and with limited resources, but that changed for 1988. The media pressure for results and a big story was being propelled by the fact that the media was looking for something in the nature of the previous success stories such as the Mahre brothers, Bill Johnson's out of nowhere win at Sarajevo or the "Miracle on Ice" at Lake Placid. This essentially became the basis for creating a success story of the first "biathlon Olympic medal" at Calgary, in a sport that the U.S. was supposedly not very good. Looking back in an interview with *The New York Times* at the next Olympic Games in 1992, Josh said he "was hardly the same fellow who was psyched into losing at Calgary, Alberta, in 1988, when *Sports Illustrated* predicted a medal for him." Josh told of being sought after at a World Cup in Europe prior to the 1988 games by a reporter from Philadelphia. Added to the distractions was the sudden appendicitis attack that teammate Raymond Dombrovsky suffered just before the Games and the questions about him remaining or being replaced on the team. Additionally, at the last minute the plans for quietly training at Whitefish, Montana were changed by a vote of the athletes, and the team management seemed out of its element. It seemed like there were too many "cooks in the kitchen." During the race, Josh said he began receiving "splits" from someone unfamiliar with the usual protocol and admitted he misinterpreted the information and redirected his focus from his performance to the outcome. Despite being in a competitive position before his last shooting, he missed three targets and fell out of contention.

The Olympics were horrible," he recalled. "I could control everything but the crowd and the press's expectations." Added to those media expectations, there were the additional distractions when others were "showing up" seeking to help, but even with their good intentions, they were getting in the way and causing a loss of focus. It was a unique position for the team in that it was the first time that there was a chance to succeed at the Olympic Games, however the athletes, coaches and all the people who came to support the effort had never experienced being in such a position and it appeared they weren't fully prepared for that opportunity.

Extremely disappointed, Josh turned to other things in 1989, marriage and pilot training, but continued to train and raced only cross-country, qualifying for the U.S. Ski Team that would compete in the FIS World Championships that year at Lahti, Finland. Due to his commitments to earning his pilot's license he declined his position on that team. By the winter of 1990 he had a renewed urge to do biathlon again, and re-energized he returned to the top of the list of U.S. athletes and had excellent results at the 1991 World Championships at Lahti finishing 9th in the individual race and 18th in the sprint race. The 1992 Olympic Games at Albertville again saw him lead the U.S. men by finishing 16th and 32nd in the individual and sprint races and having the fastest relay leg for the 13th place relay team. After Albertville, Josh focused on his family and career as a pilot but did make one last effort trying to qualify for the 1994 Winter Olympic team by participating in that year's trials at Anchorage, Alaska. However, after the 2nd race, despite acceptable performances he decided to discontinue his attempt to go to his 4th Olympic Games mostly because he felt his performance was not up to his own standard. Years later Josh commented that one of the most important memories he had from his years in biathlon was having Frank Peter Roetsch, who was widely suspected of being part of the East German doping system tell him that he was worried that Josh might beat him. He also remembered that Peter Angrer, the successful West German athlete was incredulous with Josh's answer to the question about how much money he earned for winning the silver medal at Lake Placid. Josh had a hard time trying to convince him there was no reward for his performance, unlike the Europeans. Josh, like the famous running legend Frank Shorter who was earlier denied a second gold medal in 1976 by an East German athlete, might too have won the first World Championship Gold medal for biathlon in Lake Placid if it were not for an East German.

The 1986 National Guard's program expansion not only attracted Curt Schreiner, but several other aspiring athletes who saw it as a way to extend their career. Former Olympians Lyle Nelson, Chuck Lyda and Peter Hoag were among the group with extensive experience. Laura Freeman was the first women to participate in the program and Pam Nordheim, who was among the first women to be named to the U.S. National Women's team was one of the first women to join due to biathlon. Pam was the first woman to use the National Guard as a path to success by winning a medal at the CISM Games, and despite the long wait from being named to the first U.S. Biathlon women's team in 1981, she was a member of the first U.S. Olympic team that included women in 1992. Curt Schreiner was not the only young athlete to see the National Guard as a path to success. Dave Jareckie, from Rutland, a teammate of Curt on the junior team in 1987 at Lahti, Finland and a Vermont High School state champion in cross-country running, cross-country skiing and track, had joined the National Guard's program after high school was also a 1994 Olympic team member from that program. He was Curt's partner in the many humorous episodes during team training camps and travels. At the time, the National Guard developed a very effective and closely-knit training group which also included several women.

Among that group were Tuck Miller, who was often the recipient of Curt's pranks. Curt and Dave liked to keep things humorous and thus delightfully enjoyed short-sheeting their teammate's beds on a continual basis. Curt also found another humoring way to amuse the group by using his traveling sewing kit to sew his roommate's jacket or coat pockets shut, and sometimes even the legs or arms of their pants and shirts. He even sewed Tuck Miller's pants to the bedspread. Curt bragged about the time he short-sheeted Tuck's bed on many consecutive days during a fall training camp. Tim Derrick, also a member of the National Guard team was also a target of Curt's mischiefs. Tim occasionally found his ski bag unusually heavy for skis until he found rocks that Curt had clandestinely added. Eric Wilbrecht was also involved in some of Curt's antics; one of the more famous was about a toothbrush that was used for something other than its purpose and then photographed. The photograph was then later sent to the toothbrush's owner after it was assumed he had used it for its intended purpose.

Curt kept the group laughing while at the same time becoming a model for his serious attitude about training and competition. Although always helpful and willing to share his thoughts, he was a fierce competitor who didn't like to lose at anything. Thoughtful about maximizing his strengths and limiting any weakness of his performance, he skillfully improved all the technical aspects of the sport and was exceptional at being able to ski in any condition. His strength at skiing or canoeing also served him well during NBC TV's *Survival of the Fittest* contest in Cananaskis, Alberta, Canada. A made-for-TV competition among so-called "tough athletes" that included many events, testing skills that required both strength and endurance in which both Lyle Nelson and John Ruger had previously participated, Curt captured 3rd place in 1989, winning $3,000. His annual army fitness tests, known as the APFT, that included as many pushups and sit-ups as possible in two minutes followed by a 2-mile run were legendary. Like many of the athletes in the National Guard biathlon program, they shocked their fellow soldiers with their excellent marksmanship and fitness tests. Curt's best result was 140 push-ups, 120 sit-ups and a 9:59 minute run. The maximum for the test was 100 points for each event based on age groups, which required 78 push-ups, 82 sit-ups and a run of 13:18 for a perfect score in Curt's age group at the time, which he easily surpassed. There was also an extended scale for those who were exceptional, and his extended score was in record territory.

CHAPTER 12

Professionals

Following the separation of biathlon and pentathlon in 1993 there were drastic changes in the sport that brought it onto the powerful place on the international sports stage. Leading up to the 1992 Summer Olympic Games at Barcelona, IOC President Juan Antonio Samaranch pushed hard to make the Olympic Games the world's premier sports activity which included professional basketball players to participate in what was known as the "Dream Team." The archaic amateur athlete rules ended, and athletes were finally able to be fairly compensated for their participation in sports. The IBU television contracts created a healthy European broadcasting market that increased its visibility and financial status that even caused jealousy within the FIS and other sports organizations. Although biathlon had long separated from pentathlon in the United States, it wasn't until the 1990s and the new millennium that significant progress was made by American athletes in not only their performance but also financial earnings. Earlier participants, including those in the first World Championships and Olympic Games were international competitors and are not diminished by labeling those in the 1990s and millennium professionals, but they were without the commercial, organizational support and resources, as well as the vast increase in international opportunities for financial reward that made for improved competitiveness of American athletes in the decades after 1990.

After the IBU's decision to base World Cup, World Championships and Olympic participation on the Nations Cup rankings, coupled with the USBA's financial constraints and difficulty prioritizing funding decisions, the athletes faced the difficult struggle to improve their international results. It was difficult to retain and improve the number of start positions linked to the Nations Cup criteria. In the 1994 and 1998 Olympic Games the men were allowed only two starts in the individual and sprint races and a relay team while the women had three plus a relay team. Climbing up in the IBU Nations Cup rankings proved very difficult, however as the 2002 Olympics at Salt Lake approached the goals of the decisions made by the staff and board of directors in their Long-Range Development plan had begun to make a difference. The focus on athlete development, a vibrant domestic race series and the Regional Centers of Excellence began to impact the levels of performance in international competition. The start numbers improved marginally in 2002 where both the men and women were allowed 3 individual start positions and a relay team. The 2002 season ended with the U.S. men ranked 20th in the Nations Cup standings and the women 17th and through the next decade both teams made steady progress, eventually ranking as high as 6th for the men and 11th for the women. This came as a result many elements coming together, including steady recruitment of talented athletes, great coaching and improved financial support.

Changes for the U.S. Biathlon Association began in the late 1980s and early 1990s. It gradually became more professional in coaching and administration and began to develop its own "identity." Before then, biathlon had no real distinctiveness that was easily recognizable by both the public and even within the cross-country ski community. Even though many early competitors were some of the best of the nation's cross-country skiers, its early military structure and the lack of a strong visible distinctiveness and program to the ski community, biathlon's reputation became perceived as a sport that skiers would endeavor if they weren't "fast enough" for success at the top cross-country levels. In the beginning many of the best cross-country competitors were also the best biathletes with many participating in both sports at the top international levels, however through the late 1960s to the early 1980s this did not happen. It wasn't until Josh Thompson and Jon Engen began qualifying for the cross-country FIS and Olympic teams that the perception began to change. With better coaching and leadership at the USBA and with better financial and team sponsorship biathlon began to attract interest among a wider group of cross-country skiers willing to give biathlon a try.

As the United States Ski Association began to drift away from regional development and place its focus on international strategies, and the growing National Guard's program that actually had public relations as its main objective, biathlon's visibility improved, and many new athletes were attracted, introduced and developed into the sport. As the numbers were growing, the competitive levels also improved. The National Guard's approval in 1986 for participation in CISM and anticipation for the 1992 Winter Olympic games introduction of women's events provided new potential opportunities, and this prompted greater numbers of competitive skiers to join those who were already participating. Just as the National Guard was improving its program, so too was the Canadian military. The two military programs helped to encourage a very competitive NorAm Cup program and a vibrant NorAm Championships alternating between the U.S. and Canadian national championships. This new healthy level of domestic competition between North American neighbors was a high point for a developmental process that fed both National teams for higher level international competition.

Following the former National team members who joined the National

Guard for the benefits and financial compensation there were many new competitors from both college and high school level ski experience that also joined. Tuck Miller had previous biathlon experience but then spent nearly 6 years away serving in the U.S. Army in Europe before returning to the United States and continuing his military service with the National Guard. Along with Olympians Lyle Nelson and Peter Hoag, Chuck Lyda, a summer Olympian and Rick Oliver, a college skier from central New York, they were some of the first to participate in the U.S. military's return to the CISM Games in 1986. Over the next few years they were joined by Rob Powers, Curt Schreiner, Dave Jarackie and Steve Hall. On the women's side, were Nancy Bell, Helene Arnold, Cathy Collins and Anita Olson. By 1989 the National Guard's biathlon program had begun to exert significant impact on U.S. Biathlon activities and attracted other athletes with ski experience such as Andre Frenette and Randy Sapp, both graduates of New York's St. Lawrence University ski team and stationed in Europe at the time. Andre Frenette and Nancy Bell were members of the 1989 CISM team that captured 2nd place in the cross-country team event. Many skiers had begun to see the National Guard's program as a way to continue their ski careers after college or high school. By 1992 when Art Stegen was hired, joining Steve Hall to coach the team, the National Guard had become a well-developed program with state coaches Noel Olsen of Utah, Jeff Thielen of Minnesota, Don Strom of Montana and Sara Lehto of Michigan regularly assisting and Heidi Farrington, a graduate of Springfield College's athletic trainer program providing full-time support for all training and competitive activities.

During the same period the New York State Ski Racing Association (NYSSRA) and the Minnesota Biathlon Association had developed very strong local programs that encouraged participation through a club-based system and a regular calendar of events across their state. The events were also closely associated with the National Guard. In New York Major Dennis Downing of the New York National Guard served an important role in each organization, similar to how the National Guard and the USBA functioned together. The NYSSRA program provided regular opportunities for entry and developmental levels and the emergence of a pathway from the introduction to biathlon and the steps of a developmental process towards success. At the time, it was one of the most productive programs with the introduction of future U.S. Olympic team and CISM team athletes into the sport. Curt Schreiner, Rick Oliver, Chris Norton, Tim Derrick, Rob Rosser all had experience at this level and following their college years, and all became members of the National Guard program. Curt Schreiner and Rob Rosser, along with two young skiers from strong western New York high school programs, Joan Smith and Laurie Grover were members of the U.S. Olympic Biathlon teams. Although each followed slightly different paths to the Olympic team, Grover attended and skied at St. Lawrence University and later joined the National Guard while Joan Smith was identified by the USBA coaches and an early addition to the National team while attending college part-time during her participation with the USBA team.

Following the developmental steps through the NYSSRA, NorAm and CISM programs, Joan Smith attended high school at Honeyoe Falls in western New York. She was an all-round athlete competing in soccer, track, cross-country skiing, and golf. At the time high school skiers in New York were extremely competitive and had forced the separation of New England and Mid-Atlantic into two separate USSA divisions. Joan and Laurie Grover from a nearby school in the same area of New York's high school competitive regions were both outstanding skiers at the state championships, however Joan, despite her coach's advice, began entering biathlon races while still in high school in New York and by 1984 she was the highest USBA ranked junior woman. After a 3rd and 1st place and a member of the winning relay team with Pam Weiss and Pam Nordheim at the 1985 North American Championships, she was named to the Women's National Biathlon team as a 17-year old. Joining the group of women that were among the pioneers of women's biathlon, most of whom hoped they would have a chance to participate in the 1988 Winter Olympic Games, Joan, as the youngest of the team saw their chance "slip by." In an interview with the internet's *Fasterskier.com*, she said that her "learning curve was extremely fast because she was surrounded by women who'd been doing it for so long." She became the team protégé, learning from her teammates mistakes and successes. Joan told *The New York Times* following the 1992 Olympic trials at Lake Placid, the first that included women on the Olympic team, "They used to tell me when I was younger, 'Someday you'll go to the Olympics' and now I can say it." As a 24-year-old Joan dropped out of college two years before. "I devoted my life to this." *Fasterskier* wrote, "Olympians inhabit a unique place in the imaginations of the young and there is nothing nobler in the eyes of a nine-year-old than complete dedication to the pursuit of athletic glory for flag and country." Joan achieved the goal that had eluded her teammates in 1988, the first year that she competed in the World Championships for women at Chamonix, France, and achieved the best finish for the U.S. women at 34th place.

Joan continued to be a leader on the team through the 1996 season after achieving results of 21st in 1992 at Albertville and 14th at Lillehammer in 1994. Her performance at Lillehammer in the individual race equaled the best-ever for men or women and was one shot away from a silver medal. As she related later in the interview, "It's me that missed the shot," she said matter-of-factly. I was racing so hard, feeling so good and pretty much hitting my peak. I was pushing the envelope. If I'd taken five more seconds coming into the range..." She came to the range for the standing position and one of her shots missed ever so slightly, hitting on the edge. When the bullet hits near the edge of the target, it can split in two; some of it hitting the target, and some not. "When it hits those rims, it can literally split the bullet in half... It's called a split bullet, and it happens quite a bit," she said. "Lots of the time you just follow through to the next target; you think it hits, it feels good." But the story was half right. She missed three targets in all, and one more successful shot would have gotten her a silver medal. Though it could have been so much more, the performance was still the best of Joan's career, and as any biathlete knows, it's not enough to have a good day on skis alone. The targets are there for a reason; skiing and shooting must come together at the same time. "The two disciplines are two opposites," Joan said. "To perform well in both at the same time, that's the art of the sport." Following marriage and an unsuccessful attempt to qualify for the 1998 Winter Olympic Games, Joan finished her college degree, moved to Alaska and as a coach for the area elementary and middle school students, she led the effort to set up a local biathlon venue and club from scratch. She modeled the Kenai Peninsula Biathlon Club after the relaxed environment in which she herself first learned how to shoot and ski in New York.

During the 1990s the National Guard's biathlon program became a dominant influence developing a well-coordinated and supportive program which attempted to synchronize its goals with those of the USBA. Although this sometimes led to conflicting interests and disagreements between theirs and USBA efforts; from 1988 when two members of the National Guard qualified for the Olympic team, that number increased to three in 1992, four in 1994, six in 1998 and five in 2002. Along with Curt Schreiner, the National Guard team continued to attract and develop athletes who were successful in qualifying for international competitions. Important contributions to USBA during the 1990s included full use of its Jericho facilities, including housing and the services of shooting coach Eugene Soboleski, who was a recipient of the prestigious President's 100 and the Chief's 50 awards for shooting. Soboleski served as the shooting coach for the 1992 and 1994 Winter Olympic Games. Pam Nordheim led the way for the women and won the bronze medal at the 1987 CISM Games. National team member Beth Coats, from Breckenridge, Colorado joined the National Guard in 1993 and led the U.S. team of Laurie (Grover) Tavares, Deborah Nordyke and Sonia Stanger at the 1993 CISM Games with a Silver medal and team medals in the biathlon and cross-country team competitions at Jericho. Laurie just missed qualifying for the World Championships team in 1993, and after a 3rd and 4th place at that year's National Championships, she participated in the final World Cups at Östersund, Sweden and Kontiolahti, Finland. In 1994 she raced in the Lillehammer Olympics and the IBU World Cups, achieving a best finish of 18th place at Antholz.

Deborah Nordyke who contributed to the team medals at the 1993 and 1995 CISM Games had a late start with skiing following a suggestion from a Finnish friend at the University of Alaska at Anchorage. She encouraged Deborah to take up skiing after seeing her physical potential. Originally from Arkansas, she and her sisters grew up in Alaska after her father died in an automobile accident while serving in the Air Force there. She had a strong background in gymnastics and track in high school and after joining the Air National Guard, she got her start in biathlon with the Alaska state team in 1989 when the National Guard began holding a separate class for women. Despite being new and with weak shooting skills, she finished 8th and 7th in the individual and sprint with 18 penalties and 8 misses in the races. After committing to the full-time training with the National Guard, she consistently improved her shooting percentages and ski technical skills year by year. She was the double National Guard Champion in 1994 and qualified for the World Championships in 1995, 1996 and 1997 and the 1998 Winter Olympic Games at Nagano despite the USBA coaches' concerns about her age and late start. It was during the period when USBA had decided that the senior athletes couldn't improve and were "blockers" to development, shifting their focus to juniors. It became a source of tension between the programs and when she applied for the Air Force World Class Athlete Program in 1997, USBA did not recommend her, saying that she would most likely not qualify for the Olympic team because of her age. Having been left off the National team; the Air Force program viewed it as an unusual lack of support, having already been a member of three World Championships teams, recording the highest physiological test values and having one of the fastest ski pace averages among the women. Seeing that her shooting average steadily improved from 48% in 1993 to over 80% by 1997, they approved her for their program despite the USBA's assessment. She continued to train with the National Guard program, and at the 1998 Olympic team trials at Jericho she placed 1st, 2nd and 5th in her best 3 of 4 races and qualified for the 1998 Olympic team. She then achieved the second-best result at Nagano in the women's sprint race, which brought into question the USBA's evaluation and clearly exposed a bias. The tension between the programs continued when she was left off the relay team, and it also began to have an impact on other athletes as well. The tensions gradually subsided with the change of USBA coaches and after the birth of her first child, Deborah continued to participate in the National Guard program and CISM. At the 2000 CISM Games at Hochfilzen, Austria she finished 13th in the individual race with a perfect shooting score on the range. After another break for childbirth, she returned to racing and at the 2002 Olympic trials in Soldier Hollow she twice finished 6th and 8th which did not result in a total 3 of 4 race percentage points to qualify for the Olympic team.

In 1992, National Guard athletes Pam Nordheim and Nancy Bell had qualified for the first Olympic biathlon team for women, but both had retired from competition before the 1993 CISM Games. Nancy had participated in the 1988

World Championships after joining the National Guard the previous year in anticipation that 1988 would be the first opportunity for women's Olympic participation. That year's women's World Championship team was made up of a mix of women biathlon pioneers from the early 1980s, Pam Nordheim and Patrice Jankowski and newcomers Nancy Bell and Joan Smith, all who saw the potential future Olympic opportunity. The first Olympic team for women also included Joan Geutschow, a 1988 NCSA champion from Minnetonka, Minnesota. Surprisingly she had a 16th place finish at the 1989 World University Games, qualifying her for the 1989-90 National team in her first year of competition in the sport. In addition to Joan Smith's interviews, Nancy Bell and Joan Geutschow also had some interesting comments when they spoke about their Olympic experience. It was a celebration, the culmination of eight years of lobbying to get women's biathlon into the Games, and Nancy Bell said, "The women are world class, we ski as well as the men. And some of us can even shoot as well or better than the men." An unemployed teacher from Stowe, Vermont, she said she survived on a $125-a-weekend paycheck from the Vermont National Guard, in which she was a Specialist, and a $2,500 yearly stipend from the U.S. Biathlon Association. "I'm in this for the money," she said, with a smile breaking across her face. "God, I don't know. You ask yourself out there all the time, 'Why am I doing this?' With fans along the ski tracks and Norwegian flags waving in the breeze and cowbells clanging, it was terribly exciting," she said. "Normally, there are two people at the races in America; my parents. Here, look at the crowd." Joan Geutschow said, "It won't be so strange next time. "I've had so many people ask me, 'What does it feel like to be a woman and shoot?' I just think it's a sport. It doesn't seem unusual."

During the 1990s many women competitors had transitioned to biathlon through their college ski experiences while others made the transition from racing as a junior to the senior team. Anna Sonnerup, Mary Ostergren, Joan Guetschow and Stacy Wooley were among those who came from the college ski programs. Ntala Skinner, Kristina (Viljanen) Sabasteanski and Kara (Hermanson) Salmela came from the junior ranks and Nancy Bell and Deborah Nordyke were members of the National Guard program. Laurie Grover raced for St. Lawrence and then joined the National Guard program. These women were the nucleus of the strong women's teams through the 1990s.

That period was a pivotal change for the women and helped to improve the status of the U.S. in the international environment. In 1986 many of the women "pioneers" were still active as members of that year's World Championships at Falun, Sweden. Pam Nordheim's Silver medal at the CISM Games at Autrans, France in 1987, was a first for an American woman. Improved growth and development by the women came through greater awareness within the ski community, more active recruitment and increased opportunity and coaching. The team for the 1987 World Championships at Lahti, Finland included Mary Ostergren and Anna Sonnerup, along with two of biathlon's first women competitors, Pam Weiss who had been a member of the University of Vermont's alpine ski team 1972-76 and Pam Nordheim. Both were participants in the very first women's training camp, and members of the first women's National team. Anna Sonnerup and Mary Ostergren became involved with biathlon after college skiing. Anna, in her first World Championships surprised with a 9th place finish in the sprint race.

Once the official announcement was made that women's events would be included in the 1992 Winter Olympic Games in May of 1988, hope for their Olympic dream became reality and that increased the women's interest and competitive levels. As an indication of the improvement among the U.S. women, the World Cup standings at the end of the 1988 season saw Patrice Jankowski ranked 18th with 86 points accumulated from six European races. Also on the list were Pam Nordheim, Nancy Bell, Joan Smith, Mary Ostergren and Julie Newnam, ranked 22nd, 23rd, 25th 32nd and 33rd out of a total number of 51 ranked women. The team for the 1988 World Championships at Chamonix, France, included new team members Nancy Bell and Joan Smith along with Patrice Jankowski, who had returned to competition following time away pursuing educational goals. But the impact of the announcement also led to an improvement in the numbers and level of competition at the international level. Unfortunately, the next year, the first to co-locate men and women's World Championships at Feistritz, Austria was a hiccup for the entire U.S. Biathlon program, for both women and men when the counter-productive decision, due to financial limitations, sent only a small team to participate.

With the budget limitations impacting the participation at the World Championships in 1989, athletes were limited to domestic and NorAm racing. Pam Nordheim topped the list of number of USBA points races scored that year with 18 while Nancy Bell and Mary Ostergren followed with 17, Joan Guetschow had 16 and Anna Sonnerup and Pam Weis each had 13. There was a lot of active participation by the women. The North American Championships, which began in 1984 and the robust domestic National Race Series at the time were the essential development options for the athletes coming into biathlon. Joan Smith, Anna Sonnerup and Mary Ostergren all earned some of their best early results competing against Pam Nordheim, Pam Weiss, Julie Newnam and the Canadian women. Anna Sonnerup won her first National Championships in 1986 and followed with wins in 1987, 1989 and 1991. Mary Ostergren, from St. Paul, Minnesota, a member of the Carlton College ski team, graduating in 1984 had competed in the National Collegiate Ski Association (NCSA) championships as well as competing in canoeing and marathon ski racing, began racing biathlon in 1986. She won her first National Championships sprint race in 1988 and medaled at the Polar

Biathlon Cup series in Northern Finland and won an additional National title and double North American Championships in 1990. Both Mary and Anna, along with Patrice (Jankowski) Anderson, Beth Coats, Pam Nordheim, Joan Smith and Pam Weiss were named to the 1989 Pam American team that was to be held in Argentina but was eventually cancelled. Anna made impressive progress and was voted athlete of the year in 1990 following her 2nd place finish in the World Cup at Walchsee, Austria. She had additional top ten finishes, including an 8th place at the World Championships and a 4th place overall ranking in the Polar Cup that year. She contributed a fast lap time along with Patrice (Jankowski) Anderson and Joan Smith when they finished 6th in the World Championships relay. In 1991 along with another National Championship, Anna had another excellent inter-national season that included a 7th place finish for the women's relay team at the World Championships.

When Art Stegen was hired by Colonel John Abair in July of 1992 as coach of the National Guard Program, he was asked to take some time for analysis and review of the program and then make some recommendations on how to improve all levels, especially the international performance at CISM. In September he met with Colonel Abair and suggested three main elements that would have positive impacts: they were to include more women in the program through recruiting, serious and better supervised training programs that included regular scheduled training and racing activities, and introducing coaching education with inclusion at the state levels that would widen the knowledge, provide assistant coaches and create wider support at the developmental levels within the National Guard and USBA. These suggestions were turned into a comprehensive "development plan" which guided both the National Guard Program and to some extent the USBA's as well.

The first evidence of the plan came at the 1993 World Championships team trials when the first aspects of that plan began to show themselves. The presence of a strong and coherent team of National Guard coaches and athletes displayed a positive team environment. Only three women participated in the concurrent CISM trials, but soon others began to show interest in the Guard's program. The financial support between the two programs was obvious and immediately following the trials, Beth Coats enlisted in the National Guard and later captured three medals at the 1993 CISM Games at Jericho, an individual silver and team silver and bronze. Joining the military came as a surprise to many. Beth was origi-nally from Albuquerque, New Mexico and had a strong athletic background. She got started with biathlon, working with John Underwood who served as women's team coach in 1986-87. Beth was the 10th ranked women on the USBA points list in 1989 and named to the team for the cancelled Pan American Games. In 1991 she was a member of the World Championship team finishing 39th in both the sprint and individual races and then raced at Albertville at the 1992 Winter Olympics. Extremely independent minded, Beth had a difficult relationship with the USBA coaches and decided not to train with the team in 1993. That decision left her less than adequately prepared at the start of the 1993 season. Despite her strong-willed temperament that often annoyed coaches and teammates, she found the military program a more comfortable way of continuing and by the end of the season she had won a National Championship, the CISM medals and earned World Cup points in the last two World Cup races but was not named to the National Team. Following the 1994 Winter Olympic Games and the 1995 World Biathlon Championships she turned her attention to mountain biking and was accepted into the World Class Athlete Program (WCAP) for that sport, at which she also excelled. She participated in that sport's World Championships in 1996 and 1997. She also became interested in mountain climbing and unfortunately sustained a severe spinal cord injury after a fall in 1997 that left her paralyzed from the waist down.

Several other developing athletes followed Beth's enlistment into the military, but Chad Salmela preceded her in 1992. He had begun biathlon racing in Minnesota with his brother Cory after attending a biathlon clinic. One of the best high school cross-country skiers in the mid-west, he became a member of the National Junior team in 1990 when he won the National Junior Championship and had finished 3rd in the North American Championships. He joined the National Guard in 1992 and was a member of the 1993, 94 and 95 CISM teams and due to the limited men's activity at the World Championships, wasn't a member of the World Championship team until 1996 when the National Guard sent a team to defend the IBU Nations Cup standing. Kara Hermanson-Salmela, Chad's sister-in-law, Kristina Viljanen-Sabasteanski, and Ntala Skinner all became members of the military soon after.

1993 was an important year because it saw growth of participation and improved results finally realized as a result of the hiring of Max Cobb as the Domestic Race Coordinator in 1989 and the development of a strong domestic National Race Series and North American Cup series that honed the competitive skills of those already participating and attracting new talent. Kristina Viljanen-Sabasteanski, Beth Coats, Peter Gallenz, Jay Poss and a number of junior competitors who moved up to seniors, including Ntala Skinner, Rob Rosser, Chad Salmela, Dan Westover, and Sam Cordell were among them. After 1989 the number of ranked athletes on the USBA points list continued to rise and the National Guard Championships saw over 30 states send teams to its annual championships peak with 176 men and 31 women participating; the largest of any race held in the U.S. It was a breakout year for many. Ntala Skinner had her first international experiences at the World Junior Championships in 1990 at Sodylanka, Finland achieving a best result of 21st in the women's sprint race. Chad Salmela, Dan Westover and Sam Cordell all were also members of the World Junior Championship teams in 1994 and 1995. Kristina Viljanen, Stacy Wooley, Jay Poss, Chad Salmela, Rob Rosser and Tim Derrick were members of the 1993 World University Games team that participated in Zakopane, Poland. Chad Salmela, Robert Rosser and Tim Derrick had joined the National Guard program and participated in the CISM Games that year.

Kristina Viljanen-Sabasteanski later joined the National Guard and was followed by Ntala Skinner and Kara (Hermanson) Salmela. Kristina had skied at Castleton State College in Vermont and began biathlon training with Tracy Lamb at Lake Placid before joining the National Guard program. Her brother Patrick was also a member of the National Junior Men's team and the National Guard teams. He had competed internationally at the Italian military CaSTA competition. After participating in the 1993 World University Games at Zakopane, Poland, Kristina's progress was rapid. Shortly after joining the National Guard she finished 2nd in the National Championships and qualified for the World Cup and World Championships team in 1995 with Stacy Wooley, Beth Coats and Ntala Skinner. Kristina, together with Kara (Hermanson) Salmela, became the athlete development models for the National Guard program. Kara, from Elk River, Minnesota was a 10-year veteran of competitive swimming before switching to cross-country skiing in 1990 at Northern Michigan University where she met her husband Cory. He was coaching the USOEC biathlon program there. In 1993 Kara was ranked 18th on the USBA points list and Kristina was 9th. After joining the National Guard, which vigorously supported the National Race Series and the NorAm Cups programs, Kara regularly finished in the top 10 and at the 1994 National Guard championships finished 2nd and 4th, qualifying her for the 1994 CISM Games. In 1994 the two domestic race programs offered a total of 22 race starts to North American athletes and a chance to move up to higher levels through competitive experience, which clearly showed the key ingredient to improvement was competition. In 1995 Kara used those races, winning two NorAm cups, and a National Guard Championship, to qualify for the final World Cups of the season in Finland and Norway. Named to the early World Cups in 1996, Kara's 2nd and two 3rd places at the team trials landed her a place on the World Biathlon Championships team with three other National Guard members, Deborah Nordyke, Kris Sabasteanski and Ntala Skinner. Kara continued to improve increasing her shooting percentage from the 51% in 1994 to dominate by winning two and finishing second in another with an 80% shooting average at the 1998 Olympic team trials at Jericho, Vermont, qualifying her for that year's Winter Olympic team at Nagano, Japan. Kara went on to her best World Championship finish of 28th in 1999 and was a member of the 2000 team.

However, in 2001 Kara just missed qualifying for the World Championships team but had a standout year with a 2nd place finish in the CISM Games and then qualified for the Olympic team in 2002, achieving the best finish for the women in the sprint race at Soldier Hollow.

While the influx of talented women was constantly contributing to a stronger position in the IBU's Nations Cup rankings, providing for more start positions in the World Cups, World Championships and Olympic Games, the men, after suffering from the unfair criticism of being unable to improve, also began to slowly improve their international status as well. Much of the men's improvement came from new talent as well. Newer recruits and younger athletes challenged the experienced and older athletes towards higher levels of performance much in the same way that Peter Lahdenpera's recruiting of faster skiers in 1978 had. Among the first juniors moving up to challenge the seniors was Dan Westover, a 3-sport high school champion from Colchester, Vermont who joined the National Guard in 1992. During the 2017 National Championships Dan was asked to speak to the competitors during the banquet dinner and he related his experience about getting involved in skiing by telling the audience that no one in his family, unlike most of the biathletes, had any experience with skiing. He reiterated that neither his father, grandfather or mother's relatives ever had anything to do with skiing. In fact, Dan was born in Madagascar where his English mother and American father were working for international aid agencies. Growing up in Vermont he was introduced to skiing cross-country after excelling as a cross-country and track runner. He demonstrated all the necessary talent for success, both physically and psychologically. Dan did not like to lose at anything and was extremely disciplined about his training. During his first year at the University of Vermont, he would regularly train by himself at the National Guard range at Jericho in the afternoon after classes.

Dan Westover did his first biathlon races during the trials for the 1993 CISM/World Championships at West Yellowstone and qualified for the World Junior Championships at Ruhpolding that year. After that first season, he withdrew from UVM to train biathlon full time with the National Guard. After military training during the summer of 1993 he joined the full-time National Guard training group and during the 1994 season he had several good finishes in the National Race Series, and again qualified for the World Junior Championships team and won the National Championships junior sprint and individual race titles. In his first year as a senior after he improved his shooting average from 44% to 71%, it earned him a place on the CISM team, a 3rd place in the National Guard Championships and a top-10 finish at the senior National Championships. Improving his shooting average again in 1996 to 81% and his ski speed to 2:46 per kilometer, it was Dan's breakout year winning the National Championship individual race and a team trials race. With those results, along with the other National Guard athletes Curt Schreiner, Rob Rosser and Chad Salmela, all who had finished in the top 4 positions at the trials, they made up the team to participate in that year's World Cup and World Championships after a proposal by the National Guard to support the men's team with the goal of protecting the Nations Cup score.

In 1997, which was an unusual year for the lack of snow, the team trials were held in rainy weather on a flat loop of man-made snow at Lake Placid. The trials races were short and dominated by the newer developing athletes, Sam Cordell, Jay Poss and Jeremy Teela. Dan Westover did participate in the early World Cups but failed to qualify for the World Championship team. He spent the winter racing in the NorAm Cups and finished 1st and 2nd at the National Guard Championships. He raced in the Italian military CaSTA championships and CISM where he had excellent finishes of 36th in the biathlon race and even earned excellent FIS points in the cross-country race. He was also the North American Champion for the sprint race. After a summer of focused training and skiing in South American, Dan had a fantastic start to the 1998 Olympic season by dominating the trial races at Jericho. Adjusting well to the constantly changing conditions, he won two of the races and finished 2nd and 5th in the other two. Quoted in the *Burlington Free Press*, Dan said, "a few weeks ago I thought I might have to really struggle for that 3rd or 4th spot on the team. I didn't think I'd dominate, for the lack of a better word, like I did." Joining him on the team were Jay Hakkinen, who won the first race, Robert Rosser and surprise Andy Erickson from Minnesota who also won one of the trial races. Rob Rosser told the newspaper, "Dan Westover was the big story of the trials, he kicked butt." Three-time Olympian Curt Schreiner just missed qualifying for the team with a 5th place finish and was the alternate for the team, with his best race being a 3rd place. Dan then became a member of the WCAP group and raced again in the 2002 Olympic team trials, capturing a 3rd place in the first of the four races and 2nd in the third race, but a 6th and 8th in the other two did not earn him enough percentage points to qualify for the team and was named the alternate to the team.

The 1998 Olympic team trials also witnessed a turn-over for the women as well. For the first time the team selection procedure had a pre-qualification provision. Stacy Wooley and Ntala Skinner had met that provision and were already named to the team by their World Cup results and the remaining 3 members of the team would be decided among the other women racing head-to-head in the trials. Like Dan Westover, Kara Salmela dominated the trials winning two races and finishing 2nd in another, which allowed her the ability skip the final race. Kristina Sabasteanski and Deborah Nordyke were the other two who qualified for the team. Although she didn't qualify for the team that year, Rachel Steer also represented the next generation with a 2nd place in the trials and who later finished

25th in the World Championships pursuit race, held separately from the Olympic Games at Pokljuka, Slovenia. Kara Salmela, Kristina Sabasteanski and Deborah Nordyke also finished 31st, 36th and 39th in that race. Two-time Olympian Joan Smith-Miller who had been fighting illness during the trials finished 6th among the women.

After the start of the wars in the Middle East, the National Guard's role gradually diminished, while at the same time the USBA began to find financial resources that started to make a difference in its ability to promote development and better support athletes. New athletes began to appear from the Regional Centers of Excellence who began a foundation for successful junior teams, and finally taking their place as the top U.S. athletes. Although participation on junior teams was no guarantee for achieving success as a senior athlete it was clear that successful juniors, especially those who were among the best at the international level would most likely become the best seniors as well. Two Alaskans were the best example in successfully making the move up to senior success; Jay Hakkinen and Rachel Steer.

Jay Hakkinen came from a fishing family at Kasiloff, Alaska and after learning to skate at an early age, he became involved with Nordic skiing after Joan (Smith) Miller and her husband Roger moved to Alaska. Roger took a teaching position at Skyview High School, and after some success as a junior skier, Jay became involved with biathlon in 1994 when he went on a high school exchange program to Vingrom, Norway, across the lake from Lillehammer. His host parents arranged for him to train with a local biathlon club and three years later, after returning home to Alaska, he became the World Junior Biathlon Champion, the first Gold medalist for an American athlete. Still a junior, he qualified for the 1998 Olympic team and raced three races at Nagano. He returned to the Olympic Games at Salt Lake City where he finished 13th in the pursuit competition with just one penalty. Had Jay hit the single target he missed, he would have captured the silver medal. He went on to be a four-time American Olympian, and his 10th place finish in the 20-kilometer individual race at the 2006 Winter Olympics at Torino bettered the best finish ever by an American. His best result of 10th at Torino was also a near miss, just 1 penalty away from the bronze medal. Jay's best finish at the World Championships was a 9th place at Antholz in 2007 in the mass start race. Jay also achieved nine top-10 finishes at the World Cups with a best finish of 5th at Lake Placid in 1999 and he scored World Cup points in multiple years with his best score of 97 points attained in 2010.

Growing up in Anchorage, Rachel Steer was an All-American girl with good grades and a close-knit family. She kept active sailing, skiing, swimming, hunting and doing just about anything that would get her out of doors. She began competitive swimming at age 8 and continued into high school. She also competed in track, cross-country skiing and triathlons. Rachel gravitated to biathlon while attending Service High School in 1992 when she qualified for the Arctic Winter Games for snow-shoe biathlon. That easily transferred to biathlon on skis and in her first year she made quite an impact, winning the junior trials, qualifying for her first Junior World Championships and winning both the individual and sprint National Championship junior titles. After participating in the World Junior Biathlon Championships, in 1994, 1995 and 1996 she had a breakout year in 1997 when she found her first important success at the 1997 FISU Games at Muju, Korea where she captured a bronze medal in the individual 15km race and a silver medal in the 7.5km sprint. She qualified for the World Cup starts still as a junior and after a 10th place finish in the World Junior Championships at Valcartier, Canada. She finished in 23rd and 25th places in the World Cup at Pokljuka that year. She had a 2nd place finish at the 1998 Olympic team trials and just missed qualifying for the team but did race to a 25th place in the World Championships pursuit that year held separately from the Olympic Games at Pokljuka, Slovenia. A member of the 2002 and 2006 Olympic teams she achieved bests of 31st at Salt Lake and 35th at Torino. She also reached the podium twice with a 2nd place at the IBU Cup races in 2003 at Ridnaun, Italy and a 1st place at Obertilliach, Austria in 2006.

Following the success of Josh Thompson, there were also an influx of men who made the transition through collegiate skiing, junior and National Guard programs. As the women's team was experiencing growth and improving their international standard in the 1990s, the men's team came under the perception of being too old and unable to improve, with the USBA shifting its focus on developing juniors to replace them. Much of this shift in focus came as a result of both USOC pressure to improve results and the UIPMP/IBU quota system that came into force. Based on the 1992/93 final Nations Cup scores the U.S. men were 18th and qualified to have only a team size of four with 2 start positions and a relay team at the 1994 and 1998 Olympic Games. The women were 8th and thus qualified to have a team of six with 4 start positions and a relay team. In addition to the team size quotas, only athletes who had reached a racing time in a World Championship or World Cup event within the Olympic cycle that was not more than 25% of the average time of the first three finishers or in the best half of the previous year's Junior Championships would be allowed to participate.

The men also experienced both growth in numbers and competitiveness in the late 1980s and early 1990s. As the older athletes such as Lyle Nelson, Martin Hagen, Glen Jobe and Peter Hoag retired, junior competitors Raimond Dombrovskis, Curt Schreiner, Dave Jareckie, Darin Binning, Derek Freeman, Rob Rosser, Chad Salmela, and Sam Cordell all emerged from the junior teams to take a place on the senior teams. Dartmouth alumni Glen Eberle, Willie Carow, Erich

Wilbrecht, Peter Gallenz, Ian Harvey and Tim Derrick were all Dartmouth ski team members. Robert (Duncan) Douglas had skied for St. Lawrence University while Curt Schreiner and Dave Jareckie came up from the junior team and then joined the National Guard program. Johnny Ingdal and Jon Engen came from Norway, becoming citizens and were also members of the senior men's team. Ingdal won the National Championship sprint race in 1988 and 1990 while Engen raced cross-country at the 1988 Olympic Games and then biathlon at the 1992 and 1994 Olympic Games. Curt Schreiner, Darin Benning and Raimond Dombrovskis were members of the 1988 Olympic team at Canmore and along with Josh Thompson, Willie Carow and Erich Wilbrecht, they became the dominant group of senior athletes in the early 1990s. While Josh Thompson took the 1989 season off and then limited competition in 1990, Schreiner, Dombrovskis and Carow made up the 1989 World Championships team with Duncan Douglas and Peter Gallanz and again in 1990. Peter Gallenz achieved the best results, including a breakthrough 19th place finish in the sprint race at the Minsk, USSR World Championships, for which he was named the men's Athlete of the Year.

Not only were the Olympic years of 1992 and 1994 very competitive years for U.S. athletes striving to earn a place on the U.S. teams, they were also extremely difficult years for the U.S. athletes at the World Cup and World Championships. Despite the improvement in resources, including better financial conditions, improved programs, coaching and National Guard support it was difficult to match the progress of the Europeans, and U.S. athletes struggled to catch up. Looking back at the international results in the period, one might conclude that the U.S. athletes were probably facing use of Performance Enhancing Drugs among their competitors and perhaps equipment/wax inferiorities. The two Olympic relays of 1992 and 1994 provided the best example of their predicament. At Albertville the men's relay was impacted at the start when a Slovenian racer misplaced himself on the U.S. shooting lane and Jon Engen had to go to a reserve target, disrupting the flow of his race. Despite coming through the mix-up well, Duncan Douglas, Josh Thompson and Curt Schreiner were able to finish 13th, six minutes behind the winner. The 1993 World Championship team of Curt Schreiner, Ian Harvey, Dave Jareckie and Erich Wilbrecht at Borovetz, Bulgaria weren't able to improve, finishing 16th, slightly over 7 minutes back. At Lillehammer the team of Schreiner, Jareckie, Engen and Douglas performed well, without any penalties and did improve their performance by percent behind, finishing just over 5 minutes back, but in 14th place. This contributed to the criticism that the U.S. men were too old and unable to improve, and it appeared to impact the women as well. It was an unfortunate decision not to send a men's team to the 1995 World Championships in favor of full focus on junior development.

While the men were suffering criticism and limited opportunity, the women's team was making progress, or seemed so. In their first Olympic opportunity, the women's relay team of Nancy Johnstone, Joan Smith-Miller and Mary Ostergren finished 15th almost 9 minutes behind the winning French team. In 1993 a third exchange and a fourth team member were added to the women's relay and the team of Joan Smith-Miller, Joan Geutschow, Mary Ostergren and Ntala Skinner finished 11th just over 7 minutes behind the winners. Despite falling behind by over 10 minutes at Lillehammer, the team of Beth Coats, Joan Smith-Miller, Laurie Tavares and Joan Geutschow improved to 8th place. When viewed from a "percent back," or performance perspective, the men had a much better race at 94.4% despite being only in 14th place, while the women were at 91.2%. The difference could be explained by the competitiveness and numbers between the men and women's participants, something that was not fully acknowledged in the USBA decision to shift its focus. Despite the best efforts of both the men and women, it seemed they were chasing the impossible.

Despite the frustration and disappointment, improvement seemed unattainable, but that was not completely true. The normal four-year Olympic cycle between 1994, 1998 and 2002 did experience gradual but slow progress as new groups of athletes emerged along with new coaching and improved support that produced a better understanding about development and high-performance progression. It was also the pivotal period that saw changes in the USBA Board of Directors structure, administration and funding. Perhaps the most important impact was the greater opportunities for racing that were developed during the period. The National Race Series and the NorAm Cup events as well as the National Guard's program of support to both domestic race series and international racing at military events in Europe and South American provided greater experience at high performance levels which developed better racing skills in a more consistent and challenging racing environment.

A good example of how these helped can be seen in how some of the athletes that came from those programs progressed. Ntala Skinner, Robert Rosser and Robert (Duncan) Douglas, each who first began racing in the late 1980s used domestic and National Guard opportunities to eventually participate in the Olympic Games. Ntala Skinner began skiing early in life in Pinedale, Wyoming where she was a member of a famous family that ran a well-known wilderness camp. Her father, Ole and his five brothers all skied for the University of Wyoming and her uncle Quentin was a member of the USMWBTC in Alaska during the 1960s. In an article by Rob Buchanan in *Sports Afield Magazine* her father related; Ntala was "skiing right out of her diapers" and remembers her bitter disappointment when he told her she'd have to wait till she was in first grade to start racing. Her mother, Karen, added; "A lot of times she was the only girl skiing in the races she entered." In another interview Ntala said that "from a very young age I always wanted to go to the Olympics" and that her father would tease her for bad behavior by asking, "Do you think this is how you get to the Olympics?" It was another former Olympic biathlete, Darren Binning, who also lived in Pinedale that introduced Ntala's older brother to biathlon and was 13 when she got handed down his old biathlon rifle. When she was 15 and a sophomore in high school, the family moved to Sun Valley, Idaho where the conditions for ski training were better. She raced in the National Junior Biathlon Championships in 1988 with a best of 4th place and just kept improving from there.

Ntala quickly rose to the top of the junior women athletes when she qualified for the 1990 World Junior Championships with clean shooting in one of the trials and meeting the criteria of 90% of the senior women's winner in any trials race. At the World Junior Championships at Sodylanka, Finland she had a best finish of 21st. She was also 1st and 3rd in the women's National Junior Biathlon Championships and ranked at the top of junior women's USBA points ranking. While still a junior at 19, she joined the National Guard in 1993 and qualified for the World Championships and World Cups. A member of the 1994 Winter Olympic team, she was not chosen for a start position, but had a best World Cup finish of 17th and was a member of the 2nd place relay team at the World Cup in Canmore. In 1995 Ntala shot clean to win a team trials race and repeated a clean race in the World Championships sprint race at Antholz to finish 32nd. As part of the strong women's team, she also entered the Army's World Class Athlete Program (WCAP). 1997 was even a better season in that she won both the sprint and individual National Championship races, which also served as team trials races and finished 2nd in another and then went on to score a best finish of 12th at the World Cup at Antholz, which pre-qualified her for the 1998 Olympic team. Antholz always appeared to be a favorite of American athletes and seemed to be Ntala's favorite site as well after she finished 17th in the World Cup there prior to the Olympic Games at Nagano. After racing the Olympic individual race and the lead-off leg of the relay, Ntala retired from active participation. In an interview after her retirement she said, ""Thank goodness for great parents that have always been interested in my success." She also related that after she returned home in 1994 after finally making her first Olympic team, about her father's question for bad behavior, "Do you think this is how you get to the Olympics?" She answered, "Yes."

Like Ntala Skinner, Rob Rosser started racing in 1988 and was the men's National Junior Champion while Duncan Douglas also started racing that year in the senior men's championship. In their first year of racing each participated in multiple races, Rosser 8 and Duncan did 10. Duncan got a later start in skiing and biathlon then Skinner and Rosser. He was older and a college student at St. Lawrence University in northern New York after being a top runner in high school and originally focused on the sport in college until the ski coach, Bob Axtell convinced him to give skiing a try. He took to the skating technique quickly and gave biathlon a try soon after. After the Olympic trials in 1988, he saw great opportunity and by 1990 he was a member of the World Championships team. With fast skiing he followed Josh Thompson's 18th place in the 1991 World Championships at Lahti, Finland by only 4 seconds in 21st place and helped the relay team finish 9th. Both Rob Rosser and Duncan were somewhat compulsive about their methods and volume of training that didn't always please the coaches. Duncan qualified for both the 1992 and 1994 Olympic teams with a best finish of 55th at Albertville and had the fastest relay leg at Lillehammer. Duncan then went on to complete medical school and left biathlon and ski racing for a time but came back for a second career after receiving his medical degree and continued to race internationally as a member of the National Guard and in the master's divisions in both biathlon and cross-country skiing.

As a junior, Rob Rosser was chosen to participate in the Polar Cup international races as one of the 10 junior athletes selected from the nationals at Giant's Ridge, Minnesota in 1988. Born in Plattsburg, New York, Rob grew up in Lake Placid and began skiing early. He started training for biathlon after high school working with John Underwood in Oregon. He joined the National Guard soon after high school graduation and eventually became an officer. He went to the Polar Cup again in 1989 and at the end of the season he was the top-ranked junior on the USBA points list with a total of 15 races. When Max Cobb was hired to develop and manage the Domestic Race Series, Rob took full advantage of every racing opportunity offered, including those of the National Guard program as well. A very high standard requiring the junior men to achieve a 90% level in the junior/senior trials prevented him and all the junior men from participating in the World Junior Championships, but by 1992 Rob had climbed his way up into the top-ten on the USBA senior men's points list and competed in the 1993 World University Games a Zakopane, Poland. In his final leg in the relay at Zakopane he cleaned his targets and just missed medaling with a 4th place for the U.S. team. He also had the best U.S. men's result with a 16th place in the 20km individual race. He then got his first World Cup starts in March at Lillehammer, Östersund and Kontiolahti and a 3rd place in the National Championships. Despite a 2nd and 3rd place finish in the trials, he narrowly missed qualifying for the 1994 Olympic team, but did race several World Cups, the CISM Games, won the National Race series by more than 50 points and was named U.S. Biathlete of the Year. The USBA did not send a men's team to the World Championships in 1995 and only to the final two World Cups so Rob's season focus was again on the NorAm Cups, for which he was overall winner. He was a member of the team of National Guard athletes at the World Cups and World Championships in 1996 after winning two of the team trials races. Despite a 2nd place in one of the 1997 team trials races, he did not qualify for the World Championships team that year but did win the overall NorAm Cup again. 1998 turned out to be his best year in that he qualified for the Winter Olympic team, the only one to qualify without winning a race, but with a consistent 5th, 2nd, 4th and 4th place in the trials races.

Rob continued, as part of the WCAP program, participating in the 2000 and 2001 World Championships but disappointing results on the shooting range in the trials for the 2002 Olympic team left him well short of going to his second Olympic Games. He did continue to race in some military events but retired to coaching after 2003, first with the adaptive skiers and eventually as a junior coach at the new facility he played a major role in developing at Casper Mountain in Wyoming.

Once Max Cobb was hired to be the program director in 1993 and Cory Salmela hired as the development coach, the National Race Series lost much of the organizational structure necessary for maintaining a good program. The focus of the Regional Centers of Excellence in the long-range development plan did not effectively provide the financial resources that would have ensured maintaining the structure of the National Race Series. The new National Coaches also placed their focus on international improvement and were less concerned with development. Fortunately, the NorAm Cup series and the North American Championships were strengthened by the National Guard's participation and the Canadian Forces which had invested in improvements at Quebec's Valcartier biathlon site and improved their program support as well. This coincided with new recruiting tactics by USBA which appeared to turn towards looking for fast skiers in the junior and college cross-country results to speed up development. Among those coming from a long line of Dartmouth skiers was Stacy Wooley. She grew up the daughter of the police chief in Lebanon, N.H. and was a 1986 graduate of the Stratton Mountain School in Vermont. A 1991 Dartmouth graduate and ski team member she became one of many in the unbroken string of Dartmouth alumni from 1980 to 2016 to have participated in the Winter Olympic Games.

Soon after starting biathlon training, Stacy was selected to the team for World University Games (FISU) at Zakopane, Poland in 1993 along with Kristina Viljanen (Sabasteanski), Kimberly Baumer, Devon Daney and Christine Boggs and Cory Fritzel. The FISU Games have been an important event in the development of transitioning athletes, as it was for Josh Thompson and Rachel Steer. At the 1993 races at Zakopane, a 6th and 14tth place by Kristina and a 17th by Stacy seemed to indicate their potential, along with Rob Rosser and Chad Salmela on the men's side. However, within the USBA it was a rather fractious and frustrating time that these athletes were beginning their biathlon careers. The unfair criticism for poor results felt by the athletes, disruptions in program priorities and funding outlined in the USBA's strategic plan and USOC revisions, along with subjective coaching decisions that seemed arbitrary worked against team cohesion and a sense of confidence within the team and among the athletes. Stacy was unafraid to voice her opinion on these issues and in an interview with the *Associated Press* just before the 1998 Nagano Olympic Games she and Ntala Skinner, both who had prequalified for the team through their World Cup results hinted at their discontent. "When you look at, say Russia, Germany, Norway, they're so focused from the grassroots on, and their countries are so behind biathletes all the time," Skinner said. "They understand the sport and respect it. In America, there's still a bit of a stigma." "It's difficult to compete with countries which have programs with so much money. I'm not trying to make excuses. That's the reality. There's definitely no money to be made being a biathlete in America." "Do I want to be poor and live out of my car or go to Wall Street, make money, buy a house?" Wooley asked herself. They commented that biathlon races in the United States were few, and it was extremely hard, especially for a woman, even to get into a national-level training camp.

Ntala admitted that things had improved with junior programs attracting talent, and the U.S. military's two-year World Class Athlete Program provided jobs and training opportunities at the same time. Four of the five women at the 1998 Nagano Olympics were members in the armed forces, a closely-knit group living Jericho, and Lake Placid, training or competing year-round. Stacy was the exception, preferring a less-regimented life and critical of the American effort. Telling Denis D. Gray in the *Associated Press* interview she said, "It's unpredictable. Every year the level of support is different. Three years ago, the men's team couldn't even go to Europe for World Cup races because the money ran out." Finding the centralized training dissatisfying she preferred training on her own and tried training outside the team environment, living in Ruhpolding where the German athletes trained.

Both Stacy Wooley and Kristina Viljanen-Sabasteanski made rapid progress after their first international races at Zakopane. Although they did not qualify for the Olympic team the next year, they moved up to 10th and 11th among the USBA ranked women. Stacy had good results in the National Race series and was named to the final 1994 World Cups in Canada and captured a 2nd and 3rd place in the National Championships. Both named to the National Team for 1995, Stacy and Kris achieved best results of 22nd and 26th and a relay 8th place at the World Championships at Antholz, Italy. The next year at Ruhpolding they switched places with Kristina finishing 20th and Stacy 26th. It was also the first time that Kara Salmela participated in the World Championships. Kristina's result came after some consideration to send her home for poor performance in the previous World Cups and growing tension within the team over the inclusion in the opening ceremonies of an athlete who had not qualified for the team, the same athlete who had been added to the National Team multiple times as a discretionary choice of the coach.

In 1997 Stacy had five top-25 World Cup finishes, including a 12th place at the World Championships at Osrblie, Slovakia, which along with Ntala Skinner's 12th place World Cup results prequalified them to the 1998 Olympic team. Kristina Sabasteanski, Kara Salmela and Deborah Nordyke qualified through the trials. Jay Hakkinen's winning performance at the World Junior Championships along with his qualification for the Olympic team, along with Minnesota's Andy Erickson's surprise seemed to indicate that USBA planning was on track. Seeing juniors move up to senior teams was a good sign, however the hoped-for results at Nagano were not realized either by the men or women. Many saw it as a disaster in face of the increasing pressure from the USOC to achieve results or lose funding. The High-Performance Plan of 1994 did not produce the progress expected, but not necessarily due to poor planning, but timing. The time necessary to take talented junior athletes to the senior levels was not clearly understood, but the ground work towards 2002 had been laid and it was a matter of time before the plan was fulfilled.

The revised mission statement in 1994 listed the goals of preparing athletes to achieve their best possible results in international competition, demonstrating steady improvement culminating with constituent top ten finishes in World Cup competition and by 1998 medal-winning performances in the Olympic Games thereafter. It also had the goal of promoting an awareness of, participation in, and the support of biathlon that would develop and maintain an athlete feeder system to support those objectives. With the USBA shift in focus and planning towards junior development following the 1994 Olympic Games a spark was created that eventually generated the next group of athletes. That planning, along with the improved program direction, support and coaching gradually led to more competitive teams and athletes through the 2002-2018 Olympic Games. One of the most important changes was the ability to retain the athletes longer, maintaining the consistency of their skills progress and competitive experiences. In a sense, the athletes had progressed from amateurs to professional athletes with many starting at a younger age and remaining in the sport for longer careers.

The efforts of Junior Coach Cory Salmela and Algis Shalna in establishing talent identification camps and inviting top junior skiers began to have a later impact. The success of juniors who then went on to senior success such as Jay Hakkinen and Rachel Steer aided in recruiting others. Jeremy Teela, who won the state championships and Junior National Championships was also from Alaska. The two identical twin Barnes sisters from Colorado were introduced to biathlon and each made a successful transition to the senior team and the Olympic

Games. From an early age through high school, Jeremy excelled in swimming and while skiing casually through the biathlon range at the 1993 Junior National Championships at Biwabic, Minnesota was invited to try shooting. The next year at the 1994 Olympic team trials and National Championships at Kincaid Park, Charlie Hostetler, who had helped coach the team at the World University Games suggested Jeremy give it a try and then had a few training sessions with him prior to the races. Although he didn't have very good results on the range, Jeremy was hooked on biathlon and was invited to a junior camp. He later joined the National Guard. Although he first dreamed of being an Olympic swimmer, he later explained that "the dream of becoming an Olympian and the thought of being the first American biathlete to win an Olympic medal" was a powerful motivating force. Similar dreams motivated twins Lanny and Tracy Barnes who grew up in Durango where, along with their older sister Christie, were part of the high school soccer team that won five consecutive Southern League titles earning all-state honors, but their ski experience was only limited to alpine slopes.

Living in Colorado, the twin sisters were exposed to guns, shooting, and hunting at an early age. Their father's passion was hunting and shooting, so he passed on his tradition teaching his daughters to shoot BB guns at age 7 and then graduating to shotguns and .22s. "We were hunters and shooters first, and then learned to ski," said Lanny in an interview with Tom McHale for *Range 365*, "which is the opposite of most competitors." They eventually ran into Allan Small, also from Durango who was a member of the USMWBTC in the 1960s and once he explained biathlon, they instantly became interested. Allan spread the word about the twins during the annual Thanksgiving ski week at West Yellowstone and they were soon invited by Corey Salmela to a junior clinic. Having little skiing background did not seem to be a problem for the talented sisters. They explained in the interview with *Range 365*, "We downhill skied, but we didn't know what cross-country skiing was. Why ski up the hill when you can ski down it? Our situation was quite the opposite. Most people who go into biathlon are skiers, and they learn how to shoot later. So, we jumped into biathlon and obviously shooting was our strong point. We picked up quickly on the skiing."

Lanny and Tracy were the opposite of Jeremy Teela. Jeremy brought an impressive ski background to biathlon and once in the National Guard he picked up the shooting skills. In an interview with Bucky Gleason just before the 2002 Salt Lake Olympic Games, Jeremy said, "the USBA sent National Coach Algis Shalna around the U.S. searching for fast skiers. He got some of the fastest and gave us rifles. That's us," referring to himself and Jay Hakkinen. Growing up in Alaska, far from any Olympic venue, Jeremy enjoyed but one of the benefits of living in Anchorage, Alaska; that winter sports are extremely popular. "We had ski trails right behind the high school, and a lot of people did it," he told Amy

Donaldson of the *Deseret News* of his time at Service High School. "Cross-country was big." Since he had also grown up around guns, combining the two sports wasn't a ridiculous suggestion when Shalna suggested he give the sport a try. After high school, Jeremy had decisions to make. Head to college and try to keep skiing, try to make the U.S. cross-country ski team or join the U.S. Biathlon team's development program. "I really had a drive to make the Olympic team," Teela said of 1996. "The road the U.S. Biathlon team had laid out was very well-planned and clear. You could see how you could get from where I was to there. Cross-country skiing didn't have anything like it at the time."

Jeremy was a member of the World Junior Biathlon Championship team in 1996 at Kontiolahti, Finland along with future Olympians Jay Hakkinen, Andy Erickson and Rachel Steer. With less than desired standing shooting, Jeremy could only manage a best of 46th place, however Jay Hakkinen gave a glimpse of the future with two top 20 finishes at 19th and 14th. The juniors also participated in final Europa Cup races in Russia where Jay Hakkinen won a sprint race at St. Petersburg, claiming his first international win and followed that with a 3rd place in the pursuit. Then a week later at Murmansk Jeremy Teela cracked the top ten with a 6th place in the individual race with only 2 penalties while Jay repeated with another win in the sprint race. It appeared that the 1994 High Performance Plan was beginning to have an impact. In 1997 Jay won the World Junior Biathlon Championships 10km sprint, the first-ever individual gold medal at a World Championships by an American athlete. Jeremy placed 3rd in the National Championships senior men's sprint race and was named to the World Cup team and finished 36th in the European Championships and placed 11th in the CISM Games 15km cross-country ski race.

Not long after these future Olympians were introduced to biathlon, a few others, younger, were experiencing their first contact with biathlon. In two articles written by Chad Salmela for *Fasterskier.com* he explained that during one of his training sessions in 1996 at the Mt. Van Hoevenberg biathlon range near Lake Placid, Kris Seymour, the New York Ski Education Foundation coach asked if he would let two young guys try shooting and talk to them a little about biathlon. Lowell Bailey and his best friend, Tim Burke, then were 15 and 14 years old. As they got ready to shoot, they were extremely quiet, but respectful and attentive. Without a left-handed rifle for Lowell, he shot Chad's right-handed rifle left-handed. From the standing position, he hit 4 out of 5 shots the first time. Chad said he had never seen a beginner hit 4 out of 5 prone, let alone standing, and adding the fact that he was shooting a right-handed rifle and already a stand-out junior skier, Chad knew someday he was going to see Lowell in the Olympics, racing biathlon. Lowell later related in an interview with *Fasterskier. com* that he had been skiing since he was young and "it was in high school that he was introduced to biathlon, a sport that retains the whole skiing thing, but adds a new element to the equation." He qualified for the Junior World Championship Biathlon Team in 1999.

Lowell, born in North Carolina, moved to upstate New York as a child before settling in Lake Placid. Tim, the younger of the two was slower to mature and grew up in near Saranac Lake, just west of Lake Placid where his father was vice president at Paul Smith's College. Growing up together in skiing, Lowell and Tim were best-friends-and-teammates. Tim always chased Lowell, trying to beat him, but rarely did. While they were training together as juniors in Lake Placid, there was a strong local ski program in the region. Among them was Bill Demong, Tim's high school teammate on the New York State cross-country running championship team from Saranac Lake and the future Olympic Gold Medal winner for Nordic Combined. Another young athlete from the area, also a Saranac Lake resident began her biathlon career at the same time was Annelies Cook. Skiing as a child at the Dewey Mountain Recreation Center in Saranac Lake, where today there is trail named after her, she was also coached by Kris Seymour in the Lake Placid NYSEF program. Annelies explained in an interview with Chris Morris of *Adirondack Life*, "We were all very lucky. Our parents always took us out skiing. We'd go up to Avalanche Lake with the pulk, my sister Marlijne would go too; it was such a family thing for all of us cross-country skiers. Then it was Bill Koch ski league, then the high-school team and NYSEF."

The emphasis and focus on junior development after 1994 had developed good junior teams in the 1990s and after recruiting another Minnesota athlete, Carolyn Treacy they achieved medal performances at the 2002 World Junior Championships. Cory Salmela was exceptionally good at recruiting talent and along with Algis Shalna and assistants, developing medal winning performances. Carolyn teamed up with the Barnes sisters to win the bronze medal in the women's relay. Although the development of successful juniors had the goal of creating a path for aspiring and talented young athletes and a feeder system to the senior teams, there was often a lag in that progression as the senior athletes began a tendency to participate in the sport for longer durations. This sometimes left the younger athletes with no place to continue their transition from the junior to senior teams and resulted in the loss of some and the delayed development of others. Most mainstream U.S. sports had clear step by step age, for example; baseball. Starting with Little League up through high school, college or minor leagues, athletes had progressive development in their sport that could guarantee a steady stream of Major League players. No such "system" existed in biathlon. The goal of the 1994 plan as well as the previous efforts in 1978 was to create a path for the sport from the entry level to the Olympic and World Championships teams.

Without a high school option for biathlon, clubs and the Regional Centers of

Excellence became a replacement for the entry levels, however after that options were also limited. Biathlon did not exist as a colligate sport. The USOC plans for Community and Collegiate programs in Minnesota and at the Northern Michigan University were attempts to create the next step in the development progression, but still only a limited effort. Many juniors saw the option of the National Guard's program as the best place to continue their development. The National Guard's funding and the growth of juniors and graduating collegians looking for a way to continue skiing boosted its All-Guard team to a high of 26 members at the 1997 team trials. But joining the military wasn't an acceptable option for everyone. Some, like the Barnes sisters and Tim Burke joined the Maine Winter Center group that provided a similar program as the National Guard with coaching and competitive participation in domestic events until they were able to move up to the senior team. Annelies Cook and Lowell Bailey decided to attend college on ski scholarships at the University of Utah and the University of Vermont. Both did well at the NCAA championships with Lowell achieving podium finishes and a National Championship in cross-country.

This issue of transitioning from junior to senior levels became an important concern for USBA. There was an ongoing debate within USBA about the best options for keeping potentially talented athletes in the sport. The website, *Faster-skier.com* had a multi-part article about this concern. After the robust development teams of the 1990s and early 2000s was diminished in a budget crunch, and a greater focus on high-performance at the senior level, there were fewer juniors showing up for the World Junior team trials and fewer numbers of juniors on the USBA points lists. James Upham, who along with his sister Hannah competed in the World Junior Biathlon Championships, became the shared Maine Winter Center's coach and USBA's Development Coach, at the time told reporter Chelsea Little, "We had pretty much pushed those guys onto the [senior] national team. So, we said, well, we've got to have some more people because there aren't enough clubs in America producing the high-end biathletes that we're looking for." There was already a model of what he and Max Cobb where thinking about; looking for talent in the collegiate ski programs. Lawton (Travis) Redman was the perfect example.

Lawton was a 3-sport high school champion from Rutland, Vermont who had challenged Dan Westover when Dan was a senior and Lawton an under-classman. Lawton went on to run and ski at St. Lawrence University in New York earning All-American honors in skiing, track and cross-country running. After graduation he entered a summer running biathlon race at Jericho and ran away from the field despite little experience with shooting. As an example of his talent, that summer he finished in the top ten at the prestigious Utica Boilermaker 15km road race with a time of under 47 minutes. After joining the National Guard in

1999 he captured a 2nd place in the Nationals Championships sprint race that year, 2nd place in the individual race in 2000 and both the sprint and individual races in 2001. He qualified for the World Championships team in 2001 and then the Olympic team at Soldier Hollow in 2002 as a member of the WCAP program. Lawton's quick progression seemed to be just the additional source for development that Upham and Cobb were considering. They felt that even in their early 20s, with the right physiological requirements, talent and attitudes, within four or five years they could have a World Champion.

They were also perhaps emboldened by the success of Sarah Konrad, who at age 37 and after just two years in biathlon finished 50th in the individual race at 2005 World Championships. Sarah was originally from California and hadn't begun skiing seriously until after attending Dartmouth College where she did not participate in college skiing. Once taking up the sport she found immediate success and despite qualifying for and racing in the FIS Championships at Sapporo, the USSA program did not show an interest in her due to her age. Peter Hale encouraged her to give biathlon a try. Despite her age, Max Cobb and Algis Shalna invited her to join the program and after winning national championship titles in 2004 and 2005 she went on to the 2006 Torino Olympics, where she became the first U.S. woman to compete in two winter sports at the same Olympic Games: skiing and biathlon.

The strategy of developing athletes already in their 20s was also confirmed by Catlin Compton-Gregg. Upham and Pytor Bednarski convinced Catlin to give biathlon a try after having won five Super Tour wins and represented the U.S. at FIS World Championships in Sapporo, Japan. In her very first year, she showed that the development program could work. She finished 37th in the individual race in the World Championships at Östersund, Sweden, hitting 16 of 20 targets and skiing the 29th fastest time. She was the top American in the race. She left the team to return to skiing after just one season and was a member of the cross-country ski team at the 2006 Torino Olympic Games, but her success surely reinforced USBA's confidence in its plan.

The strategy of transitioning college skiers over to biathlon continued when Dartmouth graduates Sara Studebaker, Carolyn Treacy, and Laura Spector made a successful transition after college. Each had some experience before enrolling at Dartmouth, especially Carolyn Treacy and Laura Spector who were members of the junior team and competed in the World Junior Championships with excellent results. Carolyn, along with the Barnes sisters, were medal winners in the women's relay and Laura had finished 9th in 2006. Sara Studebaker, from Idaho had tried some biathlon races in high school. Like Lowell Bailey and Annelies Cook, each felt the college skiing would help their biathlon efforts. While at Dartmouth Laura and Carolyn fixed up the old biathlon range and restarted the Biathlon

Club that was a part of the school's Outdoor Programs Office. Although both had been members of the junior team, and like Ntala Skinner in 1993, Laura qualified for the junior and senior teams in the same season in her final year as a junior, the transition to the senior teams was not without hiccups. Although the USBA embraced the strategy of recruiting graduating skiers, it was less supportive of top juniors opting for college skiing. Many of the junior skiers looking towards the future as seniors hadn't enjoyed a lot of support during their junior years, and looked to college skiing as a way forward, while the USBA coaches feared that athletes leaving biathlon for college skiing would train less, stop shooting, and never return to the sport at a high level.

First- or second-year senior athletes had a difficult decision between finding a program and resources for continuing biathlon until they could move up to the senior teams or go to college skiing and later to a career. There were other alternatives. Opting out of the college choice, Jeremy Teela joined the National Guard and used it and the WCAP program with good success making his first World Championships team in 1999 and participating in three Olympic Games, 2002, 2006 and 2010. He finished 20th and 23rd at Soldier Hollow and an American best-ever with his 9th place at Vancouver. He also achieved a 9th and 10th place at the World Championships in 2001 and 2003 at Pokljuka, Slovenia and Khanty-Mansiysk, Russia and became an integral part of the men's relay team. The military option allowed Jeremy to continue through the 2016 season when he lost the final selection to the Olympic team to the developing junior star Sean Doherty. Other juniors taking the military option were Minnesotans Jill Krause, Andrea Nahrgang, Sarah Riley and Jacob Beste, moving up from the junior World Championships team to the senior teams. Other juniors, also from Minnesota, Grant Ernhart and Dan Campbell moved up from the junior to senior levels successfully outside of the college or military programs with the limited support of the Olympic Community Development Program. Russell Currier was a product of the Maine Winter Sports Center who progressed through that program to be a member of two Olympic teams. Still others came from college skiing with and without prior biathlon experience. Haley Johnson, a Lake Placid native with some junior biathlon experience and a Bowdoin ski team member advanced through the entire development process to race in the World Championships and Olympic Games. Hannah Dreissigacker, another Dartmouth graduate, along with her sister Emily and brother Ethan, who had top 20 finishes at the World Junior Championships used the Ethan Allen Biathlon Club at Jericho, Vermont and the Green Racing Project at Craftsbury, Vermont to develop their biathlon skills, and both Hannah and Emily participated in the Winter Olympic Games. Erin Graham, from the same high school as Joan Smith and one of New York's top high school teams at Honeyoe Falls and a Williams College skier, joined the military program to extend her ski career. Clare Egan from Maine started skiing in middle school for Cape Nordic and was a Maine high school state champion and two-time member of the New England Junior National team. While attending Wellesley College, she ran cross-country and track and started the Wellesley Ski Team. After graduating she spent a year at the University of New Hampshire, where she competed in Division I cross-country, track, and Nordic skiing while pursuing a master's degree in linguistics. She later also joined the Green Racing Project and at the age of 25 Algis Shalna invited her to try biathlon. Seeing that Hannah Dreissigacker and Susan Dunklee had made the transition she also became a member of the USBA Development team, World Championships and Olympic Team.

Another diamond in the rough that was invited to join the team was Joanne Reid. She is the daughter of 1980 Olympic speedskating bronze medalist Beth (Heiden) Reid who attended the University of Vermont and became the NCAA champion in cross-country skiing, and the niece of Eric Heiden, a five-time Olympic gold medalist in speedskating. Joanne started skiing early as a child in California and followed her mother, also becoming an NCAA champion cross-country skier for the University of Colorado, and participated on the U.S. Ski Team's squad for Under-23 World Championships, where she was the top American skier in both the 10km skate and the 15km skiathlon. Using her grandfather's biathlon rifle, she participated in the Auburn Ski Club and the Colorado Biathlon Club's programs and after a meeting with Bernd Eisenbichler, she was invited to train with the development team and Coach Jean Paquet at Lake Placid. At the IBU Cup trials at Canmore she qualified for the team and then finished 16th with a single penalty in her first race, then followed that up with a clean-shooting 23rd-place finish in the second at Novo Mesto. Impressed with her ski speed and mental attitude, Eisenbichler and the coaches elevated her, just after her 8th race, to the World Cup races in 2016.

During the 2017 season training and racing, Joanne began experiencing supraventricular tachycardia, a similar condition that Joan Geutschow had also experienced. After repeated heart rates that exceeded a high of 275 beats per minute it was determined that there was an extra pathway in the AV node that was allowing current to loop backwards and giving the heart a signal to beat again. Two and a half weeks before August World Cup trials at Jericho, cardiologists at the Massachusetts General Hospital did a catheter ablation to destroy the extra pathway in the AV node. It took a second procedure to solve the problem and sent Joanne back to the start of the trials procedure, first at Utah, Minnesota IBU Cup Trials, four IBU Cups, one World Cup, before she met the Olympic team criteria for the Olympic Games at Pyeonchang where she finished 22nd in the individual race with only one penalty.

Recruiting Joanne, Clare Egan and Susan Dunklee into biathlon without any previous biathlon experience, but because of their ski potential, became an important part of the USBA strategy. Supporting the junior development of Leif Nordgren, Sean Doherty, Maddie Phaneuf, Anna Kubek and Chloe Levins, talented athletes with impressive junior results, was also an integral part. The USBA concepts towards athlete recruiting and development evolved into a multi-directional approach that considered all potential sources that could potentially improve its ability to find high performance athletes. Although support was still limited, it paid greater attention to the juniors, especially those that could achieve the benchmark performances of top 20 finishes in the World Junior Championships as well as talented athletes discovered at the talent ID clinics. It created special supported teams such as "Development" and "X team" that could hold and give athletes time and experience for progress to high performance levels. The talent identification camps attracted a range of athletes who were interested in biathlon and the transition of the IBU's European Cup races into the IBU Cup which provided a place for developing athletes in a sort of "minor league" to the World Cup. Bernd Eisenbichler and the coaches used this level for both development and cleverly, a part of a better trials criteria for the World Championships and Olympic Games. As American athletes began to achieve podium and top-ten results at the IBU Cup, it became their stepping stone to the highest levels. When the Barnes sisters and Erin Graham swept the podium at an IBU Cup race in Switzerland, it became a clear signal to American athletes, showing a pathway to success. All the developing athletes, including Tim Burke, Lowell Bailey and Susan Dunklee gained important experience at the IBU Cup races.

CHAPTER 13

The Coaches

Before the Civil War (1860) the word coach was not even used in connection with games or athletic competition in the United States. Up until that time "coach" was an English term used to describe a private tutor responsible for teaching manners or academic subjects. It was not until the 1870s that the coaching of sport emerged as a specialized profession. The values underlying this new profession were shaped by the growth of organized competitive sports rather than by the field of physical education. The specialized roles of a coach, trainer, and sport physician simply did not exist until physical activities took the form of competitive sport. In other words, the job of a coach has always been to help athletes get ready for competition, and unlike physical education, is it directly related to competition and competitive success.

The first real coaches in the United States were associated with established schools and wealthy private athletic clubs in the New England states. Although coaches were not regarded as a teacher, they were sometimes given academic status in universities and prep schools. This was done so the faculty and administration in those schools could officially keep the athletic programs of the students under their control, but coaches contributed little or nothing to academic programs.

Coaches, along with the trainers who assisted them, became the new management experts in the field of sport and sport competition. As team records and the achievements of individual athletes became more important for the reputations of the sponsoring schools and clubs, the importance and status of coaches increased. Because of their position, coaches have become a significant part of the sport experience.

Most assumptions about coaching tend to view the role of a coach as a technical one; however, there is a big difference between coaching and knowing what to coach. Knowing what should be done for training and practiced, and then executing that in a way that is productive, keeping the athletes active, motivated and improving their skills is the critical issue. The key word is *effective*. After the athlete, the coach is the most important figure in all of biathlon's human resources because that individual is the one who interacts with all levels of the sport. This highly dynamic nature of responsibilities means that human and conceptual skills are equally important as a coach's technical skills.

A dictionary defines a coach as "a person who instructs, directs or trains athletes or athletic teams." Coaches do generally teach techniques, determine training, conduct practices, and develop strategies and tactics. However, a successful coach also serves many other roles and responsibilities and they are far more important than it may seem at first glance. Coaches working with athletes, especially older athletes, often develop close relationships with them over extended periods of time. They can influence their athletes' educational plans, occupational choices and help shape general value orientations. Often coaches become genuinely concerned with the overall well-being of their athleteswho confide in them about personal problems and important decisions. As a result, the impact and responsibility of the coach extends well beyond instructing, training, and directing athletes.

Coaches must be able to understand and manage the inter-relationship of personal and organizational success, goal setting and methods of motivation, problem solving, analytical evaluation and creative decision making. The technical skills including the ability to use the techniques, methods, procedures and knowledge of the sport will be useless if the human skills of dealing effectively with other people are absent. The ability to effectively motivate, communicate and lead individuals and teams to successful outcomes is equally, if not more important. The conceptual skills that are required for planning, coordination and integrating the programs and activities are also important. It is the capacity to find clarity from the abstract, and retain a tolerance for ambiguity, and the ability to withstand confusion until things become clear. It is the ability to conceptualize, organize and integrate different ideas into a coherent frame of reference. It is also the capacity to use intelligence for the abstract but also to be practical and use good judgement, and having the ability of knowing when to act.

Thus, there are three primary aspects of coaching, one that is related to the methods and techniques of training and performance, a second that is related directly to persons and interpersonal relationships and a third that requires the conceptual skills or ability to plan, coordinate and integrate all the interests and activities required for success. To say it differently, effective coaching requires a balance between technical, human and conceptual skills. A critical balance between expertise or skills in working with people and the knowledge of the concepts, methodology and techniques of the sport.

The most frequent path to developing a coach's technical skills comes from participation in the sport. Many coaches were athlete's themselves prior to becoming a coach. This implies that much of the required learning was self-inspired, especially since most athletes seek knowledge and ways of improving their performance as an athlete. Arthur Lydiard, the famous New Zealand running coach acted as his own "guinea pig" in his marathon running before putting to practice his principles of "long distance training" for his successful athletes. Although never a coach himself, Bill Koch was an athlete who was willing to try innovative ideas in his quest to be a faster skier, and his successes led to important evolutions in aspects of equipment and ski technique. It is both through experimentation and formal scientific study that coaches accumulate the technical knowledge of physiology, psychology, biomechanics, recruiting and talent identification, goal setting and motivation, planning and organization of training, instructing and understanding learning, and the skills of leadership that are all essential for successful coaching.

During the early years (roughly 1950s), knowledge of biathlon training and techniques was based on traditional long-held ideas and local trial-and-error methods of the nordic ski environment. The efforts from that period had been developed by coaches and athletes seeking to improve their performances by borrowing methodologies, technical knowledge and practices from other similar sports. When new rules or changes in equipment altered the conditions under which the sport demands, and skills involved were performed, coaches and athletes responded by trying many different techniques and adopted the ones that seemed to produce the best results. In most cases the technique and training methodologies adopted were most often close to the optimum for the demands and skills concerned.

With the introduction of biathlon in the U.S., only a few coaches or athletes had an acceptably sound understanding of the training principles and techniques for the sport. There were also limitations in the ways by which any knowledge could be shared. There were few participants and even fewer competitions. Coaching clinics and literature on training methodology or sport techniques were non-existent. With the introduction of the U.S. Army's biathlon training center and the introduction of foreign coaching, an awareness of better training methodology and sport techniques began to develop. Gradually, from one decade to the next, the value of special training in related sciences was realized and the connection of those sciences to sport was improved. Cooperation between coaches and scientists gradually improved so that knowledge from related physical sciences began to be applied to sport. Two important published works, *Scientific Principles of Coaching*, by John Bunn (1955) and *The Mechanics of Athletics*, by Geoffrey Dyson (1962) introduced the preliminary concepts of sports science.

Hans Wagner can be viewed as the first biathlon-specific coach in the U.S. He was born in Germany where he was a member of Germany's 1928 Winter Olympic team. He emigrated to the U.S. in 1935 and received his citizenship at Ft. Dix, New Jersey. As a First Sergeant in the 10th Mountain Division he served in Italy and Austria and had worked with Colonel Ken Floto on various projects while serving together in the 10th Mountain Division. Following WWII, he was employed as a civilian with the Dept. of the Army in Europe and later in the U.S. as a Weather-Mountain-Glacier instructor and Rescue Chief from 1946 to 1969. In 1957, he was selected to be the first U.S. Army's biathlon coach, a position he held through 1961. After fulfilling many advisory duties with the army, including observing NATO exercises in Northern Norway in the spring of 1968, he retired in 1969. Spending his retirement in Colorado he continued to work part-time for seasonal winter sports establishments and participated in Senior Ski Competitions as well as shooting events.

Assisting Wagner was Captain Arvo Vikström, one of the group of former Finnish Army officers who escaped Soviet capture and joined the U.S. Army, teaching and developing winter tactics, survival skills, and skiing. After serving in Korea and Vietnam he was assigned to the USMWBTC as the rifle coach, but he also had extensive ski experience. In 1961, he was reassigned to the Ft. Leavenworth Military Academy and later to Iran where he was a military advisor, eventually retiring as a Lieutenant Colonel. After both Hans Wagner and Arvo Vikström left the USMWBTC, the army hired Sven Johanson, a native of Sweden who had immigrated to the U.S. in 1951. Sven followed Hans Wagner as the coach with Master Sergeant Marvin Fitzpatrick, a veteran of WWII, Korea and Vietnam and recipient of the Purple Heart, who was reassigned from the U.S. Army Marksmanship Unit in Georgia to Ft. Richardson, to be the shooting coach.

Sven was born in Neder-Kalix, Sweden, one of 10 children who worked on the family farm. At an early age, he and his brothers exhibited extraordinary athletic talent and on one occasion he was to help his brother, one of Sweden's best middle-distance runners, set a new record by pacing him until the final few laps and then dropping out of the race. As the story was told, despite working all day on the farm and riding his bike to town, Sven felt pretty good after the early laps while his brother was having trouble keeping up. So, forgetting his "rabbiting duties" he just kept going. It was Sven who, totally unexpectedly, beat his brother and set the new record. He had finished 4th in the Swedish biathlon championships and held national championship status in four other different sports in Sweden: cross-country skiing, cycling, track and field and speed skating. He arrived in the U.S. in 1951 and in 1955, he won the North American Ski Championships in St. Paul, Minnesota. In 1956, he earned a position on the U.S. Olympic Cross-Country Team but was not allowed to participate because of an administrative error in obtaining his citizenship. In 1957, he won the National Cross-Country Ski Championship in Lyndonville, Vermont. In 1958, he was a member of the U.S. FIS Team, and in 1960 was a member of the U.S. Olympic Cross-Country Team. From 1954 to 1959 he won the famous Mount Marathon race in Seward, Alaska a record six straight times.

Although he had helped Alaskan skiers and even trained with the early Ft.

Richardson biathletes, he became a legend in the biathlon and ski communities after he was hired as a civilian coach for the USMWBTC, where he became the central figure in U.S. Biathlon until the Army discontinued the center in 1973. His coaching philosophy was best described as "old school" in that he felt that winning required harder and more training than the competitors. He had a tremendous impact on the athletes that cycled through the unit and there were many legendary stories about him, such as building the three different sauna buildings at Independence Mines and threatening wayward snowmobilers who were about to destroy his manicured ski trails with one of his athlete's biathlon rifle. In the face of the criticism about not being "real soldiers" that occasionally came from the Ft. Richardson leadership, Sven was a strong advocate for his athletes and would often challenge that criticism by offering to have his athletes compete against the "Artic Rangers" in winter military skills of skiing and shooting, which were naturally never accepted. With the help of his athletes and shooting coach, he authored the first training manual for biathlon. Although "old-school" and sometimes stubborn, he always stayed abreast of the latest training information and brought many innovations to training and trail preparation. He guided many athletes who would later go on to great athletic careers both as skiers and coaches after their departure from the army. He was the coach of the 1964 and 1968 Olympic teams as well as all of the World Championships and CISM Games of that period. In 1975, Sven was the first Alaskan skier to be inducted into the U.S. Ski Hall of Fame and unfortunately met an untimely death at age 51 in an industrial accident in 1976.

Sven had worked with multiple shooting coaches, most coming from the Army Marksmanship Unit from Ft. Benning, Georgia. Master Sergeant Marvin Fitzpatrick was assigned to the USMWBTC when Sven was hired, and coached the team at the 1964 Winter Olympic Games. He left in 1964 when he was replaced by Master Sergeant Clyde Burns. Originally from Brandon, Mississippi, he had served in WWII in the Pacific Theater and was a two-time National Rifle 1,000-yard shooting champion. In 1959, he coached the National Military Championship Rifle Team. Well-liked by the athletes he was assigned to the USMWBTC in 1964 and served as the coach until 1968. He was the coach for the U.S. Olympic Biathlon Team in 1964 and 1968. He collaborated with Sven in writing the technical aspects and training for biathlon marksmanship for the first *Handbook of Biathlon Training*. Retiring from the military he worked as the general sales manager for Alaska Sales and Service, a General Motors dealership in Alaska where he managed the top GM sales dealership for the Northwest Region of the United States. Following his final retirement in 1993 he returned to Mississippi.

For a short period after Burns left the biathlon unit, Richard Barlow was the marksmanship coach, but soon after, Sergeant First Class Arvil Hunter was reassigned to the unit from Ft. Benning. Although he, like Fitzpatrick and Burns was from the south, he was the first marksmanship coach that had prior biathlon experience. He had previously been assigned to the Northern Warfare Training Center at Ft. Greely where he learned to ski and became a ski instructor. After leaving the army for a short period, he returned and was again assigned to Alaska where he applied to become a member of the biathlon training center. In 1966, he qualified for the World Biathlon Championships at Garmisch-Partenkirchen, Germany.

The following year he was assigned to Vietnam where he received the Purple Heart after being severely wounded from a grenade blast. After recovery, he served with the ROTC department at Norwich University in Vermont and then at Ft. Benning, when he was reassigned to the USBA as the marksmanship coach. His previous time at the center as an athlete gave him the unique ability to fully understand the demands and subtleties of biathlon shooting and to teach them to the athletes. He was well-liked by the athletes, especially because both he and Sven defended and protected the athletes from the ongoing and growing criticism among the leadership at USARAL that had even begun to creep into the USMWBTC office staff. It was a time when the army seemed divided between older career soldiers and the massive numbers of draftees who did not appear to fully support the efforts in Vietnam. The career soldiers were seen as "lifers" by the draftees who often appeared less than respectful of them. The career soldiers also frequently appeared to resent the less than "gung-ho" attitude of the athletes who were either junior officers from ROTC programs or draftees that often appeared to have minimal respect of the normal military environment.

That resentment and jealousy eventually saw the reassignment and replacement of the USMWBTC's commander and USMCJ actions against the supply sergeant and operations NCO. Hunter left the USMWBTC in the spring of 1971 for a recruiting post in Mississippi near his hometown and at the USMWBTC 2003 reunion, as the group reminisced, he revealed that he had been suffering from PTSD for many years.

During the final years of the USMWBTC, the army assigned Master Sergeant Lloyd Crow to the shooting coach position. A four-time world shooting champion for running (boar) targets, he immediately understood the difficulties of biathlon shooting. Crow was a very helpful and skilled coach who could detect shooting errors and advise how to correct them with an easy approach that was well received by the athletes. A great storyteller, he often had the athletes suffer bouts of laughter in the hot sauna after training at Independence Mines. An expert shooter himself, he sought to find ways to improve biathlon shooting by subjecting himself to its demands by exercising on the ergometer cycle in the basement range at the biathlon building and then attempting to shoot with a high pulse rate. He even took up skiing. His wide experience also gave him the ability to solve last minute problems during the zeroing just prior to a race, that occasionally required rifle repair work.

After the closure of the USMWBTC there was a series of part-time coaches who were named by the USMPBA to serve during the trials and World Championships. Usually former athletes themselves, Jim Shea was the first. He was named as the 1972 Olympic team coach along with Lloyd Crow and both followed up the next year for the World Biathlon Championships held in Shea's home town of Lake Placid. In 1974 Peter Karns and Bill Spencer were named and served those positions through the 1976 Winter Olympic Games. Although unpaid positions, both Peter and Bill tried to organize some sort of training program and maintain contact with the athletes. Bill was highly respected by the team and had a mild manner and much experience. He also served as the first U.S. member of the UIPMB Technical Committee which gave him excellent connections to the international biathlon community. He was especially helpful during the 1974 season in solving difficulties when there were severe budget shortages that threatened the participation in that year's World Biathlon Championships at Minsk. Bill also had a vibrant relationship with Dieter Anschütz who began manufacturing biathlon rifles in 1976 in anticipation of the change to small bore. On multiple occasions Bill took all the team members' rifles back to the factory to be checked and to be upgraded to any new modifications that had been made. Just before the 1980 Olympic Games he took all the team's rifles to the Cold Weather testing center at Hanover, NH to test both the rifles and ammunition for cold weather performance. By that time, it was known that some rifles and ammunition combinations did not perform well in low temperatures. Bill continued to make many contributions to the development of biathlon as a coach or team leader and as a member of the new U.S. Biathlon Association after its separation from pentathlon. He also served many years on the UIMPB's technical committee.

Ken Alligood served two periods as the U.S. team's coach that were interrupted by a return to competition in anticipation of qualifying for the 1980 Olympic Games. His first period as coach was in the final year of the large bore rules in 1977 that followed his first retirement after the 1976 Olympic trials. He spent only that season as coach and Joe-Pete Wilson was hired as the part-time coach for 1978 when Ken returned to competitive racing. Joe-Pete held the first training camps at the new Olympic Training Center that used the facilities from the 1960 Olympic Games at Squaw Valley. This represented an important step forward in organized and supported training, so long as the athletes could find a way to get there. One of the most important things that Joe-Pete did, with the help of Peter Lahdenpera, was to invite Heikki Ikola, a World Champion and Olympic medal winner and his coach to a training camp with the U.S. team at Squaw Valley. During that training camp, there was a lot of important information exchanged. It also provided the chance to have Ikola and the U.S. athletes compare themselves with a VO2 test. During these tests both the U.S. athletes and Ikola managed to stay on the treadmill for approximately the same time and grade, however Ikola's result was about 10 ml/kg/min higher and he was able to sustain a faster speed on the treadmill. This clearly showed his ability to maintain a higher rate of work through his higher values of VO2 uptake and anaerobic threshold, something that Art Stegen had learned a few years earlier when he was tested at Jyväskylä.

1978 proved to be a pivotal year with the move to small bore rifles and the 50m range. The cold weather problem of the .22 caliber rifles was unknown and advances were coming quickly in skis and equipment. An unfair trials selection procedure hampered Ken Alligood and a few other expected athletes from earning selection to the team that year. In an effort towards increasing domestic partic-ipation the USMPBA Biathlon Committee decided to require athletes to score points through a new scoring system in 6 of 8 possible races across the country. They were required to have at least one race from each of three regions that included the west, mid-west and northeast. The criteria not only forced athletes to fund their own travel to the race sites, but also subjected them to the new point system that appeared to favor some athletes over others. The system was developed in 1977 by Walter Williams and the concept was structured so that racers could be evaluated against each other even when they did not actually race head-to-head. The mechanics of the system averaged the top five racers finish times and their previous race points which had been developed from the racing the previous year, to find a race base for the race which then was divided by each competitor's finish to find a percentage that was converted to points. A problem was soon discovered by the athletes when they saw that each time the top ranked athletes did not finish in the top five ranking for a race their points were lowered. Effectively Ken Alligood and others in the top ten previous season's rankings often received lower points for a second-place finish than for an eighth place, which did appear unfair. Some of the more astute highly ranked competitors also saw a way of manipu-lating the points by dropping out of the race if they thought they would appear to finish behind lower ranked athletes but they still might be in the top five finishers, thereby lowering the race base. This situation appeared to protect the top five ranked athletes if they should not be in the base calculations and deny rewarding a lower ranked athlete for a high finish place. Rusty Scott, Ken Alligood and Art Stegen were essentially impacted by this system as well as the loss of good results when two of the trial races were not counted due to cold weather problems with some rifles. Without yet knowing about this problem, the race jury discarded the two races when the affected targets were thought to be a mix-up of identifica-tion. The cold weather caused great inaccuracy by the bullets that made normal performance impossible and it wasn't until later that it was learned the equipment caused the problem and not the athlete.

Ken Alligood did return to qualify for the team in 1979 and Rusty Scott returned in 1980 for an attempt to qualify for the Lake Placid Olympic team, but Art Stegen retired as a competitor and was hired as the first full-time coach. Art was the coach for the 1979-80 seasons and was hired as the first program director in 1981. Ken Alligood returned to coach the team through the 1982 to 1984 seasons along with Marie Alkire as the shooting coach and first woman to serve as a biathlon coach in the U.S. and international community. Marie had an unusual background for a biathlon coach. "I grew up in Kansas," she said. "I've never really lived where you can ski." So, she "did things little girls in Kansas do, like shoot." Her father, Robert D. Thompson, coached Marie and her sister, Margaret Murdock, in marksmanship. Margaret joined the army and became one of the world's premier shooters, winning a silver medal at the 1976 Olympics. Marie became National Women's Air Rifle Champion in 1975, served as the U.S. shooting team's manager in the late '70s and coached in the National Rifle Association's Junior Olympics program. When the biathlon team began to have its training camps at the newly opened Squaw Valley Olympic Training Center, Bill Spencer invited a few well-known shooting competitors and coaches to speak to the team there and to provide shooting advice during the training. He invited Marie and things just seemed to fall into place for her role in biathlon. Both the men and the newly established women's team showed great improvement in their results and her time with the team resulted in the first World Championships success when the women won the bronze medal at the first World Championships for women in 1984. Marie and Ken Alligood were the 1984 Olympic coaches at Sarajevo. Interestingly Ken had been to Sarajevo in 1980 when he served as the assistant coach at the World Junior Championships held there that year.

Following the 1984 Olympic Games, both Marie Alkire and Ken Alligood resigned and the following summer the athletes began without any specifically named coaches or planned activities. By mid-June Dale Rogers was hired as the USBA Program Director with a wide range of expected responsibilities. Bill Spencer had just retired from the army as the National Guard's coordinator for biathlon was selected as the USBA Development Coordinator. Bill's replacement at the National Guard Biathlon office was Major John Abair. A few training camps were announced and were to be staffed by Spencer and Rogers with help from volunteer coaches and available National Team members. By the fall a number of training camps were held with volunteer coaches and guest speakers, such as Steve Gaskill of the U.S Ski Team, and John Morton of Dartmouth College. Major Abair had begun to expand the National Guard program by organizing regional camps in Wisconsin, California, Utah and Vermont with Bill Spencer and Lyle Nelson as principle instructors. By December the National Team was still without a full-time coach and as a result, Dale Rogers lined up "project coaches" and guest speakers on subjects related to sports science that were helpful for improving performance for the National team's fall training camps and the international competitions. Tracy Lamb of Lake Placid and Dave Logan from Harrisburg, PA handled the initial responsibilities.

Plans to hire a full-time coach by January 1st, 1985 went unfulfilled. After the team trials were moved to Valcartier, Canada, due to the lack of snow at Lake Placid, a team was named, and the staff of Bill Spencer, John Engen and Troy Baker were selected to be the team leader, ski coach and rifle coach. Chuck Lyda and Charlie Hostetler, from Alaska were to later join the group for the women and junior teams that were held separately from the Senior World Championships. Both Jon Engen, who finished 2nd in the National Championship sprint race and Chuck Lyda had participated in the trials but did not qualify for the team. Jon was from Rælingen, Norway where he started skiing as a toddler, and his first competition was at the age of 5 and in a ski jumping competition. After immigrating to the U.S., he settled in Bozeman, Montana, where he had a lot of success in ski racing, but not in high school or college. In the mid-1980s, familiar with biathlon, he purchased a rifle and began to participate in biathlon races just as there was growing development and activity by the U.S. program in the Bozeman and Jackson, Wyoming areas. When asked why he started doing biathlon he responded, "I had previous knowledge of and affinity to the sport." Interestingly Jon later became a member of three Olympic teams, one for cross-country skiing and two for biathlon. Bill Spencer credited Jon for "quickly picking-up on the new skating technique" that impacted skiing and surprised the team that year at the World Championships, and he helped to incorporate it into the training and racing strategy. Years later he commented that biathlon is "an awesome sport" and for him "pursuing the dream" and "being with the best people you could ever find and chasing the Olympic dream" were his best memories. He characterized his time spent with biathlon by saying, "we were a developing amateur team in a more advanced circuit and we made strides one step at the time." He was a member of the 1988 Winter Olympic team for cross-country and the 1992 and 1994 team for biathlon. Jon later spent 14 years on the BOD of the USSA, 12 years as national chairman for U.S. cross-country as well as numerous involvements in coaching, industry, sports leadership and organizational work in USSA, U.S. Olympic Alumni, Special Olympics and local organizations. He also felt that "U.S. Nordic Sports have for a host of good reasons made incredible progress in the last decade and a half. The paradigm has shifted, we are a power to be reckoned with, and U.S. Biathlon is a big part of it."

In May of 1985 the USBA Board approved the hiring of a full-time coaching staff and selected Jim Young of Tabernash, Colorado as the team's coach. He had been the U.S. Ski team's Domestic Development Coach prior to taking the position with the biathlon team. During the summers between 1981-84 he had also been the U.S. Sailing team's coach. Joining him was Sigvart Bjontegaard from Elverum, Norway. Sigvart had been a top-level racer in Norway and after receiving his coaching certifications from the Norges Idrettshogskole (Norwegian Sports Institute) he worked as the National Junior Biathlon coach there. His first training camp with the U.S. team was in September of 1985 at Lake Placid. In his first assessment of the U.S. athletes he felt that their shooting skills were good but that they needed to work on improving their ski technique which had completely transitioned to skating. Sigvart's arrival seemed to energize and coincide with much progress in the development of biathlon in all areas of activity in the U.S., with the National Guard holding its first officials and trainers seminar's and having athletes participate in the Camp Perry National Shooting matches. Jim Young held a few well-attended junior camps and there appeared to be growing organizational efforts in state and local programs with New York taking the lead role on a state-wide basis.

One of Sigvart's most important immediate contributions was that of creating a culture of expectations and success. He did this by focusing on and evaluating performance, which was something that Art Stegen had begun earlier. Looking at the ski speed, range times and shooting averages was a method that provided athletes a more productive feedback. Of the two important types, knowledge of performance was more valuable than simple knowledge of results which allowed them to understand the relationship between the two and to develop goals and expectations as well as focal points for training and improvement. Although average ski speeds and range times as well as shooting averages are subject to variations due to conditions, it is similar to batting averages in baseball where hitters are always facing different pitchers and types of pitches, but regardless, the best averages are still valuable indication of the best performers. As the coaches improved the feedback to athletes, they showed improvements and began to develop better goals and expectations. This led to an impressive step forward in their performances evidenced by Josh Thompson's silver medal performance at the 1987 World Championships, and despite his disappointment in Canmore, the 1988 World Cup season ended with three men and six women attaining World Cup points with Josh topping the group at 17th place in the overall standings with 73 points. Both Josh and Curt Schreiner raced in 11 of the possible 12 World Cup events with Curt finishing 55th and Lyle Nelson capping his biathlon career at 76th place. For the women, out of a field of 51 women earning points, Patrice Jankowski was 18th with 86 points from six races. Pam Nordheim was 22nd, Nancy Bell 23rd, Joan Smith 25th, Mary Ostergren 32nd and Julie Newnam 33rd.

Following Sigvart's departure after the 1988 Olympic Games, the National team went once again without a designated full-time coach. The team was on its own during the summer of 1988. Lyle Nelson retired and some of the athletes were taking some time away from the sport. There was a lot of second-guessing about the disappointing results in Canmore and with a poor snow winter, a team of only three men and two women were chosen to participate in the World Championships at Feistritz, Austria that year. A lot of momentum of the previous two years seemed lost. Dennis Donahue took up the coaching duties and the National Guard continued its development towards a stronger program after hosting the CISM Games at Jericho for the first time. The National Guard had at first named Peter Hoag and Rob Powers as athletes-coaches, but then got the positions approved as full-time coaches with Steve Hall, one of California's team members from the Air National Guard taking the place of Rob Powers. Peter Hoag retired from the competitive aspect and accepted the full-time coaching position. Leo Girouard became the operations NCO for the Guard program.

The letdown after the 1988 Winter Olympics lasted only into the summer of 1990 when things appeared to turn around. One important event that summer was the invitation for three 1984 Olympic biathlon medalists, Algis Shalna of Lithuania, Matthias Jacob of East Germany and Walter Pichler of West Germany to spend a month touring the U.S. together as guests of the 1990 Kingsbury Summer Biathlon Series. Summer biathlon had grown rapidly, and they were recruited to help promote the running and shooting events that were scheduled across the country. Lyle Nelson was the driving force behind its rapid expansion and after the recent political changes in the Soviet Union and reunification of Germany, and with Bill Spencer's international role with the UIPMB technical committee, he made the extraordinary effort to bring the three to the United States. Not long after that visit, Walter Pichler was hired as the U.S. National Team coach to work with Dennis Donahue, having the responsibility for designing, implementing, and monitoring the National Team's training program while Dennis was to devote more attention to developing regional programs. In January of 1991 Algis joined Walter as an assistant to coach the National Team and later in the spring of 1992 they were hired as the National Team's coaches.

Walter Pichler was born in Bad Reichenhall, Germany and spent his early years in Ruhpolding where he began skiing and eventually getting involved with biathlon. Walter's uncle Claus was the local mayor and one of those responsible for developing Ruhpolding as one of the biathlon's annual World Cup premier events. He grew up in a family of woodcutters and together with his cousin Wolfgang, who was also a renowned biathlon coach, organized a biathlon club in their hometown. He had his best competitive years as a member of the West German (Federal Republic) team in the mid-1980s, winning an Olympic bronze medal in the relay in 1984 and a bronze at the 1985 World Championships in

Ruhpolding. In 1986, he was German Champion in the 10km sprint event. When he took over the responsibilities for the U.S. National team, the USBA Board of Directors had made the decision to provide centralized training at the U.S. Olympic Training Center at Lake Placid. Walter immediately set about to transform the U.S. team's training and approach to the sport, looking to develop a more professional and committed approach by the athletes. After initial acceptance by the athletes, gradual resistance to his rather autocratic leadership and blunt assessments of ability and more importantly, his tendency to "pick the winners before the races" began to weaken his support. These particular issues came to near crisis level during the 1992 Olympic team trials at Lake Placid when one of the athletes everyone expected to qualify for the team did not, and he made an effort to replace an athlete who had successfully qualified by the criteria with the one who hadn't. It led to some difficult discussions and the potential of creating a rather unfortunate situation involving athletes' rights. Voiding the trials criteria would have certainly led to legal complications. Walter later shifted to the title of women's coach where he had great success with some of the women, however ongoing issues of Walter's tendency to want to "select" the athletes he would work with and discount the potential of others eventually developed serious frustrations and ultimately to his departure from the program.

Algis Shalna grew up in Ignalina, the winter capital of Lithuania. He first started skiing in 1969 while in the 3rd grade at the local sport school and skied there through his middle and high school years. He first began biathlon during his first year in college in 1978 where he also ran cross-country. Lithuania was a part of the Soviet Union during those years and after taking 4th place at the USSR Junior Championships he was promoted to the Soviet development team in 1980. Two years later he became a member of the national team and finished 4th in the individual race at Sarajevo and was a member of the Soviet team that won the gold medal in the relay. He studied at the Institute of Physical Culture in Lithuania's second largest city of Kaunas, which is today known as the Lithuanian Sports University where he earned a degree as a physical education teacher and biathlon coach. After failing to qualify for the Soviet Calgary Olympic team he retired the following spring and was hired to be the USSR's women's national team coach responsible for shooting. He went to all world cups and world championships in 1989 and at Feistriz his team won two gold medals and several other podium places. With two young children at home, he left the position due the extensive travel and became a program director for the local military sport club. After the dissolution of the Soviet Union and Lithuanian independence he was named as the vice president of the Lithuanian Biathlon Association before he took the position of U.S. National Team coach in the spring of 1991. In 1992, he became the coach for the men's team. After the departure of Walter Pichler in 1997 he became the head coach for both the men's and women's team.

The hiring of Walter and Algis as the national team coaches was a highly anticipated step forward for the U.S. Biathlon community. That, along with the centralized training concept for Lake Placid, appeared to change the dynamics, however the excitement began to gradually diminish when some of the athletes began to feel uncomfortable with the restrictive nature of centralized training and somewhat autocratic style of the coaches. There appeared to be a certain degree of a cultural conflict between the expectations of the European coaches and their methodology and those of some of the athletes. Some fully embraced the European methodologies and limited social structure of the centralized training environment while others began to struggle with it. Probably the biggest cultural misunderstanding was the athletes' need to know the goals and reasons, and the "why" behind their training sessions, which was often seen by the coaches as a questioning of their authority and knowledge. Explaining the goals of learning are from early school days routinely given to American children and thus when what seemed to some as commands to "do this training" did not meet this expectation, some athletes became rebellious and unwilling to embrace the "system" that the coaches were trying to establish. Some also felt they were beyond the fundamental skills that the coaches were trying to re-establish and became critical of the coaching efforts. At the same time the National Guard program became more successful and financially able to provide training opportunities unavailable to the national training program. That caused professional jealousy to creep into the relationships, despite efforts to work together. Eventually Walter Pichler left and Algis gradually began to understand the cultural subtleties with the help of his own children who were assimilating into the American culture at school. Following the 2006 Winter Olympic Games, Algis asked to step down to a development role and was named the U.S. Biathlon Development coach working out of Jericho, Vermont where he has continued develop many successful younger athletes.

Faced with the discontentment of some athletes and frustrations that had developed over the methodologies of the European coaching, which coincided with the USBA's 1994 Strategic Plan for International Success, Algis stepped down as the men's coach to focus on junior development and worked with junior coach Cory Salmela. Cory had initially started working as a biathlon coach after a brief period as a competitor in 1989, and in 1991 he became an assistant coach to Willie Carow at the USOEC at Northern Michigan University. He was later hired to be USBA's National Race Series director and domestic coordinator for the 1992 season. In 1993 he was promoted to the development coach. He, with Algis served as a junior coach after the Strategic Plan eliminated funding for the National Race Series and the two led the junior team to their first successful results with Jay Hakkinen's gold medal performance at the World Junior Championships at Forni Avoltri, Italy in 1997. Algis moved back up to become the National Team coach in 1998 and Cory continued as the designated National Junior team coach.

Cory was initially attracted to biathlon following a visit by Dennis Donahue and Walter Pickler to Giant's Ridge. They were conducting a junior talent search. Cory and his brother Chad attended the clinic and then began biathlon racing. After the 1989 season Cory became increasingly interested in the physiological aspects of ski racing and turned his attention to learning all he could in that area. More successful, Chad continued biathlon racing while Cory convinced the local Mesabi Junior College in Virginia, Minnesota to start up a ski team with Cory as its coach. He also spent time at Bend, Oregon, working with John Underwood, who had served a short time as the women's coach but was better known for his work at the Central Oregon Community College and coaching individual athletes, Beth Coats and Rob Rosser. Underwood had spent time in Finland studying the physiological aspects of endurance training and had applied that knowledge to the athletes he was coaching. After Cory completed his degree at the University of Minnesota at Duluth, he began working at the USOEC at NMU and then with the U.S. Biathlon Association together with Algis Shalna until 1998. It was during that time, Jay Hakkinen won the Junior World Championships gold medal for the sprint in 1997. After assuming the role as the junior team coach, he recruited a number of volunteer coaches and developed well-supported teams for the Junior World Championships that included Bernd Eisenbichler's first efforts as a wax-technician. In 2003 Lanny Barnes won the silver medal in the individual race and together with her sister and Tracy and Carolyn Treacy, they won silver medals in the junior women's relay at the Junior World Championships at Ridnaun, Italy.

When Cory took the position of the National Junior coach he discovered many of the problems of recruiting and developing a junior program. As a non-sponsored high school sport in the U.S., and a low public awareness, biathlon is a hard sport for recruiting young athletes. Most of any junior development is at club levels in areas where there is a Nordic ski presence. Cory made good contacts with the high school coaches in Minnesota and elsewhere by assuring them that he was not trying to "steal their athletes" but wished to help them become better skiers and show them other options. One of the things he first tackled was the lack of any consistency or a planned program for recruiting and training juniors. At the time, the USOC as one of their "markers" for funding, required all sports to develop a Coaches Education Program, and since Art Stegen had already written two National Guard pamphlets (VT 350-10 Training for Biathlon and VT 350-11 Coaching Biathlon) the USBA president at the time, Don Edwards tasked Art and Cory to develop a USBA Coaches Education program that would meet the USOC funding benchmark. Cory and Art created a three-level program that included recruiting, coaching methodologies, tasks and standards, and supporting materials that was suitable for computer learning. With the help of the USOTC physiologist, Ken Rundel, Cory also developed a series of physical tests to screen and evaluate the potential of juniors that he invited to junior "try-biathlon" camps. His efforts began to give some consistency to recruiting and coaching as it was gradually shared among the biathlon community. Cory also played a key role in coaching his wife Kara, a member of the National Guard, which resulted in her qualification to the 2002 Olympic team and a silver medal performance at the 2003 CISM Games. He was also the FISU coach to the 1997 Winter Games at Jeonju, Korea where Rachel Steer won two medals.

After Cory Salmela left the program and Algis Shalna had stepped down to serve as the developmental coach, Swedish coaches Per Nilsson and Mikael Lofgren were hired to take over the National Team duties in June of 2006. The pair of Swedes had worked together in Sweden for several years where Per was the coach of biathlon and skiing at the sports academy in Solleftea and had previously worked for one year at the Maine Winter Sports Center. He had been identified in Sweden as a top candidate to be the National Team Coach after 2010 but instead took the position in the U.S. He had worked hard to create a system of athlete development in Sweden and was known for his passion for excellence and hard work. Mikael Lofgren had been coaching biathlon and skiing at the sports academy in Torsby, Sweden and was a double Olympic bronze medal winner from the 1992 Olympic Winter Games and overall World Cup Champion in 1992-93. He was widely regarded as one of the best biathlon shooting coaches anywhere in the world. Together these coaches had impressive knowledge, experience and passion that everyone hoped would lead to improved international results. They assembled their first training camp in July at Lake Placid, and were well received by the athletes, with the camp focused on evaluating the strengths and weaknesses of each athlete and developing individual training plans. They then planned the summer's training that included competition in the Swedish rollerski races in Östersund which would host the World Championships in 2008 and began to integrate their program with the newly hired ski service chief, Bernd Eisenbichler for skiing and ski testing at the new ski tunnel in Torsby, Mikael's hometown. It was also during this time when the USBA scheduled a summer roller-ski festival at Jericho that became a traditional part of the summer training, attracting the best U.S. athletes from across the country. Mikael left after two years to return to Sweden, and Armin Auchentaller of Italy was hired to replace him.

Vladimir Cervenka was hired as the junior coach filling the position left vacant by long-serving Cory Salmela's resignation. From the Czech Republic, Vladimir had previous coaching experience with some smaller European teams and then was hired by the MWSC and later as the University of Colorado ski coach before taking a position with the Mt. Itasca Biathlon Club in Coleraine, Minnesota. Mt. Itasca had built an impressive biathlon complex at the local ski hill and wanted to staff it with full-time coaching. Vladimir would continue to coach at Mt. Itasca along with his USBA Junior Team responsibilities. At the same time James Upham, a former competitor and member of the junior team was hired as an additional development coach, and he would share his responsibilities with the Maine Winter Sport Center with support shared by the MWSC and the USBA. Algis Shalna remained as the development coach working out of the National Guard's facility at Jericho, along with the Ethan Allen Biathlon Club's coaches. It was clear that by 2006, and the hiring of nearly a completely new coaching and team support staff, that a new sense of excitement was created.

The women's team had a coach of their own for the first time in 2010. Jonne Kähkönen who had spent the previous four years as the head coach of the Finnish biathlon team was hired to be the women's national team coach. He joined the team's international staff, who were from Sweden, Italy, the Czech Republic, and Germany. Having become the director of sport, Bernd Eisenbichler told *Faster-skier.com*, "We knew that if we wanted to build up a strong women's program, we needed to have a dedicated coach for them. Really just focused on their development and putting the group together to make it a really good environment." Jonne worked along with the men's coach, Jonas Johansson of Sweden, who took over from Per Nilsson and Mikael Lofgren. Per continued in a part-time basis and returned full time for the 2018 Olympic season. In 2009, the U.S. women were ranked 20th in the World Cup's Nations Cup standings. In the eight years Jonne guided the team, they had numerous top-20 performances from multiple athletes, World Youth and Junior Championships flower ceremonies, and World Cup podiums and a World Championships silver medal by Susan Dunklee. Annelies Cook, who retired in 2016 told *Fasterskier.com*, "I think that having a women's coach changed something in the heart of the women's team, because it felt like a validation that we were improving and deserved someone that was there specifically for us. He was always positive for us, and that is something you really need in a sport that can really get you down sometimes. Biathlon is different from cross-country skiing in where the differences in performances from day to day don't change that drastically. Biathlon can change instantly from good to bad, and that can be really emotional sometimes."

In May of 2018 the USBA announced two new coaches for the National Team. Armin Auchentaller of Antholz, Italy, who had worked five years with the U.S. team from 2009-2014 returned to the team after coaching the Swiss women's biathlon team for several years, and the German Olympic champion Michael Greis, who also worked for the Swiss biathlon team had joined the U.S. team as the men's head coach. Armin would take over from Jonne Kähkönen for the women's team and Michael would be responsible for the men's team. Jean Paquet and Algis Shalna would continue in their positions and for the first time two new members of the sport development staff were added. Retiring athlete Tim Burke would serve as athlete development manager and Danika Frisbie as sport program manager. Tim would be responsible for leading efforts to increase the quality of training and performance for developing athletes and clubs across the U.S., including youth and junior elite athletes, post-collegiate athletes, and existing and aspiring coaches and program leaders. He would be the main interface between USBA and regional coordinators and clubs, facilitating stronger collaboration in creating more competitive opportunities for developing athletes. Working closely with Danika, who competed in biathlon as a junior and has held various coaching positions since, including being the U.S. Biathlon coach intern since June 2017, would focus USBA initiatives and resources on strategic development goals. Danika, as the sport program manager, would be responsible for promoting the sport by supporting development of programs and events to increase athlete-coach participation and engagement in the sport. She would also be responsible for sport education resources, organization of domestic racing events and festivals, and establishing regular communications to members, athletes, and coaches. Danika would also serve as a coaching assistant supporting national and development team training and work with National Team staff, including Jean Paquette, Algis Shalna and Tim Burke, to plan and execute strategic development goals.

When Max Cobb became the USBA Executive Director after the reorganization of the Association, he saw the value of Bernd Eisenbicler's passion and at first, Bernd was just waxing skis; then, he oversaw stone-grinding and waxing; then he was put in charge of some team logistics. Eventually he became high performance director and chief of sport. Since that time, the team went from a mediocre 'also-ran' to one of the best. That success is largely due to Bernd's role and his tireless drive to win by out-maneuvering instead of out-spending. He assembled a coaching team from Sweden, Finland, and Canada, a service team that included Germans, Czechs, and an Italian, and brought in a shooting advisor from Austria, and of course, Americans. They all worked very hard towards one goal, over nearly a decade for some of the staff members. Bernd told Susan Dunklee that his goal was to see someone on the team bring home an Olympic gold medal, but that he would eventually gauge his work with the team as successful if in 20 years the team and staff decide to travel to Munich for an Oktoberfest reunion together.

CHAPTER 14

The Administrators and Organizers

At the heart of the U.S. Biathlon's mission and goals is the athlete. It is with the results of those participating individuals that success is measured. At the core of the program are the activities designed to achieve success and for any organization success is dependent upon having sound plans, the required resources and using them effectively. Those resources can be divided into three categories; human, financial and physical. The U.S. Biathlon Association's human resources are its people, including the athletes, coaches and its administrators and organizers who share the goals and aspirations of success. This includes all the individuals, staff and volunteers with the knowledge, skills and abilities that perform all the necessary activities in a manner that contribute to the success of the athletes.

The basis of all actions within the U.S. Biathlon community is to produce winning results that will satisfy the aspirations of its participants and the needs of its supporters. The community exists because its members have common interests which interact, are dependent on each other and create satisfaction in some way. At the heart of biathlon is the athlete, however it isn't the athlete alone who is responsible for the outcomes. Any success is only possible when the athlete is supported by the organization, including having the right facilities and equipment, financial resources, coaching and guidance. Quite often when the conditions aren't so perfect, or there are "hiccups" in the race organization such as problems with the results or target malfunctions, course misdirection or unexpected problems that impact a race, the athletes can be heard to complain about "they," such as "they don't know what they're doing." When travel gets disrupted or there is a problem with hotel accommodations or food, it is again the "they" that get blamed. But who are "they" exactly? It is those who have the responsibilities for planning and arranging races, who are the directors, administrators, team leaders, coaches and volunteers who make the decisions of "what, when, who, where and why" as well as "how" biathlon programs operate from the entry and developmental levels to the high performance international levels.

The initial organizational efforts for biathlon can be attributed to General Omar Bradley when he gave official organization structure to military competitions when he officially established the ISSC in February 1948. The initial efforts of establishing biathlon were taken by the U.S. Army at Camp Hale and it can be said that Colonel Erkki Lahdenpera was the advocate for the development of biathlon skills among the soldiers stationed there. Although his motivation was military training, he was aware that Finland's historic sports personality Lauri Pihkala's efforts towards establishing biathlon racing and the training effect of those biathlon skills had a profound impact during Finland's wars with the Soviet Union. While at Camp Hale he introduced cross-country ski races and biathlon skills among the troops for more appropriate winter tactical training. Even as a company commander he created and participated in biathlon-like training events. At one such exercise, soldiers marched 6 miles to a shooting range and then fired at targets that had a potential score of 100, which was followed by a mile race to the finish. Lahdenpera participated in the exercise himself, shooting a score of 96 and finishing 4th overall. Although not in any formal sense, he and others like MSG Brown at Ft. Greely and later at Dartmouth College helped to develop an informal framework that got things started. Colonel Donald Woolley, the commanding officer of the Cold Weather Training Command then took the next steps by organizing the first U.S. Biathlon competition in December 1956. His analysis that biathlon encompasses the two main characteristics required of a soldier who fights in snowy conditions; being not only a good skier but also a good marksman, and this fulfills the requirements for a first-rate biathlon competitor. He wrote in the December issue of the *American Rifleman* magazine; "The tie-in with military training and the biathlon is obvious and it is hoped the Army will continue to support and encourage this event."

The steps taken by the U.S. Army at Camp Hale and Colonel Donald Woolley were the catalyst of turning Colonel Erikki Lahdenpera's ski training exercises into official competition by organizing the first biathlon race held at Camp Hale in 1956. From 1958 to 1973, biathlon was totally managed and supported by the military and had a training center at Ft. Richardson, Alaska. This was a natural result of the military origins of the sport and its international governance. During that time, there were no domestic races or development of athletes outside the military environment at the USMWBTC in Alaska. The military appointed the directors, or commanders of this training center and hired or assigned the coaching staff, either from the civilian ski community or the U.S. Army's Marksmanship Training Unit. George Wilson, who was the secretary and then president of the United States Modern Pentathlon and Biathlon Association from 1961 to 1980 and the manager of the sports programs for the U.S. Army and Department of Defense from 1946 to 1980 played a major role in the administration of the USMWBTC during the time of its duration.

With the introduction of international military ski competitions, Colonel

Woolley's hopes were realized when the U.S. Army whole-heartedly embraced biathlon and created the organizational structure and assembled qualified candidates for biathlon training at Ft. Richardson, Alaska. The U.S. Army's Modern Winter Biathlon Training Center was initially staffed by Colonel Ken Floto, and coaches Captain Arvo Vikstrom and Hans Wagner. Each of these individuals had experience with the military applications of skiing in winter warfare, Floto and Wagner knew each other as members of the 10th Mountain Division and Vikstrom, a native of Finland was one of the 40 Finnish soldiers who were involved in the Weapons Cache Case. Colonel Floto had helped set up the Garmisch Recreation Area right after WWII and coached the USAREIR to 1-2 finishes in the championships. He did a second tour of duty in Garmisch from 1956-59. After his assignment to head up the USMWBTC, Floto became very active in trying to recruit skiers into the new training center in Alaska by not only visiting Ft. Greeley looking for skiers but also contacting college skiers who were identified by those already at the center. Colonel Floto was especially passionate about his role in building the biathlon program at Ft. Richardson. In an article written shortly after his success in encouraging a few collegiate skiers to join the army for skiing he said, "they were the first of what I hoped would be a flood of dedicated young skiers who want to join the army biathlon unit. It is possible now for interested men to join the army specifically for biathlon training. They must take the normal basic training first, but if they meet the qualifications for biathlon training they will then be assigned to the training center at Ft. Richardson. To do this they must write to the commanding general of the United States Army, Alaska expressing their interest in enlisting for U.S. Modern Winter Biathlon Training Center and listing their experience and qualifications." He was also very proactive in getting the athletes training at the center to European competition and in 1961 and 62, with Sven Johanson as coach, he took extended training and competition tours to Scandinavia where the athletes achieved surprising results.

Over the years of its presence the USMWBTC was staffed by a series of army commanders who were passionate about skiing and biathlon. They included Lt. Colonel Olavi Alakupi, who was a Finnish cross-country skier who competed in the 1930s, winning a gold medal in the 4 x 10km cross-country relay at the 1939 FIS Nordic World Ski Championships in Zakopane. An impressive personality, during the Russo-Finnish Continuation War, he served in the Finnish army, and was awarded the Mannerheim Cross, the equivalent of the U.S. Medal of Honor. In 1945 as one of the famous 40 junior officers he escaped Soviet capture during the Weapons Cache Case by skiing to Sweden and later arranged for his wife Eevi, their son Vesa, and him to travel to the United States where he, like Erikki Lahdenpera and Arvo Vikstrom, joined the United States Army. As a company commander in West Germany in the 1950s he had Elvis Presley as his driver. Following an assignment in Korea he was sent to Alaska in 1961 and later assigned as the commander of the USMWBTC and was the team leader for the 1964 Olympic biathlon team.

After Lt. Colonel Alakupi left, Major Norman Helinski was assigned the position of the USMWBTC commander and although he lacked the prior experience of his predecessors, his limited experience was not a handicap. He embraced his role and made an important contribution in supporting and aiding Walter Williams in establishing a National Championships for biathlon in 1965. However, even from the beginning of the USMWBTC it was the next higher level in the biathlon bureaucracy that made many program decisions of the Army's biathlon program. That control came through both the office of George Wilson, who was the deputy sports director for the Department of Army and secretary of the U.S. Modern Pentathlon Association in Washington and the local leadership at Ft. Richardson. At Ft. Richardson Colonel Donald Rubottom, the G-3 or logistic officer, helped to expand the USMWBTC. He served in the army from 1941 to 1972 and participated in the Battle of the Bulge during World War II and the Chosin Reservoir campaign during the Korean War. He attended the University of Nebraska, where he was a member of the football team that played in the 1941 Rose Bowl. George Wilson was also the USMPBA representative on the USOC Board of Directors and chairman of the Olympic Biathlon Committee. As the president, he was a major influence behind the development of biathlon and the guiding influence for integrating biathlon into the USMPBA. In the late 1970s and 1980, along with Walter Williams, he helped to separate the sports into two separate governing bodies.

Walter Williams became an important key figure in the development of biathlon, its transition and recognition into an independent national sports organization. As the major influence behind the Rosendale Nordic Ski Club, he encouraged biathlon participation and held biathlon races regularly at Williams Lake. His interest began when his son, Edward, was assigned to the USMWBTC following graduation from Dartmouth College in 1964. Walter had been associated with skiing ever since the 1930s when he participated in the Telemark Ski Club races held at his father's resort hotel in Rosendale, New York. Learning more about biathlon from Ed's participation in Alaska, Walter proposed holding the first U.S. National Biathlon Championships at Williams Lake, the resort his father had developed and later owned and operated by him. His proposal was accepted by George Wilson and Major Helinski. Without any sanctioning authority, biathlon was technically outside the control of the National Ski Association and had been administrated by the U.S. Army. Without any real sanctioning guidance Walter started from the beginning by organizing and developing the infrastructure for what would become an annual National Championships by bringing together various interested parties, which highlighted the need to develop a guiding authority for the sport. Once the National Ski Association declined to accept biathlon under its control, Walter saw the sport as primarily military and became involved with the USMPA as a member of its board of directors. The USMPA was the organizational authority for pentathlon, another military sport and as the UIPMB was the international governing body for the two, it seemed logical to follow the same path in the U.S. and the USMPA accepted authority for biathlon as the USMPBA.

When the Army's decision to discontinue the USMWBTC, Walter began an effort to fight that decision but ultimately failed. He then was instrumental in supporting the Vermont National Guard's interest and working on solutions to transfer the equipment from the USMWBTC to the National Guard. Soon after, he recognized the need for independence from the USMPBA and worked on developing a strategy and the path towards an independent U.S. Biathlon Association. Together with Howard Buxton of the National Guard and his son Edward who worked on the Amateur Sports Act which forced National Governing Bodies for sports to become independent and responsible for only one sport, they effectively achieved the goal of separation from the USMPBA in 1980. Walter's strong interest and advocacy for biathlon continued through the remainder of his life and included many contributions such as securing the 1973 World Championships for Lake Placid in 1972 during the Sapporo Olympic Games against competitive bids from Norway and other European sites. He developed the first USBA race points system and as treasurer of the Association, he managed the difficult and stressful financial situations that were a continual hardship for the young organization. He was an advocate for the athletes and with appreciation for their financial sacrifices, he created a trust fund for junior athletes. Walter was the first person to be inducted into the USBA's Hall of Fame.

Working in cooperation with Walter Williams, Howard Buxton and George Wilson on the financial hardships that faced the biathlon program while still under control of the USMPBA was Peter Lahdenpera. After a long and very successful athletic career that included participation in three Olympic Games, two in which he qualified for both biathlon and cross-country skiing he was elected to be the USMPBA vice president for biathlon. As the owner of a highly successful sports retail business in Colorado he helped to provide team uniforms for the 1974 World Championships team. From 1975 through 1982 he served as the team leader and was instrumental in finding ways to financially and materially support the athletes and the overall programs' goals. Finding a way around the strict amateur athlete rules, he established a "broken-time payment system" whereby the athletes could collect support money that would be channeled through the USMPBA and be withdrawn through a voucher and receipt program for their training expenses.

From the time when the Army discontinued its support for biathlon until the separation of biathlon from the USMPBA it was Howard Buxton who became the most important leadership figure within the biathlon community. When asked to attend a meeting about biathlon by General Reginald Cram, years later he recalled that he didn't know what the word meant and had to consult a dictionary to find out what the meeting was about. Originally tasked to create a biathlon range for training at the Ethan Allen Firing Range at the Vermont National Guard's facilities near Jericho, Vermont, Buxton's role continued to grow through the next few decades, becoming the most influential person within the sport during that period. Easily recognized as a natural leader in 1973, he was tasked with moving the U.S. Army biathlon training facility from Alaska to Vermont. With this, he began a relationship with the sport of biathlon that would last for more than 30 years. He along with Walter Williams guided the establishment of an independent National Governing Body, separate from the USMPBA and continued to develop the National Guard's biathlon program. His National Guard role with biathlon gradually pushed him to the forefront of biathlon growth during the difficult periods of limited funding once outside the military supportive environment. Through his work with the U.S. Biathlon Team, Howard served as the first president of the U.S. Biathlon Association and as a delegate to the U.S. Olympic Committee and the UIPMB. He had the honor of participating as an official in four Winter Olympic games and served as the biathlon chief of competition for the 1980 Olympics in Lake Placid and as the U.S. Olympic Team chef de mission for the 1994 Olympics in Lillehammer, Norway. Howard was also responsible for hiring Max Cobb who would become the next key leadership figure for U.S. Biathlon.

After Howard Buxton, who retired as a brigadier general, was promoted up the chain of command, his replacement as the chief of facilities at the Vermont National Guard was Colonel Alan Nye. Understanding the need to cultivate experience and knowledge and who would continue to lead biathlon development, Buxton had taken great care to include such individuals as Nye to take over after him. Alan was also an army engineer and was keen to turn the Ethan Allen biathlon site into one of the best. Working closely with Colonel John Abair, who was the director of the National Guard program, the two cleverly developed "shovel-ready" plans for the site and then found the resources to turn the plans into projects. Abair also worked at getting military authority for biathlon within the Department of Defense and the legal opinions needed for returning to CISM participation by the National Guard. Building on that effort, came increased funding for Nye's plans for constant improvements at the site at Jericho, Vermont. Those plans were accelerated in 1989 when Jericho hosted its first CISM Games. With each successive hosting of CISM in 1993 and 2001 at Jericho, the site was constantly improved so that it became the most utilized current U.S. Biathlon training site. Like Howard Buxton, both John Abair and Alan Nye also played important roles on the USBA Board of Directors with Nye serving as the vice president and president during the difficult years of USBA funding shortages. When Major General Donald Edwards became the adjutant general of the Vermont National Guard, he too took biathlon as a personal project and served as the president of the USBA and fully supported finding ways to support the USBA. The extensive support staff and budget for the National Guard activities, especially from Vermont and Minnesota where Leo Girouard and Jack Lang organized the annual competitions and training camps together with supportive leadership. They found ways to expand biathlon in all areas, both military and civilian, including athlete support, development of race officials, facilities and programs, yet despite those efforts there was a sense that biathlon needed to develop a stronger civilian base and to that end a stronger financial base rather than dependency on the military.

To achieve stronger financial health the USBA Board of Directors believed that after a few years of leadership by what might have been considered "insiders" it needed to go outside to the corporate world to find a leader that had ties and contacts in the commercial environment that could enhance funding and bring the appearance of greater professionalism. Jed Williamson tried to encourage the Association in that direction, as had the interim leadership of John Morton and Dennis Donahue. This eventually led to hiring Dusty Johnstone who tried his best at creating a more professional environment that had a clearly stated mission and organizational hierarchy in the new office at the USOTC at Lake Placid. He worked hard at establishing long-range plans with coaches' input and emphasis on developing successful athletes. Dusty's efforts were met by some resistance within the various constituencies of the biathlon community and BOD members. Out of the National Guard's influence, and growing athlete frustration with continual shortage of adequate funding, he attempted to hold the board of directors responsible for fundraising. With little success in fundraising by BOD members, mostly because they had no experience, limited contacts or the ability to spend time on fundraising, and with the athletes increasing frustration due to the USOC's changed conditions of athlete support, the environment for success that Dusty had envisioned seemed distant. When the USBA funding share of the budget for administration expenses appeared to continually rise at the expense of athletes, both in high performance and development programs, Dusty appeared increasingly frustrated and became confrontational, which led to his resignation.

Once again, the National Guard became the answer. Major General Donald Edwards, the president of the board of directors, offered to have Steve Sands, the very successful director of the National Guard program to serve as the executive director of USBA. A colonel, Steve Sands came at no cost to the USBA.

The USBA office was moved back to Vermont adjacent to the Vermont National Guard headquarters to an inexpensive office at the former Camp Ethan Allen army base. Steve served with distinction in numerous command and staff assignments throughout his military career and was honored with numerous awards including the Legion of Merit, U.S. Army Meritorious Service Medal with Oak Leaf, and the U.S. Army Commendation Medal. He culminated his career as the National Guard sports coordinator when he was appointed the executive director for USBA.

The strong support and leadership provided by the National Guard during the later 1980s and early 1990s helped the USBA through critical times, however the extended wars in Afghanistan and Iraq began to impact the ability of the National Guard to sustain its biathlon efforts, especially regarding athlete support. Joining the military for its support of biathlon became less attractive and recruiting became a difficult issue. At the same time, after the USBA restructuring of the board of directors, new members on that Board began to have a slow and steady impact on the sport. Most importantly, in February 2005 Larry Pugh of Yarmouth, Maine who was the former chairman and CEO of VF Corp., the largest apparel company in the world (with clothing brands that included Wrangler and Lee Jeans, The North Face, Jantzen and Vans Footwear), was elected chairman of the USBA Board of Directors. The reorganization was encouraged by the re-organization of the USBA Board of Directors and the encouragement of the USOC to have "independent directors" on the board of directors for the National Governing Bodies. Larry was a trustee of the Maine Winter Sports Center, a non-profit economic development foundation that hosted the 2004 Biathlon World Cup in Fort Kent, Maine.

Larry Pugh's professional leadership had an immediate impact on the USBA in its effectiveness and efficiency, and in July 2006 he announced long-time USBA employee Max Cobb as the new executive director, praising his work reorganizing USBA operations and programs, while also transitioning the Association's move from Vermont to Maine. Max, a 1987 Dartmouth graduate, for many years USBA Program Director and more recently the marketing director, was highly respected in both the domestic and international biathlon communities and was a catalyst in the original HPP that saw the U.S. develop internationally competitive athletes including 1997 World Junior Champion Jay Hakkinen, Rachel Steer and World Junior Medalists Lanny and Tracy Barnes. Max also assisted in the development of the newest biathlon facilities in the U.S. including the two in Maine at Fort Kent and Presque Isle, Mount Itasca in Minnesota and the 2002 Olympic venue at Soldier Hollow, Utah. Internationally, he was serving as secretary of the International Biathlon Union (IBU) Technical Committee, was chief of competition for biathlon at the 2002 Salt Lake Olympic Winter Games and later was an international referee at the 2006 Torino Olympic Winter Games.

Max Cobb was originally hired in 1989 to be a domestic race series coordinator with the duties of putting together a series of domestic races and supporting it with aspiring athletes as a "domestic team" in a similar way as the previous attempts of developing a regional race series that included the National Team members. He was then promoted to be a "team manager" in assisting the new National Team coaches hired from Europe in 1990 in addition to his domestic race series responsibilities.

From the time of his first role as a domestic race series coordinator, Max Cobb continued to have an impact on the U.S. Biathlon Association. Demonstrating outstanding administrative skills at every additional role, Max became an exceptional leader not only in the U.S. Biathlon Association but also within the IBU. While at Dartmouth College, Max also studied Olympic Sport Leadership at the Kellogg School of Management. He started working full time with U.S. Biathlon in 1991 and always felt it was a big help to have a close connection with the athletes and the trainers. Max fell in love with biathlon at an early age, but admitted he wasn't very good at the sport. His first contact with biathlon was at high school. John Morton came and talked to his school about their ski team. It wasn't until then that he knew what biathlon was. But his high school ski team got interested in the sport as soon as they heard about it. He entered Dartmouth College in 1983, which at the time was the only college with its own biathlon club. He joined the ski team and was intrigued by his experience at a training camp in October 1983 at Lake Placid where some members of the National Team helped him to shoot. It was during his college days assisting John Morton with the Dartmouth ski team and doing organizational duties with the club that kept him involved.

Max's rise from his days on Dartmouth's club team is impressive. What he thought would be a nice job before graduate school had become a career in one of the world's most popular winter sports. It was not long after Dartmouth that he began working at the U.S. Biathlon Association in the position of domestic race coordinator. It basically involved driving around with targets and a few athletes all over the country, setting them up for a domestic race, with the goal of exposing more people to biathlon and providing a racing opportunity. What was initially planned as a six-month job grew into more when USBA hired German Walter Pichler as National Team coach in 1989. Walter needed support, especially with the language and the limited biathlon program so Max became national team manager, assistant coach and part-time ski technician all at once. In 1992 at Albertville he experienced his first Olympic Winter Games and walking in the opening ceremony committed him to focus on that sport and not go back to grad school as initially planned. He was captured by the sport and the whole Olympic spirit.

He worked as the program director under Dusty Johnstone and Steve Sands until 1999 when he was named the chief of competition for biathlon at the Salt Lake City 2002 Winter Olympic Games. After the Winter Games he went back to the USBA as half-time marketing director and an interlude as part-time executive director of the New England Nordic Ski Association. Being very successful in helping to augment USBA's financial resources he accepted the position as executive director for the USBA in March 2006 after the reorganization of the USBA Board of Directors and moving the USBA's office to Maine. With responsibilities for the operational side of the USBA, care of hiring the staff, finances, insurance, marketing, fundraising and the contact to the U.S. Olympic Committee, his title was later changed to that of president and CEO. Max became the face of the USBA and as such, his interaction with the USOC and the IBU began to have a positive impact. With the excellent guidance from the USBA's chairman of the BOD, Larry Pugh, the USOC reacted to the changes with increases in financial support that resulted in improved results at the international level. The respect that Max developed within the IBU led to his election to the IBU's Technical Committee and eventually as its chair in 2010. He served as the technical delegate at many World Cups and that role at the 2014 Sochi Winter Olympic Games. As head of the Technical Committee, he pushed through comprehensive reforms on qualifying for World Cup, IBU Cup, and championship events. With his experience and as a vocal proponent of anti-doping efforts, criticizing the handling of the Russian doping scandal by the International Olympic Committee and the World Anti-Doping Agency, in 2016 he became the first American elected to the IBU Executive Board as the vice president for sport since the governing body came into being in 1993.

Although some thought Max's election to the executive board was controversial in that it put two North Americans on that level, [Dr. Jim Carrabre, a Canadian who serves as vice president for Medical Issues and lives in Minnesota was the other] most were familiar and appreciated how hard working, fair and independent he was, something that people even within the powerful European group recognized. Despite the elevation to the IBU Executive Board he felt that it actually provided more time to continue his close relationship with the U.S. team, coaches and staff. He told *Fasterskier.com* that, "I'm thinking about sport development in the United States and now really thinking about sport development on the global scale as well." Commenting on his first efforts in his new position, he said, "I'm really, really proud that the IOC accepted our proposal exactly as we presented it and that included more accreditations for biathletes so to have a balance of men and women. So now we have 115 men and 115 women, achieving gender equity." He continued to work hard at strengthening the IBU Cup points system to keep it open to for weaker nations for continued access and opportunity to strengthen their programs. Max's efforts have continued to earn the confidence and trust of his leadership within the IBU and USBA and he has probably been the individual responsible for most of the impressive progress made by the U.S. Biathlon Association and its athletes since joining as the domestic race coordinator more than 25 years before.

Perhaps one of the most important figures in the early development of biathlon in the U.S., Walter Williams organized the first U.S. National Biathlon Championships and charted the path that led the separation from pentathlon and establishment of the autonomous U.S. Biathlon Association.

Seen here at Independence Mines, Sven Johanson became the long-time coach of the U.S. Army Modern Winter Biathlon Training Center at Ft. Richardson. (USMWBTC).

Many of the successful early skiers came from the farms and woods where their hard, physical labor prepared them for their success. Much of the early training methodology attempted to imitate or copy aspects of their lives and the hard work of those champions, as an example of what it took to become a champion. Tales of prior athletes using sledge hammers to beat on rubber tires, imitating wood cutting were thought to be a myth by those of the later USMWBTC years, however this picture of Peter Lahdenpera confirms the early method of strength training.

Peter Lahdenpera heads to a 26th place finish at the 1962 World Biathlon Championships held at Hameenlinna, Finland. Peter's uncle was the Race Chairman for the event.

A time-trial race on Alaska's Eklutna glacier in 1963. From left to right are Charlie Akers, Wayne Flemming, Dean Richardson and Jim Shea.

Participants at the shooting range during the 1964 Winter Olympic Games. Competitor number 23 can be seen with a spare ski tip around his waist for an emergency repair of a broken ski.

The members of the USMWBTC in front of their assigned building at Ft. Richardson in Alaska in 1964.

Charlie Kellogg receives his target number from a range official during the first U.S. National Biathlon Championships held at Rosendale, New York in 1965.

Charlie Kellogg, Bill Spencer, and Ford Hubbard are congratulated by the Rosendale Nordic Ski Club's president William Curran and Catherine O'Leary of the Rosendale Women's Club for their 1st, 2nd, and 3rd places in the first U.S. National Biathlon Championships in 1965. Kellogg and Hubbard had been released from the army and the USMWBTC only a month earlier.

USMWBTC team members in 1965. From left to right, Charles Kellogg, William (Bill) Spencer, Major Norman Helinski, Linwood Bean, and Otto Robsahm.

The Rosendale Nordic Ski Club again hosted the National Biathlon Championships in 1966, but poor snow conditions necessitated moving the event to Lake Placid. Left to right are John Ehrensbeck (2nd place), Ed Williams (3rd place), Bill Spencer (1st place) and Allan Small.

The 1966 U.S. Biathlon team. Left to right: Bill Spencer, Arvil Hunter, Gary Varnum, John Ehrensbeck, Allan Small, Victor Privastsky and Ed Williams.

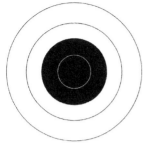

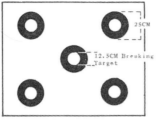

Breakable target for prone
position in relay event

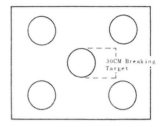

Breakable target for standing
position in relay event

The biathlon target first used at the single 150m range in 1965.

The biathlon target frames used for the relay race in 1966.

The 1968 Winter Olympic Biathlon team boards the airplane on their way to Grenoble, France. Top to bottom are Jon Chaffe, Sven Johanson, Clyde Burns, Jay Bowerman, Ralf Wakely, Bill Spencer and Ed Williams.

Bill Spencer on the ski course during the 1968 Winter Olympics at Grenoble, France.

Coaches Sven Johanson and Master Sergeant Clyde Burns wrote the first comprehensive training guidance for biathlon in 1968.

As shooting coach Arvil Hunter (on the right) readies his list of targets, the team prepares for summer training of running and shooting at the Artic Valley biathlon site.

218

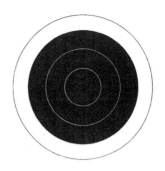

A traditional part of summer training was the annual Mt. Marathon race in Seward, Alaska. At the summit of the climb, coach Sven Johanson and George Tuthill take a moment to enjoy the view.

In 1970 the aiming area of the target was expanded however the scoring rings remained the same for the one- and two-minute penalties.

John Hall, fondly known as the "Frogman," on the shooting range at Independence Mines. Susan Stegen, who, along with other wives often visited on Friday afternoons for some skiing and to give their husbands a ride back to Ft. Richardson.

The CISM Games were held in the unusual location of Lebanon twice. Seen here with the famous cedar trees in the background are (left to right) Dennis Nelson, Scott Leake, Mike Devecka, Art Stegen and Dave Bristol.

The 1972 Olympic team achieved impressive results at Sapporo with a 6th place relay finish and equaling the all-time best individual finish of 14th place finish by Peter Karns. Holding the flag in front is Dennis Donahue with (left to right) Dexter (Terry) Morse, Peter Karns, and Jay Bowerman in the second row, John Morton in the 3rd row and Jim Shea, Bill Spencer and Lloyd Crow in the last row.

The 1973 World Championships team at Lake Placid was the first to include U.S. juniors. Seen here are (from the bottom, left to right) Marvin Macabe, Dennis Donahue, Ken Alligood, John Morton, George Tuthill, Art Stegen, Jay Bowerman, with Peter Karns, Rusty Scott and Martin Hagen at the top.

PART III.

"What Does It Take?"

In their book, *Ski Cross-Country*, authors M. Michael Brady and Lorns O. Skjemstad describe "training" as any "physical activity that improves or maintains physical ability." However, any physically demanding sports competition such as biathlon implies much more serious training efforts, or the techniques and behavior practiced, to improve performance. By imposing the human body to patterns of activity and controlled stresses, strength, endurance and coordination are improved. But what every athlete and coach would like to know, and perhaps preventing rivals from knowing, is what methods and duration of training are most effective.

Long before champion athletes begin training and reaching the podium steps where a medal is placed around their neck many prerequisites are necessary. The first of these is having the inherent abilities or talent, the right genetics, intellectual ability, personality, health and motivation to reach that success. Ideally these athletes come from a ski background with well-developed physiologies and intuitive abilities to solve and understand, without much thought, the complex mechanics of skiing and shooting. The other most important things are providing those athletes with the right opportunities, or the correct environment for participation in training and competition and offering them the right guidance through coaching, planning, direction and support for their training.

Although training for sport has become very specific and complex in the last century, a professional trainer and sport-specific training was a part of ancient Greece. Often the trainer, or coach had been champions themselves, like Iccus of Tarentam who won the pentathlon at Olympia during the fifth century BC. He is said to have been the first to write a book on training, but unfortunately it has not survived. It was the trainers like Iccus and modern-day coaches and physiologists that developed training plans and methodologies for athletes that have over the last century enabled the high performance levels of today's standards. They knew that diet was important and ensured that the athlete's day was taken up by eating, sleeping and training. They also appreciated the importance of psychology in winning races, identifying the 'ideal' athlete as one able to face hard work, possessing a healthy lifestyle and who was rarely ill, recovering quickly from stress.

At the turn of the last century when ski competitions first began to emerge, the most successful athletes came from the farms and woodlands where the hard, physical labor prepared them for their success. Most followed those early champions by imitating or copying aspects of the successful champions' lives and routines as an example of what it took to become a champion. Because of the daily labor of a woodsman or farmer, the general training was not excessively strenuous, frequent, or specific. The fact that skiing in that period was a method of transportation in the rural areas made it a natural bridge to becoming a ski champion. Working in the woods or farm added strength and endurance.

It is easy to consolidate into a single word the task for any aspiring athlete to gain further excellence. That word, "training," however embraces a multiplicity of complex requirements. Athletes, experienced coaches and scientists have tried for a long time to find optimal solutions to the training methods. There is no doubt that ability and training are the major elements, but success or failure is also dependent on other factors. Among those are one's equipment for training and racing, the appropriate environment for that training to take place and the guidance of creative leadership, sound management and available resources. When examined over the course of biathlon's introduction onto the world stage, certain tendencies can be discovered and divided into decades. This section is about the evolution of training for biathlon as it progressed from the first international competitions to the highly competitive sport it has become and to provide a review of other important elements that are a critical part of athletic success.

CHAPTER 15

The Locations

The physical resources, the facilities, buildings, equipment and supplies are critical to the success of and especially important for biathlon. Without available biathlon ranges and ski trails for training and racing to take place, biathlon couldn't exist. Without facilities and other physical requirements and tools that can adequately facilitate the development of programs and athletes at the right time, sequence, location and designed for the specific purposes or functions, nothing can be achieved. Along with these requirements, technology can also be included. Environmental interruption, specifically the loss of snow is often a frequent occurrence and the technology of snow-making can have an important impact on the consistency of training and racing.

The United States is a large country but enjoys multiple major and important biathlon facilities and training locations. With generally half of the United States covered with snow during winter, these biathlon facilities naturally developed near areas of known ski activity, especially cross-country skiing. The earliest biathlon facilities were temporary in nature, constructed for the team trials and national championships, usually with the shooting ranges located in an open field or as in the case of the first national championships in 1965 at Rosendale, New York, across a frozen lake adjacent to the ski trails. The first permanent site was the Arctic Valley biathlon range at Ft. Richardson, Alaska, however, it was primarily a training site that was never really used for competition other than USMWBTC's team activities. The area was gradually improved by the athletes themselves, first when they cleared the shooting range with hand saws and axes as part of their training. Later the trio of Lahdenpera, Wilson and Taylor managed to upgrade the facilities by convincing the engineering company to lend them a bulldozer for improving the trails and range. After persuading them to lend him the equipment, Wilson had the extraordinary skills at convincing those in charge of the engineer's bulldozers to lend him a second one to help pull out the first from the mud, after his "on-the-job" training managed to get it stuck. A rudimentary range was also constructed at the Independence Mines site for training purposes.

Many years later, when the U.S. Army turned over its missile site near the Anchorage airport to the City of Anchorage, it was developed into Kincaid Park.

With the development of the park's ski trails and biathlon range, it became a center of ski and biathlon activity in Alaska. National Championships were held there in 1992 and the Olympic team trials followed in 1994. Later the shooting range was moved and upgraded through the contributing efforts of former biathletes Dick Mize and Rachel Steer with a modern target system, and today is frequently the location of the team trials for the World Junior/Youth Championships. A small shooting range was also developed in Fairbanks adjacent to Ft. Wainwright which sees occasional use, especially during the early winter.

Once the rules centralized the shooting at a single range of 150m, holding biathlon competitions at traditional cross-country venues became easier, however the first range constructed for international competition came in 1973 for the World Championships at Lake Placid. That range had 30 firing points and butts behind the target line that provided the ability to lower and change the paper targets during the race. It was located in the current cross-country ski lodge's parking lot and linked to the trails on both sides of the entrance road through the tunnels under the road. The start/finish area was in the cross-country stadium and included climbs up to the highest part of the ski course. Shortly following that World Championships, the entire shooting range including the butts and target system was moved across the entrance road to become a biathlon complex separate from the cross-country ski stadium, but still sharing the ski trails. Further improvements were made in 1978 ahead of the 1980 Olympic Games. The firing line was moved forward to comply with the rule change to a 50m range, and metal, immediate response mechanical targets for the sprint and relay races were installed. They were called the falling plate or so-called "guillotine" type targets designed by UIPMB Technical Committee member Dr. Josef Deflorian of Austria. These new type targets had been tested for use in the 1978 World Championships at Hochfilzen and could be reset from the butts or the firing line by long ropes. Paper targets were still used for the individual race. Also, due to the lack of natural snow just prior to the 1980 Olympic Games, the Organizing Committee called on specialists for "snow-making" from the Hunter Mountain Ski Area in New York's Catskill mountains. They made a mountain of snow on the field near the shooting range and then spread it, covering the ski trails on both sides of the roads for both cross-country and biathlon. That effort was successful and laid a foundation for the natural snow that arrived just in time before the racing, however the technology remained and has been utilized for many other events ever since.

Following the Olympic Games, a new target system developed by Ilmo Kurvinen of Finland replaced the falling plate targets and could be changed between prone to standing by a sliding front plate and reset from the firing line with a rope. The new Kurvinen system eliminated the need for butts and allowed control of several targets at time by a range official. The Mt. Van Hoevenberg venue hosted the World Championships again in 1987 and later improved the site for hosting World Cup events. After the Olympic Games at Nagano in 1998 the Olympic Regional Development Authority, that had been established to manage the former Olympic facilities at Lake Placid, purchased the Hora 2000E target system from the Japanese and installed this new electronic system at Mt. Van Hoevenberg. This Hora system had been developed in Germany and was totally electronic. Hits on the target were detected by an electronic sensor which triggered an electronic motor to move a white plate over the aiming ring to indicate a hit. The system was first used at the World Championships in 1989 at Feistritz, Austria and later at the 1992 Olympic Games at Albertville.

The Mt. Van Hoevenberg biathlon range at Lake Placid has remained an important site for biathlon ever since. It was the location for IBU Biathlon World Cups in 1999, 2001 and 2004. In addition to the ski trails and biathlon range at Mt. Van Hoevenberg the USOC moved its "winter training center" from its original location at Squaw Valley, California to Lake Placid following the 1980 Olympic Games. After several temporary locations, it was finally located in newly constructed facilities near the ski jumps. With state of the art sports science and training equipment, it became a centerpiece in the U.S. Biathlon programs. In 2010 ORDA built a small shooting range with a roller ski loop behind the ski jumps that now serves as a specific training site for intensive training by the national team.

Coinciding with the development of the Lake Placid facility, Major General Reginald Cram instructed then Major Howard Buxton to begin development of biathlon facilities at the Ethan Allen Firing Range near Jericho, Vermont. At the time, there were no buildings along West Hill road and it wasn't plowed during winter, so he chose a site near the sharp bend in the road at the base of a steep climb that rises to the present biathlon range. Using the road and the lower fields, he charted out a ski course to and from the site of the range. The woods were cleared and a temporary 150m range was constructed near the turn in the road, which is still in use by the military today. This range was used for team trials and training through 1977, however he also began developing a 50m range at the plateau at the top of West Hill road for the National Guard's use in anticipation of the rule changes in 1978. With the help of the National team members he mapped and cut the trees that eventually developed into the current ski trails. This National Guard site eventually became the training center for the National Guard program and continued to go through constant upgrading through the continued efforts of Colonel Buxton and his successor Colonel Alan Nye. Both Colonels were the directors of the National Guard facilities in Vermont and continued to find funding for improvements to the site. With the support of the leadership of the Vermont National Guard and that of the National Guard Bureau, the facility at Jericho evolved into one of the most important locations for biathlon in the U.S. and hosted the international CISM Games on three occasions as well as multiple U.S. team trials and National Championships. Ever since the athletes helped Howard Buxton clear the ski trails in 1976, annual improvements eventually developed this site that today includes specifically purposed buildings, paved and lighted ski trails and a 30-point automatic shooting range for year-round training, including roller ski and biathlon training with lighting for after sunset training during the winter. An IBU licensed facility that includes dedicated athlete quarters for National Guardsmen, training facilities, accompanying buildings, snow-making and grooming equipment and as host to the very active Ethan Allen Biathlon Club it is currently the most utilized training and racing site in the country.

While Colonel Buxton was developing the biathlon site at Jericho, another National Guard site was being developed at Camp Ripley, near Little Falls, Minnesota. A skiing advocate, Colonel Clinton "Buck" Johnson was involved with the Minnesota National Guard's Norwegian exchange and in charge of the marksmanship matches at Camp Ripley. He encouraged the development of a biathlon range and began hosting competitions at the site in 1975. Following the rule changes in 1978 the firing line was moved forward and with National Guard funding, Camp Ripley's site continued to evolve with the addition of buildings and a paved roller ski loop. The National Guard Championships began to rotate between the Jericho and Camp Ripley sites annually and Camp Ripley welcomed civilian events and training by the vibrant Minnesota Biathlon Association from the Twin Cities area.

As the National Guard began to ramp up its program to higher standards it began making improvements in all areas of training and participation and that included facilities, both at Camp Ripley and Jericho, but it also began to aid development of facilities outside of military property. The first such effort came in the early 1980s and coincided with their annual training camp at West Yellowstone, Montana. In the early years of this camp which provided the opportunity for early season ski training, the National Guard would set up and staff a temporary range adjacent to the existing ski trails on the U.S. Forest Service land just outside the town. After years of beginning the early season ski training at Jackson, Wyoming, West Yellowstone became the early on-snow training site for the U.S. Ski team and the U.S. Biathlon team in the late 1970s for its reliable early snowfall and excellent grooming as well as an event that brought business to the local community during the Thanksgiving week, between the autumn closure of Yellowstone Park and its reopening for the snowmobile season. After a few years of setting up a temporary range and warming tents, it was decided to have National Guard engineers construct a permanent range. After obtaining the permits from the Forest Service and the funding from the National Guard headquarters, a permanent range was built as a part of the existing ski trail network and with the help of the U.S. Biathlon Association and local volunteers a building was later added, replacing the tents. The site is used regularly every winter with National Guard staffing during the annual Thanksgiving week's training, which frequently hosts the initial first race of the season. On occasions the site has hosted the National Championships and in 1988 the Olympic team trials which were relocated from McCall, Idaho, where the National Guard had also constructed a biathlon range. In 2012 after receiving a grant, the shooting range at West Yellowstone was improved once again. With biathlon participant and biathlon shooting equipment specialist and supplier Marc Sheppard located there, West Yellowstone has continued to be a very active location.

While the National Guard was aiding in expanding the available biathlon facilities there were other efforts taking shape outside the Guard efforts. One of the earliest was the private development of the Saratoga Biathlon Club's facility on the private property of Jim Schreiner near Day, New York. After the 1980 Olympic Games at Lake Placid had sparked the interest of his two sons, Jim and Curt, he brought them and a few other young boys to Rosendale, New York where they were introduced to the sport on the semi-permanent biathlon range on the baseball field at the Williams Lake Hotel, home of the Rosendale Nordic Ski Club. In 1982 Jim started the Saratoga Biathlon Club and, in the spring of 1983, he invited Art Stegen to help in mapping out a biathlon range and ski trails on his extensive property near his home in the southern Adirondack mountains near the Great Sacandaga lake. The rudimentary range and trails were continually improved and today the facility is one of the key locations for both the cross-country and biathlon community and home of the largest biathlon club in the New York State Ski Racing Association.

Other private development of biathlon sites also continued through the 1980s and the 1990s. Some of these became important semi-permanent locations while others saw only limited use and eventually disappeared. Of those also located in New York was the Syracuse Biathlon Club's site at Osceola, New York in the "Lake-effect snow belt" of the Tug Hill Plateau. Located at a Nordic ski center, targets are put up in the late fall for winter racing and then stored during the summer months. Another similar site is located at Old Forge, New York and managed by the local Polar Bear Ski club. With a long history of skiing in the village, this semi-permanent range is located at the community-owned ski area and adjacent to an extensive network of cross-country ski trails near the alpine area with its lodge and facilities. A small range, the targets are also stored during the summer and there is current planning to expand the shooting range for hosting larger events. With the international level facilities at Lake Placid, the

Saratoga Biathlon Club's range and the two at Old Forge and Osceola, New York has multiple options for racing within a few hours of driving.

The Minnesota Biathlon Association had use of a semi-permanent range in the suburban community of Hamel in the late 1970s and even held the National Championships there in 1980, however housing development eventually prevented further use of the range located there. In the later 1980s the state government in Minnesota provided grants to develop the facilities including an international level biathlon range at Giant's Ridge at Biwabik as a way to inject economic stimulus into the Iron Range after the closure of many of the mines in Northern Minnesota. That location even included a dormitory-style hotel and food service for the activities that included high school state championships and USBA Junior trials and the National Guard Championships on one occasion. Once the government grants ended it was difficult to sustain the facility and the biathlon range was dismantled and the area was turned into a golf course.

The 2002 Winter Olympic Games at Salt Lake City required the development of a first-class international range and ski trails for both cross-country and biathlon. At first it was a very contested choice as to where these should be, and it was eventually decided to be located at Soldier Hollow near Heber City in the Wasatch Mountain State Park. The location was chosen by the Salt Lake Organizing Committee (SLOC) as an Olympic venue in October 1997, over several other possible locations, with construction beginning in 1999. The range and trails were to share a ski stadium next to the official press and timing buildings with the shooting range into an adjacent hill. With Hora targets, snow-making and paved ski trails this site has remained in use and is a popular training site in the fall for both specialized biathlon and altitude training prior to the season's first competitions. There are plans to upgrade the facilities for use in potential World Cup competitions.

Of the three additional, high quality biathlon training and race sites that were developed after 2000, two are in Maine and one in Minnesota. The small Mt. Itasca ski area near Coleraine, Minnesota evolved out of local efforts to develop the site that has consistently been an integral part of the USBA development program and has frequently hosted early season races due to its snow-making capacity. The modern shooting range of Kurvinen targets and challenging ski trails are all within a compact area and utilized by a very active biathlon club. The two facilities located in Maine at Ft. Kent and Presque Isle are in the very northern part of the state. Both were developed by the Maine Winter Sports Center with the aid of the Libra Foundation and are the state of the art biathlon facilities that have hosted both the World Junior/Youth Biathlon Championships and IBU World Cups. Ft. Kent hosted World Cups in 2004 and 2011 while Presque Isle held World Cup, in 2011 and 2016 as well as the World Junior/Youth Championships in 2006 and 2014. Both sites have beautifully designed administrative and service buildings, automatic Kurvinen targets and snow-making ability on their John Morton-designed ski trails.

Unlike the early days when biathlon activity was confined to the U.S. Army's biathlon training center, today there are biathlon ranges near all the centers of cross-country ski activity, either in a temporary situation or completely modern multi-target ranges. And as U.S. Biathlon activity gains awareness, these facilities provide introduction and development opportunities for young skiers. The present USBA intentions to develop a highly effective development plan that makes use of these facilities is beginning to accelerate the progress towards finding and developing athletes that will continue to be competitive at the international levels.

CHAPTER 16

Training

Sports training through the years has had many influences, but the most ideal training concepts for preparing athletes for competition is unclear. There exist nearly as many different types of training programs as there are athletes. Most of these programs are based upon tradition, copied from the ideas of successful athletes and/or founded upon a combination of scientific theories and philosophies. It is rather unlikely that any one type of training will produce the most perfect results since the combination of anatomical, physiological, and psychological factors which compose the successful athlete are too divergent. Nevertheless, it is not unrealistic to expect to identify common training methodologies and procedures which will generally produce desired outcomes.

The impressive advances in sport performance over the years can be said to be the result of improved understanding and methods of athlete training, improved technologies and improvements in sports equipment. The Summer Olympic Games of 1912 can be seen as the moment in time that specific training for sport became important. Those games in Stockholm were the first truly modern version of the quadrennial event for which Sweden could claim a pioneer role in promoting sport. The Swedish Olympic Games made possible the coming of age of a sport country which at the time was not yet a nation in the political and formal sense. Finland, which was still a limited autonomy of the Russian Empire, stole the limelight with the first of many distance running stars of the first three decades of the 20th century. Johnnes Kolehmainen had discovered sport at an early age, first as a cross-country skier and then in running. Having already run a marathon at the early age of 17 in 3 hours and 6 minutes, he followed a brother's advice who was in the U.S., not to "neglect speed." The Finnish sport newspaper *Suomen Urheilulehti* extolled the virtues of his training with the words: "Work, healthy life, good sleep, fresh air, suitable nourishment, regular sauna baths, gymnastic exercises, massage, lots of moving about in the open air and a running training based on theoretical and empirical research."

This early impact on the concept of training for sport was the first of many contributions of the small Scandinavian nation whose love of sports is seen as a necessity to fight the harshness of their Nordic climate. Few countries had skiing and athletics so closely intertwined with their culture and the spectacular successes of their distance runners like the incomparable Paavo Nurmi created a great interest in their training. His early training was similar to that of the best skiers of the period. It consisted of running various distances no more than four times a week with long walks in between for rest. This was after working hours. When he had to serve in the army for 18 months he turned it into an advantage having more time to train. His training gradually became more systematic, always running with a stopwatch and his successes led the sports world to view his methods with greater interest. His more disciplined approach to training would also have an impact on the way skiers were training as well.

By the time of the first Winter Olympic Games in 1924 training for ski racing had become more than casual physical exercise. Cross-country skiing required endurance, muscular fitness, technique and psychological strength and competitors had by then begun to focus their training efforts on those requirements. Most of the written training information for skiing was rather elementary with advice such as "by October one should quit smoking and begin longer walks and running in the woods." There was little empirical study that provided guidance on how to train for skiing. Even though scientists have studied how the body works, for centuries, it wasn't until 1889 that *Physiology of Bodily Exercise* by Fernarnd LaGrange was the first book published on exercise physiology and it wasn't until the 1920s that physiologists began to apply important physiological research to sports performance. In the United States David (D.B.) Dill directed the earliest research of exercise physiology at the Harvard Fatigue Laboratory in 1927 and continued his research as deputy director of medical research for the army in 1947, and Indiana University until 1966.

Exercise physiology studies how our bodies' structures and functions are transformed and respond to acute and chronic bouts of exercise. Sport physiology further applies these concepts to athlete training and enhancing performance levels. In the 1930s D.B. Dill invited some Danish physiologists to the Harvard Fatigue Laboratory and after returning to Scandinavia they established their own laboratories. In 1941 the Gymnastik och Idrottshogskolan (GIH) was established in Stockholm and during the 1950s and 1960s it was where Per Olaf Åstrand and Bengt Saltin became leading contributors to the understanding of physical fitness, endurance capacity and muscle metabolism during exercise and sports performance.

Whether today's or yesterday's skiers, the development of their training begins with an analysis of the demands of the sport and their individual abilities and needs to best meet those demands. Even during the early days of competition, it was understood that the basic requirements were endurance, strength, technique and good psychological capacities. Through time these fundamentals became better understood through the research of coaches and physiologists, thus developing into well-known basic principles. Training to develop endurance, which is the dominant requirement for cross-country or biathlon racing has been gradually identified as general and specific endurance and is a complex function of many variables. Today's athletes are familiar with these complex functions that include both aerobic and anaerobic muscle fibers, the cardio-vascular oxygen transport system, the energy release systems in the muscle cells and the various impact that exercise intensity has on performance. Training for maximal endurance is generally categorized by coaches and athletes today as *distance or fundamental training* and is essentially continued exercise specifically designed to stress the aerobic capacities. It involves a major loading on the oxygen transport system and energy-releasing processes by activating the large muscle groups at even and moderate intensity through steady hiking, cycling, running, skiing, etc., inducing a training effect. Such effects are produced at sub-maximal levels, with stress becoming increasingly progressive. Longer sessions will be of lower intensity than shorter ones, usually at training intensities.

Over time it was also learned that shorter training sessions at higher intensities also improved performance. Athletes have always known this difference which physiologists have labeled as aerobic and anaerobic endurance. It was also well known in earlier years as the fact that adaptation to training that moderately exceeds present capacities gradually improves performance. However, it wasn't until 1966 when the biochemistry of muscle tissues fully explained what happened in the muscle cells before, during and after aerobic and anaerobic exercise. Over recent years, research in the exercise and sport sciences has provided a wealth of information concerning what happens within the muscle cells and cardio-vascular system during physical performance. This information helped to create a basis for which a physiological profile for potential biathletes and training evaluation was developed.

Perhaps the single most important measurement of physical condition and fitness in the 1970s was that of oxygen delivery to the muscle cells during exercise. Since biathlon skiing is an extremely intense and demanding physical activity, this measurement and its values determine the demands of the activity. In the laboratory and in the field, measurements of the volume of oxygen consumed (VO2) are used to evaluate the efficiency of the cardio-vascular or oxygen delivery system and its limitations. At the point where the VO2 reaches a plateau is known as VO2 max. Normally, active 18- to 22-year-old college students have been reported to have average VO2 max values of 44 to 50 ml/kg/min (milliliters per kilogram per minute) for men and 38 to 42 ml/kg/min for women. The highest values ever recorded were 94 ml/kg/min by a male cross-country ski champion and 74 ml/kg/min for a female cross-country racer. World Champion and Olympic gold medalists usually record values over 80 ml/kg/min for men and over 60 ml/kg/min for women. Age is a factor in the development of VO2, with little difference between trained and untrained children, with improvements as a responsive adaptation to training through puberty and early adulthood, and a gradual decline after age 40.

The maximum oxygen uptake or VO2, the acronym for the volume of oxygen used during maximum exertion, is a function of many physiological variables. Among the most important is the muscle fiber "types" of the individual. Microscopic and biochemical analyses can be used to identify various metabolic properties of muscle samples. The two main fiber types found in skeletal muscles are typically labeled "fast twitch" and "slow twitch" types. The fast twitch fibers have faster contractile properties and higher glycolytic (anaerobic) potential, while the slow twitch fibers have slower contractile properties and demonstrate higher oxidative (aerobic) ability. There is substantial evidence that demonstrates successful biathletes have relatively greater slow twitch (ST) than fast twitch (FT) muscle fibers. Within each individual the percentage of muscle fiber types is a function of genetics and only marginally a function of training adaptation. A microscopic determination of muscle fiber types is possible through a muscle biopsy and staining techniques; however, assessments of general fiber types can also be made through performance evaluations and tests for speed and endurance.

It was known early on that the most important factor in the ability to maintain and increase the levels of intensity of racing is a continuous supply of energy and oxygen for metabolism in the muscle cells. Bio-chemical analysis eventually revealed that this supply comes in the form of high-energy phosphate, ATP (adenosine triphosphate), chemically released from carbohydrates, fats, and proteins, stored in the muscles. Enzymes help to release the energy compounds (phosphates) and store them in the muscle cells. Since the ATP level in the cells is limited and can only sustain the energy needs of muscle for a few seconds, two other sources for ATP production fill the needs. The two sources are: 1) glycolysis; ATP production from glycogen stored in muscles, without the use of oxygen; and, 2) oxidation; formation of ATP from carbohydrates, fats, and protein molecules, with the aid of oxygen. Thus, these two sources are commonly known as anaerobic and aerobic metabolism.

The primary data that is helpful to monitor the level of exercise or training intensity are the heart rate and the production of lactic acid in the muscle cells. Lactic concentrations can be measured in the blood and along with the heart rate, provides finer control over training intensity available to the coaches and athletes. These cellular responses of lactate production along with heart rate as well as other measurements of endurance-related variables such as oxygen uptake helped to develop a greater understanding of exercise physiology and how to apply it to training.

The development of the anaerobic capacities, or exercise beyond the level at which oxygen can be adequately supplied to the muscle cells for high intensity exercise or speed, inducing concentrations of lactates, became what is generally known as *interval training*. This well-known form of doing speed-work in which bursts of fast paced running or skiing are interspersed with intervals of recovery, dates back to Nazi Germany. In the late 1930s, a coach and cardiologist in Freiburg teamed up to study the effectiveness of speed repetitions on 3,000 subjects. The cardiologist, Br. H. Reindell used exercise to strengthen the hearts of his patients and after careful measurements showed that the most effective method was for the patient to run repetitive short distance with short rest periods between each. This would increase both the size of the heart and the volume of blood expelled by the heart during each beat, or stroke/volume. The coach, Woldemar Gerschler, soon systematically applied the findings of this training to Germany's Rudolf Harbig, who broke two world records in the 400m and 800m in athletics in 1939. Interval training then became the rage in Europe and was the major part of Roger Bannister's success in becoming the first runner to run a mile in under four minutes. Hungarian coaches Mihaly Igloi and Laszlo Tabori brought this training method to the United States in the late 1950s and successfully used it in training Jim Beatty, the first runner to run a mile under four minutes indoors and the Olympic 5000m champion Bob Schul. The traditional five characteristics of interval training; the distance or length (time) of each repetition, the number of the repetitions to be done, the intensity of the repetitions, the time allocated to recovery and the mode of the recovery is today undisputed as most essential for improving the anaerobic muscle capacity and therefore an overall higher rate of speed.

Although much of the early physiological research was applied to running at first, its influence eventually began to impact training for skiing. Through the early years of skiing in the United States, training was not well organized and focused primarily on ski techniques rather than performance physiology. There was little information available on training for cross-country skiing. Most of what was available came from "hotspots" of activity such as Gunnison, Colorado or Putney, Vermont which were centers of activity around the Olympic and National team coaches. In his pamphlet *"Cross-Country Skiing – Training and Racing"* printed in 1964, Western State College ski coach and 1960 Olympic team coach Sven Wiik wrote: "Twenty to thirty years ago, Scandinavian cross-country skiers consisted primarily of lumberjacks and farmers. In those days, the lumberjack and farmer had a great advantage over the skier from the city… their daily work provided plenty of excellent conditioning training… (in) their daily routine, we find that, without knowing it, their workout was very well balanced." This pamphlet was developed with the help of his college skiers Jim Mahaffey, Dick Mize, Mack Miller and John Burritt; all who went on to become early pioneers in the ski and biathlon environment of the late 1950s and early 1960s. It was one of the first efforts towards providing an organized training plan for aspiring cross-country and biathlon skiers.

In the introduction to Sven Wiik's training pamphlet he suggests that the training during both practice and competitive seasons be divided into two parts; *Conditioning* training that will systematically build up the working capacity of the lungs, heart, muscles and ligaments and *Special* training which improves coordination, rhythm, relaxation, reflexes and technique. He broke down the training year into monthly increments from April to the end of the ski season and advised that before starting training not to allow "bad habits such as smoking or drinking," and develop good sleeping and eating habits. Wiik wrote that since the time of the Scandinavian woodsman and farmers, training methods had become more scientific and that an organized training program must provide a well-balanced combination of the two parts of training, and gone were the days of a casual or haphazard manner that began when the snow came.

When viewed by today's standards, the training of the Western State ski team and that suggested by their coach Sven Wiik was less specific and less focused than that of today, however it was clearly adequately stressful, especially when evaluated by the fact that neither the athletes nor the coaches had unlimited time to train. The athletes had classes and homework as well as the ski team practice, and Wiik's main goal was to have successful students as well as competitive skiers. Like many good coaches, he also had teaching responsibilities and stressed that getting a good education along with achieving athletic success would develop the skills and abilities necessary to achieve and live a healthy lifestyle. His training plan for the fall of 1956 began with a 2½ mile hike on Tuesday followed by gymnastics and soccer on Wednesday, Thursday and Friday and a long 4-hour hike on Saturday. The length of the hikes gradually increased, and running was added to the schedule by October and skiing at the higher elevations such as Kebler Pass, and Crested Butte began in November. The first ski racing began in early December with weekends of a morning Slalom race and afternoon cross-country race on Saturday with a jumping competition in the morning and a downhill race in the afternoon on Sunday. This same group of Western State skiers added a biathlon race to that schedule during their visit to Camp Hale that winter.

Soon after graduation many of the Western State skiers found themselves in the army and at Ft. Richardson under the coaching guidance of Hans Wagner. Other than the addition of marksmanship training, their training didn't differ much from that of their college days except there was more time and more of it. Hans Wagner decided the week's training, and did allow for some individual variation. During the summer and fall it consisted of long day hikes to Arctic Valley, Pioneer Peak and in the Chugach Mountains. They also did gym workouts and indoor marksmanship training with .22 rifles. Summer training also included training for the USARAL track and field championships and spent several weeks training for marksmanship with the Army Marksmanship Unit at Ft. Benning, Georgia with Arvo Vickström and Marvin Fitzpatrick as their shooting coaches. Imitating the Scandinavian woodcutters, for strength training they cleared the Arctic Valley biathlon range by hand, using axes and hand saws, as well as the first ski trail at the biathlon venue. Once the snow fell their training switched to skiing on a 9-mile loop around the Ft. Richardson golf course or from Ft. Richardson up to Arctic Valley and back. They did some short skiing intervals and helped each other with their ski technique but did their marksmanship training at the Ft. Richardson shooting ranges.

Following the 1960 Winter Olympic Games and the arrival of Peter Lahdenpera, Joe-Pete Wilson and Dick Taylor at the biathlon unit, the training began a gradual change. Although these eastern skiers shared the same basic ideas about training, Hans Wagner gradually allowed them more input to the training, and the knowledge gained from the Olympic Games and previous World Championships in 1958 and 1959 helped improve and add new perspectives to the training for skiing and biathlon. In the beginning biathlon was regarded as two separate sports, shooting and cross-country skiing, which saw a change to a new training strategy away from that concept and a new entity of a combined sport. One of the first things the trio of Lahdenpera, Wilson and Taylor did was to "borrow" a big bulldozer from the engineer company to work on the design and improvement of the ski trails, and building a shooting range at Arctic Valley. With Taylor scouting out potential trails and Lahdenpera, who had worked for the Alaska Road Department on a survey crew during the college summer breaks, surveying the trails and range, and Wilson operating the D-8 bulldozer, they created a biathlon training site that would allow for much more specific biathlon training. They also scouted out greater ski training opportunities and after visiting Independence Mines, it became a regular early and late ski training location for the unit.

The improved training site at Arctic Valley and expanded ski training on the early and late snow at Independence Mines moved the biathlon training towards a more specific and biathlon focused direction. Although the biathletes were good runners, with many having achieved impressive marathon race results, a greater focus on running began to replace the long hikes, and shooting was being coordinated with the physical training and became known as *combination training*. During the summers of 1962-63 army helicopters flew the group to the Eklutna Glacier for ski training two times per week, weather permitting. New coach Sven Johanson brought a new level of training demands and as a legendary successful athlete himself, he applied his thoughts and those learned from his Swedish connections to the biathlon training. Believing his own success came from harder and more training than his rivals, he included the famous Mt. Marathon race at Seward as a regular feature of the summer training, spending two weeks at the Army's Recreational Center there and climbing Mt. Marathon two times per day. With the help of Jed Williamson and rifle coach Clyde Burns, Sven wrote the *USMWBTC Handbook of Biathlon Training*, the first publication of any kind for biathlon training. The introduction explained that "there are many types of training programs for cross-country skiing, but very few for biathlon." The handbook also pointed out that the training methods described were not meant to fit the skier to the training but fitting the training methods to the skier. The handbook was the first to include marksmanship training as applied to biathlon as well as all aspects of progressive ski training, ski waxing, summary of rules and competition duties of race officials. Dick Taylor wrote years later, "The US Army Biathlon Unit at Ft. Richardson was the only place a skier could continue to train and ski seriously in the 1960s."

The 1960s also began a period when the understanding of exercise physiology, due to improvements in technology, impacted the advancement of training concepts. Much of this technology was a result of the U.S. space program. With the development of electronic analyzers to measure respiratory gases the study of energy metabolism was more productive. Radiotelemetry or radio transmitted signals were used to measure heart rate and body temperature during exercise. New techniques of needle muscle biopsy allowed bio-chemists to study muscle structure, muscle characteristics and cell nutrition. Knowledge of these studies became known in the athletic environment and most of the athletes arriving at the USMWBTC in the later 1960s had a rudimentary knowledge of the complicated physiological responses and chronic adaptation to training. The use of monitoring the heart rate during exercise and rest became a common practice. Sven Johanson obtained a cycle ergometer and began to use it to assess the fitness levels of the athletes at the unit. He was also one of the first to import roller skis for more specific summer training. Training methodologies and terminology gradually improved the understanding and overall training by the athletes. *Resistance training*, *circuit training*, and variations of interval training such as *fartlek* training all became well-known among the coaches and athletes. Although Sven Johanson was aware of the newly developing training methods, his own experiences of training "harder and more" than his competitors were still an important focus of the team.

One important influence of this period, like the earlier impact of interval training, was the concepts of New Zealand's legendary track coach Arthur Lydiard. He broke up the training year into distinct periods consisting of 10 weeks of marathon or distance training to build a strong aerobic base, and prescribed running 100 miles per week for the period. This was open to misinterpretation since no timeframe for the pace of the training was described. At a coaching seminar in New York City some years later, Lydiard was asked about this. The question focused on how "fast" should the pace be for the distance period, or at what pace this "marathon" training should be done. His response was that it should be at "conversational pace" meaning an easy running pace that would allow the participants to carry on a conversation and enjoy the effort. Lydiard's plan also called for 6 weeks of hill running to build strength and technique, and 4 weeks of interval training on the track to improve the aerobic/anaerobic threshold before the racing season. This concept of "*periodization*" was easily adapted to training for skiing, however many coaches and athletes misunderstood the purpose of the 10 weeks of "marathon" training, further increasing the volume, making it far more stressful which diminished its value, and often leading to injury and loss of motivation. An example of Sven's thoughts on training during this period was illustrated in a story often told by those at the USMWBTC in advance of the 1968 Olympic Games. In preparation for the Equinox Marathon race at Fairbanks, he proposed a plan whereby the athletes would run to Fairbanks in daily 20-mile training efforts with a support group to follow with tents and supplies. After a rest day or two they would then do the race. The athletes immediately protested to the commander and with some sarcasm suggested that they might also "swim" to Europe for the international competitions. Sven eventually came to recognize that training "harder" was not training "smarter" and the athletes forced concessions with the statement that they wanted to train to "be a race horse, not a plough horse."

The 1970s also ushered in a greater attention to ski technique, especially with the arrival of fiberglass skis, and improved ski bindings. Like Gunnison, Colorado in the late 1950s, Putney, Vermont became the hot-spot for cross-country skiing in the early 1970s. Like Sven Wiik's presence at Western State College, it was at the Putney School where John Caldwell taught, that the U.S National and Olympic team cross-country ski coach was the catalyst that helped promote recreational cross-country skiing in the United States. Author of *The Cross-Country Ski Book*, which was published in eight editions from 1964 to 1987 with a half-million copies, it became one of the most widely distributed skiing books and helped to popularize and develop understanding of ski training, technique and recreational skiing in the United States. Innovative, Caldwell placed a greater emphasis on ski technique analysis and relied on repeated technique drills to manage athletes and develop good technical skiers. He felt it important to establish the significance of technique and was at the forefront of knowledge about equipment and waxing. The significant numbers of athletes from the eastern ski colleges at the USMWBTC in the 1970s brought much of Caldwell's ideas and knowledge with them and those concepts began to creep into the biathlon training at Ft. Richardson.

The 1970s was also a period when authority of all kinds was questioned, and athletes' rights became an important issue. Although Sven Johanson and the shooting coaches kept control of the central, most focused and specific combination and ski training, he gradually relaxed the supervision over the general training, allowing the athletes greater individualization of their training. The highly motivated athletes planned and executed their training taking advantage of the perceived free time, however the basic routines and events that filled the summer continued. In July, the team trained at Seward for the Mt. Marathon race and then ran the Gold Discovery race in Fairbanks. In September was the Equinox marathon race, also at Fairbanks. By October the team went to Independence Mines for early ski training with lots of shooting included. Running time trials were held during the late summer and once skiing began at Arctic Valley, biathlon time trials were held there. After the team for the World Championships and CISM was selected and went on to participate in those events, the remaining athletes returned to Ft. Richardson for training and local racing. After the international group returned from Europe, the team would continue to ski and even race in the far north at Inuvik, in the Northwest Territory of Canada in April. The biathlon schedule was the longest extended ski program of any in the United States.

Following the closure of the USMWBTC at Ft. Richardson in 1973, the athletes were suddenly left without a facility, coaching or even adequate training resources, such as ammunition. Having to leave their rifles behind and without centralized training at a biathlon venue, they were left to their own resources and training efforts. Many returned to their home areas, most of which allowed them continued access to skiing activity. The loss of military support limited any opportunities for biathlon training and during the winter leading into the 1973 World Biathlon Championship at Lake Placid the athletes still competing had only the four selection races plus the potential for another two races for those who qualified for the World Championships during the entire racing season. Some athletes began to solve the problem by moving and finding temporary work in locations to be near former teammates still active. Ken Alligood moved to Jackson, Wyoming where he frequently trained together with juniors Martin Hagen and Rusty Scott with Peter Karns occasionally guiding their training. Peter Hale moved back to Minneapolis where he introduced biathlon to junior skiers, Peter Hoag among them. Dennis Donahue returned to teaching and coaching in Vermont, as did John Morton who stayed in Alaska as a teacher and coach, which allowed some sort of continued training among young athletes. Art Stegen took a more thorough direction by moving to Norway.

After a summer session of studying French at Besançon, France where he visited the French team at Chamonix, Art moved to Oslo and enrolled in the University of Oslo language program and the Norsk Idrettshogskole (Norwegian

Sports Institute, NIH) where he studied under the guidance of Anders Besseberg. After training and racing more than a dozen early season biathlon races in Norway, he returned for the U.S. team selection races in 1974 with better preparation and confidence. While learning more about physiology and psychology as they impact athletic performance at the NIH, Art and Bill Spencer attended a UIPMB Trainers Conference at Storlien, Sweden in the fall of 1974 where they heard lectures and were involved with discussions on the subjects from experts in the field, including Per Olaf Åstrand, and how this information applied to biathlon. After that year's World Championships Art was invited to participate in the biathlon races held during the Finnish Ski Games at Lahti and following those races was invited to Jyväskylä for some physiological testing by Dr. Maki, a physiologist who was doing the research on the Finnish biathletes.

The tests included a VO2 test by running on a treadmill after having a muscle biopsy taken from his thigh muscle. A second test for VO2 was done to evaluate arm strength and endurance by turning an arm ergometer. There were also tests for body fat, speed, flexibility and horse power. It ended up being a very instructive day with lots of discussion as to the purpose and meaning of the tests. The following day Dr. Matti Hanu went over some of the results and later sent a complete analysis. His motive for testing an American was to have some comparison with athletes outside his own group as it was difficult to engage the nearby neighbors from Sweden, Norway or Russia since they were cautious about letting the Finns test them. Art had 6.9% body fat and completed a total of 8 minutes of running at 17.1km/hr. at a 3% grade on the treadmill at 175b/min heart rate. Dr. Hanu's complete analysis showed the value of 75.5ml/kg/min for Art's VO2 and a muscle biopsy from his upper leg showed a distribution of 69% slow and 31% fast-twitch muscle fibers. He made some recommendations for better training of the arms due to a lower value for the arms only VO2, and because the new fiberglass skis created a higher demand for arm endurance and strength. In each case, Art's values were below those of the elite Finnish athlete Heikki Ikola. Dr. Hanu also suggested increased training for better endurance because of the slightly higher value in the percentage of fast or anaerobic fibers than the norm for cross-country skiers of that period. Art thought that those percentages matched his own experience from running in that his best results were in the middle distances of a mile or half mile, but wasn't fast enough for the sprints, and performance gradually dropped off as the distance became longer.

The years following the army's closure of the USMWBTC at Ft. Richardson the training became completely de-centralized with each of the continuing athletes developing their own plans and training routines without much guidance or supervision. Most had been involved in high level training and participation for many years, so they were not without complete understanding of the training principles, however without appropriate facilities, the training became less specific, with less shooting and more of a general nature. At first, Peter Karns was named the coach, but only on a part-time basis for the trials and World Championships. As a very successful athlete, Peter knew the training methodologies required for biathlon success and tried to monitor that by long-distance correspondence with the athletes. Bill Spencer provided guidance on shooting and created a "postal competition" to encourage marksmanship training, however extremely limited resources prevented the athletes from getting together at appropriate facilities for any formal group training. In 1977 Ken Alligood coached for a year and was followed by Joe-Pete Wilson in 1978. These former athletes also faced the same problems and the lack of extended focused training and extremely limited resources, preventing any real progress. Successful results were a distant and seemingly unachievable goal.

The opening of the U.S. Olympic Training Center at Squaw Valley and the hiring of Art Stegen as the first full-time coach for the biathlon team in the summer of 1978 gave new hope. With the upcoming 1980 Olympic Winter Games scheduled for Lake Placid, new revenues began to make a difference. Art and assistant coach Bill Spencer who had become the first full-time director of the National Guard Biathlon program brought much of what they had learned from the UIPMB's Trainers Seminar and the knowledge from the NIH where Art had achieved Norwegian coaching certification for both cross-country and biathlon. By then many of the training myths and guidance were affirmed or transformed by scientific study, especially, regarding nutrition and hydration. The athletes were very aware of the various training methodologies such as "*training zones*" and "*periodization*" as well as the use of monitoring one's heart rate for training and recovery purposes. Training for biathlon had become more specific. They had also seen the East Germans training with gauze sticking to their ears from the lactate samples taken during their training and although heart rate and lactate monitors were not yet generally available, the athletes and coaches were aware of the importance of these functions on training. With the opening of the U.S. Olympic Training Center at Squaw Valley the ability for centralized training camps with specialized biathlon training and the first VO2 tests on U.S. team members provided more useful, helpful feedback to both the coaches and athletes. Strength testing discovered strengths and weaknesses. Bill Spencer's invitations to champion shooters to the Squaw Valley training camps helped the athletes develop a better understanding of the principles needed for improved results. New training methods such as *plyometrics*, explosive, energy-homing exercises became well-known as a way of converting strength into speed and power by involving a fast, high intensity, involuntary eccentric contraction of the muscles and tendons, following by an immediate, powerful concentric contraction. The later 1970s also saw the introduction and greater use of sport psychology as well. The USOC's

sport psychologist Jerry May helped develop a better understanding of the importance of sports and performance psychology. Athletes and coaches had a rudimentary knowledge of sports psychology, but Jerry May explained and helped them to
better understand and manage the impact of goal setting, the influence of arousal
and levels of tension on performance, motivation and visualization. However,
despite all the advances made in their training and coaching, the U.S. athletes still
found themselves struggling to keep up with their Eastern European competitors.
Rather than a lack of ability, effort or motivation, suspicions of cheating through
the use of Performance Enhancing Drugs (PEDs) was later shown to be an
important basis behind the phenomenal success of the Eastern European nations.

Ever since the beginnings of athletic competition in the ancient Olympic
Games athletes and coaches have been trying to find an "edge" or a secret method of
improving performance. The use of "*ergogenic*" aids, or the use of special substances
or treatments as an attempt to improve physiological, psychological or biomechanical functions as related to sports, was even an issue in the original Olympic
Games when the Athenians complained that the Spartans cheated because they
ate meat. Ergogenic is a Greek word derived from the words *ergon* (work) and
gennan (to produce). In the beginning, much of the focus on ergogenic aids was
focused on nutrition and eventually athletes began experimenting with such drugs
as alcohol, caffeine and cocaine in efforts to improve their performance. Once
scientists began to explain the biochemistry of energy production at the cell levels
the focus on nutrition and hydration led to such developments as sports drinks,
energy bars and carbohydrate loading. However, starting as early as the 1930s the
political and economic motivation of winning at all costs led to the use of stimu-
lants and following WWII, blood doping and the use of synthetic hormones for
increasing strength, speed and endurance became a factor in sports performance.
Eventually these efforts became an important ethical consideration for sport that
eventually led to legal means to ban the use of PEDs.

With the access of the USOTC at Squaw Valley, the movement away from
pentathlon and the development of an independent structure under the guidance
of Peter Lahdenpera, Howard Buxton and Walter Williams, the U.S. Biathlon
efforts began to find its way back to a more focused program with leadership and
direction. The Olympic training center provided the needed professional training
resources sorely missing in the biathlon community following the army's discontinuation of its program. After the USOTC built a shooting range on site that
allowed for roller-skiing in combination with shooting, Squaw Valley provided
a training environment that seemed ideal. With specialists available in sports
medicine, physiology and psychology the athletes and coaches made astonishing
improvements. With feedback from the physiology lab and from the coaches'
analysis of shooting, range times and ski pace, the athletes began to see themselves

in a different light. Peter Lahdenpera's efforts towards finding equipment and supplies, including training gear, uniforms and most importantly ammunition provided a sense of professionalism that even exceeded that experienced at Ft. Richardson.

The turn-around began to emerge during the winter of 1979. After assuming the position as the first full-time coach during the summer of 1978, Art Stegen immediately began to create better communication with the athletes through correspondence and area visits where several team members would gather for a few days of dry-land training and ongoing discussions about new directions for the team and individual goals as well as recruiting. One of the most important things to have occurred during that summer was Peter Lahdenpera's recruitment of a few fast skiers into the biathlon group and the UIPMB transition to .22LR small bore shooting which also led to a surprising number of junior skiers interested in biathlon. With drastically improved results at the 1979 World Biathlon Championships, the biathlon team also participated in other important ski races that winter in which the results for the biathlon team members earned improved respect among their peers in the ski community. With both the team's maximized use of the USOTC and the upcoming Winter Olympic Games bringing improved financial resources, it translated into better training, improved motivation and a greater commitment by the athletes.

In the years following the 1980 Winter Olympic Games at Lake Placid, the U.S. athletes continued to show improvement, however so did their European cohort. The training for both groups was similar and this was confirmed with athlete and coaching exchanges with Finland's Heikki Ikola when he visited the USOTC training camps at Squaw Valley along with his coach. Bill Spencer had invited Marie Alkire to assess and advise the athletes on their shooting which later led to hiring her as the shooting coach. She facilitated improvements in both accuracy and consistency on the shooting range. By 1985 and 1986, the skating technique became the dominate one used for biathlon and as this new technique evolved, so too did the training. Although the basic physiological requirements were the same, the new technique placed greater demands on power and new technical directions. The ski waxing also became less of an issue when classical wax was replaced by glide waxes. Despite the success of U.S. skiers Bill Koch and Dan Simoneau, like some other European teams, the U.S. athletes were at first caught off guard with the fast-paced changes of ski technique at the international level. Years later, Art Stegen, Rusty Scott and Ken Alligood recalled racing with each other at the 1979 American Birkebeiner race in Wisconsin. After skiing the 55 kilometers race together most of the way they found themselves following each other across the large lake near the finish, which was groomed with a few classical tracks and a wider groomed adjacent area without tracks. As the three crossed the flat lake they each continually stepped out of the tracks and "skated" past the others and then returned to the track, double poling with kicks. They joked about how they each failed to see how much faster the skating was as they kept leap-frogging each other towards the finish, and never realizing that continued skating would be the fastest way to the finish. Hiring the Norwegian coach Sigvart Bjontegaard brought the U.S. team much needed experience and a new approach to training that put the U.S. athletes, especially Josh Thompson at the forefront of the technical evolution of the new skating ski technique.

The traditional method of skiing developed over centuries in Scandinavia and is currently referred to as "*classical*," "*traditional*," and/or "*diagonal*" technique. The new ski style or technique developed after the 1984 season evolved out of equipment changes and improved course (ski track) preparation. It is referred to as both "*skating*" and "*freestyle*" technique. It represented a revolution in the nordic ski world that has seen the time of all ski race distances drastically decreased, including all the biathlon distances. The older technique requires waxed skis, which alternate between kicks and glides for forward movement. The wax which was developed over a century had specific qualities that allowed the snow crystals to penetrate it while the ski momentarily stopped during the kick phase and overcame friction during the glide phase. The kick waxes had to be matched to the conditions of the snow that allows both the kick and gliding characteristics of the technique. The movements are straight forward, alternating the kicks and glides of opposite skis and poles, hence, the name diagonal because the arms and legs were diagonally opposite in their movements for the sake of balance. The skis were guided by a set of parallel ski tracks which were generally machine-prepared in the later years.

The skating technique does not depend on wax for kicks and glides but, instead, uses the inside edges of the skis for the same purpose, much in the same way the blades of ice skates are used. This technique is more side-to-side in its movements as the weight is transferred from the edged ski to the opposite gliding ski. It essentially increased overall ski speed because the kick is made from a moving ski rather than the momentarily stopped ski for the grip of the ski wax needed for the classic technique. This new technique requires a wider trail and hard-packed snow to become efficient. An increased ski speed of approximately 11% to 16%, depending upon the individual is achieved without significant difference in physiological parameters (heart rate, VO2, etc.). The change to skating technique also ushered in a focus on biomechanical analysis to determine the most efficient movements. Biomechanics is concerned with the forces that act on a human body and the effects these forces produce. It utilizes the application of the scientific principles of mechanics and physics to understand the movement and actions of the human body. Biomechanics is concerned with two major areas, the first involves the biological aspects of movement, including the skeletal and muscular systems and the second is how the laws and principles of Newtonian physics applies to human motion. For example, movement occurs as a result of forces applied to bones, contraction of muscles, and bones acting as levers. Bones, muscles, and nerves work together in producing motion. A principal part of *kinesiology* (the science of movement), biomechanics became an important component to understanding ski technique, both skating and classical. With the help of video analysis that became available in the mid-1980s, coaches and athletes were better able to establish what techniques were effective and correcting faults in athlete's performance. Although the skating technique created an overall advantage in ski speed, it did have some disadvantages in that it was very inefficient at low speeds, especially on uphills. This demanded a high physical price and therefore a slightly different approach to training.

Because of the more explosive and energy demanding nature of skating over conventional skiing, new ideas began to influence the training for cross-country skiing. With the continuing search for greater speed over the snow came some basic changes in the way coaches and athletes were constructing and arranging their training programs. Cardiovascular endurance still played a major role, however muscular endurance became much more important because skating was more taxing causing the muscles to become exhausted before the cardiorespiratory system exhausted its ability to supply oxygen. This was due to lactic acid, so improvement in one's ability to continue working in the presence of lactic acid became an important training concept. A greater focus was placed on what became known as the *anaerobic threshold*, or the point at which the body can no longer provide adequate oxygen to the muscle cells to produce energy aerobically and must begin to produce energy anaerobically. Physiologists determined that the best training adaptations occur just below the point at which high levels of lactic acid are produced and therefore heart rate and lactate monitors became standard tools for monitoring the levels of training.

The later 1980s and early 1990s also were the periods when training became more specific to the changing demands of biathlon, especially during the summer months. As the discipline evolved from a race that took nearly two hours for the 20 kilometers individual race to one that today is sometimes completed in less than 50 minutes, biathlon training moved from the general conditioning for endurance through long hikes and easy running to specific roller-skiing and other strength training devices such as roller boards and arm ergometers. Dry land training, as it is called, included ski bounding and plyometric exercises to develop specific strength for the muscles used for skiing. Planning also became an important concept which wasn't all that different from the Lydiard methodology of the 1960s but planning now included phases or periods with monthly and weekly guidelines that built many hours of training for basic components through the summer and concluding with an orientation towards more intensity in the fall before a tapering or recovery in advance of the first races of the season. The U.S. National Team coaches hired from Europe in the 1990s and more recently (Walter Pichler, Algis Shalna, Per Nilsson, Jonne Kähkönen and Jonas Johansson) brought with them expert knowledge and installed a well-planned and effective training methodology among the national team members that led to ever-increasing success.

Today's best athletes are physically training 260-290 days a year, with 60-80 days of rest. On the average, they spend 600-1,000 hours per year following well organized and monitored plans. Beginning with lactate profiles for each athlete developed in lab or field testing which match the production of lactic acid according to the athlete's heart rate, their training is then divided up into training zones that are designed to best meet individual needs for the high performance required for successful racing. The four or five training zones are determined by a percentage of one's maximum heart rate and level of lactate concentrations in the blood (measured in parts per million, or mMol). The lower levels of training are designed to improve the cardiovascular system's ability to provide oxygen to the muscles cells through development of capillary structure, oxygen transport and energy production by training below 75% of the maximal heart rate and keeping lactate concentrations below 4-5 mMol. The training levels above that are designed to develop race sustaining values above 90% of the maximal heart rate and more than 8 mMol of lactates. Supplemented with specific strength training, much of the training is also combined with shooting at the range on roller skis.

Another important development in the athlete's training that began in the 1980s was that of women's participation. At first, the women pioneers of the sport trained just as the men did, following similar methodologies with similar volume and intensities. Yet despite the discussion of gender equality in the social environment, it was clearly apparent that women and men were not equal in sports performance. There is variation between all individuals. Some athletes start off with better genetic ability, better training, better equipment, etc. To separate all the potential variables would be impossible, but to achieve a degree of fairness, competitors are separated into different classes, according to age for example. Similarly, women compete against women and men against men, but the fundamental training remains the same despite the differences in performance abilities.

Contrary to the social and political discussion on gender, women and men are not physically equal. The most important and primary biological role of child birth and lactation creates anatomical and physiological differences that prevent women from achieving the same power output as men. The main differences between males and females that affect athletic women's performance are well known and rather obvious, but those factors having the strongest impact are that women generally have a smaller heart and 10% less in cardiac output, about 20% less blood volume and 10% less hemoglobin, smaller lungs and 10% lower vital capacity, and a wider pelvis decreasing mechanical efficiency by increasing the angle of the femur, which bring the knees closer together. Average females possess about 10% more body fat than the average male, thus increasing the load to be carried, and of course there is the well-known differences in hormonal levels, especially of testosterone, that impact muscular strength.

There is a separate category for women because without it, women would have a difficult struggle to even qualify for the Olympic Games. Elite performances in nearly all sports by women range from 10 to 12% lower than that of men, however this doesn't change things for the training required for success by women. The IBU did reduce the distance for the women's relay from its original distance of 7½ kilometers, which was the same for men, down to 6 kilometers. This also does not change the training methodologies between men and women, but the fact that the distance for all the women's biathlon races is less than that of the men takes the performance discrepancy into account and equalizes the races times, making for more exciting and for closer race finishes. The most important training requirement difference between men and women is fundamentally the same for that between age-groups which require the volume and intensities or *"training load"* to be matched to the individual based on their age, physical maturation and skills development.

Another change in the evolution of training over the years has been the use of summer ski training. Although the USMWBTC used the early and late snow at the Independence Mines site near Palmer, Alaska as early as 1961, skiing during the summer months was limited to a few visits to local Alaskan glaciers by army helicopters. In the late 1970s summer ski training on European glaciers become a normal part of European teams training. Using their own resources U.S. athletes began to include summer skiing as a part of their training, traveling to Austria or Switzerland to train among the European teams. The U.S Biathlon Association made an initial investment into setting up a training site on Alaska's Eagle glacier but had to withdraw from further support due to financial limitations. In the 1980s the National Guard built a biathlon range at West Yellowstone, Montana and helped to develop that location as an early snow training site that provided both altitude and early snow training. Regular training at higher altitudes had also become a serious part of the athletes training in that it provided short term boosts to the levels of blood hemoglobin that improved the oxygen-carrying capacity of the blood, leading to a short-term improvement in race performance. After the experience of the 1968 Summer Olympic Games at Mexico's City's over 7,300 ft. elevation, more research went into performance at higher altitudes and the changes that occurred in the blood hemoglobin levels and how it translated to an improvement in performance at competitions both at higher altitudes as well as boosting performance at sea levels. Regular visits for training at higher altitudes helped to maintain that advantage.

By the 1990s the National Guard had developed a sequence of events that allowed continual visits to on-snow training throughout the summer months. After the competitive season, a month of recovery and passive training was planned for April. May began the next training year by increasing the training volume, mixing dry-land training with two weeks of on-snow skiing at Bend, Oregon. In the last weeks of June and the beginning of July the team spent three weeks in Norway and Finland where they skied in the mountains and in the innovative Ski Tunnel at Voukatti, Finland. August saw the team travel to South America for training and military races in the Southern Hemisphere's winter at Ushuaia and Bariloche, Argentina and Portillo, Chile. After an October training camp at altitude near Utah's Olympic site, the team began its winter training on early snow at West Yellowstone. As the U.S. Biathlon Association's resources improved, the U.S. National team followed a similar training routine using the Ski Hall at Oberhof, Germany or Torsby, Sweden.

While the physical training saw many changes through the years, so too did the marksmanship training. In the early years the shooting demands of different distances of targets out to 250 meters with large bore rifles and two-minute penalties for misses saw a much more methodical and slower approach to shooting. Early rifle training followed similar patterns as that of normal shooting disciplines and was often done separated from the ski or physical training. For the most part, biathlon was viewed as two separate disciplines combined or "fit together" in the same time frame. The coupling of the two sports into one was different than the other multi-sport events such as triathlon, pentathlon or decathlon. The various disciplines of those sports were in sequence and did not directly impact each other except for the accumulation of fatigue. The skiing and shooting of biathlon are simultaneous, done concurrently and thus both have a direct impact on the other and the final outcome. This view gradually changed in the later 1960s when the shooting distance was standardized at 150 meters and the time spent on shooting was reduced through more specific marksmanship training related to the demands of biathlon. By the middle 1970s following the example of the Finns, the shooting times were reduced to 45 seconds and soon after even faster with the change to small bore caliber rifles at 50 meters targets.

The closely interrelated sequence of actions: assuming the proper position, establishing the sight picture or aiming, holding, releasing the trigger, and following through with the shot were always a requirement for biathlon success, however for shooting a series of accurate shots, these actions had to become a focus of the training and made to be routine and timely. This is the difficult and intriguing part of biathlon in that beyond establishing a good solid shooting position, the remainder of these actions are psychological rather than physical. The mental aspect of shooting is essentially the processing of information. Despite the difficulty in accurately measuring psychological elements, current research has been able to discover some of the key elements that now allow top biathlon participants to attain high degrees of accuracy in shooting five shoots in under 30 seconds despite the physical stress.

The basic principles for biathlon marksmanship success fundamentally involve the basic prone and standing positions, aiming at the target through the rifle sights (sight alignment and sight picture), holding the respiration (breath control), trigger pressure and follow-through. The first of these are made in such rapid sequence that they appear to be made simultaneously and may be described as acts of observation, analysis, and judgment. The position is established with the help of sensory perception or the ability to provide an adequate degree of balance and equilibrium. This complex process, called *kinesthesia*, involves the evaluation of every muscle in the face, neck, shoulders, arms, hands, back, stomach, legs, and feet. Exactly how this process of sensory feedback is learned is unknown, but the ability to perform it seems to come with experience and training and is dependent upon the functions of the sensory and internal organs. Aiming is what might be considered the first real mental task involved in biathlon shooting by the competitor. It begins with the selection of the right target frame and goes on to the selection of the right target, the evaluation and correction of the sight alignment, and continues to the right instant when the aiming point is close enough to the center of the target, or sight picture.

Once the athlete's shooting position is established, the remaining other factors of successful shooting become more difficult. The hold can be judged from two aspects. Is it steady and is it durable? The hold is steady when it is free from oscillation or movements, and it is durable when it remains long enough to insure a proper trigger release and follow-through. A hold may be steady but not durable. The athlete judges this by what is seen through the sights and what the body senses, or if the muscles will maintain the steadiness long enough to allow the proper execution of the shot. Releasing the trigger is simply a final semi-conditioned physical act of increased pressure on the trigger, without disturbing or creating movement in the rifle. Once the shot has been fired, concentration then shifts immediately to evaluating the process. Often called follow-through, it is more than simply "holding on" to the rifle until the bullet has left the barrel. It is a concentrated effort to sense and analyze every aspect of the performance up to completion of the recoil, so that the strike of the bullet on the target can almost be predicted with accuracy. The moment the shot is fired has been described as "the psychological moment in which the entire mind and body blend in a fully coordinated act." The difficulty of this act is compounded by the physical stress placed on the body during skiing. Under this condition, it becomes an internal struggle as well, in order to control the involuntary heart and breathing frequencies.

How the amazing success of elite athletes is accomplished is best explained by understanding the sensory register, which is capable of holding large amounts of sensory information for a very brief amount of time and the amount of the information to be processed as it relates to concentration and attention. The role of concentration is critical to biathlon shooting success. Concentration is a state of consciousness, but due to the overwhelming complexity of the neurophysiological system, it is difficult to describe exactly. It is known that, in this state, one's attention must be limited to or concentrated on performance, and anything not part of the positive shooting process must be excluded. Concentration is therefore, limiting one's attentional focus to the required and relevant sensory information and cues for successful results. Attention thus plays a key role in shooting.

Concentration or attentional focus can also become confused or distracted. Elite athletes are able to devote total attention focused on the act of shooting, shot by shot. It cannot be on the hits or misses, the competitors, skiing or time spent on the range, or anything else that is not directly related to the shooting performance. Selective attention must screen out irrelevant sensory information and focus on performance-based cues. These cues are the semi-automatic sensory responses controlled from inside the consciousness. They are the semi-automated acts of shooting technique that develop during training and effort. The entire process can only be marginally controlled by the thought process, where thought control is used only to avoid errors caused by negative thoughts, diverted attention or distractions, disrupted rhythm or cadence, and changes in environmental conditions (wind).

A big difference between biathlon and marksmanship shooting is the athlete's arousal rate, as in a race environment. Arousal, stress or tension causes an increased narrowing of the attentional focus, with a progressive elimination of input from the more "peripheral" aspects. One effect of high arousal is the deterioration in the quality of discrimination between relevant and irrelevant cues during shooting performance. Increased narrowing of attentional focus and increased distractibility to irrelevant cues seem to be common from many different sources of arousal such as loud, continuous noise, increased motivation to succeed or fear of failing. When stress conditions become even more severe, *hypervigilance* or panic cause even greater disruptions in performance. This is often the case during a biathlon race when the cardio-vascular stress causes CO_2 accumulation in the blood, disrupted respiration, etc., and ultimately causing an intense stimulus in which time is quickly running out before the appropriate response must be taken. It appears that perhaps the attention is so narrowed that no alternative actions can be considered or that the alternative of restarting the shooting sequence can be initiated. The fact that maximum concentration lasts for only a few seconds under the circumstances of the physical stress, and visual acuity of the eye reduces its focusing capacity quickly, the whole process of biathlon shooting uses only 15 to 20 seconds in actual shooting time. The total time, or range time by elite athletes today from the time they remove their ski poles until they pick them up again is normally less than 30 seconds, more than a minute and a half quicker than those in the early days when sometimes the athletes even removed their skis (it was later made against the rules to remove the skis). The early participants in biathlon also did not have to deal with the loud distractions by the spectators, and a vastly different set of competition pressures.

In the five decades that biathlon has been contested at the World Championships and Olympic Winter Games there have been impressive developments. In 1960, it took the medalists over an hour and half to complete the individual race which included about 8 minutes for the time on the range for shooting. In 2014 that shooting time had been reduce to 2 minutes and the race total time just under 50 minutes. For the average of the 20 shots taken by the competitors, the average number of misses went from 8.3 in 1960, with more than a third of the competitors missing half of their targets, to 2.7 in 2014, despite that the number of competitors in the race tripled. The reasons for these developments are partly due to the changes in the rules, technologies and most importantly training methodologies. Athletes, coaches and scientists have tried to find optimal solutions to the training methods to the point where athletes today are skiing up to 10,000 kilometers per year, training over 700 hours, shooting ten thousand rounds, not including the many hours of dry-firing (training the elements of shooting without live firing). Training is continuous, year-round, broken into periods of focus on specific training goals and competitions beginning in November and lasting until April. As biathlon experienced a change to professionalism, maximizing performances based on uniform training systems has led to higher degrees of perfection. The number of athletes capable of extraordinary performances in important events has grown significantly over the years. The number of nations who send athletes to competitions with a chance to win medals has also improved considerably. Athletes now have a more thorough knowledge of the demands of the competition as well as the knowledge of the complex outcomes of their training. With the continual advancement of their training and support, U.S. athletes are now within the top group of international competitors and regularly in a position to be successful and win medals.

CHAPTER 17

The Equipment

As similar in all areas of modern life, technology, advancement in knowledge and the development of new materials has dramatically improved the athletic performance in biathlon. The two most important items critical to biathlon racers are their skis and rifle. The 10th Mountain Division soldier's skis were made by the Northland Ski Company of Laconia, New Hampshire for WWII, but the Western State College skiers of the early to mid-1950s who were among the participants in the first biathlon race at Camp Hale in 1956 were using Groswold cross-country skis which were made in Denver. Thor Groswold grew up in Norway and was later encouraged by friends and associates to begin to manufacture skis, starting his company in 1932, and developed his ski-making techniques by trial and error and from the little knowledge he had brought from Norway. He continued to produce the Groswold Skis from late 1932 until the spring of 1952. Both the Northland's military skis and the Groswolds were manufactured from a single piece of wood.

In the early 1950s the Western State ski team bought most of their equipment from Bill Copper, owner of Bill's Sport Shop in Leadville, Colorado. He was eventually able to purchase Sundins cross-country skis from Sweden for the team. The Sundins Ski Factory was started by Eric Sundins in 1925 in Hudiksvall, Sweden where he produced laminated skis with the right features by designing the Sundin hydraulic presses. In 1954 when Tony Mendez, who had a clothing store in Gunnison (Western Toggery), took an interest in the Western State ski program, he started ordering Järvinen skis and equipment for the team. Järvinen skis were manufactured in Lahti, Finland by the Finnish nordic combined skier, Esko Järvinen who competed in the late 1920s and early 1930s. He won an individual bronze at the 1929 FIS Nordic World Ski Championships in Zakopane, Poland. Järvinen skis became highly respected as some of the best racing skis right through to the 1970s when wood skis were replaced by skis constructed of synthetic materials, forcing the company into bankruptcy in 1991. Most of the 1960 Squaw Valley Olympic team raced on Järvinen skis, however Norwegian Bonna skis were also popular during that period. For their boots and bindings, they used leather boots and 4 pin Rottefella bindings. Karhu boots from Finland were common and were fastened to the bindings by drilling holes in the toe of the sole for the 4 pin bindings. For ski poles, they used bamboo-cane with good-sized baskets. They drilled small holes in each joint, injected glue and taped each joint to make them last longer. In the early 1950s they wore wool knickers with knee length cable stockings and light sweaters for tops. They used buckskin leather gloves with a liner. By the mid 1950-60s they wore the poplin Swedish white or blue racing suits. In the days before the rules for racing in cold temperatures were restricted, the leather boots and gloves made for an unpleasant experience, not to mention lying on the cold snow in poplin uniforms that tended to absorb the moisture and refreeze it in the clothing.

By the mid-1960s new fabrics found their way into athletic, aerobic, and exercise apparel. These were responsible for improving both the warmth and wicking features of sports clothing and with the introduction of Spandex and Lycra, known for their exceptional elasticity, they modernized cross-country racing uniforms. First in kickers and tops, they eventually became one-piece suits and eventually with full-length legs. The one-piece suits were an inconvenience when a last-minute toilet visit required a "sit-down," especially for the women, and they eventually lost popularity to two-piece top and pants versions. With a base layer that has a wicking property such as polypropylene that was designed to remove moisture from the skin into the fabric where it will evaporate and warmups of insulating layers of fleece, wool or other synthetic fibers such as Polartec®, which maintained insulating abilities, were designed into the clothing, cross-country and biathlon racing was made much more pleasant than the uncomfortable and sometimes biting cold experiences of the early times.

The gradual development of synthetic insulating fabrics also found their way into ski boots and gloves. At the 1976 Winter Olympic Games at Innsbrück the famous sport shoe manufacturer Adidas introduced a new ski boot and binding combination that was modeled after running shoes with a toe extension that fit a new narrow 38mm binding, replacing the 75mm bindings that had been the standard Rottefella binding since they were developed in 1927. The Rottefella 75 mm binding, which became the Nordic Norm system, had four small pins that stick up from the binding to the toe of the boot which had opposing holes into which the pins were inserted, then clamped down by a bail. The binding was asymmetrical, having left and right foot orientations. The new Adidas binding had no right or left which allowed the skis to be indifferent to right or left. Rottefella soon followed with a scaled-down version of the traditional binding which forced ski boot manufacturers to choose which system they would use. In 1979 the French boot company Salomon introduced the SNS system that had a "U-shaped" metal bar protruding from the front of the boot and a ridged plate under the sole for better turning control. The toe bar was locked under a lever on the ski binding.

Nike also briefly produced a ski boot using the Rottefella toe, but with a grooved sole that hung over the edge of the ski giving the boot great turning control. Jay Bowerman had previously used a ski boot made by his father at the 1972 Olympic team trials with the famous "waffle" sole. Adidas also redesigned their system (SDS) with a binding that worked well for both the classical technique and the newly developing skating technique. The introduction of skate technique forced both Rottefella and Salomon to redesign their boots and binding combinations. Although Rottefella did not produce ski boots, their binding system (NNN and NIS), which was similar to the competing Salomon system (SNS) in which both featured an integrated binding plate on the top of the ski to which the bindings attached by a metal bar under the toe of the boot and used one or two ridges extending backwards from the toe latch that matched corresponding channels in the boot's sole. The boots for skating also provided better stability with over the ankle support and featured construction that included new products such as Thinsulate® and Gore-tex® to protect the feet from cold temperatures.

Through the 1960s there was little change in the clothing other than the development of better warmups and the introduction of better synthetic fabrics for the clothing such as nylon tricot racing suits. Gloves and boots were still basic leather and in the extreme cold, leather mittens replaced the gloves and wool socks were worn over the boots to provide an extra layer of insulation for the feet. However, skis and ski wax witnessed more dramatic improvements. Strong competition among the many ski manufacturers in Norway led to several technical improvements and consequentially faster ski speeds. It wasn't until 1939 that laminated skis were produced when chemists invented glues strong enough to hold the various laminations together permanently. Skis were constructed with thin layers of wood that were glued together in narrow strips called "cane" throughout the entire length of the ski. The Splitkein ski factory was established by Peter Østby in 1935 and moved to Honefoss in 1950 where it produced Splitkein skis. Literally Splitkein means "split cane" in Norwegian, referring to the laminations of the ski. Splitkein skis became a dominant force in Norwegian skiing and in the early 1960s the USMWBTC provided the team members with these skis.

By the late 1960s other Norwegian and Swedish ski manufacturers began to challenge Splitkien's dominance. Among those were Sweden's Edsbyn which became the largest Swedish ski producer in the mid-1970s and were a favorite of coach Sven Johanson at the USMWBTC in that period. Two other brands of Norwegian skis that became favorites of the U.S. competitors during the period, up to the demise of wood skis, were Blå Skia (Blue Skis) and Landsem. Ivar Halvorsen opened his ski shop in 1952 and most of the skis made during that time were dark brown and utilitarian. A friend and fellow coach Gunnar Finstad returned from the 1956 Winter Olympics in Cortina, Italy and mentioned to

Ivar that the winning skis at the Olympics were colored. Both thought that it would be a good idea to color Ivar's skis in his factory, so Ivar used traditional Norwegian blue paint to color the skis the next day. The results were amazing. The skis were no faster, they just looked like they were. After giving them to local ski racers, including the 16-year old Odd Martinsen, they all returned with good results and created a demand for his skis. Odd Martinsen used a pair of wooden Blå Skias in the 1968 Winter Olympics in Grenoble, France to win a silver medal in the 30km and a gold medal in the relay. Martinsen's skis weighed a mere 1300 grams (2.86 lbs.) however weight alone was not the only factor; Blå Skias were some of the first skis to have purposely built camber for specific snow conditions. Halvorsen used birch, beech, fir, hickory, and balsa in special combinations for his skis. When Norwegian ski racers Odd Martinsen, Ivar Formo, and Jan Istad took Olympic and World Championship medals on Blå Skia skis the demand for them intensified, but Halvorsen's small factory in Nittedal, Norway with 8 employees was strained to keep up with demand and at its best could only produce 8,000-pair a year. During the late 1960s and early 1970s most of the U.S. cross-country and biathlon competitors were using Jarvinen and Splitkein skis while a few of the USMWBTC athletes ordered Landsem and Blå Skia, shipped by air from Norway to Alaska.

Landsem was somewhat in the same category as Blå Skias and became popular among some of the U.S. athletes in the early 1970s. Started in 1918 in Rindal, Norway by Ole Jonsen Haltli, he produced skis under another name until 1948 when he changed the name to Landsem. Producing over 100,000 pairs in that first year of production they became Norway's most popular brand and still hold the record for Olympic medals won with most of the champion skiers using Landsem skis through the 1970s. Everyone, from Norway's many gold medal skiers to Norway's King Olav, used Landsem skis. However, they too faced the change away from wood to synthetic materials. Making the switch better than most with their innovative "honeycomb core" the factory was sold to Madshus in 1987. Madshus had produced wooden skis since 1906 when there was little distinction between Nordic and Alpine styles of skiing and was a leader in innovation. Taking advantage of glued laminated skis in 1934 led Madshus to produce multiple-layered construction that gave more strength, lighter weight and more mobility to skis. Laminated skis allowed Madshus to produce more specialized skis, and eventually for specialized track skiing and cross-country racing which had become the backbone of the growing Winter Olympic Games movement. The Madshus factory flourished in the heart of Norway becoming a specialist after 1964. Madshus built a leadership role in the many types of cross-country skiing. In 1968 and 1972 Magnar Solberg of Norway, with Madshus skis repeated winning gold medals in biathlon at the Winter Olympics in Grenoble and Sapporo. In the early 1970s Madshus created the Skilom brand name and together with Norwegian boot, binding, pole and cross-country clothing manufacturers under the Skilom name, carried Nordic skiing to an unprecedented number of countries worldwide. Many of the famous wood ski manufacturers tried to make the switch from wood to composite skis, however the ski market was briefly dominated by the Austrian ski manufacturer Kneissl, made popular due to the multiple Swedish World Champion and Olympic medalist Gunde Svan. In a market with small margins many failed to make a profitable business, however, Madshus after acquiring the technologies of cellulose surfaces, and then polyethylene and aluminum technologies, notably the aluminum "honeycomb core" from Landsem, was able to make the transition to composite ski production. Madshus, along with Rossignol of France, Fischer and Atomic of Austria, are the few remaining competitive cross-country racing manufacturers providing high level racing skis.

Despite the movement towards early metal alpine skis in the late 1940s, it was interesting that the properties of wood actually delayed that development in cross-country skis. It was the natural characteristics of wood and ski waxing that was the major problem slowing that development. Wood is designed by nature to soak up water transporting it through the cellular structure visible in the wood grain. Ski waxing long predates the development of alpine skiing and it arose naturally, in the early days of Scandinavian skiing, from the fact that waterproofing wood also helped it to glide on snow. The earliest applications were of pine tar, often called pitch. For skis to have good glide, the important issue is that the wood repels water. The technical term for water repellency is "hydrophobic" (the opposite is hydrophilic). Pine tar glides on snow because it's insoluble in water. Water beads on it nicely, forming droplets instead of sheets. This means that at a microscopic level, the ski glides not on a sheet of water, nor on hard-point snow crystals, but on the equivalent of tiny liquid ball bearings between the sharp edges of snow crystals and the ski gliding surface. At the same time, pine tar on wood isn't perfectly smooth, so when you kick back, the surface links up mechanically with the snow surface to provide traction. It is that combination of characteristics, a durable wood preservative, with good kick and decent glide, that made pine tar the standard choice as a permanent base treatment for several centuries. The pleasant and sharp resinous scent of boiled pine tar was a common odor in ski shops and around cross-country and biathlon races in the 1950-1960s.

The first actual ski waxes for cross-country appeared in 1913 when Norwegian Peter Østbye patented Østbye Klister. The word is of German origin and means glue or adhesive. It was a mix of paraffin, pine resin, venetian turpentine and shellac, packaged in tubes and meant specifically to improve kick in wet snow. A pretty good racer himself, with his klister, Østbye beat favorite Lauritz Bergendahl to win the 18-kilometer race at Holmenkollen in 1914. At the time, his friends were blending their own klisters using beeswax, resin, melted phonograph records and bicycle innertubes, and occasionally blowing up a kitchen. Østbye's Klister became a sensation.

By World War II, North American firms had begun packaging rub-on ski waxes, usually applied from metallic tubes. The 10th Mountain Division was issued waxes for three or four temperature ranges, each imprinted with the warning that they should not be applied with heat. The waxes were clearly the byproducts of industrial processes. One of the manufacturers had, as its main business, the production of torpedo fuses while another was manufactured by a company specializing in grease. A breakthrough in ski wax technology came in 1943, when the Swedish chemical firm Astra AB hired Martin Matsbo, 1937 winner of the Holmenkollen 18-kilometer race and bronze medalist in the 1936 Winter Olympic Games and 1935 and 1938 World Ski Championships 4×10 relay, to develop a commercial ski wax based entirely on controlled, synthetic waxes. By that time synthetic waxes were predictable, stable, plentiful and cheap byproducts of petroleum refining. By mixing paraffin with microcrystalline waxes to make harder and more flexible formulas, Matsbo produced a series of three hard waxes and two klisters designed to provide a good combination of kick and glide across the entire range of cross-country snow conditions. A new company founded in 1946 by Börje Gabrielsen began producing waxes in Sweden and at Fjellhamar, near Oslo, under the brand name Swix, a blend of the words ski and wax. Because synthetic waxes were colorless, tasteless and odorless, Swix added pigments, with warm reddish colors for warm wet snow and cool blue-green colors for cold dry snow. The principle was simple enough: soft waxes, with low melting temperature around 110°C were very hydrophobic and worked well for wet snow, especially when the snow crystals had gone soft and round; and hard waxes, with melting temperatures around 140°C, were less hydrophobic but resisted penetration by the hard-sharp corners of cold snow crystals. Blending the soft and hard waxes covered the intermediate conditions. The brand quickly grew popular and inspired competition. In time for the Oslo Winter Olympic games in 1952, a group of young Finnish chemists established the Rex brand and gained wide acceptance. German, Italian and Swiss companies, Holmenkol, Rode and Toko that had been working with alpine waxes soon followed producing their own color-coded synthetic waxes.

In 1974 a revolution in the cross-country and biathlon racing environment occurred. That year fiberglass construction and plastic bases had arrived, thanks largely to Kneissl and Fischer. The Austrian factories successfully promoted fiberglass race skis to top competitors, among them Swede Thomas Magnusson, who won the 30km race at the Falun World Championships and Finn Juhani Suutarinen who won both the sprint and individual biathlon races at the World Biathlon Championships that year. The design engineers in Austria had learned their craft in alpine racing, and they naturally tested their skis with alpine glider waxes at the tip and tail, resorting to a softer kick wax, even a klister in the camber "pocket."

This development came from Austrian manufacturers of alpine skis because they had been experimenting with plywood-core, pressure-bonded aluminum metal skis since 1949 after American Howard Head had developed the first successful ski made of very different components. It had a plywood core glued under pressure and heat between top and bottom aluminum sheets with plastic sidewalls. By 1960 Head skis, along with competitors and imitators, supplanted at least half the wood alpine skis. In 1954 the first skis with a polyethylene base were introduced in Austria by Kofler and shortly after a similar material made by InterMontana in Switzerland was marketed under the brand name P-tex. With this polyethylene being widely adopted by ski factories, and supplanted earlier plastic bases and with the addition of a polyethylene base, Howard Head introduced the final version of the Head Standard ski. In the fall of 1963 he decided to bring his technology to cross-country skis and provided the cross-country skiers preparing for the 1964 Olympic team trials some prototype Head cross-country skis. Ed Williams and Mike Elliot were two of the skiers who were provided the skis, however both found difficulty in making the cross-country wax appropriately adhere to the ski base. After Ed Williams broke one of the skis under the binding while powering through a dip in the track, they abandoned them. A pair was still present in the team room at the USMBTC in Alaska in 1970, however no one ever tried to use them because "they couldn't hold the wax." Improvements in a P-tex running surface by graphite additives, the waxes and waxing applications gradually solved that problem.

Although 1974 was the breakthrough year, there had been a few earlier examples of the coming revolution. A preview came at the 1973 World Championships at Lake Placid when Daniel Claudon of France used a pair of early Fischer skis in the relay race. In extremely warm and wet conditions he moved the French team right towards the front of the competition on his leg and clearly had much better downhill speed than the other racers. Following the race, he admitted that he himself was so surprised at the difference and how light the skis remained, in comparison to wood skis that always became heavier and slower in such conditions due to the wood soaking up moisture from the wet snow. Landsem and Järvinen made good efforts to maintain their position with plastic surfaces on their skis, but the final victory for wood skis came at the same year's 1974 World Ski Championships in Falun when Norway's Magne Myrmo won the 15km race on Landsems. Both companies and others in Scandinavia tried to convert to composite constructions with Landsem having some success prior to being sold to Madshus, but eventually only Madshus remained competitive.

Much like what had happened in track and field where landing surfaces for the vertical jumps dramatically improved and allowed for the technical evolution of the high jump, composite skis dramatically changed ski speed. Landing pits allowed competitors the ability to safely land on one's back, changing jumping technique with the "Fosbury flop" becoming the new technical way to jump, and improving the world record by an impressive margin, presently at 8 feet. The same was true for the pole vault which also had the technological advancement of the vaulting pole. The world record stood just over 15 feet with only minor improvements from the 1940-50s, achieved with bamboo and metal poles, with landing pits of sawdust. With the introduction of the foam landing surfaces and fiberglass and carbon fiber vaulting poles in the late 1960s, it allowed for much higher hand holding position and reducing the fulcrum through the pole's compression with the return of recoil energy helping to push the athlete higher. Pole vaulters now attain heights over 20 feet. To the same extent, the development of skis and ski poles constructed of composite materials along with the mechanical improvements in grooming and preparation of the ski tracks, the new skating technique and two big advances in ski wax chemistry with the development of surfactants and fluorocarbons saw the times for ski racing reduced to half the time of earlier years. The Swix chief chemist Leif Torgersen was behind the advances of fluorocarbon ski waxes. Looking for something to repel dirt which progressively slowed the ski through the course of the race, he began experimenting with a form of fluorocarbon that could be ironed into the ski base for both cross-country and alpine race courses and found that it improved glide by about 2% over the best non-fluorocarbon waxes and in 1990 the company introduced a commercial version called Cera F. Other companies soon followed with their own versions which are combinations of fluorinated hydrocarbon waxes and fluorocarbon overlays in powder forms. Fluorocarbons decrease surface tension and surface area of the water between the ski and the snow, increasing speed and glide of the ski under specific conditions. Fluorocarbons are now also produced in liquid forms.

The priority of ski waxes is quite high for the top level international races. At the current international competitive levels, most athletes have access to the best equipment available. However, of all the equipment required for biathlon, their skis and their rifles are equally important and one's performance on the shooting range often makes the difference between being on the podium or not. Even though over the years the shooting penalties have been reduced and the target distances and calibers have changed, the fact remains that one cannot win a biathlon race without successfully hitting the targets, and therefore the quality of the rifle and ammunition and the marksmanship skills of the athlete are as important as the ski equipment and the athlete's physical abilities on skis.

In the early World Biathlon Championships and Winter Olympic Games the

20km race required shooting at four distances, 200m prone at 6.5km, 250m prone at 9.5km, 150m prone at 12.5km, and 100m standing at 15km and then another 5km ski to the finish. The sport was still evolving, and military rifles were the standard, mostly using 6mm, 6.5mm or 7.62mm calibers. The rifles were conventional bolt actions with aperture iron sights, although some used the open post for the front sight. The rifles used at the first biathlon race at Camp Hale in 1956 were standard U.S. Army M1 rifles, except for Jim Mahaffey and John Burritt who used their 30-06 hunting rifles. The American team soon switched to purposely-built target rifles using the Winchester Model 70 in 30.06, .308 and .243 calibers. A rifle's caliber is a unit of measurement related specifically to the bullet's diameter. Each of those used were military based with primary ballistic considerations given to the target distance, velocity and bullet weight. The complexities of ballistics and accuracy were a much greater part of biathlon shooting before the change to rim-fire small bore, .22 caliber in 1978 and are the basis for many misconceptions about rifles and shooting today.

Within the general public there is a general misunderstanding about guns and rifles. Biathlon uses specialized "rifles"; not guns. The technical difference is that rifles have "rifling" or spiral grooves in the barrel to give the bullet a spin as it leaves the barrel. This "twist" can be measured normally as a 10-, 12- or 14-inch twist, meaning that the bullet will be completely rotated every 10, 12 or 14 inches. A gun has no rifling and, like "shotguns," have smooth barrel interiors, because no spinning of a shotgun's "pellets" is required. (Also, the use of the term gun as in "handguns" is inaccurate; they are "pistols"). The spinning of a bullet from a rifle gives it greater accuracy. Today's biathlon rifles use a 16-inch twist and standard velocity rimfire .22 caliber ammunition with lead bullets of 40 grains and have a muzzle velocity of about 345 meters per second. Yesterday's large bore biathlon rifles were usually .223 or .243 calibers with a centerfire primer and much heavier, metal jacketed bullets because the distance of the targets was much greater. The speed of the older calibers used was much faster than that of today's small-bore caliber at about 930 meters per second for the .243 caliber with a 100-grain bullet. Due to target distance, accuracy was more difficult because the angle of error of the sighting could have a greater impact over the longer distance, therefore higher velocity and heavier bullets could diminish the impact of small sighting errors and the impact of the environment, especially the wind.

The 308 Winchester (7.62 NATO) and the 30-'06 Springfield were both military cartridges well suited for long range shooting and have very similar ballistics. The bullets are available in 100 to 220 grains and optimize with 150-168 grain in both cartridges. Recoil is robust and ear protection is a must. The 243 Winchester, introduced in 1953, was developed by necking down a 308 case to 6mm. This very accurate cartridge uses bullets in the range of 70 to 100 grains.

With a modest recoil, it became a very popular rifle and an excellent choice for biathlon and a strong challenge to the European and Soviet 6.5mm calibers. When the rules changed to a single 150m range the U.S. competitors moved to the .223 (5.56×45mm NATO) Remington cartridge with the Remington Model 700 or 40X being the most used rifles. The cartridge is loaded with a 0.224-inch (5.7 mm) diameter jacketed bullet, with weights ranging from 40 to 90 grains, with 55 grains being the most common. The balance of light recoil and velocity of 960 m/sec gradually made it the choice of many nations outside the Soviet sphere of influence and ultimately the envy of those athletes who were confined to the Soviet 6.5mm rifles that used rimmed cartridges.

The 1972 U.S. Olympic team at Sapporo had impressed the international environment with their shooting results and Dennis Donahue had enhanced the reputation of the rifle with perfect shooting at the 1973 World Biathlon Championships at Lake Placid. On the practice range at the 1974 World Championships at Minsk Art Stegen offered the Soviet star Alexander Tihknov an opportunity to shoot his Remington 40X .223 caliber rifle that had a stainless-steel barrel and thumbhole stock. As others gathered around to watch Tihknov shoot the "American" rifle, he achieved an impressive, very tight group of five shots that were certainly indicative of his ability. However, he felt he had to diminish the quality and performance of the rifle by saying through translators that he wouldn't use it because the stainless-steel barrel would reflect the sunlight. Others winked, knowing that he was impressed but couldn't dare complement superior quality from the United States. During that week, there was a parade of Eastern European athletes to the U.S. athletes' rooms to have a look at their rifles and feel them in the standing shooting position. The East Germans, who appreciated quality were particularly interested in looking them over. Other nations began the switch to .223 caliber and the Norwegian coach Martin Stokken had arranged for Art Stegen to eventually bring six Remington 40X stainless-steel barreled actions to Norway along with large quantities of Sierra 55 grain bullets for the cartridges. The Finnish team also used the .223 caliber in their Sako brand rifles and were very successful in the middle 1970s by increasing the accuracy and speed of the shooting. It was a comforting feeling for the U.S. athletes to know they had the best large bore rifles available.

The UIPMB change to small bore .22 rimfire rifles at 50 meters saw J.G. Anschütz GmbH & Co. KG, a German arms manufacturer specializing in rimfire and centerfire competitive rifles used by many competitive shooters participating in the 50m rifle event at the Summer Olympics become interested in biathlon. Founded in 1856, the company had moved its entire factory and operations from Thüringen, in East Germany (DDR) following World War II to Ulm in southern West Germany (BRD). Dieter Anschütz began development on a biathlon rifle before the change took effect and he brought them, offering for sale to some of the competitors at the 1976 Winter Olympics. A few of the U.S. athletes, knowing the change was coming purchased one.

Before biathlon changed rules to small bore caliber, the majority of .22 rimfire target rifles were relatively heavy, up to 7.5 kg with a cylinder action and a lateral bolt handle which is lifted and pulled back for loading single cartridges by hand. Anschütz designed the Model 1427 biathlon rifle which was based on their Model 54 Bolt Action but with a 64 Action style extractor and a 5-shot magazine. They also reduced the weight of the rifle to 4.5 kg. Knowing it is not possible to permanently keep the rifle motionless during the aiming process in biathlon and that the bullet should leave the barrel as fast as possible after releasing the trigger, reducing the impact of aiming mistakes, the design included a bolt with an extremely light firing pin with only 4 mm travel. This provided for an extremely short lock time of 4 milliseconds, meaning that the bullet left the barrel extremely quick after being struck by the firing pin. Unlike the large bore rifles, this became a very important issue due to the slower velocity of the .22 caliber.

The Anschütz Model 1427 was later improved with the Model 1827B and since the faster shooting times started to play an important role in the result, Anschütz engineers looked for a way to reduce the time needed for the repeating process. In 1981 Heikki Ikola won the World Championships individual race using a Finn-Biathlon rifle with lateral toggle action that was developed and manufactured by a Finnish company, Tampereen Asepaja Oy. Although the loading process could be slightly accelerated compared to the cylinder action, this action had the disadvantage that the lateral cocking lever was very far away from the center axis of the rifle and the travel of the cocking lever was very long so that the trigger hand had to leave the pistol grip for reloading. This slightly impaired the stability of the shooter and rifle, especially in the standing position. The Finn-Biathlon ceased production and only survived for a short time. Shortly after the Russians developed a small-bore biathlon rifle which had several improvements similar to the Finn-Biathlon, but this design also required the shooter's hand to leave the center of aiming while repeating due to the lateral cocking mechanism. In addition, the Russian rifle had a firing pin that extended the lock time. To reduce the disadvantages of a lateral toggle action the former GDR (East Germany) also developed a so-called pistol grip repeater. Repeating was carried out by tilting the pistol grip axially to the barrel axis. With this system, the rifle did not leave the center axis by loading but there was the danger that the tilting of the pistol grip would result in transferred motion on the butt plate and thus on the shoulder of the shooter which made aiming difficult after repeating. A relatively small number of these pistol grip repeaters were manufactured under the name Suhl and they also vanished from the market.

In the mid-1980s Anschütz introduced the 1827BT Fortner. This rifle with its patented Fortner straight pull action, operates very smoothly and can be opened quickly with the index finger and closed with the thumb. Essentially the bolt is pulled back with the trigger finger to eject the spent round and pushed forward with the thumb to bring another round into the chamber. The axial action facilitates aiming after repeating because the loading process is carried out by the wrist making it unnecessary to move the hand from the pistol grip. Therefore, the rifle stays very stable in the position. The elbow does not move which is a great advantage especially in prone position. In addition, the lock time was improved to 3.5 milliseconds. Additional versions of the 1827BT were later introduced as 1827F Sprint Fortner and different barrel options and receiver profile were offered with these rifles. They are currently the most popular with 97% of the biathletes who take part in international competitions using them.

As another big issue that needed to be resolved in the development of small bore biathlon rifles was their performance in cold temperatures. In the United States the first indication of the problem occurred at the U.S. team trials for the 1978 World Championships team. Using one of the new Anschütz rifles, John Hall had a terrible shooting score in an individual race at Lake Placid during a cold day for racing. Still using the paper targets, his shots were scattered all over the target with many in the white. When the targets were sent from the butts, which were still used, John immediately protested and insisted they were not his targets. Without a clear answer on the situation, Dennis Donahue, who oversaw the group changing targets in the butts, couldn't assure the athletes that there hadn't been a mistake and the targets could have been wrongly numbered during the scoring, however that explanation couldn't be reconciled with the other targets. Eventually the race was discarded, denying some athletes a good performance while giving others a second chance, especially John.

As the winter of 1978 progressed, other examples of poor shooting in cold weather began to surface. The previous summer Art Stegen and Peter Hoag made a visit to the Remington Arms research and design team at the factory at Illion, New York. Art had contacted them about developing a .22 rimfire biathlon rifle to comply with the new UIPMB rules. Taking his .223 large bore rifle for an explanation of biathlon and discussion, their team decided to take on the project and built four .22 caliber prototype rifles for biathlon. The rifles were modifications of the Remington M540X .22LR Target Rifle and were quite unusual in that they had a 19-inch barrel with an extended sleeve at the front to maintain the normal distance between the front and rear sights. The magazines were made of plastic and inserted under the bolt action. Their explanation was that a .22 bullet begins to deaccelerate after 19 inches and the shorter barrel would allow the bullet to exit the barrel at a higher velocity and shorter lock time. It was true and when the athletes began testing the rifles everyone seemed to think their standing shooting improved. However, whenever the temperature dropped below 10^0F the accuracy became unreliable, like what was also happening with some of the other rifles. When this feedback was relayed back to the Remington research team, they sent one of their staff to verify the problem. He came to Jericho, Vermont during one of that year's many team trial races and on a day when the temperature was below that when accuracy deteriorated. He went to the range and discovered the problem for himself. He had no explanation and indicated that since most competitive shooting was done indoors during the winter; this problem had never exposed itself. Later, meeting with the Remington marketing department, the question came up early; How many athletes participate in the sport and what kind of market exists for this type of rifle? With the answer of approximately 500, the Remington effort quickly died, since to the marketing staff, that potential small demand did not justify production. It was a great disappointment for U.S. Biathlon since the prototypes were light, with the short 19-inch barrel, a fast lock time and when the temperature wasn't below 10^0F they were very accurate. They also looked quite unique with the front "hood" looking like a silencer, and actually made a "popping sound" when the shot exited the rifle. It would have been a great boost to have an American supplier of biathlon rifles. It was also a shame in that other early biathlon .22 calibers, including Anschütz also experienced the cold weather problems and eventually worked on resolving the problem. It appeared random at first, but testing did discover it was both a rifle and ammunition problem. Testing to sort out those variables eventually led to eliminating the problem by replacing the barrel or eliminating those rifles that experienced the cold weather issues and cold testing precision barrels manufactured according to specific procedures that were developed for improving accuracy in the cold.

Even though Anschütz and the other rifle manufacturers produced a ready to use rifle, including the stock that allows for many adjustments, many of the top-level athletes replaced it with their own custom-made stock. This trend started in the early years when the standard military rifles were modified for better fitting and biathlon use. By the 1970s both Norway and Finland had woodworkers who were producing custom-made stocks. Stein Erik Bredvold of Gjesåsen, Norway became well known for his crafted laminated rifle stocks used by the Norwegian and Swedish athletes. Asepaja Loukonen OY of Aura, Finland made theirs from a single piece of wood and were extremely popular as well. But it was an American athlete who helped develop one most used by the U.S. athletes in the 1980-90s and concepts that were adapted by others. Like Ken Alligood who created the two-piece supporting arm band from his own experience, Glenn Eberle, a 1984 Olympic team member also used his competitive experiences to develop highly specialized biathlon rifle stocks. He had been through the transition from large bore rifles to small bore and from classical skiing to skating and his initial thoughts were to develop a stronger rifle stock to prevent the frequent occurrence of having the stock break at the pistol-grip during a fall backwards on skis. After consulting with engineers and obtaining a grant from the USOC he developed a composite Sitka Spruce/carbon fiber stock that was over 3.5 pounds lighter than anything on the market at the time. The weight reduction and eliminating the fear of breaking a stock was immediately popular with the athletes. To emphasize the strength of his carbon fiber laminated stock Glenn related the story of being hit by a car at a road crossing during a race in Italy. After checking the rifle, it had no damage and he finished the race, but the car was a bit worse off as several pieces of plastic chrome littered the road.

The Eberle Stock soon became the standard for rifle stocks. Virtually every biathlon rifle stock since that time is either an Eberle or a variation on the theme. His lightweight rifle stock even transformed international rules, as it became the standard for the IBU's 3.5 kg minimum rifle weight. Nearly every country at the World Cup level has a producer of their own versions of biathlon rifle stocks, some made of wood and others of composite materials. In 2006 Glenn created a new series made entirely from rarefied aluminum and carbon fiber. Jay Hakkinen, Rachel Steer, and Jeremy Teela became the "guinea pigs" for this "futuristic" look in rifles, using them in the 2006 Olympics Games at Torino. Although he made his first stocks as a hobby, he turned that into a business that now focuses on an entire line of high performance outdoor equipment.

In the early years, the athletes carried their large calibers rounds in loaded clips in ammunition belts with tabbed pockets around their waist. Once the rifle was loaded on the range, the clip was usually returned to the ammunition belt or the rear pocket of their uniform. The athletes at the USMWBTC used such belts that were made of military canvas. Art Stegen decided to fabricate his own from a nylon web belt and nylon tent fabric with a soft leather tab on the pockets. Once the switch was made to small caliber John Morton's wife made similar belts from nylon materials for the Anschütz magazines which were soon copied by the Anschütz factory, like what they had done with the earlier two-piece arm sling of Ken Alligood. The ammunition belts were eventually replaced with magazine cassettes on the rifle stock. The relay rules at the time required the reserve rounds to be put in a cup at the shooting position but were later dropped and were allowed to be placed on the shooting mat. When stock-maker Bredvold watched athletes sometimes scramble around the mat to pick up and load the reserve rounds he inserted a place on the stock to easily reach the reserve rounds without having to break the shooting position. Today, all the rounds, both in the magazines and reserve rounds for the relays are carried in the rifle stock.

When viewed over time, the technological changes in biathlon have been rather dramatic. The equipment, clothing, ski trails preparation and rule changes have all witnessed extraordinary changes since the sport's early days. In his recent book, *Game Changer: The Technoscientific Revolution in Sports*, Rayvon Fouché asserts that since ancient Greek times, athletes have always sought an edge, and argues that physical difference between competitors "may become so infinitesimal that athletic performances may cease to determine the outcomes," and thus technological advances are gradually eroding sport's authenticity. A common solution has been to ban such advances, as did the International Swimming Federation (FINA) by banning full-length swim suits in 2009. Sports federations are often hasty to ban innovations that change the balance of a sport, and are often prone to dithering, as happens with the use of performance enhancing drugs, however changes in the technologies within sport such as baseball's aluminum bats replacing wood, or skiing's synthetic skis and waxing technologies, and the ongoing search for better equipment make the sport more exciting and can provide for more competitive outcomes. With all things being equal, technological advances will not abolish the difference between individual talent, training and ability.

Howard Buxton was a central figure in the transition of biathlon from the U.S. Army to the National Guard and the development of the independent U.S. Biathlon Association. He served as the first president and was also the chief of competition for the 1980 Olympic Games, a member of the U.S. Olympic Committee and Chief of Mission for the 1994 Lillehammer Olympic Games.

U.S. Juniors achieved excellent results after their introduction to international competition. Rusty Scott finished 10th at the World Championships in 1974, with Martin Hagen following close behind in 14th.

The U.S. team at the 1974 World Championships in Minsk, U.S.S.R. included (left to right) Ken Alligood, Dennis Donahue, Peter Dascoulias, John Morton, Lyle Nelson, Rusty Scott, Ernie Meisnser, Art Stegen, Bill Pease, and Martin Hagen.

Like many other former athletes, John Morton made many significant contributions to the sport following his competitive years. A highly successful college coach, he also served as coach or team leader to multiple World University Games, World Biathlon Championships and Winter Olympic Games. He also served on the USBA Board of Directors and as the program director. Authoring two books about biathlon, he eventually became a renowned designer of ski and recreation trails.

The 1975 U.S. World Championships team included (front row, left to right) Ken Alligood, John Morton, Peter Hoag, Peter Dascoulias, (back row) Peter Lahdenpera, Art Stegen, Mike Sallee, Martin Hagen (partially hidden), Lyle Nelson, John Harney and Rusty Scott.

The 1976 U.S. Olympic Biathlon team at Innsbrück, (left to right) Peter Lahdenpera, John Morton, Lyle Nelson, Dennis Donahue, Peter Hoag, Martin Hagen, Bill Spencer, Peter Dascoulias and Peter Karns.

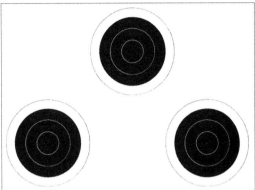

After the rule change to small bore in 1978, the target protocol was changed, requiring two shots at any two targets and one at the third. The scoring of one- and two-minute penalties remained the same. Following the 1980 Olympic Games, immediate response targets (metal) replaced paper targets and the penalty was reduced to one minute for misses in the individual races.

Lyle Nelson achieved excellent results, participating in four Olympic Games. He was elected by the athletes to carry the U.S. flag at Calgary in 1988.

The 1979 U.S. Biathlon team. (left to right) Bill Spencer, John Hall, John Ruger, Glen Ewing, Don Nielson, Rusty Scott, Peter Hoag, Lyle Nelson, Ken Alligood, Glenn Jobe, John Moody, Peter Hale, John Harney, Art Stegen and Martin Hagen.

Holly Beattie was the women's pioneer for U.S. Biathlon. She and Rae Hoisve, behind her in the start cue, were members of the first U.S. Biathlon team to include women.

The 1982 U.S. National Biathlon Team included men and women.

Winners of the first-ever U.S. World Championship medal, Holly Beattie, Kari Swenson and Julie Newnam captured a bronze medal in the relay at the first World Biathlon Championships for women in 1984 at Chamonix, France.

Josh Thompson became the first World Championship individual medalist for the United States when he captured the silver medal in 1987 at Lake Placid.

Joan Smith began her biathlon career early and was one of the first women to participate in the 1992 Olympic Games. She was also a member of the 1994 Olympic team where she achieved a best U.S. performance of 14th place.

Curt Schreiner began biathlon at a young age on a range and ski trails developed by his father. Known for his explosive relay starts he was a member of three Olympic teams, many CISM teams and won seven National Championships.

The 1996 National Guard staff and biathlon team.

The National Guard team at the 1998 Olympic trials included five members of the team that participated at the Nagano Olympic Games.

Jay Hakkinen was a World Junior Champion and a three-time Olympic team member improving the best-ever Olympic Games performance with a 13th place at Soldier Hollow.

Lanny and Tracy Barnes were known to be the fastest and most accurate shooters on the international level.

Jeremy Teela finished 9th in the World Championships and improved the best-ever Olympic performance at the Vancouver Olympic Games, also with a 9th place.

The 2010 U.S. Olympic Biathlon team and staff at the Vancouver Olympic Games.

Max Cobb has been a central figure in the USBA and a significant influence within the IBU.

Tim Burke captured the silver medal at the 2013 World Championships at Nove Mesto (CZE).

Coaches Per Nilson and Michael Löfgren were major contributors to the U.S. Biathlon team's international improvements.

Susan Dunklee finished in 2nd place at the 2017 World Championships in the mass start race capturing the silver medal.

Sean Doherty became the most medaled junior competitor with a total of 10 medals at the World Junior/Youth World Biathlon Championships.

Lowell Bailey's wife and daughter helped celebrate his 2017 World Championship gold medal on the podium at Hochflizen, Austria.

PART IV.

"What Is the Future?"

T he further development of biathlon in the United States, and the athletic values it represents must revisit the cultural values that are pivotal and primary to participation in the activity. The high premium placed on competition is as old as human existence. It began as a form of human survival. Man's ability to survive the natural world depended on his ability to overcome the lack of natural protection and to avoid extinction through his use of strength, endurance, agility and intelligence. Born of necessity, hunting skills were nourished and some hunters distinguished themselves as superior to others. In northern climates, they overcame snow and ice barriers by making crude skis and the most successful possessed better endurance, strength, speed, accuracy and skill. These are the skills inherent in the modern sport of biathlon. However, these characteristics and values are largely overlooked in today's world of productiveness, fads, explosive advertising, market manipulation and indiscriminate profit motives. Value is translated through money and marketability rather than through participation, wholesome competition and educational or social importance. This section is about the other group of participants that exert influence beyond the athletes, coaches and those who organize, manage, govern and promote events; that being the spectators, fans and the media and how that interaction impacts the goals of both those actively involved and those following the sport. As the marketplace for sports entertainment constantly grows, biathlon gradually emerges from the shadows and has taken a respected place among winter sports. As awareness and interest grows, and seeing growth both in membership and in participation in the sport, so too will the financial support and success of the athletes.

CHAPTER 18
The Media and Fans

Throughout history, sport activities have always been integrally related to the political, social and economic structures dominant at the time. Over the last century, more and more activities have been increasingly formalized in the pursuit of this interest. The military was responsible for transforming biathlon from its informal contests to its bureaucratization, or in simple terms from a participant-controlled activity to a focused military purpose which later evolved into national and international organizationally-managed featured events. Biathlon's combination of disciplined skills and personal effort gives it a powerful appeal for participants and spectators alike, however in the early years this appeal remained unknown to the general public in the United States simply because the general public lacked an awareness of its existence. Unlike the Scandinavian nations that had a strong ski culture and experienced the military value of skiing, in the U.S. that experience was mostly limited to 10th Mountain Division soldiers who were the catalyst for its development. After biathlon was embraced by the military, there was little recruiting outside the small group of skiers who entered the military and there was only limited publicity outside of a few hometown newspapers. Knowledge of the sport remained in the confinements of the military and to the limited ski communities which were the only places that informal recruiting took place.

In his 1970 book, *Sne-Ski-Skudd, Om Norsk Skiskyter*, Ole Jacob Bangstad wrote that biathlon was not "sufficiently well-established before the large audience." Other than some newspaper articles there was little media coverage of biathlon's earliest World Championships and only limited visual documentation of biathlon at the 1960 Squaw Valley Olympic Games. In the context of televised sports which has been the greatest agent of change in sports, television revenue paid to the International Olympic Committee amounted to $50,000 in 1960, none of which was shared by the UIMPB. By 1976 the IOC received $10 million for broadcasting rights and shared $16,200 with biathlon. After separation into two separate governing bodies in 1993 and through the efforts of the new International Biathlon Union's Vice President Peter Beyer, a lucrative broadcasting rights had been negotiated with the European Broadcasting Union. This important step brought biathlon into the public consciousness throughout Europe and became by measures of audience viewership, one of the most popular televised winter sports in Europe. By 1998 the IOC revenue for biathlon had increased to $4.7 million and in 2016 the IBU signed another partnership agreement which covered four more biathlon seasons, until 2021/22, extending the current agreement which was due to expire in 2018. The new contract extended the 23-year partnership dating back to 1993, when the IBU was founded.

The gradual evolution from the original biathlon 20km individual race has slowly developed the sport as we know it today. Its evolutionary changes have resulted in a profound impact on the nature of biathlon but had not altered the fundamental concepts and made the sport more suitable for television coverage, creating greater excitement for the spectators. There is no doubt that increased media and television coverage of biathlon has helped in improving public interest as well as providing important revenues.

American audiences were never treated to the exciting atmosphere generated by the World Cup events held in Europe. Although there have been Olympic, World Championships and World Cup events held in North America, on-site participation by general spectators has not been especially inspiring or widely supported. Prior to its re-introduction in 1960, Jean Catherine Conger wrote in an extensive newspaper article, "Olympic Games at Squaw Valley to see Debut of Biathlon Event," in which she described as "an unusual success story for news hounds to sniff during the VIII Winter Olympics." She wrote that the usual recipe for a sport success story begins with the unknown athlete who, after long struggles (preferably the tear-jerking kind, with a minimum of laughs), finally wins you-know-what. Her article then pointed out "that once in a blue moon does it happen that a sport itself knows triumph and a hearty pat-on-the-back from its fans." She continued her article by explaining the history of how biathlon was at first a demonstration sport called the "Military Ski Patrol" and later lost its place among the official Olympic events, but had moved from an Olympic afterthought, and on February 21, 1960 to making its debut as an official event open to all contestants. After continuing her article with many interesting historical facts about the sport, she speculated that TV should help to popularize the new Olympic sport. She suggests that "ski-marksmanship fanciers are obviously hoping to gain new brothers-at-arms by the popular TV showing of this winter's Olympics… millions of TV watchers across the country will see this sport… and in fact, they probably will have a better view than the throngs who will pay $7.50 for the day's privilege to stand beside the starting or finish line…"

However, since biathlon was re-introduced into the Olympic program in 1960, it has seen only marginal television coverage, especially outside of Europe. In 1960, 1964, and 1968 there was no coverage of Olympic biathlon in North

America. In 1972 and 1976 there was mention of biathlon and a few momentary sound bites in the general coverage, but no dedicated live coverage. Plans for live coverage of the 10km sprint race in 1980 were canceled at the last-minute due to a power outage at the Mt. Van Hoevenberg complex, however an edited recorded segment of the team relay was televised. In 1984 recorded highlights were broadcasted for all the biathlon events. In 1988 there was some live coverage mainly due to the expectations of success by Josh Thompson, however when it appeared he would not win any medal, coverage of other events replaced the biathlon event before its conclusion. In 1992 and 1994 recorded coverage for both the men's and women's relay events were televised. No World Championships or World Cup events were televised live, however in 2006 NBC gave biathlon a window in which the U.S. viewing public had a chance to see how exciting and popular the sport is around the world. At the Olympic Games of that year, former National Team and World Championships member Chad Salmela provided the color commentating in a way that continually exposed that excitement, as well as a good insight and understanding, to the viewers and his fellow commentators. All the athletes were seen in U.S. telecasts, some in special features like the Barnes twins and Sarah Konrad's "dual-team" status. NBC also covered the 2010 Games well; however, it was the 2014 Olympic Games at Sochi that provided a turning point for broadcasting biathlon in the U.S.

At Sochi the event that ushered live and increased coverage on American television was the fact that Norway's Ole Einar Bjørndalen was about to surpass Bjorn Dahlie, his countryman's record of winning the most Olympic Winter Games medals. It appeared most certainly that he would succeed and to that end, coverage of his feat would require an explanation of biathlon and extensive live coverage of the biathlon events to the American audience. This was also helped by the fact that Americans Lowell Bailey and Susan Dunklee were in the competitive mix and would give the commentators another angle to their coverage. Outside of the relatively small group of biathlon fans that followed the sport through the IBU's internet live-streaming of World Cups and World Championships there was little opportunity to view biathlon competitions through visual media. NBC's decision to telecast live biathlon events at the 2002, 2006 and 2010 Olympic Games received a positive response, especially when Chad Salmela was hired as the color commentator. His verbal and analysis skills provided expert insight and exciting commentary during the televised events and increased the public interest in the sport.

The 1973 World Championships at Lake Placid drew few competitors and little interest outside of the Nordic ski community. The 1980 Olympic Games was perhaps the most attended event prior to the 2002 Games in Salt Lake City, but the World Cup events held in Lake Placid and Maine showed only mild signs of increasing public interest. After Sochi and the medal winning performances of Lowell Bailey and Susan Dunklee during the 2017 World Championships at Hochfilzen, the athletes and those associated with the sport no longer found themselves having always to explain biathlon to those unaware. Although it took years for the European broadcasting audience to see and embrace the excitement of biathlon, making it Europe's leading televised winter sport, U.S. viewers are slowly being awakened to that excitement. With the development of the U.S. Olympic television cable and live-streaming options, fans are finally offered opportunities to view and enjoy the sport and that can only help foster a growing interest as Americans begin to find greater success at the highest levels of the sport.

CHAPTER 19

Reaching Success

There are many thoughts that occupy the athlete's mind during the many training sessions throughout their career and one of those that repeatedly visits their thoughts, especially during the lonely hours of training, alone without other social contact, is that of victory and standing on the podium. It is during this training that athletes think of their goals and dream of success. It is a reoccurring dream, especially as athletes move closer to reaching their goals at top performance levels. As they develop and learn the sport they often dream of being an Olympic or World Champion, but in the beginning their goals are more simply to acquire the skills and develop their abilities to win a local race and maybe qualify for a team or a championship start. As they improve, their goals gradually move towards ever increasing challenges, and regardless of their talent and the important external factors for success, the goal always remains "to win."

Ever since the first days of biathlon in the United States those athletes participating in training and competition have surely shared the dream and goal of achieving success, at each level of their participation. The ultimate goal of standing on the podium at major competitions, including local and national championships, CISM, World Biathlon Championships and the Olympic Games is a dream that can be realized only when the many prerequisites necessary for reaching the podium steps are met. On the day of a competition at the international level there is little that athletes and coaches can do to enhance their chances, however the priority required for the podium steps is to achieve the race results that make the potential possible and to challenge those who also have the capability to be on those steps. The dream of standing on the podium steps will always be frustrated by results that place one far behind the winner, and through the 1970s U.S. athletes often joked about making the first page of the results sheet. In the 1980s coaches Art Stegen and Bill Spencer often told the athletes that to be on the podium, regular top 15 finishes were a precondition. This was clearly achievable by U.S. athletes since their first participation at the international level. Maurice Paquette was 8th in 1959, John Burritt 15th in 1960, Dick Taylor 11th in 1961, and Peter Karns 14th in 1972. 1961 and 62 were impressive years when Peter Lahdenpera, Dick Taylor and Joe-Pete Wilson surprised their Scandinavian counterparts. Without today's international events, they raced in the Norwegian, Swedish and Finnish championships with well over 100 competitors and the U.S. athletes regularly finished high in the results. However, it was their limited opportunities as well as lacking years involved in high levels of international racing that worked against their ability to "learn how to win" and develop the consistency of good performances that could make medaling at a World Championships a more certain possibility. In fact, prior to and following the 1980 Olympic Games, the U.S. team had no international racing opportunities and only domestic racing in preparation for their Olympic races. It wasn't until the 1980s that Americans had greater access to international events and began to achieve the more consistent results that would eventually put them on the podium.

Championship medal-winning athletes are unique and have the special physical and psychological qualities that make them champions. But it goes beyond just those individual qualities. There are many elements that create the potential to win that are outside any individual's abilities and characteristics. Among these are the very important team environment and the dynamic process that occurs when a group has the tendency to stick together and remain united in the pursuit of its individual and collective goals. During the times that U.S. athletes have been successful in achieving good results and winning World Championships medals there has always been what sports psychologists call a "culture for success." Each of these highly successful moments had common elements that created a culture for success. Besides the talented athletes, there was strong and effective leadership, great coaching, positive attitudes towards work and training, collective action and thinking, the right equipment and waxing decisions and a conscious discipline towards constructing and maintaining a climate favorable for success. One of the most important was that of trusting the coaches and teammates, and that the leadership had done all that was possible to create the conditions for success.

Over the years, success was often frustrated by the lack of adequate resources and the less than optimal time the athletes participated in the sport. While the U.S. Army provided strong financial support, once released from military duty, athletes lost favorable support and ability to effectively continue their participation. Rarely was there an opportunity to participate in more than two Olympic Games and a few World Championships, and unlike the Eastern European state-supported athletes, they were never able to fully develop their potential abilities, set higher goals and learn how to win. Once the army discontinued their training center, the 1970s saw talented athletes struggle as amateurs and although some managed to stay involved over longer periods, many had left the sport for periods which compromised their progression. There was a brief period of success in the 1980s when improved financial resources and the USOC training centers filled some of the required conditions that made winning World Championships possible, but still, the first occurring World Championships success came without any previous international experience at the first World Championships for women in 1984.

In the March 1984 *Biathlon Bulletin* U.S. Coach Marie Alkire began her story about the first World Biathlon Championships for women by writing "The traditional European dominance in nordic sports has been threatened by a handful of American women who are not easily intimidated. Perhaps skiing with a rifle on your back gives you the feeling that you can do anything you want; to include traveling to Europe and winning a bronze medal in the first Biathlon World Championships for women." She continued writing that "thirty-nine athletes representing twelve nations had gathered in the shadow of Mt. Blanc, Europe's highest peak at Chamonix, France. There was a constant excitement prevailing in the famous alpine village, a popular site for European jetsetters. Bozeman, Montana's Kari Swenson started the competitions in a positive fashion for the U.S. women with a 5th place in the 10km individual race with three shooting stages of two prone and one standing. Kari was nearly perfect on the range missing only one shot from the standing position. First through fourth went to the Soviet women, who evidently planned to match the success of their men's teams, which have won the Olympic Gold in the relay since 1968. Kari also lead the women in the 5km sprint event finishing 13th. Again, it was the Soviets and Norwegians who dominated the top ten."

Marie continued the story, writing that "the biathlon relay has always been a favorite for the spectators. The race is high action, quick developing, unpredictable and can be seen almost entirely from the range area. The U.S. three-woman team included Julie Newnam of Mercer Island, Washington, Kari Swenson and Squaw Valley, California's Holly Beattie. After Julie's start leg, the U.S. team was in 5th place, behind the Soviets, Norwegians, Finns and Swedes. Kari again proved she was one of the best by posting the fourth best overall time and lifting the U.S. into 3rd place. Although Holly hit all five prone targets and avoided the penalty lap, the Finnish skier did the same, and by shooting quicker she left the range ahead of Holly. Both approached the range together for the standing shooting. The wind was howling, further increasing the difficulty of shooting while gasping for air and monitoring a pounding heartbeat. Holly shot quickly, but was headed for the 150m penalty lap to ski two loops for the two targets she failed to hit. The Finn was close behind with only one penalty lap and left the penalty loop ahead of Holly for the final 1.5km to the finish. They both skied out of sight, Holly trailing the Finn by 75m. The U.S. coaches were instantly three feet in the air when they reappeared with Holly leading, battling a head-wind with the Finn drafting a ski-length behind. With only 200m of a gradual uphill to the finish and a mix of English and Finnish encouragement, Holly held off the final effort of the Finn to give the U.S. team the bronze medal by a scant foot. Even the Soviet coaching staff was so impressed by the American women's performance they rushed to the winner's circle to kiss each team member."

Marie commented, "the team's inherent enthusiasm spilled from racing to the awards banquet and the real challenge is to go forward from this glimpse of success and make it an American tradition to be on the winner's podium." Marie closed her story by writing that the rewards for Julie, Kari and Holly and others chasing them are great and asked, with the world's best marksman and a nation half covered in snow during the winter; "why shouldn't we excel in biathlon?" It was a unique occasion for those pioneer women and they made the best of it by achieving the first U.S. Biathlon World Championships medals. A major part of their success came from the fact that they had a great coach in whom they had developed a great trust. It reflected all that they together had done for three seasons to improve and gain confidence in their shooting knowledge, skills, and mental training, had worked. Quite the opposite of what the European women were doing. They had former Olympian and volunteer Coach Peter Hoag who did an outstanding job, with no money, using his own vehicle and gas, making sure that they could get training and racing experience. The American women had lived together for three seasons without major conflicts, and the men had welcomed the new women's program and helped them to learn biathlon, and follow training plans. Peter, a serious and hard trainer himself, communicated the need to represent the USA to the world, that with a ground-breaking opportunity, developed a sense of confidence and strong commitment to each other that they could succeed.

Years later when asked about her experience leading the women to a first for U.S. Biathlon, Marie answered, "In my opinion, you build a positive atmosphere by caring a great deal about your athletes, as people and as competitors. And you must care deeply about the sport itself. Your actions, day in and day out, are more important than your words, however although, years later, my biathletes repeat verbatim to me, something I said that was important to them, which they still remember."

And as often happens in similar situations they had no real expectations in this first-ever women's world championships other than to do their best. Marie explained:

> The Europeans had been racing each other all season, something we did not know until the Championships began, as 1984 was before instant Internet communication. So, it was well past the time that we could compute average scores, compare and evaluate them against ours to predict or project how we might do. I just told our women to relax and do the best they could do, and that was all we expected and all they should expect of themselves. I knew that our program was greatly inferior to those in Europe, but did not say that. We just decided to

do our best and see how we placed. Kari's fifth place in the individual race behind 3 Russians and a Norwegian, was a wonderful finish for our confidence and we were all very pleased, especially given the terrible windy conditions for that day.

The weather conditions on race day were the worst conditions, weather-wise, that I experienced in the three seasons I coached biathlon. A winter storm was moving in atop the mountain where we raced. The wind blew so hard that it was only possible to shoot in the lulls. We had 22 clicks of left windage on the rifles. I had never put that much windage on a rifle in my shooting life of twenty-eight years. We began with our zeros, they all had them marked from training, as I had asked, and counted clicks until we could group shots fairly consistently. They knew by now to check the wind flags for direction and quadrant as they entered the range. I told them I would radio any changes to the ski coaches on the trails, if we needed to change. Fortunately, the storm didn't pick up until the race was finished. Biathlon is a race, and I was very proud of their poise and patience, in waiting for the lulls on the range, the only possible chance of firing a decent score. In my room that night, just before sleeping, I thought how much they had learned in three short seasons, without any of the optimal training elements that the USA team should have. Talented athletes, they put it all together on the right day.

It took only another few years before that historic moment would be repeated when Josh Thompson won the first-ever individual medal at the 1987 World Biathlon Championships at Lake Placid. Marie also had something to do with that success as well. Josh began his participation in biathlon when he qualified for the 1983 World University Games at Sofia, Bulgaria while a student at Western State College in Gunnison, Colorado. He qualified mainly through his fast skiing at the Bohart Ranch trials in Montana but admitted years later that his shooting was something of a "hope he would hit enough targets." The coaching staff of John Morton, John Durben and Nat Brown were completely surprised when he finished 12th in the individual race after having cross-fired one complete shooting stage at the wrong target. He came back to finish 6th in the sprint and it was then that the coaches and he himself realized that he could have a future in the sport.

At the trials for the 1984 Olympic team Josh again qualified by taking the final position on the team and years later he still remembers Marie's comment with an inviting smile on her face, "You know, we can teach you how to shoot." He recalled that she gave him some "homework" to do and it worked. He raced reasonably well at Sarajevo turning in the second fastest relay leg without penalties.

He returned to finish school in 1985 but also participated in the 1985 FISU Games in cross-country skiing. When Sigvart Bjontegaard was hired as the team coach in 1986 Josh felt that Sigvart was both a skiing and shooting coach and hit it off immediately. He felt that something "clicked" with Sigvart, especially with the skating technique for skiing. Josh said years later that he found coaches over time, but never really had all the required pieces together at the same time. With Sigvart's leadership and a "home-court" advantage, everything fell into place for the World Championships at Lake Placid in 1987 where Josh finished second to the East German Frank Peter Roetsch, taking the silver medal and the first U.S. medal for an individual event. Missing one target on his final standing stage of shooting he was slightly ahead of Roetsch or equal for most of the race, but finished just over 50 seconds behind him at the finish. Roetsch also had one miss for the race on his first standing bout. There were immediate suspicions of performance enhancement drug use which was confirmed years later, but for the U.S. program, which had taken a real risk with designating limited reserve resources to the sole purpose of winning a medal, had succeeded. One of the happiest at the post race celebrations, who had uncharacteristically consumed more alcohol then ever known before, was Walter Williams who had voluntarily and tirelessly pursued that goal for more than 20 years.

In the middle of the 1990s things began to take a positive turn for multiple reasons. It began with the juniors as they began to win medals at the World Junior Championships. Much of the change was a direct result of Cory Salmela's approach to find talented athletes and instilling skills development and encouraging individual and team dynamics for success. This was augmented when Bernd Eisenbichler's firm and demanding, but fully positive influence was added to the program. Jay Hakkinen was the first to breakthrough by winning a World Junior Championship and later followed with medal winning performances by Tracy and Lanny Barnes, Carolyn Treacy, Grace Butot, and Leif Norgren. The Barnes sisters came to biathlon with a strong background in shooting and eventually were a few of the best on the biathlon ranges with their accuracy and speed. Lanny is a three-time Olympian, and a three-time national champion, eight-time North American Champion, as well as an eight-time World Championship team member. Tracy won the National Championship four times and a two-time Olympian who was famously awarded the 2014 United Nations International Fair Play Award for giving her spot to Lanny in the 2014 Olympics. Lanny won a bronze medal in the European Cup in 2003 and earned second and fourth-place finishes at the 2012 IBU Cup. At the Vancouver Olympic Games she finished 23rd, the best ever for American women at the time. In 2018 she was selected as one of four Olympic athletes from around the world by the IOC to participate in the Olympic Art Project.

Carolyn Treacy, Grace Butot and Leif Nordgren were all products of regional development programs. Carolyn and Leif in Minnesota and Grace in Maine. Leif got involved because of his older brother Eric and sister Sonne. Eric was a member of the National Guard's All-Guard team before he entered pilot training and began flying fighter jets, while sister Sonne was also a member of two World Junior Championships teams before him. Starting biathlon at 14, he later captured a bronze medal in the pursuit race at Ruhpolding in 2008. Grace was a member of the Maine Winter Sports Center and used excellent shooting, hitting 19 of 20 targets, to finish 2nd for the silver medal at the 2009 World Junior Championships in the individual race at Canmore.

As the junior athletes were beginning to collect world championship medals, the senior athletes were coming closer to the podium, scoring World Cup points and seemingly began putting themselves also closer to medal winning performances. Tim Burke led the improvement among the seniors after a few good finishes in the Junior World Championships including an 11th place in 2003 and then an 8th place IBU Cup in 2004 before moving up to the World Championship team that year. At the Torino 2006 Winter Olympic Games he had bests of 35th and 36th in the sprint and pursuit races. In 2007 he began breaking into the top 10 at the World Cups with a 10th place at Hochfilzen and 6th at Pokljuka and a 7th place at the World Championships at Antholz. As many of the board of directors were in attendance for the World Championships, Tim's improving results caused excitement to grow throughout the biathlon community. A 7th and 8th place at the World Cup in Oslo in 2008 gave continued hope that he would be on the podium in a matter of time. A great 5th place relay performance by the men's team at Ruhpolding in 2009 also indicated that the men's team had developed some depth and Tim continued to capture top-10 finishes in the World Cups. Tim finally ascended the podium at the start of 2010 with a 2nd place finish at the Oberhof World Cup mass start race, however, unlucky weather impacted the Vancouver Olympic races and Tim could only manage a best of 8th in the mass start race. Injuries impacted his results in 2011, however he still managed top-20 finishes. He bounced back in 2012 with more top-10 results including a 10th place at the World Championships at Ruhpolding and a 4th place at the World Cup in Russia. 2013 started out with impressive 4th, 7th, and 3rd places at the World Cup races at Pokljuka and then he equaled Josh Thompson's individual race silver medal performance at the World Championships at Nove Mesto. He also was the first American to wear the "Yellow Bib."

The U.S. team at the 2013 World Championships started with a solid performance in the mixed relay, just two seconds ahead of the Russians. Max Cobb characterized it as not the best, but a good result and a strong indicator that the team was ready for the World Championships. In the men's sprint race, Tim had the best result at 28th place, just a second ahead of Lowell Bailey in 32nd place; another indication of how close the competitions had become at the top level. Tim told Media Director Linda Jager, "today was definitely not the sprint that I was looking for; two penalties is simply not good enough in a field of this quality." In the pursuit race, the Lowell gave an excellent performance on the shooting range, hitting all 20 targets for the first time and moving up from 32nd to finish 13th. Tim missed four targets and dropped to 32nd. After a day of rest, the individual race proved to be the exciting one that the U.S. fans had been waiting.

After his frustrations of finishing 28th in the sprint race, Tim was still hopeful for a top result at Nove Mesto. After his 32nd place result in the pursuit, he was somewhat at a loss to explain his disappointment, saying that he "would just try to put things together in the individual race" and that is just what he did. He surprised the field by taking the silver medal with only one missed target and only 23.5 seconds behind France's Martin Fourcade and 10.2 seconds ahead of Sweden's Fredrik Lindstrom. On the near perfect evening, Tim had his best day since being on the podium earlier that year at Pokljuka World Cup. After three clean stages he missed one target in the final standing stage, just like Fourcade and Lindstrom. He skied as fast as he could around the final loop and earned the USA's second World Championships medal ever, after Josh Thompson's in 1987.

At the IBU press conference following the race Tim said that he "found it hard to figure out what was different from his 32nd in the pursuit race. I only know that today, I felt good. I thought my championships were over after the pursuit on Sunday. I felt so bad." He said he was not so sure of a medal during the last loop, knowing that Lindstrom was a fast skier. "I was not thinking so much about a medal. I was just trying to go as hard as possible." On winning the second-ever medal for the USA, he added, "I have been waiting my whole life for this; it is very special, but I think it will take a couple of days to sink in." He told Linda Jager, "I'm so proud. It's been such a big effort by our entire team and organization, and it feels great to help finally make that come together. It was one of those races where I ended up being by myself for most of the race, so I wasn't able to judge where I was from the others, but my shooting went really well so I knew I was going to be up there. I had a disappointing start to these World Championships in the first two races, so today I just wanted to be aggressive and not over-think things, and bottom line just go for it. I knew heading into the last lap that I was in second place, but in an individual race you can never tell how people are doing behind you, so I wasn't ready to start celebrating until after the finish. We had a strong team day today as well. Thanks to the fans back home for all their support. I got a lot of encouraging messages over the last few days from people telling me to keep my head up and to keep at it, and it worked."

Bernd Eisenbichler, USBA high performance director said, "we showed over the last two or three years that we are really close, and we can do it, and today everything came together," and Head Coach Per Nilsson added "this was our first World Championship podium since 1987, and Tim did it with a perfect race. Everyone here is super excited, and we feel it is so well deserved for Tim." Bernd also had praise for the supporting staff saying, "Per and our staff has bought our program up to another level." CEO/President Max Cobb said, "with Tim's medal and the three Youth World Championship medals from Sean Doherty, USBA seems headed in the right direction. It's just so exciting and a phenomenal performance by Tim. All the evidence that Tim could do this has been there for a long time, and he put it together on the most important day of the year. The whole high-performance staff has done an outstanding job, not just here but over the last six years that we've been working towards this. I couldn't be prouder of all of them. The whole group really helped Tim get this done today. It's a phenomenal milestone for Tim and biathlon in America." Later, on his personal blog, Tim thanked the many people who helped him achieve his dream and said he feels surrounded by the best team in the world. He gave special credit to his coaches and wax team for the incredible skis they prepared for him.

Between Josh Thompson's success and that of Tim Burke, there were many changes and improvements that helped to turn the corner towards the reward of Tim's silver medal and it was just the start of momentum that would gain speed. When commenting on Tim's result, Max Cobb mentioned the coming success of outstanding junior Sean Doherty. Sean had grown up among the high peaks of the White Mountains in New Hampshire. Active in outdoor activities and an early skier he had the luck of meeting Eli Walker who worked with his father at the local ski center. Eli was an avid biathlon fan and a decent biathlon competitor who often trained with the National Guard team at Jericho. Eli introduced him to biathlon when he was 12 years old and brought him to a few races at the Schreiner's Saratoga Biathlon center as a 13-year old. In his first actual biathlon race he wanted to compete in the men's class rather than the modified junior class so that he could carry the rifle and do the race as what he considered a "real race." Despite limited racing experience in biathlon, he surprisingly won the race ahead of the senior athletes, making quite an impression.

Sean joined the Saratoga Biathlon Club and his father brought him to most of its events. During the summer he came with a tent, camping out near the range and was introduced to Algis Shalna who was an instructor at one of the NYSSRA junior clinics. Sean attended the clinic along with his eventual Olympic teammate from Old Forge, New York, Maddie Phaneuf. It didn't take Algis long to see the potential that others had seen in them and to recognize Sean's exceptional talent and potential, immediately getting him and Maddie involved with the junior training group at Jericho. Sean, as a 14-year old, qualified for the World Junior/

Youth World Biathlon Championships in 2011, beginning what would become something extraordinary for U.S. Biathlon as the most medaled World Junior Champion in IBU history and a member of the U.S. Olympic team at Sochi while still a junior athlete.

Max Cobb's mentioning Sean's medal-winning performances at the World Biathlon Championship at Nove Mesto that year revealed the general enthusiasm for what Sean had just accomplished in the previous week at the World Youth/ Junior Championships. However, in 2012 at the first winter Youth Olympic Games Sean won a bronze medal in a new and interesting event, the Nordic/ Biathlon combined relay with teammates Anna Kubek and cross-country skiers Heather Mooney and Patrick Caldwell. The team took 3rd place behind the teams from Germany and Russia. Anna led off the race with the 8th fastest time on the first leg, using only 3 reserve rounds. Heather fell back slightly, but Sean came up big on his leg to make the exchange to Patrick in 2nd position. Sean had the fastest leg for the male biathletes on the 3rd leg. He used only one reserve round on each stage to catch all but the Germans who had a big lead after the first two legs. Patrick was eventually caught by the Russian, but held on to finish only .5 seconds behind the Russian team, 59.6 seconds behind the German gold medalists. Patrick had high praise for Sean's effort on the biathlon leg during which he moved from 9th putting the Americans in contention for the medal.

At the World Junior/Youth Championships in 2013 Sean became the first biathlete in U.S. history to win three individual medals in a single world championship competition by winning one gold and two silver medals. In the USBA press release following the race, Max said, "Sean proved beyond doubt that with hard work, a supportive family and coach, even big dreams can be realized. I'm sure the whole US Biathlon community takes motivation from what Sean and the staff, coaches and team achieved at these World Championships." Sean won the gold medal in the pursuit race, with four stages of shooting. Coach Algis Shalna wrote in an e-mail to *Fasterskier.com*, "Sean is especially good at not giving up or losing confidence. After the first two shooting stages I was nervous. I thought a few times the medal is gone, but believed he will stay focused and shoot well in the last stages and he did. Just watching him on the course after he missed those first shots he looked like he felt he is still in the game, but just had a late start. Coaches tell the athletes before every race to focus until the last stage of shooting because the game is not over until everyone is through the range and done shooting and results are posted. There is always a case when someone misses targets at the beginning of the race and someone at the end." For many of those who knew Sean and followed his progress it wasn't really a great surprise. Having demonstrated his potential abilities early, Algis commented that he "marveled at Doherty's resolve" in his come-from-behind effort in the individual race. He went on to say, "Overall his confidence is very stable. It's a gift, the emotions are high and me, personally, I am trying not to think what just happened but to think; what is the next thing I need to get done and do everything the same way; to stay on track for preparation for the next race. I know Sean does pretty much the same thing. He makes the plan in his head and sticks with it until it's done." Algis' step-by-step approach was something that made great progress with younger athletes and everyone felt with his guidance, it would be exciting to see what can happen the next year when the World Youth/Junior Championships were to be held at Presque Isle, Maine, in the U.S.

Still in the youth category, Sean began his progression towards success as a junior athlete with a 37th place finish in the 2011 championships at Nove Mesto and two 13th place finishes at Kontiolahti in 2012. Following his 3 medal performances in 2013, he did not disappoint the U.S. Biathlon fans at home at Presque Isle, winning three medals again; two golds and a silver medal in the sprint, pursuit and individual races. As the Olympic year approached Sean became a factor in the trials for the team that would participate at Sochi and in the final selections races it came down to the veteran Jeremy Teela and Sean, a good situation for the team because that would have ended either with the stability of a seasoned, and successful older athlete or the young, upcoming star. Sean prevailed and qualified for the 2014 U.S. Olympic team at Sochi, and did race for the team in the relay, however his main objective was again focused on the World Youth/Junior Championships. Moving up to the junior category, he started in World Cup races, earning World Cup points at four different venues and captured another medal, the bronze, for the sprint at the Championships at Minsk in 2014. Perhaps Sean's most impressive achievement was once again winning three medals at a single World Youth/Junior Championships. After capturing a Bronze medal in 2015 at Minsk, in 2016 he brought his total to 10 by winning one of each color at the World Youth/Junior Championships in Romania, becoming IBU's winningest junior athlete. It was an important accomplishment since junior athletes, aged 19 to 20 years old, are physically more mature than youths, and the competition is at a different level. Instead of being the best young biathletes, winners at the junior level are often on their way to becoming the best senior biathletes.

As Sean emerged as the brightest star in the U.S. Biathlon's future, like Jay Hakkinen before him, he quickly moved up to successfully take his place on the senior team. Already, as a junior, he participated in the World Biathlon Championships and World Cup events. At the World Championships in 2016 at Oslo he raced in all the races with a best finish of 34th in the individual race. Illness slowed him at the start of the 2017 season, but he still managed a 36th place in the sprint at the World Championships in Austria and finished the season with excellent World Cup races in Finland. But the most rewarding moment for U.S.

Biathlon and for themselves came from Lowell Bailey and Susan Dunklee at the 2017 World Championships at Hochfilzen, Austria.

Lowell grew up in Lake Placid, N.Y., where he began ski racing early and together with Tim Burke they did very well as junior racers. After winning the first individual World Championships gold medal in 2017 at Hochfilzen, Austria for the United States, Lowell told a group of young skiers at that year's national championships that he had raced in over 300 international races before he won his first. His first win was one of the most important that one could have possibly hoped to win, a World Championships. Lowell explained to the group that he embraced cross-country skiing early, loved racing and was invited to a biathlon junior talent identification camp when he was 14 years old. He enjoyed the challenge of shooting and like Josh Thompson, who chased around after the National team athletes in Montana years before, of being in the same proximity of Olympians. When asked his afterthoughts about winning the gold medal, he told the group that it was a surreal experience on the final lap of that race. The entire crowd and staff were encouraging him and that the 4km loop seemed to be 40km. With his wife and young daughter out on the course's final climb he had confidence for the final downhill kilometer to the finish. A few days before he had been upset when Ole Einar Bjørndalen skied away from him on the final climb and this time he knew he was in first place. He said he kept saying to himself "don't let the medal get away." After leaving the range with a 4-second advantage, it had shrunk to only four-tenths at the top of the final climb but he did not know how slim the margin had become. With a staff member at every corner on the final loop screaming at him and as one of the last competitors out on the course, and the whole crowd knowing that he was within grasp of the gold medal, the entire 30,000 people in attendance were also screaming. He heard his wife at the top of that final hill. Erika was right there with daughter Ophelia on her chest, running next to him, yelling over and over again, "You're winning! You're winning! You're winning!" Lowell said it was like "a lightning bolt of the knowledge that I need to do this. I just need to do this. I have 700 meters left in this race and I need to make every single meter count. The rest of my life I'll remember that moment of cresting that hill with her saying those words, screaming those words at me." Skiing the final descent with his exceptional downhill ability, he recaptured most of the lost seconds to win by just 3.3 seconds. Skiing into the arms of Bernd Eisenbichler, who had evaded the officials in the finish area, incurring a €100 fine for violating IBU rules, both Lowell and everyone watched as his emotions showed that he knew it was a truly special day.

Lowell related to the group of juniors that winning by only 3.3 seconds was something that required many factors. Winning by such a small margin meant that those factors were present on that day, as at the top level almost all the athletes are equal in terms of training and abilities. "Winning by 30 seconds is athlete talent" he said, "but winning by just a small margin means that everything was done to win, including the right wax, the right grind on the ski base, the right ammunition and all the preparation for the day was in place." At the spring board of directors meeting following the season, Max Cobb told the members that Lowell had been seen at the team van prior to the race changing his daughter's diapers. It was meant to highlight his calmness prior to the race. Lowell, who was a member of the board of directors as an athlete representative confirmed it. He told them he had decided to help his wife, Erika, get situated with their 8-month-old daughter Ophelia at the team van before getting ready for the race. While that may seem like a major distraction before such an important race, Lowell commented that he was on the brink of retiring a year ago, worried about leaving his wife at home with a newborn baby while he traveled on the world cup circuit. He was unwilling to be an absent father for the first seven months of his daughter's life. Lowell was still competing because his family could travel with him. It was definitely a logistical challenge but having his family with him provided a more mentally positive seasonal experience, because it contributed to being in a really relaxed but focused space once on the starting line. "Well, glad I didn't stop," he told German ARD broadcasting. He said that he was glad that he didn't retire and added, "I'm so thankful for the people who allowed me to continue my career," especially his wife Erika.

After being awarded the "Male Athlete of the Month for February 2017," in his interview with the *Dow Diamond Club,* Lowell once again said:

> The way I think about it is, if you win by 30 seconds, that's a huge margin. You can kind of pat yourself on the back and say, 'I did a great job in my training this year, way to go me.' But when you win by 3.3 seconds, you have to thank every single person that put wax on your skis, that put the stone grind on your skis. . . . The level of dedication from this team to our athletes, to me and this result, is staggering and I am 100-percent sure that their hard work is the reason that I was able to keep that lead, that very, very narrow sliver of a 3.3-second gap. I'm just hugely thankful to our staff of dedicated people that have sacrificed so much over, in some cases, two decades. It meant so much, obviously for me and my family, but to be able to share the result with the team, it was so emotional because we've all been working towards this for so long.

Humble and thoughtful, he saw his result as not just his effort, but that of a "team." Lowell told the audience at the National Championships that "racing at the World Cup, World Championships and Olympic Games takes focus." On the day of his World Championship win he said he was "in the zone" and that rarely happens as well as it did that day. Many successful athletes and even those beginning sports acknowledge the concept of being in the psychological "zone," saying that things seem compacted in time during a good performance, with the details of what happened almost passing without memory, however during a bad performance is seems time gets extended and everything about the race can be recalled. Lowell said that to be successful one needs to learn how to "refocus" through lots of repetition and visualization. He said that he had been thinking about the World Championships since the previous May and that the more one prepares for it, the easier it becomes to deal with the pressure and anxiety. After hitting 20 for 20 of his targets, Lowell said for him, that was when the race began, when he left the shooting mat after his final shot. What made his performance most notable wasn't just that he became the first American biathlete to ever earn the title of world champion, it was the way he did it. After a perfect result on the shooting range, he pushed hard on his skis and created a suspenseful final lap thriller, rising to meet the pressure and sealing the win with aggressive skiing on the final downhill into the stadium. Along with the many changes that brought Lowell to a competitive factor at the top level of the sport, he finally achieved a "milestone" performance for himself and for which the U.S. Biathlon community was waiting for 59 years.

As the cliché goes, "success breeds success" certainly became true a few days following Lowell's benchmark achievement. Susan Dunklee who had also been on the podium at World Cup events also reached a benchmark achievement by capturing the silver medal in the women's mass start race. Leaving the range after her final standing stage in 1st place she was caught on the final uphill by the World Cup leader from Germany, Laura Dahlmeier leaving Susan with the silver medal just 4.6 seconds behind the winner. Like Lowell, she was perfect on the range. Susan's success was probably less surprising than that of Lowell's. Susan hadn't been participating in the sport for anywhere near the number of years Lowell had and didn't have any junior experience, but when invited by the USBA coaches to give biathlon a try following her success at Dartmouth, she rose quickly among the ranks of women's biathlon. Starting at the IBU's second tier level IBU Cup races in 2009 she perfected the shooting and managed a 9th place in the 2011 European Championships at Ridnaun, Italy. She moved up to the World Cup level in 2012 and achieved an American best-ever 5th place result in the individual race at the World Championships of that year at Ruhpolding. At Sochi in 2014 she was 14th, 18th and 11th in the sprint, pursuit, and mass start races which, along with Lowell's performances, provided the NBC television coverage something on which to focus in their broadcasting. She followed the Olympic Games with multiple top-ten finishes and was on the podium at the Oslo World Cup. In 2015 and 2016 she again had multiple top-ten results in the World Championships at Oslo and a World Cup best of 2nd at Presque Isle, Maine.

Susan began the 2017 season with a new confidence and attitude. She had previously been rather deliberate with her shooting, somewhat cautious in trying to be accurate, giving away precious seconds on the range to those who she was equal in ski speed. During the summer she and the coaches focused on improving her shooting speed without compromising her accuracy and this had an immediate impact on her early season results with a 3rd place in the sprint at Nove Mesto, Czech Republic, as well as two more top-five finishes. After her powerful skiing and a clean 20-for-20 shooting performance, her first in a four-stage race at the World Championship and World Cup level that propelled her to a historic podium finish, she reflected, "repetition and discipline and training will get you to be able to shoot fast in the race, and you have to get to the point where you trust that speed is better than shooting slow. That takes a long time, to feel comfortable with that speedy rhythm. It has worked some days in races this year, and then other days it has totally fallen apart. But today it worked."

At her first World Championships in 2015 where she finished 5th in the individual race, Susan was the slowest shooter in the race, but her ski speed was nearly the best. At Hochfilzen in 2017 she was determined to shoot both quickly and accurately, and not giving up time on the range. Starting from bib 17, Susan moved into the top ten on the first loop and then, at the range for the first prone stage her moment came, taking only 26 seconds to hit the mat, clear all five targets, and jump back up again. It was the fastest time of the whole field and she left with a 5.1 seconds lead on the rest. It was a pattern that would repeat again and again: the others caught her on the top of the large climb on the back of the course, but then they would ski into the range together, and Susan would once again clear her targets quickly and go out with a gap again. At the final standing stage, she stood with three other women, Laura Dahlmeier of Germany, who had already won four gold medals at that World Championships; Gabriela Koukalova of the Czech Republic, who had won a medal in every individual race so far; and Marie Dorin Habert of France, the winningest athlete of the previous year's World Championships. Without a hiccup, Susan's first target turned white and on a roll, keeping up the speed she finally got that 20-for-20 perfect shooting result and again, she left ahead of the others. As she left the stadium, she told *Faster-skier.com*, "I kind of looked up at the scoreboard and saw that Laura [Dahlmeier] was five seconds behind." Halfway through the loop Dahlmeier had caught her. "I didn't quite have it to stick with her," Dunklee said. To avoid being caught by the others, she continued her drive to the finish, 4.5 seconds behind Dahlmeier earning the historic silver medal.

Later that season after finishing 5th in the World Cup at Pyeongchang,

South Korea, Susan reflected about her and Lowell's success, telling *Fasterskier. com*; "I think back to a few years ago when Lowell got his first podium in Kontio-lahti, Finland, and I watched him do that. I thought, he has been doing this for a long time and that's possible. Then a week later I got my first podium at Oslo. So that thought crossed my head the other day when he won. I was like, huh, maybe I can feed off this. You just need to get some positive momentum going and it makes it easier for the whole team to do well."

Susan and Lowell followed up on their medal winning performances with Lowell taking second place in the sprint at the World Cup in Pyeongchang, South Korea, the site of the 2018 Olympic Winter Games, and Susan finished 5th in both the sprint and pursuit races. However, a fitting conclusion to their crowning successful 2017 season came at the World Cup at Kontiolahti, Finland where Lowell and Susan combined to capture 2nd place in a new event, the single mixed relay. A new format, and one that is not yet contested at World Championships or the Olympics, it has the highest shooting-to-skiing ratio of any biathlon competition. The women ski and shoot twice, then tag off to the men just after shooting so the men can ski and shoot twice, then the women twice again, then the men twice, and finally the men getting to ski one last 1.5 k loop to reach the finish line. Susan told *Fasterskier.com*, "I have dreamed for a long time being able to run into the finishing pen with a bib on and a rifle, and greet my teammates as they come in," describing her new experience of winning as part of a team. "It's so cool to finally do that. It's definitely a dream come true." Lowell echoed Susan's comments by saying, "That was a first and it's a great feeling. In a lot of ways, it's better than just going out and having a great race on your own, but to have a great team result like that, it's a new experience. I shouldn't say that, we've had some great team results in both the mixed relay and the men's relay; we were fourth place last year in the mixed relay [in Canmore], but no one really wants to go out and celebrate in the finish zone with fourth place. This was the first time that you could hug your teammate in the finish zone. I've watched that phenomenon throughout my career so it's nice to finally experience it."

Sixty Years of Biathlon

The 2018 Winter Olympic Games at Pyeongchang, South Korea represented the 60th year that U.S. athletes have participated in biathlon at the World Championships and Winter Olympic Games. Following the success at the 2017 World Biathlon Championships there was great anticipation of winning the first Olympic biathlon medal by an American athlete at Pyeongchang, but that wasn't to be. Many in the biathlon community were disappointed. However, most understood what Lowell, Susan, Tim, Sean, Josh and the other medal winners had so clearly indicated many times over: that to win was something special and unique. It requires everything to be just right at the pivotal moment; the talent required of the athlete, the best possible training and timing for peak performance, the right external factors of equipment, weather and environment, the support of the staff and teammates, and the right amount of luck that the competitors will have weaknesses. Despite the success of getting everything right in 2017 at Hochfilzen, it was not so easy at Pyeongchang.

Without making excuses, an analysis of the 2018 IBU World Cup season, shows clearly that Pyeongchang presented unusual challenges that even the best athletes found difficult. France's exceptional Martin Fourcade came to Pyeonchang after dominating the World Cups with a podium finish in every race, hoping to surpass Ole Einar Bjørndalen's four gold medals from 2002. Three uncharacteristic misses in windy conditions for his first prone stage in the sprint race and a less than normal ski speed in the individual race left him short of that goal. The atypical late night starts along with the constant and difficult shifting winds made even the best athletes struggle to achieve their normal expectations and this included the Americans. Although it could be said that the conditions were the same for everyone, it was not really the case. The inconsistency of the strong winds made it somewhat of a lottery that even Fourcade and Germany's top woman Laura Dahlmaier and the favored Norwegian and German relay teams found unlucky. The U.S. athletes clearly showed they were ready and prepared for their goals, but an unlucky shooting stage ended up pushing them away from the finishes for which they hoped. Their results showed the injustice of their misfortune. Emily Dreissigacker excelled in the sprint and qualified for the pursuit while

Susan Dunklee and Joanne Reid struggled on the range and did not. Susan later led the women's relay with the 2nd fastest time on her lead-off leg and a 4th and 3rd place finish in the World Cup at Oslo immediately following the Games. Lowell and Tim also struggled on the range in the individual and sprint races but came back for good performances in the pursuit. Lowell, Tim, Leif and Sean excelled in the men's relay in which the team finished in 6th place, equaling the best-ever finish of the 1972 team. They too went on to the final World Cups and achieved good results, especially by the young Sean Doherty who began to assert himself with results within the top 15 and together with Lowell, Tim and Leif, another excellent relay finish at Oslo.

At the conclusion of the 2018 season, both Tim Burke and Lowell Bailey, along with Russell Currier, retired from the men's team. Tim and Lowell had grown up together as junior skiers and long-time members of the U.S. Biathlon team. As members of four U.S. Olympic teams and multiple World Championships teams, they probably represent the biggest difference between today's athletes and those early U.S. competitors of the sport. That difference was the opportunity and ability to stay involved and active in the sport, enjoying the support of an organizational effort that provided a program of dedicated administration and coaching staff, intensive training, as well as greater awareness by the public.

It is important to acknowledge that this story was inspired by conversations and correspondence with some of the first U.S. Biathlon team competitors, many of whom contributed their memories, pictures, newspaper reports and results. Without their help it couldn't have been written. Many are now in their elder years and felt a need to tell their story. They also wondered how the experiences they have shared compare with the experiences of today's athletes. It goes without saying that those pioneers, both men and women were the best at the time and they gave their best efforts at achieving success. To compare themselves with today's athletes would be like comparing any of today's athletes with those of previous times. Over the years the sport has changed in many ways, but the athletes have always faced the same challenges and exercised their exceptional skills to best meet those challenges with the knowledge and tools available to them at the time. They should look back at those efforts with pride and hopefully this story will provide them with some recognition for their representation of the United States in international biathlon competitions.

U.S. National Championships

Senior Men

Year	Location	Event	1st	2nd	3rd
1965	Rosendale NY	Individual	Charles Kellogg	William Spencer	Ford Hubbard
1966	Lake Placid NY	Individual	William Spencer	John Ehrensbeck	Ed Willilams
1967	Marquette MI	Individual	William Spencer	Melvyn Matis	John Ehrensbeck
1968	Upson WI	Individual	John Ehrensbeck	Jon Chaffee	William Spencer
1969	Putney VT	Individual	Jay Bowerman	John Isokangas	Dennis Donahue
1970	Jackson WY	Individual	Peter Karns	Bill Kendall	John Morton
1972	Jackson WY	Individual	Peter Karns	Dennis Donahue	Jay Bowerman
1973	Lake Placid NY	Individual	Dennis Donahue	George Tuthill	John Morton
1974	East Burke VT	Individual	John Morton	Ken Alligood	Terry Aldrich
		Sprint	Dennis Donahue	Lyle Nelson	Art Stegen
1975	Jericho VT	Individual	John Morton	Ken Alligood	Terry Morse
		Sprint	Ken Alligood	Bill Pease	Mike Sallee
1976	Lake Placid NY	Individual	Peter Dascoulias	Dennis Donahue	Lyle Nelson
		Sprint	Lyle Nelson	John Morton	Ken Alligood
1977	Jericho VT	Individual	Lyle Nelson	Peter Hoag	John Hall
		Sprint	Peter Hoag	Lyle Nelson	Rusty Scott
1978	Jericho VT	Individual	Peter Hoag	Ken Alligood	Martin Hagen
		Sprint	Martin Hagen	Peter Hoag	John Hall
1979	Squaw Valley CA	Individual	Ken Alligood	Rusty Scott	Lyle Nelson
		Sprint	Lyle Nelson	Glenn Jobe	Ken Alligood
1980	Hamel MN	Individual	Don Nielsen	Glen Ewing	Ken Alligood
		Sprint	Ken Alligood	Lyle Nelson	Glenn Jobe
1981	Bozeman MT	Individual	Glenn Jobe	Lyle Nelson	Chuck Lyda
		Sprint	Lyle Nelson	Peter Karns	Roy Pederson
1982	Bemidji MN	Individual	Willie Carrow	Peter Hoag	Tom McElroy
		Sprint	Martin Hagen	Peter Hoag	Willie Carrow
1984	Lake Placid NY	Individual	Josh Thompson	Martin Hagen	Lyle Nelson
		Sprint	Josh Thompson	Willie Carrow	Lyle Nelson
1985	Valcartier CAN	Individual	Lyle Nelson	Willie Carrow	Chuck Lyda
		Sprint	Lyle Nelson	Jon Engen	Willie Carrow
1986	Giant's Ridge MN	Individual	Ray Dombrovsky	Jon Engen	Josh Thompson
		Sprint	Ray Dombrovsky	Josh Thomspon	Jon Engen
1987	Lake Placid NY	Individual	Darrin Binning	Glen Eberle	Lyle Nelson
		Sprint	Lyle Nelson	Willie Carrow	Rich Gross
1988	Giant's Ridge MN	Individual	Ray Dombrovsky	John Ingdal	Rick Oliver
		Sprint	John Ingdal	Ray Dombrovksy	Erich Wilbrecht
1989	Royal Gorge CA	Individual	Josh Thompson	Rick Oliver	Robert Douglas
		Sprint	Josh Thompson	Rick Oliver	Willie Carrow

Year	Location	Event	1st	2nd	3rd
1990	Jericho VT	Individual Sprint	Josh Thompson Jon Ingdal	John Ingdal Tuck Miller	Dave Jareckie Josh Thompson
1991	Rumford ME	Individual Sprint	Curt Schriener Curt Schreiner	Josh Thompson Rick Oliver	Ray Dombrovsky Josh Thompson
1992	Anchorage AK	Individual Sprint	Josh Thompson Josh Thompson	Ben Michaud Erick Wilbrecht	Erich Wilbrecht Jon Engen
1993	Jericho VT	Individual Sprint	Ian Harvey Robert Douglas	Rick Oliver Ian Harvey	Robert Rosser Erich Wilbrecht
1994	Sun Valley ID	Individual Sprint	Robert Rosser Curt Schreiner	Max Saenger Jon Engen	Robert Douglas Samuel Cordell
1995	Lake Placid NY	Individual Sprint	Curt Schreiner Robert Douglas	Robert Rosser Curt Schreiner	Jesse Hansen Jay Poss
1996	Lake Placid NY	Individual Sprint	Dan Westover Curt Schreiner	Robert Rosser Robert Douglas	Sergei Vinogradov Chad Salmela
1997	Lake Placid NY	Individual Sprint	Samuel Cordell Jay Poss	Jay Hakkinen Samuel Cordell	Jeremy Teela Curt Schreiner
1998	Valcartier CAN	Individual Sprint	Curt Schreiner Robert Rosser	Rick Oliver Curt Schreiner	Dan Westover Grant Ernhart
1999	Canmore CAN	Individual Sprint	Grant Ernhart Sergei Vinogradov	Robert Rosser Travis Redman	Sergei Vinogradov Grant Ernhart
2000	Fort Kent ME Soldier Hollow UT	Individual Sprint	Jeremy Teela Curt Schreiner	Travis Redman Dan Westover	Robert Rosser Jeremy Teela
2001	W Yellowstone MT Lake Placid NY	Individual Sprint	Travis Redman Travis Redman	Curt Schreiner Dan Westover	Dan Westover Robert Rosser
2002	Fort Kent ME Soldier Hollow UT	Individual Sprint	Tim Burke Travis Redman	Jacob Beste Jay Hakkinen	Curt Schreiner Jeremy Teela
2003	Lake Placid NY	Sprint	Lowell Bailey	Jay Hakkinen	Jesse Downs
2004	Jericho VT Lake Placid NY	Individual Sprint	Mark Matheny Jeremy Teela	Jesse Downs Jacob Beste	Marc Sheppard Mark Matheny
2005	Canmore CAN	Sprint Pursuit	Tim Burke Tim Burke	Robert Rosser Robert Rosser	Robert Douglas Robert Douglas
2006	Valcartier CAN	Individual Sprint Pursuit	Brian Olsen Robert Rosser Robert Rosser	Robert Rosser Brian Olsen Brian Olsen	Adrian Harris Robert Douglas Robert Douglas
2007	Ft. Kent ME	Individual Sprint Pursuit	Robert Douglas Walter Shepard Robert Douglas	Walter Shepard Robert Douglas Walter Shepard	Bjorn Bakken Bjorn Bakken Nigel Kinney
2008	Coleraine MN	Sprint Pursuit Mass Start	Walter Shepard Walter Shepard Walter Shepard	Jesse Downs Zachary Hall Robert Douglas	Bjorn Bakken Jesse Downs Jesse Downs
2009	Ft Kent ME	Sprint Pursuit Mass Start	Bill Bowler Russell Currier Kevin Patzoldt	Jesse Downs Dan Campbell Casey Simmons	Zachary Hall Jesse Downs Russell Currier

Year	Location	Event	1st	2nd	3rd
2010	Ft Kent ME	Sprint Pursuit Mass Start	Casey Simmons Wynn Roberts Russell Currier	Walter Shepard Walter Shepard Walter Shepard	Bill Bowler Bill Bowler Casey Simmons
2011	Mt. Itasca, MN	Sprint Pursuit Mass Start	Bill Bowler Wynn Roberts Russell Currier	Russell Currier Mark Johnson Mark Johnson	Wynn Roberts Russell Currier Bill Bowler
2012	W Yellowstone MT	Sprint Pursuit Mass Start	Leif Nordgren Leif Nordgren Leif Nordgren	Mark Johnson Mark Johnson Mark Johnson	Michael Gibson Michael Gibson Michael Gibson
2013	Ft Kent ME	Sprint Pursuit	Raleigh Goessling Raleigh Goessling	Michael Gibson Michael Gibson	
2014	Jericho, VT	Individual Sprint Mass Start	Ethan Dreissigacker Raleigh Goessling Raleigh Goessling	Casey Smith Casey Smith Brian Halligan	Raleigh Goessling Sean Doherty Casey Smith
2015	Soda Springs CA	Sprint Pursuit	Patrick Johsnon Patrick Johnson	Michael Gibson Max Durtschi	Max Durtschi Michael Gibson
2016	Ft Kent ME	Sprint Pursuit Mass Start	Lowell Bailey Lowell Bailey Tim Burke	Tim Burke Tim Burke Sean Doherty	Sean Doherty Sean Doherty Leif Nordgren
2017	Jericho, VT	Sprint Pursuit Mass Start	Russell Currier Lowell Bailey Lowell Bailey	Lowell Bailey Leif Nordgren Leif Nordgren	Leif Nordgren Russell Currier Paul Schommer

1971, 1983 cancelled due to weather, 2003 Individual event not held.

Senior Women

Year	Location	Event	1st	2nd	3rd
1980	Hamel MN	Individual	Betty Stroock	Holly Beattie	Rae Hoisve
		Sprint	Betty Stroock	Holly Beattie	Rae Hoisve
1981	Bozeman MT	Individual	Betty Stroock	Patrice Jankowski	Pam Weiss
		Sprint	Betty Stroock	Pam Weiss	Patrice Jankowski
1982	Bemidji MN	Individual	Pam Weiss	Patrice Jankowski	Diana Tiahrt
		Sprint	Patrice Jankowski	Pam Nordheim	Holly Beattie
1984	Lake Placid NY	Individual	Kari Swenson	Holly Beattie	Jan Reynolds
		Sprint	Holly Beattie	Kari Swenson	Julie Newnam
1985	Valcartier CAN	Individual	Julie Newnam	Pam Nordheim	Laura Freeman
		Sprint	Kari Swenson	Julie Newnam	Pam Weiss
1986	Giant's Ridge MN	Individual	Anna Sonnerup	Kari Swenson	Pam Nordheim
		Sprint	Pam Nordheim	Kari Swenson	Pam Weiss
1987	Lake Placid NY	Individual	Anna Sonnerup	Pam Nordheim	Nancy Bell
		Sprint	Pam Nordheim	Peggy Hunter	Pam Weiss
1988	Giant's Ridge MN	Individual	Peggy Hunter	Patrice Jankowski	Pam Nordheim
		Sprint	Mary Ostergren	Joan Smith	Anna Sonnerup
1989	Royal Gorge CA	Individual	Anna Sonnerup	Mary Ostergren	Patrice Jankowski
		Sprint	Anna Sonnerup	Pam Nordheim	Beth Coats
1990	Jericho VT	Individual	Pam Nordheim	Holly Farr	Mary Ostergren
		Sprint	Mary Ostergren	Pam Nordheim	Helene Arnold
1991	Rumford ME	Individual	Anna Sonnerup	Mary Ostergren	Joan Guetschow
		Sprint	Patrice Jankowski	Helene Arnold	Pam Nordheim
1992	Anchorage AK	Individual	Angie Stevenson	Joan Guetschow	Mary Ostergren
		Sprint	Joan Guetschow	Joan Smith	Mary Ostergren
1993	Jericho VT	Individual	Beth Coats	Patrice Jankowski	Joan Guetschow
		Sprint	Angie Stevenson	Patrice Jankowski	Laurie Tavares
1994	Sun Valley ID	Individual	Joan Smith	Stacey Wooley	Mary Ostergren
		Sprint	Joan Smith	Gilian Sharp	Stacey Wooley
1995	Lake Placid NY	Individual	Beth Coats	Kris Viljanen	Stacey Wooley
		Sprint	Beth Coats	Stacey Wooley	Ntala Skinner
1996	Lake Placid NY	Individual	Kris Sabasteanski	Deborah Nordyke	Beth Coats
		Sprint	Deborah Nordyke	Cory Fritzel	Kara Salmela
1997	Lake Placid NY	Individual	Ntala Skinner	Kara Salmela	Joan Miller
		Sprint	Ntala Skinner	Kris Sabasteanski	Joan Miller
1998	Valcartier CAN	Individual	Andrea Nahrgang	Kris Sabasteanski	Deborah Nordyke
		Sprint	Kara Salmela	Kris Sabasteanski	Deborah Nordyke
1999	Canmore CAN	Individual	Jamie Meuller	Sonia Rosser	Elizabeth Pike
		Sprint	Sonia Rosser	Jamie Meuller	Tracy Dooley
2000	Fort Kent ME	Individual	Kara Salmela	Kris Sabasteanski	Jill Krause
	Soldier Hollow UT	Sprint	Rachel Steer	Kris Sabasteanski	Andrea Nahrgang
2001	W Yellowstone MT	Individual	Kris Sabasteanski	Andrea Nahrgang	Betty Stroock
	Lake Placid NY	Sprint	Rachel Steer	Stacy Wooley	Andrea Nahrgang
2002	Fort Kent ME	Individual	Rachel Steer	Deborah Nordyke	Kara Salmela
	Soldier Hollow UT	Sprint	Jill Krause	Rachel Steer	Kara Salmela

Year	Location	Event	1st	2nd	3rd
2003	Lake Placid NY	Sprint	Sarah Riley	Lanny Barnes	Denise Whitten
2004	Jericho VT	Individual	Sarah Konrad	Erin Graham	Patricia Driscoll
	Lake Placid NY	Sprint	Rachel Steer	Lanny Barnes	Jill Krause-Beste
2005	Canmore CAN	Sprint	Sarah Konrad	Erin Graham	Denise Teela
		Pursuit	Sarah Konrad	Denise Teela	Erin Graham
2006	Valcartier CAN	Individual	Haley Johnson	Denise Teela	BethAnn Chamberlain
		Sprint	Denise Teela	Haley Johnson	BethAnn Chamberlain
		Pursuit	Haley Johnson	Denise Teela	BethAnn Chamberlain
2007	Ft. Kent ME	Individual	Lanny Barnes	BethAnn Chamberlain	Tracy Barnes
		Sprint	Lanny Barnes	Annelies Cook	Tracy Barnes
		Pursuit	Lanny Barnes	Tracy Barnes	Annelies Cook
2008	Coleraine MN	Sprint	Annelies Cook	Caitlyn Compton	Sara Studebaker
		Pursuit	Caitlyn Compton	Sara Studebaker	Carolyn Bramante
		Mass Start	Annelies Cook	Sara Studebaker	Carolyn Bramante
2009	Ft. Kent ME	Sprint	Susan Dunklee	Lanny Barnes	Tracy Barnes
		Pursuit	Tracy Barnes	Lanny Barnes	Annelies Cook
		Mass Start	Tracy Barnes	Laura Spector	Annelies Cook
2010	Ft. Kent ME	Sprint	Tracy Barnes	Haley Johnson	Annelies Cook
		Pursuit	Tracy Barnes	Annelies Cook	Katrina Howe
		Mass Start	Susan Dunklee	Tracy Barnes	Annelies Cook
2011	Mt. Itasca, MN	Sprint	Susan Dunklee	Annelies Cook	Lanny Barnes
		Pursuit	Annelies Cook	Tracy Barnes	Lanny Barnes
		Mass Start	Annelies Cook	Susan Dunklee	Tracy Barnes
2012	W Yellowstone, MT	Sprint	Annelies Cook	Laura Spector	Corrine Malcolm
		Pursuit	Annelies Cook	Laura Spector	Corrine Malcolm
		Mass Start	Annelies Cook	Laura Spector	Corrine Malcolm
2013	Ft. Kent ME	Sprint	Clare Egan	Katrina Howe	
		Pursuit	Katrina Howe	Clare Egan	
		Mass Start	Clare Egan	Katrina Howe	
2014	Jericho, VT	Individual	Katrina Howe	Clare Egan	Hillary Saucy
		Sprint	Katrina Howe	Clare Egan	Hillary Saucy
		Mass Start	Katrina Howe	Clare Egan	Amanda Del Frate
2015	Soda Springs CA	Sprint	Clare Egan	Kelsey Dickinson	Katrina Howe
		Pursuit	Clare Egan	Kelsey Dickinson	Madeleine Phaneuf
2016	Ft. Kent ME	Sprint	Clare Egan	Joanne Reid	Hannah Dreissigacker
		Pursuit	Clare Egan	Joanne Reid	Annelies Cook
		Mass Start	Annelies Cook	Joanne Reid	Emily Dreissigacker
2017	Jericho, VT	Sprint	Susan Dunklee	Joanne Reid	Clare Egan
		Pursuit	Susan Dunklee	Joanne Reid	Madeleine Phaneuf
		Mass Start	Susan Dunklee	Clare Egan	Emily Dreissigacker
2018	Soldier Hollow UT	Sprint	Susan Dunklee	Clare Egan	Joanne Reid
		Pursuit	Susan Dunklee	Clare Egan	Emily Dreissigacker
		Mass Start	Susan Dunklee	Clare Egan	Emily Dreissigacker

1983 cancelled due to weather, 2003 Individual event not held.

Olympic Games and World Championships

World Championships, Saalfelden, Austria, 1958
Individual Race, Men

Rank	Name	Nation	Hits[1]	Finish
1	VIKLUND Adolf	SWE	17	1:33:44.0
2	GUNNERIUSSEN Olle	SWE	17	1:34:13.0
3	BUTAKOV Viktor	URS	14	1:34:46.0
20	DAMON Lawrence	USA	5	2:00:44.0
24	MIZE Richard	USA	3	2:02:26.0
26	JACKSON Walter	USA	4	2:04:35.0
28	JENSEN Gunnar	USA	4	2:08:52.0

World Championships, Courmayeur, Italy, 1959
Individual Race, Men

Rank	Name	Nation	Hits	Finish
1	MELANIN Vladimir	URS	15	1:41:05.0
2	SOKOLOV Dmitiri	URS	16	1:41:15.0
3	AGGE Sven	SWE	17	1:43:23.0
8	PAQUETTE Maurice	USA	15	1:48:43.0
19	COLLINS Robert	USA	10	2:01:10.0
21	BURRITT John	USA	9	2:03:37.0
25	MIZE Richard	USA	4	2:12:54.0

Winter Olympic Games, Squaw Valley, USA, 1960
Individual Race, Men

Rank	Name	Nation	Hits	Finish
1	LESTANDER Klas	SWE	20	1:33:21.0
2	TYRVÄINEN Antti	FIN	18	1:33:57.0
3	PRIVALOV Aleksandr	URS	17	1:34:54.0
14	BURRITT, John	USA	15	1:46:36.0
21	MIZE Richard	USA	9	1:55:56.0
23	HANSON, Gus	USA	11	1:58:06.0
24	DAMON Lawrence	USA	7	1:59:38.0

World Championships, Umeä, Sweden, 1961
Individual Race, Men

Rank	Name	Nation	Hits	Finish
1	HUUSKONEN Kalevi	FIN	19	1:32:11.0
2	PRIVALOV Alexandr	URS	17	1:35:07.0
3	REPO Paavo	FIN	16	1:35:20.0
11	TAYLOR Richard	USA	14	1:41:41.0
30	WILSON Joseph	USA	10	1:59:22.0
32	CRAGG	USA	11	2:02:10.0
33	LAHDENPERA Peter	USA	4	2:02:31.0

World Championships, Hameenlinna, Finland, 1962
Individual Race, Men

Rank	Name	Nation	Hits	Finish
1	MELANJIN Vladimir	URS	18	1:23:30.0
2	TYRVÄINEN Antti	FIN	19	1:24:08.0
3	PCHENTSYN Valentin	URS	19	1:24:17.0
26	LAHDENPERA Peter	USA	11	1:42:58.0
27	TAYLOR Richard	USA	11	1:44:09.0
29	AKERS Charles	USA	12	1:44:32.0
35	WILSON Joseph	USA	9	1:51:12.0

World Championships, Seefeld, Austria, 1963
Individual Race, Men

Rank	Name	Nation	Hits	Finish
1	MELANJIN Vladimir	URS	18	1:32:06.8
2	TYRVÄINEN Antti	FIN	18	1:33:46.7
3	POSTI Hannu	FIN	18	1:35:02.1
27	BOHLIN Karl	USA	15	1:50:14.2
33	SHEA James	USA	11	1:58:06.9
36	AKERS Charles	USA	11	1:58:59.0
37	ROBSAM Otto	USA	11	1:59:13.0

Winter Olympic Games, Innsbruck, Austria, 1964
Individual Race, Men

Rank	Name	Nation	Hits	Finish
1	MELANIN Vladimir	URS	20	1:20:26.8
2	PRIVALOV Aleksandr	URS	20	1:23:42.5
3	JORDET Olav	NOR	19	1:24:38.8
16	AKERS Charles	USA	18	1:32:24.9
30	SPENCER William	USA	16	1:36:49.8
36	LAHDENPERA Peter	USA	12	1:43:04.7
39	RENNE Paul	USA	14	1:46:45.9

World Championships, Elverum, Norway, 1965
Individual Race, Men

Rank	Name	Nation	Hits	Finish
1	JORDET Olav	NOR	19	1:23:34.9
2	PUZANOV Nikolay	URS	19	1:23:57.0
3	TYRVÄINEN Antti	FIN	20	1:23:57.6
	No USA Participation			

[1] *Old Program Scoring, number of targets hit, each miss added 2 minutes penalty, multiple ranges.*

World Championships, Garmisch-Part, W. Germany, 1966

Individual Race, Men

Rank	Name	Nation	Penalties[2]	Finish
1	ISTAD John	NOR	1+2+1+0	1:38:21.8
2	GASIENICA-SOBC J	POL	0+2+1+1	1:39:19.9
3	GUNDARTSEV Vlad	URS	0+1+0+0	1:39:53.6
30	WILLIAMS Edward	USA	1+10+2+1	1:58:01.7
31	EHRENSBECK John	USA	8+6+3+2	1:58:20.1
37	SMALL Allen	USA	1+6+3+1	2:02:35.6
40	SPENCER William	USA	4+2+10+3	2:03:07.8

[2] *Single 150m range, each miss added 1 or 2 minutes penalty.*

Team Relay, Men

1	NORWAY	0 6		2:19:53.9
	NORDKILD Ivar	0 0	35:21.8	
	JORDET Olav	0 1	34:21.7	
	ISTAD Jon	0 3	35:48.5	
	TVEITEN Ragnar	0 2	34:21.9	
2	POLAND	0 4		2:24:03.8
	RUBIS Jozef	0 2	36:25.7	
	LUKASZCZYK Stanislaw	0 0	35:04.9	
	SZCZEPANIAK Stanislaw	0 0	36:04.0	
	GASIENICA-SOBC J	0 2	36:29.2	
3	SWEDEN	0 11		2:25:38.8
	OHLIN Sture	0 2	34:57.3	
	PETRUSSON Olle	0 4	37:28.6	
	ERIKSSON Sten	0 5	38:41.2	
	OLSSON Holmfried	0 0	34:31.7	
11	USA	0 15		2:47:02.0
	SPENCER William	0 5	40:27.6	
	WILLIAMS Edward	0 3	39:41.5	
	EHRENSBECK John	0 6	43:38.4	
	VARNAM Gerald	0 1	43:41.5	

World Championships, Altenburg, East Germany, 1967

Individual Race, Men

Rank	Name	Nation	Penalties	Finish
1	MAMATOV Viktor	URS	0+1+2+3	1:28:34.1
2	SZCZEPANIAK Stanisl	POL	1+3+1+0	1:29:21.3
3	ISTAD Jon	NOR	0+3+3+6	1:30:03.7
	No USA Participation			

Team Relay, Men

1	NORWAY	2 11		2:52:41.5
	WERHAUG Ola	0 4	42:42.0	
	JORDET Olav	1 3	43:10.2	
	ISTAD Jon	1 1	40:38.0	
	TVEITEN Ragnar	0 3	44:01.7	
2	SOVIET UNION	5 11		3:03:11.8
	TICHONOV Alexandr	1 0	39:45.2	
	PUSANOV Nikolai	4 4	47:25.5	
	SAFIN Rinat	0 4	45:14.4	
	MAMATOV Viktor	0 3	49:14.9	
3	SWEDEN	0 11		2:25:38.8
	OHLIN Sture	0 1	41:14.9	
	ERIKSSON Sten	2 2	45:51.4	
	PETRUSSON Olle	2 3	47:31.8	
	OLSSON Holmfried	1 2	45:41.7	

World Biathlon Championships, Zakopane, Poland, 1969

Individual Race, Men

Rank	Name	Nation	Penalties	Finish
1	TICHONOV Alexandr	URS	2+1+1+1	1:22:46.2
2	SAFIAN Rinat	URS	0+1+1+1	1:22:49.0
3	SOLBERG Magnar	NOR	1+1+1+2	1:24:00.7
44	KARNS Peter	USA	2+3+2+2	1:37:27.7
45	DONAHUE Dennis	USA	2+0+0+3	1:38:26.1
51	BOWERMAN William	USA	1+5+1+0	1:41:42.5
53	WILLIAMS Edward	USA	5+5+2+3	1:43:43.1

Team Relay, Men

1	SOVIET UNION	0 0		1:57:55.1
	TIKHONOV Alexandr	0 0	28:46.7	
	MAMATOV Viktor	0 0	29:25.9	
	GUNDARCEW Vladislav	0 0	29:59.8	
	SAFIAN Rinat	0 0	29:42.7	
2	NORWAY	0 3		2:03:58.6
	TVEITEN Ragnar	0 1	29:24.3	
	GIELTEN Esten	0 0	30:58.6	
	ISTAD Jan	0 1	32:06.4	
	SOLBERG Magnar	0 1	31:29.3	
3	FINLAND	0 4		2:05:04.1
	VAHAKYLLA Kalevi	0 1	30:15.7	
	MARTTINEN Esko	0 0	30:51.8	
	PELTONEN Mauno	0 3	32:56.6	
	RÖPPÖNEN Mauri	0 0	31:00.0	
13	USA	0 5		2:17:41.2
	DONAHUE Dennis	0 0	32:18.2	
	BOWERMAN William	0 1	35:39.6	
	MORTON John	0 1	33:41.9	
	KARNS Peter	0 3	36:01.5	

World Championships, Östersund, Sweden, 1970

Individual Race, Men

Rank	Name	Nation	Penalties	Finish
1	TICHONOV Alexandr	URS	0+1+0+1	1:23:42.1
2	SVENDSBERGET Tor	NOR	0+0+0+2	1:24:36.1
3	MAMATOV Viktor	URS	1+1+0+0	1:25:00.4
21	DONAHUE Dennis	USA	1+2+0+1	1:31:39.8
38	KARNS Peter	USA	3+4+0+0	1:35:10.2
40	KENDALL William	USA	0+1+2+2	1:35:29.2
52	MORTON John	USA	2+2+1+2	1:39:32.3

Team Relay, Men

1	SOVIET UNION	1 0		2:07:49.0
	TIKHONOV Alexandr	0 0	30:32.0	
	SAFIN Rinnat	1 0	32:54.0	
	USHAKOV Alexandr	0 0	32:04.0	
	MAMATOV Viktor	0 0	32:19.0	
2	NORWAY	1 4		2:13:25.0
	TVEITEN Ragnar	0 1	32:33.0	
	SVENDSBERGET Tor	0 2	33:02.0	
	SOLBERG Magnar	0 0	32:36.0	
	GJELTEN Esten	1 1	35:14.0	
3	EAST GERMANY	0 4		2:14:45.9
	JAHN Hans G.	0 1	34:02.0	
	KNAUTHE Hans J.	0 0	32:10.0	
	SPEER Dieter	0 2	33:56.0	
	KOSCHKA Horst	0 1	34:37.9	
10	USA	0 4		2:22:02.7
	DONAHUE Dennis	0 2	35:33.0	
	ALDRICH Terry	0 1	36:48.0	
	MORTON John	0 0	34:24.0	
	KARNS Peter	0 1	35:17.7	

World Championships, Hameenlinna, Finland, 1971

Individual Race, Men

Rank	Name	Nation	Penalties	Finish
1	SPEER Dieter	GDR	1+1+0+0	1:18:20.2
2	TIKHONOV Alexandr	URS	1+1+0+1	1:18:48.4
3	SOLBERG Magnar	NOR	0+0+0+0	1:20:00.9
28	DEXTER Morse	USA	1+2+1+0	1:27:41.8
46	DONAHUE Dennis	USA	1+1+3+0	1:34:40.8
49	ALDRICH Terry	USA	2+2+2+1	1:37:13.7
52	ROMINE Michael	USA	4+7+3+3	1:45:14.8

Team Relay, Men

1	SOVIET UNION	2 0		2:09:42.0
	TIKHONOV Alexandr	2 0	34:08.0	
	MUHITOV Nazim	0 0	32:10.0	
	SAFIN Rinnat	0 0	31:45.0	
	MAMATOV Viktor	0 0	31:39.0	
2	NORWAY	1 0		2:10:13.0
	SVENDSBERGET Tor	1 0	31:44.0	
	TVEITEN Ragnar	0 0	31:14.0	
	SOLBERG Magnar	0 0	32:46.0	
	NORDKILD Ivar	0 0	33:30.0	
3	POLAND	0 2		2:14:57.0
	ROZAK Jozef	0 0	32:20.0	
	RAPACZ Andrzej	0 1	33:43.0	
	KLIMA Alexander	0 0	33:23.0	
	STOPKA Jozef	0 1	35:32.0	
11	USA	2 1		2:28:06.0
	ALDRICH Terry	0 1	36:57.0	
	ROMINE Michael	1 0	37:52.0	
	MORSE Dexter	0 0	35:58.0	
	DONAHUE Dennis	1 0	37:19.0	

Winter Olympic Games, Sapporo, Japan, 1972

Individual Race, Men

Rank	Name	Nation	Penalties	Finish
1	SOLBERG Magnar	NOR	0+1+1+0	1:15:55.5
2	KNAUTHE Hansjörg	GDR	1+0+0+0	1:16:07.6
3	ARWIDSON Lars-Göran	SWE	0+0+2+0	1:16:27.0
14	KARNS Peter	USA	0+0+0+2	1:20:59.7
24	DONAHUE Dennis	USA	1+0+3+0	1:23:20.4
41	MORSE Dexter	USA	1+1+4+1	1:28:40.1
45	BOWERMAN Jay	USA	1+3+1+2	1:29:13.7

Team Relay, Men

1	SOVIET UNION			1:51:44.9
	TIKONOV Alexandre	0-2	28:54.5	
	SAFIN Rinnat	0-0	26:48.5	
	BIAKOV Ivan	0-1	28:15.9	
	MAMATOV Victor	0-0	27:46.0	
2	FINLAND			1:54:37.2
	SAIRA Esko	0-1	28:52.0	
	SUUTARINEN Juhani	1-1	29:37.3	
	IKOLA Heikki	0-0	28:45.8	
	ROPPANEN Mauri	0-0	27:22.1	

3	GERMAN DEM REPUBLIC			1:54:57.7
	KNAUTHE Hans Jorg	0-0	28:11.7	
	MEISCHNER Joachim	0-0	28:36.9	
	SPEER Dieter	0-2	29:02.0	
	KOSCHKA Horst	0-2	29:19.4	
6	USA			1:57:24.3
	KARNS Peter	0-0	28:50.4	
	MORSE Dexter	0-0	28:43.6	
	DONAHUE Dennis	0-0	29:02.0	
	BOWERMAN Jay	0-1	30:48.4	

World Championships, Lake Placid, USA, 1973
Individual Race, Men

Rank	Name	Nation	Penalties	Finish
1	TIKHONOV Alexandr	URS	0+0+1+1	1:24:30.2
2	KOVALEV Gennadi	URS	0+0+1+0	1:27:17.2
3	SVENDSBERGET Tor	NOR	1+0+2+2	1:28:08.2
19	DONAHUE Dennis	USA	0+0+0+0	1:34:30.3
24	MORTON John	USA	2+2+1+2	1:37:02.0
35	ALLIGOOD Kenneth	USA	1+1+1+2	1:42:37.3
38	STEGEN Arthur	USA	2+3+1+5	1:50:42.6

Team Relay, Men

1	SOVIET UNION	1 0		2:27:02.2
	KOVALEV Gennadi	0 0	36:11.5	
	SAFIN Rinnat	1 0	36:45.2	
	KOLMAKOV Yuri	0 0	36:35.5	
	TIKHONOV Alexandr	0 0	37:29.9	
2	NORWAY	1 3		2:27:07.2
	HOVDA Kjell	0 2	37:31.5	
	ESTEN Gjelten	1 0	35:34.2	
	TVEITEN Ragnar	0 1	36:51.1	
	SVENDSBERGET Tor	0 0	37:10.2	
3	EAST GERMANY	0 4		2:28:26.4
	SPEER Dieter	0 3	37:31.7	
	GEYER Manfred	0 0	35:13.6	
	WIEGANG Herbert	0 0	38:09.5	
	BARTNIK Günther	0 1	37:31.5	
9	USA	0 4		2:41:04.9
	MORTON John	0 1	37:52.7	
	BOWERMAN Jay	0 1	38:58.5	
	TUTHILL George	0 2	42:46.8	
	DONAHUE Dennis	0 0	41:26.8	

World Championships, Minsk, USSR, 1974
Individual Race, Men

Rank	Name	Nation	Penalties	Finish
1	SUUTARINEN Juhani	FIN	0+1+0+0	1:12:04.7
2	GIRNITA Gheorge	ROM	0+0+0+1	1:13:28.9
3	SVENDSBERGET Tor	NOR	0+3+0+0	1:13:37.1
21	DONAHUE Dennis	USA	0+1+2+0	1:19:44.1
30	NELSON Lyle	USA	0+2+2+2	1:21:50.4
39	MORTON John	USA	1+5+0+1	1:23:19.6
56	STEGEN Arthur	USA	2+2+0+4	1:31:39.1

Sprint Race, Men

Rank	Name	Nation	Penalties	Finish
1	SUUTARINEN Juhani	FIN	0+2	37:42.4
2	BARTNICK Günther	GDR	1+3	38:30.7
3	WADMAN Torsten	SWE	2+0	38:44.0
34	MORTON John	USA	3+3	41:28.0
36	ALLIGOOD Ken	USA	2+1	41:47.7
56	DASCOULIAS Peter	USA	4+4	44:56.0
57	DONAHUE Dennis	USA	3+3	44:59.0

Team Relay, Men

1	SOVIET UNION	3 1		2:02:48.7
	USHAKOV Alexandr	0 0	29:31.2	
	TIKHONOV Alexandr	0 0	29:37.5	
	KOLMAKOV Juri	0 0	30:55.9	
	KRUGLOV Nikolai	3 1	32:44.0	
2	FINLAND	0 2		2:04:08.8
	HALONEN Simo	0 0	30:46.1	
	FLOJT Heikki	0 1	31:54.3	
	SUUTARINEN Juhani	0 0	29:33.2	
	IKOLA Heikki	0 1	31:55.1	
3	NORWAY	0 4		2:05:15.3
	HANSEN Terje	0 1	30:50.7	
	HOVDA Kare	0 2	31:43.9	
	HOVDA Kjell	0 1	32:13.9	
	SVENDSBERGET Tor	0 0	30:26.6	
14	USA	3 6		2:18:17.5
	DONAHUE Dennis	0 0	31:27.6	
	NELSON Lyle	3 3	35:06.6	
	ALLIGOOD Kenneth	0 1	35:25.4	
	MORTON John	0 2	36:17.8	

World Championships, Antholz, Italy, 1975

Individual Race, Men

Rank	Name	Nation	Penalties	Finish
1	IKOLA Heikki	FIN	0+2+0+0	1:13:52.3
2	KRUGLOV Nikolai	URS	0+1+2+0	1:14:31.3
3	SAIRA Esko	FIN	0+1+2+0	1:15:08.8
29	MORTON John	USA	1+4+0+0	1:22:19.7
41	STEGEN Art	USA	1+2+1+0	1:24:42.0
51	NELSON Lyle	USA	2+4+3+2	1:26:15.6
54	DASCUOLIUS Peter	USA	2+1+2+2	1:26:25.1

Sprint Race, Men

Rank	Name	Nation	Penalties	Finish
1	KRUGLOV Nikolai	URS	1+0	35:27.7
2	ELISAROV Alexandr	URS	1+0	35:56.2
3	SIEBERT Klaus	GDR	0+2	36:27.4
34	MORTON John	USA	1+3	39:23.9
56	NELSON Lyle	USA	2+5	41:51.8
59	ALLIGOOD Kenneth	USA	3+1	43:01.4
63	DASCOULIAS Peter	USA	3+5	44:34.4

Team Relay, Men

Rank	Name		Finish
1	FINLAND	3 0	1:55:10.6
	FLOJT Heikki	0 0	28:37.0
	HALONEN Simo	0 0	30:44.3
	SUUTARINEN Juhani	3 0	28:27.5
	IKOLA Heikki	0-0	27:21.8
2	SOVIET UNION	2 6	1:55:36.2
	USHAKOV Alexandr	0 3	28:38.6
	ELISAROV Alexandr	3 1	29:39.6
	TIKHONOV Alexandr	0 0	27:26.4
	KRUGLOV Nikolai	1 2	27:26.4
3	POLAND	0 2	1:57:12.2
	SZPUNAR Jan	0 1	29:44.5
	RAPACZ Andrzej	0 0	29:00.9
	ZIEBA Ludwig	0 0	29:18.1
	TRUCHAN Wojciek	0 1	29:08.7
14	USA	2 4	2:10:19.5
	MORTON John	0 0	30:06.7
	ALLIGOOD Kenneth	0 1	34:45.2
	STEGEN Arthur	1 2	34:00.7
	NELSON Lyle	1 1	31:26.9

Winter Olympic Games, Innsbruck, Austria, 1976

Individual Race, Men

Rank	Name	Nation	Penalties	Finish
1	KRUGLOV Nikolay	URS	1+0+0+1	1:14:12.3
2	IKOLA Heikki	FIN	0+0+0+2	1:15:54.1
3	YELIZAROV Aleksandr	URS	1+0+0+2	1:16:05.6
35	NELSON Lyle	USA	1+4+3+2	1:25:27.5
47	HAGEN Martin	USA	2+4+1+4	1:28:49.2
	DASCOULIAS Peter	USA		DNF

Team Relay, Men

Rank	Name			Finish
1	SOVIET UNION	3 0		1:57:55.6
	ELISAROV Aleksandr	0-0	29:47.4	
	BIAKOV Ivan	0-0	30:16.8	
	KRUGLOV Nikolay	0-0	29:04.8	
	TIKHONOV Aleksandr	0-0	28:46.6	
2	FINLAND			2:01:45.6
	FLOJT Henrik	0-2	32:00.2	
	SAIRA Esko	0-0	29:12.5	
	SUUTARINEN Juhani	0-0	30:52.2	
	IKOLA Heikki	0-0	29:40.7	
3	GERMAN DEM REPUPLIC			2:04:08.6
	MENZ Karl-Heinz	0-0	31:02.2	
	ULLRICH Frank	1-1	32:47.3	
	BEER Manfred	0-2	31:30.0	
	GEYER Manfred	0-0	28:49.1	
14	USA			2:10:19.5
	NELSON Lyle	0-0	30:29.2	
	DONAHUE Dennis	0-2	33:11.8	
	MORTON John	0-1	33:09.1	
	DASCAULIAS Peter	0-1	33:27.7	

World Championships, Antholz, Italy, 1976

Sprint Race, Men *(10km, prone and standing with penalty laps)*

Rank	Name	Nation	Penalties	Finish
1	TIKHONOV Alexandr	URS	1+3	36:48.2
2	ELISAROV Alexandr	URS	1+0	36:51.5
3	KRUGLOV Nikolai	URS	2+0	37:19.9
19	NELSON Lyle	USA	2+1	39:49.0
38	HAGEN Martin	USA	3+2	41:44.2
45	DASQUOLLAS Peter	USA	2+4	42:45.6
50	MORTON John	USA	0+4	43:38.7

World Championships, Vingrom, Norway, 1977

Individual Race, Men

Rank	Name	Nation	Penalties	Finish
1	IKOLA Heikki	FIN	0+0+0+1	1:10:51.8
2	JOHANSEN Sigleif	NOR	0+0+1+1	1:11:16.3
3	TIKHONOV Alexandr	URS	2+0+0+2	1:11:18.1
31	NELSON Lyle	USA	2+2+3+0	1:18:27.3
38	HOAG Peter	USA	1+1+1+1	1:20:27.0
40	EWING Glen	USA	1+2+1+1	1:22:05.2

Sprint Race, Men

Rank	Name	Nation	Penalties	Finish
1	TIKHONOV Alexandr	URS	0+0	32:47.8
2	KRUGLOV Nikolai	URS	1+0	33:45.1
3	USHAKOV Alexandr	URS	0+1	34:12.4
32	HOAG Peter	USA	1+1	37:03.8
34	NELSON Lyle	USA	2+1	37:20.8
44	EWING Glen	USA	2+2	41:39.0
45	DOXSEE Brian	USA	2+3	42:43.9

Team Relay, Men

1	SOVIET UNION	0 0		1:48:10.8
	ELISAROV Alexandr	0 0	27:50.9	
	USHAKOV Alexandr	0 0	27:52.9	
	KRUGLOV Nikolai	0 0	26:01.6	
	TIKHONOV Alexandr	0 0	26:25.4	
2	FINLAND	0 2		1:49:55.9
	ANTILA Erkki	0 2	27:53.4	
	SEPPÄNEN Raimo	0 0	27:11.3	
	HALONEN Simo	0 0	27:26.7	
	IKOLA Heikki	0 0	27:24.5	
3	GERMAN DEM REPUBLIC	0 0		1:50:52.5
	BEER Manfred	0 0	28:11.2	
	SIEBERT Klaus	0 0	27:09.2	
	ULLRICH Frank	0 0	27:02.5	
	GEYER Manfred	0 0	28:29.6	
10	USA	3 1		2:02:33.5
	NELSON Lyle	2 0	31:39.2	
	HOAG Peter	0 1	30:13.4	
	FOOTE Robert	1 0	30:52.8	
	SCOTT Rusty	0 0	29:48.1	

World Championships, Hochflizen, Austria, 1978

Individual Race, Men

Rank	Name	Nation	Penalties[3]	Finish
1	LIRHUS Odd	NOR	1+0+0+0	1:05:26.3
2	ULLRICH Frank	GDR	1+1+0+0	1:05:35.7
3	RÖSCH Eberhard	GDR	0+1+0+1	1:06:04.2
50	HALL John	USA	1+4+0+0	1:17:32.4
51	EWING Glen	USA	0+4+1+0	1:18:46.1
61	HOAG Peter	USA	1+0+3+3	1:21:26.0

[3] *Single 50m range, .22 rim fire caliber, each miss added 1 or 2 minutes penalty.*

Sprint Race, Men

Rank	Name	Nation	Penalties	Finish
1	ULLRICH Frank	GDR	0+0	32:17.4
2	ROESCH Eberhard	GDR	0+0	32:38.1
3	SIEBERT Klaus	GDR	0+0	33:02.8
55	HAGEN Martin	USA	2+4	38:38.5
63	HOAG Peter	USA	3+2	39:48.4
64	HALL John	USA	4+1	39:51.0
66	EWING Glen	USA	1+3	40:21.4

Team Relay, Men

1	GERMAN DEM REPUBLIC	0 1		1:37:47.6
	BEER Manfred	0 0	25:31.1	
	SIEBERT Klaus	0 0	23:55.7	
	ULLRICH Frank	0 0	23:45.8	
	RÖSCH Eberhard	0 1	24:34.9	
2	NORWAY	0 1		1:40:28.5
	SVENSBERGET Tor	0 0	26:31.4	
	NILSEL Roar	0 1	25:26.3	
	LIRHUS Odd	0 0	24:32.1	
	JOHANSEN Sigleif	0 0	23:58.6	
3	FEDERAL REP GERMANY	0 1		1:40:35.1
	MEHRINGER Heinrich	0 0	25:30.4	
	ESTNER Hansi	0 1	25:52.9	
	SCHWEIGER Andreas	0 0	25:01.3	
	WINKLER Gerd	0 0	24:10.3	
17	USA	0 3		1:50:42.4
	HALL John	0 3	28:46.7	
	EWING Glen	0 0	27:17.8	
	JOBE Glenn	0 0	26:37.8	
	HOAG Peter	0 0	27:59.9	

World Championships, Rupholding, Germany, 1979

Individual Race, Men

Rank	Name	Nation	Penalties	Finish
1	SIEBERT Klaus	GDR	0+0+1+0	1:07:40.1
2	TIKHONOV Alexandr	URS	0+0+2+0	1:09:22.1
3	JOHANSEN Sigleif	NOR	0+0+0+1	1:09:37.4
34	ALIGOOD Ken	USA	1+0+0+0	1:15:45.9
35	NELSON Lyle	USA	3+2+2+0	1:16:06.0
39	HAGEN Martin	USA	0+2+1+1	1:17:22.6
58	JOBE Glen	USA	1+2+2+3	1:21:57.3

Sprint Race, Men

Rank	Name	Nation	Penalties	Finish
1	ULLRICH Frank	GDR	0+0	40:35.3
2	LIRHUS Odd	NOR	1+2	41:28.5
3	WEISS Luigi	ITA	0+2	41:46.3
33	HAGEN Martin	USA	1+2	45:21.7
41	NELSON Lyle	USA	2+4	46:00.4
42	JOBE Glen	USA	3+2	46:01.7
52	NIELSEN Don	USA	3+3	47:01.2

Team Relay, Men

1	GERMAN DEM REPUBLIC	0 1		1:54:48.5
	BEER Manfred	0 0	29:32.5	
	SIEBERT Klaus	0 0	28:39.8	
	ULLRICH Frank	0 0	27:46.8	
	RÖSCH Eberhard	0 1	28:49.3	
2	FINLAND	0 1		1:56:26.7
	HALONEN Simo	0 0	29:58.1	
	ANTILA Erkki	0 1	29:00.4	
	SEPPÄNEN Raimo	0 0	29:18.0	
	IKOLA Heikki	0 0	28:10.1	
3	SOVIET UNION	0 3		1:58:14.6
	ALIKIN Vladimir	0 0	28:57.5	
	BARNASHOV Vladimir	0 0	28:34.9	
	KRUGLOV Nikolai	0 2	31:05.4	
	TIKHONOV Alexandr	0 1	29:36.6	
15	USA	0 5		2:09:05.2
	NELSON Lyle	0 0	30:14.4	
	NIELSEN Donald	0 4	32:45.1	
	HAGEN Martin	0 0	32:34.5	
	JOBE Glen	0 1	33:31.1	

Winter Olympic Games, Lake Placid, USA, 1980

Individual Race, Men

Rank	Name	Nation	Penalties	Finish
1	ALYABYEV Anatoly	URS	0+0+0+0	1:08:16.3
2	ULLRICH Frank	GDR	1+0+1+1	1:08:27.8
3	RÖSCH Eberhard	GDR	2+0+0+0	1:11:11.7
36	HAGEN Martin	USA	0+4+4+0	1:21:02.9
38	JOBE Glenn	USA	1+0+0+5	1:21:36.5
45	RUGER John	USA	8+4+6+3	1:33:30.8

Sprint Race, Men

Rank	Name	Nation	Penalties	Finish
1	ULLRICH Frank	GDR	0+2	0:32:10.7
2	ALIKIN Vladimir	URS	0+0	0:32:53.1
3	ALYABYEV Anatoly	URS	0+1	0:33:09.2
19	NELSON Lyle	USA	1+1	0:35:45.8
44	NIELSEN Donald	USA	2+4	0:38:51.0
45	HOAG Peter	USA	2+2	0:38:53.4

Team Relay, Men

1	SOVIET UNION	0-0		1:34:03.3
	ALIKIN Vladimir	0-0	22:40.7	
	TIKHONOV Alexander	0-0	23:44.6	
	BARNASCHOV Vladimir	0-0	23:48.3	
	ALJABIEV Anatoli	0-0	23:49.6	
2	GERMAN DEM REPUBLIC	1-2		1:34:57.0
	JUNG Mathias	0-0	23:03.8	
	SIEBERT Klaus	1-1	24:47.6	
	ULLRICH Frank	0-0	24:01.2	
	RÖSCH Eberhard	0-1	24:04.2	
3	FEDERAL REP GERMANY	0-2		1:37:30.3
	BERNREITER Franz	0-2	24:53.5	
	ESTNER Hansi	0-0	24:31.9	
	ANGERER Peter	0-0	23:31.2	
	WINKLER Gerd	0-0	24:33.5	
8	USA	0-0		1:39:24.2
	HAGEN Martin	0-0	24:25.4	
	NELSON Lyle	0-0	24:43.6	
	NIELSON Donald	0-0	24:31.2	
	HOAG Peter	0-0	25:43.9	

World Championships, Lahti, Finland, 1981

Individual Race, Men

Rank	Name	Nation	Penalties	Finish
1	IKOLA Heikki	FIN	0+0+0+0	1:13:07.2
2	ULLRICH Frank	GDR	0+0+2+0	1:14:09.6
3	ANTILA Erkki	FIN	1+1+1+0	1:14:51.1
40	NELSON Lyle	USA	1+1+2+2	1:23:55.1
41	HOAG Peter	USA	1+0+1+0	1:24:06.9
54	MC'GUIRE Rick	USA	1+2+1+4	1:28:25.8
62	RUGER John	USA	3+2+4+2	1:32:52.3

Sprint Race, Men

Rank	Name	Nation	Penalties	Finish
1	ULLRICH Frank	GDR	0+1	33:08.5
2	ANTILA Erkki	FIN	0+0	33:10.1
3	MOUGEL Yvon	FRA	0+0	33:13.5
29	NELSON Lyle	USA	1+1	36:20.9
52	HOAG Peter	USA	3+1	38:27.1
56	LYCY Nat	USA	4+2	38:52.7
57	RUGER John	USA	3+2	38:58.5

Team Relay, Men

1	GERMAN DEM REPUBLIC	0 0		1:42:37.8
	JUNG Mathias	0 0	26:33.2	
	JACOB Matthias	0 0	25:30.7	
	ULLRICH Frank	0 0	25:02.2	
	RÖSCH Eberhard	0 0	25:31.5	
2	FEDERAL REP GERMANY	0 0		1:44:50.0
	BERNREITER Franz	0 0	27:13.9	
	SCHWEIGER Andreas	0 0	26:58.0	
	ANGERER Peter	0 0	25:03.0	
	FISCHER Fritz	0 0	25:35.0	
3	SOVIET UNION	0 1		1:46:17.9
	ALIKIN Vladimir	0 1	27:12.7	
	BARNASHOV Vladimir	0 0	26:58.1	
	GAVRIKOV Vladmir	0 0	25:56.3	
	ALJABJEV Anatoli	0 0	26:10.6	
14	USA	0 10		1:59:55.7
	HOAG Peter	0 0	28:38.9	
	MC'GUIRE Rick	0 5	31:53.9	
	LUCY Nat	0 3	30:37.9	
	NELSON Lyle	0 2	28:44.8	

World Championships, Minsk, Soviet Union, 1982

Individual Race, Men

Rank	Name	Nation	Penalties	Finish
1	ULLRICH Frank	GDR	0+0+1+0	1:07:17.0
2	KVALFOSS Eirik	NOR	0+0+2+0	1:07:50.3
3	KROKSTAD Terje	NOR	0+0+0+1	1:10:48.6
42	CAROW William	USA	1+0+0+0	1:17:40.7
47	NIELSEN Donald	USA	3+2+2+0	1:19:33.0
48	RUGER John	USA	0+2+1+1	1:22:22.3

Sprint Race, Men

Rank	Name	Nation	Penalties	Finish
1	KVALFOSS Eirik	NOR	1+1	33:03.2
2	ULLRICH Frank	GDR	0+1	33:09.1
3	ALIKIN Vladimir	URS	2+0	33:21.6
44	NIELSEN Donald	USA	1+2	37:44.1
45	CARROW William	USA	2+2	37:45.4
52	RUGER John	USA	3+1	38:43.5
55	LUCY Nathaniel	USA	1+3	39:29.3

Team Relay, Men

1	GERMAN DEM REPUBLIC	0 0		1:39:45.2
	JUNG Mattias	0 0	24:39.1	
	JACOB Matthias	0 0	25:12.9	
	ULLRICH Frank	0 0	24:49.5	
	HELMIN Bernd	0 0	25:03.6	
2	NORWAY	2 0		1:40:53.0
	KVALFOSS Eirik	0 0	24:14.4	
	SÖBAK Kjell	0 0	24:48.8	
	STORSVEEN Rolf	2 0	26:44.0	
	LIRHUS Odd	0 0	24:42.7	
3	SOVIET UNION	0 1		1:41:09.5
	ALIKIN Vladimir	0 0	24:39.9	
	BARNASHOV Vladimir	0 1	26:02.4	
	SEMENOV Viktor	0 0	25:29.2	
	ALIABYEV Anatoli	0 0	24:57.9	
13	USA	2 1		1:53:49.2
	HAGEN Martin	2 0	29:17.2	
	NIELSEN Donald	0 0	27:16.6	
	RUGER John	0 1	29:54.2	
	CARROW William	0 0	27:31.8	

World Championships, Antholz, Italy, 1983

Individual Race, Men

Rank	Name	Nation	Penalties	Finish
1	ULLRICH Frank	GDR	0+1+0+0	1:05:00.9
2	RÖTSCH Frank Peter	GDR	1+0+0+0	1:05:17.8
3	ANGERER Peter	FRG	1+0+0+1	1:06:57.3
44	CAROW William	USA	3+1+1+2	1:16:11.0
46	LUCY Nat	USA	3+1+2+1	1:16:28.1
53	RUGER John	USA	3+3+2+0	1:19:10.5
62	HOAG Peter	USA	1+4+2+0	1:22:48.4

Sprint Race, Men

Rank	Name	Nation	Penalties	Finish
1	KVALFOSS Eirik	NOR	0+2	31:12.3
2	ANGERER Peter	FRG	0+0	31:31.2
3	EDER Alfred	AUT	0+0	31:45.5
36	HAGEN Martin	USA	0+2	35:36.9
57	CAROW Willie	USA	3+2	37:09.2
59	RUGER John	USA	2+4	37:18.8
63	LUCY Nat	USA	4+1	37:36.9

Team Relay, Men

1	SOVIET UNION	0 0		1:36:48.5
	BULIGYN Sergei	0 0	25:06.0	
	SHALNA Algemantas	0 0	23:27.1	
	KASCHKAROV Juri	0 0	24:17.0	
	MILORADOV Peter	0 0	23:58.2	
2	GERMAN DEM REPUBLIC	0 1		1:38:04.7
	JUNG Matthias	0 0	24:48.5	
	ROETSCH Frank Peter	0 0	24:13.0	
	ULLRICH Frank	0 1	24:38.8	
	JACOB Mathias	0 0	24:24.3	
3	NORWAY	0 3		1:41:27.1
	NERHAGEN Oeyvind	0 0	25:42.5	
	SOEBAK Kjell	0 0	25:00.4	
	KVALFOSS Eirik	0 0	25:02.8	
	LIRHUS Odd	0 3	25:41.2	
9	USA	1 1		1:48:31.4
	CAROW Willie	0 0	26:43.3	
	LUCY Nat	1 1	29:01.4	
	HAGEN Martin	0 0	26:45.1	
	RUGER John	0 0	26:01.5	

Winter Olympic Games, Sarajevo, Yugoslavia, 1984

Individual Race, Men

Rank	Name	Nation	Penalties	Finish
1	ANGERER Peter	FRG	0+1+1+0	1:11:52.7
2	ROETSCH Frank Peter	GDR	0+0+2+1	1:12:05.5
3	KVALFOSS Erik	NOR	2+1+1+1	1:14:02.4
26	NELSON Lyle	USA	2+3+1+1	1:21:05.4
33	EBERLE Glen	USA	2+2+0+0	1:22:15.0
53	HAGEN Martin	USA	2+4+2+4	1:30:19.0

Sprint Race, Men

Rank	Name	Nation	Penalties	Finish
1	KVALFOSS Erik	NOR	1+1	30:53.8
2	ANGERER Peter	FRG	0+1	31:02.4
3	JACOB Matthias	GDR	0+0	31:10.5
20	CAROW William	USA	0+0	33:05.8
40	THOMPSON Josh	USA	2+2	35:10.0
42	NIELSEN Donald	USA	2+1	35:23.0

Team Relay, Men

1	SOVIET UNION	0+2		1:38:51.7
	VASSILLIEV Dmitry	0+0	24:52.4	
	KACHKAROV Youry	0+0	24:34.8	
	SHALNA Alguimantas	0+5	25:17.8	
	BOULIGUIN Serguey	0+0	24:06.7	
2	NORWAY	0+1		1:39:03.9
	LIRHUS Odd	0+2	26:56.2	
	KVALFOSS Erik	0+0	23:27.6	
	STORSVEEN Rolf	0+0	24:46.5	
	SOEBAK Kjell	0+0	23:53.6	
3	FEDERAL REP GERMANY	0+1		1:39:05.1
	REITER Ernst	0+0	26:01.9	
	PICHLER Walter	0+1	25:13.5	
	ANGERER Peter	0+0	23:39.3	
	FISCHER Fritz	0+0	24:10.4	
11	USA	1+0		1:44:31.9
	CAROW William	0+0	27:23.9	
	NIELSEN Donald	1+0	26:42.7	
	NELSON Lyle	0+0	24:58.2	
	THOMPSON Josh	0+0	25:27.1	

World Championships, Chamomix, France, 1984

Individual Race, Women

Rank	Name	Nation	Penalties	Finish
1	TCHERNYCHOVA Venera	URS	2+2+0	44:21.7
2	ZABOLOTNIAIA Liudmila	URS	0+2+1	44:30.9
3	BRYLINA Tatiana	URS	2+1+1	44:50.0
5	SWENSON Kari	USA	0+1+0	45:49.6
15	REYNOLDS Jan	USA	0+1+2	48:19.9
27	NEWNAM Julie	USA	2+2+2	51:01.4
29	BEATTIE Holly	USA	3+2+1	51:41.4

Sprint Race, Women

Rank	Name	Nation	Penalties	Finish
1	TCHERNYCHOVA Venera	URS	1+2	23:00.1
2	GRONLID Sanna	NOR	0+1	23:35.0
3	GROSSEGGER Andrea	AUT	0+2	23:39.5
13	SWENSON Kari	USA	0+2	25:53.4
16	REYNOLDS Jan	USA	0+4	26:23.2
22	NEWNAM Julie	USA	3+1	27:32.4
26	BEATTIE Holly	USA	1+4	28:06.9

Team Relay, Women

1	SOVIET UNION	2+9		1:23:26.2
	ZAPOLOTNIAIA Ludmila	0+2	28:43.0	
	PARVE Kaija	2+5	29:41.0	
	TCHERNYSCHOVA Venera	0+2	23:27.6	
2	NORWAY	2+8		1:26:22.0
	OESTVIK GRY	1+2	29:00.8	
	BRAATEN Siv	0+4	28:12.9	
	GROENLID Sanna	1+2	28:00.5	
3	U.S.A.	4+4		1:27:10.6
	NEWNAM Julie	2+1	31:31.4	
	SWENSON Kari	1+1	27:22.1	
	BEATTIE Holly	0+2	28:05.1	

World Championships, Ruhpolding, Germany, 1985

Individual Race, Men

Rank	Name	Nation	Penalties	Finish
1	KASCHKAROV Yuri	URS	0+0+0+0	57:30.3
2	ROETSCH Frank-Peter	GDR	0+1+0+1	59:18.6
3	PIIPPONEN Tapio	FIN	0+0+0+0	59:45.0
40	CAROW Willie	USA	0+1+2+1	1:06:25.1
51	NELSON Lyle	USA	1+3+1+2	1:09:49.6
55	DOMBROVSKY Raimond	USA	0+2+3+2	1:11:00.7
59	EBERLE Glen	USA	3+0+3+2	1:12:13.1

Sprint Race, Men

Rank	Name	Nation	Penalties	Finish
1	ROETSCH Frank-Peter	GDR	0+1	30:25.2
2	KVALFOSS Eirik	NOR	1+0	31:16.1
3	PASSLER Johann	ITA	0+0	31:33.7
33	NELSON Lyle	USA	0+1	34:29.9
51	EBERLE Glen	USA	1+2	36:27.6
58	DOMBROVSKY Raimond	USA	0+0	37:12.9
74	HOAG Peter	USA	0+1	40:49.1

Team Relay, Men

1	SOVIET UNION	0 2		1:33:12.7
	KASCHKAROV Juri	0 0	23:20.8	
	SHALNA Algemantas	0 2	23:51.1	
	ZENKOV Andrei	0 0	22:59.2	
	BULIGYN Sergei	0 0	23:01.6	
2	GERMAN DEM REPUBLIC	0 0		1:34:57.5
	SEHMISCH Andre	0 0	24:18.0	
	JACOB Matthias	0 0	23:00.8	
	GÖTHEL Ralf	0 0	24:21.4	
	ROETSCH Frank Peter	0 0	23:17.3	
3	FEDERAL REP GERMANY	1 1		1:35:44.9
	FRITZENWENGER Herb	1 0	23:47.9	
	PICHLER Walter	0 1	25:35.6	
	ANGERER Peter	0 0	22:24.4	
	FISCHER Fritz	0 0	22:57.0	
13	USA	0 0		1:47:54.6
	EBERLE Glen	0 0	27:21.3	
	DOMBROVSKY Raimond	0 0	27:30.1	
	CAROW Willie	0 0	26:59.7	
	NELSON Lyle	0 0	26:03.5	

World Championships, Egg, Switzerland, 1986

Individual Race, Women

Rank	Name	Nation	Penalties	Finish
1	PARVE Kaya	URS	2+1+1	43:21.4
2	GROENLID Sanna	NOR	0+3+1	44:20.8
3	KORPELA Eva	SWE	2+0+0	44:40.5
20	NORDHEIM Pam	USA	1+3+0	51:08.6
22	WEISS Pam	USA	2+1+2	53:56.3
23	NEWMAN Julie	USA	0+4+3	53:57.3
27	SWENSON Kari	USA	3+3+3	57:30.5

Sprint Race, Women

Rank	Name	Nation	Penalties	Finish
1	GROENLID Sanna	NOR	0+0	21:58.9
2	PARVE Kaya	URS	2+1	22:03.7
3	TCHERNYCHOVA Venera	URS	3+0	22:52.3
15	NORDHEIM Pam	USA	1+2	25:45.1
18	WEISS Pam	USA	2+1	25:55.6
24	NEWMAN Julie	USA	2+1	27:44.7
26	SWENSON Kari	USA	2+4	28:56.7

Team Relay, Women

1	SOVIET UNION	0+2		1:12:43.0
	CHERNYSHOVA Venera	0+2	26:43.0	
	GOLOVINA Elena	0+0	22:53.0	
	PARVE Kaija	0+0	23:06.0	
2	NORWAY			1:12:51.0
	GROENLID Sanna			
	OESTVIK GRY			
	BRAATEN Siv			
	FINLAND			1:21:00.0
	MATTILA Pirjo			
	VOUKSIALA Tuija			
	NIEMINEN Teija			
3	UNITED STATES	2+1		1:24:07.0
	WEISS Pam	0+0	27:49.0	
	NEWMAN Julie	0+1	28:45.0	
	NORDHEIM Pam	2+0	27:30.0	

World Championships, Oslo, Norway, 1986

Individual Race, Men

Rank	Name	Nation	Penalties	Finish
1	MEDVEDTSEV Valeriy	URS	1+0+0+1	57:05.3
2	SEHMISCH Andre	GDR	0+1+0+0	57:19.2
3	EDER Alfred	AUT	0+0+0+0	58:38.1
12	THOMPSON Josh	USA	0+1+0+1	1:01:04.3
33	NELSON Lyle	USA	0+2+1+0	1:03:51.9
49	CAROW Willie	USA	1+2+2+1	1:06:57.1
57	EBERLE Glen	USA	3+1+1+0	1:09:24.7

Sprint Race, Men

Rank	Name	Nation	Penalties	Finish
1	MEDVEDTSEV Valeriy	URS	0+0	28:02.8
2	SCHULER Franz	AUT	0+1	28:55.3
3	SEHMISCH Andre	GDR	0+1	28:59.9
39	THOMPSON Josh	USA	1+2	31:00.8
44	NELSON Lyle	USA	3+0	31:22.4
59	DOMBROVSKY Raimond	USA	3+1	32:24.1
62	EBERLE Glen	USA	2+0	32:32.5

Team Relay, Men

1	SOVIET UNION	1 0		1:39:23.2
	VASILIEV Dimitri	0 0	24:52.8	
	KASHKAROV Juri	0 0	24:28.3	
	MEDVETSEV Valeri	0 0	24:56.4	
	BULYGIN Sergej	1 0	25:05.7	
2	GERMAN DEM REPUBLIC	0 1		1:40:02.3
	WIRTH Jürgen	0 0	24:51.3	
	ROETSCH Frank Peter	0 0	24:49.2	
	JACOB Matthias	0 1	24:57.6	
	SEHMISCH Andre	0 0	24:24.2	
3	ITALY	1 0		1:41:07.0
	KIEM Werner	1 0	26:23.0	
	TASCHLER Gottlieb	0 0	25:23.7	
	PASSLER Johann	0 0	24:25.3	
	ZINGERLE Andreas	0 0	24:55.0	
12	USA	3 0		1:49:16.5
	DOMBROVSKY Raimond	1 0	28:09.6	
	THOMPSON Josh	2 0	27:30.5	
	CAROW Willie	0 0	26:51.9	
	NELSON Lyle	0 0	26:44.5	

World Championships, Falun, Sweden, 1986

Individual Race, Women

Rank	Name	Nation	Penalties	Finish
1	KORPELA Eva	SWE	0+0+1	37:46.9
2	BRAATEN Siv	NOR	0+0+0	38:47.3
3	GRÖNLID Sanna	NOR	1+1+0	39:19.6
21	NORDHEIM Pam	USA	1+2+4	47:05.8
22	SWENSON Kari	USA	2+2+0	47:10.3
25	WEISS Pam	USA	2+1+1	47:30.3
32	BEATTIE-FARR Holly	USA	2+4+3	51:21.8

Sprint Race, Women

Rank	Name	Nation	Penalties	Finish
1	PARVE Kaya	URS	1+0	20:07.0
2	BELOVA Nadezda	URS	1+0	20:53.2
3	KORPELA Eva	SWE	0+2	21:25.0
17	NORDHEIM Pam	USA	2+1	23:14.0
20	WEISS Pam	USA	0+1	23:54.8
25	SWENSON Kari	USA	3+1	24:52.8
34	BEATTIE-FARR Holly	USA	5+3	27:39.3

Team Relay, Women

1	SOVIET UNION	0 2		1:05:52.0
	BELOVA Nadezda	0 0	23:27.6	
	PARVE Kaya	0 2	21:27.9	
	TCHERNYCHOVA Venera	0 0	20:56.5	
2	SWEDEN	0 0		1:06:09.4
	BJÖRKBOM Inger	0 0	23:39.7	
	KARLSSON Sabiene	0 0	21:32.9	
	KORPELA Eva	0 0	20:56.8	
3	NORWAY	2 0		1:06:27.6
	ELVEBAAK Anne	2 0	24:26.8	
	BRAATEN Siv	0 0	21:26.3	
	GROENLID Sanna	0 0	20:44.5	
7	USA	0 3		1:14:47.3
	WEISS Pam	0 2	27:38.5	
	SWENSON Kari	0 1	24:38.0	
	NORDHEIM Pam	0 0	22:30.8	

World Championships, Lake Placid, 1987

Individual Race, Men

Rank	Name	Nation	Penalties	Finish
1	ROETSCH Frank Peter	GDR	0+1+0+0	1:00:00.4
2	THOMPSON Josh	USA	0+0+0+1	1:00:51.0
3	MATOUS Jan	TCH	0+0+0+0	1:01:15.3
26	DOMBROVSKY Raimond	USA	1+0+0+0	1:06:39.5
47	CAROW Willie	USA	1+2+3+2	1:10:55.0
50	EBERLE Glen	USA	1+1+1+3	1:11:38.6

Sprint Race, Men

Rank	Name	Nation	Penalties	Finish
1	ROETSCH Frank Peter	GDR	0+1	29:49.6
2	JACOB Matthias	GDR	0+2	30:38.8
3	SEHMISCH Andre	GDR	1+1	30:55.4
18	THOMPSON Josh	USA	1+2	32:28.0
24	CAROW Willie	USA	2+2	33:09.6
57	WILBRECHT Erich	USA	3+3	38:40.9
DSQ	OLIVER Rick	USA		

Team Relay, Men

1	GERMAN DEM REPUBLIC	0 2		1:25:02.3
	WIRTH Jürgen	0 0	20:59.9	
	ROETSCH Frank Peter	0 1	20:59.7	
	JACOB Matthias	0 1	21:21.9	
	SEHMISCH Andre	0 0	21:40.8	
2	SOVIET UNION	2 1		1:27:12.1
	VASSILIEV Dmitri	0 0	21:03.1	
	POPOV Alexandre	0 0	22:10.9	
	KASHKAROV Juri	2 1	23:09.5	
	MEDVETSEV Valery	0 0	20:48.6	

3	FEDERAL REP GERMANY	0 3		1:27:21.1
	REITER Ernst	0 0	21:04.9	
	FRITZENWENGER Herb	0 0	22:09.8	
	ANGERER Peter	0 2	22:30.4	
	FISCHER Fritz	0 1	21:36.0	
10	USA	0 1		1:32:43.2
	EBERLE Glen	0 0	24:23.2	
	DOMBROVSKY Raimond	0 0	24:14.6	
	CAROW Willie	0 1	22:46.7	
	THOMPSON Josh	0 0	21:18.7	

World Championships, Lahti, Finland, 1987

Individual Race, Women

Rank	Name	Nation	Penalties	Finish
1	GRÖNLIND Sanna	NOR	2+0+0	42:42.8
2	PARVE Kaija	URS	0+0+2	43:31.1
3	VUOKSIALA Tuija	FIN	0+2+0	44:56.8
16	NORDHEIM Pam	USA	1+3+2	49:45.5
20	SONNERUP Anna	USA	2+3+1	50:11.2
24	OSTERGREN Mary	USA	1+2+3	51:26.6
34	WEISS Pam	USA	1+1+3	54:29.2

Sprint Race, Women

Rank	Name	Nation	Penalties	Finish
1	GOLOVINA Elena	URS	0+0	21:14.7
2	TSERNYSOVA Venera	URS	0+1	21:51.9
3	LINN ELVEBAKK Anne	NOR	0+2	22:12.1
9	SONNERUP Anna	USA	0+1	22:57.8
23	NORDHEIM pam	USA	2+2	24:07.9
33	OSTERGREN Mary	USA	3+2	25:35.2
38	WEISS Pam	USA	1+2	26:28.9

Team Relay, Women

1	SOVIENT UNION			1:02:55.0
	GOLOVINA Elena			
	CHERNYCHOVA Venera			
	PARVE Kaija			
2	SWEDEN			1:03:40.0
	BJORKBOM Inger			
	STADIG Mia			
	KORPELA Eva			
3	NORWAY			1:04:03.0
	ELVEBEKK Anne			
	GROENLID Sanna			
	BRAATEN Siv			
7	USA			1:13:39.0
	SONNERUP Anna			
	OSTERGREN Mary			
	NORDHEIM Pam			

Winter Olympic Games, Calgary, Canada, 1988
Individual Race, Men

Rank	Name	Nation	Penalties	Finish
1	ROETSCH Frank Peter	GDR	1+1+0+1	56:33.3
2	MEDVEDTSEV Valeriy	URS	0+1+0+1	56:54.6
3	PASSLER Johann	ITA	1+0+0+1	57:10.1
25	THOMPSON Josh	USA	1+1+0+3	1:01:29.4
42	BINNING Darin	USA	1+1+2+0	1:03:54.8
49	CAROW Willie	USA	0+3+0+2	1:05:10.2
52	SCHREINER Curt	USA	1+1+1+2	1:05:22.7

Sprint Race, Men

Rank	Name	Nation	Penalties	Finish
1	ROETSCH Frank Peter	GDR	0+1	25:08.1
2	MEDVEDTSEV Valeriy	URS	0+0	25:23.7
3	TCHEPIKOV Sergei	URS	0+0	25:29.4
27	THOMPSON Josh	USA	2+2	27:27.7
30	NELSON Lyle	USA	0+1	27:34.3
49	CAROW Willie	USA	1+3	28:19.6
50	SCHREINER Curt	USA	2+1	28:19.9

Team Relay, Men

1	SOVIET UNION	0 0		1:22:30.0
	VASSILIEV Dmitry	0 0	21:04.3	
	TCHEPIKOV Sergei	0 0	20:12.0	
	POPOV Alexandr	0 0	20:35.1	
	MEDVEDTSEV Valeriy	0 0	20:38.6	
2	FEDERAL REP GERMANY	0 0		1:23:37.4
	REITER Ernst	0 0	21:05.7	
	HÖCK Stefan	0 0	21:18.0	
	ANGERER Peter	0 0	20:33.9	
	FISCHER Fritz	0 0	20:39.8	
3	ITALY	0 0		1:23:51.5
	KIEM Werner	0 0	20:57.9	
	TASCHLER Gottlieb	0 0	21:31.1	
	PASSLER Johann	0 0	20:38.6	
	ZINGERLE Andreas	0 0	20:43.9	
9	USA	2 0		1:29:33.0
	NELSON Lyle	1 0	22:43.3	
	SCHREINER Curt	0 0	21:39.7	
	BINNING Darin	0 0	22:17.3	
	THOMPSON Josh	1 0	22:52.7	

World Championships, Chamonix, France, 1988
Individual Race, Women

Rank	Name	Nation	Penalties	Finish
1	ELVEBAAK Anne	NOR	0+2+0	36:53.0
2	KRISTIANSEN Elin	NOR	0+1+0	37:35.3
3	TCHERNYCHOVA Vernera	URS	1+0+0	38:01.7
34	SMITH Joan	USA	1+1+2	43:28.9
35	NORDHEIM Pam	USA	1+2+2	43:33.2
37	ANDERSON Patrice	USA	3+2+1	44:34.4
40	BELL Nancy	USA	4+2+1	46:51.0

Sprint Race, Women

Rank	Name	Nation	Penalties	Finish
1	SCHAAF Petra	FRG	0+0	19:33.0
2	KORPELA Eva	SWE	0+1	19:47.3
3	ELVEBAKK Anne	NOR	1+1	19:55.6
25	NORDHEIM Pam	USA	1+2	22:10.8
31	BELL Nancy	USA	1+3	23:12.4
36	ANDERSON Patrice	USA	2+3	23:52.7
38	SMITH Joan	USA	2+2	24:19.3

Team Relay, Women

1	SOVIET UNION	0 0		0:57:17.1
	GOLOVINA Elena	0 0	20:01.9	
	PARVE Kaya	0 0	18:17.8	
	TCHERNYCHOVA Venera	0 0	18:57.4	
2	NORWAY	0 3		0:57:56.0
	KRISTIANSEN Elin	0 1	20:16.2	
	BOLLERUD Mona	0 0	18:23.4	
	ELVEBAKK Anne	0 2	19:16.4	
3	SWEDEN	0 2		0:58:11.1
	BJÖRKBOM Inger	0 2	23:10.9	
	KARLSSON Sabiene	0 0	16:53.1	
	KORPELA Eva	0 0	18:07.1	
9	USA	3 1		1:04:07.1
	BELL Nancy	3 0	24:29.5	
	NORDHEIM Pam	0 0	19:34.2	
	ANDERSON Patrice	0 1	20:03.4	

World Championships, Fiestritz, Austria, 1989
Individual Race, Men

Rank	Name	Nation	Penalties	Finish
1	KVALFOSS Erik	NOR	0+0+0+1	58:13.0
2	FENNE Gisle	NOR	0+0+0+0	59:20.8
3	FISCHER Fritz	FRG	0+2+0+0	1:00:48.1
41	DOMBROVSKY Raimond	USA	1+2+0+0	1:07:37.3
57	SCHREINER Curt	USA	2+0+0+1	1:09:45.8
64	CAROW Willie	USA	2+1+2+1	1:10:45.7

Sprint Race, Men

Rank	Name	Nation	Penalties	Finish
1	LUCK Frank	GDR	0+0	28:08.7
2	KVALFOSS Eirik	NOR	1+0	28:14.1
3	KASCHKAROV Juri	URS	0+1	28:32.7
46	CAROW Willie	USA	2+0	31:20.0
47	DOMBROVSKY Raimond	USA	1+1	31:23.3
50	SCHREINER Curtis	USA	0+0	31:29.3

Team Relay, Men

1	GERMAN DEM REPUBLIC	0 1		1:29:05.0
	LUCK Frank	0 0	22:29.6	
	SEHMISCH Andre	0 0	21:59.0	
	ROETSCH Frank Peter	0 0	21:48.1	
	ANDERS Birk	0 1	22:48.3	
2	SOVIET UNION	0 0		1:29:40.0
	KASCHKAROV Juri	0 0	22:35.5	
	TCHEPIKOV Sergei	0 0	21:44.1	
	POPOV Alexandr	0 0	22:06.3	
	BULYGIN Sergei	0 0	23:14.1	
3	NORWAY	0 0		1:29:53.0
	EINANG Geir	0 0	22:51.4	
	GLIMSDAL Sylvest	0 0	22:40.2	
	FENNE Gisle	0 0	22:35.3	
	KVALFOSS Eirik	0 0	21:46.1	
DNS	USA			

Team Race, Men

1	SOVIET UNION	0+1+1+1	59:36.9	
	KASHKAROV Juri			
	TCHEPIKOV Sergei			
	POPOV Alexandr			
	BULYGIN Sergei			
2	FED.REPUBLIC OF GERMANY	2+0+0+0	59:44.2	
	FRITZENWENGER Herbert			
	WUDY Franz			
	FISCHER Georg			
	FISCHER Fritz			
3	GERMAN DEM REPUBLIC	0+1+0+3	1:01:27.1	
	DITTRICH Raik			
	HEYMANN Andreas			
	HOOS Steffen			
	SEHMISCH Andre			
DNS	UNITED STATES OF AMERICA			

Individual Race, Women

Rank	Name	Nation	Penalties	Finish
1	BEHLE Petra	FRG	0+0+1+1	1:06:11.2
2	LINN ELVEBAKK Anne	NOR	1+0+1+1	1:06:31.6
3	DAVIDOVA Svetlana	URS	1+1+1+0	1:07:25.2
33	JANKOWSKI Patrice	USA	2+3+0+2	1:17:34.7
36	MILLER SMITH Joan	USA	1+0+1+3	1:19:17.0

Sprint Race, Women

Rank	Name	Nation	Penalties	Finish
1	LINN ELVEBAKK Anne	NOR	0+2	27:12.3
2	KRASTEVA Zwetlana	BUL	1+1	27:15.4
3	PRIKOSTSCHINKOVA Nat	URS	2+1	27:24.8
28	JANKOWSKI Patrice	USA	1+0	30:14.3
33	MILLER SMITH Joan	USA	1+1	30:59.4

Team Relay, Women

1	SOVIET UNION	0 0		1:23:15.5
	PRIKOSTSCHIKOVA Natali	0 0	28:02.5	
	DAVIDOVA Svetlana	0 0	27:23.1	
	GOLOVINA Elena	0 0	27:49.9	
2	BULGARIA	0 0		1:25:29.9
	KRASTEVA Zwetana	0 0	28:48.7	
	MANOLOVA Maria	0 0	27:53.3	
	ALEXIEVA Nadeza	0 0	28:47.9	
3	CZECHOSLOVAKIA	0 0		1:26:07.5
	BURESOVA Eva	0 0	29:12.8	
	NOVOTNA Renata	0 0	29:14.5	
	ADAMICKOVA Jirina	0 0	27:40.2	
	USA			DNS

Team Race, Women

1	SOVIET UNION	0+1+1+2	1:05:38.8	
	PRIKOSTSCHIKOVA Natali			
	DAVIDOVA Svetlana			
	TCHERNYCHOVA Venera			
	GOLOVINA Elena			
2	NORWAY	1+2+0+1		
	THORESEN S			
	KRISTIANSEN E			
	LINN ELVEBAKK Anne			
	BOLLERUD M			
3	GERMAN DEM REPUBLIC	1+0+0+1		
	KESPER I			
	HÖRBURGER D			
	PIEPER D			
	BEHLE P			
DNS	UNITED STATES OF AMERICA			

World Championships, Minsk, Soviet Union, 1990

Individual Race, Men

Rank	Name	Nation	Penalties	Finish
1	MEDVEDTSEV Valeri	URS	0+0+0+0	1:06:39.7
2	TCHEPIKOV Sergei	URS	0+0+0+0	1:07:03.0
3	SHOANOVITSCH Anatoli	URS	0+0+0+0	1:08:39.3
42	GALLENZ Peter	USA	0+0+1+2	1:16:13.4
57	DOUGLAS Robert	USA	1+2+1+3	1:19:43.7
62	DOMBROVSKY Raimond	USA	2+2+0+1	1:20:29.5

Sprint Race, Men

Rank	Name	Nation	Penalties	Finish
1	KIRCHNER Mark	FRG	0+0	25:48.9
2	KVALFOSS Eirk	NOR	1+1	25:59.8
3	TCHEPIKOV Sergei	URS	1+1	26:20.9
19	GALLENZ Peter	USA	0+0	27:32.4
44	DOUGLAS Duncan	USA	0+3	28:50.3
56	WILBRECHT Erich	USA	1+3	29:20.0
58	DOMBROWSKI Raimond	USA	2+1	29:26.2

Team Relay, Men

1	ITALY	1 0		1:30:54.7
	CARRARA Pieralbert	1 0	24:17.9	
	PALLHUBER Wilfried	0 0	22:31.6	
	PASSLER Johann	0 0	22:13.2	
	ZINGERLE Andreas	0 0	21:52.0	
2	FRANCE	0 0		1:33:08.8
	BLOND Xavier	0 0	24:08.0	
	GERBIER Thierry	0 0	22:42.0	
	DUMONT Christian	0 0	22:55.4	
	FLANDIN Herve	0 0	23:23.4	
3	GERMAN DEM REPUBLIC	0 0		1:34:02.2
	LUCK Frank	0 0	23:38.9	
	SEHMISCH Andre	0 0	23:16.3	
	KIRCHNER Mark	0 0	23:49.4	
	ANDERS Birk	0 0	23:17.6	
DNS	USA			

Team Race, Men

1	GERMAN DEM REPUBLIC	1+0+1+1	1:04:24.1
	DITTRICH Raik		
	KIRCHNER Mark		
	ANDERS Birk		
	LUCK Frank		
2	CZECHOSLOVAKIA	0+1+0+0	1:04:36.5
	KOS Tomas		
	MASARIK Ivan		
	HOLUBEC Jiri		
	MATOUS Jan		

3	FRANCE	1+2+0+1	1:05:14.2
	DUMONT Christian		
	BOUTHIAUX Stephane		
	FLANDIN Herve		
	GERBIER Thierry		
11	USA	0+2+0+2	1:10:16.8
	DOUGLAS Duncan		
	GALLENZ Peter		
	WILBRECHT Erich		
	DOMBROWSKI Raimond		

Individual Race, Women

Rank	Name	Nation	Penalties	Finish
1	DAVYDOVA URS	URS	0+1+0+1	51:53.4
2	GOLOVINA Elena	URS	1+2+0+0	53:48.2
3	SCHAAF Petra	FRG	0+1+0+0	53:54.6
15	SONNERUP Anna	USA	0+1+2+2	56:15.1
20	SMITH Joan	USA	0+1+1+2	57:10.0
33	ANDERSON Patrice	USA	0+2+2+1	59:24.2
36	BELL Nancy	USA	1+2+0+3	1:00:18.3

Sprint Race, Women

Rank	Name	Nation	Penalties	Finish
1	ELVEBAKK Anne	NOR	0+1	27:12.8
2	DAVYDOVA Svetlana	URS	1+1	27:16.1
3	KRISTIANSEN Elin	NOR	1+0	27:44.9
8	SONNERUP Anna	USA	1+2	28:33.4
13	ANDERSON, Patrice	USA	1+2	29:08.4
23	SMITH Joan	USA	3+1	30:01.2
26	BELL Nancy	USA	1+1	30:14.1

Team Relay, Women

1	SOVIET UNION	0 0		1:33:14.1
	BATSEVITSCH Elena	0 0	32:04.5	
	GOLOVINA Elena	0 0	30:37.3	
	DAVIDOVA Svetlana	0 0	30:32.3	
2	NORWAY	1 1		1:34:28.0
	NYKKELMÖ Grete	1 1	32:10.7	
	ELVEBAKK Anne	0 0	31:07.1	
	KRISTIANSEN Elin	0 0	31:10.2	
3	FINLAND	2 0		1:35:12.9
	VUOKSIALA Tuija	2 0	33:41.4	
	HYYTIÄINEN Seija	0 0	31:22.7	
	MATTILA Pirjo	0 0	30:08.8	
6	USA	1 0		1:39:19.1
	ANDERSON Patrice	1 0	33:40.3	
	SMITH Joan	0 0	34:00.0	
	SONNERUP Anna	0 0	31:38.8	

Team Race, Women

1	SOVIET UNION	1+1+0+0	56:30.3
	BATSEVITSCH Elena		
	GOLOVINA Elena		
	PARAMYGUINA Svetlana		
	DAVIDOVA Svetlana		
2	FEDERAL REPRULIC GERMANY	1+1+2+2	1:01:18.3
	SCHROLL Irene		
	HÖRBURGER Daniela		
	KESPER Inga		
	BEHLE Petra		
3	BULGARIA	1+1+4+3	1:02:09.4
	ALEXIEVA Nadejda		
	SHKODREVA Iva		
	MANOLOVA Maria		
	KRASTEVA Zwetlana		
4	USA	1+3+1+1	1:02:38.6
	BELL Nancy		
	SONNERUP Anna		
	ANDERSON Patrice		
	SMITH Joan		

World Championships, Lahti, Finland, 1991

Individual Race, Men

Rank	Name	Nation	Penalties	Finish
1	KIRCHNER Mark	GER	0+1+0+1	1:03:05.7
2	POPOV Alexandr	URS	0+0+1+0	1:03:33.3
3	KVALFOSS Eirik	NOR	0+1+1+0	1:03:38.3
9	THOMPSON Josh	USA	1+0+1+0	1:05:16.3
48	DOUGLAS Robert	USA	2+1+1+1	1:11:10.1
56	OLIVER Rick	USA	2+1+1+0	1:12:51.1
65	INGDAL Johnny	USA	0+1+1+0	1:15:33.2

Sprint Race, Men

Rank	Name	Nation	Penalties	Finish
1	KIRCHNER Mark	GER	0+0	30:48.1
2	LUCK Frank	GER	1+0	31:12.8
3	KVALFOSS Eirik	NOR	2+0	31:27.9
18	THOMPSON Josh	USA	0+0	32:33.8
21	DOUGLAS Robert	USA	1+1	32:37.8
32	SCHREINER Curt	USA	0+1	33:09.8
55	WILBRECHT Erich	USA	1+3	34:58.2

Team Relay, Men

1	GERMANY	0 0		1:33:33.5
	GROSS Ricco	0 0	23:49.5	
	LUCK Frank	0 0	22:50.5	
	KIRCHNER Mark	0 0	23:31.1	
	FISCHER Fritz	0 0	23:22.2	

2	SOVIET UNION	0 0		1:35:01.3
	KASHKAROV Juri	0 0	24:23.5	
	POPOV Alexander	0 0	23:50.5	
	TARASOV Sergei	0 0	23:11.6	
	TCHEPIKOV Sergei	0 0	23:35.5	
3	NORWAY	0 0		1:35:08.3
	EINANG Geir	0 0	23:36.2	
	KVALFOSS Eirik	0 0	23:22.7	
	TYLDUM Jon Age	0 0	24:11.9	
	FENNE Gisle	0 0	23:58.4	
9	USA	0 1		1:38:55.4
	DOUGLAS Robert	0 1	25:32.8	
	SCHREINER Curt	0 0	24:38.3	
	THOMPSON Josh	0 0	23:38.8	
	WILBRECHT Erich	0 0	25:05.4	

Team Race, Men

1	ITALY	0+0+0+1	1:00:59.8
	LEITGEB Hubert		
	TASCHLER Gottlieb		
	DEMETZ Simon		
	PALLHUBER Wilfried		
2	NORWAY	0+1+1+1	1:01:14.0
	ISTAD Sverre		
	TYLDUM Jon Age		
	ULEKLEIV Ivar		
	LÖBERG Frode		
3	SOVIET UNION	0+3+1+0	1:01:40.8
	ZHDANOVITSH Anatoli		
	MEDVETSEV Valeri		
	TARASOV Sergei		
	TSHEPIKOV Sergei		
DNS	UNITED STATES OF AMERICA		

Individual Race, Women

Rank	Name	Nation	Penalties	Finish
1	SCHAAF Petra	GER	0+0+0+0	55:14.9
2	NYKKELMÖ Grete I.	NOR	1+2+0+1	57:13.4
3	SCHKODREVA Iva	BUL	0+0+1+0	57:43.3
22	OSTERGREN Mary	USA	0+2+0+1	1:02:44.6
38	SONNERUP Anna	USA	2+3+1+3	1:07:20.9
39	COATS Beth	USA	0+2+3+3	1:08:47.3
41	ANDERSON Patrice	USA	2+2+0+2	1:08:52.2

Sprint Race, Women

Rank	Name	Nation	Penalties	Finish
1	NYKKELMO Grete I.	NOR	0+1	30:01.9
2	DAVIDOVA Svetlana	URS	0+1	30:32.7
3	GOLOVINA Elena	URS	0+0	30:35.1
16	ANDERSON Patrice	USA	0+1	33:07.3
16	GUETSCHOW Joan	USA	1+0	33:07.3
19	OSTERGREN Mary	USA	1+1	33:10.4
39	COATS Beth	USA	0+0	34:59.9

Team Relay, Women

Rank	Name	Penalties		Finish
1	SOVIET UNION	0 2		1:24:54.3
	BELOVA Elena	0 2	28:49.2	
	GOLOVINA Elena	0 0	28:18.9	
	DAVIDOVA Svetlana	0 0	27:46.1	
2	NORWAY	0 2		1:25:52.0
	NYKKELMO Grete Inge	0 2	28:02.4	
	ELVEBAKK Anne	0 0	28:30.2	
	KRISTIANSEN Elin	0 0	29:19.3	
3	GERMANY	0 7		1:28:15.9
	DISL Uschi	0 1	28:37.1	
	MORING Kerstin	0 3	29:28.0	
	MIESERSKY Antje	0 3	30:10.8	
7	USA	0 1		1:31:09.7
	OSTERGREN Mary	0 0	30:58.7	
	SONNERUP Anna	0 0	29:11.5	
	GUETSCHOW Joan	0 1	30:59.4	

Winter Olympic Games, Albertville, France, 1992

Individual Race, Men

Rank	Name	Nation	Penalties	Finish
1	REDKIN Evgenij	EUN	0+0+0+0	57:34.4
2	KIRCHNER Mark	GER	0+1+1+1	57:40.8
3	LÖFGREN Mikael	SWE	0+1+0+1	57:59.4
16	THOMPSON Josh	USA	0+2+0+0	1:00:05.4
51	SCHREINER Curt	USA	1+0+0+2	1:03:34.2
59	DOUGLAS Robert	USA	1+2+2+1	1:04:17.5
70	ENGEN Jon	USA	0+1+2+2	1:06:18.4

Sprint Race, Men

Rank	Name	Nation	Penalties	Finish
1	KIRCHNER Mark	GER	0+0	26:02.3
2	GROSS Ricco	GER	0+1	26:18.0
3	ELORANTA Harri	FIN	0+0	26:26.6
32	THOMPSON Josh	USA	0+1	27:53.2
37	SCHREINER Curt	USA	0+0	28:08.4
49	WILBRECHT Erich	USA	1+1	28:41.1
55	DOUGLAS Robert	USA	0+2	28:49.2

Team Relay, Men

Rank	Name	Penalties		Finish
1	GERMANY	0 0		1:24:43.5
	GROSS Ricco	0 0	22:37.4	
	STEINIGEN Jens	0 0	21:00.9	
	KIRCHNER Mark	0 0	20:17.5	
	FISCHER Fritz	0 0	20:47.7	
2	RUSSIAN FEDERATIONS	0 0		1:25:06.3
	MEDVEDTSEV Valeriy	0 0	21:56.3	
	POPOV Alexandr	0 0	21:01.2	
	KIRIENKO Valeri	0 0	21:11.7	
	TCHEPIKOV Sergei	0 0	20:57.1	
3	SWEDEN	0 0		1:25:38.2
	JOHANSSON Ulf	0 0	21:53.3	
	ANDERSSON Leif	0 0	21:03.1	
	WIKSTEN Tord	0 0	22:05.5	
	LÖFGREN Mikael	0 0	20:36.3	
13	USA	0 1		1:30:44.0
	ENGEN Jon	0 0	22:55.1	
	DOUGLAS Duncan	0 1	23:21.2	
	THOMPSON Josh	0 0	22:12.0	
	SCHREINER Curt	0 0	22:15.7	

Individual Race, Women

Rank	Name	Nation	Penalties	Finish
1	HARVEY Antje	GER	0+0+0+1	51:47.2
2	PETCHERSKAIA Svetlana	EUN	0+1+0+0	51:58.5
3	BEDARD Myriam	CAN	0+1+1+0	52:15.0
34	BELL Nancy	USA	0+2+0+3	57:55.2
42	JANKOWSKI Patrice	USA	1+1+0+0	58:59.6
47	COATS Beth	USA	0+0+1+1	59:36.1
55	MILLER SMITH Joan	USA	1+2+0+2	1:01:15.2

Sprint Race, Women

Rank	Name	Nation	Penalties	Finish
1	RESTZOVA Anfisa	EUN	0+3	24:29.2
2	HARVEY Antje	GER	0+2	24:45.1
3	BELOVA Elena	EUN	2+0	24:50.8
21	MILLER SMITH Joan	USA	0+0	26:54.5
25	OSTERGREN Mary	USA	0+2	27:05.7
44	BELL Nancy	USA	1+2	28:20.6
64	GUETSCHOW Joan	USA	1+2	31:30.6

Team Relay, Women

Rank	Name	Penalties		Finish
1	FRANCE	0 0		1:15:55.6
	NIOGRET Corinne	0 0	25:54.7	
	CLAUDEL Veronique	0 0	25:30.7	
	BRIAND Anne	0 0	24:30.2	

2	GERMANY	1 0		1:16:18.4
	DISL Uschi	1 0	26:33.7	
	HARVEY Antje	0 0	24:28.9	
	BEHLE Petra	0 0	25:15.8	
3	RUSSIAN FEDERATION	1 1		1:16:54.6
	BELOVA Elena	0 1	26:21.9	
	RESTZOVA Anfisa	1 0	24:33.5	
	MELNIKOVA Elena	0 0	25:59.2	
15	USA	0 2		1:24:36.9
	JOHNSTONE Nancy	0 1	29:15.7	
	MILLER SMITH Joan	0 0	27:47.7	
	OSTERGREN Mary	0 1	27:33.5	

World Championships, Borovetz, Bulgaria, 1993

Individual Race, Men

Rank	Name	Nation	Penalties	Finish
1	ZINGERLE Andreas	ITA	0+1+0+0	53:05.4
2	TARASOV Sergei	RUS	0+1+0+1	53:49.9
3	TCHEPIKOV Sergei	RUS	1+0+0+0	54:38.3
32	HARVEY Ian	USA	0+1+0+1	57:55.0
82	SCHREINER Curt	USA	1+3+1+0	1:03:02.5
85	DOUGLAS Robert	USA	1+2+2+1	1:03:30.1
91	JARECKIE Dave	USA	1+3+1+2	1:04:58.4

Sprint Race, Men

Rank	Name	Nation	Penalties	Finish
1	KIRCHNER Mark	GER	0+0	27:30.5
2	TYLDUM Jon Age	NOR	1+0	27:44.9
3	TARASOV Sergei	RUS	1+0	27:46.7
49	SCHREINER Curt	USA	0+2	29:46.3
68	HARVEY Ian	USA	1+1	30:23.0
72	WILBRECHT Erich	USA	1+1	30:53.6
73	DUGLAS Robert	USA	3+2	30:59.2

Team Relay, Men

1	ITALY	0 0		1:32:18.3
	PALLHUBER Wilfried	0 0	23:41.4	
	PASSLER Johann	0 0	22:35.8	
	CARRARA Pieralberto	0 0	22:56.2	
	ZINGERLE Andreas	0 0	23:04.9	
2	RUSSIA	0 0		1:32:55.0
	MEDVEDTSEV Valeriy	0 0	23:45.2	
	KIRIENKO Valeri	0 0	22:36.7	
	TARASOV Sergei Sen.	0 0	22:47.6	
	TCHEPIKOV Sergei	0 0	22:45.5	

3	GERMANY	0 0		1:32:57.9
	FISCHER Sven	0 0	23:16.4	
	LUCK Frank	0 0	23:01.8	
	KIRCHNER Mark	0 0	23:19.7	
	STEINER Toni	0 0	23:20.0	
16	USA	1 0		1:39:24.7
	SCHREINER Curt	1 0	25:20.5	
	HARVEY Ian	0 0	24:58.5	
	JARACKIE David	0 0	24:34.1	
	WILBRECHT Erich	0 0	24:31.6	

Individual Race, Women

Rank	Name	Nation	Penalties	Finish
1	SCHAAF Petra	GER	0+0+0+1	50:32.9
2	BEDARD Myriam	CAN	0+0+1+0	50:47.6
3	PARAMIGINA Svetlana	BLS	0+1+2+0	52:16.6
49	STEVENSON Angie	USA	0+2+1+3	59:12.5
55	SKINNER Ntala	USA	4+1+1+1	1:00:08.0
64	GUETSCHOW Joan	USA	0+3+2+3	1:01:15.5
68	OSTERGREN Mary	USA	3+1+2+3	1:02:23.1

Sprint Race, Women

Rank	Name	Nation	Penalties	Finish
1	BEDARD Myriam	CAN	0+0	21:01.9
2	TALANOVA Nadezda	RUS	0+1	21:18.5
3	BELOVA Elena	RUS	0+1	21:21.7
29	GUETSCHOW Joan	USA	0+2	22:44.5
49	SKINNER Ntala	USA	1+1	23:17.5
51	OSTRGREN Mary	USA	1+2	23:23.5
52	SMITH Joan	USA	2+1	23:32.8

Team Relay, Women

1	CZECH REPUBLIC	0 1		1:52:08.6
	VAPENIKOVA Jana	0 0	27:48.7	
	PELCOVA Jirina	0 0	28:00.5	
	ROUBICKOVA Iveta	0 1	28:38.9	
	HAKOVA Eva	0 0	27:40.5	
2	FRANCE	1 0		1:52:56.2
	NIOGRET Corinne	0 0	27:14.6	
	CLAUDEL Veronique	1 0	29:23.8	
	BURLET Delphyne	0 0	28:00.8	
	BRIAND Anne	0 0	28:17.0	
3	RUSSIA	0 1		1:52:58.9
	PANIUTINA Svetlana	0 0	28:30.6	
	TALANOVA Nadejda	0 0	28:03.8	
	SIMUSHINA Olga	0 0	27:44.7	
	BELOVA Elena	0 1	28:39.8	

11	USA	1 5		1:59:34.1
	MILLER SMITH Joan	1 0	28:58.8	
	GUETSCHOW Joan	0 0	28:04.8	
	OSTERGREN Mary	0 2	30:46.2	
	SKINNER Ntala	0 3	31:44.3	

Winter Olympic Games, Lillehammer, Norway, 1994
Individual Race, Men

Rank	Name	Nation	Penalties	Finish
1	TARASOV Sergei	RUS	2+0+1+0	57:25.3
2	LUCK Frank	GER	0+2+0+1	57:28.7
3	FISCHER Sven	GER	0+2+0+0	57:41.9
64	ENGEN Jon	USA	2+2+0+0	1:06:39.7
65	SCHREINER Curt	USA	1+1+2+2	1:07:41.6

Sprint Race, Men

Rank	Name	Nation	Penalties	Finish
1	TCHEPIKOV Sergei	RUS	0+0	28:07.0
2	GROSS Ricco	GER	0+0	28:13.0
3	TARASOV Sergei Sen.	RUS	1+0	28:27.4
64	JARACKIE David	USA	2+2	33:15.6
65	DOUGLAS Robert	USA	1+2	33:29.2

Team Relay, Men

1	GERMANY	0 0		1:30:22.1
	GROSS Ricco	0 0	22:32.3	
	LUCK Frank	0 0	22:06.0	
	KIRCHNER Mark	0 0	22:49.5	
	FISCHER Sven	0 0	22:54.3	
2	RUSSIA	0 2		1:31:23.6
	KIRIENKO Valeri	0 1	23:34.6	
	DRACHEV Vladimir	0 1	23:14.4	
	TARASOV Sergei Sen.	0 0	21:54.0	
	TCHEPIKOV Sergei	0 0	22:40.6	
3	FRANCE	1 0		1:32:31.3
	DUSSERRE Thierry	0 0	23:22.2	
	BAILLY-SALINS Patrice	1 0	22:51.6	
	LAURENT Lionel	0 0	23:04.5	
	FLANDIN Herve	0 0	23:13.0	
14	USA	0 0		1:35:43.7
	SCHREINER Curt	0 0	23:37.1	
	JARACKIE David	0 0	23:58.9	
	ENGEN Jon	0 0	24:42.8	
	DOUGLAS Robert	0 0	23:24.9	

Individual Race, Women

Rank	Name	Nation	Penalties	Finish
1	BEDARD Myriam	CAN	0+1+0+1	52:06.6
2	BRIAND Anne	FRA	1+1+0+1	52:53.3
3	DISL Uschi	GER	2+0+0+1	53:15.3
14	MILLER SMITH Joan	USA	0+1+1+1	54:46.7
32	TAVARES Laurie	USA	1+1+1+1	57:04.3
33	COATS Beth	USA	1+1+1+1	57:20.0

Sprint Race, Women

Rank	Name	Nation	Penalties	Finish
1	BEDARD Myriam	CAN	0+2	26:08.8
2	PARAMYGUINA Svetlana	BLR	2+0	26:09.9
3	TSERBE Valentina	UKR	0+0	26:10.0
24	MILLER SMITH Joan	USA	0+2	27:39.1
51	COATS Beth	USA	3+0	29:24.3
52	GUETSCHOW Joan	USA	1+3	29:26.7

Team Relay, Women

1	RUSSIA	0 0		1:47:19.5
	TALANOVA Nadejda	0 0	27:21.1	
	SNITINA Natalia	0 0	27:25.4	
	NOSKOVA Luiza	0 0	26:59.0	
	RESTZOVA Anfisa	0 0	25:34.0	
2	GERMANY	3 3		1:51:16.5
	DISL Uschi	0 0	26:56.8	
	HARVEY Antje	0 0	26:38.5	
	GREINER-PETTER-M. Sim	3 3	30:43.1	
	BEHLE Petra	0 0	26:58.1	
3	FRANCE	0 1		1:52:28.3
	NIOGRET Corinne	0 0	27:32.5	
	CLAUDEL Veronique	0 0	28:15.3	
	BURLET Delphyne	0 0	28:30.2	
	BRIAND Anne	0 1	28:10.3	
8	USA	0 3		1:57:35.9
	COATS Beth	0 3	31:25.2	
	MILLER SMITH Joan	0 0	27:34.7	
	TAVARES Laurie	0 0	28:15.4	
	GUETSCHOW Joan	0 0	30:10.6	

World Championships, Antholz, Italy, 1995
Individual Race, Men

Rank	Name	Nation	Penalties	Finish
1	SIKORA Tomasz	POL	0+0+0+0	1:01:36.0
2	TYLDUM Jon Age	NOR	0+0+0+0	1:02:10.6
3	RYZHENKOV Oleg	BLR	1+0+0+1	1:02:16.4
	No USA Participation			

Sprint Race, Men

Rank	Name	Nation	Penalties	Finish
1	BAILLY-SALINS Patrice	FRA	0+1	29:23.8
2	MOUSLIMOV Pavel	RUS	0+0	29:25.7
3	GROSS Ricco	GER	0+0	29:29.0
	No USA Participation			

Team Relay, Men

1	GERMANY	0 0		1:23:29.9	
	GROSS Ricco	0 0	21:23.9		
	KIRCHNER Mark	0 0	21:18.9		
	LUCK Frank	0 0	20:33.0		
	FISCHER Sven	0 0	20:14.1		
2	FRANCE	0 0		1:23:41.9	
	LAURENT Lionel	0 0	21:24.7		
	BAILLY-SALINS Patrice	0 0	20:23.1		
	DUSSERRE Thierry	0 0	21:36.6		
	FLANDIN Herve	0 0	20:17.5		
3	BELARUS	0 0		1:24:06.0	
	KHOKHRIAKOV Igor	0 0	22:08.0		
	POPOV Alexandr	0 0	20:34.2		
	RYZHENKOV Oleg	0 0	20:41.4		
	SASHURIN Vadim	0 0	20:42.4		
	No USA Participation				

Individual Race, Women

Rank	Name	Nation	Penalties	Finish
1	CLARET Emmanuelle	FRA	1+0+0+1	46:43.1
2	MELNIK Olga	RUS	0+1+0+0	47:55.3
3	PETROVA Olena	UKR	0+0+0+1	48:15.7
20	SABASTEANSKI Kristina	USA	0+0+0+1	51:35.6
26	WOOLEY Stacey	USA	0+1+1+0	52:06.0
53	MILLER SMITH Joan	USA	0+2+0+1	55:21.6

Sprint Race, Women

Rank	Name	Nation	Penalties	Finish
1	ROMASKO Olga	RUS	0+0	22:30.5
2	SKJELBREID Ann Elen	NOR	0+1	22:49.9
3	FORSBERG Magdalena	SWE	0+0	22:52.5
22	WOOLEY Stacey	USA	0+0	24:06.8
32	SKINNER Ntala	USA	0+0	24:25.4
39	MILLER SMITH Joan	USA	0+1	24:46.3

Team Relay, Women

1	GERMANY	0 0		1:37:05.0	
	DISL Uschi	0 0	23:52.0		
	HARVEY Antje	0 0	24:31.1		
	GREINER-PETTER-M. Simone	0 0	24:06.5		
	BEHLE Petra	0 0	24:35.4		
2	FRANCE	0 0		1:37:38.4	
	NIOGRET Corinne	0 0	24:37.6		
	CLAUDEL Veronique	0 0	24:42.8		
	BAVEREL Florence	0 0	24:26.3		
	BRIAND Anne	0 0	23:51.7		
3	NORWAY	0 2		1:39:31.3	
	SKJELBREID Ann Elen	0 1	25:29.2		
	MIKKELSPLASS Hildegunn	0 0	25:14.0		
	SIKVELAND Annette	0 1	24:31.5		
	ANDREASSEN Gunn Margit	0 0	24:16.6		
8	USA	1 0		1:42:00.8	
	SABASTEANSKI Kristina	1 0	26:36.5		
	WOOLEY Stacey	0 0	25:08.9		
	COATS Beth	0 0	24:56.3		
	SKINNER Ntala	0 0	25:19.1		

World Championships, Ruhpolding, Germany, 1996

Individual Race, Men

Rank	Name	Nation	Penalties	Finish
1	TARASOV Sergei	RUS	0+0+0+0	52:03.2
2	DRACHEV Vladimir	RUS	0+0+0+2	54:09.3
3	SASHURIN Vadim	BLR	0+1+0+0	54:13.9
71	WESTOVER Dan	USA	0+3+0+0	1:02:48.4
78	ROSSER Robert	USA	2+3+0+1	1:04:09.9

Sprint Race, Men

Rank	Name	Nation	Penalties	Finish
1	DRACHEV Vladimir	RUS	0+1	26:52.3
2	MAIGOUROV Viktor	RUS	0+0	27:02.0
3	CATTARINUSSI Rene	ITA	0+0	27:31.0
61	SCHREINER Curt	USA	0+0	30:23.6
82	SALMELA Chad	USA	2+3	32:06.3

Team Relay, Men

1	RUSSIA	0 0		1:19:50.8
	MAIGOUROV Viktor	0 0	20:19.1	
	DRACHEV Vladimir	0 0	19:47.4	
	TARASOV Sergei Sen.	0 0	19:55.3	
	KOBELEV Alexei	0 0	19:49.0	
2	GERMANY	0 1		1:20:50.9
	GROSS Ricco	0 0	20:52.3	
	SENDEL Peter	0 0	19:53.9	
	LUCK Frank	0 0	19:49.2	
	FISCHER Sven	0 1	20:15.5	
3	BELARUS	0 0		1:21:05.9
	AIDAROV Alexei	0 0	20:52.6	
	RYZHENKOV Oleg	0 0	19:29.3	
	SASHURIN Vadim	0 0	19:55.3	
	POPOV Alexandr	0 0	20:48.7	
21	USA	1 0		1:28:29.8
	SCHREINER Curt	1 0	22:43.5	
	WESTOVER Dan	0 0	21:54.6	
	ROSSER Robert	0 0	22:36.3	
	SALMELA Chad	0 0	21:15.4	

Team Race, Men

1	BELORUS	BLR	0+0+0+0
	IWASCHKO Petr		
	RYSHENKOV Oleg		
	POPOV Alexandr		
	SASHURIN Vadim		
2	RUSSIA	RUS	0+0+1+1
	DRATSHEV Vladimir		
	MOUSLIMOV Pavel		
	MAIGUROV Viktor		
	ROJKOV Sergei		
3	ITALY	ITA	0+0+2+1
	CATTARINUSSI Rene		
	LEITGEB Hubert		
	CARRARA Pier Alberto		
	FAVRE Patrick		
5	UNITED STATES	USA	0+0+2+1
	ROSSER Robert		
	WESTOVER Dan		
	SALMELA Chad		
	SCHREINER Curtis		

Individual Race, Women

Rank	Name	Nation	Penalties	Finish
1	CLARET Emmanuelle	FRA	1+0+0+1	46:43.1
2	MELNIK Olga	RUS	0+1+0+0	47:55.3
3	PETROVA Olena	UKR	0+0+0+1	48:15.7
20	SABASTEANSKI Kristina	USA	0+0+0+1	51:35.6
26	WOOLEY Stacey	USA	0+1+1+0	52:06.0
53	MILLER SMITH Joan	USA	0+2+0+1	55:21.6
59	NORDYKE Deborah	USA	3+0+2+1	57:10.4

Sprint Race, Women

Rank	Name	Nation	Penalties	Finish
1	ROMASKO Olga	RUS	0+0	22:30.5
2	SKJELBREID Ann Elen	NOR	0+1	22:49.9
3	FORSBERG Magdalena	SWE	0+0	22:52.5
22	WOOLEY Stacey	USA	0+0	24:06.8
32	SKINNER Ntala	USA	0+0	24:25.4
39	MILLER SMITH Joan	USA	0+1	24:46.3
57	SALMELA Kara	USA	0+3	25:44.1

Team Relay, Women

1	GERMANY	0 0		1:33:59.8
	DISL Uschi	0 0	24:05.4	
	GREINER-PETTER-M. Simone	0 0	23:23.7	
	APEL Katrin	0 0	23:21.1	
	BEHLE Petra	0 0	23:09.6	
2	FRANCE	0 3		1:36:44.8
	NIOGRET Corinne	0 0	23:52.8	
	BAVEREL Florence	0 0	24:09.1	
	CLARET Emmanuelle	0 2	24:01.4	
	BRIAND Anne	0 1	24:41.5	
3	UKRAINE	1 0		1:36:48.1
	VODOPYANOVA Tetyana	1 0	26:04.3	
	TSERBE NESSINA Valentina	0 0	23:54.4	
	PETROVA Olena	0 0	23:25.2	
	ZUBRILOVA Olena	0 0	23:24.2	
14	UNITED STATES	0 0		1:43:21.4
	SKINNER Ntala	0 0	25:25.9	
	SABASTEANSKI Kristina	0 0	27:27.9	
	MILLER SMITH Joan	0 0	25:51.7	
	WOOLEY Stacey	0 0	24:35.9	

Team Race, Women

1	GERMANY	GER	0+1+1+0
	APEL Katrin		
	GREINER-PETTER-M. Simone		
	BEHLE Petra		
	DISL Uschi		
2	UKRAINE	UKR	1+1+1+0
	LEMESH Nina		
	PETROVA Olena		
	WODOPJANOVA Tatiana		
	ZUBRILOVA Olena		
3	FRANCE	FRA	0+0+2+1
	CLARET Emmanuelle		
	BRIAND Anne		
	BAVEREL Florence		
	NIOGRET Corinne		
5	USA	USA	1+0+0+2
	SKINNER Ntala		
	WOOLEY Stacey		
	VILJANEN S. Kristin		
	NORDYKE Deborah		

Team Relay, Men

1	GERMANY	0 0		1:17:42.5
	GROSS Ricco	0 0		
	SENDEL Peter	0 0		
	FISCHER Sven	0 0		
	LUCK Frank	0 0		
2	NORWAY	0 0		1:17:48.2
	GJELLAND Egil	0 0		
	TYLDUM Jon Age	0 0		
	BJOERNDALEN Dag	0 0		
	BJOERNDALEN Ole Einar	0 0		
3	ITALY	0 1		1:19:10.4
	CATTARINUSSI Rene	0 0		
	PALLHUBER Wilfried	0 0		
	FAVRE Patrick	0 1		
	CARRARA Pieralberto	0 0		
20	USA	0 7		1:26:30.0
	HAKKINEN Jay	0 1		
	CORDEL Sam	0 0		
	TEELA Jeremy	0 0		
	SCHREINER Curt	0 0		

World Championships, Osrblie, Slovakia, 1997

Individual Race, Men

Rank	Name	Nation	Penalties	Finish
1	GROSS Ricco	GER	0+0+0+0	52:04.6
2	RYZHENKOV Oleg	BLR	1+0+0+1	52:40.1
3	GREDLER Ludwig	AUT	0+0+2+0	53:13.0
37	HAKKINEN Jay	USA	0+2+0+1	56:18.1
47	CORDEL Sam	USA	2+1+0+1	57:32.3
59	SCHREINER Curt	USA	0+1+0+2	58:31.6

Sprint Race, Men

Rank	Name	Nation	Penalties	Finish
1	PALLHUBER Wilfried	ITA	0+0	26:24.4
2	CATTARINUSSI Rene	ITA	1+0	26:41.2
3	RYZHENKOV Oleg	BLR	0+2	26:42.7
38	CORDEL Sam	USA	1+2	28:11.8
53	SCHREINER Curt	USA	1+1	28:42.9
85	POSS Jay	USA	4+3	31:36.9

Pursuit Race, Men

Rank	Name	Nation	Penalties	Finish
1	MAIGOUROV Viktor	RUS	0+0+0+0	33:21.9
2	TARASOV Sergei	RUS	0+1+0+0	33:28.8
3	BJOERNDALEN Ole Einar	NOR	0+1+0+1	33:32.1
44	CORDELL Sam	USA	3+1+2+3	39:49.0

Team Race, Men

1	BELARUS	1+0+0+0	27:22.4
	RYZHENKOV Oleg		
	IVASHKO Petr		
	POPOV Alexandr		
	SASHURIN Vadim		
2	GERMANY	0+1+0+1	27:47.3
	HEYMANN Carsten		
	KIRCHNER Mark		
	LUCK Frank		
	SENDEL Peter		
3	POLAND	0+0+2+1	28:15.8
	ZIEMIANIN Wieslaw		
	ZIEMIANIN Jan		
	KOZUB Wojciech		
	SIKORA Tomasz		
14	USA	1+0+2+2	29:34.0
	POSS Jay		
	TEELA Jeremy		
	HAKKINEN Jay		
	SCHREINER Curt	1+0+0+0	27:22.4

Individual Race, Women

Rank	Name	Nation	Penalties	Finish
1	FORSBERG Magdalena	SWE	0+1+0+0	48:17.3
2	ZUBRILOVA Olena	UKR	2+0+0+0	49:52.0
3	DAFOVSKA Ekaterina	BUL	0+1+1+0	50:41.1
37	WOOLEY Stacey	USA	1+2+3+0	55:48.3
41	SABASTEANSKI Kristina	USA	2+1+2+0	56:14.7
53	SALMELA Kara	USA	1+2+0+2	57:22.1
74	SKINNER Ntala	USA	3+2+2+4	1:03:09.0

Sprint Race, Women

Rank	Name	Nation	Penalties	Finish
1	ROMASKO Olga	RUS	0+0	22:30.5
2	SKJELBREID Ann Elen	NOR	0+1	22:49.9
3	FORSBERG Magdalena	SWE	0+0	22:52.5
22	WOOLEY Stacey	USA	0+0	24:06.8
32	SKINNER Ntala	USA	0+0	24:25.4
39	MILLER SMITH Joan	USA	0+1	24:46.3
71	NORDYKE Deborah	USA	2+1	25:32.4

Pursuit Race, Women

Rank	Name	Nation	Penalties	Finish
1	FORSBERG Magdalena	SWE	0+0+0+0	33:16.1
2	ZUBRILOVA Olena	UKR	0+0+0+0	33:21.1
3	ROMASKO Olga	RUS	0+0+0+1	33:34.5
16	WOOLEY Stacy	USA	0+1+0+1	35:57.3

Team Relay, Women

1	GERMANY	0 0		1:28:36.9
	DISL Uschi	0 0		
	GREINER-PETTER-M. Simone	0 0		
	APEL Katrin	0 0		
	BEHLE Petra	0 0		
2	NORWAY	0 0		1:30:06.7
	SKJELBREID Ann Elen	0 0		
	SIKVELAND Annette	0 0		
	POIREE Liv Grete	0 0		
	ANDREASSEN Gunn Margit	0 0		
3	RUSSIA	0 0		1:30:09.7
	MELNIK Olga	0 0		
	KOUKLEVA Galina	0 0		
	TALANOVA Nadejda	0 0		
	ROMASKO Olga	0 0		
9	USA	0 0		1:33:45.5
	SKINNER Ntala	0 0		
	WOOLEY Stacey	0 0		
	NORDYKE Deborah	0 0		
	SABASTEANSKI Kristina	0 0		

Winter Olympic Games, Nagano, Japan, 1998

Individual Race, Men

Rank	Name	Nation	Penalties	Finish
1	HANEVOLD Halvard	NOR	0+0+0+1	56:14.4
2	CARRARA Pieralberto	ITA	0+0+0+0	56:21.9
3	AIDAROV Alexei	BLR	0+0+0+1	56:46.5
42	HAKKINEN Jay	USA	1+1+0+2	1:02:10.3
69	ROSSER Robert	USA	1+4+1+1	1:08:35.7

Sprint Race, Men

Rank	Name	Nation	Penalties	Finish
1	BJØERNDALEN Ole Einar	NOR	0+0	27:16.2
2	ANDRESEN Frode	NOR	1+1	28:17.8
3	RÄIKKÖNEN Ville	FIN	0+1	28:21.7
49	WESTOVER Dan	USA	1+0	30:39.5
60	HAKKINEN Jay	USA	1+2	31:31.6

Team Relay, Men

1	GERMANY	0+4 0+2	0+6	1:21:36.2
	GROSS Ricco	0+0 0+1	20:09.3	
	SENDEL Peter	0+0 0+0	19:56.6	
	FISCHER Sven	0+2 0+0	20:18.0	
	LUCK Frank	0+2 0+1	21:12.3	
2	NORWAY	0+4 0+3	0+7	1:21:56.3
	GJELLAND Egil	0+1 0+1	20:33.8	
	HANEVOLD Halvard	0+1 0+0	20:08.7	
	BJOERNDALEN Dag	0+2 0+2	21:25.0	
	BJOERNDALEN Ole Einar	0+0 0+0	19:48.8	
3	RUSSIA	0+3 0+4	0+7	1:22:19.3
	MOUSLIMOV Pavel	0+0 0+1	20:35.9	
	DRACHEV Vladimir	0+0 0+2	19:56.6	
	TARASOV Sergei Sen.	0+3 0+0	21:01.4	
	MAIGOUROV Viktor	0+0 0+1	20:45.4	
17	USA	0+8 0+7	0+15	1:28:13.9
	HAKKINEN Jay	0+2 0+2	20:37.7	
	WESTOVER Dan	0+3 0+1	22:14.0	
	ERICKSON Andrew	0+2 0+3	22:57.2	
	ROSSER Robert	0+1 0+1	22:25.0	

Individual Race, Women

Rank	Name	Nation	Penalties	Finish
1	DAFOVSKA Ekaterina	BUL	0+0+1+0	54:52.0
2	PETROVA Olena	UKR	1+0+0+0	55:09.8
3	DISL Uschi	GER	0+0+0+1	55:17.9
55	WOOLEY Stacey	USA	1+1+0+0	1:03:57.3
56	SALMELA Kara	USA	1+0+3+1	1:04:43.7
61	SKINNER Ntala	USA	1+0+0+2	1:09:09.0

Sprint Race, Women

Rank	Name	Nation	Penalties	Finish
1	KOUKLEVA Galina	RUS	1+0	23:08.0
2	DISL Uschi	GER	0+1	23:08.7
3	APEL Katrin	GER	0+1	23:32.4
33	SABASTEANSKI Kristina	USA	1+0	25:12.2
48	NORDYKE Deborah	USA	0+2	25:50.5
58	WOOLEY Stacey	USA	1+2	27:03.0

Team Relay, Women

1	GERMANY	0+5 0+6	0+11	1:40:13.6
	DISL Uschi	0+2 0+3	25:20.3	
	ZELLNER Martina	0+1 0+0	24:46.1	
	APEL Katrin	0+0 0+2	24:39.8	
	BEHLE Petra	0+2 0+1	25:28.0	
2	RUSSIA	0+7 0+2	0+9	1:40:25.2
	MELNIK Olga	0+1 0+2	25:32.1	
	KOUKLEVA Galina	0+3 0+0	24:27.4	
	AKHATOVA Albina	0+2 0+0	24:59.8	
	ROMASKO Olga	0+1 0+0	25:25.8	
3	NORWAY	1+4 1+6	2+10	1:40:37.3
	SKJELBREID Ann Elen	0+1 1+3	25:47.2	
	SIKVELAND Annette	1+3 0+1	24:55.0	
	ANDREASSEN Gunn Mar	0+0 0+0	25:20.8	
	POIREE Liv Grete	0+0 0+2	24:34.3	
15	USA	0+6 1+6	1+12	1:48:30.2
	SKINNER Ntala	0+1 0+2	28:35.0	
	WOOLEY Stacey	0+0 0+1	27:12.1	
	SALMELA Kara	0+3 0+0	26:21.2	
	SABASTEANSKI Kristina	0+2 1+3	28:21.9	

World Championships, Pokljuka, Slovenia, 1998
Pursuit Race, Men

Rank	Name	Nation	Penalties	Finish
1	DRACHEV Vladimir	RUS	0+1+1+0	36:30.3
2	BJOERNDALEN Ole Einar	NOR	1+1+0+0	36:44.3
3	POIREE Raphael	FRA	1+1+0+0	37:11.9
39	HAKKINEN Jay	USA	3+0+2+1	40:55.3

Pursuit Race, Women

Rank	Name	Nation	Penalties	Finish
1	FORSBERG Magdalena	SWE	0+1+1+0	37:58.6
2	NIOGRET Corinne	FRA	0+0+1+0	39:05.5
3	ZELLNER Martina	GER	0+0+0+0	39:24.4
25	STEER Rachel	USA	0+1+0+1	43:10.6
31	SALMELA Kara	USA	1+1+1+2	43:44.3
36	SABASTEANSKI Kristina	USA	2+0+3+3	44:31.7
39	NORDYKE Deborah	USA	1+1+2+1	44:45.1

World Championships, Hochflizen Austria, 1998
Team Race, Men

1	NORWAY	0+0+1+1	29:17.6
	GJELLAND Egil		
	GLIMSDAL Sylfest		
	HANEVOLD Halvord		
	BJØRNDALEN Ole Einar		
2	GERMANY	0+0+3+1	30:01.3
	GROSS Rico		
	HEYMAN Carsten		
	FISCHER Sven		
	LUCK Frank		
3	RUSSIA	0+1+1+1	30:38.9
	DRACHEV Vladimir		
	KOBELEV, Alexei		
	RAIKOV, Sergei		
	MAIGOUROV Viktor		
10	UNITED STATES	1+0+3+0	32:01.4
	WESTOVER Daniel		
	ROSSER Robert		
	HAKKENIN, Jay		
	SCHREINER Curt		

Team Race, Women

1	RUSSIA	0+0+1+1	30:21.4
	SPRUNG A		
	ROMOSKO A		
	ISHMOURATOVA S		
	AKHATOVA A		
2	NORWAY	0+0+2+3	30:38.7
	MIKKELSPLASS H		
	SKJELBREID A		
	SIKVELAND A		
	POIREE L		
3	FINLAND	0+0+1+1	31:00.2
	HOLANTI K		
	MIKKOLA T		
	LAMPINEN M		
	PERUNKA S		
10	UNITED STATES	1+0+3+0	31:54.0
	SKINNER N		
	SABSTEANSKI K		
	SALMELA K		
	NORDYKE D		

World Championships, Kontiolahti, FIN/Oslo, NOR, 1999

Individual Race, Men

Rank	Name	Nation	Penalties	Finish
1	FISCHER Sven	GER	1+0+0+0	53:53.2
2	GROSS Ricco	GER	0+0+0+0	54:01.9
3	SASHURIN Vadim	BLR	0+0+0+0	54:30.5
48	HAKKINEN Jay	USA	0+2+1+1	1:00:02.2
75	TEELA Jeremy	USA	0+1+3+4	1:05:46.0
76	OLIVER Richard	USA	1+2+1+2	1:05:51.1
78	GIECK David	USA	2+3+2+1	1:07:20.4

Sprint Race, Men

Rank	Name	Nation	Penalties	Finish
1	LUCK Frank	GER	0+0	26:24.4
2	FAVRE Patrick	ITA	0+0	26:41.2
3	ANDRESEN Frode	NOR	1+1	26:42.7
16	HAKKINEN Jay	USA	0+4	28:11.8
39	TEELA Jeremy	USA	2+1	28:42.9
54	GIECK David	USA	1+2	31:36.9

Pursuit Race, Men

Rank	Name	Nation	Penalties	Finish
1	GROSS Ricco	GER	0+0+0+0	35:37.8
2	LUCK Frank	GER	0+0+1+2	36:05.0
3	FISCHER Sven	GER	1+0+1+1	36:18.7
24	HAKKINEN Jay	USA	0+1+3+2	38:27.6
58	TEELA Jeremy	USA	3+1+3+2	43:09.9

Mass Start Race, Men

Rank	Name	Nation	Penalties	Finish
1	POIREE Raphael	FRA	0+0+1+0	39:31.5
2	ROSTOVTSEV Pavel	RUS	0+1+1+0	39:40.9
3	BJØRNDALEN Ole Einar	NOR	0+2+1+0	39:49.9
	No USA Qualifiers			

Team Relay, Men

1	BELARUS	0+1	1	1:23:19.3
	AIDAROV Alexei	0+0	20:53.3	
	IVASHKO Petr	0+0	20:39.6	
	SASHURIN Vadim	0+0	20:11.4	
	RYZHENKOV Oleg	0+1	21:35.0	
2	RUSSIA	1+1	2	1:23:42.4
	MAIGOUROV Viktor	0+0	20:46.5	
	DRACHEV Vladimir	1+0	20:41.5	
	ROZHKOV Sergei	0+1	21:29.2	
	ROSTOVTSEV Pavel	0+0	20:45.2	

3	NORWAY	3+1	4	1:23:56.3
	HANEVOLD Halvard	0+0	20:32.3	
	BJOERNDALEN Dag	0+0	20:17.9	
	ANDRESEN Frode	0+1	20:53.9	
	BJOERNDALEN Ole Einar	3+0	22:12.2	
18	USA	1+4	5	1:30:52.7
	HAKKINEN Jay	0+0	21:08.8	
	TEELA Jeremy	1+1	22:43.1	
	GIECK David	0+3	22:51.4	
	ERNHART Grant	0+0	24:09.4	

Individual Race, Women

Rank	Name	Nation	Penalties	Finish
1	ZUBRILOVA Olena	UKR	0+0+0+0	43:28.1
2	NIOGRET Corinne	FRA	0+0+0+0	45:32.0
3	AKHATOVA Albina	RUS	0+0+1+0	46:41.7
29	STEER Rachel	USA	0+1+0+0	50:25.2
46	SALMELA Kara	USA	2+1+1+1	52:18.3
59	TROUTNER Jill	USA	1+1+2+1	55:10.1
60	SABASTEANSKI Kris	USA	1+1+2+1	55:10.7

Sprint Race, Women

Rank	Name	Nation	Penalties	Finish
1	ZELLNER Martina	GER	0+2	26:59.9
2	FORSBERG Magdalena	SWE	0+1	27:04.4
3	ZUBRILOVA Olena	UKR	1+2	27:08.2
28	SALMELA Kara	USA	0+2	29:05.3
48	STEER Rachel	USA	2+1	30:28.8
48	SABASTEANSKI Kris	USA	0+3	30:28.8

Pursuit Race, Women

Rank	Name	Nation	Penalties	Finish
1	ZUBRILOVA Olena	UKR	0+1+1+0	32:17.5
2	HALINAROVA Martina	SVK	0+1+0+0	33:19.5
3	ZELLNER Martina	GER	1+0+0+1	33:25.1
34	SALMELA Kara	USA	1+1+2+1	38:26.9
40	STEER Rachel	USA	0+0+0+1	39:16.0

Mass Start Race, Women

Rank	Name	Nation	Penalties	Finish
1	ZUBRILOVA Olena	UKR	0+2+2+0	40:08.2
2	PETROVA Olena	UKR	0+0+1+1	40:11.3
3	FORSBERG Magdalena	SWE	1+0+2+0	40:16.9
	No USA Qualifiers			

Team Relay, Women

1	GERMANY	2+2		1:36:56.0
	DISL Uschi	0+ 0+4	23:59.5	
	GREINER-PETTER-M. S	0+ 0+3	24:12.1	
	APEL Katrin	0+ 0+1	23:05.7	
	ZELLNER Martina	1+ 0+4	25:38.7	
2	RUSSIA	1+3		1:37:34.3
	TALANOVA Nadejda	0+ 2+3	25:13.5	
	KOUKLEVA Galina	0+ 1+4	24:23.8	
	ROMASKO Olga	0+ 0+2	23:45.8	
	AKHATOVA Albina	0+ 0+1	24:11.2	
3	FRANCE	0+9		1:37:42.9
	BURLET Delphyne	0+ 0+3	24:42.0	
	BAVEREL-ROBERT Flore	0+ 0+3	25:09.4	
	GROS Christelle	0+ 0+1	24:07.7	
	NIOGRET Corinne	0+ 0+2	23:43.8	
12	USA	1+7		1:44:51.3
	STEER Rachel	0+ 0+2	25:28.9	
	SALMELA Kara	0+ 2+3	26:17.6	
	SABASTEANSKI Kristina	0+ 1+4	26:08.4	
	TROUTNER Jill	0+ 0+5	26:56.4	

World Championships, Oslo, Norway, 2000

Individual Race, Men

Rank	Name	Nation	Penalties	Finish
1	ROTTMANN Wolf	AUT	0+0+0+1	53:36.2
2	GREDLER Ludwig	AUT	0+1+0+1	54:11.2
3	LUCK Frank	GER	0+0+0+1	54:58.1
31	HAKKINEN Jay	USA	0+1+2+1	58:46.5
41	SCHREINER Curt	USA	0+0+0+1	59:54.5
71	ROSSER Robert	USA	1+3+1+0	1:02:56.1
86	TEELA Jeremy	USA	4+4+0+2	1:07:32.2

Sprint Race, Men

Rank	Name	Nation	Penalties	Finish
1	ANDRESEN Frode	NOR	0+1	23:51.2
2	ROSTOVTSEV Pavel	RUS	0+0	24:00.7
3	CATTARINUSSI Rene	ITA	0+0	24:10.4
32	HAKKINEN Jay	USA	1+1	25:15.7
62	TEELA Jeremy	USA	2+2	26:34.7
76	ROSSER Robert	USA	1+2	27:10.2

Pursuit Race, Men

Rank	Name	Nation	Penalties	Finish
1	LUCK Frank	GER	1+0+0+1	33:21.9
2	ROSTOVTSEV Pavel	RUS	0+1+1+0	33:25.2
3	POIREE Raphael	FRA	0+1+1+1	33:37.0
30	HAKKINEN Jay	USA	1+1+1+2	36:05.2

Mass Start Race, Men

Rank	Name	Nation	Penalties	Finish
1	POIREE Raphael	FRA	0+0+1+0	39:31.5
2	ROSTOVTSEV Pavel	RUS	0+1+1+0	39:40.9
3	BJØRNDALEN Ole Einar	NOR	0+2+1+0	39:49.9
	No USA Qualifiers			

Team Relay, Men

1	BELARUS	1+1	1	1:23:19.3
	AIDAROV Alexei	0+ 0+3	20:53.3	
	IVASHKO Petr	0+ 0+2	20:39.6	
	SASHURIN Vadim	0+ 0+2	20:11.4	
	RYZHENKOV Oleg	0+ 1+3	21:35.0	
2	RUSSIA	2+2	2	1:23:42.4
	MAIGOUROV Viktor	0+ 0+1	20:46.5	
	DRACHEV Vladimir	1+ 0+4	20:41.5	
	ROZHKOV Sergei	0+ 1+5	21:29.2	
	ROSTOVTSEV Pavel	0+ 0+1	20:45.2	
3	NORWAY	4+4	4	1:23:56.3
	HANEVOLD Halvard	0+ 0+1	20:32.3	
	BJOERNDALEN Dag	0+ 0+1	20:17.9	
	ANDRESEN Frode	0+ 1+4	20:53.9	
	BJØRNDALEN Ole Einar	3+ 0+5	22:12.2	
18	USA	3+2	5	1:30:52.7
	HAKKINEN Jay	0+ 0+4	21:08.8	
	TEELA Jeremy	1+ 1+6	22:43.1	
	GIECK David	0+ 3+3	22:51.4	
	ERNHART Grant	0+ 0+5	24:09.4	

Individual Race, Women

Rank	Name	Nation	Penalties	Finish
1	NIOGRET Corinne	FRA	0+0+0+0	45:30.9
2	YU Shumei	CHN	0+0+0+0	46:24.2
3	FORSBERG Magdalena	SWE	0+1+0+1	46:47.8
34	STEER Rachel	USA	0+2+0+0	50:58.0
55	SALMELA Kara	USA	0+1+3+2	54:19.5
61	SABASTEANSKI Kris	USA	1+1+0+2	55:53.8
62	NAHRGANG Andrea	USA	2+1+1+1	56:07.5

Sprint Race, Women

Rank	Name	Nation	Penalties	Finish
1	POIREE Liv Grete	NOR	0+0	20:51.9
2	APEL Katrin	GER	0+1	21:21.7
3	ZELLNER Martina	GER	1+0	21:22.5
50	STEER Rachel	USA	1+1	23:55.6
57	SABASTEANSKI Krist	USA	0+0	24:17.7
67	SALMELA Kara	USA	3+3	25:21.2
71	NAHRGANG Andrea	USA	1+1	27:14.0

Pursuit Race, Women

Rank	Name	Nation	Penalties	Finish
1	ZUBRILOVA Olena	UKR	0+1+1+0	32:17.5
2	HALINAROVA Martina	SVK	0+1+0+0	33:19.5
3	ZELLNER Martina	GER	1+0+0+1	33:25.1
34	SALMELA Kara	USA	1+1+2+1	38:26.9
40	STEER Rachel	USA	0+0+0+1	39:16.0

Mass Start Race, Women

Rank	Name	Nation	Penalties	Finish
1	FORSBERG Magdalena	SWE	1+0+0+1	31:53.8
2	DISL Uschi	GER	0+1+2+0	32:25.7
3	BAVEREL Florence	FRA	0+0+0+0	32:36.2
	STEER Rachel	USA	2+1+1+1	DNF
	SABASTEANSKI Kris	USA	1+2	DNF

Team Relay, Women

1	RUSSIA		0+5 1+9		1:32:19.8
	PYLEVA Olga		0+0 0+3	22:54.5	
	CHERNOUSOVA Svetl		0+0 0+3	22:58.9	
	KOUKLEVA Galina		0+3 1+3	23:16.3	
	AKHATOVA Albina		0+2 0+0	23:10.1	
2	GERMANY		1+6 0+9		1:32:42.5
	DISL Uschi		0+0 0+3	22:54.1	
	APEL Katrin		0+2 0+2	22:24.2	
	HENKEL Andrea		0+1 0+2	23:38.0	
	ZELLNER Martina		1+3 0+2	23:46.2	
3	UKRAINE		1+7 0+5		1:34:07.9
	ZUBRILOVA Olena		1+3 0+3	24:09.3	
	PETROVA Olena		0+1 0+2	23:10.7	
	LEMESH Nina		0+1 0+0	23:12.7	
	VODOPYANOVA Tety		0+2 0+0	23:35.2	
	USA		1+8 0+3		DNF
	STEER Rachel		0+2 0+0	24:47.7	
	SALMELA Kara		1+3 0+3	25:41.5	
	NAHRGANG Andrea		0+3 0+0	26:01.4	
	SABASTEANSKI Kris				

World Championships, Pokljuka, Slovenia, 2001
Individual Race, Men

Rank	Name	Nation	Penalties	Finish
1	PUURUNEN Paavo	FIN	0+0+0+1	55:05.6
2	SASHURIN Vadim	BLR	0+0+0+1	55:33.8
3	BRICIS Ilmars	LAT	0+0+0+0	55:35.1
39	HAKKINEN Jay	USA	1+1+1+1	00:39.9
55	TEELA Jeremy	USA	1+3+0+2	1:03:01.8
58	ROSSER Robert	USA	1+2+1+1	1:03:39.9
63	REDMAN Lawton	USA	0+2+0+2	1:04:05.4

Sprint Race, Men

Rank	Name	Nation	Penalties	Finish
1	ROSTOVTSEV Pavel	RUS	0+0	24:40.3
2	CATTARINUSSI Rene	ITA	0+0	25:26.9
3	HANEVOLD Halvard	NOR	1+0	25:28.2
9	TEELA Jeremy	USA	1+0	25:48.6
31	HAKKINEN Jay	USA	0+1	26:44.0
88	REDMAN Lawton	USA	3+4	30:15.0

Pursuit Race, Men

Rank	Name	Nation	Penalties	Finish
1	ROSTOVTSEV Pavel	RUS	1+0+2+0	34:21.3
2	POIREE Raphael	FRA	0+1+0+1	34:27.2
3	FISCHER Sven	GER	0+1+1+0	35:06.9
20	TEELA Jeremy	USA	1+0+2+0	37:37.1
41	HAKKINEN Jay	USA	0+2+4+0	39:10.9

Mass Start Race, Men

Rank	Name	Nation	Penalties	Finish
1	POIREE Raphael	FRA	1+0+1+0	39:28.2
2	BJØRNDALEN Ole Einar	NOR	3+1+0+0	39:32.0
3	FISCHER Sven	GER	1+1+0+1	39:46.6
	No USA Qualifiers			

Team Relay, Men

1	FRANCE	FRA	0+1 0+5	1:12:56.7
	MARGUET Gilles		0+1 0+2	18:24.3
	DEFRASNE Vincent		0+0 0+2	18:22.9
	ROBERT Julien		0+0 0+0	18:22.0
	POIREE Raphael		0+0 0+1	17:47.5
2	BELARUS	BLR	0+2 0+4	1:13:28.6
	AIDAROV Alexei		0+0 0+1	18:00.7
	SYMAN Alexandr		0+1 0+1	18:43.2
	RYZHENKOV Oleg		0+0 0+2	18:36.0
	SASHURIN Vadim		0+1 0+0	18:08.7
3	NORWAY	NOR	1+7 2+8	1:13:29.7
	GJELLAND Egil		0+0 0+3	18:04.8
	ANDRESEN Frode		0+3 2+3	18:49.5
	HANEVOLD Halvard		0+1 0+1	18:29.5
	BJØRNDALEN Ole Einar		1+3 0+1	18:05.9
	USA	USA		DNS

Individual Race, Women

Rank	Name	Nation	Penalties	Finish
1	FORSBERG Magdalena	SWE	0+0+0+1	45:13.0
2	POIREE Liv Grete	NOR	0+1+0+2	45:50.3
3	ZUBRILOVA Olena	UKR	1+0+0+1	46:22.2
51	WOOLEY Stacey	USA	0+1+2+1	52:43.9
56	KRAUSE Jill	USA	1+2+0+3	53:09.1
61	NAHRGANG Andrea	USA	3+2+1+1	53:53.0
71	STEER Rachel	USA	2+2+0+3	55:24.5

Sprint Race, Women

Rank	Name	Nation	Penalties	Finish
1	WILHELM Kati	GER	0+1	21:56.2
2	DISL Uschi	GER	1+0	22:23.1
3	POIREE Liv Grete	NOR	1+1	22:37.6
27	STEER Rachel	USA	0+1	24:22.7
45	NAHRGANG Andrea	USA	1+2	24:57.5
53	WOOLEY Stacey	USA	1+1	25:22.0
64	KRAUSE Jill	USA	2+2	25:58.9

Pursuit Race, Women

Rank	Name	Nation	Penalties	Finish
1	POIREE Liv Grete	NOR	1+1+2+1	32:13.5
2	NIOGRET Corinne	FRA	0+0+0+1	32:38.5
3	FORSBERG Magdalena	SWE	0+2+1+0	32:48.5
23	STEER Rachel	USA	0+0+1+0	35:42.2
41	WOOLEY Stacey	USA	0+3+0+0	37:50.7
48	NAHRGANG Andrea	USA	1+0+1+4	38:50.2

Mass Start Race, Women

Rank	Name	Nation	Penalties	Finish
1	FORSBERG Magdalena	SWE	0+0+1+0	38:38.6
2	BECK Martina	GER	0+0+0+0	39:43.0
3	POIREE Liv Grete	NOR	0+2+2+0	39:44.4
	No USA Qualifiers			

Team Relay, Women

1	RUSSIA	0+5 1+8	1+13	1:29:02.8
	PYLEVA Olga	0+1 0+2	21:32.5	
	BOGALIY-TITOVETS Anna	0+1 0+0	22:08.0	
	KOUKLEVA Galina	0+2 0+3	22:23.2	
	ISHMOURATOVA Svetlana	0+1 1+3	22:59.1	
2	GERMANY	2+4 0+3	2+7	1:29:28.3
	DISL Uschi	0+1 0+1	21:20.8	
	APEL Katrin	0+0 0+2	22:11.1	
	HENKEL Andrea	0+0 0+0	22:34.3	
	WILHELM Kati	2+3 0+0	23:22.1	

3	UKRAINE	0+1 0+4	0+5	1:29:55.2
	ZUBRILOVA Olena	0+1 0+1	21:36.8	
	PETROVA Olena	0+0 0+0	22:34.7	
	LEMESH Nina	0+0 0+2	22:59.8	
	VODOPYANOVA Tetyana	0+0 0+1	22:43.9	
	USA			DNS

Winter Olympic Games, Salt Lake City, USA, 2002

Individual Race, Men

Rank	Name	Nation	Penalties	Finish
1	BJØRNDALEN Ole Einar	NOR	0+1+1+0	51:03.3
2	LUCK Frank	GER	0+0+0+0	51:39.4
3	MAIGOUROV Viktor	RUS	0+0+1+0	51:40.6
14	TEELA Jeremy	USA	1+1+0+0	53:56.5
26	HAKKINEN Jay	USA	0+2+0+1	55:13.8
76	CAMPBELL Dan	USA	2+1+2+1	1:00:58.6

Sprint Race, Men

Rank	Name	Nation	Penalties	Finish
1	BJØRNDALEN Ole Einar	NOR	0+0	24:51.3
2	FISCHER Sven	GER	0+1	25:20.2
3	PERNER Wolfgang	AUT	0+0	25:44.4
20	TEELA Jeremy	USA	0+2	26:36.6
26	HAKKINEN Jay	USA	1+0	26:43.5
54	REDMAN Lawton	USA	1+1	27:43.4

Pursuit Race, Men

Rank	Name	Nation	Penalties	Finish
1	BJØRNDALEN Ole Einar	GER	1+0+0+1	32:34.6
2	POIREE Raphael	FRA	0+1+0+0	33:17.6
3	GROSS Ricco	GER	0+0+0+2	33:30.6
13	HAKKINEN Jay	USA	0+0+0+1	34:11.8
23	TEELA Jeremy	USA	0+1+2+0	35:18.1
52	REDMAN Lawton	USA	1+0+3+2	38:59.0

Team Relay, Men

1	NORWAY	0+5 0+3	0+8	1:23:42.3
	HANEVOLD Halvard	0+1 0+0	22:09.1	
	ANDRESEN Frode	0+2 0+1	20:17.2	
	GJELLAND Egil	0+0 0+1	20:45.7	
	BJOERNDALEN Ole Ein	0+2 0+1	20:30.3	
2	GERMANY	1+4 0+5	1+9	1:24:27.6
	GROSS Ricco	0+0 0+3	22:20.2	
	SENDEL Peter	0+1 0+1	20:47.5	
	FISCHER Sven	1+3 0+1	21:13.9	
	LUCK Frank	0+0 0+0	20:06.0	

3	FRANCE	0+3 0+3	0+6	1:24:36.6
	MARGUET Gilles	0+1 0+0	22:25.1	
	DEFRASNE Vincent	0+1 0+1	20:22.1	
	ROBERT Julien	0+1 0+2	21:36.3	
	POIREE Raphael	0+0 0+0	20:13.1	
15	USA	0+8 2+9	2+18	1:30:27.1
	TEELA Jeremy	0+3 1+3	23:06.9	
	HAKKINEN Jay	0+3 0+1	21:55.0	
	CAMPBELL Dan	0+1 1+3	23:01.0	
	REDMAN Lawton	0+1 0+3	22:24.2	

3	RUSSIA	0+6 2+7	2+13	1:29:19.7
	MEDVEDTSEVA Olga	0+1 0+1	21:32.4	
	KOUKLEVA Galina	0+3 2+3	23:05.8	
	ISHMOURATOVA Svetlana	0+1 0+1	22:00.1	
	AKHATOVA Albina	0+1 0+2	22:41.4	
15	USA	1+7 2+9	3+16	1:41:16.0
	NAHRGANG Andrea	0+0 1+3	25:23.7	
	SALMELA Kara	1+3 0+3	25:45.6	
	STEER Rachel	0+2 0+0	24:21.1	
	SABASTEANSKI Kris	0+2 1+3	25:45.6	

Individual Race, Women

Rank	Name	Nation	Penalties	Finish
1	HENKEL Andrea	GER	0+1+0+0	47:29.1
2	POIREE Liv Grete	NOR	0+1+0+0	47:37.0
3	FORSBERG Magdalena	SWE	0+0+0+2	48:08.3
31	STEER Rachel	USA	0+1+1+0	51:50.6
55	SABASTEANSKI Kris	USA	0+1+0+3	55:00.9
59	SALMELA Kara	USA	1+1+2+4	57:25.9

Sprint Race, Women

Rank	Name	Nation	Penalties	Finish
1	WILHELM Kati	GER	0+0	20:41.4
2	DISL Uschi	GER	0+1	20:57.0
3	FORSBERG Magdalena	SWE	1+0	21:20.4
49	SALMELA Kara	USA	1+2	23:44.1
50	NAHRGANG Andrea	USA	1+0	23:48.7
60	STEER Rachel	USA	2+1	24:41.7

Pursuit Race, Women

Rank	Name	Nation	Penalties	Finish
1	MEDVEDTSEVA Olga	RUS	1+0+0+0	31:07.7
2	WILHELM Kati	GER	3+0+1+0	31:13.0
3	NIKULCHINA Irina	BUL	0+0+0+2	31:15.8
45	SALMELA Kara	USA	2+0+1+2	37:07.7
47	NAHRGANG Andrea	USA	0+1+1+1	38:08.5
DNF	STEER Rachel	USA	2+4+ +	

Team Relay, Women

1	GERMANY	0+0 1+7	1+7	1:27:55.0
	APEL Katrin	0+0 1+3	22:15.6	
	DISL Uschi	0+0 0+2	21:19.2	
	HENKEL Andrea	0+0 0+0	22:13.8	
	WILHELM Kati	0+0 0+2	22:06.4	
2	NORWAY	0+3 0+6	0+9	1:28:25.6
	SKJELBREID Ann Elen	0+0 0+3	22:01.0	
	GRUBBEN Linda	0+1 0+0	22:07.7	
	ANDREASSEN Gunn	0+1 0+1	22:18.5	
	POIREE Liv Grete	0+1 0+2	21:58.4	

World Championships, Khanty-Mansiysk, Russia, 2003
Individual Race, Men

Rank	Name	Nation	Penalties	Finish
1	HANEVOLD Halvard	NOR	0+0+0+1	53:39.4
2	HIETALAHTI Vesa	FIN	0+0+2+0	55:04.1
3	GROSS Ricco	GER	1+0+2+0	55:05.3
45	BAILEY Lowell	USA	1+1+1+0	59:18.0
66	CAMPBELL Dan	USA	0+2+3+1	1:01:23.0
76	TEELA Jeremy	USA	1+3+1+3	1:03:43.9

Sprint Race, Men

Rank	Name	Nation	Penalties	Finish
1	BJØRNDALEN Ole Einar	NOR	0+0	26:52.1
2	GROSS Ricco	GER	0+1	27:42.8
3	VITEK Zdenek	CZE	0+1	27:45.0
10	TEELA Jeremy	USA	1+0	28:30.8
44	CAMPBELL Dan	USA	1+0	30:08.7
59	BAILEY Lowell	USA	2+1	30:58.7

Pursuit Race, Men

Rank	Name	Nation	Penalties	Finish
1	GROSS Ricco	GER	0+0+1+1	37:37.5
2	HANEVOLD Halvard	NOR	0+0+1+0	37:49.5
3	PUURUNEN Paavo	FIN	1+0+0+0	38:33.7
17	TEELA Jeremy	USA	1+1+1+2	40:19.2
44	CAMPBELL Dan	USA	2+0+1+1	43:32.8

Mass Start Race, Men

Rank	Name	Nation	Penalties	Finish
1	BJØRNDALEN Ole Einar	FRA	1+0+1+0	40:49.7
2	FISCHER Sven	GER	1+0+1+1	41:38.9
3	POIREE Raphael	FRA	1+0+1+2	41:54.0
28	TEELA Jeremy	USA	0+1+3+4	44:51.7

Team Relay, Men

1	GERMANY	GER	0+2 0+6	1:18:38.0
	SENDEL Peter		0+0 0+0	19:12.5
	FISCHER Sven		0+2 0+2	19:42.5
	GROSS Ricco		0+0 0+1	19:26.1
	LUCK Frank		0+0 0+3	20:16.9
2	RUSSIA	RUS	0+4 0+4	1:18:45.3
	MAIGOUROV Viktor		0+1 0+1	19:41.5
	ROSTOVTSEV Pavel		0+1 0+0	19:13.8
	ROZHKOV Sergei		0+1 0+1	19:40.9
	TCHEPIKOV Sergei		0+1 0+2	20:09.1
3	BELARUS	BLR	0+6 0+6	1:18:59.2
	AIDAROV Alexei		0+2 0+2	20:10.7
	DRACHEV Vladimir		0+0 0+2	19:54.8
	VALIULLIN Rustam		0+1 0+2	19:30.7
	RYZHENKOV Oleg		0+3 0+0	19:23.0
17	USA	USA	0+3 1+10	1:24:07.9
	HAKKINEN Jay		0+1 0+3	20:30.2
	BAILEY Lowell		0+2 0+2	20:51.2
	CAMPBELL Dan		0+0 0+2	21:08.9
	TEELA Jeremy		0+0 1+3	21:37.6

Individual Race, Women

Rank	Name	Nation	Penalties	Finish
1	HOLUBCOVA Katerina	CZE	0+0+0+0	48:28.4
2	ZUBRILOVA Olena	BLR	0+1+0+0	48:36.4
3	ANDREASSEN Gunn	NOR	0+0+0+0	49:05.9
44	KAMILEWICZ Sarah	USA	1+2+0+1	55:35.0
59	STEER Rachel	USA	1+0+3+2	57:59.6
64	KRAUSE Jill	USA	1+2+3+2	59:02.2

Sprint Race, Women

Rank	Name	Nation	Penalties	Finish
1	BECAERT Sylvie	FRA	0+1	23:46.3
2	PETROVA Olena	UKR	0+0	24:13.2
3	HOLUBCOVA Katerina	CZE	0+0	24:19.0
25	KRAUSE Jill	USA	0+1	25:55.3
43	KAMILEWICZ Sarah	USA	0+1	26:48.5
50	BARNES Tracy	USA	0+0	27:01.7
51	STEER Rachel	USA	1+1	27:03.1

Pursuit Race, Women

Rank	Name	Nation	Penalties	Finish
1	BAILLY Sandrine	FRA	1+0+0+1	35:15.6
1	BECK Martina	GER	0+0+1+1	35:15.6
3	ISHMOURATOVA Svet	RUS	2+1+1+0	36:07.9
42	KRAUSE Jill	USA	1+1+4+2	42:01.7
44	STEER Rachel	USA	0+1+1+2	42:16.1
51	KAMILEWICZ Sarah	USA	2+0+4+1	43:15.6
54	BARNES Tracy	USA	1+3+0+1	44:37.3

Mass Start Race, Women

Rank	Name	Nation	Penalties	Finish
1	AKHATOVA Albina	RUS	0+0+0+0	37:15.8
2	ISHMOURATOVA Svetl	RUS	0+0+0+0	37:18.5
3	BAILLY Sandrine	FRA	0+1+0+0	37:26.7
	No USA Qualifiers			

Team Relay, Women

1	RUSSIA	RUS	1+6 0+5	1:24:34.4
	AKHATOVA Albina		0+0 0+0	20:19.8
	ISHMOURATOVA Svetlan		0+2 0+0	20:34.6
	KOUKLEVA Galina		1+3 0+2	22:12.9
	CHERNOUSOVA Svetlana		0+1 0+3	21:27.1
2	UKRAINE	UKR	0+7 0+7	1:25:58.2
	KHVOSTENKO Oksana		0+0 0+0	20:42.0
	MERKUSHINA Irina		0+2 0+3	21:44.0
	YAKOVLEVA Oksana		0+3 0+3	22:09.7
	PETROVA Olena		0+2 0+1	21:22.5
3	GERMANY	GER	4+7 4+9	1:26:39.7
	HAUSWALD Simone		0+0 2+3	21:50.1
	DISL Uschi		1+3 2+3	22:26.9
	WILHELM Kati		3+3 0+2	22:14.3
	BECK Martina		0+1 0+1	20:08.4
	USA	USA	3+9 3+9	DNF
	STEER Rachel		1+3 0+3	23:51.9
	KRAUSE Jill		2+3 2+3	25:22.6
	KAMILEWICZ RILEY Sarah		0+3 1+3	23:39.8
	BARNES Tracy			

World Championships, Oberhof, Germany, 2004

Individual Race, Men

Rank	Name	Nation	Penalties	Finish
1	POIREE Raphael	FRA	0+0+0+1	51:37.9
2	SIKORA Tomasz	POL	1+0+0+0	52:33.4
3	BJØRNDALEN Ole Einar	NOR	1+1+0+0	52:38.4
61	BURKE Tim	USA	0+2+1+1	59:11.5
70	HAKKINEN Jay	USA	0+2+2+3	1:00:24.3
75	TEELA Jeremy	USA	1+1+1+4	1:01:34.7
87	BESTE Jacob	USA	3+1+1+1	1:02:54.9

Sprint Race, Men

Rank	Name	Nation	Penalties	Finish
1	POIREE Raphael	FRA	0+0	30:11.9
2	GROSS Ricco	GER	0+0	30:21.0
3	BJØRNDALEN Ole Einar	NOR	2+0	30:56.9
47	HAKKINEN Jay	USA	1+1	34:08.8
60	TEELA Jeremy	USA	3+0	34:54.1
71	BURKE Tim	USA	3+1	35:43.9
99	BESTE Jacob	USA	3+1	38:41.8

Pursuit Race, Men

Rank	Name	Nation	Penalties	Finish
1	GROSS Ricco	GER	1+0+0+1	38:53.8
2	POIREE Raphael	FRA	0+1+0+1	39:07.1
3	BJØRNDALEN Ole Einar	NOR	0+2+2+2	40:10.4
DNF	HAKKINEN Jay	USA	4+1+4+	
DNS	TEELA Jeremy	USA		

Mass Start Race, Men

Rank	Name	Nation	Penalties	Finish
1	POIREE Raphael	FRA	1+0+1+0	40:31.7
2	BERGER Lars	NOR	2+1+2+0	41:04.1
3	KONOVALOV Sergei	RUS	0+1+0+1	41:07.9
	No USA Qualifiers			

Team Relay, Men

1	GERMANY	GER	0+1 0+1	1:17:50.3
	LUCK Frank		0+0 0+0	19:44.1
	GROSS Ricco		0+0 0+0	19:08.3
	FISCHER Sven		0+1 0+0	19:01.0
	GREIS Michael		0+0 0+1	19:56.9
2	NORWAY	RUS	0+4 2+4	1:18:06.0
	HANEVOLD Halvard		0+0 0+0	19:34.0
	BERGER Lars		0+1 2+3	20:02.4
	GJELLAND Egil		0+0 0+1	19:36.7
	BJOERNDALEN Ole Einar		0+3 0+0	18:52.8

3	FRANCE	BLR	0+2 0+0	1:18:23.6
	CANNARD Ferreol		0+0 0+0	20:15.3
	DEFRASNE Vincent		0+1 0+0	19:14.3
	ROBERT Julien		0+0 0+0	20:00.5
	POIREE Raphael		0+1 0+0	18:53.4
18	USA	USA	1+4 2+8	1:25:18.2
	HAKKINEN Jay		1+3 0+0	20:55.5
	TEELA Jeremy		0+0 0+2	20:01.6
	BURKE Tim		0+1 1+3	21:55.4
	BESTE Jacob		0+0 1+3	22:25.6

Individual Race, Women

Rank	Name	Nation	Penalties	Finish
1	MEDVEDTSEVA Olga	RUS	0+0+0+1	49:43.0
2	AKHATOVA Albina	RUS	1+0+0+0	50:24.0
3	PETROVA Olena	UKR	0+2+0+1	51:24.5
62	STEER Rachel	USA	1+0+4+2	59:20.2
66	KRAUSE Jill	USA	3+1+2+1	1:00:21.8
73	TEELA Denise	USA	4+1+3+1	1:02:13.7
76	GRANROTH Sara	USA	1+5+2+2	1:03:47.7

Sprint Race, Women

Rank	Name	Nation	Penalties	Finish
1	POIREE Liv Grete	NOR	1+0	25:51.0
2	BOGALIY-TITOVETS An	RUS	0+0	26:11.6
3	VINOGRADOVA Ekater	BLR	0+1	26:44.2
20	STEER Rachel	USA	1+1	28:31.9
65	TEELA Denise	USA	2+2	30:56.2
66	GRANROTH Sara	USA	1+3	30:59.2
70	KRAUSE Jill	USA	1+4	31:45.9

Pursuit Race, Women

Rank	Name	Nation	Penalties	Finish
1	POIREE Liv Grete	NOR	0+0+1+3	37:39.3
2	BECK Martina	GER	0+0+2+1	38:00.6
3	BOGALIY-TITOVETS A	RUS	1+1+3+0	38:42.6
34	STEER Rachel	USA	1+3+0+2	43:06.7

Mass Start Race, Women

Rank	Name	Nation	Penalties	Finish
1	POIREE Liv Grete	NOR	0+0+2+0	39:46.1
2	APEL Katrin	GER	0+0+0+2	41:10.0
3	BAILLY Sandrine	FRA	0+0+2+1	41:51.8
	No USA Qualifiers			

Team Relay, Women

1	NORWAY	NOR	0+6 0+6	1:16:59.8
	GRUBBEN Linda		0+1 0+0	19:16.8
	KRISTIANSEN Gro Marit		0+3 0+2	19:26.8
	ANDREASSEN Gunn Marg		0+0 0+1	19:06.2
	POIREE Liv Grete		0+2 0+3	19:09.9
2	RUSSIA	RUS	0+0 0+9	1:18:08.0
	MEDVEDTSEVA Olga		0+0 0+3	19:23.8
	ISHMOURATOVA Svetlan		0+0 0+3	19:37.8
	BOGALIY-TITOVETS Anna		0+0 0+1	19:17.6
	AKHATOVA Albina		0+0 0+2	19:48.7
3	GERMANY	GER	0+4 2+8	1:18:18.4
	BECK Martina		0+0 0+0	18:53.0
	APEL Katrin		0+1 1+3	20:01.5
	HAUSWALD Simone		0+0 0+2	19:18.2
	WILHELM Kati		0+3 1+3	20:05.5
14	USA	USA	1+7 0+4	1:22:25.5
	STEER Rachel		0+0 0+0	19:37.6
	KRAUSE Jill		0+2 0+3	20:44.4
	TEELA Denise		1+3 0+0	21:18.3
	GRANROTH Sara		0+2 0+1	20:45.0

World Championships, Hochflizen, Austria, 2005

Individual Race, Men

Rank	Name	Nation	Penalties	Finish
1	DOSTAL Roman	CZE	0+0+0+1	1:00:24.0
2	GREIS Michael	GER	0+0+0+0	1:00:33.9
3	GROSS Ricco	GER	1+0+0+1	1:00:51.4
54	TEELA Jeremy	USA	3+1+1+2	1:08:39.0
63	BURKE Tim	USA	1+1+2+1	1:09:46.2
69	HAKKINEN Jay	USA	1+2+2+2	1:11:15.8
	SHEPARD Walter	USA		DNS

Sprint Race, Men

Rank	Name	Nation	Penalties	Finish
1	BJØRNDALEN Ole Einar	NOR	1+0	24:37.5
2	FISCHER Sven	GER	1+0	24:48.0
3	BRICIS Ilmars	LAT	0+0	25:01.5
18	HAKKINEN Jay	USA	1+1	26:00.9
22	TEELA Jeremy	USA	1+1	26:06.1
66	BURKE Tim	USA	0+2	27:10.9
97	SHEPARD Walter	USA	2+1	30:06.6

Pursuit Race, Men

Rank	Name	Nation	Penalties	Finish
1	BJØRNDALEN Ole Einar	NOR	0+1+1+1	36:41.4
2	TCHEPIKOV Sergei	RUS	0+0+0+0	37:20.6
3	FISCHER Sven	GER	2+0+1+0	37:32.1
23	HAKKINEN Jay	USA	0+1+2+3	40:30.9
36	TEELA Jeremy	USA	2+2+1+2	41:18.1

Mass Start Race, Men

Rank	Name	Nation	Penalties	Finish
1	BJØRNDALEN Ole Einar	NOR	1+0+2+0	40:51.9
2	FISCHER Sven	GER	0+1+1+1	41:03.8
3	POIREE Raphael	FRA	0+0+1+1	41:12.5
	No USA Qualifiers			

Team Relay, Men

1	NORWAY	NOR	0+3 0+4	1:21:59.2
	HANEVOLD Halvard		0+2 0+3	21:52.3
	ECKHOFF Stian		0+0 0+1	20:03.1
	GJELLAND Egil		0+1 0+0	20:20.6
	BJØRNDALEN Ole Einar		0+0 0+0	19:43.2
2	RUSSIA	RUS	0+3 0+2	1:22:25.2
	ROZHKOV Sergei		0+0 0+0	21:25.5
	KRUGLOV Nikolay		0+0 0+1	20:15.5
	ROSTOVTSEV Pavel		0+1 0+0	20:33.7
	TCHEPIKOV Sergei		0+2 0+1	20:10.5
3	AUSTRIA	AUT	0+0 0+4	1:22:42.5
	MESOTITSCH Daniel		0+0 0+2	21:35.7
	PINTER Friedrich		0+0 0+0	20:40.2
	ROTTMANN Wolfgang		0+0 0+1	20:25.3
	SUMANN Christoph		0+0 0+1	20:01.3
18	USA	USA		

Individual Race, Women

Rank	Name	Nation	Penalties	Finish
1	HENKEL Andrea	GER	0+1+0+0	52:37.5
2	SUN Ribo	CHN	0+1+0+1	53:07.7
3	GRUBBEN Linda	NOR	1+0+0+0	53:11.8
44	BARNES Lanny	USA	2+0+0+0	59:31.9
50	KONRAD Sarah	USA	3+1+1+3	00:05.4
60	STEER Rachel	USA	4+1+1+1	01:10.3
82	KRAUSE Jill	USA	3+1+1+5	1:03:41.7

Sprint Race, Women

Rank	Name	Nation	Penalties	Finish
1	DISL Uschi	GER	0+0	21:58.6
2	ZAITSEVA Olga	RUS	0+0	22:01.1
3	ZUBRILOVA Olena	BLR	0+0	22:25.2
23	STEER Rachel	USA	1+1	23:33.3
50	KRAUSE Jill	USA	2+2	24:54.6
66	KONRAD Sarah	USA	3+4	25:46.7
80	BARNES Lanny	USA	2+2	27:02.2

Pursuit Race, Women

Rank	Name	Nation	Penalties	Finish
1	DISL Uschi	GER	1+0+2+1	33:32.5
2	LIU Xianying	CHN	0+1+1+2	33:50.4
3	ZAITSEVA Olga	RUS	0+1+1+2	34:13.1
17	STEER Rachel	USA	1+1+2+1	36:02.9
54	KRAUSE Jill	USA	3+1+2+4	40:46.6

Mass Start Race, Women

Rank	Name	Nation	Penalties	Finish
1	KRISTIANSEN Gro Mar	NOR	0+1+0+3	41:40.3
2	ZIDEK Anna Carin	SWE	0+1+1+1	41:44.0
3	MEDVEDTSEVA Olga	RUS	1+1+1+0	41:48.7
20	STEER Rachel	USA	1+0+1+2	43:44.4

Team Relay, Women

Rank	Name	Nation	Penalties	Finish
1	RUSSIA	RUS	0+6 0+1	1:13:44.4
	MEDVEDTSEVA Olga		0+1 0+0	18:51.6
	ISHMOURATOVA Svetla		0+2 0+1	18:29.9
	BOGALIY-TITOVETS Anna		0+0 0+0	17:57.8
	ZAITSEVA Olga		0+3 0+0	18:25.1
2	GERMANY	GER	0+8 1+4	1:14:25.8
	DISL Uschi		0+3 1+3	19:59.0
	APEL Katrin		0+2 0+0	17:50.4
	HENKEL Andrea		0+1 0+0	18:16.4
	WILHELM Kati		0+2 0+1	18:20.0
3	BELARUS	BLR	0+0 1+9	1:14:37.6
	VINOGRADOVA Ekaterina		0+0 1+3	19:45.2
	NAZAROVA Olga		0+0 0+2	18:18.8
	ANANKO Liudmila		0+0 0+1	18:27.0
	ZUBRILOVA Olena		0+0 0+3	18:06.6
16	USA	USA	3+7 6+6	1:21:27.0
	STEER Rachel		0+2 0+0	19:35.4
	BARNES Lanny		0+1 0+0	19:14.0
	KRAUSE Jill		0+1 1+3	19:29.9
	KONRAD Sarah		3+3 5+3	23:07.7

Winter Olympic Games, Torino, Italy, 2006

Individual Race, Men

Rank	Name	Nation	Penalties	Finish
1	GREIS Michael	GER	0+1+0+0	54:23.0
2	BJØRNDALEN Ole Einar	NOR	1+1+0+0	54:39.0
3	HANEVOLD Halvard	NOR	1+1+0+0	55:31.9
10	HAKKINEN Jay	USA	2+0+1+0	56:10.9
27	BAILEY Lowell	USA	2+1+0+0	58:45.1
51	TEELA Jeremy	USA	1+0+1+3	1:01:03.3
58	BURKE Tim	USA	3+3+1+0	1:01:55.0

Sprint Race, Men

Rank	Name	Nation	Penalties	Finish
1	FISCHER Sven	GER	0+0	26:11.6
2	HANEVOLD Halvard	NOR	0+0	26:19.8
3	ANDRESEN Frode	NOR	0+1	26:31.3
35	BURKE Tim	USA	1+2	28:27.8
46	BAILEY Lowell	USA	1+2	29:02.0
60	TEELA Jeremy	USA	2+2	29:32.7
78	HAKKINEN Jay	USA	5+1	31:22.2

Pursuit Race, Men

Rank	Name	Nation	Penalties	Finish
1	DEFRASNE Vincent	FRA	0+0+0+2	35:20.2
2	BJØRNDALEN Ole Einar	NOR	0+1+1+1	35:22.9
3	FISCHER Sven	GER	2+2+0+0	35:35.8
36	BURKE Tim	USA	0+2+2+0	39:17.6
48	BAILEY Lowell	USA	3+1+1+1	41:31.3

Mass Start Race, Men

Rank	Name	Nation	Penalties	Finish
1	GREIS Michael	GER	0+0+1+0	47:20.0
2	SIKORA Tomasz	POL	0+0+0+1	47:26.3
3	BJØRNDALEN Ole Einar	NOR	0+0+1+2	47:32.3
13	HAKKINEN Jay	USA	0+0+1+0	48:29.6

Team Relay, Men

Rank	Name	Nation	Penalties	Finish
1	GERMANY	GER	0+3 1+5	1:21:51.5
	GROSS Ricco		0+0 0+1	0:20:47.1
	ROESCH Michael		0+0 0+0	0:19:42.5
	FISCHER Sven		0+1 1+3	0:21:11.6
	GREIS Michael		0+2 0+1	0:20:10.3
2	RUSSIA	RUS	0+6 0+0	1:22:12.4
	TCHEREZOV Ivan		0+3 0+0	0:21:10.0
	TCHEPIKOV Sergei		0+0 0+0	0:20:09.7
	ROSTOVTSEV Pavel		0+2 0+0	0:20:40.0
	KRUGLOV Nikolay		0+1 0+0	0:20:12.7

3	FRANCE	FRA	0+2 0+4	1:22:35.1
	ROBERT Julien		0+0 0+0	0:21:33.8
	DEFRASNE Vincent		0+1 0+0	0:19:45.3
	CANNARD Ferreol		0+1 0+1	0:21:02.1
	POIREE Raphael		0+0 0+3	0:20:13.9
9	USA	USA	0+6 1+11	1:24:23.4
	HAKKINEN Jay		0+1 0+2	0:20:40.8
	BURKE Tim		0+3 0+3	0:21:05.9
	BAILEY Lowell		0+1 0+3	0:21:17.1
	TEELA Jeremy		0+1 1+3	0:21:19.6

Individual Race, Women

Rank	Name	Nation	Penalties	Finish
1	ISHMOURATOVA Sve	RUS	0+0+1+0	49:24.1
2	BECK Martina	GER	0+1+0+1	50:34.9
3	AKHATOVA Albina	RUS	1+0+0+1	50:55.0
41	STEER Rachel	USA	1+1+1+0	55:48.3
57	BARNES Tracy	USA	1+0+0+0	57:58.0
62	KONRAD Sarah	USA	2+2+4+2	59:33.1
64	BARNES Lanny	USA	1+2+0+1	59:46.2

Sprint Race, Women

Rank	Name	Nation	Penalties	Finish
1	BAVEREL Florence	FRA	0+0	22:31.4
2	ZIDEK Anna Carin	SWE	1+0	22:33.8
3	VAYGINA Lilia	UKR	0+0	22:38.0
35	STEER Rachel	USA	1+0	24:29.6
71	BARNES Tracy	USA	2+0	26:47.9
75	KONRAD Sarah	USA	4+4	27:30.6
80	BRAMANTE Carolyn	USA	1+3	28:18.7

Pursuit Race, Women

Rank	Name	Nation	Penalties	Finish
1	WILHELM Kati	GER	0+0+1+0	36:43.6
2	BECK Martina	GER	1+1+0+0	37:57.2
3	AKHATOVA Albina	RUS	0+1+0+0	38:05.0
39	STEER Rachel	USA	0+0+1+1	43:32.8

Mass Start Race, Women

Rank	Name	Nation	Penalties	Finish
1	ZIDEK Anna Carin	SWE	0+0+0+1	40:36.5
2	WILHELM Kati	GER	0+0+1+0	40:55.3
3	DISL Uschi	GER	1+0+1+1	41:18.4
	No USA Qualifiers			

Team Relay, Women

1	RUSSIA	RUS	0+1 0+1	1:16:12.5
	BOGALIY-TITOVETS Anna		0+0 0+1	19:06.3
	ISHMOURATOVA Svetlan		0+1 0+0	18:56.2
	ZAITSEVA Olga		0+0 0+0	19:06.8
	AKHATOVA Albina		0+0 0+0	19:03.2
2	GERMANY	GER	0+3 1+5	1:17:03.2
	BECK Martina		0+1 0+2	19:18.8
	HENKEL Andrea		0+2 0+0	19:15.9
	APEL Katrin		0+0 1+3	19:45.5
	WILHELM Kati		0+0 0+0	18:43.0
3	FRANCE	FRA	0+6 0+2	1:18:38.7
	PERETTO Delphine		0+2 0+1	20:46.5
	BAVEREL Florence		0+1 0+0	19:02.6
	BECAERT Sylvie		0+1 0+1	19:50.2
	BAILLY Sandrine		0+2 0+0	18:59.4
15	USA	USA	0+5 0+6	1:25:20.3
	STEER Rachel		0+1 0+3	20:31.1
	BARNES Tracy		0+2 0+0	22:07.0
	BARNES Lanny		0+1 0+1	21:21.7
	BRAMANTE Carolyn		0+1 0+2	21:20.5

World Championships, Anthloz, Italy, 2007

Individual Race, Men

Rank	Name	Nation	Penalties	Finish
1	POIREE Raphael	FRA	0+0+0+0	56:14.5
2	GREIS Michael	GER	0+1+0+1	56:41.4
3	SLESINGR Michal	CZE	0+2+0+0	56:52.0
7	BURKE Tim	USA	0+1+0+1	57:42.0
31	HAKKINEN Jay	USA	0+2+0+1	1:01:02.0
41	BAILEY Lowell	USA	1+0+1+1	1:02:34.2
44	TEELA Jeremy	USA	1+1+0+2	1:02:40.6

Sprint Race, Men

Rank	Name	Nation	Penalties	Finish
1	BJØRNDALEN Ole Einar	NOR	0+1	26:18.8
2	SLESINGR Michal	CZE	0+0	26:23.6
3	DERYZEMLYA Andriy	UKR	0+0	26:44.6
35	BURKE Tim	USA	1+3	28:16.6
38	HAKKINEN Jay	USA	2+1	28:29.4
46	TEELA Jeremy	USA	2+2	28:50.4
48	BAILEY Lowell	USA	2+2	29:04.1

Pursuit Race, Men

Rank	Name	Nation	Penalties	Finish
1	BJØRNDALEN Ole Einar	NOR	1+0+1+0	32:21.2
2	TCHOUDOV Maxim	RUS	1+0+2+0	33:31.0
3	DEFRASNE Vincent	FRA	0+0+1+0	33:31.1
18	HAKKINEN Jay	USA	0+0+1+0	34:45.3
32	BURKE Tim	USA	0+1+2+2	36:06.5
46	TEELA Jeremy	USA	2+0+3+2	38:05.2

Mass Start Race, Men

Rank	Name	Nation	Penalties	Finish
1	GREIS Michael	GER	0+0+2+0	37:52.1
2	BIRNBACHER Andreas	GER	0+0+0+0	38:07.5
3	POIREE Raphael	FRA	1+0+0+0	38:20.2
9	HAKKINEN Jay	USA	1+0+0+1	38:45.0
24	BURKE Tim	USA	1+2+2+1	40:28.7

Team Relay, Men

1	RUSSIA	RUS	0+1	1:14.36.1
	TCHEREZOV Ivan		0+0 0+0	18:50.7
	TCHOUDOV Maxim		0+0 0+1	18:23.2
	IAROCHENKO Dmitri		0+0 0+0	18:39.7
	KRUGLOV Nikolay		0+0 0+0	18:42.5
2	NORWAY	NOR	1+11	1:15:36.6
	HANEVOLD Halvard		0+2 0+1	19:24.5
	BERGER Lars		0+2 0+2	18:31.1
	ANDRESEN Frode		0+0 1+3	19:21.1
	BJOERNDALEN Ole Einar		0+0 0+1	18:19.9
3	GERMANY	GER	2+13	1:16:08.6
	GROSS Ricco		0+0 0+2	19:30.3
	ROESCH Michael		0+0 0+1	19:00.0
	FISCHER Sven		0+1 0+2	18:53.5
	GREIS Michael		0+0 0+1	18:44.8
9	USA	USA	0+15	1:18:03.0
	HAKKINEN Jay		0+0 0+3	19:22.3
	BURKE Tim		0+1 0+1	18:42.0
	BAILEY Lowell		0+3 0+3	20:17.4
	TEELA Jeremy		0+2 0+2	19:41.3

Individual Race, Women

Rank	Name	Nation	Penalties	Finish
1	GRUBBEN Linda	NOR	0+0+0+0	46:24.3
2	BAVEREL-ROBERT Flor	FRA	0+0+0+0	47:30.8
3	GLAGOW Martina	GER	1+0+0+0	47:59.9
50	BARNES Tracy	USA	0+2+1+0	53:22.5
53	BARNES Lanny	USA	1+0+2+0	53:58.1
65	BRAMANTE Carolyn	USA	0+1+0+2	55:25.2
85	GRAHAM Erin	USA	1+3+2+1	1:01:12.5

Sprint Race, Women

Rank	Name	Nation	Penalties	Finish
1	NUENER Magdalena	GER	1+1	22:46.9
2	OLOFSSON Anna Carin	SWE	1+1	22:49.2
3	GUSEVA Natalia	RUS	0+1	23:06.5
40	BARNES Lanny	USA	0+1	25:05.5
41	BARNES Tracy	USA	1+0	25:07.6
54	KONRAD Sarah	USA	2+2	25:38.5
83	BRAMANTE Carolyn	USA	0+5	29:01.1

Pursuit Race, Women

Rank	Name	Nation	Penalties	Finish
1	NEUNER Magdalena	GER	1+0+1+2	33:01.6
2	GRUBBEN Linda	NOR	0+1+0+0	33:08.7
3	OLOFSSON Anna Car	SWE	2+0+1+2	33:09.2
38	BARNES Tracy	USA	1+0+1+1	37:40.0
49	BARNES Lanny	USA	1+0+2+3	39:04.5
DNF	KONRAD Sarah	USA	4+3+ +	

Mass Start Race, Women

Rank	Name	Nation	Penalties	Finish
1	HENKEL Andrea	GER	1+0+1+0	37:13.1
2	GLAGOW Martina	GER	1+0+0+0	37:17.7
3	WILHELM Kati	GER	0+1+1+0	37:23.7
	No USA Qualifiers			

Team Relay, Women

1	GERMANY	GER	0+7	1:14.19.1
	BECK Martina		0+0 0+1	18:57.2
	HENKEL Andrea		0+2 0+1	18:27.6
	NEUNER Magdalena		0+0 0+3	18:23.7
	WILHELM Kati		0+0 0+0	18:30.6
2	FRANCE	FRA	1+7	1:15:26.9
	BAVEREL-ROBERT Flore		0+1 0+2	18:55.7
	PERETTO Delphine		0+1 1+3	19:32.7
	BECAERT Sylvie		0+0 0+0	18:30.0
	BAILLY Sandrine		0+0 0+0	18:28.5
3	NORWAY	NOR	1+6	1:15:48.8
	BERGER Tora		0+0 1+3	19:35.5
	FLATLAND Ann Kristin		0+0 0+2	18:45.6
	MOERKVE Jori		0+0 0+0	19:15.3
	GRUBBEN Linda		0+0 0+1	18:12.4
	USA	USA		DNS

Team Relay, Mixed

1	SWEDEN	SWE	0+13	1:20:04.7
	JONSSON Helena		0+1 0+1	19:56.6
	OLOFSSON Anna Carin		0+1 0+2	19:07.2
	FERRY Björn		0+2 0+3	20:39.1
	BERGMAN Carl Johan		0+2 0+1	20:21.8
2	FRANCE	FRA	0+2	1:20:32.3
	BAVEREL-ROBERT Floren		0+0 0+0	20:04.9
	BAILLY Sandrine		0+1 0+1	19:49.7
	DEFRASNE Vincent		0+0 0+0	20:12.9
	POIREE Raphael		0+0 0+0	20:24.8
3	NORWAY	NOR	0+11	1:20:41.1
	BERGER Tora		0+1 0+1	19:38.9
	MOERKVE Jori		0+0 0+1	20:18.1
	SVENDSEN Emil Hegle		0+1 0+1	19:59.3
	ANDRESEN Frode		0+3 0+3	20:44.8
	USA	USA		DNS

World Championships, Östersund, Sweden, 2008

Individual Race, Men

Rank	Name	Nation	Penalties	Finish
1	SVENDSEN Emil Hegle	NOR	0+1+0+0	51:51.9
2	BJØRNDALEN Ole Einar	NOR	1+1+0+0	52:23.3
3	MAKSIMOV Maxim	RUS	0+0+0+0	52:26.7
29	BURKE Tim	USA	1+2+0+0	56:24.9
47	TEELA Jeremy	USA	2+1+0+1	58:08.7
56	BAILEY Lowell	USA	1+1+2+1	58:59.7
79	CURRIER Russell	USA	3+2+1+0	1:02:09.2

Sprint Race, Men

Rank	Name	Nation	Penalties	Finish
1	TCHOUDOV Maxim	RUS	0+0	22:25.4
2	HANEVOLD Halvard	NOR	0+0	22:45.2
3	BJØRNDALEN Ole Einar	NOR	0+2	22:55.4
9	BURKE Tim	USA	0+1	23:30.4
61	BAILEY Lowell	USA	0+2	24:57.0
73	TEELA Jeremy	USA	2+1	25:26.3
89	HAKKINEN Jay	USA	3+1	26:31.4

Pursuit Race, Men

Rank	Name	Nation	Penalties	Finish
1	BJØRNDALEN Ole Einar	NOR	0+1+1+0	31:04.5
2	TCHOUDOV Maxim	RUS	2+0+2+0	31:14.6
3	WOLF Alexander	GER	0+0+1+0	31:47.3
10	BURKE Tim	USA	0+0+2+0	32:23.1

Mass Start Race, Men

Rank	Name	Nation	Penalties	Finish
1	SVENDSON Emil Hegle	NOR	1+0+0+0	36:12.6
2	BJØRNDALEN Ole Einar	NOR	0+0+1+0	36:13.0
3	TCHOUDOV Maxim	RUS	0+1+2+0	36:37.5
25	BURKE Tim	USA	1+1+1+2	38:54.8

Team Relay, Men

1	RUSSIA	RUS		1:21:00.7
	TCHEREZOV Ivan		0+0 0+1	19:29.9
	KRUGLOV Nikolay		0+0 0+2	20:53.5
	YAROSHENKO Dmitri		0+0 0+1	20:29.2
	TCHOUDOV Maxim		0+0 0+1	20:08.1
2	NORWAY	NOR		1:21:49.9
	SVENDSEN Emil Hegle		0+0 0+1	19:30.3
	BRATSVEEN Rune		0+0 0+3	21:18.0
	HANEVOLD Halvard		0+1 0+2	20:58.4
	BJOERNDALEN Ole Einar		0+0 0+0	20:03.2
3	GERMANY	GER		1:22:43.2
	ROESCH Michael		0+0 1+3	20:12.9
	WOLF Alexander		0+0 0+1	20:12.9
	BIRNBACHER Andreas		0+2 1+3	21:41.9
	GREIS Michael		0+3 0+2	20:31.4
15	USA	USA		1:26:39.
	BAILEY Lowell		0+1 0+1	20:09.5
	HAKKINEN Jay		0+0 2+3	22:18.7
	BURKE Tim		1+3 1+3	22:49.3
	TEELA Jeremy		0+1 0+1	21:21.7

Individual Race, Women

Rank	Name	Nation	Penalties	Finish
1	IOURIEVA Ekaterina	RUS	0+0+0+0	44:23.8
2	BECK Martina	GER	1+0+0+0	45:37.1
3	KHVOSTENKO Oksana	UKR	0+0+1+0	46:48.2
37	COMPTON Caitlin	USA	1+2+0+1	51:44.1
49	BARNES Lanny	USA	1+1+0+0	52:54.3
62	SPECTOR Laura	USA	2+1+0+2	54:15.8
78	JOHNSON Haley	USA	1+3+1+3	57:05.4

Sprint Race, Women

Rank	Name	Nation	Penalties	Finish
1	HENKEL Andrea	GER	0+0	19:43.1
2	AKHATOVA Albina	RUS	0+0	19:55.8
3	KHVOSTENKO Oksana	UKR	0+0	20:06.3
53	JOHNSON Haley	USA	1+1	22:14.4
63	BARNES Lanny	USA	1+0	22:51.0
70	COMPTON Caitlin	USA	3+2	23:13.2
88	BARNES Tracy	USA	1+3	24:39.6

Pursuit Race, Women

Rank	Name	Nation	Penalties	Finish
1	HENKEL Andrea	GER	0+0+0+0	28:56.0
2	IOURIEVA Ekaterina	RUS	0+0+0+0	29:16.5
3	AKHATOVA Albina	RUS	0+0+0+0	29:34.5
52	JOHNSON Haley	USA	1+1+1+2	36:00.3

Mass Start Race, Women

Rank	Name	Nation	Penalties	Finish
1	NEUNER Magdalena	GER	0+0+2+2	39:36.5
2	BERGER Tor	NOR	1+0+0+0	39:39.5
3	IOURIEVA Ekaterina	RUS	1+0+1+0	40:06.0
	No USA Qualifiers			

Team Relay, Women

1	GERMANY	GER		1:10:12.6
	BECK Martina		0+0 0+0	16:50.5
	HENKEL Andrea		0+0 0+0	17:16.4
	NEUNER Magdelena		0+2 1+3	18:00.1
	WILHELM Kati		0+2 0+2	18:05.6
2	UKRAINE	UKR		1:10:43.5
	YAKOVLEVA Oksana		0+0 0+0	17:10.7
	SEMERENKO Vita		0+0 0+2	17:48.5
	SEMERENKO Valj		0+0 0+2	18:12.0
	KHVOSTENKO Oksana		0+0 0+0	17:32.3
3	FRANCE	FRA		1:11:48.3
	PERETTO Delpine		0+1 0+1	17:44.1
	BRUNET Marie Laure		0+0 1+3	18:03.9
	BECAERT Sylvie		0+1 1+3	18:35.6
	BAILLY Sandrine		0+2 0+2	17:24.7
18	USA	USA		1:17:59.3
	BARNES Tracy		0+2 0+0	19:07.6
	BARNES Lanny		0+0 0+0	19:28.8
	JOHNSON Haley		0+2 0+1	19:07.5
	COMPTON Caitlin		0+3 1+3	20:15.4

Team Relay, Mixed

1	GERMANY	GER		1:12:20.5
	BUCHHOLZ Sabrina		0+0 0+0	17:53.8
	NEUNER Magdelena		0+0 0+2	17:19.1
	BIRNBACHER Andreas		0+1 0+2	18:46.4
	GREIS Michael		0+0 0+1	18:21.2
2	BELARUS	BLR		1:13:13.1
	KALINCHIK Liudmila		0+0 0+1	17:59.6
	DOMRACHEVA Darya		0+0 0+1	18:17.1
	VALIULLIN Rustam		0+0 0+0	18:15.1
	NOVIKOV Sergey		0+0 0+2	18:41.3

3	RUSSIA	RUS		1:13:23.4
	SLEPTSOVA Svetlana		0+0 0+0	17:31.7
	NEUPOKOEVA Oksana		0+0 0+2	18:36.3
	KRUGLOV Nikolay		1+3 0+2	19:13.2
	YAROSHENKO Dmitri		0+0 0+2	18:02.2
16	USA	USA		1:22:25.8
	BARNES Tracy		0+1 0+0	19:42.0
	SPECTOR Laura		0+2 0+2	20:50.6
	TEELA Jeremy		0+0 1+3	19:36.5
	CURRIER Russell		1+3 0+3	22:16.7

World Championships, Pyeong Chang, Korea, 2009
Individual Race, Men

Rank	Name	Nation	Penalties	Finish
1	BJØRNDALEN Ole Einar	NOR	0+0+2+1	52:28.0
2	STEPHAN Christoph	GER	1+0+0+0	52:42.1
3	FAK Jakov	CRO	0+0+0+1	52:45.1
14	BURKE Tim	USA	0+1+0+2	54:25.9
22	BAILEY Lowell	USA	1+0+0+1	55:06.3
44	TEELA Jeremy	USA	1+1+0+2	56:48.4
DNF	HAKKINEN Jay	USA	2+0+ +	

Sprint Race, Men

Rank	Name	Nation	Penalties	Finish
1	BJØRNDALEN Ole Einar	NOR	1+1	24:16.5
2	BERGER Lars	NOR	1+1	24:17.7
3	HANEVOLD Halvard	NOR	0+0	24:29.0
11	BURKE Tim	USA	0+2	25:36.4
55	BAILEY Lowell	USA	2+2	27:04.1
57	CURRIER Russell	USA	3+1	27:12.2
69	TEELA Jeremy	USA	3+1	27:29.6

Pursuit Race, Men

Rank	Name	Nation	Penalties	Finish
1	BJØRNDALEN Ole Einar	NOR	0+2+0+2	31:46.7
2	TCHOUDOV Maxim	RUS	0+0+1+2	32:28.4
3	OS Alexander	NOR	0+0+2+1	32:39.5
21	BURKE Tim	USA	1+2+4+1	35:59.8
22	BAILEY Lowell	USA	2+1+1+0	36:01.0
56	CURRIER Russell	USA	2+3+2+5	40:42.2

Mass Start Race, Men

Rank	Name	Nation	Penalties	Finish
1	LANDERTINGER Dominik	AUT	2+0+0+1	38:32.5
2	SUMANN Christoph	AUT	2+0+0+1	38:41.4
3	TCHEREZOV Ivan	RUS	2+0+0+0	38:46.4
18	BAILEY Lowell	USA	2+0+2+1	40:54.0
28	BURKE Tim	USA	2+2+2+4	42:52.5

Team Relay, Men

1	NORWAY	NOR	0+2 2+7	1:08:04.1
	SVENDSEN Emil Hegle		0+0 1+3	17:09.2
	BERGER Lars		0+0 1+3	17:02.5
	HANEVOLD Halvard		0+0 0+0	17:16.5
	BJOERNDALEN Ole Einar		0+2 0+1	16:35.9
2	AUSTRIA	AUT	0+2 0+5	1:08:16.7
	MESOTITSCH Daniel		0+0 0+1	16:49.8
	EDER Simon		0+1 0+0	16:57.2
	LANDERTINGER Dominik		0+1 0+2	17:29.7
	SUMANN Christoph		0+0 0+2	17:00.0
3	GERMANY	GER	0+3 0+7	1:08:36.8
	ROESCH Michael		0+1 0+1	16:36.8
	STEPHAN Christoph		0+1 0+3	17:47.7
	PEIFFER Arnd		0+0 0+1	17:05.4
	GREIS Michael		0+1 0+2	17:06.9
21	USA	USA	2+6 2+9	1:15:07.0
	BAILEY Lowell		0+2 1+3	18:26.7
	BURKE Tim		0+1 1+3	18:11.8
	TEELA Jeremy		0+0 0+3	17:30.6
	CURRIER Russell		2+3 0+0	20:57.9

Individual Race, Women

Rank	Name	Nation	Penalties	Finish
1	WILHELM Kati	GER	0+1+0+0	44:03.1
2	GREGORIN Teja	SLO	0+0+0+1	44:42.6
3	BERGER Tora	NOR	0+0+0+1	44:49.6
23	JOHNSON Haley	USA	0+0+0+1	47:27.0
42	BARNES Lanny	USA	1+0+0+0	49:31.6
59	BARNES Tracy	USA	0+0+0+2	51:13.1
64	BRAMANTE Carolyn	USA	1+2+0+0	51:55.1

Sprint Race, Women

Rank	Name	Nation	Penalties	Finish
1	WILHELM Kati	GER	0+0	21:11.1
2	HAUSWALD Simone	GER	0+0	21:21.0
3	ZAITSEVA Olga	RUS	0+0	21:38.2
46	BARNES Lanny	USA	0+0	24:04.6
56	BARNES Tracy	USA	0+1	24:34.1
58	SPECTOR Laura	USA	0+2	24:41.4
92	JOHNSON Haley	USA	4+2	26:44.1

Pursuit Race, Women

Rank	Name	Nation	Penalties	Finish
1	JONSSON Helena	SWE	2+0+0+0	34:12.3
2	WILHELM Kati	GER	1+1+3+1	34:30.6
3	ZAITSEVA Olga	RUS	0+3+1+2	34:36.4
39	BARNES Lanny	USA	0+0+0+1	38:32.8
55	BARNES Tracy	USA	1+0+1+3	40:57.5
58	SPECTOR Laura	USA	2+3+2+3	43:30.0

Mass Start Race, Women

Rank	Name	Nation	Penalties	Finish
1	ZAITSEVA Olga	RUS	0+0+1+1	34:18.3
2	KUZMINA Anastasiya	SVK	0+0+1+1	34:25.8
3	JONSSON Helena	SWE	0+0+1+1	34:30.6
	No USA Qualifiers			

Team Relay, Women

1	RUSSIA	RUS		1:13:12.9
	SLEPTSOVA Svetlana		0+2 0+0	18:17.7
	BOULYGINA Anna		0+0 0+3	19:16.1
	MEDVEDTSEVA Olga		0+1 0+2	18:03.2
	ZAITSEVA Olga		0+0 0+1	17:35.9
2	GERMANY	GER	0+6 3+8	1:14:28.0
	BECK Martina		0+1 0+1	18:22.0
	NEUNER Magdalena		0+2 2+3	18:57.8
	HENKEL Andrea		0+1 0+1	18:01.0
	WILHELM Kati		0+2 1+3	19:07.2
3	FRANCE	FRA		1:14:40.4
	BRUNET Marie Laure		0+0 0+1	18:01.7
	BECAERT Sylvie		0+2 0+3	18:48.7
	DORIN Marie		0+0 0+3	18:38.7
	BAILLY Sandrine		0+1 1+3	19:11.3
10	USA	USA		1:18:42.4
	BARNES Lanny		0+0 0+2	19:43.3
	JOHNSON Haley		0+2 0+3	20:18.9
	SPECTOR Laura		0+2 0+1	19:19.8
	BARNES Tracy		0+0 0+0	19:20.4

Team Relay, Mixed

1	FRANCE	FRA	0+2 0+4	1:10:30.0
	BRUNET Marie Laure		0+0 0+1	17:40.6
	BECAERT Sylvie		0+0 0+1	17:23.4
	DEFRASNE Vincent		0+2 0+0	18:04.4
	FOURCADE Simon		0+0 0+2	17:21.6
2	SWEDEN	SWE	0+0 0+3	1:10:36.2
	EKHOLM Helena		0+0 0+0	17:33.0
	ZIDEK Anna Carin		0+0 0+1	17:41.0
	EKHOLM David		0+0 0+0	17:56.0
	BERGMAN Carl Johan		0+0 0+2	17:26.2

3	GERMANY	GER	0+3 0+8	1:10:39.0
	HENKEL Andrea		0+0 0+2	17:41.2
	HAUSWALD Simone		0+2 0+1	18:10.3
	PEIFFER Arnd		0+0 0+2	17:21.4
	GREIS Michael		0+1 0+3	17:26.1
16	USA	USA	0+4 0+8	1:17:59.8
	BRAMANTE Carolyn		0+0 0+1	19:57.7
	SPECTOR Laura		0+1 0+2	19:55.0
	TEELA Jeremy		0+1 0+3	18:18.4
	CURRIER Russell		0+2 0+2	19:48.7

Winter Olympic Games, Vancouver, Canada, 2010

Individual Race, Men

Rank	Name	Nation	Penalties	Finish
1	SVENDSEN Emil Hegle	NOR	0+0+0+1	48:22.5
2	BJØRNDALEN Ole Einar	NOR	0+1+0+1	48:32.0
2	NOVIKOV Sergey	BLR	0+0+0+0	48:32.0
45	BURKE Tim	USA	1+1+0+3	53:22.6
57	BAILEY Lowell	USA	0+2+1+1	54:23.1
76	HAKKINEN Jay	USA	2+1+2+2	57:01.8
86	ROBERTS Wynn	USA	3+2+0+3	58:49.2

Sprint Race, Men

Rank	Name	Nation	Penalties	Finish
1	JAY Vincent	FRA	0+0	24:07.8
2	SVENDSEN Emil Hegle	NOR	1+0	24:20.0
3	FAK Jakov	CRO	0+0	24:21.8
9	TEELA Jeremy	USA	1+1	25:21.7
36	BAILEY Lowell	USA	0+0	26:26.6
47	BURKE Tim	USA	1+2	26:54.8
54	HAKKINEN Jay	USA	0+0	27:17.4

Pursuit Race, Men

Rank	Name	Nation	Penalties	Finish
1	FERRY Björn	SWE	0+0+0+1	33:38.4
2	SUMANN Christoph	AUT	0+0+1+1	33:54.9
3	JAY Vincent	FRA	0+0+1+1	34:06.6
24	TEELA Jeremy	USA	0+0+2+2	35:45.4
36	BAILEY Lowell	USA	0+2+1+0	36:34.0
46	BURKE Tim	USA	0+2+1+2	37:26.8
57	HAKKINEN Jay	USA	1+2+3+0	40:33.2

Mass Start Race, Men

Rank	Name	Nation	Penalties	Finish
1	USTYUGOV Evgeny	RUS	0+0+0+0	35:35.7
2	FOURCADE Martin	FRA	2+0+0+1	35:46.2
3	HURAJT Pavol	SVK	0+0+0+0	35:52.3
18	BURKE Tim	USA	0+0+3+1	36:44.7
29	TEELA Jeremy	USA	1+1+0+2	38:36.1

Team Relay, Men

1	NORWAY	NOR		1:21:38.1
	HANEVOLD Halvard		0+1 0+0	20:15.6
	BOE Tarjei		0+1 0+1	20:26.8
	SVENDSEN Emil Hegle		0+1 0+1	20:31.3
	BJOERNDALEN Ole Einar		0+2 0+0	20:24.4
2	AUSTRIA	AUT		1:22:16.7
	EDER Simon		0+0 0+1	20:10.0
	MESOTITSCH Daniel		0+2 0+1	20:38.0
	LANDERTINGER Dominik		0+1 0+0	20:25.9
	SUMANN Christoph		1+3 0+0	21:02.8
3	RUSSIA	RUS		1:22:16.9
	TCHEREZOV Ivan		0+0 0+1	20:07.5
	SHIPULIN Anton		0+0 0+0	21:05.0
	TCHOUDOV Maxim		0+0 0+0	20:23.2
	USTYUGOV Evgeny		0+0 0+3	20:41.2
6	USA	USA		1:27:58.3
	BAILEY Lowell		0+0 0+1	20:51.8
	HAKKINEN Jay		0+0 1+3	21:47.0
	BURKE Tim		0+0 2+3	22:01.7
	TEELA Jeremy		0+2 1+3	23:17.8

Individual Race, Women

Rank	Name	Nation	Penalties	Finish
1	BERGER Tora	NOR	0+0+0+1	40:52.8
2	KHRUSTALEVA Elena	KAZ	0+0+0+0	41:13.5
2	DOMRACHEVA Darya	BLR	0+1+0+0	41:21.0
23	BARNES Lanny	USA	0+0+0+0	43:31.8
34	STUDEBAKER Sara	USA	0+0+1+0	44:27.3
65	SPECTOR Laura	USA	0+0+0+2	47:19.3
66	JOHNSON Haley	USA	2+1+0+1	47:19.4

Sprint Race, Women

Rank	Name	Nation	Penalties	Finish
1	KUZMINA Anastasiya	SVK	1+0	19:55.6
2	NEUNER Magdalena	GER	0+1	19:57.1
3	DORIN Marie	FRA	0+0	20:06.5
45	STUDEBAKER Sara	USA	0+1	22:05.3
77	SPECTOR Laura	USA	1+1	23:18.1
78	BARNES Lanny	USA	1+0	23:26.0
80	JOHNSON Haley	USA	1+3	23:35.4

Pursuit Race, Women

Rank	Name	Nation	Penalties	Finish
1	NEUNER Magdalena	GER	0+0+1+1	30:16.0
2	KUZMINA Anastasiya	SVK	0+1+1+0	30:28.3
3	BRUNET Marie Laure	FRA	0+0+0+0	30:44.3
24	STUDEBAKER Sara	USA	1+0+0+1	35:00.1

Mass Start Race, Women

Rank	Name	Nation	Penalties	Finish
1	NEUNER Magdalena	GER	1+0+1+0	35:19.6
2	ZAITSEVA Olga	RUS	0+0+1+0	35:25.1
3	HAUSWALD Simone	GER	0+0+2+0	35:26.9
	No USA Qualifiers			

Team Relay, Women

1	RUSSIA	RUS	0+2 0+3	1:09:36.3
	SLEPTSOVA Svetlana		0+0 0+0	17:24.4
	BOGALIY-TITOVETS Anna		0+1 0+1	17:17.3
	MEDVEDTSEVA Olga		0+0 0+0	17:27.7
	ZAITSEVA Olga		0+1 0+2	17:26.9
2	FRANCE	FRA	2+4 0+4	1:10:09.1
	BRUNET Marie Laure		0+0 0+2	17:22.6
	BECAERT Sylvie		0+0 0+1	17:17.6
	DORIN Marie		2+3 0+1	18:34.2
	BAILLY Sandrine		0+1 0+0	16:54.7
3	GERMANY	GER	0+2 0+3	1:10:13.4
	WILHELM Kati		0+1 0+0	17:26.0
	HAUSWALD Simone		0+0 0+0	17:16.2
	BECK Martina		0+1 0+1	18:12.0
	HENKEL Andrea		0+0 0+2	17:19.2
13	USA	USA	1+8 0+4	1:15:47.5
	STUDEBAKER Sara		0+1 0+0	17:53.2
	BARNES Lanny		0+1 0+1	18:52.5
	JOHNSON Haley		0+3 0+0	19:01.5
	SPECTOR Laura		1+3 0+3	20:00.3

World Championships, Khanty-Mansiysk, Russia 2011

Individual Race, Men

Rank	Name	Nation	Penalties	Finish
1	BOE Tarjei	NOR	0+0+1+0	48:29.9
2	MAKSIMOV Maxim	RUS	0+0+0+0	49:09.9
3	SUMANN Christoph	AUT	0+0+0+1	49:15.4
21	NORDGREN Leif	USA	0+0+0+1	51:21.1
30	BURKE Tim	USA	1+1+0+1	52:13.9
78	BAILEY Lowell	USA	1+3+2+0	56:17.3
80	HAKKINEN Jay	USA	1+1+2+2	56:29.2

Sprint Race, Men

Rank	Name	Nation	Penalties	Finish
1	PEIFFER Arnd	GER	0+1	24:34.0
2	FOURCADE Martin	FRA	2+0	24:47.0
3	BOE Tarjei	NOR	1+0	24:59.2
26	NORDGREN Leif	USA	0+1	26:03.0
31	BURKE Tim	USA	2+1	26:15.2
32	BAILEY Lowell	USA	0+1	26:16.0
42	HAKKINEN Jay	USA	0+1	26:49.8

Pursuit Race, Men

Rank	Name	Nation	Penalties	Finish
1	FOURCADE Martin	FRA	0+1+2+0	33:02.6
2	SVENDSEN Emil Hegle	NOR	0+0+1+1	33:06.4
3	BOE Tarjei	NOR	0+0+1+1	33:07.8
30	BURKE Tim	USA	2+0+3+1	36:12.6
35	HAKKINEN Jay	USA	0+1+0+1	36:25.6
38	NORDGREN Leif	USA	1+2+2+1	36:47.2
45	BAILEY Lowell	USA	0+0+3+3	37:10.0

Mass Start Race, Men

Rank	Name	Nation	Penalties	Finish
1	SVENDSEN Emil Hegle	NOR	0+0+0+1	38:42.7
2	USTYUGOV Evgeny	RUS	0+0+0+0	38:47.7
3	HOFER Lukas	ITA	0+0+0+1	38:57.0
17	NORDGREN Leif	USA	1+0+1+1	40:26.7

Team Relay, Men

1	NORWAY	NOR	0+2 2+8	1:16:13.9
	BJOERNDALEN Ole Einar		0+0 0+0	19:12.7
	OS Alexander		0+0 1+3	19:16.3
	SVENDSEN Emil Hegle		0+1 0+2	18:31.5
	BOE Tarjei		0+1 1+3	19:13.4
2	RUSSIA	RUS	0+5 0+3	1:16:27.3
	SHIPULIN Anton		0+1 0+1	19:32.8
	USTYUGOV Evgeny		0+0 0+2	18:56.9
	MAKSIMOV Maxim		0+1 0+0	18:59.9
	TCHEREZOV Ivan		0+3 0+0	18:57.7
3	UKRAINE	UKR	0+4 0+6	1:16:41.9
	BILANENKO Olexander		0+1 0+2	19:40.6
	DERYZEMLYA Andriy		0+1 0+2	19:00.1
	SEMENOV Sergey		0+0 0+1	18:57.5
	SEDNEV Serguei		0+2 0+1	19:03.7
6	USA	USA	0+6 0+8	1:16:52.0
	BAILEY Lowell		0+1 0+2	19:36.2
	HAKKINEN Jay		0+3 0+2	19:31.8
	BURKE Tim		0+0 0+2	18:55.6
	NORDGREN Leif		0+2 0+2	18:48.4

Individual Race, Women

Rank	Name	Nation	Penalties	Finish
1	EKHOLM Helena	SWE	0+0+0+0	47:08.3
2	BACHMANN Tina	GER	0+2+0+0	49:24.1
3	SEMERENKO Vita	UKR	1+0+0+2	50:00.4
17	STUDEBAKER Sara	USA	0+1+0+1	52:37.8
44	SPECTOR Laura	USA	1+2+1+2	56:19.2
67	COOK Annelies	USA	0+3+1+3	58:59.2
68	JOHNSON Haley	USA	1+3+1+3	59:02.5

Sprint Race, Women

Rank	Name	Nation	Penalties	Finish
1	NEUNER Magdalena	GER	0+0	20:31.2
2	MÄKÄRÄINEN Kaisa	FIN	0+0	20:43.4
3	KUZMINA Anastasiya	SVK	0+1	21:11.2
48	STUDEBAKER Sara	USA	1+2	23:56.6
57	COOK Annelies	USA	1+1	24:26.1
72	JOHNSON Haley	USA	2+2	24:58.8
79	SPECTOR Laura	USA	3+2	25:29.8

Pursuit Race, Women

Rank	Name	Nation	Penalties	Finish
1	MÄKÄRÄINEN Kaisa	FIN	0+0+0+0	30:00.1
2	NEUNER Magdalena	GER	0+0+0+2	30:21.7
3	EKHOLM Helena	SWE	0+0+0+0	31:43.7
38	STUDEBAKER Sara	USA	1+1+0+2	37:14.3
DNF	COOK Annelies	USA	0+1+1+2	

Mass Start Race, Women

Rank	Name	Nation	Penalties	Finish
1	NEUNER Magdalena	GER	0+1+2+1	36:48.5
2	DOMRACHEVA Darya	BLR	2+1+0+0	36:53.3
3	BERGER Tora	NOR	2+1+0+0	37:02.5
	No USA Qualifiers			

Team Relay, Women

Rank	Name	Nation	Penalties		Finish
1	GERMANY	GER	0+7	2+6	1:13:31.1
	HENKEL Andrea		0+2	0+1	18:40.8
	GÖSSNER Miriam		0+2	2+3	19:02.4
	BACHMANN Tina		0+2	0+2	18:59.6
	NEUNER Magdalena		0+1	0+0	16:48.3
2	FRANCE	FRA	0+6	0+3	1:14:18.3
	BESCOND Anais		0+2	0+1	19:17.7
	BRUNET Marie Laure		0+0	0+0	17:56.1
	BOILLEY Sophie		0+3	0+2	19:21.8
	DORIN Marie		0+1	0+0	17:42.7
3	BELARUS	BLR	0+6	0+3	1:14:18.3
	SKARDINO Nadezhda		0+0	0+1	19:08.5
	DOMRACHEVA Darya		0+1	0+0	17:44.0
	PISAREVA Nadzeya		0+0	0+0	18:49.2
	KALINCHIK Liudmila		0+1	1+3	19:36.8
13	USA	USA	1+7	2+9	1:19:55.7
	STUDEBAKER Sara		0+1	0+1	19:23.1
	SPECTOR Laura		0+0	0+2	19:41.9
	COOK Annelies		1+3	1+3	21:24.0
	JOHNSON Haley		0+3	1+3	19:26.7

Team Relay, Mixed

Rank	Name	Nation	Penalties		Finish
1	NORWAY	NOR	0+4	0+3	1:14:22.5
	BERGER Tora		0+1	0+0	18:18.3
	FLATLAND Ann Kristin		0+1	0+1	18:16.4
	BJOERNDALEN Ole Einar		0+2	0+1	19:05.5
	BOE Tarjei		0+0	0+1	18:42.3
2	GERMANY	GER	0+5	0+3	1:14:45.4
	HENKEL Andrea		0+2	0+0	18:45.0
	NEUNER Magdalena		0+0	0+0	17:25.0
	PEIFFER Arnd		0+1	0+2	19:06.3
	GREIS Michael		0+2	0+1	19:29.1
3	FRANCE	FRA	0+2	0+6	1:15:38.7
	BRUNET Marie Laure		0+2	0+2	19:36.5
	DORIN HABERT Marie		0+0	0+3	18:27.7
	BOEUF Alexis		0+0	0+1	19:14.8
	FOURCADE Martin		0+0	0+0	18:19.7
13	USA	USA	0+8	0+6	1:19:33.6
	STUDEBAKER Sara		0+3	0+2	20:09.6
	SPECTOR Laura		0+2	0+2	19:59.8
	HAKKINEN Jay		0+1	0+0	20:07.5
	NORDGREN Leif		0+2	0+2	19:16.7

World Championships, Ruhpolding, Germany, 2012
Individual Race, Men

Rank	Name	Nation	Penalties	Finish
1	FAK Jakov	SLO	0+0+0+1	46:48.2
2	FOURCADE Simon	FRA	0+0+1+0	46:55.2
3	SOUKUP Jaroslav	CZE	0+1+0+0	47:00.5
31	HAKKINEN Jay	USA	1+0+0+1	50:06.0
38	BAILEY Lowell	USA	0+2+1+1	50:27.8
56	BURKE Tim	USA	0+2+1+2	51:26.3
81	NORDGREN Leif	USA	0+1+2+3	54:07.1

Sprint Race, Men

Rank	Name	Nation	Penalties	Finish
1	FOURCADE Martin	FRA	1+1	24:18.6
2	SVENDSEN Emil Hegle	NOR	1+1	24:33.7
3	BERGMAN Carl Johan	SWE	0+0	24:36.3
10	BURKE Tim	USA	0+1	25:17.4
20	BAILEY Lowell	USA	0+0	25:33.8
63	CURRIER Russell	USA	1+2	27:07.0
91	HAKKINEN Jay	USA	4+1	28:37.0

Pursuit Race, Men

Rank	Name	Nation	Penalties	Finish
1	FOURCADE Martin	FRA	1+1+0+2	33:39.4
2	BERGMAN Carl Johan	SWE	0+1+1+0	33:44.6
3	SHIPULIN Anton	RUS	1+0+0+0	34:01.5
20	BAILEY Lowell	USA	0+0+1+2	35:28.2
28	BURKE Tim	USA	1+1+2+1	35:47.7

Mass Start Race, Men

Rank	Name	Nation	Penalties	Finish
1	FOURCADE Martin	FRA	0+1+1+0	38:25.4
2	FERRY Bjoern	SWE	0+0+0+0	38:28.4
3	LINDSTROEM Fredrik	SWE	0+1+1+0	38:28.8
23	BURKE Tim	USA	2+1+1+0	40:07.9
25	BAILEY Lowell	USA	0+1+3+1	40:17.6

Team Relay, Men

1	NORWAY	NOR	0+1	1+6	1:17:26.8
	BJOERNDALEN Ole Einar		0+0	1+3	20:13.5
	BRATTSVEEN Rune		0+0	0+2	19:19.5
	BOE Tarjei		0+1	0+1	19:02.4
	SVENDSEN Emil Hegle		0+0	0+0	18:51.4
2	FRANCE	FRA	0+5	0+5	1:17:56.5
	BEATRIX Jean Guillaume		0+1	0+1	19:23.4
	FOURCADE Simon		0+1	0+1	19:35.1
	BOEUF Alexis		0+1	0+0	19:18.1
	FOURCADE Martin		0+2	0+3	19:39.9
3	GERMANY	GER	0+4	0+6	1:18:19.8
	SCHEMPP Simon		0+0	0+1	19:33.6
	BIRNBACHER Andreas		0+1	0+3	19:35.8
	GREIS Michael		0+2	0+0	19:34.0
	PEIFFER Arnd		0+1	0+2	19:36.4
10	USA	USA	0+5	0+9	1:20:32.9
	BAILEY Lowell		0+0	0+1	19:35.8
	HAKKINEN Jay		0+3	0+3	20:37.3
	BURKE Tim		0+2	0+2	19:59.5
	NORDGREN Leif		0+0	0+3	20:20.3

Individual Race, Women

Rank	Name	Nation	Penalties	Finish
1	BERGER Tora	NOR	1+0+0+0	42:30.0
2	BRUNET Marie Laure	FRA	0+0+0+1	43:26.4
3	EKHOLM Helena	SWE	1+0+0+0	43:41.1
5	DUNKLEE Susan	USA	0+1+0+0	43:48.2
37	BARNES Lanny	USA	0+1+0+0	48:06.2
38	STUDEBAKER Sara	USA	0+1+1+1	48:11.2
66	COOK Annelies	USA	2+3+1+0	50:27.4

Sprint Race, Women

Rank	Name	Nation	Penalties	Finish
1	NEUNER Magdalena	GER	0+0	21:07.0
2	DOMRACHEVA Darya	BLR	0+0	21:22.2
3	SEMERENKO Vita	UKR	0+0	21:44.6
49	STUDEBAKER Sara	USA	1+1	24:15.8
55	DUNKLEE Susan	USA	3+1	24:23.8
62	COOK Annelies	USA	2+1	24:43.2
67	BARNES Lanny	USA	1+0	24:55.6

Pursuit Race, Women

Rank	Name	Nation	Penalties	Finish
1	DOMRACHEVA Darya	BLR	0+1+1+0	29:39.6
2	NEUNER Magdalena	GER	0+1+0+2	30:04.7
3	VILUKHINA Olga	RUS	0+0+1+0	30:55.0
36	DUNKLEE Susan	USA	0+1+2+0	34:22.4
41	STUDEBAKER Sara	USA	0+0+0+0	34:56.4

Mass Start Race, Women

Rank	Name	Nation	Penalties	Finish
1	BERGER Tora	NOR	0+0+1+0	35:41.6
2	BRUNET Marie Laure	FRA	0+0+0+1	35:49.7
3	MÄKÄRÄINEN Kaisa	FIN	0+0+0+1	35:54.3
16	DUNKLEE Susan	USA	1+0+0+0	37:10.3

Team Relay, Women

1	GERMANY	GER	0+6	1+4	1:09:33.0
	BACHMANN Tina		0+1	0+0	17:09.6
	NEUNER Magdalena		0+3	1+3	17:28.4
	GÖSSNER Miriam		0+2	0+1	17:37.8
	HENKEL Andrea		0+0	0+0	17:17.2
2	FRANCE	FRA	0+4	0+3	1:10:01.5
	BRUNET Marie Laure		0+1	0+0	17:09.0
	BOILLEY Sophie		0+1	0+0	17:19.7
	BESCOND Anais		0+1	0+2	18:04.6
	DORIN HABERT Marie		0+1	0+1	17:28.2
3	NORWAY	NOR	0+4	0+8	1:10:12.5
	HORN Fanny		0+1	0+3	18:12.0
	RINGEN Elise		0+1	0+2	17:28.4
	SOLEMDAL Synnoeve		0+1	0+3	17:39.2
	BERGER Tora		0+1	0+0	16:52.9
11	USA	USA	0+4	0+5	1:13:33.1
	STUDEBAKER Sara		0+2	0+1	18:12.6
	DUNKLEE Susan		0+2	0+3	18:19.7
	COOK Annelies		0+0	0+1	18:29.1
	BARNES Lanny		0+0	0+0	18:31.7

Team Relay, Mixed

1	NORWAY	NOR	0+3 1+8	1:12:29.3
	BERGER Tora		0+0 0+0	16:29.1
	SOLEMDAL Synnoeve		0+1 0+3	17:42.8
	BJOERNDALEN Ole Einar		0+2 1+3	19:38.5
	SVENDSEN Emil Hegle		0+0 0+2	18:38.9
2	SLOVENIA	SLO	0+5 0+2	1:12:29.3
	MALI Andreja		0+1 0+0	18:04.2
	GREGORIN Teja		0+1 0+0	16:58.1
	BAUER Klemen		0+3 0+2	19:04.4
	FAK Jakov		0+0 0+0	18:42.8
3	GERMANY	GER	0+4 1+6	1:13:02.1
	HENKEL Andrea		0+2 0+1	17:43.8
	NEUNER Magdalena		0+1 0+2	16:46.6
	BIRNBACHER Andreas		0+0 0+0	18:37.6
	PEIFFER Arnd		0+1 1+3	19:54.1
12	USA	USA	0+2 1+7	1:15:08.7
	STUDEBAKER Sara		0+0 1+3	19:00.2
	DUNKLEE Susan		0+1 0+2	17:30.4
	BURKE Tim		0+1 0+2	19:25.6
	BAILEY Lowell		0+0 0+0	19:12.5

World Championships, Nove Mesto, Czech Republic, 2013

Individual Race, Men

Rank	Name	Nation	Penalties	Finish
1	FOURCADE Martin	FRA	0+0+0+1	49:43.0
2	BURKE Tim	USA	0+0+0+1	50:06.5
3	LINDSTROEM Fredrik	SWE	0+0+0+1	50:16.7
22	NORDGREN Leif	USA	1+0+1+0	52:49.8
29	BAILEY Lowell	USA	0+2+0+1	53:09.3
59	CURRIER Russell	USA	1+1+1+2	56:13.1

Sprint Race, Men

Rank	Name	Nation	Penalties	Finish
1	SVENDSEN Emil Hegle	NOR	0+1	23:25.1
2	FOURCADE Martin	FRA	0+1	23:33.2
3	FAK Jakov	SLO	0+0	23:36.3
28	BURKE Tim	USA	1+1	25:01.3
32	BAILEY Lowell	USA	1+0	25:02.8
43	CURRIER Russell	USA	2+0	25:30.4
52	NORDGREN Leif	USA	1+0	25:43.8

Mass Start Race, Men

Rank	Name	Nation	Penalties	Finish
1	BOE Tarjei	NOR	0+0+0+0	36:15.8
2	SHIPULIN Anton	RUS	0+0+1+0	36:19.5
3	SVENDSEN Emil Hegle	NOR	0+1+0+0	36:23.2
13	BAILEY Lowell	USA	0+0+0+2	37:25.2
30	BURKE Tim	USA	2+3+0+0	41:15.5

Pursuit Race, Men

Rank	Name	Nation	Penalties	Finish
1	SVENDSEN Emil Hegle	NOR	0+0+0+1	32:35.5
2	FOURCADE Martin	FRA	0+1+1+0	32:35.6
3	SHIPULIN Anton	RUS	0+0+1+0	32:39.1
13	BAILEY Lowell	USA	0+0+0+0	33:56.4
32	BURKE Tim	USA	0+1+2+1	35:33.8
43	NORDGREN Leif	USA	2+2+2+0	37:08.3
52	CURRIER Russell	USA	3+1+2+1	38:06.2

Team Relay, Men

1	NORWAY	NOR	0+2 0+3	1:15:39.0
	BJOERNDALEN Ole Einar		0+1 0+2	18:34.9
	L'ABEE-LUND Henrik		0+0 0+0	18:50.2
	BOE Tarjei		0+1 0+0	18:52.4
	SVENDSEN Emil Hegle		0+0 0+1	19:21.5
2	FRANCE	FRA	0+0 0+7	1:16:51.8
	FOURCADE Simon		0+0 0+3	18:58.8
	BEATRIX Jean Guillaume		0+0 0+1	19:10.4
	BOEUF Alexis		0+0 0+1	19:35.3
	FOURCADE Martin		0+0 0+2	19:07.3
3	GERMANY	GER	0+0 2+3	1:16:57.5
	SCHEMPP Simon		0+0 0+0	18:30.8
	BIRNBACHER Andreas		0+0 0+0	18:54.6
	PEIFFER Arnd		0+0 0+0	19:08.7
	LESSER Erik		0+0 2+3	20:23.4
12	USA	USA	0+3 0+9	1:19:40.8
	BAILEY Lowell		0+0 0+3	19:13.2
	BURKE Tim		0+2 0+2	19:47.8
	CURRIER Russell		0+0 0+1	20:21.4
	NORDGREN Leif		0+1 0+3	20:18.4

Individual Race, Women

Rank	Name	Nation	Penalties	Finish
1	BERGER Tora	NOR	0+0+0+0	44:52.5
2	HENKEL Andrea	GER	0+0+0+0	45:45.2
3	SEMERENKO Valj	UKR	1+0+0+0	46:35.0
15	DUNKLEE Susan	USA	1+0+1+0	48:22.8
27	STUDEBAKER Sara	USA	0+0+0+1	49:44.7
38	COOK Annelies	USA	0+3+0+1	50:54.1
56	DREISSIGACKER Hanah	USA	1+1+1+2	53:00.7

Sprint Race, Women

Rank	Name	Nation	Penalties	Finish
1	PIDHRUSHNA Olena	UKR	0+0	21:02.1
2	BERGER Tora	NOR	0+1	21:08.5
3	SEMERENKO Vita	UKR	0+0	21:24.9
45	COOK Annelies	USA	0+2	23:05.4
49	DUNKLEE Susan	USA	2+2	23:09.5
65	STUDEBAKER Sara	USA	2+0	23:35.5
71	DREISSIGACKER Hanah	USA	0+3	24:01.0

Pursuit Race, Women

Rank	Name	Nation	Penalties	Finish
1	BERGER Tora	NOR	0+1+2+0	28:48.4
2	PALKA Krystyna	POL	0+0+1+1	29:06.9
3	PIDHRUSHNA Olena	UKR	0+0+2+0	29:09.9
47	DUNKLEE Susan	USA	1+1+2+1	33:01.0
51	COOK Annelies	USA	2+0+1+2	33:23.7

Mass Start Race, Women

Rank	Name	Nation	Penalties	Finish
1	DOMRACHEVA Darya	BLR	1+0+0+1	35:54.5
2	BERGER Tora	NOR	1+0+1+0	36:03.2
3	HOJNISZ Monika	POL	0+0+1+0	36:22.1
	No USA Qualifiers			

Team Relay, Women

1	NORWAY	NOR	0+2 1+7	1:08:11.0
	FENNE Hilde		0+2 1+3	17:18.1
	FLATLAND Ann Kristin		0+0 0+2	17:29.1
	SOLEMDAL Synnoeve		0+0 0+1	16:53.5
	BERGER Tora		0+0 0+1	16:30.3
2	UKRAINE	UKR	0+3 0+2	1:08:18.0
	DZHYMA Juliya		0+0 0+1	16:49.5
	SEMERENKO Vita		0+2 0+0	17:03.3
	SEMERENKO Valj		0+1 0+0	17:12.6
	PIDHRUSHNA Olena		0+0 0+1	17:12.6
3	ITALY	ITA	0+2 0+2	1:08:22.6
	WIERER Dorothea		0+0 0+0	16:30.8
	GONTIER Nicole		0+2 0+0	17:07.7
	PONZA Michela		0+0 0+2	17:48.5
	OBERHOFER Karin		0+0 0+0	16:55.6
11	USA	USA	1+6 0+4	1:11:15.5
	COOK Annelies		0+2 0+3	17:37.5
	STUDEBAKER Sara		0+1 0+0	17:54.5
	DUNKLEE Susan		0+0 0+0	16:59.0
	DREISSIGACKER Hanah		1+3 0+1	18:44.5

Team Relay, Mixed

1	NORWAY	NOR	0+1 0+3	1:12:04.9
	BERGER Tora		0+0 0+0	15:45.6
	SOLEMDAL Synnoeve		0+0 0+2	17:16.2
	BOE Tarjei		0+1 0+0	19:29.4
	SVENDSEN Emil Hegle		0+0 0+1	19:33.7
2	FRANCE	FRA	0+1 0+7	1:12:24.9
	BRUNET Marie Laure		0+0 0+2	16:29.3
	DORIN HABERT Marie		0+1 0+2	16:45.8
	BOEUF Alexis		0+0 0+2	19:47.1
	FOURCADE Martin		0+0 0+1	19:22.7
3	CZECH REPUBLIC	CZE	0+3 0+2	1:12:37.2
	VITKOVA Veronika		0+2 0+1	16:30.0
	SOUKALOVA Gabriela		0+1 0+0	16:56.4
	SOUKUP Jaroslav		0+0 0+1	19:46.1
	MORAVEC Ondrej		0+0 0+0	19:24.7
8	USA	USA	0+3 0+4	1:13:37.7
	COOK Annelies		0+0 0+3	16:58.0
	DUNKLEE Susan		0+0 0+1	16:38.9
	BAILEY Lowell		0+2 0+0	20:01.1
	NORDGREN Leif		0+1 0+0	19:59.7

Winter Olympic Games, Sochi, Russia, 2014

Individual Race, Men

Rank	Name	Nation	Penalties	Finish
1	FOURCADE Martin	FRA	0+1+0+0	49:31.7
2	LESSER Erik	GER	0+0+0+0	49:43.9
3	GARANICHEV Evgeniy	RUS	0+1+0+0	50:06.2
8	BAILEY Lowell	USA	0+1+0+0	50:57.4
43	BURKE Tim	USA	0+2+0+2	54:21.2
49	CURRIER Russell	USA	2+2+0+0	55:07.5
82	NORDGREN Leif	USA	1+0+5+0	58:47.6

Sprint Race, Men

Rank	Name	Nation	Penalties	Finish
1	BJØRNDALEN Ole Einar	NOR	0+1	24:33.5
2	LANDERTINGER Dom	AUT	0+0	24:34.8
3	SOUKUP Jaroslav	CZE	0+0	24:39.2
19	BURKE Tim	USA	0+1	25:23.3
35	BAILEY Lowell	USA	1+1	26:04.1
44	NORDGREN Leif	USA	0+0	26:17.4
60	CURRIER Russell	USA	4+0	26:58.5

Pursuit Race, Men

Rank	Name	Nation	Penalties	Finish
1	FOURCADE Martin	FRA	0+0+1+0	33:48.6
2	MORAVEC Ondrej	CZE	0+0+0+0	34:02.7
3	BEATRIX Jean Guillaum	FRA	0+0+1+0	34:12.8
22	BURKE Tim	USA	1+0+0+1	35:37.0
38	BAILEY Lowell	USA	0+1+1+1	36:34.8
53	NORDGREN Leif	USA	3+2+1+1	39:31.4

Mass Start Race, Men

Rank	Name	Nation	Penalties	Finish
1	SVENDSEN Emil Hegle	NOR	0+0+0+0	42:29.1
2	FOURCADE Martin	FRA	1+0+0+0	42:29.1
3	MORAVEC Ondrej	CZE	0+0+0+0	42:42.9
21	BURKE Tim	USA	2+0+2+0	44:55.9
23	BAILEY Lowell	USA	2+1+1+1	45:19.2

Team Relay, Men

1	RUSSIA	RUS	0+4 0+4	1:12:15.
	VOLKOV Alexey		0+1 0+1	17:19.5
	USTYUGOV Evgeny		0+1 0+2	18:15.9
	MALYSHKO Dmitry		0+0 0+1	18:04.8
	SHIPULIN Anton		0+2 0+0	18:35.7
2	GERMANY	GER	0+1 0+1	1:12:19.4
	LESSER Erik		0+0 0+0	17:13.7
	BOEHM Daniel		0+0 0+1	18:17.4
	PEIFFER Arnd		0+0 0+0	17:54.5
	SCHEMPP Simon		0+1 0+0	18:53.8
3	AUSTRIA	AUT	0+4 0+3	1:12:45.7
	SUMANN Christoph		0+1 0+0	17:26.7
	MESOTITSCH Daniel		0+2 0+0	18:11.4
	EDER Simon		0+0 0+2	18:04.1
	LANDERTINGER Dominik		0+1 0+1	19:03.5
16	USA	USA	3+8 0+4	1:17:39.1
	BAILEY Lowell		0+0 0+0	17:20.7
	CURRIER Russell		3+3 0+2	20:11.3
	DOHERTY Sean		0+3 0+0	19:37.3
	NORDGREN Leif		0+2 0+2	20:29.8

Individual Race, Women

Rank	Name	Nation	Penalties	Finish
1	DOMRACHEVA Darya	BLR	0+1+0+0	43:19.6
2	GASPARIN Selina	SUI	0+0+0+0	44:35.3
3	SKARDINO Nadezhda	BLR	0+0+0+0	44:57.8
23	DREISSIGACKER Hannah	USA	1+0+0+1	47:51.7
35	DUNKLEE Susan	USA	1+1+2+1	48:54.1
55	STUDEBAKER Sara	USA	2+1+1+0	50:53.4
64	BARNES Lanny	USA	1+0+1+1	53:02.2

Sprint Race, Women

Rank	Name	Nation	Penalties	Finish
1	KUZMINA Anastasiya	SVK	0+0	21:06.8
2	VILUKHINA Olga	RUS	0+0	21:26.7
3	SEMERENKO Vita	UKR	0+0	21:28.5
14	DUNKLEE Susan	USA	0+1	21:48.3
44	STUDEBAKER Sara	USA	1+0	22:59.5
53	COOK Annelies	USA	0+2	23:23.4
65	DREISSIGACKER Hannah	USA	1+3	23:55.0

Pursuit Race, Women

Rank	Name	Nation	Penalties	Finish
1	DOMRACHEVA Darya	BLR	0+0+0+1	29:30.7
2	BERGER Tora	NOR	0+0+0+1	30:08.3
3	GREGORIN Teja	SLO	0+0+1+0	30:12.7
18	DUNKLEE Susan	USA	0+1+0+3	31:11.6
51	STUDEBAKER Sara	USA	3+1+0+1	35:00.0
54	COOK Annelies	USA	2+1+1+1	36:20.9

Mass Start Race, Women

Rank	Name	Nation	Penalties	Finish
1	DOMRACHEVA Darya	BLR	0+0+0+1	35:25.6
2	SOUKALOVA Gabriela	CZE	0+0+0+1	35:45.8
3	ECKHOFF Tiril	NOR	0+1+0+0	35:52.9
12	DUNKLEE Susan	USA	0+1+1+1	36:57.9

Team Relay, Women

1	UKRAINE	UKR	0+1 0+4	1:10:02.5
	SEMERENKO Vita		0+0 0+1	16:56.4
	DZHYMA Juliya		0+0 0+0	17:16.3
	SEMERENKO Valj		0+0 0+3	17:40.9
	PIDHRUSHNA Olena		0+1 0+0	18:08.9
2	RUSSIA	RUS	0+1 0+3	1:10:28.9
	ROMANOVA Yana		0+0 0+1	16:56.3
	ZAITSEVA Olga		0+1 0+1	17:43.2
	SHUMILOVA Ekaterina		0+0 0+0	17:43.3
	VILUKHINA Olga		0+0 0+1	18:06.1
3	NORWAY	NOR	0+1 0+4	1:10:40.1
	HORN Fanny Welle		0+1 0+2	17:40.5
	ECKHOFF Tiril		0+0 0+1	16:57.9
	FLATLAND Ann Kristin		0+0 0+0	17:43.6
	BERGER Tora		0+0 0+1	18:18.1
7	USA	USA	0+7 0+6	1:12:14.2
	DUNKLEE Susan		0+2 0+1	17:02.6
	DREISSIGACKER Hannah		0+3 0+3	18:08.3
	STUDEBAKER Sara		0+0 0+0	17:55.6
	COOK Annelies		0+2 0+2	19:07.7

Team Relay, Mixed

1	NORWAY	NOR	0+0 0+2	1:09:17.0
	BERGER Tora		0+0 0+2	15:55.6
	ECKHOFF Tiril		0+0 0+0	16:11.9
	BJOERNDALEN Ole Einar		0+0 0+0	17:50.9
	SVENDSEN Emil Hegle		0+0 0+0	19:18.6
2	CZECH REPUBLIC	CZE	0+4 0+3	1:09:49.6
	VITKOVA Veronika		0+0 0+1	16:01.9
	SOUKALOVA Gabriela		0+3 0+0	16:04.5
	SOUKUP Jaroslav		0+1 0+1	18:35.1
	MORAVEC Ondrej		0+0 0+1	19:08.1
3	ITALY	ITA	0+1 0+5	1:10:15.2
	WIERER Dorothea		0+0 0+1	15:57.9
	OBERHOFER Karin		0+0 0+1	16:28.0
	WINDISCH Dominik		0+1 0+3	18:46.6
	HOFER Lukas		0+0 0+0	19:02.7
8	USA	USA	1+7 0+6	1:12:20.1
	DUNKLEE Susan		0+1 0+1	16:02.5
	DREISSIGACKER Hannah		1+3 0+1	17:55.5
	BURKE Tim		0+3 0+1	19:02.9
	BAILEY Lowell		0+0 0+3	19:19.2

World Championships, Kontiolahti, Finland, 2015

Individual Race, Men

Rank	Name	Nation	Penalties	Finish
1	FOURCADE Martin	FRA	0+1+0+0	47:29.4
2	SVENDSEN Emil Hegle	NOR	0+0+0+0	47:50.3
3	MORAVEC Ondrej	CZE	0+1+0+0	48:09.9
24	BAILEY Lowell	USA	2+0+0+0	50:39.4
31	BURKE Tim	USA	1+1+0+2	51:22.1
33	NORDGREN Leif	USA	0+1+1+1	51:25.5
47	DOHERTY Sean	USA	0+1+2+0	52:44.9

Sprint Race, Men

Rank	Name	Nation	Penalties	Finish
1	BOE Johannes Thingnes	NOR	0+1	24:12.8
2	SMITH Nathan	CAN	0+1	24:24.9
3	BOE Tarjei	NOR	0+0	24:38.1
15	BURKE Tim	USA	1+1	25:12.4
17	BAILEY Lowell	USA	0+1	25:14.3
45	NORDGREN Leif	USA	0+3	26:09.4
55	DOHERTY Sean	USA	2+1	26:41.7

Pursuit Race, Men

Rank	Name	Nation	Penalties	Finish
1	LESSER Erik	GER	0+0+0+0	30:47.9
2	SHIPULIN Anton	RUS	0+1+0+0	31:04.9
3	BOE Tarjei	NOR	0+0+1+0	31:06.6
20	BURKE Tim	USA	0+0+2+2	32:36.0
36	BAILEY Lowell	USA	0+0+4+1	33:50.5
45	DOHERTY Sean	USA	1+1+0+1	34:43.8
51	NORDGREN Leif	USA	2+2+0+2	35:14.1

Mass Start Race, Men

Rank	Name	Nation	Penalties	Finish
1	FAK Jakov	SLO	0+0+1+0	36:24.9
2	MORAVEC Ondrej	CZE	1+0+0+0	36:25.9
3	BOE Tarjei	NOR	0+0+1+0	36:28.6
13	BAILEY Lowell	USA	1+0+0+0	36:59.9
14	BURKE Tim	USA	1+0+1+1	37:10.5

Team Relay, Men

1	GERMANY	GER	0+0 0+3	1:13:49.5
	LESSER Erik		0+0 0+0	18:33.9
	BOEHM Daniel		0+0 0+2	18:50.8
	PEIFFER Arnd		0+0 0+0	18:24.7
	SCHEMPP Simon		0+0 0+1	18:00.1
2	NORWAY	NOR	0+0 0+6	1:14:04.9
	BJOERNDALEN Ole Einar		0+0 0+0	18:27.5
	BOE Tarjei		0+0 0+3	19:05.3
	BOE Johannes Thingnes		0+0 0+2	18:31.9
	SVENDSEN Emil Hegle		0+0 0+1	18:00.2
3	FRANCE	FRA	0+3 0+1	1:14:23.1
	FOURCADE Simon		0+0 0+0	18:28.8
	BEATRIX Jean Guillaume		0+1 0+1	18:52.8
	FILLON MAILLET Quentin		0+1 0+0	19:08.3
	FOURCADE Martin		0+1 0+0	17:53.2
14	USA	USA	0+5 2+6	1:17:21.1
	BAILEY Lowell		0+0 0+2	18:57.8
	NORDGREN Leif		0+1 0+1	18:58.5
	BURKE Tim		0+1 2+3	20:15.1
	DOHERTY Sean		0+3 0+0	19:09.7

Individual Race, Women

Rank	Name	Nation	Penalties	Finish
1	YURLOVA Ekaterina	RUS	0+0+0+0	41:32.2
2	SOUKALOVA Gabriela	CZE	0+0+0+1	41:55.4
3	MAKARAINEN Kaisa	FIN	0+1+1+0	41:56.6
12	DUNKLEE Susan	USA	2+0+0+1	44:15.2
47	COOK Annelies	USA	0+0+0+4	46:59.0
51	EGAN Clare	USA	0+0+2+2	47:17.9
67	DREISSIGACKER Hannah	USA	2+1+1+1	48:21.9

Sprint Race, Women

Rank	Name	Nation	Penalties	Finish
1	DORIN HABERT Marie	FRA	0+1	22:16.8
2	NOWAKOWSKA-ZIEMNIA	POL	0+0	22:26.4
3	SEMERENKO Valj	UKR	0+1	22:36.5
40	EGAN Clare	USA	2+2	24:47.2
42	DUNKLEE Susan	USA	1+2	24:52.0
61	DREISSIGACKER Hannah	USA	4+2	25:30.1
68	COOK Annelies	USA	2+3	25:45.3

Pursuit Race, Women

Rank	Name	Nation	Penalties	Finish
1	DORIN HABERT Marie	FRA	0+0+2+1	30:07.7
2	DAHLMEIER Laura	GER	1+0+0+1	30:23.0
3	NOWAKOWSKA-ZIEMNIA	POL	0+1+2+0	30:39.3
34	DUNKLEE Susan	USA	1+1+2+2	34:05.8
52	EGAN Clare	USA	1+1+3+2	36:36.9

Mass Start Race, Women

Rank	Name	Nation	Penalties	Finish
1	SEMERENKO Valj	UKR	0+0+0+0	34:32.9
2	PREUSS Franziska	GER	0+0+0+1	34:39.1
3	OBERHOFER Karin	ITA	1+1+0+0	34:45.5
20	DUNKLEE Susan	USA	1+1+2+1	36:33.9

Team Relay, Women

1	GERMANY	GER	0+1 0+5	1:11:54.6
	HILDEBRAND Franziska		0+0 0+2	18:18.8
	PREUSS Franziska		0+1 0+2	18:04.9
	HINZ Vanessa		0+0 0+1	18:17.7
	DAHLMEIER Laura		0+0 0+0	17:13.2
2	FRANCE	FRA	1+6 0+3	1:12:54.9
	BESCOND Anais		0+0 0+1	18:13.8
	LATUILLIERE Enora		0+1 0+1	18:24.3
	BRAISAZ Justine		1+3 0+1	19:22.1
	DORIN HABERT Marie		0+2 0+0	16:54.7
3	ITALY	ITA	0+3 0+6	1:13:00.7
	VITTOZZI Lisa		0+0 0+0	18:11.2
	OBERHOFER Karin		0+1 0+3	18:03.2
	GONTIER Nicole		0+2 0+2	19:26.2
	WIERER Dorothea		0+0 0+1	17:20.1
12	USA	USA	0+7 0+7	1:15:39.4
	DUNKLEE Susan		0+2 0+0	18:10.0
	DREISSIGACKER Hannah		0+3 0+2	19:10.4
	COOK Annelies		0+2 0+2	19:26.4
	EGAN Clare		0+0 0+3	18:52.6

Team Relay, Mixed

1	CZECH REPUBLIC	CZE	0+3 0+5	1:20:27.2
	VITKOVA Veronika		0+2 0+2	19:50.5
	SOUKALOVA Gabriela		0+0 0+0	19:44.8
	SLESINGR Michal		0+0 0+2	20:42.1
	MORAVEC Ondrej		0+1 0+1	20:09.8
2	FRANCE	FRA	0+1 0+7	1:20:47.4
	BESCOND Anais		0+1 0+3	20:35.6
	DORIN HABERT Marie		0+0 0+1	19:16.2
	BEATRIX Jean Guillaume		0+0 0+3	21:24.4
	FOURCADE Martin		0+0 0+0	19:31.2
3	NORWAY	NOR	0+0 1+3	1:20:54.9
	BIRKELAND Fanny Horn		0+0 0+0	20:20.3
	ECKHOFF Tiril		0+0 1+3	20:21.7
	BOE Johannes Thingnes		0+0 0+0	20:08.6
	BOE Tarjei		0+0 0+0	20:04.3
8	USA	USA	1+5 0+3	1:22:13.8
	DUNKLEE Susan		0+1 0+1	20:01.2
	DREISSIGACKER Hannah		1+3 0+2	21:10.6
	BAILEY Lowell		0+0 0+0	20:54.6
	NORDGREN Leif		0+1 0+0	20:07.4

World Championships, Oslo, Norway, 2016

Individual Race, Men

Rank	Name	Nation	Penalties	Finish
1	FOURCADE Martin	FRA	0+1+0+0	49:13.9
2	LANDERTINGER Dominik	AUT	0+0+0+0	49:19.0
3	EDER Simon	AUT	0+0+0+0	49:28.3
15	BAILEY Lowell	USA	0+1+0+0	51:57.6
27	NORDGREN Leif	USA	0+1+0+1	52:54.5
34	DOHERTY Sean	USA	1+0+1+0	53:27.5
44	BURKE Tim	USA	0+1+0+3	54:28.1

Sprint Race, Men

Rank	Name	Nation	Penalties	Finish
1	FOURCADE Martin	FRA	0+0	25:35.4
2	BJØRNDALEN Ole Einar	NOR	0+0	26:02.3
3	SEMENOV Sergey	UKR	0+0	26:03.0
14	BURKE Tim	USA	0+1	26:44.5
18	NORDGREN Leif	USA	0+0	26:52.2
29	BAILEY Lowell	USA	1+0	27:10.2
43	DOHERTY Sean	USA	1+1	27:31.9

Pursuit Race, Men

Rank	Name	Nation	Penalties	Finish
1	FOURCADE Martin	FRA	0+0+1+2	32:56.5
2	BJØRNDALEN Ole Einar	NOR	1+0+0+1	33:16.6
3	SVENDSEN Emil Hegle	NOR	0+0+0+1	33:27.7
17	BURKE Tim	USA	0+0+1+2	34:23.8
36	BAILEY Lowell	USA	0+0+2+3	35:53.7
45	DOHERTY Sean	USA	0+2+1+2	36:48.6
52	NORDGREN Leif	USA	2+2+1+2	38:07.3

Mass Start Race, Men

Rank	Name	Nation	Penalties	Finish
1	BOE Johannes Thingnes	NOR	0+0+1+0	37:05.1
2	FOURCADE Martin	FRA	1+0+0+0	37:07.9
3	BJØRNDALEN Ole Einar	NOR	0+0+0+0	37:11.8
10	BAILEY Lowell	USA	0+0+0+1	37:46.8
12	BURKE Tim	USA	0+0+1+1	37:58.5
DNF	NORDGREN Leif	USA	2+2+2+	

Team Relay, Men

1	NORWAY	NOR	0+1	0+5	1:13:16.8
	BJOERNDALEN Ole Einar		0+0	0+2	18:09.3
	BOE Tarjei		0+1	0+1	18:01.9
	BOE Johannes Thingnes		0+0	0+0	18:03.1
	SVENDSEN Emil Hegle		0+0	0+2	19:02.5
2	GERMANY	GER	0+2	0+3	1:13:28.3
	LESSER Erik		0+0	0+0	18:00.2
	DOLL Benedikt		0+1	0+1	18:11.3
	PEIFFER Arnd		0+1	0+1	18:32.2
	SCHEMPP Simon		0+0	0+1	18:44.6
3	CANADA	CAN	0+1	0+4	1:13:40.2
	GOW Christian		0+0	0+0	18:14.9
	SMITH Nathan		0+1	0+1	17:57.5
	GOW Scott		0+0	0+3	18:36.3
	GREEN Brendan		0+0	0+0	18:51.5
8	USA	USA	0+3	0+2	1:14:44.1
	BAILEY Lowell		0+0	0+1	18:07.4
	NORDGREN Leif		0+1	0+1	19:09.0
	BURKE Tim		0+1	0+0	18:33.0
	DOHERTY Sean		0+1	0+0	18:54.7

Individual Race, Women

Rank	Name	Nation	Penalties	Finish
1	DORIN HABERT Marie	FRA	0+0+0+1	44:02.8
2	BESCOND Anais	FRA	0+0+0+1	44:15.0
3	DAHLMEIER Laura	GER	1+0+1+0	45:20.6
18	DUNKLEE Susan	USA	1+1+1+0	46:32.3
32	DREISSIGACKER Hannah	USA	1+0+0+1	47:48.0
66	EGAN Clare	USA	0+3+0+1	50:44.7
77	COOK Annelies	USA	4+2+1+0	52:52.2

Sprint Race, Women

Rank	Name	Nation	Penalties	Finish
1	ECKHOFF Tiril	NOR	0+0	21:10.8
2	DORIN HABERT Marie	FRA	0+0	21:25.8
3	DAHLMEIER Laura	GER	1+0	21:30.6
8	DUNKLEE Susan	USA	0+1	21:59.0
18	DREISSIGACKER Hannah	USA	0+0	22:28.8
63	COOK Annelies	USA	0+1	23:42.8
84	EGAN Clare	USA	0+1	24:58.3

Pursuit Race, Women

Rank	Name	Nation	Penalties	Finish
1	DAHLMEIER Laura	GER	0+0+0+0	30:49.2
2	WIERER Dorothea	ITA	0+1+1+0	31:37.5
3	DORIN HABERT Marie	FRA	0+0+2+1	31:46.5
10	DUNKLEE Susan	USA	0+1+3+0	32:41.7
36	DREISSIGACKER Hannah	USA	2+0+1+1	34:32.4

Mass Start Race, Women

Rank	Name	Nation	Penalties	Finish
1	DORIN HABERT Marie	FRA	0+0+0+0	35:28.5
2	DAHLMEIER Laura	GER	0+0+1+0	35:35.8
3	MAKARAINEN Kaisa	FIN	0+0+1+0	35:36.6
11	DUNKLEE Susan	USA	2+0+0+1	36:28.9
27	DREISSIGACKER Hannah	USA	0+2+1+1	38:43.9

Team Relay, Women

1	NORWAY	NOR	0+3	0+3	1:07:10.0
	SOLEMDAL Synnoeve		0+0	0+0	16:39.0
	BIRKELAND Fanny Horn		0+1	0+1	17:02.9
	ECKHOFF Tiril		0+0	0+0	16:19.4
	OLSBU Marte		0+2	0+2	17:08.7
2	FRANCE	FRA	0+5	0+3	1:07:15.3
	BRAISAZ Justine		0+3	0+2	17:26.9
	BESCOND Anais		0+0	0+0	16:10.9
	CHEVALIER Anais		0+0	0+1	16:52.1
	DORIN HABERT Marie		0+2	0+0	16:45.4

3	GERMANY	GER	0+0 0+4	1:07:38.6
	PREUSS Franziska		0+0 0+2	16:49.2
	HILDEBRAND Franziska		0+0 0+0	16:42.8
	HAMMERSCHMIDT Mari		0+0 0+2	16:52.6
	DAHLMEIER Laura		0+0 0+0	17:14.0
13	USA	USA	0+2 0+6	1:10:57.1
	DUNKLEE Susan		0+0 0+2	16:53.7
	DREISSIGACKER Hannah		0+2 0+1	17:47.3
	EGAN Clare		0+0 0+2	18:17.6
	COOK Annelies		0+0 0+1	17:58.5

Team Relay, Mixed

1	FRANCE	FRA	0+2 0+6	1:14:01.0
	BESCOND Anais		0+0 0+3	18:10.7
	DORIN HABERT Marie		0+0 0+1	17:34.2
	FILLON MAILLET Quentin		0+2 0+1	19:04.5
	FOURCADE Martin		0+0 0+1	19:11.6
2	GERMANY	GER	0+5 0+2	1:14:05.3
	PREUSS Franziska		0+2 0+0	17:51.8
	HILDEBRAND Franziska		0+2 0+0	17:52.9
	PEIFFER Arnd		0+0 0+1	19:04.9
	SCHEMPP Simon		0+1 0+1	19:15.7
3	NORWAY	NOR	0+7 0+3	1:14:15.4
	OLSBU Marte		0+1 0+0	17:37.1
	ECKHOFF Tiril		0+2 0+2	18:07.4
	BOE Johannes Thingnes		0+1 0+1	19:05.7
	BOE Tarjei		0+3 0+0	19:25.2
10	USA	USA	0+3 0+2	1:16:20.6
	DUNKLEE Susan		0+0 0+0	17:35.5
	DREISSIGACKER Hannah		0+2 0+1	19:00.3
	BAILEY Lowell		0+0 0+0	19:46.9
	DOHERTY Sean		0+1 0+1	19:57.9

World Championships, Hochfilzen, Austria, 2017
Individual Race, Men

Rank	Name	Nation	Penalties	Finish
1	BAILEY Lowell	USA	0+0+0+0	48:07.4
2	MORAVEC Ondrej	CZE	0+0+0+0	48:10.7
3	FOURCADE Martin	FRA	1+0+1+0	48:28.6
23	NORDGREN Leif	USA	1+0+0+1	51:01.0
36	BURKE Tim	USA	1+1+0+2	52:21.8
53	DOHERTY Sean	USA	1+1+2+0	54:11.8

Sprint Race, Men

Rank	Name	Nation	Penalties	Finish
1	DOLL Benedikt	GER	0+0	23:27.4
2	BOE Johannes Thingnes	NOR	0+0	23:28.1
3	FOURCADE Martin	FRA	1+1	23:50.5
4	BAILEY Lowell	USA	0+0	23:56.9
26	NORDGREN Leif	USA	0+1	24:51.7
39	DOHERTY Sean	USA	2+0	25:05.1
40	BURKE Tim	USA	0+2	25:06.0

Pursuit Race, Men

Rank	Name	Nation	Penalties	Finish
1	FOURCADE Martin	FRA	0+0+0+1	30:16.9
2	BOE Johannes Thingnes	NOR	1+1+1+0	30:39.7
3	BJØRNDALEN Ole Einar	NOR	0+0+0+1	30:42.5
6	BAILEY Lowell	USA	0+0+1+0	30:51.6
32	BURKE Tim	USA	1+0+1+1	33:02.3
49	NORDGREN Leif	USA	2+0+2+1	34:28.0
55	DOHERTY Sean	USA	2+3+3+1	35:32.1

Mass Start Race, Men

Rank	Name	Nation	Penalties	Finish
1	SCHEMPP Simon	GER	0+0+0+0	35:38.3
2	BOE Johannes Thingnes	NOR	0+0+0+1	35:47.3
3	EDER Simon	AUT	0+0+0+0	35:48.4
6	BAILEY Lowell	USA	0+0+0+0	36:11.8

Team Relay, Men

1	RUSSIA	RUS	0+1 0+2	1:14:15.0
	VOLKOV Alexey		0+1 0+1	18:49.2
	TSVETKOV Maxim		0+0 0+0	18:35.0
	BABIKOV Anton		0+0 0+0	18:57.7
	SHIPULIN Anton		0+0 0+1	17:53.1
2	FRANCE	FRA	0+4 0+0	1:14:20.8
	BEATRIX Jean Guillaume		0+0 0+0	18:34.6
	FILLON MAILLET Quentin		0+1 0+0	18:40.9
	DESTHIEUX Simon		0+3 0+0	19:18.9
	FOURCADE Martin		0+0 0+0	17:46.4
3	AUSTRIA	AUT	0+4 0+6	1:14:35.1
	MESOTITSCH Daniel		0+0 0+1	18:50.3
	EBERHARD Julian		0+2 0+2	18:39.3
	EDER Simon		0+1 0+2	18:52.8
	LANDERTINGER Dominik		0+1 0+1	18:12.7
7	USA	USA	0+4 0+4	1:16:05.5
	BAILEY Lowell		0+1 0+0	18:41.6
	NORDGREN Leif		0+0 0+1	18:51.6
	BURKE Tim		0+1 0+3	19:49.9
	DOHERTY Sean		0+2 0+0	18:42.4

Individual Race, Women

Rank	Name	Nation	Penalties	Finish
1	DAHLMEIER Laura	GER	1+0+0+0	41:30.1
2	KOUKALOVA Gabriela	CZE	1+0+0+0	41:54.8
3	RUNGGALDIER Alexia	ITA	0+0+0+0	43:15.7
6	DUNKLEE Susan	USA	1+0+0+1	43:36.9
22	EGAN Clare	USA	0+0+0+2	45:25.1
56	REID Joanne	USA	1+2+1+0	48:06.8
87	PHANEUF Madeleine	USA	0+2+0+2	51:08.4

Sprint Race, Women

Rank	Name	Nation	Penalties	Finish
1	KOUKALOVA Gabriela	CZE	0+0	19:12.6
2	DAHLMEIER Laura	GER	0+0	19:16.6
3	CHEVALIER Anais	FRA	0+0	19:37.7
20	EGAN Clare	USA	0+0	20:25.0
29	DUNKLEE Susan	USA	1+2	20:40.0
49	REID Joanne	USA	1+1	21:10.2
78	PHANEUF Madeleine	USA	0+2	22:09.2

Pursuit Race, Women

Rank	Name	Nation	Penalties	Finish
1	DAHLMEIER Laura	GER	0+0+0+1	28:02.3
2	DOMRACHEVA Darya	BLR	0+0+0+0	28:13.9
3	KOUKALOVA Gabriela	CZE	2+0+1+0	28:18.9
22	DUNKLEE Susan	USA	1+0+1+2	29:47.0
38	REID Joanne	USA	0+0+0+1	30:39.6
41	EGAN Clare	USA	1+0+2+0	31:03.6

Mass Start Race, Women

Rank	Name	Nation	Penalties	Finish
1	DAHLMEIER Laura	GER	0+0+0+0	33:13.8
2	DUNKLEE Susan	USA	0+0+0+0	33:18.4
3	MAKARAINEN Kaisa	FIN	1+0+0+0	33:33.9
24	EGAN Clare	USA	1+0+1+2	36:17.9

Team Relay, Women

Rank	Name	Nation	Penalties		Finish
1	GERMANY	GER	0+2	0+7	1:11:16.6
	HINZ Vanessa		0+0	0+2	18:03.6
	HAMMERSCHMIDT Mar		0+1	0+3	17:58.5
	HILDEBRAND Franziska		0+0	0+0	18:13.9
	DAHLMEIER Laura		0+1	0+2	17:00.6
2	UKRAINE	UKR	0+2	0+2	1:11:23.0
	VARVYNETS Iryna		0+0	0+1	18:25.3
	DZHIMA Yuliia		0+1	0+1	17:56.5
	MERKUSHYNA Anastasi		0+1	0+0	18:03.9
	PIDHRUSHNA Olena		0+0	0+0	16:57.3

Rank	Name	Nation	Penalties		Finish
3	FRANCE	FRA	0+3	0+4	1:11:24.7
	CHEVALIER Anais		0+0	0+1	17:53.0
	AYMONIER Celia		0+0	0+3	18:31.8
	BRAISAZ Justine		0+3	0+0	18:14.9
	DORIN HABERT Marie		0+0	0+0	16:45.0
14	USA	USA	0+3	0+10	1:14:53.6
	EGAN Clare		0+1	0+3	19:13.5
	DUNKLEE Susan		0+0	0+2	17:19.3
	REID Joanne		0+1	0+3	19:15.8
	PHANEUF Madeleine		0+1	0+2	19:05.0

Team Relay, Mixed

Rank	Name	Nation	Penalties		Finish
1	GERMANY	GER	0+2	0+5	1:09:06.4
	HINZ Vanessa		0+0	0+2	16:37.4
	DAHLMEIER Laura		0+2	0+2	16:26.6
	PEIFFER Arnd		0+0	0+0	18:05.7
	SCHEMPP Simon		0+0	0+1	17:56.7
2	FRANCE	FRA	0+1	1+7	1:09:08.6
	CHEVALIER Anais		0+0	0+2	16:41.5
	DORIN HABERT Marie		0+0	0+2	16:23.3
	FILLON MAILLET Quentin		0+1	1+3	18:51.4
	FOURCADE Martin		0+0	0+0	17:12.4
3	RUSSIA	RUS	0+1	0+3	1:09:09.6
	PODCHUFAROVA Olga		0+0	0+0	17:03.9
	AKIMOVA Tatiana		0+1	0+0	16:22.1
	LOGINOV Alexander		0+0	0+3	18:31.1
	SHIPULIN Anton		0+0	0+0	17:12.5
16	USA	USA	1+7	1+6	1:12:26.6
	DUNKLEE Susan		0+2	0+2	16:35.2
	EGAN Clare		0+1	1+3	18:29.8
	BAILEY Lowell		0+1	0+1	18:28.9
	DOHERTY Sean		1+3	0+0	18:52.7

Winter Olympic Games, Pyeongchang, Korea, 2018

Individual Race, Men

Rank	Name	Nation	Penalties	Finish
1	BOE Johannes Thingnes	NOR	1+0+0+1	48:03.8
2	FAK Jakov	SLO	0+0+0+0	48:09.3
3	LANDERTINGER Dominik	AUT	0+0+0+0	48:18.0
41	BURKE Tim	USA	1+1+0+2	52:07.2
44	DOHERTY Sean	USA	2+0+1+0	52:25.6
53	BAILEY Lowell	USA	2+1+0+1	54:11.8
66	NORDGREN Leif	USA	1+1+3+0	54:31.1

Sprint Race, Men

Rank	Name	Nation	Penalties	Finish
1	PEIFFER Arnd	GER	0+0	23:33.8
2	KRCMAR Michal	CZE	0+0	23:43.2
3	WINDISCH Dominik	ITA	0+1	23:46.5
33	BAILEY Lowell	USA	0+1	24:54.4
47	BURKE Tim	USA	2+2	25:26.3
58	NORDGREN Leif	USA	1+1	25:49.0
65	DOHERTY Sean	USA	4+0	25:55.2

Pursuit Race, Men

Rank	Name	Nation	Penalties	Finish
1	FOURCADE Martin	FRA	1+0+0+0	32:51.7
2	SAMUELSSON Sebastian	SWE	0+0+1+0	33:03.7
3	DOLL Benedikt	GER	0+0+1+0	33:06.8
17	BURKE Tim	USA	0+1+1+0	35:11.3
32	BAILEY Lowell	USA	0+0+3+2	36:43.3
50	NORDGREN Leif	USA	2+2+0+1	38:40.4

Mass Start Race, Men

Rank	Name	Nation	Penalties	Finish
1	FOURCADE Martin	FRA	1+0+0+1	35:47.3
2	SCHEMPP Simon	GER	0+0+0+1	35:47.3
3	SVENDSEN Emil Hegle	NOR	1+0+1+0	35:58.5
	No USA Qualifiers			

Team Relay, Men

1	SWEDEN	SWE	0+2 0+5	1:15:16.5
	FEMLING Peppe		0+0 0+1	18:50.9
	NELIN Jesper		0+1 0+3	18:59.9
	SAMUELSSON Sebastian		0+1 0+0	18:31.5
	LINDSTROEM Fredrik		0+0 0+1	18:54.2
2	NORWAY	NOR	0+7 1+8	1:16:12.0
	BIRKELAND Lars Helge		0+1 0+1	18:48.1
	BOE Tarjei		0+3 0+3	19:17.5
	BOE Johannes Thingnes		0+0 0+1	18:16.3
	SVENDSEN Emil Hegle		0+3 1+3	19:50.1
3	GERMANY	GER	0+3 3+7	1:17:23.6
	LESSER Erik		0+0 0+1	18:23.6
	DOLL Benedikt		0+0 2+3	19:48.2
	PEIFFER Arnd		0+0 0+0	18:23.8
	SCHEMPP Simon		0+3 1+3	20:48.0
6	USA	USA	2+6 0+8	2+14
	BAILEY Lowell		0+2 0+2	19:14.2
	DOHERTY Sean		0+1 0+0	19:14.0
	BURKE Tim		0+0 0+3	19:32.5
	NORDGREN Leif		2+3 0+3	21:06.0

Individual Race, Women

Rank	Name	Nation	Penalties	Finish
1	OEBERG Hanna	SWE	0+0+0+0	41:07.2
2	KUZMINA Anastasiya	SVK	0+1+1+0	41:31.9
3	DAHLMEIER Laura	GER	1+0+0+0	43:48.4
19	DUNKLEE Susan	USA	0+1+0+1	44:33.5
22	REID Joanne	USA	0+1+0+0	44:41.3
62	EGAN Clare	USA	0+3+0+1	48:00.8
67	DREISSIGACKER Emily	USA	2+1+0+1	48:16.4

Sprint Race, Women

Rank	Name	Nation	Penalties	Finish
1	DAHLMEIER Laura	GER	0+0	21:06.2
2	OLSBU Marte	NOR	1+0	21:30.4
3	VITKOVA Veronika	CZE	0+1	21:32.0
51	DREISSIGACKER Emily	USA	0+1	23:27.2
61	EGAN Clare	USA	1+2	23:51.6
66	DUNKLEE Susan	USA	1+4	24:13.1
86	REID Joanne	USA	4+3	26:18.8

Pursuit Race, Women

Rank	Name	Nation	Penalties	Finish
1	DAHLMEIER Laura	GER	0+1+0+0	30:35.3
2	KUZMINA Anastasiya	SVK	0+1+2+1	0:58.7
3	BESCOND Anais	FRA	0+0+1+0	31:04.9
47	DREISSIGACKER Emily	USA	0+1+1+2	5:36.7

Mass Start Race, Women

Rank	Name	Nation	Penalties	Finish
1	KUZMINA Anastasiya	SVK	0+0+0+1	35:23.0
2	DOMRACHEVA Darya	BLR	0+0+1+0	35:41.8
3	ECKHOFF Tiril	NOR	1+0+1+0	35:50.7
	No USA Qualifiers			

Team Relay, Women

1	BELARUS	BLR	0+3 0+6	1:12:03.4
	SKARDINO Nadezhda		0+0 0+2	17:35.2
	KRYUKO Iryna		0+1 0+0	18:08.2
	ALIMBEKAVA Dzinara		0+2 0+1	18:52.4
	DOMRACHEVA Darya		0+0 0+3	17:27.6
2	SWEDEN	SWE	0+5 0+7	1:12:14.1
	PERSSON Linn		0+2 0+2	17:35.1
	BRORSSON Mona		0+3 0+3	19:16.8
	MAGNUSSON Anna		0+0 0+2	18:25.9
	OEBERG Hanna		0+0 0+0	16:56.3
3	FRANCE	FRA	0+7 0+9	1:12:21.0
	CHEVALIER Anais		0+2 0+2	17:20.8
	DORIN HABERT Marie		0+1 0+1	18:25.6
	BRAISAZ Justine		0+3 0+3	18:40.6
	BESCOND Anais		0+1 0+3	17:54.0
13	USA	USA	1+5 0+5	1:14:05.3
	DUNKLEE Susan		0+0 0+1	16:56.6
	EGAN Clare		0+0 0+0	18:42.4
	REID Joanne		1+3 0+1	18:29.1
	DREISSIGACKER Emily		0+2 0+3	19:25.2

Team Relay, Mixed

1	FRANCE	FRA	0+1	0+3	1:08:34.3
	DORIN HABERT Marie		0+0	0+0	15:51.1
	BESCOND Anais		0+1	0+3	16:46.4
	DESTHIEUX Simon		0+0	0+0	17:58.4
	FOURCADE Martin		0+0	0+0	17:58.4
2	NORWAY	NOR	0+6	1+6	1:08:55.2
	OLSBU Marte		0+2	0+1	16:16.9
	ECKHOFF Tiril		0+2	1+3	16:55.1
	BOE Johannes Thingnes		0+0	0+1	17:24.4
	SVENDSEN Emil Hegle		0+1	0+1	18:18.8
3	ITALY	ITA	0+1	0+6	1:09:01.2
	VITTOZZI Lisa		0+0	0+0	15:44.1
	WIERER Dorothea		0+0	0+3	16:34.4
	HOFER Lukas		0+0	0+1	18:17.4
	WINDISCH Dominik		0+1	0+2	18:25.3
15	USA	USA	1+3	3+6	1:12:05.4
	DUNKLEE Susan		0+2	0+0	16:07.9
	REID Joanne		0+0	3+3	18:50.7
	BURKE Tim		0+0	0+3	18:28.9
	BAILEY Lowell		0+1	0+0	18:37.7

Glossary and Biathlon Terminology

ability   A concept that refers to a hypothetical basis that underlies (or supports) performance in a number of tasks or activities. Ability is usually thought to be a relatively stable characteristic or trait that is usually thought of as being either genetically determined or developed through the processes in growth and maturation.

acceleration   Refers to the change in velocity involving speed or direction of a moving body.

acidosis   The production and accumulation of lactic acid and hydrogen ions (H++) that impairs energy metabolism and reduces the contractile force of the muscles.

aerobic capacity   A person's maximum level of oxygen uptake per kilogram of body weight per minute (VO2), or the ability to utilize oxygen for the release of energy during moderate and high intensity physical activities.

aerobic endurance   One's ability to perform physical activity of high intensity over a relatively long period using the aerobic process.

aerobic process   The energy-releasing process which depends upon the presence of oxygen.

aerobic training   Training designed to sustain or increase the level of one's aerobic capacity.

altitude training   Training designed to acclimatize oneself to the metabolic changes that will occur during prolonged physical activity at higher altitudes.

ammo   Ammunition.

ampumahiihtolitto   The Finnish term for biathlon.

anaerobic capacity   A person's maximum level to sustain an oxygen debt, or the ability to produce energy through a chemical reaction without the use of oxygen during high intensity physical activities.

anaerobic endurance   One's ability to perform physical activity of high intensity over a relatively long period using the anaerobic process.

anaerobic process   The energy releasing process occurring through a chemical reaction within the muscle cells without the use of oxygen.

anaerobic training   Training designed to sustain or increase the level of one's anaerobic capacity.

autogen training   Training designed to reduce the level of muscular tension through the mental powers of suggestion.

biathlon   Word of Greek origin, meaning "two tests," modern term for the winter sport of nordic skiing and rifle marksmanship.

biomechanics The application of the scientific principles of mechanics and physics to understand the movement and actions of the human body.

capacity analysis An analysis (testing and evaluation) of an athlete's capacities that have a meaningful effect on the performance level and of the ability to meet the demands of physical and psychological stresses.

center of gravity (COG) refers to the gravitational pull through the center of weight or mass of an object.

CISM Abbreviation: for Conseil International du Sport Militaire (French), International Union of Military Sport.

click One part of a minute in elevation or windage of the rifle sights.

cognition The psychological processes which cause thinking and knowing as well as conscious reactions.

combo training Acronym for combination training, designed to bring together shooting with the stress of physical training.

concurrent training Training designed so as to sustain or improve more than one component of athletic performance simultaneously during the same training session, such as combinations of skiing and shooting.

competition training Training that closely imitates competition, or taking part in a competition, so as to familiarize one with competitive strategies and tactical situations.

condition Physical as well as psychological training state in relation to the demands of the sport or the stress of bodily activity.

concentration Fixing or focusing one's thoughts and efforts as well as attention on a given task or idea.

confidence The belief in one's own abilities.

coordination The behavior of two or more joints and the nerve-muscle systems' interrelation in the performance of a set of movements.

diagonal stride The classical or traditional ski stride used in forward movement, coordinating the use of diagonally opposite arms and legs.

distance training Training of a constant, moderate intensity over a relatively long period which is designed to induce a training adaptation on the aerobic capacity.

double-poling The ski technique for forward movement using the arms and ski poles.

dynamic muscle contraction Muscle contraction caused by a shortening or lengthening of the muscle fibers.

effector anticipation Estimating the difference between how long a response or movement will take and allowance for the interval in initiating the actions so that some critical aspect of the movement occurs at the proper time.

electromyography (EMG)   The measure the electrical discharge from a muscle, which indicates the action potential of that muscle.

elevation (rifle sights)   The term used of and for the rear sight part which determines the strike of the bullet on a vertical axis.

emotion   The psychological processes which are the background for and influences on one's experiences of love, gladness, fear, hate, anger and other reactions of feelings.

endurance   One's level or capacity to sustain physical and/or activity of high intensity over a relatively long period.

energy   Concerning biomechanical study, it relates to the capacity of a body to perform work, of the two types utilized most important for biathlon is kinetic, or the energy a body has because it is moving, such as skier whose weight and velocity determine kinetic energy. It also refers to the fuel used by muscles to create movement of which there are two main types, aerobic and anaerobic.

erogenic   Derived from Greek, usually interpreted as "work producing" or "work enhancing" and used today to mean "increasing work output."

exteroceptors   Sensory information or feedback that provides information about the movements of objects in the environment.

extrinsic feedback   Verbalized or verbalizable information provided in post-response outcome of a task.

eye relief   The distance between the eye and the rear sight aperture.

fartslek   (Swedish term meaning "speed play") A term for a type of interval training, alternating between fast and slow speeds.

feedback   Response produced information that is received, both internal and external that provides both the knowledge of results (KR) and knowledge of performance (KP).

FIS   Abbreviation: Federation Internationale de Ski (French), the international governing authority for ski sports.

follow-through   Concentration on every detail of performance after a shot has been released.

force   It is the effect that one body has on another. It is always present when motion occurs. In relationship to body force, its production, application and absorption of force are important concerning movement skills. The production of force is produced by the actions of muscles, force must be applied in the same direction and in proper sequence to realize the greatest force. The application of force should be applied through the COG or mass of the object and in a forward direction to project an object or the body forward most efficiently. And the concepts of absorption of force are: the more muscles that are used, the greater force that is produced, the more elasticity or stretch a muscle is capable of, the more force it can supply and when an object is moved, the weight should be pushed or pulled through the COG and in the direction that they are to be moved.

foundation (base) training   Training designed to sustain or increase the capacity of the basic organisms used in a general athletic performance, meaning all of the organisms that are actually used in conjunction with a general athletic performance.

front sight   The front aperture through which the target is sighted and aligned with the rear sight.

functional training   Training that is distinctly designed to achieve the physical and psychological stress that a specific activity requires.

herringbone   The ski stride which is used in climbing very steep hills which characteristically leaves a herringbone pattern of marks in the snow. It is achieved by turning the skis outward and using the inside edges against backward slipping and moving forward.

hold   The phase between sighting and releasing a shot in which one strives to attain a totally motionless, without oscillation, position through the kinesthetic senses.

hypervigilance   Often seen as panic, it is the result of sudden and intense stimulus that causes severe narrowing of attention and increased distractibility of attention prior to initiating a response, and usually caused by CO_2 buildup in the blood.

IBU   Abbreviation: International Biathlon Union, the current international governing body responsible for biathlon.

IOC   Abbreviation: International Olympic Committee, the governing authority of the Olympic Movement, ensuring the regular celebration of the Olympic Games.

intensity   The amount of stress or energy demand placed on an organism during physical activity, often seen in terms of speed.

interval training   Training according to the interval principle that is designed to have a sustaining or improving effect on the aerobic and anaerobic processes.

interoceptors   Sensory information or feedback that tell about the states of our internal organs.

intrinsic feedback   Information about many aspects of one's own movements gained through various sensory "channels".

isometric contraction   Muscle contraction in which the contractile unit remains the same, generally resulting in no limb movement because the weight is too heavy.

isotonic contraction   A concentric or eccentric contraction of the muscles that results in limb movement.

kinesiology   The scientific study of human motion, dealing with the anatomical, mechanical, nervous and muscular aspects of motion.

kinesthesia   The sense in one's body that feels the positions of its various parts in relation to one another.

kinetic energy   The energy resulting from movement or motion.

lactic acid   A clear syrupy acid produced in the souring of milk and in the muscles during the anaerobic energy-releasing process.

large bore   A rifle barrel for which the caliber or diameter of the metal jacketed bullet exceed 5.6mm and shall be centerfired.

linear and angular motion   The angular velocities at the joints determine final linear velocity or motion.

level of performance   One's ability to produce a good result.

maximal strength   A muscle or group of muscles maximal level of tension development.

mental training   Training designed to develop the psychological factors which can influence the level of performance.

mirage   An optical illusion caused by the refraction of light.

model training   Picking out models of competition situations and including them in training.

motivation   The psychological processes which incite one's impulse to do something and which decides how and with what intensity he/she will do it in a given situation.

motor development   As age progresses to about 18 years, large and systematic increases in motor performance, such as fitness and strength, capacities to anticipate and predict, ability to process information from complex displays, speed of decision and movement, accuracy in movements, etc., occur. Past the age of 25, a progressive decline occurs in just about every measurable aspect of motor development.

muscle contraction   The nerve-muscle process which takes place to produce muscle tension.

muscle strength   A muscle or group of muscles ability to produce the chemical reaction required for mechanical tension.

objectives   The ends towards which all actions and activities are aimed. Often called goals, they flow from the needs and wants of an individual or the purpose or mission of an organization, but are much more specific.

over-training   Over-stress of the physical or psychological organism that causes a negative impact on the level of performance.

patrol race   A ski race combining the biathlon skills as a group, military in character, consisting of one officer and three soldiers.

perception   The psychological process which, through preliminary work of sensory interpretation, have a stronger or weaker direct effect on the experiences which influences oneself, the knowledge attained through the senses.

perceptual anticipation   The predictably of environmental events due to practice and experience.

planning   The process of setting objectives and then determining the actions needed to attain them.

plyometrics   Explosive, energy-homing exercises designed to improve strength, speed and power by involving a fast, high intensity, involuntary eccentric contraction of the muscles and tendons, followed by an immediate, powerful concentric contraction.

power   The amount of work accomplished in one unit of time.

pressure   Concerning biomechanics, it refers to the ratio of force to the area over which the force is applied.

program   A complex of objectives, policies, procedures, rules, resources, and other elements necessary to carry out a given plan of action.

proprioception   The term used to mean the perception of movement of the body, both of the limbs with respect to one another and also of the body as a whole, which contribute to kinesthetic capabilities.

proprioceptors   Sensory information or feedback that provides information about one's own movement.

quality training   Training of higher intensity and generally shorter periods or duration.

quantity training   Training of lower intensity and relatively long periods or duration.

range procedure   The movements one uses in shifting from skiing to shooting and from shooting to skiing during a biathlon competition.

rear sight   The rear aperture of the sighting system through which the target is sighted and aligned with the front sight. Control of the elevation and windage should be possible in fine gradations of one-quarter minute-of-angle per click adjustment.

receptor anticipation   Detecting upcoming events with various sensory receptors.

sensory feedback   Sources of sensory information that originates from three kinds of receptors: interoceptors, proprioceptors and exteroceptors.

shooting position   The way in which one is placed or arranged for shooting.

sighting   The act of aligning the target with the front and rear sight.

sight picture   The mental process involved in evaluating and correcting the sight alignment.

skifeldtskyting   A Scandinavian biathlon competition during which the shooting takes place at figure targets at unknown distances.

small bore   A rifle barrel for which the caliber or diameter of the bullet shall not exceed 5.6mm and shall be rimfired. (Long rifle)

specific training   Training designed to develop the factors which affect the level of performance in specific athletic conditions.

speed   An organism's nerve-muscle system's level of attainment or possibility of acceleration.

speed training   Training of short periods and maximal intensity (stress) of the nerve-muscle systems, which is designed to develop the ability to accelerate.

stability   The concept of stability is related to equilibrium, or a state of equalized forces on the body. It may be static, in which the center of gravity (COG) is in a stable position or dynamic, when the COG is in motion. Stability is often referred to as "balance." It is governed by 3 principles: The lower the COG is to the base of support, the greater will be the stability. The nearer the COG is to the center of the base of support, the more stable the body. The larger or wider the base of support, the more stable the body.

strategy   The development of specific actions and implied emphasis of resources and efforts to attain comprehensive and specific objectives.

strength training   Training designed to improve a muscle or group of muscles ability to produce mechanical tension.

stress   Strain caused by physical and psychological tensions or activities.

stress demand analysis   An analysis of the physical and psychological demands that an activity places on an athlete.

style   A personal form or solution to a specific technique or set of movements, adapted to accommodate one's own abilities.

tactics   The strategic patterns one follows in different athletic situations to achieve the best level of performance.

tactical training   Training designed to increase the level of adequacy and the number of choices in the handling of different athletic situations.

technique   A solution to the task of a coordination of movements.

technique training   Training designed to gain an effective solution to the coordination of movements.

tempo training   Training after the interval principle of such a high intensity that it has an increasing or sustaining effect on the aerobic and anaerobic capacities.

training   All activity that is designed to increase or maintain the level of athletic performance.

training diary   A journal of all training and competitive activities.

training dosage (amount)   The total amount of physical and psychological stress achieved in a certain training period.

training forms (methods)   The different forms (methodologies) that training can take.

trigger-pull   The physical and mental process of releasing a shot by increasing tension on the trigger.

UIPMB   Abbreviation: International Union of Modern Pentathlon and Biathlon, the original international governing body for biathlon.

USBA   Abbreviation: The United States Biathlon Association, which is the governing authority for biathlon in the United States.

USMPBA   Abbreviation: The original authority for biathlon and pentathlon in the United States prior to 1980.

USOC   Abbreviation: The United States Olympic Committee, the governing authority for Olympic sports in the United States.

V1   Common label for the skating (freestyle) technique that is characterized by one poling stroke for each two ski steps. Generally used for going up steeper hills.

V2   Common label for the skating (freestyle) technique that is characterized by one poling stroke for each ski step. Generally used on flat or slight uphill section of the ski course.

velocity   Refers to the speed and direction of a body and involves the change of position of a body per unit of time.

VO2 Max   The volume of oxygen uptake during maximum exertion, expressed in Liters/minute/kilogram. A measure of aerobic one's capacity.

WBC, WC   Abbreviation: World Biathlon Championships, World Cup Biathlon Race

warming-up   The processes of engaging the physical and psychological process prior to athletic competition or training.

windage   The term applied to the rear sight and to the strike of a bullet on a horizontal plane usually caused by wind.

WOG   Abbreviation: Winter Olympic Games

Zero(ing)   The term used for a sight setting (or the act of establishing it) that indicates that the horizontal and vertical axis are set exactly on the point of impact on a target at a given distance under given conditions.

References

Bø, Olav; *Skiing Traditions in Norway*, (Oslo, Det Norske Samlaget, 1968) 126 pgs.

Coakley, Jay J.; *Sport in Society, Issues and Controversies*, (St. Louis, MO, Times Mirror/ Mosby College Publishing, 1990) 417 pgs.

Cratty, BJ; Psychology and Physical Activity, (Englewood Cliffs, NY, Prentice Hall, Inc. 1968) 214 pgs.

Fangel, Greg; *Classic Skis, 1800s to 1980s*, www.woodenskis.com

Knutsen, Odd-Sverre, editor; *Sne, Ski, Skudd, on Norsk skiskyttere*, (Oslo, Norway, H Aschehaug & Co., 1970) 114 pgs.

Masia, Seth; *Gripe and Glide, a Short History of Ski Wax*, International Ski History, www. skiinghistory.org

Niinimaa, Veli M; *Double Contest, Biathlon History and Development*, (Salzburg, Austria, International Biathlon Union, 1998) 134 pgs.

Lehotan, Ivor; Magyar, Jozsef; Lange, Peer; editors; *50 Years of Biathlon*, (Salzburg, Austria, International Biathlon Union, 2008) 401 pgs.

Lund, Morten, Mesia, Seth; *A Short History of Skis*; International Ski History, www. skiinghistory.org

Rogers, Chris, editor; *Sport Psychology, Concepts and Applications*, (Dubuque, IA, Wm C. Brown Publishers, 1985, 1990) 469 pgs.

Stegen, Arthur; *Biathlon* (Washington, D.C., NRA Books, 1979) 128 pgs.

Willmore, Jack H., Costill, David L.; *Physiology of Sport and Exercise*, (Champaign, IL, Human Kinetics, 1988) 420 pgs.

Willmore, Jack H., Costill, David L.; *Training for Sport and Activity*, (Dubuque, IA, Wm C. Brown Publishers, 1985, 1990) 469 pgs.

Yur'yev, A. A., English translation edited by Anderson, Gary L.; *Competitive Shooting*, (Fizkul'tura I Sport, Moscow, USSR, 1973; English version National Rifle Association, Washington D.C., 1985) 399 pgs.

Index